Canadian Business Law

THIRD EDITION

Tamra Alexander
Pat Papadeas
Kathryn Filsinger
Laurence Olivo
Nora Rock
Camilla Wheeler

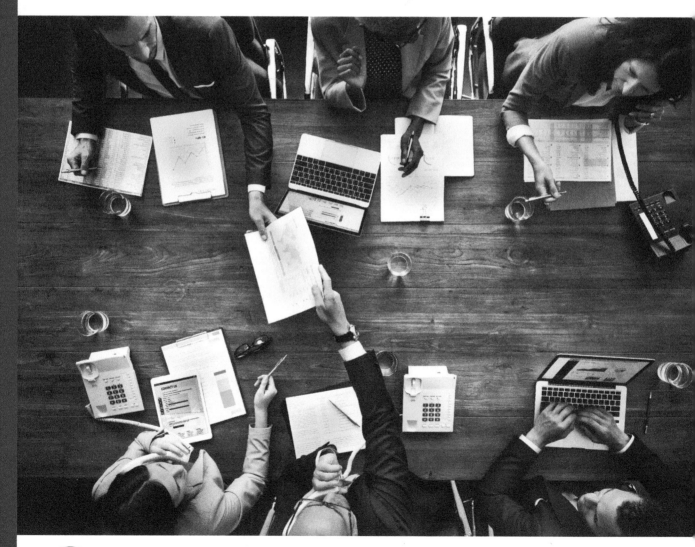

emond ▪ Toronto, Canada ▪ 2018

Emond Montgomery Publications Limited
60 Shaftesbury Avenue
Toronto ON M4T 1A3
http://www.emond.ca/highered

Printed in Canada.

We acknowledge the financial support of the Government of Canada. Canada

Vice president, publishing: Anthony Rezek
Publisher: Mike Thompson
Director, development and production: Kelly Dickson
Developmental editor: Sarah Fulton
Production supervisor: Laura Bast
Copy editor: Alison Jacques
Typesetter: SPi Global
Text designer: Tara Agnerian
Permissions editor: Monika Schurmann
Proofreader: Craig Bateman
Indexer: Karen Hunter
Cover image: Rawpixel.com/Shutterstock

Library and Archives Canada Cataloguing in Publication

Alexander, Tamra, 1967-, author
Canadian business law / Tamra Alexander [and five others]. Third edition.

Includes index.
Revision of Canadian business law. 2nd ed. Toronto : Emond Montgomery Publications, 2012.
ISBN 978-1-77255-281-2 (softcover)

1. Commercial law--Canada--Textbooks. 2. Textbooks. I. Title.
KE919.A75 2018 346.7107 C2017-908073-3
KF889.A75 2018

Brief Contents

Contents

Preface

There are several Canadian business law texts available, each with its merits. So when planning began for this third edition of *Canadian Business Law*, the authors and publisher had to seriously consider what would make this text an appealing option for instructors. After gathering extensive feedback from professors and listening carefully to their concerns, it was clear that for many, the *right* business law text had not yet been written. They are looking for a student-friendly text with a risk-management emphasis that covers core subjects well and has a clear focus on business applications. Perhaps most importantly, they are looking for a resource that provides introductory level students with what they most need: thorough, practical coverage of the core content that these courses require—particularly at the college level—while avoiding excessive detail or unnecessary legal complexity that can bog students down.

We believe that this third edition has achieved that goal, by building on the strengths of the second edition, refining and streamlining that content while adding relevant updates and pedagogy. There are several important features, retained from the second edition, that make *Canadian Business Law* an indispensable resource both in the classroom and beyond. It allows students to:

- quickly review the material covered in each chapter, and prepare for tests and exams, using helpful chapter summaries and exercises.
- reinforce critical business lessons through "Case in Point" features.
- apply what they have learned to real-world business scenarios using the "Apply Your Knowledge" material at the end of each chapter.

Key Features and Structure of the Third Edition

While the core content of the second edition remains largely intact, this third edition features some important revisions and new features, most notably:

- a new, recurring case-study, focussing upon a small, fictional start-up (Val-Nam Generation Limited), that evolves over the 11 chapters of the book, addressing different aspects of business law as the company grows and faces new challenges.
- a new chapter examining many central business considerations that have emerged in the 21st century: Intellectual Property and Business Law in the Digital Age.

- a new presentation of contract law material; the lengthy chapter in the second edition has now been divided into two shorter, more focused chapters.
- an increased emphasis on a risk management perspective
- streamlined coverage of certain legal matters, with excessive details removed.
- more visual appeal, photos, and graphics.

The book's structure has also been revamped from 9 to 11 chapters, meaning that it now maps better to a typical one-semester course, while remaining relatively concise. The order of material has also been fine-tuned, to create a smoother and more logical flow:

Chapter 1, renamed Foundations of Business Law in Canada, retains a focus on laws, lawmakers, and the sources of law, providing a valuable introduction to Canada's legal system and the key legal aspects of business, as well as introducing the concept of legal risk management.

Chapter 2, Resolving Disputes and Navigating Canada's Court System, describes the court system and legal processes, and explores the value of various forms of alternative dispute resolution to businesses.

Chapter 3, Tort Law, explains the legal risks associated with negligence and other types of harms that can result from business activity, and addresses various ways to protect one's business.

Chapter 4, Understanding Contracts, provides a basic understanding of the elements of a legal contract, noting pitfalls to avoid and potential legal risks.

Chapter 5, Working with Contracts, builds on the previous chapter while addressing the most common types of issues that arise from business agreements, and discusses how to handle various legal scenarios and mitigate risks.

Chapter 6, Facilitating Business, Protecting Consumers, and Safeguarding the Marketplace, expands on the scope of coverage in the second edition. It not only discusses how businesses comply with consumer protection legislation such as the *Sale of Goods Act*, the *Consumer Protection Act*, and the *Competition Act*, but also explains the role of key federal and provincial statutes.

Chapter 7, Forms of Carrying On Business, explains the advantages and disadvantages of the different types of business organizations, such as sole proprietorship, partnership, and corporation.

Chapter 8, Banking, Financing, and Debtor–Creditor Law, explains the legal aspects of financing a business and debt collection.

Chapter 9, Workplace Law, introduces the many laws governing the employment relationship, including union and non-union workplaces, and with particular attention given to issues such as equity, privacy, and wrongful dismissal.

Chapter 10, Property Law, focuses on personal property and real property, examining a company's various rights and obligations in both owning and being in possession of property, and describing how businesses can protect their legal interests.

Chapter 11, Intellectual Property and Business Law in the Digital Age, picks up where the previous chapter left off, presenting the legal issues and business considerations of contemporary businesses, including protecting trademarks, copyrights and patents, avoiding infringements, safeguarding confidential business information, and complying with new regulations dealing with customer information and privacy.

Acknowledgments

We authors, along with the publisher, wish to thank the following people who provided their constructive feedback and suggestions during the development stages of this revised text and its supplemental teaching materials: Peter Bowal, University of Calgary; Mike Bozzo, Mohawk College; Audel Cunningham, Humber College; Richard Gasparini, Seneca College; Christine Gigler, Sheridan College; David Hughes, Thompson Rivers University; Peter Inkpen, College of the North Atlantic; Kristine Jeffels, Bow Valley College; Ilias Kiritsis, Barrister and Solicitor; Tammy Kiss, College of the Rockies; Greg Libitz, St. Lawrence College/Queen's University; Susan Lieberman, Humber College; Eric Pelot, Algonquin College; Dan Shear, University of Toronto; Elaine Smith, Humber College; Bruce Stewart, IBT College; and Deirdre Way, Loyalist College.

The text is greatly enhanced by the contributions of Nora Rock, Camilla Wheeler, Laurence Olivo, and Kathryn Filsinger. Their collective expertise is a strength maintained from the second edition. We wish to thank them for their continued collaboration. We would also like to express our appreciation to the team at Emond Publishing that continually encouraged us and kept us on task—thanks to Mike Thompson, Kelly Dickson, Sarah Fulton May, Alison Jacques, and Laura Bast. Thanks also to Margaret Buchan and Dionne Coley for their contributions to earlier editions.

Finally, thank you to our students who inspire us to continue to develop better resources, our colleagues who share new ideas and approaches, and our families who support us through it all.

Tamra Alexander, Algonquin College
Pat Papadeas, St. Clair College

For Instructors

A full package of supplemental teaching materials is available to any instructor who has adopted this text for his or her course. These include an expanded test bank; PowerPoint presentations; instructor's guide with answers to end-of-chapter questions and exercises; and an expanded offering of "Apply Your Knowledge" business scenario questions, in addition to those in each chapter, that appear only in the teaching supplements, thereby allowing instructors to present and challenge their students with fresh, unseen scenarios.

For more information and additional teaching resources, including live links to the "Dig Deeper" material that is highlighted in the margins of selected passages in the text, please visit the accompanying website for this book at **www.emond.ca/cbl3** or contact your Emond Publishing representative.

About the Authors

Tamra Alexander coordinates the Paralegal program and teaches in the Paralegal and Law Clerk programs at Algonquin College. Prior to joining the faculty at Algonquin, she taught law at the University of New Brunswick and the University of Ottawa, and was a competition law and international trade law lawyer with Stikeman Elliott. She has a BA (Hons) from the University of Toronto in International Relations and Economics and an LLB, also from the University of Toronto, as well as a Master of Law from McGill University. She has represented clients before appellate courts, federal tribunals, and binational panels constituted under NAFTA.

Pat Papadeas has an LLB from the University of Windsor (1990) and was in private practice prior to joining the faculty at St. Clair College in 2002. She is the course developer and instructor of Business Law, Employment Law, and Law and Ethics in the Information Age, and is a Coordinator of International Business Studies. She developed the curriculum for the Paralegal Program, and developed an applied learning model that was awarded the Law Foundation of Ontario's Community Leadership in Justice Fellowship. She has been a member of Academic Council, Chair of the Academic Integrity Committee, and St. Clair College's Board of Governors. Pat has led numerous faculty-training workshops and has been an academic advisor to many student clubs, including varsity athletics, for which she received the Jack Costello Exceptional Service Award.

Contributors

Kathryn J. Filsinger (Chapter 9) is a professor in Humber College's Human Resources Management Degree Program. She teaches employment law in the HR degree and postgraduate HRM programs, as well as labour relations and human resources management. Previously she has taught employment law at both Ryerson and York Universities. Kathryn holds a BA (magna cum laude) from Queen's University, an LLB from the University of Toronto, and an LLM from Osgoode Hall Law School.

Laurence M. Olivo, BA, MA, JD (Chapters 2 and 8), is a lawyer and was a professor in the Faculty of Business, Seneca College, for over 30 years, with experience in post-secondary teaching in a variety of college programs, and in the Law Society of Ontario's Bar Admission program. His legal practice experience included civil litigation and family law, as well as policy development work with the Ontario Ministry of the Attorney General. He is the author of more than 15 texts in various areas of law and has developed specialized online courses for use by post-secondary institutions. He currently sits as a Small Claims Court Judge in Richmond Hill.

Nora Rock (Chapter 3) is an Ontario JD (lawyer) working as the corporate and policy writer for LawPRO, the Lawyers' Professional Indemnity Company. Nora is author/co-author of several texts for high school, community college and university, as well as two novels for young adults.

Camilla Wheeler (Chapters 4 and 5) is a faculty member at Toronto's George Brown College in its Office of Academic Excellence. Following a successful career as a litigation lawyer she transitioned into post-secondary education, initially teaching law courses and then moving into curriculum support and quality assurance roles. Currently, she leads comprehensive reviews of a range of George Brown vocational programs, resulting in evidence-based recommendations designed to ensure government standards and the changing needs of students, industry, and community partners are met. Camilla has a Bachelor of Laws degree from the University of Toronto and a Master of Education (IT) degree from Memorial University.

Foundations of Business Law in Canada

1

LEARNING OUTCOMES

After reading this chapter, you should be able to:

- Describe how law relates to business and its significance to business decision-making.
- Describe the process for developing a legal risk management plan and explain its importance.
- Explain the concept of legal precedent in Canada's common law system.
- Explain the function of the three branches of government and identify the source of law that is derived from each.
- Explain the significance of Canada's Constitution for the government's law-making powers.
- Describe how the federal, provincial, and municipal governments regulate business activity.
- Explain the significance of the *Canadian Charter of Rights and Freedoms* to business activity.
- Classify law as either substantive or procedural.
- Differentiate public law from private law and identify legal terminology associated with each.
- Explain how administrative law affects businesses.
- Discuss the difference between business law and business ethics.
- Describe the benefits of studying business law.

Business and the Law

From a business perspective, the law can be a tool that, when used effectively, enhances business. However, law can also pose a risk that, when improperly managed, can significantly damage a business. An understanding of the legal aspects of doing business is crucial to business success. The law can facilitate business by setting reliable ground rules for everyone to follow, protect business assets and other interests, and provide a mechanism for resolving disputes in an efficient and predictable manner. However, the law can also impose liability on businesses—for both their actions and their inactions.

Becoming familiar with the number and scope of laws that are applicable to one's business may seem a daunting task. This textbook has been developed to provide those involved in business activity with sufficient knowledge of business law to achieve the following objectives:

- Identify legal risks associated with business activity and business relationships.
- Apply knowledge of law in developing strategies to minimize legal risks.
- Recognize when the assistance of a legal professional is prudent.
- Utilize the services of a legal professional effectively.

Learning the basic principles that underlie business law will benefit anyone involved in business today. Whether you are a business owner, manager, employee, or consumer, knowledge of business law can help minimize legal risk by ensuring that legal implications are considered as part of the business decision-making process.

Managing Legal Risk

Good business decisions cannot be made without consideration of the legal risk associated with business choices. Legal risk management allows you to plan for and reduce, or even prevent, many business losses. There is no handy list of legal risks. Anticipating what can go wrong and developing strategies to prevent the risk from being realized is an ongoing process.

As you approach the study of business law, consider how the concepts we discuss apply to the business operations relevant to you. A proactive approach to minimizing risk is to implement a **legal risk management plan**. This means identifying the legal risks associated with every facet of your business activity and developing comprehensive measures to address them. Here is a basic overview of the steps involved in a legal risk management plan:

legal risk management plan
plan that allows businesses to take action to prevent or reduce loss

1. Identify the legal risks. This is a comprehensive process that requires assessing the entire operation of the business, including functional areas of the business as well as internal and external relationships. It requires a basic familiarity with the laws that will govern your business.
2. Evaluate the legal risks. For each risk identified, assess the probability of the risk occurring and the severity of potential losses, should the risk occur. (Refer to Table 1.1.) This requires an understanding of the consequences of legal breaches and the options for resolving disputes.
3. Manage the legal risk by devising and implementing a legal risk strategy. This will require you to devise proactive and reactive measures to address the risks that you have identified. Conscientious implementation of the plan should reduce or eliminate significant legal risk.

Table 1.1 Evaluating Severity and Probability of Legal Risk

Probability of Risk Occurring	Consequence of Risk Occurring				
	Very low	Low	Moderate	High	Critical
Very low					
Low					
Moderate					
High					
Very high					

4. Review and revise your legal risk strategy. Monitor its implementation to ensure it is effective—and if it is not, amend it. Track changes to your business strategy and goals and to the law to ensure your legal risk strategy keeps pace with those changes. Revise your legal risk strategy to reflect changes in your business and the legal environment.

There are four main strategies in managing legal risk (Step 3, above):

1. **Risk avoidance.** This involves the decision to stop a particular business activity because the risk is too great; this might be of particular importance where the probability and the severity of the risk are high.
2. **Risk transference.** This approach involves transferring the risk to another; the two most common ways to transfer risk are by contract (where another party agrees to assume the risk) or acquisition of insurance (where your risk is pooled with that of others).
3. **Risk reduction.** This is an extensively used strategy in legal risk management plans that involves putting practices in place to lower the probability and/or severity of the risks.
4. **Risk retention.** This is a decision to simply risk it; this approach may be appropriate where the impact of the risk on the business is lower than the cost of avoiding or transferring the risk.

Legal risk management requires a comprehensive approach to each legal issue that may arise for a particular business. We will explore the laws that commonly apply to Canadian businesses from the perspective of legal risk management. Throughout the text, you will find suggestions on how you can most effectively address the risks posed by various business activities in Minimizing Your Risk boxes. In addition to the overview provided here, legal advice can be of significant assistance in identifying legal risks, appreciating their potential severity, and developing and reviewing your legal risk management plan.

Preparing to Learn About Canadian Business Law

Before launching into an examination of the many laws that apply to Canadian businesses, it is helpful to ensure that all businesses start with the same base understanding of the Canadian legal system. This is important for businesses because:

- examining the different sources of law allows businesses to appreciate the wide range of laws that affect Canadian businesses;

- familiarity with government bodies and their respective roles allows businesses to identify which government bodies can assist them in interpreting law, changing ineffective law, or resolving legal disputes;
- identifying the legal limitations on government action allows businesses to properly protect their interests; and
- recognizing the different categories of law allows businesses to better understand the purpose and objectives of particular laws.

Because an examination of Canadian business law can be difficult to grasp in the abstract, you will find practical examples of the legal principles being discussed throughout the text. In addition, a running fact scenario will be used to allow for more in-depth and sustained discussion and analysis. This fact scenario is introduced in the Scenario box, below.

SCENARIO

Valery Garza has a PhD in chemical and biological engineering from the University of British Columbia. She studied how enzymes (naturally occurring chemicals) in the larvae of a certain type of moth are able to biodegrade plastics. She saw a great opportunity to create a potentially valuable, eco-friendly product, so she developed a synthetic version of the enzyme that is able to perform the same task. When this synthetic enzyme comes into contact with plastic, it creates a chemical reaction that degrades 96 percent of the plastic material into carbon dioxide and water. The degradation process releases a significant amount of heat, and the heat produced can be used to power turbines and generate electricity.[1]

Valery envisions many applications for her invention. It could be used to reduce landfill volume while generating power; plastics companies could use their scrap materials to power their buildings; environmental cleanup firms could use portable generators to eliminate plastic pollution on the spot and store the energy produced in batteries for later use; and even remote communities could benefit from consumer-sized generators powered by the plastic that wraps all of the products delivered to them.

Valery has enlisted the help of her best friend from university, Namid Blackburn. Namid is a chemical processing engineer and is working with Valery to improve the efficiency of the degradation process. With the help of Mitchell Wu, a mechanical engineer, they have developed a prototype for a small portable electricity generator that uses plastic (exposed to the synthetic enzyme) as the fuel rather than gasoline. Although it is a bit bulky, and they continue to work on its efficiency, their current prototype can produce a 2,000-watt charge that can run for one hour on a 50 percent load from the equivalent of 48 water bottles of plastic as the fuel.

Valery, Namid, and Mitchell are considering going into business together to further develop and market the portable generators and then to expand to larger-scale

1 The idea for this research project and the subsequent business venture arose from Ian Sample, "Plastic-Eating Worms Could Help Wage War on Waste," *Guardian* (25 April 2017), online: <https://www.theguardian.com/science/2017/apr/24/plastic-munching-worms-could-help-wage-war-on-waste-galleria-mellonella>; and Matthew Sedacca, "Plastic-Eating Worms Could Inspire Waste-Degrading Tools," *Scientific American* (8 June 2017), online: <https://www.scientificamerican.com/article/plastic-eating-worms-could-inspire-waste-degrading-tools/>. However, the inventions described do not currently exist, nor does the business venture.

generators, perhaps joining forces with environmental cleanup firms or municipal waste firms. They are excited about the potential of their business concept.

Valery views this venture as her "baby"; she developed the initial invention and business concept and she wants to be involved in all aspects of the evolving business. She is considering a number of names for the business but currently favours Val-Nam Generation (hereafter referred to as Val-Nam), which uses the first three letters of her name and Namid's name. Namid is more interested in continuing to work on the research and development side of the business and, given the potential he sees for the business, would like to invest in it. Mitchell has some start-up experience: he has commercialized a few of his own inventions and is currently involved in two other business ventures. He is interested in using his experience to help the business develop and also in investing in the business.

As the three (individually and collectively, as the business Val-Nam) consider their next steps, they have a number of issues to address, including the following:

- Valery wonders how best to protect her invention so that she receives appropriate compensation for it and so that it doesn't fall into the hands of a competitor.
- Val-Nam is concerned about product safety regulations that may restrict the sale and use of its generators. It believes it can convince concerned parties that the generators are safe, even though they do not technically comply with some of the current regulations.
- Val-Nam was recently turned down for a government grant aimed at green energy start-up ventures. It wants to investigate why it was turned down and perhaps challenge the decision.
- Val-Nam would like to arrange for WeSolve Manufacturing Solutions Incorporated (WeSolve) to produce an initial batch of the generators but doesn't want to be locked into a long-term arrangement because Val-Nam would like to eventually do its own manufacturing.
- Namid has a young family and he has heard that business owners can sometimes lose their personal assets, like their house, if their products cause injury to customers and there is significant court-ordered compensation. He is concerned, given that this is a new, untested product, that he could lose everything if things go wrong. He wants to know how best to protect his family while still becoming involved in the business.
- Given his other business interests, Mitchell is wondering how best to set up his relationship with this new business. Should he invest? Become an employee? Simply provide contracted services? Or should he engage in some combination of the three?
- Together, the three have some capital to contribute to the new business but they will need more. They are wondering which financing options would be best, given the nature of the business and their respective tolerances for risk.
- Val-Nam is looking at location options for both a business head office and potential future manufacturing facilities. It is concerned about the debt burden of purchasing land but also does not want to be locked into long-term leasing arrangements. It wonders how best to proceed.

All of these questions, and many more that the business will face, require an understanding of the law to answer. For some questions, it will be important for Valery, Namid, and Mitchell to obtain legal advice before making a decision; for others, however, they may be able to find sufficient information on their own if they have an adequate base knowledge of Canadian business law.

In providing the base from which further discussion of Canadian business law can develop, we will look at the legal systems that exist in Canada, different sources of law, including the institutions that create law, key categories of law, and an overview of the main topics in Canadian business law.

The Canadian Legal System: A Framework for an Orderly Society

Law consists of the rules that are established and enforced by society to regulate the conduct of its members. By establishing rules of conduct, society (through government) seeks to create a stable environment in which its members can interact peaceably and productively. Law governs the relationships of individuals and organizations, including businesses and governments. At the same time, law functions to safeguard individuals and organizations, by providing protection not only from others, but also from government itself.

Not all rules that set expectations on the conduct of individuals and organizations are law. The feature that distinguishes law from other rules is enforceability; law is the body of rules enforceable using the authority of the state. Courts and other government agencies have the power to enforce law.

The authority of government and its institutions to create and enforce law, however, is not without limits. The **rule of law** is a fundamental legal principle that no one is above the law. The rule of law prevents the arbitrary use of government power. Judges, government officials, and the government itself cannot act outside their respective **jurisdictions**—the legal authority granted to them by law. In this chapter, we will examine the authority (and limits) of government action in Canada as we take a closer look at the Canadian Constitution. A **constitution** is the foundation upon which government is granted its authority to govern. Before proceeding to study the substantive areas of law that impact business, it is important to have a solid understanding of the basis upon which all law is founded and how it is applied. The material that will be examined in this chapter, therefore, establishes the context in which to consider the content in later chapters.

In Canada, the Constitution establishes a federal government structure that incorporates two different legal systems or traditions: the British common law system and the European civil law system.

rule of law
legal principle that every person has equal rights before the law and that the law is supreme; it safeguards citizens from arbitrary actions of government

jurisdiction
authority to make or enforce the law

constitution
supreme law that establishes the basis upon which all other laws are created

civil law system
system of law where all rules are established in statute and courts lack authority to act without a statute; judges in civil law systems are not bound by the doctrine of precedent and have the freedom to interpret statutes independently of previous decisions; another way to refer to "private law"

common law system
system of law that recognizes court decisions with the same force of law as statutes, where statutes mean what courts interpret them to mean and where courts have the authority to make law where no legislative statute exists and to establish precedent

Canada's Two Legal Systems

There are two main legal systems in the world, which have developed from differing historical origins: the civil law system and the common law system.

The **civil law system** is a system of codified law. This means that the source of law comes from the rules that are set, or codified, by statute. Judges in a civil law system do not have to consider how other judges may have decided similar cases. While they may be persuaded by how a decision was reached in other, similar cases, they are not required to follow them; they only have to apply the written law before them. France has a civil law system and thus the province of Quebec, having French roots, adopted the civil law system for matters within Quebec's provincial jurisdiction.

All other provinces and territories in Canada, as well as the federal government, follow the system of law derived from Britain, called the **common law system**. This system was developed by judges over time, using previously decided similar cases to determine how to apply the law to the case before them. Gradually, a system of rules emerged from these cases, thus creating "common law" or "judge-made" law. The principle that a rule established in a previous case is binding on subsequent cases is known by the Latin term ***stare decisis***, which means to follow that which has already been decided. It is also known as the **doctrine of precedent**.

stare decisis
principle that requires judges to follow decisions of higher courts in similar cases

doctrine of precedent
principle requiring that a rule set out by a court in a decided case be applied to a new case

Having a common law system in Canada means that in all common law jurisdictions, judges are required to follow the interpretation given to the law by higher courts in the same jurisdiction. The Supreme Court of Canada is the highest court in the land and so its rulings must be followed by all lower court judges. We will take a closer look at the hierarchy of courts and how the doctrine of precedent applies in Chapter 2. Practically, however, what it means for businesses examining legal issues is that it is not enough to know what the legislation says. In order to have a firm grasp of the law, it is important to know the legal principles and application of the law established in previous court cases. The doctrine of precedent is an important part of Canadian legal tradition and helps provide a degree of certainty in how judges will decide similar cases. The drawback is that it often requires the assistance of a legal professional to research the relevant case law.

If Val-Nam operates in both Quebec and other Canadian provinces, it will have to consider whether the different legal systems (civil law and common law) affect its legal relationships and arrangements differently.

In both the civil law system and the common law system, "law" is found in constitutional documents and in statutes created by legislatures, but only in the common law system will you find "law" in case law. The next section looks at these three sources of law and the institutions that create law.

The Canadian Constitution and Other Sources of Law in Canada

For businesses trying to determine how to comply with the law in their day-to-day dealings, it is important to know where to look for "law." In Canada, law is found in the Constitution, in statutes, regulations, and by-laws, and in the common law. The Constitution also establishes which bodies have the jurisdiction to create these different types of law and protects citizens against improper government action. The two main documents of Canada's Constitution are the *Constitution Act, 1867* and the *Constitution Act, 1982*, which includes the *Canadian Charter of Rights and Freedoms*. This section provides a brief overview of each act.

www.emond.ca/CBL3/links

DIG DEEPER
See the full text of the *Civil Code of Quebec* on the Quebec government's website.

The Constitution Act, 1867 (formerly the British North America Act, 1867)

A constitution is the foundation upon which a government is organized and its powers are defined, thus establishing the extent (and limits) of government authority. The Canadian Constitution establishes the basic framework under which all other laws are created and the basic principles to which all other laws must conform. The Constitution is the supreme law of Canada.

Canada was created by an act of the Parliament of the United Kingdom called the *British North America Act, 1867.* This act was transferred from the authority of the UK Parliament to the authority of the Canadian federal Parliament and provincial legislatures in 1982 (it was "patriated") and was renamed the *Constitution Act, 1867.* However, the Canadian Constitution is not a single document; it includes many statutes, judicial decisions that interpret these documents, and unwritten rules called constitutional conventions.

Although we begin the study of Canada's legal framework in 1867, when the Dominion of Canada was established, we do so with deference to the original inhabitants of these lands who were here for many thousands of years before explorers arrived from Europe. Indeed, Canada's Constitution recognizes the rights of Indigenous peoples to preserve customs and traditions as continuing cultural practices, and it reaffirms treaty rights set out in agreements between the government and particular Indigenous communities.

federal system of government
system whereby law-making powers are divided between the federal and provincial governments according to subject matter

The *Constitution Act, 1867* creates a **federal system of government** in Canada. This means that there are two levels of government: the federal level and the provincial level. Both levels of government have similar institutional structures.

The Three Branches of Government

The Constitution establishes that Canada has three branches of government: the legislative branch, the executive branch, and the judicial branch. The three branches operate at both the federal and provincial levels. In other words, there is a legislative, executive, and judicial branch of government at the federal level and in each province.

A brief overview of these three branches, below, provides the basic framework of how government is structured. This is significant because each of the branches serves a different function and is a source of law. See Table 1.2.

Table 1.2 Branches of Government and Sources of Law

	Legislative Branch	Executive Branch	Judicial Branch
Function	Introduce, vote on, and pass legislation (statutes)	Administer day-to-day business of government	Adjudicate legal matters and disputes
Composition	Federal: Parliament (elected) Provincial: Legislative assemblies (elected)	Federal: Prime minister, Cabinet ministers, and each department's civil servants Provincial: Premier, Cabinet ministers, and each department's civil servants Federal and provincial administrative tribunals	Federally and provincially appointed judges
Sources of law	Statutes	Regulations	Case law

Figure 1.1

The House of Commons in Ottawa is where democratically elected officials debate and vote on statute law as part of the legislative branch of government.

LEGISLATIVE BRANCH

The **legislative branch** of government is the branch that is democratically elected and whose function it is to legislate—to introduce, vote on, and pass legislation, also known as statute law. The legislative body, or legislature, at the federal level is Parliament. Provincial legislative bodies are known as legislative assemblies. The term "statutory" refers to something that is required or permitted as a result of enacted legislation. For example, a statutory holiday or statutory minimum wage requirements are rights or obligations established by legislation. Refer to Table 1.3 for examples of statutes that affect business.

legislative branch branch of government at both the federal and provincial levels that has the power and responsibility to pass legislation

The legislative process refers to the manner in which a bill (proposed law) becomes a statute. The process involves several steps before a statute is enacted, including a vote by elected representatives. If passed, the bill will become law on the date that it is proclaimed to be in force. The power to create legislation is divided between Parliament and the provincial legislative assemblies. The powers of Parliament are set out in section 91 of the *Constitution Act, 1867*, and the powers of the provincial legislatures are set out in section 92. The two levels of government are assigned separate law-making authority, or jurisdiction, according to subject matter.

◇ Law-Making Authority of Parliament (Section 91)

Parliament is based in Ottawa, Canada's capital. It has jurisdiction over matters of national interest, and federal legislation applies to all people in Canada, from coast to coast to coast. For example, the federal government regulates the importation and exportation of goods in and out of Canada because it was deemed important

Table 1.3 A Sampling of Statutes That Affect Business

Area of Law	Name of Statute	Sample Rules
Business organizations	*Business Corporations Act*	Rules for incorporating companies that do business in Ontario
Intellectual property	*Copyright Act*	Rules protecting rights in property such as music, art, books, and theatre productions
Contracts	*Sale of Goods Act*	Rules that imply terms and conditions into commercial contracts, unless the contracting parties opt out
Employment	*Employment Standards Act, 2000*	Rules that provide minimum standards for wages, hours of work, and pregnancy leave
Bankruptcy	*Bankruptcy and Insolvency Act*	Rules determining when an act of bankruptcy has occurred
Property	*Mortgages Act*	Rules outlining the steps a creditor must take before foreclosing on a mortgage
Marketing and promotion	*Competition Act*	Rules forbidding unacceptable pricing schemes
Torts	*Occupiers' Liability Act*	Rules establishing a high duty of care owed to anyone who enters business premises with permission

to have the same legal standards apply across the country. Other matters that fall under federal jurisdiction, as set out in section 91 of the of the *Constitution Act, 1867*, include citizenship, criminal law, military and national defence, banking and printing of money, postal services, intellectual property, taxation of any kind, shipping, and interprovincial trade and commerce.

Section 91 also provides that the federal government shall make laws for the "peace, order and good government of Canada." This represents the federal government's residual powers to make law in respect of all matters that do not fall within provincial jurisdiction. In other words, matters that are not exclusively allocated to the provinces under section 92 are matters over which the federal government has jurisdiction, even if they are not specifically mentioned in section 91. Many matters requiring regulation today were not even imagined in 1867. Over time, the federal government has, by way of application of this residual clause, come to govern matters such as radio, television, nuclear energy, aeronautics, and control of drugs.

www.emond.ca/CBL3/links

DIG DEEPER

The authority of Canada's federal parliament is outlined in section 91 of the *Constitution Act, 1867*, which includes numerous areas directly related to conducting business, including banking, intellectual property, and regulating trade.

A government agency can often be identified as federal by the inclusion of "Canada" in its name: for example, Canadian Human Rights Commission, Canadian Environmental Assessment Agency, Canada Revenue Agency, Canada Employment Insurance Commission, and Canadian Radio-television and Telecommunications Commission.

The federal government also has law-making jurisdiction over Canada's three territories, the Northwest Territories, Yukon, and Nunavut, but has delegated some law-making powers to the territorial governments.

◇ Law-Making Authority of Provincial Legislatures (Section 92)

The work of government is divided between, and assigned to, the two levels in a federal system. Whereas the *Constitution Act, 1867* assigned matters of national interest to the federal government, it assigned jurisdiction over all matters of local interest to the provincial level of government.

In many ways, the provincial governments have greater authority over matters of concern in the day-to-day life of people and businesses. As set out in section 92 of the *Constitution Act, 1867*, provincial governments are responsible for legislating in matters that affect the welfare of people, such as education, hospital administration, the administration of justice, social services, property rights, and natural resources such as minerals, gas, and oil; they also have the power of direct taxation. Provincial governments regulate commercial activities carried out at the provincial level, including incorporation, real estate, consumer protection, sale of goods, business and other licensing, and employment. The expression "Canadian business law" can be misleading. More often than not, when it comes to matters that directly impact most businesses, it is provincial law that will be applicable.

Each province in Canada has its own government, with law-making authority over the matters set out in section 92. This is why matters such as minimum wage, the percentage of sales tax applied to goods, and the age of majority for the service of alcohol are not uniform across the country.

Municipal governments get their power from the provincial level of government. Provinces create these smaller governing bodies of cities and towns for more localized delivery of government services by delegating responsibilities to them. For example, municipal governments are responsible for local infrastructure, including roads and sewers, fire and police services, water services, local transit, libraries, garbage collection, and parks. Unlike federal and provincial governments, which have the power to create legislation in their respective areas of jurisdiction, municipal governments are granted the power to make by-laws. Generally, municipal by-laws regulate those things that impact the safety or enjoyment of property in the community. For instance, by-laws may regulate parking, speed limits on local roads, noise limits, food inspection, animal control, zoning of commercial and residential areas, building codes, and construction permits. A municipality may require businesses to obtain permits, licences, or other manner of approvals. For example, a business may need a permit to erect a sign. Municipalities need revenue to operate; their main source of revenue comes from the collection of tax on property. By-laws are included in our definition of law as they are part of the body of rules that can be enforced by the courts and other government agencies, including municipal officials and by-law enforcement officers.

Refer to Figure 1.2 for a summary of the legislative jurisdiction of Parliament, the provincial and territorial governments, and municipalities.

◇ Shared Power: Concurrent Jurisdiction

The areas of law-making authority set out in sections 91 and 92 largely represent the exclusive jurisdiction of the federal and provincial levels of government. Where the Constitution sets out an exclusive jurisdiction, the other level of government is excluded from enacting legislation. For example, a provincial government cannot enact criminal law. Also, a government cannot directly delegate its exclusive law-making authority to the other level. Sometimes, however, the federal and provincial governments will share law-making authority. This is known as having

Figure 1.2 Law-Making Jurisdiction of Federal and Provincial Governments

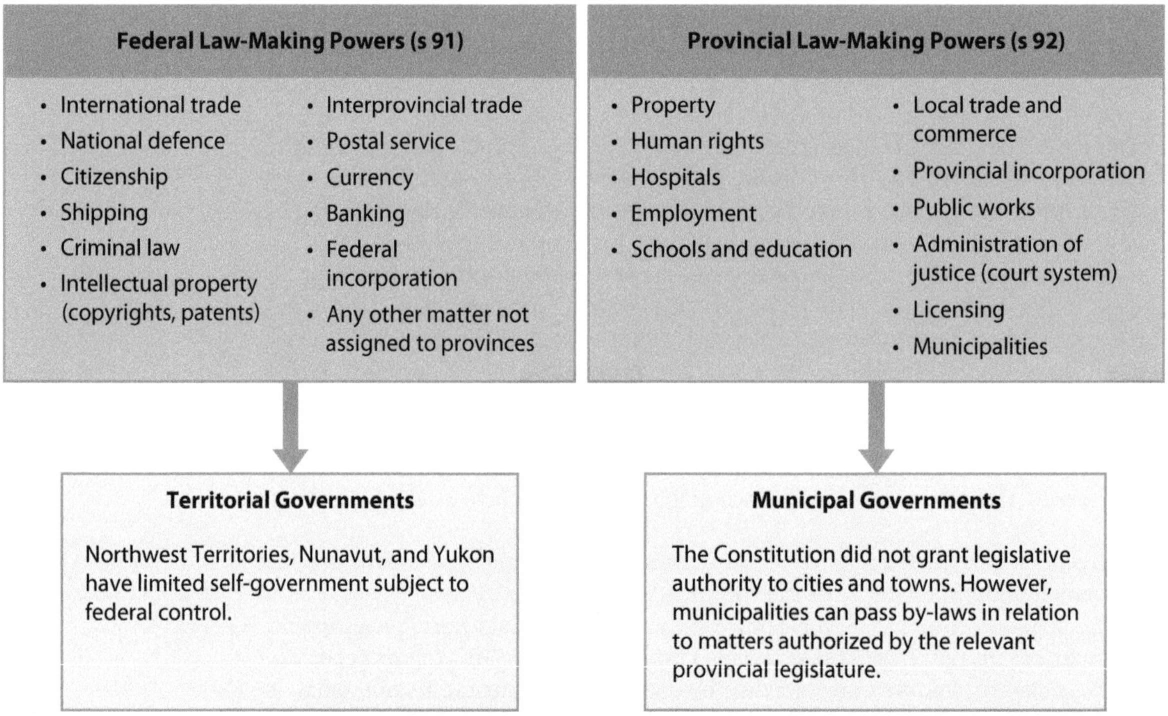

Federal Law-Making Powers (s 91)		Provincial Law-Making Powers (s 92)	
• International trade • National defence • Citizenship • Shipping • Criminal law • Intellectual property (copyrights, patents)	• Interprovincial trade • Postal service • Currency • Banking • Federal incorporation • Any other matter not assigned to provinces	• Property • Human rights • Hospitals • Employment • Schools and education	• Local trade and commerce • Provincial incorporation • Public works • Administration of justice (court system) • Licensing • Municipalities

Territorial Governments

Northwest Territories, Nunavut, and Yukon have limited self-government subject to federal control.

Municipal Governments

The Constitution did not grant legislative authority to cities and towns. However, municipalities can pass by-laws in relation to matters authorized by the relevant provincial legislature.

concurrent jurisdiction. Agriculture and the environment are examples of areas where both levels share law-making authority. The risk in having concurrent jurisdiction is that enactment of different laws may conflict with one another. This is not common, but in the rare case that there is an express contradiction between the laws, the **doctrine of paramountcy** will apply. This means that the federal law will prevail.

doctrine of paramountcy rule that establishes that where there is a conflict between federal and provincial law, the federal law will prevail and, where it conflicts, the provincial law will be inoperative

EXECUTIVE BRANCH

The **executive branch** of government is the one that carries out the day-to-day function of government; it formulates and executes government policy and administers all the departments of government. The chief executive is the prime minister at the federal level and the premier at the provincial level. The executive branch includes the Cabinet, made up of the ministers who head the departments of government; civil servants; and agencies, boards, commissions, and tribunals. Cabinet establishes government policy. The departments of government provide Cabinet members with policy recommendations. As the members of Cabinet are also members of the legislative branch, it is through them that most legislation is introduced into the legislature. Typically, because the executive branch carries out the operations of government, it is the branch with the greatest practical relevance to business and with which business people will most commonly interact.

executive branch branch of government at both the federal and provincial levels responsible for implementing and enforcing the laws made by the legislative branch

Statutes enacted by the legislative branch of government often empower the executive branch to create the detailed rules to complement the legislation. These rules are called **regulations** and provide us with another source of law that can be enforced by the courts and other government agencies.

regulations rules created by the executive branch of government that have the force of law

SCENARIO

If Val-Nam is concerned with the application of product safety regulations to its generators, it will want to:

- determine which level of government regulates product safety,
- review the relevant product safety legislation and regulations,
- consult with the executive branch—the ministry responsible for implementing the legislation in question, and
- consider lobbying for change. If a change to the legislation is required, Val-Nam should consider lobbying the executive branch (where policy is developed) and then members of the legislative branch in order to obtain the necessary support to pass an amending bill through the legislature. If a change to the regulation is required, Val-Nam need only lobby the executive branch, as both the policy- and regulation-making functions rest with that branch.

JUDICIAL BRANCH

The **judicial branch** of government is comprised of judges whose function it is to adjudicate; they do so by interpreting and applying the law to disputes that are brought before the courts. Judges are appointed by federal and provincial governments, but they function independently from both the legislative and executive branches. In our common law system, the interpretation and application of law by judges can lead to the creation of precedent. In essence, precedents create "rules" that must be followed by other judges. By this method of making law, the judicial branch of government provides another source of law known as common law (or case law).

judicial branch
courts at the federal and provincial levels responsible for interpreting and applying the law passed by the legislative branch; also responsible for determining that law is valid within the authority set out in the Constitution

Figure 1.3

The Supreme Court of Canada is the highest level of the judicial branch of government.

judiciary
term used to describe judges, collectively

ultra vires
beyond the level of power of a government or corporation

The **judiciary** is also responsible for ensuring the constitutionality of the law. Judges have the power to declare law unconstitutional, thus having no force or effect, if created without proper jurisdiction. When government creates law that is outside its authorized jurisdiction, it is acting unconstitutionally. Judges will declare such law ***ultra vires***—a Latin term meaning that the government acted "beyond the scope of its power"—and strike down the legislation.

PARLIAMENTARY SUPREMACY

parliamentary supremacy
constitutional convention that holds the legislative branch of government supreme over the other branches, thus allowing new legislation to override judge-made law

The judicial branch of government has a significant amount of power, and it may appear perplexing that judges, who are appointed, can trump the work of the legislature, which is an elected body. Judges, for instance, may interpret legislation in a way that the legislature did not intend. Or, judges may strike down legislation because the legislature overstepped its authority. Although judges have the authority to act in this manner, it is important to recognize that the legislature has parliamentary supremacy. **Parliamentary supremacy** is a constitutional convention that allows the legislature to override judge-made law. This means that the legislative branch of government can respond to court rulings or interpretations of the law by creating new law to give effect to what they wish to do (provided they are acting constitutionally within their jurisdiction).

The three branches of government are distinct, but together they provide the framework that guides the democratic governance of Canada. Canadian businesses are well served by understanding the roles and responsibilities of each branch.

The Constitution Act, 1982 and the Canadian Charter of Rights and Freedoms

When the Constitution was patriated in 1982, Canada took the opportunity to include the *Canadian Charter of Rights and Freedoms* in the *Constitution Act, 1982*. By its inclusion in the Constitution, the Charter was made "supreme law of the land." The Charter proclaims important rights and freedoms of people in Canada including equality rights, legal rights, democratic rights, and fundamental freedoms. The Charter has had a profound impact on law in Canada because it has broadened the judiciary's ability to strike down legislation. Up until 1982, the examination of the constitutionality of legislation by judges was limited to issues of jurisdiction that pertained to sections 91 and 92 and that ensured each level of government had the lawful authority to enact the legislation at issue. Since 1982, the constitutionality of legislation can be challenged for violating fundamental rights and freedoms as set out in the Charter as well. Canadian courts, therefore, are empowered to strike down any law that violates the Charter. Keeping in mind the doctrine of parliamentary supremacy, this nonetheless represents a considerable expansion of the court's powers.

It must be stressed that the Charter protects rights and freedoms from *government* interference. It places a limit on the power of government and applies to both levels and all branches of government, including the actions of government officials and law enforcement agents. It does not apply to discriminatory actions by individuals or businesses (for that we must look to human rights legislation, which we will examine in Chapter 9). Note that property rights (rights to own and enjoy property) and economic rights (rights to carry on business activity) are not protected in the Charter. Table 1.4 presents a sampling of ways in which the Charter has the potential to affect business activity in Canada.

Table 1.4 Charter Rights and Business Activities

Charter Right	Meaning of Right	Business Activity Affected
Equality (s 15)	Freedom from discrimination in the application and protection of the law based on specified grounds (such as age, gender, race, and religion)	Laws permitting mandatory retirement policies have been challenged
Freedom of expression (s 2(b))	Freedom to state opinions openly	Laws limiting advertising and marketing strategies have been challenged
Freedom of association (s 2(d))	Freedom to establish and belong to associations	Laws limiting the rights of workers to organize and join trade unions have been challenged
Freedom of religion (s 2(a))	Freedom to practise sincerely held beliefs of a religious or spiritual nature	Laws limiting Sunday shopping have been challenged
Mobility (s 6)	Freedom to pursue a job anywhere in Canada	Laws limiting the rights of provincially certified professionals to work in other provinces have been challenged

Canada is a representative democracy in which people vote for politicians who represent them. If people do not like the laws passed or the policies of the government, the election process provides the opportunity to choose differently in the next election. The democratic principle of "majority rule," however, may at times come into conflict with other important principles, such as protecting minority rights or individual freedoms. The Charter protects rights that are seen as fundamental and that should not be infringed by the public opinion of the day.

Section 1 of the Charter provides that all rights and freedoms are subject to "such reasonable limits prescribed by law as can be demonstrably justified in a free and democratic society." This means that although rights and freedoms are guaranteed by the Charter, they are not without limits. Each time a court hears a constitutional challenge about whether a law has violated the Charter, the court must consider whether the law imposes a *reasonable* limit on the right or freedom. Only when the court finds that the law violates a Charter right *and* cannot be justified as reasonable in the circumstances will the court strike down the legislation. For example, although the Charter protects freedom of expression, this freedom may be reasonably limited by laws regulating pornography, hate speech, advertising, copyright, defamation, and even noise by-laws.

www.emond.ca/CBL3/links

DIG DEEPER

Various viewpoints on how the *Canadian Charter of Rights and Freedoms* has changed many aspects of Canadian society, including business.

Categories of Law

In addition to recognizing the different sources of business law in Canada, it is important to understand key categories into which the law is divided; this will enable you to better understand the function and purpose of the laws that affect your business. All laws can be identified as either substantive or procedural in nature and can also be divided into public law or private law. These categorizations are explored below.

Substantive Law Versus Procedural Law

substantive law
rules that establish rights and limits

Substantive law refers to the law that sets out the rights and obligations of individuals. As the name suggests, this is the "substance" of the rules that establish what we can and cannot do. For example, the law that sets the speed limits on roads is substantive law. Exceeding the speed limit is an offence that violates this substantive rule.

procedural law
rules that establish the process of how substantive law will be enforced

Procedural law refers to the rules that set out how substantive laws will be enforced. There are often numerous rules of procedure on how to enforce a single substantive rule. For example, in the case of exceeding the speed limit, there are many rules in place that must be followed, by law, before someone can be convicted of that offence: a ticket must be issued, the driver may dispute the ticket, there is a time limit within which to dispute the ticket, and if the driver wishes to dispute the ticket, a court hearing will be held to determine whether the driver is guilty of violating the substantive rule. The rules governing the court process are also procedural rules: who will preside at the hearing, how the hearing will be conducted, how witness testimony and other evidence will be admitted—these are just a few examples of the many procedural rules that must be followed in order to enforce the substantive rule that set out what the driver could and could not do. The main purpose of procedural law is to ensure a fair process and consistency in the enforcement of substantive law.

Most of the chapters in this book will present the substantive aspects of business law. These rules that establish rights and obligations relevant to business activity are of primary importance in managing legal risk. In most cases where the risk is realized, legal counsel—whose concern it is to follow the procedural rules—will be retained. The rules of evidence, for example, provide the procedure for the establishment of proof in legal proceedings. While reference to procedural law will be made to provide additional context in instances throughout this textbook, the focus on procedural law will take place largely in Chapter 2.

Public Law Versus Private Law

Law can also be categorized as either public or private. The distinction between public law and private law is foundational and will provide context for understanding how to categorize all the areas of business law addressed in later chapters. Public law governs the relationship between persons and the state. Private law governs the relationship between persons; the relationships between persons can be personal, social, or business relationships. Government is not a party to the relationship in private law.[2]

public law
rules that govern the relationship between individuals (including corporations) and government

"Public" refers to something that concerns the people as a whole. In our society, the public are represented by government. **Public law** describes all the areas of law that concern the people as a whole, and thus, public law regulates the relationship between individuals and government at all levels. Tax law, criminal law, administrative law, environmental law, and constitutional law are examples of public law.

2 The exception to this statement is where government is acting as a person rather than in its capacity as a government. For example, when a government department hires an employee, which it does in the same manner and to the same effect as a business would hire an employee, the employment agreement is governed by contract law principles, which are private law.

From the perspective of business activity, any time a business is involved with a regulatory body or government official, it is a matter of public law. Examples include health and safety officials, food inspection agencies, municipal building departments, the federal competition bureau, labour relation boards, human rights tribunals, and privacy commissions. Public law disputes may end up in court or may be dealt with by an administrative tribunal (discussed later in this chapter).

Another term commonly used in relation to public law is **Crown**. Canada is a constitutional monarchy with the Queen as the symbolic head of state. Crown is another word used to refer to the state, or government. For example, Crown lands refer to lands belonging to the government.

Crown
all aspects of the state in a commonwealth nation; the Monarch is the symbolic embodiment

Private law relates to the legal relationships between persons, including corporations. The focus of this text is on business interactions and, to the extent that these are person-to-person relationships, the legal aspects of business are most often private law matters. The law of torts, property, and contracts, for example, are categorized as private law. Although we will not be addressing it in our examination of business law, family law is another example of private law. See Table 1.5 for examples of public and private laws.

private law
rules that govern the relationship between individuals (including corporations) where there is no government involvement

Another way to refer to private law is as **civil law**. The terms "private law" and "civil law" can be used interchangeably. Private law disputes may result in a lawsuit; the lawsuit process, which we will examine in Chapter 2, is also known as civil litigation. The term "civil" in these instances refers to the fact that the matter is one of private law. Note, however, that this reference to civil law should not be confused with the civil law system, which is explained above and refers to the type of *system* of law used by some countries (and the province of Quebec).

civil law
another way to refer to private law; concerned with the private relations of individuals

Public Law Offences Versus Lawsuits

Public law and private law differ in several ways, including the process by which cases move through the courts. They also differ in purpose. When the state creates rules to be followed by its members, it can make it an offence to break the rules. Criminal law is an example of law that establishes a set of offences. The purpose of criminal law is to punish offenders. Its purpose is different from that of civil law, whose purpose it is to compensate the victim for the harm done. Because criminal and civil law have different purposes, it is possible for one set of events to lead to both kinds of proceedings. This section will introduce you to the distinct terminology used in respect of criminal and civil matters.

Table 1.5 Examples of laws categorized as public or private

Public Law	Private Law
Administrative law	Contract law
Constitutional law	Tort law
Criminal law	Corporate and commercial law
Tax law	Property law

TERMINOLOGY OF PUBLIC LAW OFFENCES: CRIMINAL AND PROVINCIAL OFFENCES

criminal law
rules established by the federal government that govern the standard of acceptable behaviour in society, the breach of which results in fines and imprisonment

prosecutor
representative of the government who is responsible for presenting the government's case in public law matters against an accused person charged with an offence; also known as Crown attorney

defendant
party who is sued in a lawsuit; person accused of an offence

regulatory offence
breaking of a rule contained in a statute that can result in fines or other penalties but is not a criminal offence

Criminal law refers to the rules of the state that are designed to protect society as a whole. In Canada, criminal law is regulated by the federal government, which means that criminal offences are uniformly applicable across Canada. Criminal law is enforced by the state. Police and other law enforcement officials have the power to bring charges against offenders. When someone is charged with an offence, the proceeding will be one of public law. In these legal proceedings, society is represented by the Crown attorney, also known as the **prosecutor**. The prosecutor does not represent the victim. The prosecutor's role is to "see justice done." Proceedings in the criminal justice system are about determining whether the accused person, known as the **defendant**, is guilty of the charges. The victim's role is to be a witness in the case. A defendant who is found not guilty is acquitted of the charges. A defendant who is found guilty is convicted. Following a conviction, a judge will punish, or sentence, the defendant for the crime. The terminology used here is reserved for criminal (or provincial offence) cases.

Provincial governments do not have the authority to make criminal law. While only the federal government can make an offence a "crime," provincial governments do have powers to create **regulatory offences**. For example, provincial governments can develop health and safety, fishing, environmental, and traffic laws. Individuals charged under these provincial offences will go through a process similar to that of less serious criminal offences (known as summary conviction offences). Conviction for a provincial offence will not result in a criminal record or qualify as a criminal act. The individual who is convicted, however, can be punished with fines or even imprisonment. The terminology of criminal law is used for regulatory offences as well. Provincial offences are sometimes referred to as quasi-criminal matters because of their similarity to criminal law.

TERMINOLOGY OF PRIVATE LAW: LAWSUITS

The terminology of civil law cases, or lawsuits, is different from that of public law cases. We do not say that someone is "charged" with breach of contract or is "guilty" of a tort. It is not the purpose of a lawsuit to punish the person sued, so there will be no fines or imprisonment as a result. The civil litigation process will be explored in more detail in Chapter 2. The objective here is to introduce you to the terminology and how it differs from criminal law cases.

plaintiff
party who commences a lawsuit (the party who is suing)

liable
legally responsible

damages
losses suffered as a result of the commission of a tort or a breach of contract, or monetary compensation awarded for those losses

Categorized as private law, lawsuits involve disputes between persons. A person who has been wronged, in private law, can sue the person responsible for the harm. Rather than punishing the wrongdoer, the purpose of the lawsuit will be to compensate the person who has been wronged. There is no government involvement and thus no prosecutor. The person bringing the lawsuit and making the claim is called the **plaintiff**. The person being sued is called the defendant. A civil case is concerned with whether the defendant is **liable**, or legally responsible, in the matter before the court. If the defendant is found liable, the most common remedy imposed by the court is monetary compensation, also known as **damages**. The study of business law will most often use this terminology because the law that primarily concerns businesses falls under the category of private law.

BURDEN OF PROOF AND STANDARD OF PROOF

As noted above, one set of events can lead to both a public law trial and a lawsuit. For example, a person can be charged with fraud (a crime) in public law and be

Table 1.6 Civil Counterparts of Criminal Offences

Criminal Offences	Civil Counterparts
Criminal negligence	Tort of negligence
Attempted murder	Tort of battery
Fraud	Tort of deceit or fraudulent misrepresentation
Theft	Tort of conversion
Assault	Tort of assault/battery
Impaired driving causing death	Tort of negligence
Arson	Tort of trespass and/or tort of conversion

sued (a lawsuit) in private law. See Table 1.6 above for some examples of where the same set of events can lead to two different proceedings—one in criminal law and one in civil law.

Burden of proof refers to the responsibility to prove the case in court. In the criminal case, the burden of proof will be on the prosecutor. Consider that it is society who is accusing the defendant of the crime, so it will be society's representative who must prove the charges. In contrast, the burden of proof in the lawsuit will be on the plaintiff, because it is the plaintiff who is claiming that the defendant should be held liable for the harm done.

burden of proof requirement that a certain party prove a particular fact at trial

The outcome of one case is not dependent on the other, not only because the purpose of the proceedings is different, but because the standard of proof used to establish the facts is different. **Standard of proof** refers to the degree of proof that must be provided in order to satisfy the court that the allegations are proven. The serious nature of an accusation by the state against an individual results in a higher standard of proof in criminal cases. In a criminal case, the prosecutor will have to establish the defendant's guilt **beyond a reasonable doubt**. In the example above—of a person both charged with fraud in public law and sued in private law—the defendant in the fraud case will be convicted only if the court is satisfied, without any reasonable doubt, that the crime was committed by the defendant. In the lawsuit, the plaintiff has a lower standard of proof. In order to be successful in the lawsuit, the plaintiff must satisfy the court that the defendant is liable on a **balance of probabilities**. The court will be satisfied of a defendant's liability if it accepts the sufficient likelihood of the plaintiff's claims. A person who *probably* committed a crime (but there is reasonable doubt) will not be found guilty; but a person who *probably* wronged the plaintiff will be found liable for the harm.

standard of proof degree to which a party must convince a judge or jury that the allegations are true

beyond a reasonable doubt standard of proof that the prosecutor must meet in a criminal trial in order for a defendant to be found guilty

balance of probabilities standard of proof in civil (as opposed to criminal) law indicating that one version of events is more probable than another

See Table 1.7 for a summary of the key differences between criminal and civil court proceedings.

But what does it mean to "prove" something either beyond a reasonable doubt or on a balance of probabilities? Establishing proof depends upon evidence. The law of evidence involves a complex set of rules that determine what is admissible and therefore can be considered by a court or tribunal in its decision. An examination of the

Table 1.7 Contrasting Criminal and Civil Proceedings

	Criminal Proceedings	Civil Proceedings
Category	Public law	Private law
Case name	R* v Defendant	Plaintiff v Defendant
Terminology	Accused is charged	Defendant is sued
Issue in the case	To determine whether the defendant is guilty	To determine whether the defendant is liable
Purpose	To punish the guilty party	To compensate the wronged party (plaintiff)
Burden of proof	Prosecutor	Plaintiff
Standard of proof	Beyond a reasonable doubt	Balance of probabilities
Judgment	If the defendant is convicted of the crime, the judge will pass sentence.	If the defendant is held to be liable for the harm caused, the judge will order a remedy.
Consequences	Examples of types of sentence include fines, imprisonment, and other requirements that are part of a probation order. The accused will have a criminal record.	Example of types of remedies include an order for damages, injunction, and specific performance, as well as an order to pay the other side for legal costs.

* "R" in the case title of a criminal proceeding stands for the Crown, in reference to the Latin term for King (Rex) or Queen (Regina).

law of evidence is outside the focus of the material in this textbook, as it is generally a matter to be addressed by the legal professionals representing the parties. However, a short answer to the question of what is proof is that evidence is required to establish or prove the facts. If a fact cannot be established by the admissible evidence, it is as if the fact did not exist. If a fact that is germane to the legal issue cannot be proven, it may not be treated as fact for the purposes of the legal proceeding and, consequently, it cannot alter the legal outcome.

Administrative Law

administrative law body of rules applied to monitor decision-making powers of government agencies

One area of public law that warrants specific attention is **administrative law**. Administrative law refers to the body of law that is concerned with the regulation of business and other activities by government, including the rules created and applied to government agencies and their decision-making powers. It is an area of public law with growing importance to business, as government agencies, boards, and commissions expand regulation of economic and commercial activity. See Table 1.8 for examples of administrative agencies that affect business.

administrative agency government body that administers and enforces a particular area of law

Administrative agencies are government bodies established by legislation to regulate or oversee a particular activity that requires specialized knowledge. Administrative agencies have three broad functions: advisory (providing information to help develop government policy), operational (running day-to-day operations), and regulatory. We will focus on the regulatory aspects of administrative agencies. Administrative agencies function as regulatory bodies when they oversee and regulate

Table 1.8 Administrative Agencies That Affect Business

Administrative Agency	Function
Provincial alcohol commissions	Grant licences to bars and restaurants, allowing them to serve alcohol to patrons
Canadian Radio-television and Telecommunications Commission (CRTC)	Grants operating licences to television and radio stations across the country
Provincial workplace safety and insurance boards	Grant compensation to injured workers
Federal and provincial human rights tribunals	Determine whether human rights legislation has been violated
Canadian Food Inspection Agency	Issues decisions regarding food inspection and safety
Provincial professional societies or governing bodies	Grant licences to particular professionals (for example, lawyers, accountants, architects, nurses, and pharmacists) to practise their profession
Federal Competition Tribunal	Issues decisions regarding anti-competitive and dishonest conduct in business
Municipal building departments	Conduct inspections of buildings and grant permits to alter premises

the operation of private activity. A business that is licensed, for instance, will have to be aware of its relationship to the regulatory body that is responsible to ensure that the requirements of the licence are met.

ADMINISTRATIVE TRIBUNALS

In some instances, government will use the court system to enforce its rules (see coverage of regulatory offences above). But in many other instances, government establishes other government bodies to help enforce its rules. Whether they are called tribunals, boards, or commissions, these government agencies work alongside government departments and ministries to enforce regulatory rules (you will recall that they fall under the executive branch, just like government departments and ministries). An **administrative tribunal** is any government body (even if it is called something else) that has a decision-making function. The rules that provide the authority, procedure, and limits to tribunal actions are all part of administrative law. There are countless examples of government bodies that function as tribunals. Look at Table 1.8 and consider the context in which those administrative agencies would act as tribunals in exercising decision-making discretion.

administrative tribunal government body that has decision-making power regarding an administrative matter

PROCEDURAL FAIRNESS IN ADMINISTRATIVE TRIBUNALS

In order to exercise decision-making powers, an administrative body must be authorized to do so by legislation (or regulation). It must exercise that authority properly and fairly. Circumstances vary depending on the type of administrative

rules of natural justice principle encompassing the right to be heard, the right to hear the case against you, and the right to reply to the case; also known as fundamental fairness

tribunal but, at a minimum, procedural fairness means that the administrative tribunal must respect the following **rules of natural justice**:

- The person affected by the decision must be notified that a decision is going to be made.
- All the information, or evidence, that will impact the decision must be disclosed to the person it will affect.
- The person affected by the decision must be provided with an opportunity to address or refute the evidence provided.
- The decision must be made by the body that hears the evidence.
- The decision-makers must be impartial (free from any bias or conflict of interest in the case).

When Val-Nam reviews the decision of the government body that turned down its grant application, it will want to consider whether the body adhered to the principles of natural justice in coming to its decision.

If Val-Nam has reason to believe that the decision did not comply with these principles, it may decide to challenge the decision through judicial review, described below.

ADMINISTRATIVE TRIBUNAL VERSUS JUDICIAL PROCESS

Hearings before administrative tribunals differ depending on the type of tribunal and the authorizing statute that created it. Administrative tribunals are similar to courts in the sense that they make binding decisions that affect legal rights, but they differ from the judicial branch of government in some significant ways. The decision-makers of administrative tribunals are rarely judges; they are usually people with some relevant expertise in the subject matter of the dispute. Administrative tribunals also differ from courts in the following significant ways:

- Administrative tribunals are not bound by the strict rule of *stare decisis* that requires courts to follow previously decided cases.
- They can take public policy into account when applying the law.
- Their procedural rules are more informal and flexible.
- The rules of evidence are much more permissive, such that evidence that would not be admissible in court may be accepted at a hearing before an administrative tribunal.
- There is often no appeal process that would bring the substantive legal matter dealt with by an administrative tribunal into the court system; generally, the opportunity to involve the court system is limited to challenging whether the administrative body had legal authority to make the decision or whether it properly followed the rules of procedural fairness. The means of challenging a tribunal decision in this manner is a process known as **judicial review**.

judicial review process whereby a court reviews the decision of an administrative tribunal

It is advisable to seek legal advice before submitting to, or appearing before, an administrative tribunal. Although they are not courts, administrative tribunals have decision-making powers that can profoundly impact an individual or business.

With this background in the structure of the Canadian legal system and in key categories of law, you now have the foundation on which to build your understanding of the substantive areas of business law and, from there, to consider how you will manage the legal risks inherent in your business.

Legal Aspects of Business Activity

Law functions to create stable environments in which members of society can plan their affairs with some certainty and predictability. Applying this function to business activity, law enables people to go about their business with a measure of confidence in the enforceability of the established rules. Business is a very large arena. It should not come as a surprise that no academic course, or single textbook, can comprehensively address every possible instance of the law's reach when it comes to business matters. There are, however, key areas of law that are common to all types of businesses, regardless of industry. The following key areas will be addressed in the subsequent chapters.

First, while law functions to minimize conflict in society, where legal conflict does occur the law's role is to facilitate the resolution of disputes through the establishment of processes and procedures. Generally, the details involved in navigating the court system can be left to legal professionals. However, even where legal representation is needed, a basic understanding of these processes, the terminology used, and the relevant court structure provide for more effective communications between legal representative and client. We will explore the basic elements of the systems of dispute resolution, including alternatives to court action, in Chapter 2.

Should Val-Nam's arrangements with WeSolve for the manufacture of Val-Nam's generators not meet Val-Nam's expectations, Val-Nam may want to negotiate some form of compensation or concession from WeSolve. An understanding of the options for dispute resolution will assist Val-Nam in this process.

The law of torts (Chapter 3) provides compensation to those harmed by the intentional or negligent acts (or omissions) of others. A business could be either the person harmed or the person who has caused the harm. Of legal significance for any business is the potential for injury to those who interact with the business, including injury to a person harmed on the property, harm caused by an employee's actions or by a product or service, losses suffered because of misrepresentations made during the negotiation of an agreement, and damage to the reputation of a person or business caused by false statements. We will examine the legal principles that are applied to these and other types of torts.

Agreements made in the course of business are governed by the law of contracts (Chapters 4 and 5), and understanding the basic underlying principles of contract law is important for every business person. Extensive government regulation addresses many business practices. Key areas of regulation include regulation related to contract formation, consumer protection, and the protection of a fair and open marketplace (Chapter 6). Laws also govern how business is formed and carried out. We will consider the legal advantages and disadvantages of the most common forms of carrying on business: sole proprietorships, partnerships, and corporations (Chapter 7).

Product liability issues may be an area of significant legal risk for Val-Nam. An understanding of the elements of the tort of negligence, of contractual protections that are available to a business, and of consumer protection legislation will help Val-Nam properly evaluate and manage this risk.

Further, an understanding of the legal protections, costs, and risks associated with the different forms of carrying on business (sole proprietorships, partnerships, and corporations) will help Valery, Namid, and Mitchell decide whether the form of business chosen will sufficiently protect their personal assets from product liability claims.

It is advantageous to business people to have a basic understanding of law that governs banking, financing, and the law of debtor-creditor (Chapter 8). The legal responsibilities involved in the employment relationship, and awareness of the legal risks that arise from it, are essential in today's business environment (Chapter 9). Similarly vital is an understanding of the law surrounding property (Chapter 10). Property is not limited to tangible assets. We will examine law as it relates to intangible forms of property such as copyrights, trademarks, and patents. Intellectual property is exceedingly important in today's digital world, as is the expanding nature of a business's legal responsibility in protecting the personal information and privacy of others (Chapter 11).

An understanding of the legal forms of business, of contract law, and of employment law will help Mitchell decide what the nature of his relationship to the business should be.

An appreciation for the different forms of financing available to the business and their relative legal risks will help Val-Nam determine the appropriate mix of financing options for the business.

An understanding of financing law, contract law, and property law will help Val-Nam determine how best to obtain a head office location and land for future manufacturing facilities.

Familiarity with intellectual property law, both common law and statutory law, will allow Valery to protect her invention and the business concept she has created.

The foundational knowledge that will be gained in the study of these areas of the law has applications to all types of business. Knowledge of business law forms the basis upon which to assess legal risk and, in turn, to develop important skills for avoiding legal risk. Before a legal risk can be managed, it must be recognized. The ability to identify and anticipate legal risk is a valuable and necessary skill for anyone whose goal it is to succeed in business.

The Answer to Every Legal Question

As you work your way through the materials in this text, be alert to the complexity that can be hidden in what may appear to be a simple legal question. One of the frustrating aspects of the study of law for some students is that it may appear that there are no definitive answers to even what seem to be simple legal questions. There is a running joke that the answer to every legal question is "It depends." While it is probably accurate that "It depends" is the first response to most questions, the inquiry must then continue. The issue is generally in the incompleteness of the facts available to answer the question. More information is usually needed for an answer that is relevant and applicable.

Consider this question: Can the staff at a restaurant lawfully serve an alcoholic beverage to a 19-year-old patron? Answer: It depends.

What other information is needed before we can reach the answer?

- Is the restaurant licensed to serve alcohol? (This is a threshold question, as without a liquor licence, no alcohol can be served.)
- In what province is the restaurant located? (Different provinces have different age restrictions for the service of alcoholic beverages.)

In practice, assessing a legal question requires applying the applicable law and relevant facts to the issue at hand. The fact that it is provincial law that regulates the service of alcohol is relevant but only partially helpful. The facts of the case are critical. *Change the facts and you change the answer.* In the scenario above, if the restaurant is licensed to serve alcohol, and if it is located in the province of Ontario, where the age of majority for the service of alcohol is 19, then it would appear that the answer to the original question is yes and that the patron can be lawfully served. Remember, however, that if the facts are changed, the answer can change. For instance, if we add an additional fact that it is 3:00 a.m., then it would not be permissible to serve the patron. What if the patron is impaired? What if the staff person is 17 years old? What other factors or issues might affect the answer?

The study of law requires the ability to identify the legal issue and apply the facts and the law to that issue. In order to concentrate on learning the law and identifying legal issues, the facts will be provided to you in case scenarios and examples used in this textbook. The facts presented throughout this textbook to illustrate each legal principle should be accepted as the facts that are to be applied to the legal concept under review; you need not concern yourself with "what if" questions about the existence of other facts. This guideline also applies to answering review questions (unless the question asks you to explore additional facts). Remember that taking into consideration facts that are not part of the discussion or scenario may lead to a different answer when applying the law. Although you will be provided with facts in the discussions of legal concepts for the purpose of applying the law, when faced with real legal questions, ensuring a thorough exploration of facts is critical.

Business Law and Business Ethics

Legal principles and ethical values often intersect, but they are not the same thing: complying with the law is not equivalent to being ethical; conversely, violating the law is not necessarily equivalent to being unethical. It may not be illegal to betray a friend, but many would condemn it as unethical. Likewise, it may be illegal to drive with expired license plates, but few people would categorize it as unethical.

Should a business outsource manufacturing of a product to a country where it is legal to use child labour? Should a business recycle even if it is not required to do so by law? Should a business advertise using images that are degrading to women? From the perspective of reputation and, indeed, risk to a business' profitability, it may not be enough for a business to be legally compliant—the business may also need to reflect the moral standards of its community.

Business ethics are the values and moral principles that help to identify right and wrong in a business context. Legal standards may be the minimum requirements. People in business are well advised to have an understanding of both the legal and ethical environments in which their business operates and to consider the ethical as well as legal risks in business decision-making.

CHAPTER SUMMARY

The law can be a valuable tool to enhance your business but it can also impose costly liability on a business. A legal risk management plan can allow you to reduce or even prevent many business losses. The development of a legal risk management plan is an ongoing process that requires you to anticipate what can go wrong and to develop strategies to prevent legal risks from being realized.

A basic understanding of the Canadian legal system provides an important foundation for the examination of legal risk. Canadian law stems from a number of sources. The Constitution is the highest law: it provides the framework and principles to which all other laws must adhere. It contains the *Constitution Act, 1867* and the *Canadian Charter of Rights and Freedoms*. The latter sets out the rights and freedoms of Canadians and prohibits government and legislation from interfering with those rights and freedoms. All Canadian provinces and territories use the British-based common law (except Quebec, which uses the French-based civil law). The name "common law" stems from the fact that the laws have been applied many times and, now, courts are required to make decisions according to these precedents. Statute law is created by the federal, provincial, and territorial governments. Many statutes formalize and clarify the common law. As well, municipalities pass by-laws on matters such as local taxes, land zoning, and licensing for the region and municipality for which they are responsible.

Substantive law is the "substance" of the rules that establish what we can and cannot do. Procedural law tells us how to enforce the substantive rules. Public law regulates the relationship between persons and government at all levels. Private law regulates individual-individual, individual-business, and business-business relationships. There are many differences between public and private law: in the terminology used, the process by which disputes proceed through the courts, and the standard and burden of proof in proceedings.

Given the increased prevalence of government regulation of business, an understanding of administrative law is important for business. Administrative law governs the fairness of decisions made by government agencies and protects the public and businesses from government action that overreaches its statutory jurisdiction.

Assessing a legal issue requires applying the applicable law and relevant facts. The facts of the case are critical. *Change the facts and you change the answer.*

Adherence to legal requirements may not be enough for a business to develop a positive reputation in the community. While legal standards tend to establish a base level of acceptable behaviour, community morals may demand a higher level of ethical behaviour from businesses.

KEY TERMS

REFERENCES

Bankruptcy and Insolvency Act, RSC 1985, c B-3.
Business Corporations Act, RSO 1990, c B.16.
Canadian Charter of Rights and Freedoms, Part I of the *Constitution Act, 1982*, being Schedule B to the *Canada Act 1982* (UK), 1982, c 11.
Competition Act, RSC 1985, c C-34.
The Constitution Act, 1867, 30 & 31 Vict, c 3.
The Constitution Act, 1982, being Schedule B to the *Canada Act 1982* (UK), 1982, c 11.
Copyright Act, RSC 1985, c C-42.
Employment Standards Act, 2000, SO 2000, c 41.
Mortgages Act, RSO 1990, c M.40.
Occupiers' Liability Act, RSO 1990, c O.2.
Sale of Goods Act, RSO 1990, c S.1.

EXERCISES

True or False?

____ **1.** Laws promote certainty and predictability because they never change.

____ **2.** One of the purposes of the criminal justice system is to ensure that the victim of the crime will be compensated for the harm done by the offender.

____ **3.** A purpose of a legal risk management plan is to reduce the risk of being sued and to reduce the amount of liability in the event of a lawsuit.

____ **4.** The *Canadian Charter of Rights and Freedoms* replaced human rights legislation in 1982, when Canada's Constitution was brought home from England.

____ **5.** The courts are empowered to strike down any law that violates the Charter.

____ **6.** The Charter does not prohibit businesses from discriminating against racial minorities if they so choose.

____ **7.** Administrative tribunals have less expertise than courts.

____ **8.** Public laws govern actions of individuals and businesses when those actions occur in public places such as parks, roads, waterways, and the air.

____ **9.** Canada and all its provinces and territories operate under a common law legal system.

____ **10.** Judicial review is a process whereby a court reviews a tribunal's decision for errors of law, errors involving fairness, or errors involving the tribunal's exercise of power.

Multiple Choice

1. Which definition or definitions best describe "the rule of law"?

a. Everyone has equal rights before the law, and nobody is above the law, including government.
b. The wealthy and educated are more likely to benefit from the law than are the poor and uneducated, and all societies are ruled by law.
c. Punishment for breaking the law is imposed according to rules of conduct.
d. All of the above.

2. Which of the following best describes the protections afforded by the *Canadian Charter of Rights and Freedoms*?

a. Freedom from discrimination and harassment in the workplace.
b. Freedom from unreasonable government interference with respect to rights and freedoms such as equality, religion, and expression.
c. The legal right to sue a person or company for discrimination.
d. The legal rights and freedoms of Canadians are guaranteed and cannot be limited by legislation in any way.

3. Which of the following best describes substantive law?
   a. It defines international legal status.
   b. It defines relationships between governments.
   c. It defines the process by which to enforce legal protections set out in the Charter.
   d. It defines rights and sets limits on conduct.
4. What does the division of powers found within Canada's Constitution dictate?
   a. Which powers are statutory and which are derived from the common law.
   b. Which powers are territorial, provincial, and municipal.
   c. Which powers are provided to Quebec through the civil law and to the rest of Canada through the common law.
   d. Which powers are federal and which powers are exclusively provincial.
5. In which of the following legal proceedings is Barney appearing in a matter categorized as private law?
   a. Barney appears as a witness for the prosecution in Fred's fraud trial.
   b. Barney appears as a witness at a hearing where Fred is appealing the decision of a worker's compensation tribunal.
   c. Barney appears as a witness in a proceeding where Fred is suing a business associate for breach of contract.
   d. Barney appears as a witness at Fred's trial on a municipal noise by-law infraction.
6. Which of the following is an example of procedural law?
   a. The rule that prohibits a restaurant from serving alcohol to persons under the age of 19.
   b. The rule that requires the operator of a vehicle to drive within the prescribed speed limit.
   c. The rule that prevents songs protected by copyright from being uploaded onto the Internet without permission.
   d. The rule that requires that a lawsuit must be personally served on the defendant in the case.
7. Which of the following is not a legal term normally associated with civil law proceedings?
   a. liability
   b. prosecutor
   c. plaintiff
   d. damages
8. Which of the following is *not* an example of how tribunals are different from courts?
   a. Tribunal decisions are not binding on the parties in the same way as are court decisions.
   b. Tribunals usually have more informal and flexible procedures than do courts.
   c. Tribunals may consider public policy to a degree that courts usually do not.
   d. Tribunals may admit evidence that would never be admitted in a court.
9. The judicial branch of government creates case law when it interprets the law. However, Canada has a constitutional principle that allows the legislative branch of government to override judge-made law. What is this constitutional principle known as?
   a. *ultra vires*
   b. *stare decisis*
   c. rule of law
   d. parliamentary supremacy

Short Answer

1. Define "law" and describe its purpose.
2. Describe the steps to take in devising a legal risk management plan.
3. Explain why the most common answer to many legal questions is "It depends." What factors affect the analysis of a legal issue?
4. What is meant by "jurisdiction"? Provide examples to explain your answer.
5. Describe the advantages and disadvantages of Canada's common law legal system.
6. Explain how the protections of equality rights under the Charter differ in application from provincial human rights codes.
7. Explain how business law differs from business ethics.
8. Describe two reasons for which a court may determine legislation to be unconstitutional.

Apply Your Knowledge

1. Review the following scenarios and identify whether the legal matter at issue will be categorized as public law or private law. Discuss the terminology used in the scenario and how that helps determine how the matter is categorized.
   a. Jessica must attend a hearing before an immigration tribunal regarding her status to live and work in Canada.
   b. George has been fired from his job and plans to sue his employer for wrongful dismissal.
   c. Anastasia got a ticket for talking on her cellphone while driving and intends to fight the ticket in court.
   d. Maria is bringing a legal proceeding against her competitor for patent violation.
   e. Sarah has been fined for fishing without a licence.
   f. Kosta is commencing legal proceedings against his business associate for breach of contract.
   g. Sami has filed a complaint with the Canadian Human Rights Commission alleging discrimination by his employer.
   h. Rino's company has been fined by the provincial Ministry of Labour following a workplace accident.
   i. Sonya has received several notices from the Canada Revenue Agency about failing to report income.
   j. Olga has applied for a liquor licence for a new nightclub, but the neighbours are opposing it.
   k. Kira has made a complaint to the Privacy Commissioner about the disclosure of her personal financial information by a bank manager without authorization.
2. Refer to sections 91 and 92 of the Constitution and identify which level of government, federal or provincial, has the power to make law in relation to the following topics:
   a. Protection of an invention.
   b. Disposal of waste products by hospitals.
   c. Fees payable to register a real estate transaction.
   d. Conspiring to commit fraud.
   e. Minimum wage for liquor servers.
   f. Safety standards for trucking companies that carry goods between provinces.
3. Review the following matters and comment on whether the Charter applies:
   a. A taxi company refuses to hire a Sikh because he wears a turban.
   b. A city by-law prohibits the rental of community spaces to religious organizations.
   c. The federal government enacts legislation authorizing police to seize computer data of anyone suspected of a computer crime without needing to apply for a warrant.
   d. A software development company fires an employee for expressing political views on social media.

Resolving Disputes and Navigating Canada's Court System

2

LEARNING OUTCOMES

After reading this chapter, you should be able to:

- Identify circumstances when it may be advisable to obtain legal advice or assistance.
- Explain what distinguishes a paralegal and a lawyer in Ontario with respect to what services each can offer.
- Describe Canada's hierarchy of courts.
- List and describe five roles of Canadian courts.
- Explain the litigation process in the Small Claims Court and the Superior Court.
- Describe negotiation and suggest circumstances under which various types of negotiation can assist in resolving business disputes.
- Describe various types of mediation and suggest how they can assist business people in resolving disputes.
- Describe arbitration and its role in resolving commercial disputes.
- Distinguish between the roles of mediators and arbitrators.
- Describe how administrative boards and tribunals operate and how they are different from courts.

Understanding When Legal Assistance Is Required

In the operation of any business, there will be times when you will require assistance to deal with issues that involve the law and require the expertise of legal professionals who can give advice and provide services. Legal issues for business people fall into two broad categories.

The first category involves dealing with legally regulated processes that do not involve disputes, many of which are covered in this textbook. Examples include buying or selling land or other property (Chapter 10), dealing with contracts and agreements (Chapters 4 and 5), complying with government regulations (most chapters), and creating entities to carry on a business (Chapter 7).

The second category involves dealing with and resolving disputes. This chapter deals with how legal disputes are dealt with by businesses.

SCENARIO

Val-Nam Generation Limited's ("Val-Nam") business has been expanding quickly but not without a few bumps along the road. Three disputes have arisen that Val-Nam must deal with:

- Val-Nam has a contract with WeSolve Manufacturing Solutions Incorporated ("WeSolve"). Under the contract, WeSolve manufactures the portable electricity generators that Val-Nam develops so that Val-Nam can then sell them to retailers and, through its online operations, to end-users. WeSolve was supposed to have a new prototype manufactured and delivered to a recent trade show but production difficulties delayed its completion and the prototype was not ready in time for the trade show. Val-Nam likely lost the opportunity to attract a number of sales contracts with national equipment retailers because of this. Val-Nam feels that WeSolve should compensate it for some of this loss of business and for the delayed supply of the new prototype.
- Kaya Sun was injured while using one of Val-Nam's earlier models of the portable electricity generator. It appears that the generator overheated and Kaya was burned when she tried to move the unit. Kaya has sent a letter of complaint to Val-Nam and is asking for compensation for her medical expenses.
- Val-Nam sold 100 generators to Dubious Distributors Corporation ("Dubious Distributors") nine months ago. Pursuant to the terms of the contract, Dubious Distributors had 30 days from the date of sale to pay in full. Val-Nam has yet to receive any payment. Val-Nam has sent numerous letters and emails demanding payment, but has had no response from Dubious Distributors.

As we examine how legal disputes are dealt with by businesses, consider how Val-Nam should deal with these disputes.

Providers of Legal Services: Lawyers and Paralegals

In Ontario you have a choice of the type of legal service provider you employ. You can use a licensed paralegal or a licensed lawyer, depending on your needs and the services to be provided. Note that the term "paralegal," when used in other provinces or in the United States, refers to someone who is not licensed and who does some legal work, but only under the supervision and control of a lawyer; these paralegals do not appear in court for clients. In some places, such as Ontario, individuals who do some legal work under a lawyer's supervision are usually referred to as "law clerks."

Lawyers

A business person should avoid becoming embroiled in legal disputes, if possible. Knowledge of the law can help you to develop guidelines for your business's policies, procedures, and interactions. If you do become involved in a dispute, you may need to hire someone knowledgeable to give you advice about your options for dispute resolution and to predict the likelihood of success or failure if you proceed with litigation.

Qualified lawyers who are experienced in the subject matter of your dispute may be able to assist you because of their special training in identifying and resolving legal problems.

Many business law lawyers are quite capable of advising you about the various issues that will arise in your business's day-to-day operations. However, some lawyers specialize in different areas of law, such as corporate law, labour relations law, and bankruptcy law. When your legal problem is complex and specific, it may be wise for you to seek specialized legal advice. To find appropriate legal counsel, business people should seek referrals from trustworthy colleagues, contact their local law society office, or interview several lawyers to determine the one that can best meet their immediate and long-term needs. It is important to find a lawyer whose approach fits the organization's vision and goals.

Paralegals in Ontario

You may also benefit from the services of licensed paralegals, which are generally less expensive than those of lawyers. Like lawyers, paralegals in Ontario are regulated by the Law Society of Ontario (LSO),[1] and have to carry liability insurance to protect their clients from negligence.

Unlike lawyers, who may practise in any area of law, paralegals are restricted to practising in certain areas only. Most notably, they may appear in the Small Claims Court and in the lower criminal courts dealing with provincial offences and less serious offences under the *Criminal Code*. They may also appear before administrative tribunals. They may advise their clients with respect to matters heard in these courts and tribunals, and draft the necessary documents for litigation or settlement.

The Small Claims Court hears matters involving claims of $25,000 or less, although the monetary limit in Ontario is expected to be increased to $50,000, sometime in 2018, following the trend of other provinces. Many businesses will have to deal from time to time with issues in this court, such as bill collections, minor contract disputes with suppliers, and wrongful dismissal claims made by fired employees.

A number of administrative tribunals relate to various businesses, including

- Liquor Control Board of Ontario
- Ontario Labour Relations Board
- Environmental Review Tribunal
- Ontario Human Rights Commission

1 In November 2017, the Law Society of Upper Canada (LSUC) changed its name to the Law Society of Ontario. The new name is being phased in during 2018.

www.emond.ca/CBL3/links

DIG DEEPER
The website of the Law Society of Ontario (formerly Law Society of Upper Canada) provides a lawyer referral service and information on the regulation of lawyers and paralegals in Ontario. The LSO also certifies lawyers to carry on practice as specialists. You can use the LSO's database to search for a lawyer or paralegal according to area of practice or specialization.

- Ontario Municipal Board
- Landlord and Tenant Board
- Ontario Securities Commission
- Workplace Safety and Insurance Board
- Financial Services Commission.

Hiring a paralegal with experience and expertise to advocate before one of these tribunals may be a cost-effective alternative to hiring a lawyer.

Customizing Legal Services

Many businesses choose to have an ongoing relationship with a lawyer or law firm. Larger businesses may have a legal department, which employs in-house lawyers and licensed paralegals. Both in-house and outside lawyers can assist businesses by reviewing their operations to uncover and minimize legal risks, by simplifying everyday issues such as employee relations, and by examining new ventures to ensure that new legal risks are identified and addressed.

Retaining a Lawyer's Services

If you wish to retain the services of a lawyer to deal with a specific issue or legal problem, you will usually obtain the lawyer's services by paying a deposit against the cost of the work to be done. This deposit, called a retainer, is paid before the work actually starts. The lawyer will deposit your retainer into a trust account to your credit. As the work is completed, it is billed out to you, at which point funds equal to the amount billed are transferred from the trust account to the lawyer.

You will also probably be asked to sign a contract for services, also called a retainer, in which the lawyer will set out the fees to be charged, using either an hourly rate or a fixed fee for a particular service. Hourly rates are usually charged for cases involving litigation and court appearances. However, some work, such as incorporating a business or preparing a lease, may be done for a fixed fee. The rate charged will be based in part on the lawyer's expertise and years of experience. In some cases, a lawyer will charge a contingency fee, which is based on a percentage of the amount the client obtains, either on a judgment or through a settlement of the case. If the lawyer fails to obtain an amount of money for the client, a contingency fee arrangement will usually stipulate that the client pays no fees to the lawyer. In addition to arrangements about the fees charged, a retainer will also stipulate that the client must pay disbursements. These will include expenses incurred by the lawyer in acting for the client. Examples include court fees, photocopying expenses, long-distance phone charges, examination for discovery transcripts, fees of expert witnesses, and trial transcripts.

SCENARIO

Knowing When to Call for Legal Help

Val-Nam is still a young, developing business, so it is unlikely that it will have a legal department to consult about the three disputes that have arisen. Should it find a lawyer or paralegal to assist it with these disputes? This depends on a number of considerations:

- How complex are the legal issues involved?
- What information is available publicly (through government websites, etc.) to help Val-Nam understand the issues?

- How time-consuming would it be for Val-Nam to deal with the issue on its own?
- Is there a potential for significant liability?
- Is litigation the most likely route to solving the issue or is it more likely that it can be solved through negotiation with the other party?
- If the issue is likely to be litigated, which court or administrative body will be deciding the issue? How complex are its proceedings?
- Is this likely to be a recurring situation/issue or is this a one-off occurrence?
- Does the issue suggest there are more systemic problems with the business that need to be addressed?

The more complex the issues, the greater the potential for significant liability, the less likely it is that Val-Nam and the other party can resolve the dispute through negotiation, the more likely it is that consulting a lawyer or paralegal would be the best course of action. Further, proactive consultations with a lawyer to develop procedures and processes that minimize legal risk and enhance legal compliance can not only be cost effective but can also enhance Val-Nam's reputation.

Lawyers are prohibited by their professional rules of conduct from disclosing confidential client information to third parties. Communications between clients and lawyers are also protected by **solicitor–client privilege**, a rule that prevents these communications from being used as evidence in court. This is very important in promoting open communication between lawyers and their clients. Without full and accurate information, lawyers are not able to effectively advise or represent their clients. For example, if the management of a business is concerned that it might be violating the *Canadian Environmental Protection Act*, it may wish to retain a lawyer to assess potential **liability**. It may also wish to have the lawyer draft policies and procedures to prevent violations from occurring. The protection provided by the solicitor–client privilege encourages this proactive approach because management has no concern about revealing problems to its lawyers. Communications to lawyers, generally, cannot be used as evidence.

solicitor–client privilege
protection that prevents a solicitor from revealing in court communications between that lawyer and the client

liability
legal responsibility for injuries or losses suffered by another

There are some lawyer–client communications for which the client cannot claim privilege. For example, if the client told the lawyer he was going to lie under oath when giving evidence, the lawyer would be obliged—as an officer of the court—to inform the court or, at the very least, to stop representing that client.

MINIMIZING YOUR RISK

Find a Lawyer or Paralegal

- Consult colleagues or the law society to find lawyers or paralegals who practice in areas of concern to your business.
- Interview lawyers and/or paralegals until you find one with whom you can work.
- Add specialists if and when the need arises.

How Are Business Disputes Resolved?

As a business person in Canada, you are entitled to have any legal dispute resolved in accordance with the law in a final and binding manner. People with little experience of the law tend to think that most disputes in Canada are resolved by the courts, and certainly courts do settle many matters between opposing parties through the process of litigation.

litigation
process of resolving disputes through a formal court process

Litigation begins when a party launches a lawsuit; it proceeds through a standard series of steps that eventually lead to a hearing before an impartial judge. When engaging in litigation, the parties to the lawsuit resolve their dispute as adversaries. Opposing lawyers usually present evidence on behalf of each party to a presiding judge. The judge determines the facts, applies the law, and eventually decides the case in favour of one party and against the other. In theory, with both parties presenting opposing points of view to the best of their abilities, the truth will emerge and justice will be done.

Litigation, however, is not the only process for resolving disputes, and courts are not the only forums. The parties themselves can gather their facts, present their points of view, and negotiate a solution to their dispute either on their own or with the assistance of a **neutral individual**, called a mediator, whom they have chosen. The parties may also select a third party to hear their evidence and arguments, and the latter will decide in favour of one side or the other. In this case, the third party is called an arbitrator. Arbitration is similar to litigation.

neutral individual
a person who has no personal interest in a dispute between the parties and can help them resolve a dispute, such as a mediator or arbitrator

Negotiation, mediation, and arbitration are the three most widely used forms of **alternative dispute resolution (ADR)**. The term "alternative" refers to the fact that these forms provide an alternative to litigation. These methods are becoming increasingly popular among members of the business community.

alternative dispute resolution (ADR)
settlement of conflict through a process other than the court system

In this chapter, we begin our consideration of dispute resolution with a discussion of the structure of the Canadian legal system and the litigation process. We then turn to the alternative methods, which in many instances can prove to be the most efficient, most flexible, and least expensive ways of settling conflicts that arise in the course of doing business.

Canada's Court System

As a business person, you will never need the extensive knowledge of the Canadian court system that a lawyer, a paralegal, or a court administrator needs. However, because you may find yourself using Canada's court system to resolve your legal disputes, some knowledge may be useful.

Each province and territory in Canada has its own court system to try all civil and criminal cases. While the systems differ slightly from province to province, they are similar in most respects. All systems arrange courts in a hierarchy. A court's relative position in the hierarchy depends on how much authority it has to decide legal issues. Generally, the more extensive its authority, the higher the court is perceived to be. Also, the procedure in higher courts is more formal and complex.

The Hierarchy of Courts in Ontario

The lowest court in the province is the Ontario Court of Justice, which deals with less serious criminal matters. The lowest civil court, the Small Claims Court, however, is now part of the Superior Court.

The trial court with the greatest powers is the Superior Court of Justice. It is staffed, for the most part, by federally appointed judges and consists of several divisions, which are described below in the section entitled "The Superior Court of Justice."

At the top of Ontario's court hierarchy are the appellate courts, which hear appeals from decisions of lower courts. The appellate courts occupy two tiers in the

Figure 2.1 Hierarchy of Courts in Ontario

Hierarchy of Courts in Ontario
Supreme Court of Canada A federally established national appeal court that hears appeals from all provincial court systems; its decisions are binding on all courts in Canada.
↑
Ontario Court of Appeal The highest court in the province; it hears appeals from lower provincial courts, and its decisions are binding on all other courts in the province.
↑
Superior Court of Justice The highest trial court in the province; it includes specialized courts, such as Divisional Court and Small Claims Court; its decisions are not binding on any other courts.
↑
Ontario Court of Justice Includes the lower criminal courts.

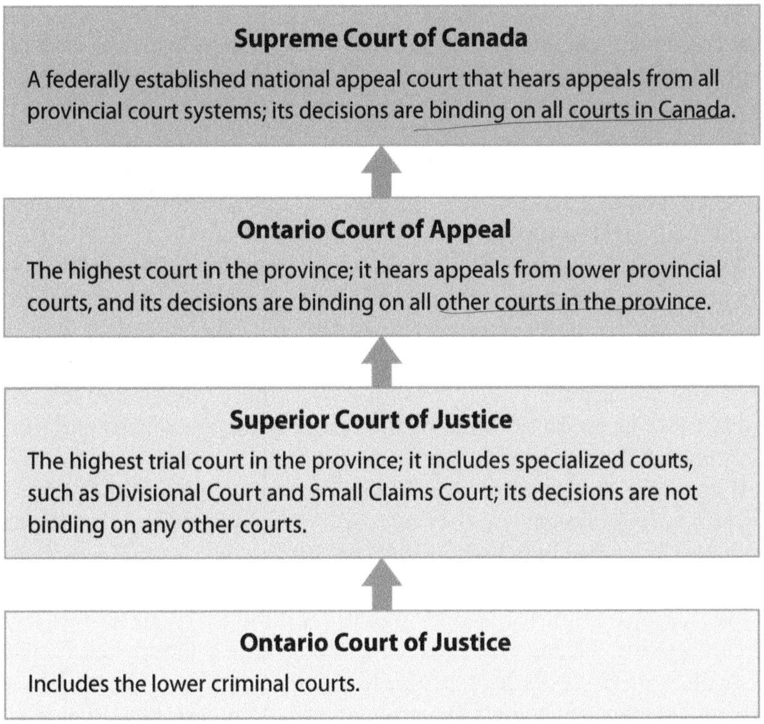

hierarchy: the highest provincial court is the Ontario Court of Appeal; above that, at the federal level, is the Supreme Court of Canada.

Figure 2.1 sets out the hierarchy of courts in Ontario. In the following sections, we briefly describe the function and composition of these courts.

The Ontario Court of Justice

The Ontario Court of Justice is often referred to as an inferior or lower court because its power is limited by statute. (This is also true for the Small Claims Court, even though it is technically part of the Superior Court system.) The court consists of several different courts that are defined by the type of law they deal with. The criminal court deals with young offenders and with offences under the *Criminal Code* that are not reserved for hearing by the Superior Court. The family court deals with adoptions, child custody, and family support, but not divorce, which is reserved for the Superior Court. Lastly, there is a provincial offences court, staffed largely by justices of the peace who exercise judicial functions but who are not lawyers. They deal with provincial offences such as traffic offences, which are relatively minor, but also with provincial offences such as breaches of environmental or workplace safety legislation, which carry very heavy penalties.

The Ontario Superior Court of Justice

The Ontario Superior Court of Justice consists of three divisions of interest to business persons:

1. *Trial Division.* The trial division of the Superior Court of Justice is the highest trial court in Ontario. Judges of this court are federally appointed to hear criminal and civil cases in larger cities and towns across Ontario. As far as business people are concerned, you can sue for any amount in this court and ask the court for any civil remedy recognized by law.

   Because procedures in this court are complex, the court also provides for some specialized procedures. If you are suing for between $25,000 and $100,000, you can make use of a simpler and quicker court process that will reduce your legal **costs**.

   costs
   court fees and the fees and expenses charged by a legal representative

   If you are suing about certain types of commercial matters in Toronto, you may file the claim on what is called the Commercial List. Commercial List cases are handled separately from other civil cases by judges with specialized knowledge of such disputes. The procedure is somewhat streamlined, and the dispute is likely to be dealt with more quickly and efficiently, and at a lower cost, than would be the case in a less specialized and focused trial court in the Superior Court.

   If you have brought a proceeding in Toronto, Windsor, or Ottawa, and it is very complex, you may ask (or a judge may order) that the case be moved into case management. An action that is case-managed will usually have a judge or a junior judicial official called a Master assigned to oversee and monitor the steps in a proceeding up to and including the trial. Normally, the lawyers themselves determine the pace at which a case moves forward, or how legal procedures are carried out, but in this case the court supervises the process more closely than would be the case in an ordinary trial.

2. *Divisional Court.* The Divisional Court hears applications for judicial review of decisions made by government agencies, such as the Ontario Human Rights Commission, the Ontario Labour Relations Board, and the Liquor Control Board of Ontario. If, for example, the Ontario Human Rights Commission finds the hiring policies of a business to be in contravention of the Ontario *Human Rights Code*, the business can apply to the Divisional Court for judicial review of the decision.

   Generally, the Divisional Court does not substitute its own judgment for the judgment of a governmental agency whose decision is under review and whose members often have specialized expertise in dealing with the issues before them. Rather, the Divisional Court identifies an agency's procedural error or misapplication of the law and sends the matter back to the agency to make an appropriate decision.

3. *Small Claims Court.* The Small Claims Court has authority to hear cases where the claim is for $25,000 or less. Although any federally appointed Superior Court judge can hear such a case, these judges rarely do so. Instead, the Small Claims Court is staffed primarily by deputy judges (lawyers who work part-time as judges).

   The rules of procedure and the court forms in the Small Claims Court are much simpler than they are in the trial division of the Superior Court of Justice. As well, guides are available from the government to assist people who wish to represent themselves in the Small Claims Court. The idea is to create a quick and inexpensive process to try small claims so that the cost of trying the case does not exceed the worth of the claim itself.

The Ontario Court of Appeal

Immediately above the Superior Court of Justice is the Ontario Court of Appeal. Its job is to review the decisions of lower courts for errors, not to try or retry cases. It hears appeals from decisions about criminal and civil cases made in the Superior Court of Justice.

As a business person, you might find yourself in the Court of Appeal if you are dissatisfied with the result you obtain from the Superior Court of Justice. For example, if you think the trial court misinterpreted a contract that was being disputed, you might want to argue in the Court of Appeal that the wrong rules of contract interpretation were applied. Or if the trial court decided an issue that had been decided differently by other trial judges in other cases, you might want the court to rule on which interpretation is correct.

www.emond.ca/CBL3/links

DIG DEEPER

Find help on representing yourself in Small Claims Court on the Attorney General's website and the Law Help Ontario website.

The Supreme Court of Canada

At the highest level sits the Supreme Court of Canada. This court is the most powerful court in the land and the court of last resort. It hears appeals from the provincial courts of appeal and from the highest federal courts.

The Supreme Court does not hear every appeal that is filed with it. If you want the court to hear your case, you must persuade it that your case raises issues of general public significance, or reflects opposing decisions by provincial courts of appeal. Therefore, the court would not likely hear your appeal from a decision that went against you in the Ontario Court of Appeal on the interpretation of an ordinary business contract that was of no real interest to anyone but yourself and the other contracting party. It might, however, be interested in hearing your appeal if your contract had unusual implications that affected many other business contracts, or if the law in the area was not yet settled.

Figure 2.2 The Ontario Court of Appeal

The Court of Appeal for Ontario is located in historic Osgoode Hall in downtown Toronto.

Like most appeal courts, the Supreme Court of Canada does not hear witnesses or original evidence. The Supreme Court's job is to review the decisions of the provincial courts of appeal for errors made by judges. The court does not try or retry cases. It relies on transcripts of trials and hearings and on arguments from lawyers in reaching its decisions. The decisions of the Supreme Court, once made, are binding on all other courts in Canada.

Reducing Cost and Delay

As we have noted already, the people who administer Ontario's courts are very concerned about how long it takes to try a case and how expensive the process can be. Efforts have been made to reduce cost and delay to make justice more easily available to everyone. Reformers have streamlined the civil trial process, established shorter time lines, created specialized courts to deal with complex cases, simplified procedures for certain types of cases, and diverted cases away from an adversarial framework where appropriate. Unfortunately, these efforts have had limited success, and the cost of using formal litigation is still prohibitive for many.

The Role of Canadian Courts

Courts have five essential roles to fulfill in Canada's judicial–political system. They resolve disputes, interpret legislation, answer constitutional questions, protect the rights and freedoms of individuals, and review the actions of government agencies. Although these functions often overlap, we examine them individually in the following sections.

Dispute Resolution

As we have noted, a principal role of the courts is to settle disputes between parties who have been unable to settle their differences themselves. Because the courts provide a forum for resolving conflicts peacefully, the parties have no need to resort to remedies that involve force or fraud. The very existence of courts prevents, or at least limits, the social disorder and violence that can result when people engage in "do-it-yourself" justice.

A party who is dissatisfied with a judge's decision may appeal to a higher court, whose job it is to decide if the judge made an error. Once all rights of appeal have been exhausted, the decision is final and binds the parties. Thus, the parties' dispute is resolved.

Interpretation of Legislation

In the course of deciding a dispute, a court may be called upon to determine the meaning of a statute or a regulation made under a statute. When a statute is drafted, the drafters cannot take into account every possible situation to which the statute might apply. In some cases, it is unclear how a statute is to be applied. In cases such as these, the parties will ask a court to interpret the statute to decide what it means in relation to a particular set of facts. The court's interpretation will resolve the matter for the parties to the lawsuit. It also provides guidance to others affected by the statute by allowing them to arrange their affairs so that they can predict, with reasonable certainty, the legal consequences of their actions.

CASE IN POINT

Government Policy and Interpreting Statutes

Barrie Public Utilities v Canadian Cable Television Assn, [2003] 1 SCR 476

Facts

The Canadian Radio-television and Telecommunications Commission (CRTC) granted an order under section 43(5) of the *Telecommunications Act* permitting cable television companies to attach their cable lines to the power poles of Barrie Public Utilities.

Section 43(5) delegates such authority to the CRTC where a provider of public services is refused access to "the supporting structure of a transmission line" constructed on public property. On the basis of this wording, the CRTC decided that it had authority over the utility's poles. The CRTC relied on the telecommunications policies contained in the *Telecommunications Act* and the broadcasting policy contained in the *Broadcasting Act* to interpret the section and concluded that "transmission line" included lines used to distribute electricity.

The case was appealed and eventually heard by the Supreme Court of Canada.

Result

The Supreme Court disagreed with the CRTC's interpretation of section 43(5) for many reasons. It held that the phrase "constructed on a highway or other public place" qualified the phrase "transmission line," and therefore the CRTC did not have jurisdiction over transmission lines on private property. Also, section 43(5) referred to "transmission lines," not "distribution lines," and because the utilities' power poles supported distribution lines, the CRTC did not have jurisdiction.

The Supreme Court also objected to the CRTC's heavy reliance on the policy objectives of the *Telecommunications Act* and the *Broadcasting Act*. While consideration of policy and legislative objectives is a legitimate approach to statutory interpretation, the CRTC wrongly used policy objectives to override the plain meaning of the statutory provisions.

Business Lesson

Government policies may be useful tools for filling in the gaps left by vague statutory provisions. However, they sometimes conflict with a strict reading of the statute. When this happens, it is the statute that prevails. Seek legal advice if you are uncertain about the meaning of a section or about whether to rely on a government policy, and if getting it wrong could have a significant consequence to your business.

Constitutional Interpretation and Protection of Rights and Freedoms

The Constitution, like other legislation, must be applied to many different situations. It is the role of the courts to determine how to interpret and apply it. This can be a particularly weighty responsibility. Unlike ordinary legislation, which can always be changed and clarified if the government is dissatisfied with how the courts are interpreting and applying it, the Constitution is not so easily amended. A Supreme Court of Canada ruling on the interpretation of a particular section of the Constitution is generally the final word on the matter.

Constitutional decisions usually involve resolutions of disputes about the powers of the federal and provincial governments and interpretations of the *Canadian Charter of Rights and Freedoms*. As we discussed in Chapter 1, the creation of the Charter greatly expanded the role of Canadian courts by giving them the power to strike down laws that violate rights and freedoms such as equality, freedom of expression, and freedom of religion. Pursuant to the Charter, the courts are responsible for safeguarding the rights and liberties of individuals against unlawful encroachments by the state. This responsibility sometimes pits courts against the state on issues that are often considered political and controversial.

Review of Government Agencies

As we observed in Chapter 1 under the heading "Administrative Law," administrative boards and tribunals now resolve many disputes that arise in the course of doing business. The statutes that establish these adjudicative agencies of government often have provisions that exclude interference from courts. However, the courts have maintained their power to review the decisions of these agencies to ensure that they act fairly and do not make major legal errors in deciding cases.

Courts generally defer to the expertise of specialized government agencies and do not interfere unless the agency makes a clear and obvious error. For example, if the Ontario Labour Relations Board, after listening to both union and management representatives, comes to the conclusion that an employer has engaged in an unfair labour practice, a court will generally not interfere. The board is clearly using its expertise in considering subject matter with which it deals every day. If, however, the board comes to its conclusion without hearing from both parties or without considering a matter that is of vital importance to the issue before it, a court may order a re-hearing and a new decision.

Litigation

Litigation in a Superior Court is costly and time-consuming, particularly if the case is complex and the parties are entrenched in their positions and not disposed to settle at an early stage. A lawsuit can easily take two years or more from start to finish. The costs can run from several thousand dollars to well over $100,000, depending on the complexity of the case. In addition to paying your own legal costs, you may have to pay between one-third and two-thirds of your opponent's legal costs if you lose. The idea behind this rule is to make you think twice before launching or defending a weak or dubious case, and to encourage you to settle your differences rather than litigate. Should you decide to litigate, however, you will need to be aware of the many steps involved.

www.emond.ca/CBL3/links

DIG DEEPER
The Court Services section of the Attorney General's website provides an introduction to civil legal actions in the Superior Court.

The Pre-Litigation Process

A lawsuit begins long before a case arrives at the doorstep of a courthouse for trial. As in the case of some ADR procedures, such as arbitration, a court proceeding usually requires a party to find a lawyer. We discussed this matter at the beginning of this chapter under the heading "Lawyers."

Consulting the Lawyer

The client will meet with the lawyer to give them the factual details of the case and provide documents, such as invoices, memos, and emails. On the basis of this information, the lawyer will advise the client about the pros and cons of proceeding with a lawsuit. On the basis of this advice, the lawyer will ask the client for instructions to proceed.

When you consult a lawyer about a problem, negotiations will often take place to try to settle the dispute without going to court. The parties, through their lawyers and on their lawyers' advice, may exchange written or oral communications where they state their views and make offers to settle that might imply admissions of liability or acknowledgment of damage. To encourage parties to have frank discussions that might lead to settlement, lawyers are permitted to make offers or statements on a **without prejudice** basis, indicated verbally or in writing at the top of any written communication. If something is stated on a without prejudice basis, it means that the matter cannot be referred to or disclosed to the court if the case does not settle.

Val-Nam may be able to quickly settle its dispute with Kaya Sun if an appropriate settlement offer is made early on. However, Val-Nam will not want Kaya to file the settlement offer as evidence in any later court case, should the issue not be resolved. Val-Nam will not want it to appear that it was admitting some degree of liability for her injuries. Sending a settlement offer to Kaya on a "without prejudice" basis allows Val-Nam to try to settle early without compromising its ability to defend itself should the case go to court.

without prejudice
stipulation indicating that statements made either orally or in writing may not be disclosed to the court if attempts at settlement are unsuccessful

limitation period
time period in which a lawsuit must be commenced, after which the right to sue is lost

Avoiding Delay: Limitation Periods

Procedural rules establish that lawsuits must be brought within a certain period of time. However, the law has also established **limitation periods**, that is, time periods during within which lawsuits must be brought. To establish whether a limitation period has expired, the client and the client's lawyer must determine when the client's right to sue the defendant first arose. If the client is suing in Ontario, for example, the *Limitations Act, 2002* gives the client two years from the time it first had a reason for suing the defendant to start its lawsuit. Obtaining legal advice early is recommended so that a legal professional can inform the client on the limitation period that applies in a given situation. If a lawsuit is not commenced before the expiration of the limitation period, the right to sue can be lost.

Limitation periods also have some relevance for arbitrations. Some arbitration clauses provide that a proceeding must be started within a specific time period and may not be arbitrated if the specified time has elapsed.

Selecting Court Jurisdiction for Lawsuits

- The Superior Court (Trial Division) has monetary jurisdiction for any amount. It has the power to award compensation in the form of money and also to make a variety of other orders. For example, it can grant injunctions ordering parties to behave or to refrain from behaving in certain ways. The court's powers to grant remedies is discussed in more detail later in this chapter.
- If an individual is suing for less than $25,000, the person may wish to do so in the Small Claims Court if seeking *only* monetary compensation or the return of personal property worth $25,000 or less.
- If an individual is suing for less than $25,000 but is also seeking remedies *other than monetary compensation* (for example, because the person wishes to obtain an injunction to stop the defendant from doing something), then it is necessary to sue in the Superior Court, as this court has very broad powers to grant remedies above and beyond the payment of money. The Small Claims Court's powers are much more limited.
- If an individual is suing for an amount between $25,000 and $100,000, it is wise to sue in the Superior Court using a simplified civil procedure that limits

some of the time-consuming and expensive pre-trial steps. The procedure also simplifies the trial process, thereby reducing the cost and delay for the parties so that the lawsuit is not overly costly given the amount of the claim.

- If an individual is suing for over $100,000, then it is necessary to sue in the Superior Court using the ordinary civil process.

The Litigation Process in Superior Court (Trial Division)

If the client is suing in the Superior Court (Trial Division), the client must follow the multi-step process set out in the Ontario *Rules of Civil Procedure*. The most important of these steps are set out in the following sections. In our fact scenario, Val-Nam may decide to sue WeSolve in the trial division of the Superior Court if the losses it incurred from the non-delivery of the prototype exceeded $25,000; similarly, Val-Nam may be forced to defend an action in the trial division of the Superior Court if Kaya's medical expenses exceed $25,000.

Exchange of Pleadings

statement of claim
court document notifying a defendant of a lawsuit against him or her and the reasons for the proceedings

statement of defence
court document notifying the plaintiff in a lawsuit that the defendant is denying the claim and identifying the defendant's arguments

Once the plaintiff's lawyer has reviewed the facts and researched the law, the lawyer prepares a **statement of claim**, which is brought to a court office or filed electronically. The lawyer pays a fee, and the court officially starts the process. The statement of claim is served on (delivered to) the defendant. The statement of claim tells the defendant that they are being sued and gives the reasons for the lawsuit. The defendant then has a short period of time to file a **statement of defence**. If the defendant fails to act in time, the plaintiff is entitled to judgment by default, which brings an early end to the lawsuit. However, defendants usually file statements of defence. At this point, the legal position of the parties has been set out, as have the basic facts on which they rely. The exchange of the statement of claim and the statement of defence usually completes the pleadings stage of procedure.

Discovery

discovery
procedure after exchange of pleadings where both parties disclose all information, including producing documents, relevant to the case

Once the plaintiff and defendant have exchanged pleadings, they each have an outline of the facts and legal rules or principles on which the other relies. They are now entitled to find out more details about the evidence against them through a process called discovery. **Discovery** requires that each party disclose and produce all relevant documents, except for those that they no longer have in their possession, power, or control and cannot produce or that are privileged. Both parties must appear at an examination for discovery to answer questions about the case posed by the opposing lawyer. As the production of documents may involve the production of masses of electronic data and files, discovery can be very time-consuming and complicated. The parties largely run the discovery process themselves, following the *Rules of Civil Procedure*. No judge is present.

Preparation for Trial

At the conclusion of the discovery process, the parties will usually attend a pre-trial conference, where a judge reviews the case, explores options for settlement with the parties, and tries to narrow the issues and facts in dispute to shorten the trial. Many parties settle their dispute at this stage. If they do not settle, they summon witnesses, prepare their evidence, and get ready for trial.

Trial

Most trials take a day or two, but a complex one with many witnesses may take months. Because of the challenges in scheduling lawyers, parties, witnesses, and judges, a trial lasting several days may be spread over many months. It begins with the lawyers for each party making opening statements, in which they present the judge with their version of what the case is about. The plaintiff's lawyer examines, or questions, its witnesses first. By examining the plaintiff's witnesses, the plaintiff's lawyer is presenting the judge with the evidence necessary to win the case. The defendant's lawyer will then cross-examine these witnesses in an effort to discredit their evidence. When the plaintiff has finished presenting its case, the defendant will call and examine its witnesses, and the plaintiff's lawyer will then cross-examine them. At the end, each lawyer will present an oral summary to the judge.

In a civil (non-criminal) case, the plaintiff bears the **burden of proof**. This means that the plaintiff's lawyer must convince the judge on a **balance of probabilities** that the plaintiff's version of facts and law has more merit than the defendant's version. If the plaintiff is only able to establish that its version of facts and law is equally meritorious as the defendant's, the plaintiff loses the lawsuit.

burden of proof
requirement that a certain party prove a particular fact at trial

balance of probabilities
standard of proof in civil (as opposed to criminal) law indicating that one version of events is more probable than another

After hearing all the evidence and arguments of the parties' lawyers, the judge—if sitting without a jury—gives judgment. Jury trials in civil cases are rare in Canada. If there is a jury, however, it is the jury's job to sift through the evidence to draw factual conclusions. The judge then instructs the jury on how to apply the law to its factual conclusions. After deliberating in secret, the jury renders its verdict.

The Litigation Process in the Small Claims Court

If a claim is relatively small—under $25,000 in Ontario (the amount is expected to rise to $50,000 in 2018)—the plaintiff may choose to take the case to the Small Claims Court. This court is designed to provide a forum where small claims can be heard quickly, efficiently, and inexpensively. Plaintiffs and defendants can conduct their cases themselves, without being represented by lawyers. The Small Claims Court also permits paralegal agents to represent parties in court, providing a presumably less expensive alternative to lawyers.

CASE IN POINT

Can I Get the Remedy I Need from the Small Claims Court?

936464 Ontario Ltd (cob as Plumbhouse Plumbing & Heating) v Mungo Bear Ltd, 2003 OJ 3795 (QL) (Sup Ct J)

Facts

936464 sued Mungo Bear for an unpaid account. 936464 had given Mungo an estimate to repair a boiler. The estimated price was $30,000. 936464 rendered an invoice for $30,000 on the contract, which was paid. It then also invoiced Mungo for $14,500 for extras that were connected to the performance of the contract that was paid. This invoice was not paid and was the subject of a breach of contract action in the Small Claims Court. The trial judge noted that there was no formal contract that could be recognized at common law. Nonetheless, she awarded damages of $10,000 on the equitable principle of *quantum meruit*, which provides that work actually done must be paid for even where there is no formal contract. Here, the work was done and the account was not challenged in any way. Mungo claimed that the court did not have jurisdiction to award damages based on *quantum meruit*, which is an equitable form of relief. Mungo also argued that the judge had improperly awarded damages since 936464 did not raise *quantum meruit* as a basis for the claim.

Result

The appeal was dismissed. As part of the Superior Court, the Small Claims Court could consider and apply equitable principles, such as *quantum meruit*, as part of the exercise of its jurisdiction to hear and decide cases. However, statute law clearly barred the court from doing more than ordering the payment of money or the return of goods that did not exceed its monetary jurisdiction of $10,000 (now $25,000). Thus, it could not invoke equitable remedies such as injunctions.

The court also held that it did not matter if the plaintiff formally included the *quantum meruit* claim in its case. The claim was clear, and the court was not going to require a party to meet the higher procedural requirements of the Superior Court, as these would be unworkable in the Small Claims Court where litigants were usually unrepresented.

Business Lesson

While the Small Claims Court is fast and inexpensive to use, it does not have the range of power of the Superior Court. If the plaintiff wants a remedy like an injunction that goes beyond the payment of money, it may not be able to use the Small Claims Court and may instead have to sue in the Superior Court, which is slower and more expensive.

Because parties often represent themselves, judges tend to intervene in the process more frequently than they do in the Superior Court to assist and guide parties in presenting their cases. The procedure in this court is based on that of the trial division of the Superior Court, but is much simpler in form and operation.

- Let us suppose that the claim against the defendant was for only $20,000 (that is, within the limit of the Small Claims Court's monetary jurisdiction), so that the plaintiff would sue in the Small Claims Court instead of the Superior Court. The plaintiff's lawsuit would begin when a claim is filed and served on the defendant. If the defendant intends to defend the case, it files a defence within the time allowed. If the defendant fails to file a defence, the plaintiff may obtain a default judgment.
- There is no discovery process; if there are relevant documents, parties attach them to the claim and defence, respectively, and file them with the court. In most instances, the case proceeds to a settlement conference, where the parties are encouraged to settle, and if there is no settlement, the case goes on to trial.
- Court forms are relatively easy to use, requiring a party to simply follow instructions and fill in the blanks rather than to engage in complicated legal drafting, which would require a lawyer's skills.
- The rules about what may be used as evidence are less complicated, less formal, and less restrictive than in the Superior Court.
- Judgments are enforced in the Small Claims Court in the same way that they are in the Superior Court.

The Small Claims Court is a high-volume court, with many cases involving debt collections for relatively small amounts of money, such as unpaid phone, gas, or credit card bills. However, commercial parties often use this court to resolve disputes that can be quite complex, legally, even though large amounts of money are not involved.

MINIMIZING YOUR RISK

Litigate Only When Necessary

- Choose the Small Claims Court over the Superior Court if your claim qualifies.
- Consult a lawyer, or a paralegal, or take other action to advance your claim as quickly as possible to avoid missing a limitation period.
- Seek representation from a lawyer who specializes in litigation if your case must be heard in the Superior Court.

Civil Court Remedies: Damages

Once a plaintiff has proven that a defendant is liable to rectify the harm done to the plaintiff, the goal of the law is to provide a suitable remedy. By fashioning a remedy, a court seeks, as far as is practicable, to put the plaintiff back into the position in which it was before the defendant caused the harm the law recognizes.

Remedies take a variety of forms. By far, the most common remedy is damages, which we discuss in the following sections.

Damages

Damages awards have two main purposes. The primary purpose is to compensate the victim/plaintiff for past and future losses caused by the defendant. But **damages** may also be used to punish the defendant for inappropriate behaviour, although this is done only in cases where the defendant's conduct has been exceptionally outrageous. The "compensatory" elements of a damage award are divided into three categories of damages: special, general, and aggravated damages. **Special damages** are awarded to compensate the plaintiff for specific, precise, easily calculated pre-trial losses. They are well defined and easily expressed in terms of money because the losses have already occurred and the exact amounts involved are known. **General damages** compensate the plaintiff for losses that are more subjective and cannot be precisely calculated. They include pecuniary losses (future care costs and loss of earning capacity) that represent monetary losses and non-pecuniary losses like pain and suffering or loss of expectation of life that are not based on actual, specific monetary losses and are therefore harder to quantify. **Aggravated damages** also compensate the plaintiff for non-pecuniary losses. They cover further harm to the plaintiff's reputation or well-being caused by the outrageous nature of the defendant's conduct.

More rarely, conduct that is outrageous may also attract sanction through punitive damages. Punitive damages are not awarded to compensate the plaintiff for any past or future harm but are meant to punish the defendant and deter others from behaving in the same manner. They are only awarded in situations where the defendant's conduct was intolerable or outrageous in the circumstances.

Providing the evidence to substantiate a damage award can be costly and time-consuming. Business people negotiating a contract can proactively address this issue by including a liquidated damages clause in the contract. See Chapter 4 for more on liquidated damages.

damages
losses suffered as a result of the commission of a tort or the breach of a contract, or monetary compensation awarded for these losses

special damages
pecuniary damages that have already been incurred and that can be precisely measured (out-of-pocket losses)

general damages
pecuniary damages for pain, suffering, and future economic loss, including future loss of life expectancy or quality of life

aggravated damages
a subcategory of non-pecuniary damages awarded for intangible harm, such as harm to reputation or humiliation

Non-Pecuniary Damages

Non-pecuniary damages attempt to address losses not based on money. They are more difficult to quantify than **pecuniary damages**. For example, how should a court award compensation for the loss of a limb, damage to a reputation, or lingering debilitating pain? Since it is impossible to return a severed limb or to erase pain and suffering, a court must determine a fair dollar figure to award instead.

Awards for non-pecuniary losses are, of necessity, somewhat arbitrary. To promote consistency in the administration of justice, courts refer to the awards that other courts have made in cases involving similar suffering. In general, awards for non-pecuniary damages tend to be much higher in the United States than in Canada, although awards in Canada have increased significantly since approximately 1980.

Aggravated damages are a subcategory of non-pecuniary damages. They are typically used in two categories of cases. The first includes cases that involve

non-pecuniary damages
damages that cannot be readily quantified in financial terms

pecuniary damages
damages that are actual monetary losses

intangible harm, such as damage to reputation or humiliation. If, for example, a competitor defames your business in a particularly high-handed way, you may claim aggravated damages. Second, aggravated damages may be awarded to reflect that the defendant's actions deviated so seriously from the required standard of care that the harm suffered by the plaintiff was more serious than that which would flow from "ordinary" negligence. For example, in a medical negligence case based on post-operative infection, the failure to prescribe post-operative antibiotics as a preventative measure might be "ordinary" negligence; whereas performing plastic surgery in a clinic where treatment rooms are not kept sterile and instruments are not cleaned between procedures might be deemed to be a departure from the standard of care so extreme as to warrant aggravated damages.

punitive damages sum added to a damage award that is intended to punish a defendant and discourage similar behaviour by others where the behaviour is particularly outrageous

Another subcategory of non-pecuniary damages is **punitive damages**. While aggravated damages are designed to compensate a plaintiff for loss, punitive damages are designed to punish a defendant and to discourage similar behaviour by others where the behaviour is particularly outrageous.

A strip search of a suspected shoplifter by an employee of a retail business would probably justify an award of punitive damages. The case of *Whiten v Pilot Insurance Co* provides another example of conduct sufficiently outrageous to attract punitive damages.

Mitigation of Damages

Plaintiffs are expected to mitigate—or minimize—their damages. For example, after Kaya is burned when moving the generator she purchased from Val-Nam, she is expected to seek appropriate medical treatment to avoid infection and complications. Where a plaintiff fails to make reasonable efforts to minimize their losses, and the result is a more serious loss, such as amputation of a finger due to an infection acquired after sustaining a burn, their compensation may be limited. We discuss the topic of mitigation more fully in Chapter 5 under the heading "Duty to Mitigate Damages."

CASE IN POINT

Punitive Damages: A Million-Dollar Message

Whiten v Pilot Insurance Co, 2002 SCC 18, [2002] 1 SCR 595

Facts

On a freezing night in January, the plaintiff discovered a fire in the addition attached to her house. The family fled, in pajamas, into the night. The father suffered frostbite serious enough to place him in hospital. The house burned to the ground, and the family lost three cats, some valuable antiques, and many items of sentimental value.

The family, who were suffering serious financial difficulties at the time, moved into a winterized cottage and received an initial $5,000 living expenses payment from the defendant insurance company. After a few months, the insurer stopped paying the rent on the cottage and began an aggressive campaign to challenge the family's insurance claim.

The company forced the family to trial in an effort to deny the claim. The insurer alleged arson, despite the fact that none of the many investigators who had examined the fire scene found any evidence that the fire was deliberately set. The family had to pay $320,000 in legal fees to recover the $345,000 in insurance money that was owed to them. By the time the case reached the Court of Appeal, the insurer had conceded that there was no basis for its arson allegations.

Result

At trial, the jury found that the insurer was required to pay the insurance claim. It also made a $1 million punitive damages award against the insurer.

The Supreme Court of Canada affirmed the jury's award of $1 million in punitive damages. The court stated that punitive damages are "imposed only if there has been high-handed, malicious, arbitrary, or highly reprehensible misconduct that departs to a marked degree from ordinary standards of decent behaviour."

Business Lesson

Ensure that your conduct always meets or exceeds the ordinary standards of decent behaviour.

Other Remedies

Injunctions are a remedy designed to prevent future harm or the escalation/worsening of present harm by prohibiting a party from engaging in certain conduct, or by ordering the party to cease conduct already begun. Injunctions are commonly ordered in cases of passing off. A plaintiff that has discovered a defendant is passing off its wares as those of the plaintiff will often immediately seek an injunction that prevents the defendant from selling those goods to avoid further damage to the reputation of the plaintiff's goods and to its business.

injunction
court order requiring a party to discontinue an action or prohibiting a party from taking a proposed action

An order for **specific performance** may be made where the plaintiff alleges that the defendant breached a contract and caused damage, and where the result of the breach is a consequence not readily compensated for by the payment of money. For example, if you wished to buy a piece of land on which to build a hotel and the property has a spectacular view that could not be duplicated, which was essential to your business plan, if the seller breached the contract, the court might grant an order for specific performance requiring the vendor who refuses to complete the sale to actually perform its contractual obligations by completing the property sale rather than simply paying damages for failing to complete the sale.

specific performance
requirement by a court that a party complete its obligations under a contract

Legal Costs

In addition to any claims for remedies, parties in a civil suit ask for legal costs as part of their pleadings. This is a request that the other party pay for the legal costs associated with the litigation. Many people choose to represent themselves in Small Claims Court matters but there are still costs incurred in the process. Although parties do have the option to represent themselves in higher courts, lawyers are often essential. Whether self-represented or represented by counsel, a successful party is usually entitled to an award of costs, although a cost award is generally higher for a party represented by a legal professional. Judges review a claim for costs following the trial of the matter to determine whether a judgment should include an award of costs to the successful party. The amount of legal costs a party may be ordered to pay is determined by guidelines established in each province. The calculation of costs using the guidelines does not normally cover the full extent of the costs of the lawsuit. As a result, even successful parties to a lawsuit will not recover all of their costs. Even with an award for costs, successful litigants may end up paying one-third to one-half of their legal expenses. The costs associated with litigation need to be considered as part of the decision to initiate a lawsuit in the first place. In cases to recoup payment, for instance, some creditors may decide to write off the debt rather than incur the costs of the action, particularly where the amount of the judgment is likely to be low relative to the costs likely to be incurred in obtaining it.

www.emond.ca/CBL3/links

DIG DEEPER

The Attorney General's website provides past and current pre- and postjudgment interest rates.

Post-Trial Enforcement

As noted in the previous section discussing remedies, in most business cases, the court awards monetary damages for the wrongful actions of the defendant. The judge will also award the plaintiff pre- and postjudgment interest. Generally, a winning plaintiff is entitled to prejudgment interest on the amount of monetary damages awarded, from the time the right to sue arose until judgment, and then postjudgment interest, from judgment until payment. If the parties had agreed to an interest rate in a contract or otherwise, the court will usually use that rate. If not, the court will use pre- and postjudgment interest rates set by statute. These statutory rates reflect actual market rates. The purpose of including pre- and postjudgment interest is to compensate a plaintiff for monetary loss if payment is not made for a long time. If, for example, you were owed $120,000 and went without payment for several years, it would be reasonable to receive interest to compensate you for the loss of opportunity to have and use the money owed to you.

If the defendant refuses to pay the judgment award voluntarily, the plaintiff must bring further proceedings to enforce its judgment, the most common of which are set out below:

- *Judgment debtor examination.* The plaintiff can require a defendant, if an individual, or a representative of the defendant, if it is a company, to appear before a court or at a court reporter's office to answer questions about its assets, debts, and ability to pay.
- *Writ of seizure and sale.* The plaintiff can obtain a document from the court (also called a writ of execution) and file it with the sheriff. This writ enables the sheriff to seize property belonging to the defendant and sell it at public auction. The proceeds of the sale (minus the costs of conducting it) are then available to the plaintiff to pay the judgment.
- *Garnishment.* If a third party, such as a customer of the defendant, owes money to the defendant, the plaintiff can obtain a garnishment order, which requires the third party to pay the money it owes the defendant into court so it is available to the plaintiff.

SCENARIO

Considerations Before Enforcing a Judgment

Val-Nam commenced an action in Small Claims Court against Dubious Distributors for payment of the purchase price for the 100 generators (plus accrued interest). Dubious Distributors did not file a defence within the set timeframe. Val-Nam obtained default judgment in the amount of $7,598 plus postjudgment interest. Dubious Distributors has not paid the judgment. What should Val-Nam do?

- Find out if Dubious Distributors has any assets by conducting a judgment debtor examination and conducting asset searches (discussed in detail in Chapter 8).
- If Dubious Distributors owns assets (for example, inventory, computer equipment, vehicles) that could satisfy the judgment, consider filing a writ of seizure and sale, but
  - recognize that additional costs are involved in seizing and selling the assets, which must be paid before Val-Nam will receive any proceeds; and
  - be aware that, if other creditors have filed writs of seizure and sale, they will be entitled to a portion of the proceeds of any sale as well. This may significantly reduce the amount of money that Val-Nam can recover.

- If individuals or businesses owe Dubious Distributors money, consider filing a Notice of Garnishment with the relevant court. For example:
  - If Dubious Distributors is owed money by its customers, a garnishment order can direct the customers to pay the amount owed into court until Val-Nam is paid in full.
  - If Dubious Distributors has licensed its intellectual property to a third party, a garnishment order can direct the third party to pay the licence fees into court until Val-Nam is paid in full.
- However, if the judgment debtor examination and searches reveal that Dubious Distributors doesn't have the assets or funds to pay the judgment (or it would cost too much to enforce), it may make business sense for Val-Nam to simply walk away and leave the judgment unpaid.

Alternatives to Litigation

While courts and tribunals provide structures to resolve legal conflicts and settle issues, there are alternatives to going to court.

For some time now, the people involved in the administration of justice in Canada have been concerned about the costs of, and delays in, taking cases to court. Experienced business people are also aware of the difficulties presented by lawsuits, in addition to the high cost of hiring lawyers. Issues that lie at the heart of a dispute—and that are most in need of peaceful, efficient, and lasting resolution—can often become lost in the procedural delays and complexity of litigation.

Business people have therefore sought out dispute resolution techniques that are cheaper, quicker, simpler, less formal, and less adversarial than those provided in Canada's court system. As we have mentioned, contemporary methods of dispute resolution fall within three main approaches: negotiation, mediation, and arbitration.

Interests and Rights

In the sections that follow, we use the terms "interests" and "rights." Interests are short- and long-term business goals as well as business concerns, priorities, and aspirations. In general, interests tend to be subjective—that is, particular to individual businesses and business people. For example, where one business might place a high priority on expansion when the market for its product is hot, another might be equally concerned about limiting its operations to a level that is manageable for its existing staff. Interests are flexible: they change over time and evolve as a business evolves.

Rights, on the other hand, are entitlements. Although subject to change, they are much less flexible than interests. Rights are objective, rather than subjective—that is, they are identified through rational analysis or by reference to some authority. They include privileges enjoyed by individuals and businesses as a result of laws, agreements, policies, and practices. For example, the entitlement of workers to a safe workplace is a right under the *Workplace Safety and Insurance Act, 1997*. The various entitlements that business people have negotiated and incorporated into binding contracts are rights under the common law of contract. Freedom of assembly is a right under the *Canadian Charter of Rights and Freedoms*.

Dispute resolution usually focuses on either interests or rights. Often, a focus on rights tends to be simpler than a focus on interests. Though subject to interpretation, rights can usually be determined by reference to a law or to another authority. Dispute resolution that involves interests, however, broadens the field of discussion. Consideration of such matters as a business person's hopes, fears, and plans for the future of their business can require different—and often more subtle—skills than a logical analysis of rights.

In the following sections, we examine negotiation, mediation, and arbitration as vehicles for settling both interest- and rights-based conflicts.

1. For each of Val-Nam's disputes, identify the interests that Val-Nam should protect.
2. For each of Val-Nam's disputes, identify the rights that Val-Nam is entitled to.
3. For each of Val-Nam's disputes, consider whether Val-Nam should focus on its interests or its rights when seeking to resolve the dispute.

Negotiation

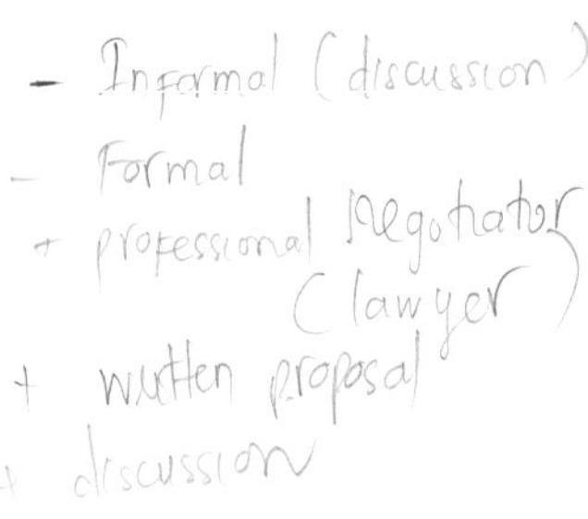

Negotiation is a process in which parties interact in an attempt to reach an agreement about their respective rights or interests. It can be extremely informal, involving a discussion over a cup of coffee. It can also be relatively formal, involving professional negotiators—often lawyers—with a written agenda, formal exchange of written proposals, and a formal discussion of the respective positions of the parties. As noted earlier in this chapter, when parties speak to their own lawyers in the context of potential litigation, the content of their discussions is subject to solicitor–client privilege. This means that the lawyer may not reveal anything that has been said without the client's consent. If, however, a client makes a comment to a non-lawyer who is assisting them with negotiations, the comment is not privileged. The non-lawyer might be forced to reveal the comment made by the client in a subsequent legal proceeding. It is therefore important that a client take extreme care when making comments to non-lawyers.

The key feature that distinguishes negotiation from other forms of dispute resolution is that the parties control the process themselves. There is no third-party intervenor with authority to influence or settle the dispute, to referee the discussion, or to set the rules for holding it. This means that the parties are totally responsible for what occurs and must exercise more self-control and discipline than would be the case in mediation or arbitration.

When and When Not to Choose Negotiation

Negotiation is a useful tool in the following circumstances:

1. *You are establishing rules for resolving potential conflicts, but no actual conflict exists*. For example, assume that you are negotiating a contract with a parts supplier for your computer-servicing business. Both you and the parts supplier see the potential for an enjoyable and profitable long-term business relationship. It is wise to consider matters that could cause conflict between you while you still have a good relationship. Negotiate ground rules

that will govern any future problems, such as late deliveries or late payments. This may involve the inclusion of an arbitration clause, as discussed in Chapter 4 under the heading "Reading the Fine Print: Typical Terms in Business Contracts."

2. *You and the other party are interested in advancing each other's business interests as well as your own and are willing to seek win–win solutions.* For example, your computer-servicing business might experience a temporary cash-flow problem because of an overdue customer account. As a result, your business might be unable to pay its bills on time, including payment owed to the parts supplier. It is not likely in the parts supplier's interest to exercise its legal rights by repossessing parts or petitioning your business into bankruptcy. The parts supplier's interests are more likely to be served when your business is operating successfully. By negotiating with you to allow additional time to pay your bill, the parts supplier can support this shared goal.

Negotiation should be avoided in the following circumstances:

1. *The power balance is tipped unevenly, and you are the weaker party.* There can be any number of reasons why one party has less bargaining power than the other. For example, in a vendor–purchaser relationship, the vendor may have only a few purchasers for its goods, while the purchaser may have many vendors to choose from. This makes the vendor dependent on the purchaser and places the purchaser in a superior bargaining position. Whatever the reason for the power imbalance, the weaker party is likely to suffer in the negotiation process, particularly in a positional negotiation where the stronger party is prepared to take advantage of their power position.
2. *Your concern about maintaining a business relationship with the other party greatly exceeds the other party's concern about maintaining a business relationship with you.* Where one party is concerned with maintaining a relationship and the other is less concerned, negotiation is often not very useful. In these cases, the party that values the business relationship more is likely to make too many concessions at the negotiating table. The result is an agreement that favours one party at the expense of the other, not something that will be good for the relationship in the long run.

SCENARIO

A negotiated solution may be a good fit for the dispute between Val-Nam and WeSolve, based on the factors identified above:

- Although a conflict already exists, Val-Nam and WeSolve are early on in their relationship and both will significantly benefit from a continued development of the relationship. Negotiation can be used as an opportunity to further clarify their relationship.
- Both parties are better off if they are able to continue their relationship.
- There do not appear to be any significant imbalances in power or in the value that each party attaches to the relationship.

A negotiated solution may not be a good fit for the dispute between Val-Nam and Dubious Distributors, from Val-Nam's perspective, for the following reasons:

- Dubious Distributors' obligation to pay is a clear legal requirement, so Val-Nam may not feel there is a need or justification for accepting anything other than full payment.
- Val-Nam's interest in maintaining a relationship with a small purchaser that does not pay bills in a timely manner is unlikely to be high.
- Val-Nam may want to "send a message" that it deals quickly with delinquent accounts so other purchasers take their payment obligations seriously.

In addition to the concerns related to resolving the dispute, Val-Nam must be aware of how the form of dispute resolution it chooses will reflect back on it. Consider how consumers might view hard-fought litigation in Val-Nam and Kaya's dispute, regardless of whether Val-Nam is actually at fault for her injuries.

MINIMIZING YOUR RISK

Use Negotiation Wisely

- Develop negotiation skills and use them before disputes arise in your business dealings.
- Be creative in seeking win–win solutions for yourself and the other party.
- In the event of a dispute, be cautious about choosing negotiation if your position is weaker than that of the other party.
- Remember that any communication you have with a non-lawyer might later be subject to disclosure.

Enforcing a Negotiated Settlement

A negotiated settlement is a contract and may be enforced in court like any other contract. Failure to comply with the terms of the negotiated settlement is a breach of contract. We discuss these matters in Chapter 5 under the headings "Consequences of a Breach of Contract" and "Damages."

Mediation

Mediation is a dispute-resolving process in which the parties to the dispute invite a neutral individual—a mediator—to supervise or oversee their negotiations. Mediators often set rules about how the parties are to interact with each other, schedule meetings, and set the agenda for meetings. They may try to persuade the parties to move from a win–lose process toward a win–win process. Mediators may choose to bring the parties together in face-to-face negotiations or may place the parties in separate rooms and shuttle back and forth between them. It is the job of the mediator to ensure that all parties necessary in resolving a dispute are present, including experts, if required.

Types and styles of mediation vary widely, and you should do some research before choosing a mediator. It is important that the mediator's style and approach meet your needs.

CASE IN POINT

Mediation: Do We Have To?

IBM Canada Ltd v Kossovan, 2011 ABQB 621

Facts

One defendant was an IBM employee who, with a non-employee posing as an outside contractor, pretended to perform contract work that was billed to IBM and for which IBM paid. No work was actually done. IBM sued the defendants for fraud. IBM was determined to go to trial to obtain judgment. It had a strong case based on law, was keen to proceed to trial, and had no interest in mediating. It regarded compulsory and mandatory mediation as a waste of time. It brought an application for an order permitting it to bypass the mandatory mediation process.

Result

IBM's application was dismissed. The court held that the mandatory mediation rule was designed to ensure that all parties were exposed to the benefits of alternative dispute resolution. A waiver or bypassing of the procedure should only be granted for the most compelling reasons. In this case, a power imbalance between the parties that would make the process inappropriate did not exist. IBM's allegations of fraud were based on relatively simple facts, and certain admissions had already been made. While IBM was taking a strong position, its willingness to accept less than full payment left some room for flexibility. The result of a trial was never certain. In addition, a settlement might not require much compromise of IBM's position, and a consent judgment resulting from a mediation process was as enforceable as one made after a trial. The court also noted that good-faith commitment to the process could shorten the trial time, even if a mediated settlement were not reached.

Business Lesson

While mediation works best when it is voluntary, a business involved in a lawsuit will likely have to attempt mediation even where it would not choose to do so, as mandatory mediation has become a feature of the civil court process across Canada.

Facilitative Mediation

Facilitative mediation is appropriate when the parties to the dispute already have a strong and trusting relationship. The facilitative mediator's role is to assist the parties in communicating effectively by helping them to define and obtain the information they need to resolve their problem. This may involve facilitating brainstorming and proposing mutually beneficial exchanges. A facilitative mediator relies on the parties' mutual desire to maintain or improve their relationship while assisting them in solving whatever problem has caused the dispute. Facilitative mediation is usually interest- rather than rights-based.

Rights-Based Mediation

A typical rights-based mediator assesses which of the parties has the stronger position by determining which party's rights are most strongly supported by law. The mediator then attempts to persuade the parties to settle on that basis. Consider a claim for wrongful dismissal by an employee who was fired without legal justification or compensation. A rights-based mediation would seek a negotiated settlement that is logically connected to the rights of the parties. Using legal rules—in this case, the common law rules related to justification and compensation—the mediator would assist the parties in looking realistically at how a court would resolve their case for the purpose of promoting a settlement.

Rights-based mediation does not require a cooperative attitude between the parties. Because of its adversarial nature, it is best suited to situations where the parties do not have a close relationship and are not interested in fostering a long-term relationship. Interests tend to be ignored in this process.

Transformative Mediation

Transformative mediation encourages the parties to understand the positive aspects of their relationship and to appreciate the wisdom of each other's point of view. The mediator's goal is to have the parties see themselves and each other in a different light. From the new perspective they gain through mediation, the parties question and re-examine their own assumptions.

Transformative mediation might be used to resolve a dispute between an expanding business and the community in which it is located. For example, a transformative mediator might attempt to help the business owner understand how disruptive increased traffic and noise are to community life; the mediator would also attempt to help community members understand the business's need to grow and thus generate the revenue necessary to pay rising taxes and higher salaries. Both sides might thereby be "transformed" and able to see each other in a different light. Transformation often increases the parties' respect for each other and can lead to novel solutions to entrenched problems.

For discussion:

1. Consider why transformative mediation may be a better choice for resolving Val-Nam and WeSolve's dispute than rights-based mediation.
2. You have already identified the disputes in which Val-Nam should focus on its rights (rather than interests) when resolving. Consider whether rights-based mediation would be effective in resolving those disputes.

When and When Not to Choose Mediation

Mediation can be a useful technique in the following circumstances:

1. *You and the other party are prepared to make serious efforts to resolve your dispute.* For example, you and a supplier agree on most of the terms of a contract for the supply of material you need to make an innovative communication device. The profit potential for both of you is great, but you are unable to agree on how to determine the price of the material, and you seem to be unable to find a way to break the impasse. Nonetheless, you want to save the contract because the potential benefit to both parties is so great.
2. *You and the other party approach your dispute with a view to exploring your mutual interests and maintaining your business relationship.* For example, you have a serious dispute about the level of service you require from a service provider for your manufacturing equipment. The service provider thinks the level is adequate for the price paid, but you want a quicker response time. The quality of the service provider's work is good, and you are expanding

your business by adding other factories. The situation has great potential for both parties, but you need reassurance that the service provider can handle the increased volume. You would like to continue to use the provider's services if possible, and the service provider is interested in the business expansion that your plans represent for its company.

3. *You and the other party want to settle a rights issue, and your mutual desire to set your own rules exceeds your desire to have a neutral individual settle them for you.* You and your customer are entering into an agreement to cooperate on the joint production of a new product. You are having some problems working out contract details, but both parties realize that the cooperative venture will work best if you both participate in making the rules.

Mediation will not work in certain circumstances:

1. *You or the other party is focused entirely on power or control.* If power or control of a business relationship or a dispute is the chief concern of one or both parties, mediation will probably fail. Why? There will be nothing for the mediator to discuss with either of you, short of one party totally giving in.
2. *One or both parties require a public decision that resolves the dispute and sets a precedent by which future disputes are resolved.* Because mediation is a private process, it will not create a precedent for similar future disputes. Arbitration or litigation may be required.
3. *The legal rights clearly favour one party, and that party sees no reason to compromise.* Consider, for example, a term of a contract that unambiguously gives one party the right to terminate the agreement for any reason on giving the other party 30 days' notice. Mediation will be a fruitless exercise if that party gives the required notice and has no interest in rethinking its position.

Enforcing a Mediated Settlement

When the parties have reached an agreement through a mediator, the mediator will often help them to draft a formal contract. A contract achieved through mediation is the same as any other contract: it is an exchange of promises by the parties. Like any other contract, it is legally binding and can be enforced by the courts if necessary.

MINIMIZING YOUR RISK

Choose Your Mediator Carefully

- Research your choice: consult other business people and your lawyer; check mediator websites and directories.
- Check the credentials of all prospective mediators. Do they have a background where they have used mediation skills? Have they taken mediation courses from a reputable institution, such as a university or law school, that provides comprehensive training? There is no official certifier of mediators.
- If the issues are technical, consider choosing someone with a background in and experience with the issues. For example, someone with engineering training might be able to work more efficiently with you on a product liability dispute.
- Once you have some names, suggest them to the other parties to the mediation. If you cannot agree, consider choosing randomly from an agreed-upon list.

Arbitration

Commercial arbitration is a more formal process than negotiation or mediation. Like mediation, arbitration requires the presence of a neutral individual to oversee and steer the process. Unlike a mediator, however, an arbitrator determines the results of the process by making a binding decision at the end of the arbitration. In this way, an arbitrator's role in an arbitration hearing resembles a judge's role in a trial.

The arbitration process, in many respects, also mirrors the court process: there is a formal procedure for presenting a case and rules of evidence to govern the material that is acceptable for presentation to the arbitrator. These rules are often more relaxed than they are in a court, and the atmosphere at an arbitration hearing is usually much less formal than in court.

Parties often use lawyers to represent them during an arbitration, especially to examine expert witnesses when presenting their cases to the arbitrator. Arbitration begins with one side presenting its case through the evidence of witnesses and relevant documents. The other party cross-examines these witnesses before presenting its own case. At the end, the arbitrator makes a decision on the basis of the evidence presented. The arbitrator's decision is usually binding on the parties and enforceable in the courts if the parties do not voluntarily comply. While courts can intervene through judicial review to overturn an arbitrator's decision, they do so only in very limited circumstances.

fundamental fairness
principle encompassing the right to be heard, the right to hear the case against you, and the right to reply to the case

Most provinces have statutes that govern arbitration. These laws set minimum standards of **fundamental fairness**—the right to be heard, to hear the case against you, and to reply to the case. The statutes also provide mechanisms to enforce arbitration decisions (also called arbitration awards) in the superior courts of the provinces, as if the arbitration awards were court orders.

Arbitration is generally faster and less expensive than adjudication in the courts; however, this is not always the case. For example, proceedings in the Small Claims Court are relatively quick and inexpensive; parties can handle the cases themselves, and there is no arbitrator to pay. Retail sellers of expensive items such as automobiles often include a provision in their sales contracts that requires disputes about the product to be referred to arbitration rather than the courts. We provide a more detailed discussion of arbitration clauses in Chapter 4 under the heading "Arbitration."

When and When Not to Choose Arbitration

In general, arbitration can be useful in the following situations:

1. *You and the other party agree on an arbitration system before a conflict develops.* A preordained arbitration system can be particularly useful if your conflict is likely to concern technical matters that require both expert evidence and knowledgeable adjudicators for a just and speedy resolution. For example, if your conflict concerns whether machinery meets the specifications set out in the contract, an arbitrator with an engineering background could likely resolve the matter more quickly than a judge, who would need more explanatory evidence.
2. *You and the other party are concerned about each other's business interests and about maintaining a good business relationship.* While arbitration is adversarial and somewhat formal, it is less so than litigation. Arbitration may be less destructive to an ongoing relationship than a lawsuit would be, particularly if you had agreed on an arbitration process before your dispute

arose. If you combine arbitration with mediation as a first step, and use goodwill, you may be able to salvage the relationship.

3. *The balance of power between you and the other party is tipped against you.* Because the arbitrator controls the process and decides on the basis of rules after hearing the evidence, arbitration can prevent a more powerful party from using its power to get its way, despite the merits of the case.

Arbitration may be unhelpful in the following circumstances:

1. *The relationship is damaged beyond repair.* The more formal process of litigation might be more useful because there is less direct contact between the parties.
2. *The credibility of the parties or witnesses is an issue.* The court system may be a better place to decide the dispute since the courts have formal rules for controlling witnesses and presenting evidence.
3. *A party may be seeking a remedy or remedies that cannot be granted by arbitrators.* A remedy may be unavailable because of limitations in an arbitration clause or because only courts can grant the remedy being sought. For example, only courts can grant injunctions—that is, orders requiring a party to do or refrain from doing something.

www.emond.ca/CBL3/links

DIG DEEPER

Find information on the ADR process on the ADR Institute of Canada website and at adric.ca.

Enforcing an Arbitration Award

Where both parties have agreed to arbitrate rather than litigate, the parties are likely to comply with the arbitrator's decision. Where one side refuses to accept the decision, provincial arbitration legislation provides that an award may be registered in the Superior Court for enforcement as if it were an order or judgment of the Superior Court.

As a summary of our discussion of dispute resolution alternatives, Table 2.1 sets out some of the factors that can influence the choice of dispute resolution procedure, including the most complex procedure—litigation.

MINIMIZING YOUR RISK

Find the Dispute Resolution Mechanism That Is Right for You

- Think about the nature of your conflict, its true causes, and what you hope to achieve for your business through its resolution.
- Think about your relationship with the other party and assess your relative power positions.
- Decide on the degree of informality that will best serve your interests and those of the other party.
- Consider both your innate dispute-resolving skills and those of the other party.
- Determine whether a neutral individual would be likely to assist you. If so, choose a neutral individual who both of you trust and who has the qualities necessary to address your concerns skillfully. You can find an arbitrator or mediator by consulting others in the business community, consulting your lawyer, or searching online.
- Approach the process openly and with a view to seeing it through to an appropriate conclusion.
- Prepare to present your case thoroughly, and with as much convincing documentation as you can find.

Table 2.1 Brief Comparison of Negotiation, Mediation, Arbitration, and Litigation

	Negotiation	Mediation	Arbitration	Litigation
Participation in process	Voluntary, as both parties must agree to do this	Voluntary, unless the parties agreed in a contract or otherwise to mandatory mediation of any disputes that arise	Voluntary, unless the parties agreed in a contract or otherwise to mandatory arbitration of any disputes that arise	Voluntary for the plaintiff who decides to start litigation, but involuntary for the defendant who must defend or face judgment by default
Formality	Usually informal and unstructured, although the parties can agree to structure	Degree of formality and structure depends on the mediator and the extent to which the parties accept the mediator's proposals to formalize and structure the process	Less formal than litigation, but much more formal and structured than negotiation or mediation	Highly formal, following a process prescribed by rules of practice
Party control of process	Parties control the process and may proceed with or without establishing their own rules	Mediator and parties control the process, usually with the mediator proposing rules for the process and the parties agreeing to them	Arbitrator controls the process	Judge controls the process
Outcome	Private agreement, enforceable as a contract	Private agreement, enforceable as a contract	Private decision by arbitrator that is usually binding, unless the parties agree beforehand to non-binding arbitration. May be subject to court review and enforceable by legal action	Public decision by judge, enforceable by the court

CHAPTER SUMMARY

Business people in Canada are entitled to have any legal dispute resolved in accordance with the law in a final and binding manner. They can do this through the court system (litigation) or through alternative dispute resolution (negotiation, mediation, or arbitration).

Depending on the complexity of the case, whether or not it requires a lawyer, and the compensation being sought, businesses may sue in the Small Claims Court or the Superior Court. If they want to appeal the decisions, they may do so in the Court of Appeal and, finally, in the Supreme Court of Canada.

A business wishing to litigate may need a lawyer to review the facts, research the law, prepare a statement of claim, and manage the trial on its behalf. Most trials take a day or two, but a complex one with many witnesses may take much longer.

If a case is proceeding in the Small Claims Court in Ontario, a licensed paralegal may be used instead of a lawyer, in which case the cost of representation may be lower.

In bringing a legal case, a party must consider the type of damages it needs to claim, which may include general, special, or aggravated damages. In deciding to sue, the party will need to consider the costs of doing so in terms of fees paid to its own representative, but also the additional costs it may have to pay the other party if the case is lost.

Negotiation is a process in which parties are responsible for reaching an agreement between themselves. They can decide to deviate as little as possible from their position or they can find common ground by listening to each other.

With mediation, the parties invite a neutral individual to oversee the negotiations. The mediator guides the parties to a solution by helping them communicate and assessing which party has the stronger position in law. The mediator may also help them draw up a formal contract, which, like any other contract, is legally binding and enforceable by the courts.

Arbitration is more formal and court-like. The arbitrator makes a binding decision on the parties at the end of the arbitration.

Many factors affect what process businesses may choose. Much depends on whether the parties want to control the process and whether they trust each other to apply the solution. Generally, if one party is more powerful than the other and there is a high degree of conflict, having a third party control the process may lead to a faster and more successful solution. A lawsuit can easily take two years from start to finish, and the costs can be exorbitant; arbitration is usually faster and less expensive. In the Small Claims Court, proceedings are relatively quick and inexpensive, parties can handle the cases themselves, and there is no arbitrator to pay.

KEY TERMS

REFERENCES

936464 Ontario Ltd (cob as Plumbhouse Plumbing & Heating) v Mungo Bear Ltd, 2003 OJ 3795 (QL) (Sup Ct J).

Barrie Public Utilities v Canadian Cable Television Assn, [2003] 1 SCR 476.

Broadcasting Act, SC 1991, c 11.

Canadian Charter of Rights and Freedoms, Part I of the *Constitution Act, 1982*, being Schedule B to the *Canada Act 1982* (UK), 1982, c 11.

Canadian Environmental Protection Act, 1999, SC 1999, c 33.

Criminal Code, RSC 1985, c C-46.

Human Rights Code, RSO 1990, c H 19.

IBM Canada Ltd v Kossovan, 2011 ABQB 621.

Limitations Act, 2002, SO 2002, c 24, Schedule B.

Rules of Civil Procedure, RRO 1990, reg 194.

Telecommunications Act, SC 1993, c 38.

Whiten v Pilot Insurance Co, 2002 SCC 18, [2002] 1 SCR 595.

Workplace Safety and Insurance Act, 1997, SO 1997, c 16, Schedule A.

EXERCISES

True or False?

____ 1. In the Superior Court, you are entitled to disclosure of the other party's documents and evidence prior to trial.

____ 2. If you win a case in court, you can enforce your judgment by using garnishment to seize and sell the defendant's car.

____ 3. A decision made in the trial division of the Superior Court is binding on the Court of Appeal.

____ 4. The Small Claims Court has the power to grant injunctions.

____ 5. If you believe a decision of an administrative board was unfair and not based on evidence, you have the right to have the decision reviewed in the courts.

____ 6. If you think someone has breached your legal rights, you can sue at any time.

Multiple Choice

1. Arbitration as a process is
   - **a.** more formal than negotiation
   - **b.** more formal than litigation
   - **c.** controlled by the parties
   - **d.** none of the above
2. If the parties have a history of conflict, and one is stronger than the other, the following is probably the best alternative dispute resolution process:
   - **a.** negotiation
   - **b.** mediation
   - **c.** arbitration
   - **d.** either b or c would work equally well
3. In talking about alternative dispute resolution, we often discuss rights and interests. In this context, "rights" refers to
   - **a.** short-term goals
   - **b.** long-term goals
   - **c.** business concerns, aspirations, and priorities
   - **d.** entitlements
4. In positional negotiation, you
   - **a.** determine what outcome you want before you start, and stick to it as best you can
   - **b.** explore with the other parties what the source of the conflict is
   - **c.** accept the other side's position as legitimate and valid
   - **d.** ask open-ended questions
   - **e.** do none of the above
5. In the mediation process,
   - **a.** the mediator guides discussions and imposes a settlement after hearing both sides
   - **b.** the mediator guides discussions
   - **c.** the mediator always keeps the parties apart during discussions
   - **d.** the parties must not be in an adversarial position
6. You should use mediation if
   - **a.** both parties are prepared to make serious efforts to resolve the issues
   - **b.** both parties are prepared to explore mutual interests and wish to maintain an ongoing relationship
   - **c.** in settling a rights issue, the parties are more interested in making their own rules than in having rules imposed on them by a neutral individual
   - **d.** all of the above
   - **e.** only b and c are correct
7. You should use arbitration if
   - **a.** the other party is stronger than you are
   - **b.** you know the other party will comply with the arbitrator's decision
   - **c.** you have a good working relationship with the other party and have successfully resolved interest disputes in the past
   - **d.** all of the above
   - **e.** none of the above
8. "Solicitor–client privilege" means
   - **a.** anything your lawyer tells you cannot be repeated by you to anyone else
   - **b.** anything you write to your lawyer cannot be revealed by either of you
   - **c.** your lawyer has a right, ahead of other creditors, to payment of his or her bill for services
   - **d.** third parties who provide your lawyer with information about your case cannot reveal it to anyone else
   - **e.** your lawyer cannot reveal any information you give to him or her about the case without your permission
9. Small Claims Court cases differ from those in the trial division of the Superior Court in the following way(s):
   - **a.** There is a limit on the amount of money one can sue for in the Small Claims Court.
   - **b.** Proceedings in the trial division of the Superior Court are quicker and cheaper than those in the Small Claims Court.

c. There is no discovery process in the Small Claims Court.
d. The rules of evidence are more relaxed in the Small Claims Court than in the trial division of the Superior Court.
e. A, c, and d are correct.

Short Answer

1. In the context of ADR, what are interests and rights, and why is the distinction between them important?
2. When should you choose negotiation over other dispute settlement techniques?
3. When should you choose mediation over other dispute settlement techniques?
4. When should you choose arbitration as a dispute resolution technique?
5. What are the main steps in the litigation process in the trial division of the Superior Court?
6. How does a Small Claims Court case differ from one in the trial division of the Superior Court?
7. What is the hierarchy of courts in Ontario?
8. Why do business people increasingly opt for ADR rather than civil litigation to resolve disputes?

Apply Your Knowledge

1. Legover Industries Ltd is a custom furniture maker. Its president and only shareholder, Hieronymous Firple, recently sold the company to BlackLeather Ltd, a company that is also in the furniture business. The parties negotiated a lengthy contract of purchase and sale. One of the clauses in the contract stated, "Any tax liabilities existing at the time of the signing of the agreement shall be payable by the seller." Six months after the contract was signed, Canada Revenue Agency (CRA) sent BlackLeather a Notice of Reassessment. CRA had discovered a tax liability for a taxation year prior to the sale that it had overlooked. BlackLeather could easily pay the amount owing to the CRA but thinks that Firple is responsible for paying. Also, BlackLeather's principals found Firple difficult to deal with and their feelings about him are mostly negative. On that basis, they would not mind making him pay.

   BlackLeather accordingly demanded that Firple reimburse BlackLeather for the $8,000 it must pay to the CRA. Firple is now retired and plays golf in warm places on a year-round basis. He is a cranky, rigid individual who spends most of the year outside Canada. Firple does not want to pay, on the grounds that this tax liability did not exist when the agreement was signed. It only became a tax liability when the CRA said it was, which was after the agreement was signed. In response, BlackLeather says that the liability existed prior to the signing of the agreement. The fact that the liability was not known to exist until after does not permit Firple to dodge the responsibility of paying, as the purpose was to affix liability for taxes for the period when Firple controlled the company. When consulted, lawyers on both sides said the answer was not clear cut and arguments could be made for both positions. Discuss the applicability of negotiation, mediation, arbitration, and litigation to the facts of this case.
2. Graymetal is a mining company that has a lease on a coal mine in Bearsnout, Ontario. This small town used to have several mines, but now has only this one. The coal mined here contains a rare element called germanium, which is used to make computer chips. There is a huge market for germanium. However, germanium is extracted from the coal ash, so the coal has to be burned. Burning coal, particularly this type of coal, is very polluting. A company, CompVolt, is interested in buying the germanium from Graymetal. CompVolt has a process for burning coal to create energy and reduce pollution as it extracts the germanium from the ash. The town's current by-laws do not permit a coal-burning operation. However, should the project materialize, the town would be interested in obtaining electric power from the operation. It must also consider the increased employment opportunities and property tax income that would result. What resolution process would work best in this case?

Tort Law

3

LEARNING OUTCOMES

After reading this chapter, you should be able to:

- Recognize a tort.
- Distinguish between intentional and unintentional torts.
- Describe the concept of vicarious liability.
- Describe the elements of negligence.
- Explain strict liability.
- Identify torts that are common in the commercial world.
- Explain defences to tort actions.
- Manage business risks from a torts perspective.

What Is a Tort?

tort
civil wrong, other than a breach of contract, for which damages may be sought to compensate for any harm or injury sustained

omission
failure to act

A **tort** is an act or **omission** that causes injury to people or damage to property or economic interests, other than an injury that arises from a breach of contract. In some circumstances, the act or omission can give rise to both criminal liability and tort liability. However, unlike a crime—which the law views as harming the state—tort law focuses on the harm caused to individuals, property, and businesses by the act or omission. Examples of torts that could arise in respect of Val-Nam's business include the following:

- A Val-Nam employee fails to clean up an oil leak from one of the forklifts in the warehouse and the purchasing manager from one of Val-Nam's main customers slips on the oil, falls, and breaks her leg.
- A consulting company supplies Val-Nam with inaccurate information about marketing techniques; Val-Nam acts on the information and loses several million dollars as a result.
- Val-Nam fails to illuminate exit signs in its warehouse; a fire breaks out and a number of employees, independent contractors, and customers are injured from smoke inhalation when they cannot find the exits quickly.
- A competitor intentionally creates a product and packaging deceptively similar to Val-Nam's electrical generator in the hope that purchasers will be fooled into buying the knock-off. The knock-off product is of poor quality, and bad publicity about it harms Val-Nam's commercial reputation.

The state prosecutes crimes but does not prosecute torts. It is the injured person who must bring an action for damages arising from a tort. In the examples above, it is the purchasing manager; Val-Nam; the employees, contractors, and customers; and Val-Nam again who must bring lawsuits against, respectively, the negligent employee and Val-Nam; the consulting firm; Val-Nam; and the competitor, to obtain compensation for their injuries. By bringing a lawsuit, the purchasing manager, Val-Nam, and those who were trapped in the warehouse become **plaintiffs** in their respective **tort actions**. By being sued, the negligent employee, Val-Nam, the consulting firm, and the competing manufacturer become **defendants** in the tort actions.

plaintiff
party who commences a lawsuit (the suing party)

tort action
lawsuit based on tort

defendant
party who is sued in a lawsuit; person accused of an offence

If a tort causes very serious harm, as in the fire example, it is likely that the state would launch a criminal investigation to determine whether a criminal prosecution is warranted against the individual or business responsible for the damage. Such a prosecution would be an entirely separate matter from any tort actions that those trapped in the warehouse might choose to bring. The purpose of a criminal prosecution is to *punish* lawbreakers in the name of the state and prevent further crimes. By contrast, the purpose of a tort action is to *compensate* persons, including businesses, who have suffered injury as a result of torts committed by others.

Over time, many forms of harm traditionally recognized in tort law have been codified into various statutes. For example, the *Occupiers' Liability Act* codifies, with modifications, the common law standard of care to be provided by occupiers to visitors and business people who enter onto their property. In other cases, legislatures have created statutory offences that address harmful conduct that previously would have been dealt with through a tort action. For example, many environmental laws now cover activity that would have previously been actionable in the tort of nuisance. Once a tort evolves into a statutory offence, the state assumes responsibility for enforcing it. While individuals and businesses may still sue in tort unless the statute specifically prohibits these lawsuits, courts generally encourage the use of statutory remedies wherever possible (see the summary of *AI Enterprises* on page 76).

Predicting and minimizing the potential harm to consumers and others that a business's acts or omissions may cause is an ongoing responsibility of businesses that want to avoid legal liability.

The Importance of Tort Law for Business People

Torts can occur in all kinds of contexts; they are not unique to the business world. It is essential, however, for business people to be aware of the risks of tort-based litigation against their businesses:

- *Tort judgments are expensive.* Tort liability is perhaps the most significant potential source of unexpected expense for businesses. While fines under the criminal law are certainly unpleasant, they are usually predictable and well defined. Tort judgments, by contrast, are much less predictable, and large awards to plaintiffs can plunge a business into insolvency. Tort liability is a difficult risk to manage, but all businesses must consider it.
- *Tort judgments are a public relations nightmare.* Financial impact aside, a tort lawsuit can do irreparable damage to a business's reputation. Business people invest considerable resources into building trust in their products and services. Goodwill can evaporate in the face of bad press relating to a tort suit (even, sometimes, when the plaintiff's case is proven to be unfounded). Sensitive handling of tort matters—for example, knowing when to fight and when to settle—can help protect a business's valuable reputation.

It is also important for business people to understand that tort law is an essential business tool. When most business people think about tort liability, they think first about how to avoid it. However, businesses themselves are often plaintiffs in lawsuits based on tort. When harm is suffered by your business due to the acts or omissions of another and no breach of contract is involved, there may be a remedy for your business in tort. Later in the chapter, we consider examples such as nuisance, occupiers' liability, and passing off.

Vicarious Liability

One of the most important principles in tort law—and a principle that business people must always keep in mind—is **vicarious liability**. Because of vicarious liability, businesses can be held responsible, or liable, for injuries that result from the actions of their employees or the independent contractors who provide services in connection with the business.[1] For example, in the situation described above where

vicarious liability
liability imposed on one party (often an employer) for the harmful actions or omissions of another (often an employee)

1 For commentary on another case related to this issue, see Jeremy Daniel Schwartz, "Using Independent Contractor Not a 'Get out of Jail Free' Card," *CanLII Connects* (20 April 2017), online: <http://canliiconnects.org/en/commentaries/45422>.

the purchasing manager was injured when she slipped on oil that was not properly cleaned up by a Val-Nam employee, Val-Nam may be held vicariously liable for the employee's negligence. The purchasing manager can sue the employee for negligence, but she can also sue Val-Nam. Vicarious liability holds an employer responsible for the torts that its employees commit while doing their jobs.

CASE IN POINT

Vicarious Liability

Teskey v Toronto Transit Commission, 2003 CanLII 11726 (Ont Sup Ct J)

Facts

The Toronto Transit Commission (TTC) became concerned about a drug problem among TTC night shift operators. To address it, the TTC hired an agent through an investigation agency and trained him to work undercover, posing as a TTC employee.

In the course of his employment, the agent reported on marijuana use and a marijuana sales transaction conducted by a TTC employee. However, the agent's credibility was at issue because of his own marijuana use. The TTC employee made a defamation claim against the agent and, based on vicarious liability, against the TTC and the investigation agency.

Result

The TTC was held liable for the agent's actions. The court ruled that the contract between the TTC and the agent created an employer-employee relationship, and that more than one employer (the investigation agency and the TTC) may be vicariously liable for the actions of a single employee at the same time. It made no difference that the agent was hired to conduct an investigation.

Business Lesson

Remember that your business is vicariously liable for the actions of your employees and contractors. Whether a person is an employee or a contractor is not determinative of whether or not vicarious liability will apply—more important factors are how much control the company has over the person's work and how closely the tort was connected to that work.

MINIMIZING YOUR RISK

Train and Monitor Employees

- Prevent employees and contractors from committing torts through clear policies, sufficient training, and adequate monitoring.
- Consider including indemnification clauses (provisions that require your employee or contractor to assume liability for their own torts) in your contracts if your business carries a significant risk of vicarious liability. However, be aware that these clauses are not always enforceable, especially where the employee or contractor does not have the financial means to satisfy an award of damages (compensation).
- Consider the possibility of criminal or intentionally harmful acts by employees and contractors (even though you are not usually liable for them), and consider the use of specialized insurance (often called "fidelity bonding") against the risk of employee crime, fraud, or intentional harm.
- Carry sufficient liability insurance to cover the costs of employee and contractor accidents and other risks.

Negligence Act

Another important concept is joint and several liability. Liability is the state of being responsible to pay compensation for another party's loss. Joint liability arises in situations where there are two or more tortfeasors, such as an employee and the business that employs him, or partners in a firm (discussed in greater detail in Chapter 7), or two engineers who worked on a project. If both are held liable for the harm to the plaintiff, the *Negligence Act* provides that the plaintiff is entitled to recover the full amount of the damages from either of them. In other words, if Joe and Maria are both liable for harm to Bob, and the court awards damages of $5,000, Bob could demand the entire amount from either Joe or Maria. This allows the plaintiff, Bob, to collect from whoever has the deeper pockets. Even if the court allocates liability between Joe and Maria such that Joe is only 10 percent responsible, he may be required to pay the entire amount. The *Negligence Act* permits him to then sue Maria for the difference based on their "several" liability.

The *Negligence Act* also deals with the concept of contributory negligence. The doctrine of contributory negligence allows courts to hold the plaintiff partially responsible for his own injuries. For example, if the purchasing manager who slipped on the oil on the warehouse floor was wearing stiletto heels, particularly if she had been told that she must wear flat shoes with good grip when visiting the warehouse, she may be found to have contributed to her injury by failing to take reasonable care for her own safety. In practice, because a plaintiff will not be required to actually pay himself a portion of the compensation for the loss, a finding of contributory negligence will result in a reduction of the damages by a certain percentage; for example, the defendant may be found liable for only 80 percent of the damages.

Elements of a Tort

A tort does not exist every time a person is hurt or feels offended. An individual or business that has suffered harm as a result of the actions of another must prove the elements of a tort in order to obtain compensation in tort law. The elements may vary depending on the type of tort, but they almost always include the following:

1. *a wrongful act*—an intentional act or omission or a breach of a duty of care owed by the plaintiff to the defendant,
2. *causation*—that the wrongful act of the defendant caused the harm, and
3. *quantifiable harm*—that the harm is measurable in a manner recognized by the law (see Figure 3.1).

For example, assume that early on in their business venture, Valery and Mitchell attempt to sell prototypes of the electrical generator that Mitchell developed, from a booth at an outdoor fair, to see if there is a market for the product. It pours all day, and no one buys anything. Valery and Mitchell quarrel and have a miserable time. Mitchell cannot bring a tort action against Valery just because the unsuccessful business venture was her idea. Why not?

Figure 3.1 Elements of a Tort

WRONGFUL ACT + CAUSATION + QUANTIFIABLE HARM = TORT

First, he cannot establish that Valery has done anything wrong. Valery cannot control the weather or the commercial decisions of customers. She is not responsible in any way for ensuring Mitchell's business success. In legal terms, we would say that Valery did not owe Mitchell a duty of care (and therefore, she cannot have been in breach of that duty).

Second, the cause of Mitchell's misery had nothing to do with Valery. It was caused by rain and a lack of interest in the electrical generators, not by anything Valery did.

Third, even though Mitchell was uncomfortable and upset, he cannot prove quantifiable harm because the law does not, in general, provide compensation for discomfort and disappointment.

If, on the other hand, Valery carelessly left the roof off the booth, and the rain short-circuited the generators, Mitchell might have an action against Valery in the tort of negligence. At least he would be able to prove causation—that is, that Valery's carelessness resulted in damage to the generators. Mitchell would also be able to quantify the harm based on the value of the generators that were ruined or the cost to repair the generators. Finally, depending on his instructions to Valery or on the understanding between them when they got involved in the business venture, Mitchell may be able to prove that Valery owed him a duty of care to protect the generators while they were in her possession and that she breached that duty.

To succeed in a tort action, a plaintiff must almost always prove a wrongful act, causation, and quantifiable harm, but he may also need to prove other elements, depending on the nature of the tort in question. To take an obvious example, a plaintiff who claims to have suffered damages as a result of the tort of trespass must prove that the defendant did, in fact, trespass on premises lawfully occupied by the plaintiff. In the sections that follow, we discuss the elements that plaintiffs are required to prove when seeking compensation for injuries suffered as a result of various torts, both intentional and unintentional.

Categories of Torts

Torts can be categorized in a number of ways. We have grouped some of the most common torts in three principal categories: intentional torts, unintentional torts, and torts that can be either intentional or unintentional (see Figure 3.2).

Figure 3.2 Categories of Torts

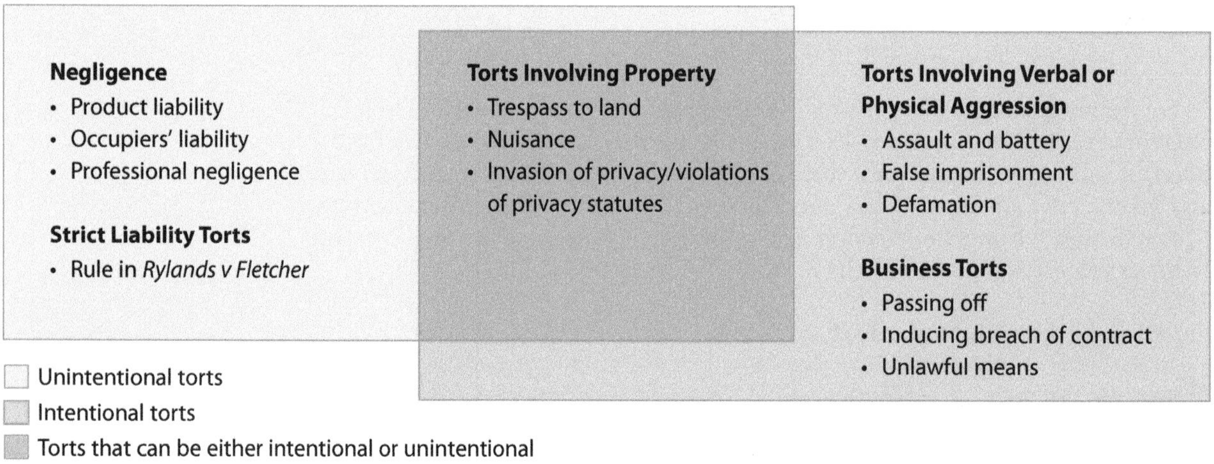

Negligence
- Product liability
- Occupiers' liability
- Professional negligence

Strict Liability Torts
- Rule in *Rylands v Fletcher*

Torts Involving Property
- Trespass to land
- Nuisance
- Invasion of privacy/violations of privacy statutes

Torts Involving Verbal or Physical Aggression
- Assault and battery
- False imprisonment
- Defamation

Business Torts
- Passing off
- Inducing breach of contract
- Unlawful means

Unintentional torts
Intentional torts
Torts that can be either intentional or unintentional

An **intentional tort** occurs when a person or business deliberately harms another. We will focus on intentional torts that fall into two large groups: torts involving verbal or physical aggression, and business torts.

An **unintentional tort** occurs as a result of careless or negligent actions that cause unintended harm to people or businesses. Most unintentional torts fall into the large group of torts known as negligence. Product liability, occupiers' liability, and professional negligence are three subcategories of negligence. Another form of unintentional tort is known as a **strict liability tort**, which requires no proof of negligence.

Certain torts may be committed intentionally or unintentionally: for example, trespass to land, nuisance, and invasion of privacy.

intentional tort
injury deliberately caused to a plaintiff by a defendant

unintentional tort
injury inadvertently caused to a plaintiff by a defendant

strict liability tort
unintentional tort that requires no proof of negligence

Intentional Torts

Intentional torts are actions by individuals or businesses that intentionally cause harm to others. Like all torts, intentional torts require proof of causation and harm. The following sections describe the intentional torts that business people should be particularly aware of.

Intentional Torts Involving Verbal or Physical Aggression

Of course, violence and defamation are not common in a business setting. When intentional torts occur in the commercial world, they are often the result of employees losing their tempers, or they may occur because of the nature of the business itself. Some businesses—for example, those that repossess assets that have been pledged as security—lead to stress, and conflict can arise with clients or service providers. Where dealings require sensitivity, business people should carefully screen and train their employees.

Intentional torts involving aggressive and defamatory conduct occur both within and outside the business arena. After examining them in the sections that follow, we will also explore three intentional torts that relate only to the commercial world: passing off, inducing breach of contract, and interference with a business by unlawful means.

Assault and Battery

The torts of assault and battery can occur in business settings. For example, a security guard may be excessively violent when detaining a suspected shoplifter, or a bouncer may be overly rough in expelling patrons from a bar. Employees may also be violent toward one another, and the business that employs them may be held responsible for the resulting injuries.

While an assault is generally understood in the criminal law to be a physical attack, an **assault** in tort law is a *threat* of imminent physical harm. Assault on its own (without contact, or "battery") is actionable but is unlikely to form the basis of a lawsuit, because the cost of the lawsuit would not be warranted given the modest award that is likely to be made absent a quantifiable harm. **Battery**, which is often claimed in conjunction with assault (as in "assault and battery"), is any intentionally harmful or socially offensive direct physical contact. When the tort of battery forms the basis of a lawsuit, it can include violent or sexual contact.

assault
tort in which the defendant threatens the plaintiff with physical harm

battery
tort in which the defendant engages in unwanted physical contact with the plaintiff

MINIMIZING YOUR RISK

Prohibit Violence and Train Employees

- Train employees to treat one another, customers, and clients with respect.
- Implement a zero-tolerance policy on workplace violence and harassment.
- If the potential for conflict is high, provide employees with advanced training in how to handle angry clients and how and when to contact appropriate authorities.
- Carry sufficient insurance to compensate victims adequately.

False Imprisonment

Retail businesses have the right to temporarily infringe on the freedom of anyone caught in the act of shoplifting. However, these detentions must be founded on reasonable grounds (see the decision in *Mann v Canadian Tire Corporation Limited* for an overview of the right to stop shoplifters). If an employee or security guard detains a suspect—by means of a threat or physical restraint—without reasonable evidence that the suspect was shoplifting, a business could be sued for false imprisonment as a result of the principle of vicarious liability.

false imprisonment tort in which the defendant unlawfully restricts the freedom of the plaintiff

False imprisonment occurs when one person unlawfully restricts the freedom of another. The "imprisoner" need not place the plaintiff in jail, but the plaintiff's freedom must be completely restricted (i.e., there must not be an alternate way out). Any complete restriction on liberty is technically a tort, though it may be difficult to prove quantifiable harm from temporary detentions and, therefore, the amount of damages awarded may be minimal.

CASE IN POINT

False Imprisonment: Set-Up Leads to Nominal Damages

Trew v 313124 Saskatchewan Ltd, 2005 SKQB 79

Facts

While shopping in a Moose Jaw grocery store, a customer observed another customer (the plaintiff Trew), dressed in a long black trench coat, behaving suspiciously. The customer alerted store staff, and when Trew approached the cash register, the cashier challenged him and asked him to empty his pockets. Trew refused. The cashier then called the police and asked Trew to remain on the scene to wait for them. Trew presented some soap refills for purchase, on which it appeared that he had changed the price stickers from $4.49 to $0.99. While the cashier noticed this, she did not challenge it. When Trew tried to leave the store, the cashier stuck her arm out to block his path, and he brushed past her. She again asked him to remain in the store, and he became very agitated and began declaring that he was going to sue the store for false imprisonment.

The police arrived and searched Trew. No merchandise was found in his possession. Trew sued the store for false imprisonment. In the evidence presented at trial, it was revealed that Trew had a long history of involvement with the court, including shoplifting convictions. He had also previously brought a claim of false imprisonment against a store and had received a cash settlement.

Result

The court found that when the cashier stuck her arm out to block Trew's path, she was relying only on the other customer's warning and therefore did not have enough grounds to detain Trew. While she used no force, sticking out her arm constituted false imprisonment. However, the court found that because of his shoplifting history, Trew's claim that the store's actions had traumatized and embarrassed him lacked credibility. He was awarded only nominal damages of $500 (likely less than his costs of bringing the litigation).

Business Lesson

Thoroughly train all retail store employees on how to deal with shoplifting suspicions. Absent very clear evidence—for example, direct observation—of shoplifting, staff should *not* detain suspects (especially in a grocery store where the quantum of loss will be much less than potential damages for false imprisonment). If a decision is made to detain, the situation should be handled discreetly and the detainee treated with respect.

MINIMIZING YOUR RISK

Teach Retail Employees to Use Minimal Force in Detaining Suspected Shoplifters

- Never conduct arbitrary fishing expeditions into the bags or coats of customers.
- Do not approach a customer unless you have actually observed a theft or the customer is clearly hiding something.
- Treat detainees with courtesy, and call the police immediately to minimize detention time.
- If someone objects to a physical search, do not touch them; wait for the police to arrive.
- Carry general liability insurance.

Defamation

Business people must be careful when commenting about their competitors. Negative statements about other companies, their management, or their products can result in a lawsuit.

Defamation is a tort that occurs when someone makes a statement, to at least one other person, about a person or business that results in a significant loss of respect or reputation in the eyes of a reasonable or right-thinking person in the community. For example, if your car rental business advertises that your competitor does not maintain its fleet to the same standards of safety that your business does, you may be making a defamatory statement. Negative advertising—that is, advertising that focuses on the negative aspects of the competition, rather than on the positive aspects of your own product—is especially open to accusations of defamation if it lowers a competitor's reputation.

defamation
tort based on harm to a person's or a business's reputation through false statements made by the defendant

Defamation in written form is sometimes referred to as "libel"; defamation in verbal form is sometimes referred to as "slander." Malicious false statements made with the intention of harming a product's reputation are sometimes referred to as "injurious falsehood" or "slander of goods."

www.emond.ca/CBL3/links

DIG DEEPER
The Cyberlibel website provides information on protecting businesses from vicarious liability for employees' defamatory remarks.

DEFENCES TO DEFAMATION

When confronted with an allegation of defamation, a number of defences can be relied upon. In the business context, two are particularly relevant: truth and fair comment.

◇ Truth

If your car rental business advertised that your competitor fails to maintain its fleet to the same safety standards that your business does, and you can prove that your statement is true—for example, by reference to maintenance records and safety tests—you have a complete defence. No defamation lawsuit can succeed against you.

MINIMIZING YOUR RISK

Avoid Potentially Defamatory Remarks

- Review all advertising and marketing material, especially if it identifies a competitor.
- Advertise the benefits of your own product; avoid criticizing the products of competitors.
- Have a lawyer review all negative advertising.
- Train employees in media relations before they speak on behalf of your business or refer to a competitor.
- Hire public relations staff if necessary.

◇ Fair Comment

The defence of fair comment is designed to encourage the expression of opinions. It is based on the notion that people can and should make up their own minds about whether a statement is true. If your statement about your competitor is an opinion—an honest criticism, based on a sincere impression formed after your review of the facts—you may be able to succeed with a defence of fair comment. Success generally depends on three things: whether the comment is made on a matter of public interest, whether there is a known or disclosed factual foundation for the opinion expressed, and whether the statement was fair—it cannot be made maliciously, with intent to harm.

Therefore, if you have informally observed the state of your competitor's fleet over a number of months and judged it to be substandard, you are in a better position to raise the defence of fair comment than if your advertisement was based on no evidence at all. If your comment was motivated, at least in part, by a genuine concern for public safety, you may raise the defence of fair comment. Unsubstantiated or purely malicious comments are unlikely to constitute fair comment.

Intentional Business Torts

Three business torts that involve intentional actions are passing off, inducing breach of contract, and the "unlawful means" tort. We discuss these torts below.

Passing Off

passing off
tort based on one party's attempt to distribute its own knock-off product or service on the pretense that it is the product or service of another party

Using a product name or design that is similar to that of a more well-known and respected brand constitutes the tort of **passing off**. This tort protects the goodwill that a business has created and provides a remedy when a competitor misrepresents the origin of its product or service. For example, a watch manufacturer that calls its watches "Rollex" can expect to be sued by Rolex, the well-known watchmaker. The similarity of names could confuse customers, who might think they are buying a quality brand when, in fact, they are buying a cheap knock-off. When the Rollex watch breaks, the reputation of Rolex is diminished in the mind of the confused customer. Similarly, when Val-Nam's competitor creates a product and packaging that is deceptively similar to Val-Nam's electrical generator, and this knock-off product does not work, it harms Val-Nam's reputation and may give rise to a remedy under the tort of passing off.

This kind of dishonesty in business is also addressed in consumer protection legislation (in provisions dealing with false, misleading, or deceptive representations) and in intellectual property law (in provisions dealing with trademarks). We discuss these topics in Chapter 6 and Chapter 11 under the headings "False, Misleading, or Deceptive Representations" and "Trademark Law," respectively.

MINIMIZING YOUR RISK

Name and Design Your Products Responsibly

- Research the marketplace before naming your products or business.
- Avoid product design so similar to competitors' products that it might confuse customers.
- Register your trademarks.
- Monitor the marketplace for product or business names that might adversely affect your business.

Inducing Breach of Contract

When one party breaches a contract it has with another, the innocent party can sue for breach under the law of contract. The tort of inducing breach of contract supports the law of contracts by providing an additional remedy—this one in tort—in cases where the breaching party has been induced to commit the breach by a third party.

Third parties can have a variety of motivations for inducing breaches of other parties' contracts. A common example arises in the context of employment. For example, one hospital, seeking to hire a specialist whose skills are rare and in high demand, may encourage that specialist to breach a term employment contract with a different hospital. In a commercial context, a manufacturer in need of scarce component parts might induce a supplier to sell to it, at a premium price, a supply of the components that were promised to another manufacturer.

The elements that establish the tort of inducing breach of contract are: (1) a contract exists (one to which the plaintiff, but not the defendant, is a party); (2) the defendant has knowledge of the contract; (3) the defendant has the intention to induce a breach of the contract; (4) the defendant employs a direct inducement in an effort to cause the breach; and (5) damage is suffered by the plaintiff.

The fourth element—that the defendant employed a direct inducement—has been the subject of many legal decisions. Courts have generally held that advising a contract party that a breach might be in its best interests is not enough to lead to liability; there needs to be something more. For example, the hospital in the above example would likely meet the threshold by actually entering into a contract of its own with the specialist.

Where the breach is provoked by the defendant's intentional unlawful act, the facts fall within the definition of a newly defined tort: interference with economic relations by unlawful means.

The Tort of "Unlawful Means"

The ways in which one business may interfere with the business of another are limited only by the human imagination. Some methods of interference, such as defamation or inducing breaches of contract, are defined as particular torts. If a form of intentional damage by a third party to the economic interests of a business is not defined as a particular tort, it may be encompassed by the tort of interference with economic relations by **unlawful means**.

unlawful means
tort based on intentional harm, through illegal acts, to a party's means of earning money

In 2014, the Supreme Court of Canada (SCC) heard the appeal of a New Brunswick case (*AI Enterprises Ltd v Bram Enterprises Ltd*) that had been decided on the basis of an emerging tort that has come to be known as "inference with economic relations by unlawful means" or, more simply, the "unlawful means tort." In dismissing the appeal, the SCC affirmed the existence and narrow scope of this tort, which has less broad application than did its predecessor, the tort of "interference with economic relations."

The "new" unlawful means tort allows a plaintiff to sue a defendant for economic loss resulting from the defendant's unlawful act against a third party. The parameters of this new tort are outlined in the text box below. In its decision, the SCC made it clear that when considering cases based on this tort, courts should keep in mind the appropriate limits of tort law as a tool to regulate economic and competitive activity. There is legislation in place in Canada to regulate business, and therefore it should only be the rare case that requires a court to turn to the common law tort to impose liability.

Instead of creating a whole separate basis for liability outside of business law statutes, the tort of unlawful means can only be used to "stretch" liability for an act that caused harm to the plaintiff and would have been actionable by the third party against the defendant.

SCENARIO

Unlawful Means: What Does It Mean?

Val-Nam had been trying to convince the national chain Canada Survival Supplies Inc (CSS) to stock its electrical generators. The two parties were going back and forth in negotiations, but Valery was certain they were close to a deal. However, just as the last details were being ironed out, CSS suddenly withdrew from negotiations. They stated they were no longer interested in doing business with Val-Nam under any conditions. Valery was perplexed and frustrated. A supply contract with CSS had the potential to very significantly expand Val-Nam's business.

Valery was determined to figure out what happened and did a little digging, asking colleagues and business acquaintances if they had heard any rumours. Valery found out from a disgruntled ex-employee of Val-Nam's main competitor, Off-Grid Real Energy Solutions Ltd (OGRES), that OGRES had threatened CSS and convinced it to drop the deal with Val-Nam. OGRES has a long-term supply contract with CSS that covers a wide range of goods. OGRES told CSS that if CSS entered into a contract with Val-Nam, OGRES would stop supplying CSS even though it would be a breach of their contract. In fact, as negotiations between Val-Nam and CSS progressed, OGRES *did* stop supplying CSS. This caused significant economic harm to CSS and so CSS withdrew from the Val-Nam negotiations.

In this situation, CSS obviously has a remedy against OGRES for breach of contract, if the chain wants to pursue it. However, what is Val-Nam's remedy? OGRES did not do anything directly to Val-Nam, but its actions against CSS were clearly designed to harm Val-Nam. This is where the newly recognized tort of unlawful means may be applicable. OGRES committed an unlawful act against CSS (the breach of contract) that intentionally caused harm to Val-Nam (OGRES meant for CSS to withdraw from the negotiations). The breach of contract meets the threshold of unlawfulness because it would be actionable by CSS against OGRES.

MINIMIZING YOUR RISK

Maintain Zero Tolerance for Illegality in Your Business

- Enact business policies that prohibit illegal practices.
- Train staff to obey the law and respect the rights of competitors.

Because the tort of unlawful means involves breaking laws or committing other torts, these actions can expose the defendant business to other lawsuits or criminal charges. The bad press that flows from a high-profile unlawful means lawsuit usually outweighs any perceived advantage gained through acting in an unethical manner. It can permanently injure the reputation of both a business and its management. These are all reasons why a business should avoid conduct that puts it at risk of being sued for interference by unlawful means.

Unfair competition is another way in which businesses can interfere with one another. The *Competition Act*, a federal statute, now largely governs this very complex area of law. A discussion of some of the main *Competition Act* provisions is found in Chapter 6.

injunction
court order requiring a party to discontinue an action or prohibiting a party from taking a proposed action

CASE IN POINT

The Mutinous Barista

Cappuccino Affair Ltd v Haraga, 2000 ABQB 750

Facts

The owner of a coffee franchise system (the franchisor) hired a director of operations who organized an association of franchisees and encouraged them to repudiate their franchise agreements by refusing to pay royalties to the franchisor, selling unapproved food items, refusing to accept shipments of approved coffee cups, and installing and upholstering unapproved furniture.

The franchisor fired the director of operations, but continued to suffer losses when 11 of its 13 outlets continued to breach their contracts. The franchisor applied for an **injunction** to stop the director from attempting to interfere with its contractual relations with the outlets.

Result

Because this was an application for an injunction and not a full trial, the court needed only to find that a serious issue was raised and there was a prospect of irreparable harm. The evidence that the director had intentionally interfered with the franchisor's contracts, and that the franchisor had suffered losses as a result, was sufficient. The court granted the injunction.

Business Lesson

Act quickly if someone is interfering with your contracts. Getting an injunction to stop losses immediately is often more effective than waiting to sue on the basis of harm already done.

Unintentional Torts

The broadest and most significant unintentional tort that affects businesses is the tort of negligence. In order to make a successful claim in negligence, a plaintiff must establish certain elements, which we explore in the sections below. Then, following a detailed discussion of negligence, we provide a brief description of strict liability, which is also an unintentional tort.

Definition and Scope of Negligence

negligence
failure of a person to act reasonably, resulting in harm to someone else

Negligence is a tort in which a business or individual commits a careless act that results in unintended harm to another. The harm is caused by either the defendant's failure to carry out a duty or the defendant's poor performance of a duty.

Negligence is an extremely broad category of tort. The torts that business people most commonly encounter fall into certain well-established subcategories of negligence. These subcategories include:

- *product liability*, which occurs when a manufacturer carelessly designs, produces, or distributes goods that injure a member or members of the public;
- *occupiers' liability*, which occurs when a business carelessly fails to keep its premises safe for its customers and other visitors to enter; and
- *professional negligence*, which occurs when a professional, such as a lawyer, accountant, or veterinarian, falls below recognized standards of practice and thereby causes loss or harm while performing their job.

Elements of Negligence

As discussed above, to prove negligence (or any subcategory of negligence), a plaintiff must prove a careless act or omission, causation, and quantifiable harm. Proof of quantifiable harm in a negligence action is the same as proof of quantifiable harm in any other tort action—the plaintiff must establish that the harm they suffered is measurable in a manner recognized in law. The element of causation in a negligence action, however, is unique. We explore it below under the heading "Causation."

To succeed in a claim based on negligence, a plaintiff must prove quantifiable harm in addition to each of the following:

- the defendant owed them a duty of care,
- the defendant breached the standard of care that was reasonable in the circumstances,
- this breach caused the plaintiff's loss or injury, and
- the defendant should have foreseen the plaintiff's loss or injury.

We discuss each of these elements in the following sections.

Duty of Care

duty of care
legal duty owed by one person to another based on a relationship or on the doctrine of foreseeability

A **duty of care** is a legal responsibility to avoid causing harm to others through carelessness. This duty lies at the base of all negligence claims.

In the commercial world, a duty of care arises whenever a business person or corporation becomes aware—or should reasonably become aware—that its actions or omissions could harm another. Businesses owe a duty of care to their customers, suppliers, and anyone else who could reasonably be expected to come into contact with their products or services. This includes the original purchaser of products or services and also others who are not the original purchasers: for example, those who buy a product second-hand from the original purchaser, or those who use goods purchased by someone else (for example, school children who use sports equipment purchased by the school board). Businesses are responsible—they have a duty—to make sure that their products or services do not harm anyone.

Standard of Care

A **standard of care** is the degree of care that a business person or corporation must take to prevent or minimize harm to others. Every time a business sells a product, harm may result from the use or misuse of the product. But how careful must a business be? For example, is Val-Nam responsible for the injuries suffered by a child who is electrocuted when the child plugs in one of Val-Nam's generators outside in the rain? Is it relevant whether the generator is labelled with warnings to keep it away from water and that it is to be used only by those over the age of 16? What if the warning label falls off the generator?

standard of care degree of care that a person must take to prevent harm to others

Courts use the reasonable person test to determine the appropriate standard of care on a case-by-case basis. A **reasonable person** is defined as a normal, prudent individual who acts according to generally accepted practices and conducts their affairs in a manner generally accepted by society. The reasonable person standard also applies to corporations because, in law, a corporation is a person. That is, a corporation has the same rights and responsibilities as an individual and is held to the same standard of care—a corporation must act in a manner that is reasonable in the circumstances.

reasonable person fictional person who, in negligence law, applies the appropriate standard of care in a given situation

If the defendant has been more careless than a reasonable person would have been in the situation, the defendant has breached the standard of care required. Appropriate standards of care vary from situation to situation. However, for consistency, courts look to previous decisions in similar cases to determine what kind of behaviour is reasonable. For example, *Jordan House Ltd v Menow* provided the judge in *Crocker v Sundance Northwest Resorts Ltd* with a precedent. In the *Jordan House* case, a hotel was found liable for injuries to a drunk customer who was ejected from the hotel and then hit by a car while walking home. The court found that the hotel had a duty to ensure that the customer got home safely, given their knowledge of his condition. This affirmative duty was applied in the *Crocker* case, where a ski resort business was found liable for injuries to an intoxicated customer whom resort staff allowed to compete in a snow-tube race. Even though the customer signed a waiver explaining that he entered the race at his own risk, the court held that a reasonable person would have foreseen that drunkenness increased the risk of injury. The resort's staff had a duty of care to their customer and the standard of care required staff to stop the man from competing once they observed that he was intoxicated. The Case in Point summarizes another example of standard of care to customers.

In many negligence cases, what is considered reasonable behaviour can be influenced by statutory standards. For instance, consumer product safety and labelling acts require warning labels on items like Val-Nam's generator. A failure to affix such a label may be evidence of a breach of the standard of care. However, breach of the statutory standard does not automatically mean there has been a breach of the standard of care. It is but one element that the court can consider when establishing what would constitute reasonable conduct. By the same token, compliance with a statutory standard does not automatically mean that the defendant met the required standard of care. It is but one element for the court to consider. In a complicated case—where, for example, someone has tampered with a label—courts will look to the principles established in earlier cases. They may ask, for example, whether Val-Nam performed tests on its product labels to ensure tamper resistance.

In cases of professional negligence, the standard of care is generally higher than that of the reasonable person test. Professionals are typically held to the standards of their profession. For example, doctors are held to the standard of a reasonable doctor, lawyers to the standard of a reasonable lawyer, and architects to the standard of a reasonable architect. We provide more information on this topic below under the heading "Professional Negligence."

CASE IN POINT

Standard of Care: The Bingo Bus

Parsons and Sons Transportation Ltd v Whelan, 2005 NLCA 52

Facts

As a free service to patrons, a charitable organization running a bingo parlour in Conception Bay, Newfoundland and Labrador, arranged to transport players to and from the parlour by bus. A tradition had arisen that when the bingo bus passed a "notorious" takeout restaurant in Avondale, unruly teenagers would pelt it with various objects (eggs were favoured in summer, ice chunks in winter—and the occasional rock). Knowing the danger, the owner of the bus company had warned its drivers to "be careful" near the restaurant and had contacted the police about the situation (to no avail, due to insufficient information about the identity of the perpetrators).

One evening, as the bingo bus passed the takeout restaurant, a beer bottle crashed through a passenger window and hit an elderly woman in the head, causing injury. The woman sued for negligence, alleging that the driver and the bus company had fallen short of the standard of care required of them in protecting her. This case relied in part on a branch of the law about "common carriers" (public transportation and shipping). Tort law recognizes an enhanced duty and standard of care for common carriers.

Result

The court agreed that the bus was a common carrier and thus subject to a high standard of care. The court acknowledged that the bus company and driver had taken *some* steps to protect passengers (passengers were sometimes warned to watch out for projectiles when passing the restaurant; the bus company owner had called the police). However, the court found that the bus company did not demonstrate that there were no viable alternatives that it could have taken to protect the passengers. The court identified a number of possible alternatives including always warning about projectiles, rerouting the bus, installing break-proof glass in the windows, and wrapping the bus in wire mesh. Therefore, the bus company had fallen short of the standard of care and was liable for the passenger's injuries.

Business Lesson

Take *all* appropriate preventive steps the moment you or an employee become aware that harm may befall a patron or client as a result of your actions or services. This may include setting clear policies and investing in protective equipment or products, even if those policies and products are not the norm for all businesses of the same type. Tailor your efforts to the unique risks of your particular business.

Causation

To obtain compensation for a defendant's negligence, a plaintiff must prove that the defendant breached the standard of care owed to her, and also that the breach caused, or contributed to, the harm that she suffered.

In some cases, proving causation is straightforward. For example, consider a computer service that attempts to repair a business's computer system but does so incompetently and renders the system unworkable. Clearly, the computer service has breached the standard of care owed to the business, and clearly this breach has caused the business's loss.

In some cases, however, the actions of the defendant are not the only cause of the harm. Consider, for example, a case in which weather conditions contribute to a car crash in which a plaintiff is harmed because a defective air bag fails to deploy; or, consider a case in which a home hair-colouring product causes a serious reaction in a customer because the customer has a rare allergy or has been newly sensitized to a component of the dye (this can occur after having had a tattoo). In these cases, problems with the defendant's product were only one factor in the eventual harm. Can the defendants in these cases be said to have "caused" the harm?

In deciding cases like these, the court uses a legal test known as the "but for" test, asking itself: But for the actions of the defendant, would the harm have occurred?

In the faulty air bag example, the court would more specifically ask: Had the defendant manufacturer's air bag deployed, would the plaintiff have been hurt in the crash? If the answer is no, then the defendant is fully liable for the harm. If the answer is yes, the plaintiff would have still been hurt but less seriously, then the situation is more complicated. Whenever the answer to the "but for" test is "no," the actions of the defendant are said to be a "cause in fact" of the plaintiff's loss. However, it is not enough to establish that the defendant's actions are the cause in fact; the actions must also pass a "remoteness of causation" test to establish that they are also the "cause in law."

Sometimes, harm occurs as a result of a chain of events so unlikely as to be unforeseeable to the party who started the chain. These cases, where the consequences are excessively remote from the wrongful act, are said to be cases in which there is no "cause in law," which is simply another way of saying that, for public policy reasons, it would not be fair to impose liability on the defendant.

The case that first established the concept of cause in law is a US case called *Palsgraf v Long Island Railroad Co.* In *Palsgraf*, a railway employee "boosted" a passenger roughly onto a train that was about to depart. The force of the boost caused the passenger to drop a parcel containing explosives. The parcel exploded, and the force of the explosion caused a heavy set of commercial scales, located many metres farther down the platform, to topple over, injuring a person standing on the platform.

While the railway employee was found to be negligent in roughly boosting the passenger, he could not have known that the passenger was carrying explosives, or that there would be an explosion that would cause an item to fall on a person standing a distance away. The court found that while the case satisfied the "but for" test (and, therefore, there was cause in fact), there was no cause in law. The railway employee was found not to be liable for the harm to the plaintiff caused by the falling scales.

Another kind of case that is complicated from a causation standpoint is one in which there are multiple causes of an injury—for example, a person breaks a leg in a slip-and-fall accident, and then the surgery to repair the break is completed incompetently, so the person needs further surgeries and a longer hospital stay; but while in hospital she contracts an antibiotic-resistant infection that leads to the amputation of her foot. In these cases, courts often find that all the parties have jointly caused the plaintiff's injury and are therefore jointly responsible. As provided by the *Negligence Act* (discussed earlier in the chapter), the court will apportion—or divide—liability among the parties.

In its 1996 decision in *Athey v Leonati*, the Supreme Court of Canada created a system of steps for analyzing complex cases. The *Athey v Leonati* steps are applied to each defendant in turn, as follows:

1. Apply the "but for" test to establish basic causation.
2. Address multiple causes:
   a. to attract liability, a defendant's actions need not be the only cause;
   b. where another cause, such as weather, was not a tort, the defendant bears the full responsibility (that is, there is no "deduction" for weather or natural causes);
   c. where another defendant contributed to the harm, liability should be divided between the defendants;
   d. where the plaintiff's actions are one of the causes, the principles of contributory negligence should be applied.
3. Make each defendant liable only for the injuries caused by that defendant.
4. Apply the "thin skull rule" (a rule that makes defendants liable for harm that happens because the plaintiff has a hidden underlying susceptibility, like an especially thin skull).
5. Make the defendant liable only for the injuries and losses that the plaintiff suffered as a result of that defendant's negligence. (In some cases, the plaintiff will have other, compounding problems that would have arisen later anyway and that cannot be attributed to the defendant.)

Remoteness of Damages

In order to establish the tort of negligence, a plaintiff must prove that the defendant could, in a general way, foresee the harm she suffered as a result of the defendant's breach of the standard of care owed to her. In other words, the harm the plaintiff suffered as a result of the defendant's breach cannot be too far removed (or "remote," as the law commonly refers to it) from the kind of harm that the defendant might anticipate.

For example, Val-Nam encloses its generators in a waterproof cover and affixes labels on each generator that warn users not to submerge the generator or to leave it out where it can get wet. It does this to protect the generator from short circuiting and to protect users from electrocution. If the waterproof cover is not properly sealed during the manufacturing process or if the warning labels are not affixed, electrocution is a foreseeable result. A plaintiff who suffers injury from electrocution would be able to establish that the harm was foreseeable to Val-Nam. A plaintiff who suffers injury after climbing on the generator to reach a high shelf would likely not.

foreseeability expectation of whether a reasonable person could predict that a certain result might follow from their actions

The issue of **foreseeability** is relevant to the kind of harm, and not usually to the degree of harm, the plaintiff suffered. That means that as long as the defendant could have anticipated harm of the general type that actually occurred, the defendant is usually held responsible for all the damage that results.

CASE IN POINT

Remoteness: The Bottle Fly

Mustapha v Culligan of Canada Ltd, 2008 SCC 27, [2008] 2 SCR 114

Facts

When changing the bottle on his home water cooler, Mr. Mustapha discovered a dead fly in the unopened bottle of water he was about to install. Although he discovered the fly before consuming any of the water, he had an extreme reaction to the sight of the fly and to the "revolting implications" of its presence for the health of his family, who had been consuming Culligan bottled water for 15 years.

Mr. Mustapha's initial shock at seeing the fly developed into an extreme psychiatric reaction characterized by severe depression, anxiety, and phobia. The mental illness caused him to lose revenue for his business. At the trial level, the court awarded the plaintiff $80,000 in general damages, approximately $24,000 in special damages, and over $200,000 in damages for loss of business.

Result

Culligan appealed the decision, and the Court of Appeal overturned the judgment, deciding that while the water company was negligent in allowing the water to be contaminated, the extreme psychiatric reaction suffered by the plaintiff from simply seeing the fly was too remote to be foreseeable. Mustapha appealed further, but the Supreme Court upheld the denial of damages.

Business Lesson

Even though courts will rarely hold defendants liable for damage caused by truly improbable contingencies, make sure you take all due care to avoid harm to customers and others and buy insurance to manage risk.

Negligence Torts Common in Business

Product liability and occupiers' liability are the two types of negligence suits that most commonly threaten businesses. Any business that designs, manufactures, or sells a product is at risk of being sued for product liability if someone alleges that the product has caused harm. Any business that invites customers or clients onto its premises is at risk of being sued for occupiers' liability if the customer or client suffers injury while on the property.

Professional negligence is a third type of unintentional tort that involves professionals such as accountants, doctors, engineers, lawyers, and veterinarians. This tort may affect businesses that deal with or employ these people. Professionals are at risk of being sued if a client or patient alleges that he suffered physical or financial harm as a result of the professional's advice or services.

Product Liability

Product liability arises out of harm caused by defective or dangerous products. The harm this tort addresses may affect both people and property. For example, if Val-Nam's electric generator is defective, it could result in injury to a person through electrocution. The defective generator could also start a fire if it short circuits, causing damage to a house or other property.

product liability
subcategory of negligence based on a defendant's liability for harm caused to others because of his or her defective or dangerous products

The designer, manufacturer, or supplier of a product owes a duty of care to anyone who can reasonably be foreseen as a user of the product. One such user is the purchaser of the product, but there are others as well. Unlike the purchaser, these other users cannot sue for breach of contract. This is because these users lack privity of contract, a matter we discuss in Chapter 4 under the heading "Identification of Parties."

www.emond.ca/CBL3/links

DIG DEEPER
The Canada Business Network offers ideas and resources for business owners to manage risk in their day-to-day operations.

Consider the example of a passenger who is injured when a seatbelt in a friend's car malfunctions during an accident. The passenger is not a party to the contract of purchase and sale between the car's owner and the dealership; nor is she a party to the contract between the car's manufacturer and the seatbelt manufacturer. She therefore cannot seek compensation for her injuries in an action for breach of contract. However, she can bring a tort action in product liability. Product liability expands the scope of plaintiffs to include all potential seatbelt users, not just those who were parties to contracts involving the sale of cars or the purchase and installation of seatbelts. Anyone who uses a seatbelt is owed a duty of care.

As in all lawsuits based on negligence, the injured passenger must still establish that the seatbelt manufacturer and/or car manufacturer breached the relevant standard of care and that the breach of this standard caused her injuries that were reasonably foreseeable.

CASE IN POINT

The Snail in the Bottle

Donoghue (M'Alister) v Stevenson, [1932] All ER Rep 1, [1932] UKHL 100

Facts

This case, identified by many as the origin of the modern concept of duty of care, would be classified as a product liability case if it arose today.

The plaintiff and her friend visited a café where the friend bought the plaintiff a ginger beer (soft drink). When she had almost finished the drink, the plaintiff discovered a partially decomposed snail in the bottom of the bottle. She was horrified, and became ill. Her condition was characterized by the court as "nervous shock," a traditional form of harm that is a hybrid between physical and psychiatric harm caused by another party's wrongful act.

In defending what it viewed as a contracts case, the defendant soda manufacturer argued that the plaintiff had no cause of action. Since she had not purchased the drink, there was no privity of contract between the plaintiff and defendant.

Result

The court overcame the privity of contract problem by treating the case as a tort case and holding that regardless of the lack of privity of contract, the defendant could reasonably foresee that parties other than the immediate buyer might consume its products and, should the products be defective, be harmed by them. As a result of this foreseeability, the defendant owed the plaintiff a duty of care. The defendant died before the case went back to court for an assessment of damages. His estate settled out of court with the plaintiff, paying her £200.

Business Lesson

If your business designs or manufactures products, keep *all* potential users in mind (in other words, foresee), not just the anticipated purchasers. Does the product pose special risks to second-hand users? What about to users with a different body type or body chemistry from the intended user? What about to people with food allergies? What about children?

An example of risk management based on foresight is the now commonplace addition of bitter flavours to poisonous household cleaning products. While these products are generally designed to be used by adults, manufacturers have foreseen the risk that toddlers might discover and attempt to drink the products. The bitter flavouring is designed to deter children from drinking the product and to encourage them to spit it out if they do.

MINIMIZING YOUR RISK

Reduce Lawsuits Based on Product Liability

- Test all products thoroughly to determine whether they pose any dangers.
- Document your testing.
- Eliminate potential dangers through redesign if possible.
- Apply clear and exhaustive warnings securely to products.
- Carry sufficient insurance to cover any potential liability.

DEFECTIVE PRODUCTS VERSUS DANGEROUS PRODUCTS

A defective product is one that is designed poorly or manufactured improperly. If a product has a design problem, the defect will affect all identical products. If, however, a product has a manufacturing problem, usually only some of a manufacturer's products will be affected. In either case, the designer, manufacturer, or supplier has a duty to take reasonable steps to prevent a defective product from finding its way into the hands of consumers.

CASE IN POINT

The Second-Hand Helmet

Thomas v Bell Helmets Inc, 1999 CanLII 9312 (Ont CA)

Facts

A motorcyclist who was wearing a second-hand helmet suffered serious brain damage after colliding with a car. The motorcyclist was thrown through the air, his helmet flew off, and he landed in a ditch, hitting his head on the ground. The motorcyclist's family commenced a lawsuit on his behalf against various parties, including the other driver and the manufacturer of the helmet. All the defendants settled the case before trial with the exception of the helmet manufacturer, which disputed its liability.

Result

The helmet manufacturer was held 25 percent responsible for the motorcyclist's injuries. In 1985 (the year the helmet was manufactured), Bell Helmets either knew or should have known that users risked injury if an ill-fitting helmet flew off on impact. This risk could be minimized if the user conducted a "roll off" fit test. Instructions on how to perform this test were not printed on the warning label that remained on the helmet at the time the motorcyclist purchased it. The court found that the manufacturer was liable to the motorcyclist based on the law of product liability.

Business Lesson

If you manufacture safety products, be especially vigilant in the design and content of warning labels, because it is foreseeable that products can be passed on to people who do not have other warning materials (such as user guides). Affix warning labels directly on your merchandise. Ensure that your labels exhaustively describe known risks and how to avoid them.

Certain products, such as poisons, chainsaws, and children's swimming pools, are inherently dangerous even if properly designed and manufactured. Manufacturers of these products have a duty to warn users of the dangers and to provide clear directions for using the products safely. For this reason, warnings are now commonplace on a variety of household items. Once a manufacturer is aware that a product can cause harm, it has two choices: eliminate the potential for harm, or clearly warn the user.

MINIMIZING YOUR RISK

Reduce Lawsuits Based on Defective Products

- Conduct regular and thorough quality inspections of your product at all stages of the manufacturing process.
- Document all inspections.
- Recall any products you discover to be defective if they have already reached distribution channels.
- Contact purchasers of defective products if possible.
- Carry insurance to cover any potential liability.

Occupiers' Liability

occupiers' liability
subcategory of negligence that imposes liability on occupiers of land or buildings for any harm caused to visitors, invitees, or trespassers

occupier
person or company that has control over land or buildings, including owners and tenants

If someone is injured on or near your business premises, you may be required to compensate them for their injuries pursuant to the doctrine of **occupiers' liability**. The most common example of this tort is the "slip and fall," in which a customer suffers an injury after slipping on a wet floor or icy steps (or a customer's purchasing manager slips on leaked oil in a warehouse!).

Occupiers' liability applies to all "occupiers" of property, whether or not the occupier is an owner. An **occupier** is a person who has control of the property and who is therefore in the best position to prevent, detect, and remedy risks. As a result, the occupier of property is responsible for keeping it safe. Canadian courts have established that businesses can even be occupiers of public property—for example, a portion of a sidewalk leading up to a business entrance—for the purpose of occupiers' liability (see *MacKay v Starbucks Corporation*).

Occupiers owe a duty of care to anyone who enters the property that they are occupying. An occupier's standard of care—that is, how much and what type of care an occupier needs to take to protect visitors—depends to some degree on the nature of the visit.

The *Occupiers' Liability Act* has superseded and simplified the common law standards of care for occupiers in Ontario. Under this Act, occupiers must take reasonable care to see that people (and their property, such as cars) are reasonably safe when entering business premises. The Act limits an occupier's liability in the case of criminals and trespassers to dangers deliberately created to cause harm (such as a trap) or dangers created with reckless disregard (such as a gaping hole not cordoned off). Where the property is of a type deemed hard to patrol for hazards (for example, a wooded property or a closed golf course in winter), a somewhat lower standard of care applies.

MINIMIZING YOUR RISK

Maintain the Safety of Your Business Premises

- Shovel snow and remove ice from walkways.
- Clean up spills immediately.
- Comply with building code requirements about handrails and guardrails.

- Conduct scheduled and regular inspections of your property.
- Remove and repair hazards immediately.
- Document the safety measures you take.
- Post warning notices to alert people to any special risks, such as wet floors.
- Obtain adequate insurance to cover your risks.

Professional Negligence

Professionals—such as lawyers, accountants, financial advisers, stockbrokers, engineers, and computer programmers—are required to meet the standard of a reasonable professional when providing their services. **Professional negligence** occurs when professionals fail to meet this standard and their shoddy service or faulty advice harms a client.

professional negligence tort based on a professional's failure to provide services that meet that profession's standards

Professional organizations often set standards of education, competence, and ethical conduct for their members. The law expects a person who holds herself out as a professional to have the training and qualifications that are standard in that profession and to follow approved practices when providing services.

The standard applied to professionals is that of a reasonable—not perfect—professional, because highly trained professionals are as human as everybody else. For example, if an architect makes an error in designing your office building and the error is one that a reasonable architect might have made, your negligence action against her will not succeed. She has not breached the standard of care of a reasonable architect. Only if the error falls outside the scope of reasonable professional competence will she be liable for professional negligence.

In determining whether or not a professional has met this standard, the court will often compare the professional's performance against industry standards and recognized best practices.

In some cases, the delivery of professional services gives rise to a special duty, called a **fiduciary duty**, owed by the professional to the client. A fiduciary duty is an enhanced standard of care that flows from a relationship of special trust. A lawyer who holds assets in trust for a beneficiary, for example, owes a fiduciary duty to his client. He, and all other professionals who owe a fiduciary duty to clients, must demonstrate a high standard of good faith and loyalty, as well as the competency required by his profession.

fiduciary duty enhanced duty of care that flows from a relationship of special trust, such as that between a doctor and a patient

CASE IN POINT

The Incurious Accountant

Bloor Italian Gifts Ltd v Dixon, 2000 CanLII 14727 (Ont CA)

Facts

The owner of a Toronto gift shop received a notice of assessment from the Canada Revenue Agency advising that the business owed over $1 million in unremitted retail sales tax, plus a 25 percent penalty. The owner brought an action based on professional negligence against its accountant, alleging that the accountant should be liable to compensate the gift shop for its losses because the accountant had apparently failed to notice that the business's annual retail sales tax remittances were far below what they should have been compared with the volume of business the store was doing.

In accounting for retail sales tax, the accountant had simply relied on the paper printouts from a cash register that was being used improperly by the store staff, so that retail sales tax, though it was being collected, was not being properly recorded. At the trial level, the court found that the accountant did not fall below the required standard of care in failing to question the low sales tax being reported; instead, it was up to the business owner to provide the accountant with correct numbers.

Result

The Court of Appeal reversed this finding, holding that in the course of his review engagement (a type of informal audit), it was the accountant's duty to challenge implausible numbers, which he did not do. Comparing the accountant's work to established industry standards, the court found that failing to question the quantum of sales tax fell below the standard of care expected of a reasonably competent accountant. The court found the accountant liable to compensate the business for half its losses (the business was liable for the other half, based on contributory negligence).

Business Lesson

When performing professional services yourself, complying with established industry standards can help you fend off a professional negligence claim. When hiring a professional to provide services to your business, inquire about their credentials and familiarity with industry standards. If you are not happy with the professional's work, take steps to determine whether that work meets the standards agreed upon by other professionals in the same industry.

MINIMIZING YOUR RISK

Take Professional Care

- If your business employs professionals, know what standards they must meet.
- Ensure your professional employees are in good standing with their regulatory associations.
- Keep abreast of any changes in professional standards.
- Monitor the work of professionals through peer reviews.
- Carry sufficient malpractice insurance to cover potential liability.

Strict Liability Torts and the Rule in Rylands v Fletcher

While the concept of strict liability is much more commonly associated with criminal and quasi-criminal statute law these days, there was a historical line of tort law that incorporated the concept.

Strict liability is liability that a court imposes on defendants without the need for proof that the defendants intended to cause harm or that they were negligent. Vicarious liability, discussed above, is an example of strict liability. Remember that Val-Nam could be held vicariously liable for the injuries to the purchasing manager after she slipped on the leaked oil. Once it is proven that Val-Nam's employee was negligent while performing his job duties (in failing to clean up the spill), Val-Nam will be vicariously liable even if Val-Nam can demonstrate that it took all reasonable steps to properly train the employee, etc.

In addition to vicarious liability, in the tort context, courts in England recognized liability for harm in the absence of intent or negligence in certain narrowly defined circumstances. Two of these circumstances were the possession of dangerous animals and blasting. In one case, the owner of a savage dog was held liable for injuries to bite victims even though he himself played no role in setting the dog loose. (In Ontario today, liability for the actions of one's dog is governed by statute.)

In other strict liability cases, contractors conducting blasting operations were held liable for blast damage on neighbouring lands even though there was no evidence that they had conducted the blasting negligently.

The branch of strict liability that has found the surest foothold in modern tort law was defined in 1868 in the case of *Rylands v Fletcher*. In that case, the defendant owned a reservoir. The reservoir burst, and water escaped through a channel of which the reservoir owner was unaware, damaging neighbouring property. The court found that the defendant was liable based on strict liability—that is, without actually being negligent.

The "rule in *Rylands v Fletcher*" now provides that a person who makes "non-natural use" of their land by bringing, storing, or using a dangerous thing on the land is liable for any damage to neighbouring lands caused by the escape of that thing, even in the absence of negligence. While case law continues to develop its meaning, "non-natural use" tends to mean that there is special use of the land that brings with it the possibility of an extraordinary danger or detriment to the community. Many applications of this rule are now a part of environmental statute law, especially those concerning the discharge of contaminants into the air and water.

MINIMIZING YOUR RISK

Exercise Due Diligence

- If you keep or use a potentially dangerous thing on your property, such as large quantities of water, chemicals, wild animals, or spark-generating machinery, keep or use it safely.
- Obey all safety guidelines and environmental laws, and work quickly to contain spills and attend to accidents.
- Because strict liability arises without negligence on your part, you may be liable even when you do everything right. Carry adequate insurance.

Intentional or Unintentional Torts

Many torts that involve business property can be committed intentionally or unintentionally. For example, a resort owner who is mistaken about the exact extent of her property's lake frontage might build a beachside bar and seating area that encroaches onto neighbouring land; in this case, the building and use of the area would constitute unintentional trespass. By contrast, if the same resort owner plays croquet on what she knows to be the neighbour's lawn, this is intentional trespass.

Common Business Torts Involving Property

Three torts that involve the use of property may be of particular interest to business people: trespass to land, nuisance, and invasion of privacy. We describe these torts in the following sections.

Trespass to Land

Trespass to land occurs when a person comes onto land without the express or implied permission of its occupier. Express permission is uncommon in the commercial world; implied permission is much more typical, as in the case of a retail store with an "open" sign that impliedly invites its customers to enter its premises as frequently as possible.

trespass to land
tort in which the defendant, without the permission of the plaintiff, comes onto land occupied by the plaintiff

Trespass usually occurs when a person refuses to leave business premises upon being asked to do so. In Ontario, the *Trespass to Property Act* now governs the tort of trespass.

Most businesses have the right to exclude whomever they want from their property. However, there are exceptions. A retail or other business that depends on dealing with the public cannot unreasonably exclude potential customers or clients.

A retail business that removes or excludes a potential customer without a valid reason could face charges under a provincial or federal human rights statute. The "look" of a person is not a valid reason for removing them, particularly if the reason is based on discriminatory criteria such as race, gender, or age. For example, an electronics outlet may not remove teenagers simply because they are teenagers. However, if some of the teenagers become belligerent, disturb other customers, or destroy product displays, for example, the store has the right to remove those particular teenagers.

In detaining or removing trespassers, business owners and employees should use the minimal level of force necessary to avoid tort suits or criminal charges based on assault and battery or false imprisonment (both discussed above).

Businesses, such as land developers, that are not open to the public and that wish to prevent trespassing on their property must post "no trespassing" signs, as described in the *Trespass to Property Act*.

MINIMIZING YOUR RISK

Manage Access to Your Premises

- Post "no trespassing" signs to minimize liability in negligence and to support your enforcement of the *Trespass to Property Act*.
- Avoid exclusion of patrons on the basis of discriminatory criteria, and train employees to respect human rights.
- Use minimal physical contact to remove trespassers or troublemakers. If patrons resist removal, call the police.

Nuisance

nuisance
tort in which the defendant interferes with the use and enjoyment of the plaintiff's property

Occupiers, both owners and tenants, have the right to use and enjoy their property without unreasonable, substantial interference. The tort of **nuisance** provides a remedy when there is interference with that right.

For example, consider the implications if Val-Nam purchases an old factory that has been dormant for a number of years and starts up round-the-clock production. During the time that the factory was closed, an entire community was built around it. For years, the neighbourhood had been a quiet retreat. However, when Val-Nam starts up production, the noise levels increase significantly due to the operation of the machines and there are constant vibrations from the machines and heavy truck traffic (which also adds engine brake noise). Neighbours are complaining about not being able to enjoy their backyards due to the noise and not being able to sleep at night due to the noise and vibrations. Neighbours closest to the factory have suggested that the vibrations are causing structural damage to their homes. In these circumstances, Val-Nam may have to defend itself against a tort action in nuisance commenced by its neighbours.

Nuisances come in many different forms: sounds, smells, spills, fumes, vibrations, and many types of pollution. Often two businesses are incompatible, such as a candy shop and a pulp mill, or a bed and breakfast and a pig farm. Municipal zoning by-laws, building codes, and environmental laws have evolved in an attempt to manage the environmental impacts of different kinds of land use; however, they have not replaced the tort of nuisance. Accidents such as broken water pipes and sewage spills can still result in nuisance lawsuits.

These examples may sound similar to the types of situations that would invoke strict liability under the rule in *Rylands v Fletcher*, discussed above. However, remember that the rule in *Rylands v Fletcher* requires that the defendant's use of their land be "non-natural." The tort of nuisance can provide a remedy where the defendant's land use falls within ordinary use of the land.

MINIMIZING YOUR RISK

Be Considerate of Your Neighbours

- Comply with all land-use laws that pertain to your business.
- Investigate technologies to control emissions such as chemicals and exhaust fumes.
- Choose a site suitable for your business.
- Maintain good relations in your community.
- Carry sufficient insurance to cover cleanup costs in the event of accidents.

www.emond.ca/CBL3/links

DIG DEEPER
The Office of the Privacy Commissioner of Canada offers tips to help businesses avoid contravening privacy laws.

Privacy Torts and Breaches of Privacy Legislation

The law requires businesses to respect the privacy of employees, customers, and clients in circumstances where these people have a reasonable expectation of privacy and where privacy of personal information is specifically protected by statute.

The torts of invasion of privacy or intrusion upon seclusion occur where there is an expectation of privacy, where that privacy is invaded in a manner that is intentional and would be highly offensive to a reasonable person, and where harm results. The harm that results can be limited to distress, humiliation, or anguish; there does not have to be a quantifiable economic loss. Clearly, the level of privacy that employees can expect in the workplace is lower than the level of privacy that they can expect in their own homes. However, a business's ability to monitor an employee's telephone and computer use and its ability to rely on video surveillance are subject to legal scrutiny. We discuss these matters in Chapter 9.

Businesses must also be aware of the right of customers and clients to the protection of their personal information, such as names, addresses, and consumer purchase history. Business owners who collect personal information must ensure that their operation complies with the *Personal Information Protection and Electronic Documents Act* and also with provincial privacy protection legislation, where requirements differ from those in federal statutes. Breaches of privacy laws, unlike the tort of invasion of privacy, need not be intentional to attract penalties. Privacy protection requirements are particularly stringent in health care settings. We discuss this legislation in Chapter 11.

MINIMIZING YOUR RISK

Respect the Privacy of Employees and Customers

- Allow employees as much privacy as possible, being mindful of the need for business security and productivity.
- Keep up to date with changes in privacy law.

- Designate a person to deal with privacy issues.
- Obtain customers' consent to the collection and use of their personal information.
- Put safeguards in place to protect customers' personal information, and do not share customer lists with other businesses.

Defending Against Tort Actions

If Val-Nam is sued by the purchasing manager for compensation for her injuries caused by slipping on the oil on the warehouse floor, what should Val-Nam do? Prior to a lawsuit being filed, Val-Nam will have a greater number of options for resolving the dispute, including negotiation and mediation (See Chapter 2 for a full discussion of alternative dispute resolution choices). Once the lawsuit has been filed, Val-Nam can either ignore it and risk having the plaintiff obtain default judgment, attempt to settle the action, or defend the action. There are three common defences to tort actions: failure to prove the tort, contributory negligence, and voluntary assumption of risk. We discuss each of these in the following sections. We also comment briefly on statutory compensation schemes, which are alternatives to tort actions.

burden of proof requirement that a certain party prove a particular fact at trial

standard of proof degree to which a party must convince a judge or jury that the allegations are true

balance of probabilities standard of proof in civil (as opposed to criminal) law indicating that one version of events is more probable than another

Failure to Prove the Tort

As the victim of an alleged wrong, a plaintiff bears the **burden of proof**. This means that the plaintiff must present evidence showing that a particular tort occurred, that the defendant was responsible for its occurrence, and that the tort resulted in quantifiable harm to the plaintiff. Unlike in a criminal case, where the **standard of proof** is very high and the prosecutor must prove the guilt of a defendant "beyond a reasonable doubt," in a civil case, a plaintiff need only prove her case on a **balance of probabilities**. This means that the plaintiff must prove that her version of events is *more likely* to be true than the version presented by the defendant.

It is the defendant's job to refute (respond to and argue against) the plaintiff's evidence in an effort to prevent the plaintiff from establishing her case. If a defendant successfully demonstrates that the plaintiff failed to show that her version of events is more likely than not to have occurred, the defendant will successfully defend his case.

SCENARIO: FOR DISCUSSION

What is the purchasing manager's burden of proof? If she makes a negligence claim against Val-Nam, what elements must she prove? What evidence will she need to collect in order to demonstrate that the elements of the tort are satisfied?

For example, when refuting a negligence claim, the defendant may argue that the plaintiff failed to prove one of the four elements of negligence. He may, for example, persuade the judge that the plaintiff failed to prove, on a balance of probabilities, that the defendant owes the plaintiff a duty of care. If the judge is persuaded by the defendant's arguments, the defendant wins the case. The defendant is not required to present any evidence of his own, and he is not required to compensate the plaintiff for her losses.

MINIMIZING YOUR RISK

Challenge the Plaintiff's Case

- Consult a lawyer (if the amount of compensation sought is within the limits of the Small Claims Court, and you are in Ontario, you may wish to consider consulting a paralegal instead).
- Research the case and the nature of the plaintiff's alleged damages.
- Present credible evidence—to the court or to your legal representative—about alternative causes for the plaintiff's harm, including people other than yourself who have contributed to it.
- In appropriate cases, raise before the court the possibility that the plaintiff has not met the burden of proof.

Contributory Negligence

contributory negligence role that a plaintiff may play in negligently contributing to the cause or aggravation of their own injury

Contributory negligence is available as a partial defence to many torts that involve negligence and, pursuant to the *Negligence Act*, to intentional torts as well. By raising the defence of contributory negligence, the defendant claims that the plaintiff contributed to, or was partially responsible for, their own injuries. For example, if the purchasing manager was wearing inappropriate footwear in the warehouse (stiletto heels), this may have contributed to her injuries.

As an additional example, consider a product liability case in which a plaintiff sues a lawn mower manufacturer after suffering an injury while mowing the lawn. The plaintiff claims that the lawn mower was defective and establishes the four elements of negligence on a balance of probabilities.

The defendant manufacturer now has an opportunity to present its defence. To establish the defence of contributory negligence, it may claim, for example, that the plaintiff was partially responsible for the injuries she suffered because she tampered with the lawn mower by removing a safety guard. Like the plaintiff, the defendant must establish its defence on a balance of probabilities. If the judge finds that it is more likely than not that the plaintiff was partially responsible for the harm she suffered, the defence of contributory negligence succeeds.

SCENARIO: FOR DISCUSSION

In the Val-Nam/purchasing manager negligence action, who will have the burden of proving that the defence of contributory negligence applies?

What will that person have to demonstrate and what type of evidence will they want to collect in order to do this?

How would you apportion liability between Val-Nam and the purchasing manager?

When a defence of contributory negligence succeeds, a judge apportions—or distributes—liability between the plaintiff and the defendant. The judge may, for example, find that the plaintiff was 25 percent responsible for the accident by tampering with the guard, and the defendant was 75 percent responsible for the accident by selling a defective lawn mower. In deciding how the plaintiff can be fairly compensated for her injuries, the judge will apportion the plaintiff's monetary damages accordingly. If the damages she suffered can be quantified at $1,000, the defendant will be required to pay $750, and the plaintiff will be required to absorb the $250 herself (see Figure 3.3).

Figure 3.3 Contributory Negligence

LIABILITY	TOTAL DAMAGES $1,000
Plaintiff is 25% liable	**Plaintiff must absorb $250**
Defendant is 75% liable	**Defendant must pay $750**

MINIMIZING YOUR RISK

Try to Establish Contributory Negligence

- Consider and raise the possibility that the plaintiff may have contributed to their own injuries or losses.
- Investigate the issue. Request that the plaintiff disclose all available medical or repair records to determine whether the plaintiff responded to the incident in an appropriate way.
- If you suspect contributory negligence, locate and call witnesses who can support your case.

Voluntary Assumption of Risk

voluntary assumption of risk
defence based on proof that a plaintiff knowingly entered into a risky situation and thereby assumed responsibility for any injuries

waiver of liability
acknowledgment of the risks in an activity and an agreement to assume them

The defence of **voluntary assumption of risk** is available to defendants who can prove, on a balance of probabilities, that a plaintiff voluntarily and knowingly put himself in a risky situation and thereby assumed responsibility for his own fate, including any injuries he suffered.

For example, a whitewater rafting company might argue voluntary assumption of risk if a customer is injured while on a rafting trip. The company might demonstrate that the plaintiff assumed the risk of injury by providing the court with a **waiver of liability**—a document signed by the customer before the rafting trip, stating that the customer was aware of the risks and had agreed to assume them. A sample waiver is reproduced on page 95.

Unlike the defence of contributory negligence, the defence of voluntary assumption of risk is a complete defence. This means that a court will not apportion the responsibility for assumption of risk between the parties. If a court determines, on a balance of probabilities, that the injured party voluntarily assumed the risk of injury, the injured party will receive no compensation. In the whitewater rafting case, the customer must bear the cost of their losses alone.

Sample Waiver

Slippery Slopes Ski Area Waiver and Release of Liability

SIGNING THIS RELEASE MAY AFFECT YOUR LEGAL RIGHTS, INCLUDING THE RIGHT TO SUE OR THE RIGHT TO CLAIM COMPENSATION IN THE EVENT OF AN ACCIDENT. PLEASE READ CAREFULLY!

Skiing is a sport with inherent risks that the staff of Slippery Slopes Ski Area cannot completely control. While we do everything in our power to promote the safety of our patrons, patrons assume the risk of injury, property loss, or death by engaging in skiing activities.

As a condition of his or her use of Slippery Slopes Ski Area facilities, each entrant onto Slippery Slopes premises assumes all risk of personal injury, death, or property loss resulting from any cause whatsoever including, but not limited to: the risks, dangers, and hazards of skiing, snowboarding, snow-tubing, and all other recreational activities; the use of ski lifts; collision with natural or man-made objects or with skiers, snowboarders, or other persons; and negligence or breach of statutory duty of care on the part of Slippery Slopes Ski Area and its directors, officers, employees, instructors, volunteers, agents, independent contractors, representatives, sponsors, successors, and assigns (hereinafter collectively referred to as "Slippery Slopes").

The entrant agrees that Slippery Slopes shall not be liable for any such personal injury, death, or property loss, and releases Slippery Slopes and waives all claims with respect thereto.

The entrant agrees that any litigation involving Slippery Slopes shall be brought solely within the Province of Ontario, and shall be within the exclusive jurisdiction of the courts of the Province of Ontario.

PLEASE ADHERE TO THE ALPINE RESPONSIBILITY CODE PRINTED ON THE REVERSE OF YOUR LIFT TICKET AND BE RESPONSIBLE FOR YOUR OWN SAFETY AT ALL TIMES.

By signing below I agree to be bound by the terms of this release:

________________	________________	________________
Entrant name (please print)	Entrant signature	Date

The defence of voluntary assumption of risk frequently arises in occupiers' liability cases. Consider, for example, a case in which a banker sues a construction company after suffering injury on a construction site. Although the site manager warns the banker that the premises are unsafe for untrained personnel, the banker insists on walking in a cordoned-off area and refuses to wear a hard hat. In a case such as this, a court may determine that the banker voluntarily assumed the risk of injury and is therefore responsible for their own injuries.

SCENARIO: FOR DISCUSSION

Could you argue that the purchasing manager voluntarily assumed the risk of slipping on the oil?

Generally, to prove that a plaintiff has voluntarily assumed a risk, you must demonstrate:

- an express or implied agreement between the plaintiff and defendant in which the plaintiff consented to accept both
  - the physical risk (the danger of injury) and
  - the legal risk (abandoning the right to sue).

What type of steps would Val-Nam have had to have taken to be able to claim that the purchasing manager voluntarily assumed the risk of slipping?

A pair of 2017 Ontario cases (*Woodhouse v Snow Valley* and *David Schnarr v Blue Mountain Resorts Limited*) considered the interplay between the provisions of the *Occupiers' Liability Act* (OLA) and the *Consumer Protection Act* (CPA) in the context of waivers.[2] Both plaintiffs were injured at ski resorts, and both argued that the broad waivers they signed were invalid because of the operation of the OLA and/or CPA. As discussed earlier in this chapter, the OLA (at s 3) allows claims against occupiers by people who are injured on the property they are occupying. The application of the CPA is not based on being a property occupier, but instead creates contract and tort rights for consumers. Section 9(1) of the CPA creates a deemed warranty (a warranty created by the operation of statute) that the services provided by a business will be of reasonably acceptable quality. The plaintiffs in the ski hill cases both argued that either or both of these statutes invalidated the waivers they signed, allowing them to recover damages for their injuries. While the two decisions were different in a number of ways, both courts found that the warranty created by the CPA has the potential to invalidate a waiver where the facts support this (for example, the person seeking damages would have to have used "services," not just have been present on the defendant's property).

While both cases are being appealed, for the time being it is important that business owners realize that having customers sign a waiver is no guarantee that the businesses will be free from liability for injuries that flow from the provision of services. We revisit these cases in Chapter 6, from the perspective of making decisions about the breadth and content of waivers.

www.emond.ca/CBL3/links

DIG DEEPER

The Insurance Bureau of Canada offers information on risk management, internal fraud, crisis preparedness, and other relevant topics.

2 This matter is discussed in Robert L. Love and Edona C. Vila, "Two Judicial Treatments of a Novel Question of Law: Invalidating an Occupier's Waiver Through the Application of Ontario's Consumer Protection Legislation," *CanLII Connects* (8 March 2017), online: <http://canliiconnects.org/en/summaries/45014>.

MINIMIZING YOUR RISK

Inform Your Customers About Risks

- If you run a business or operate a facility that poses a risk to customers, be thorough and detailed in explaining to customers the risks associated with participation.
- Use signage and handouts to communicate all foreseeable risks.
- Require and enforce the use of personal safety equipment, where appropriate.
- Require customers to read and sign liability waivers that your lawyer has prepared.
- Carry adequate insurance in case your waivers fail to hold up in court.

Figure 3.4

Where your business involves risks to customers, it is important to communicate those risks thoroughly and clearly. Post signage, distribute written material, require a signed liability waiver, and explain the hazards verbally.

CASE IN POINT

Not So Much Fun at the Water Park

Hutchison v Daredevil Park Inc, 2003 CanLII 25623 (Ont Sup Ct J)

Facts

A customer at a water park broke his ankle while using a waterslide. The top part of the slide contained a slip-resistant tub that was designed for users to sit in before launching themselves into the steep and slippery chute. Water jets obscured the users' view of the bottom of the launching tub and the chute. An attendant at the top of the slide, who was also responsible for several other slides, did not instruct the customer on the proper use of the slide, other than to indicate when it was safe for the customer to launch himself. The customer failed to sit down in the tub before entering the chute. Although he had never used such a slide before that day, he did complete several successful runs before breaking his ankle.

There was no sign close to the entry tub directing the user to sit down in the tub. There was no luminescent line at the point of transition to the slippery surface with a warning to sit behind the line. In the 12 years of the park's operation, no one had ever suffered the same sort of accident as the customer.

Result

The court found that, while the customer voluntarily assumed some risk in using the slide, not all the inherent risks of its use were communicated to him. The court also found that the customer was not fully instructed in how to use the slide safely. Because the water park failed to communicate all the risks and to fully instruct the customer, it was found liable for 80 percent of his injuries. Because he did not ask questions about how to use the entry tub, and assumed the risk of using it without full instructions, the customer was found contributorily negligent and was liable for 20 percent of his own losses.

Business Lesson

Explain all foreseeable risks of injury to your customers, and carry adequate insurance.

Statutory Compensation Schemes

In some cases, legislative schemes, such as workplace safety insurance, compensate plaintiffs for the injuries they suffer as a result of the torts of others. Compensation offered under these programs is typically paid as an alternative to lawsuits. This means that a person who accepts statutory compensation for an injury cannot also sue a defendant in tort for the same injury. We discuss some of these compensatory legislative schemes in Chapter 9 under the heading "Workplace Safety and Insurance Act, 1997."

Remedies for Torts

Once a plaintiff has proven that a defendant has committed a tort, and once the defendant has failed to raise a credible defence, the goal of the law is to compensate the plaintiff. By fashioning a remedy, a court seeks, as far as is practicable, to put the plaintiff back into the position in which he was before the defendant committed the tort.

Remedies take a variety of forms. By far, the most common tort remedy is damages. The categories of damages available to successful plaintiffs were introduced in Chapter 2 under the heading "Civil Court Remedies: Damages."

While damages are the most common remedy sought in torts cases, plaintiffs occasionally seek other remedies. These remedies are generally pursued either to prevent future harm from occurring or to clarify the parties' rights.

Injunctions, discussed in greater detail in Chapter 2, are a remedy designed to prevent future harm or the escalation/worsening of present harm by prohibiting a party from engaging in certain conduct or by ordering the party to cease conduct already begun. Injunctions are commonly ordered in cases of passing off. A plaintiff who has discovered that a defendant is passing off its wares as those of the plaintiff will often immediately seek an injunction that prevents the defendant from selling those goods to avoid further damage to the reputation of the plaintiff's goods and to its business.

CHAPTER SUMMARY

A tort is an act or omission that injures people or damages property. To succeed in a tort action, a plaintiff must almost always prove a wrongful act, causation, and quantifiable harm, in addition to other elements, depending on the tort.

One of the most important principles in tort law is vicarious liability, under which businesses can be held responsible for injuries that result from the actions of their employees or contractors. Two or more parties may also be jointly and severally liable, meaning that the plaintiff is entitled to recover the full amount of the damages from either one.

An intentional tort happens when an individual or business deliberately harms another. Assault is the threat of physical harm; it is usually claimed with battery, which is any intentionally harmful or offensive physical contact. False imprisonment occurs when one person unlawfully restricts the freedom of another, which could be a simple act like putting an arm across somebody's path. Another intentional tort, defamation, happens when someone makes a statement about an individual or business to at least one other individual that results in a significant loss of respect or reputation.

The most common intentional business torts are passing off, inducing breach of contract, and interference by unlawful means. Passing off involves using a product name or design that is similar to that of a better-known and respected brand. To prove that it is the victim of interference by unlawful means, a business must demonstrate that the defendant engaged in unlawful conduct toward another party with the intention to injure the plaintiff's business.

Unintentional torts happen as a result of careless or negligent acts or omissions that cause unintended harm. To succeed in a claim based on negligence, a plaintiff must prove quantifiable harm, a breach in a reasonable standard of care, that the breach caused loss or injury, that the defendant owed a duty of care, and that the defendant should have foreseen the loss or injury.

Certain torts may be committed intentionally or unintentionally. These include trespass; nuisance, or the interference with the right of occupiers to use and enjoy their property; and invasion of privacy.

Common defences to tort actions include contributory negligence (where the plaintiff is partially responsible for his own injuries) and voluntary assumption of risk (where the plaintiff voluntarily and knowingly assumed the risk and is therefore responsible for himself).

Once a plaintiff has proven that a defendant has committed a tort, and once the defendant has failed to raise a credible defence, the goal of the law is to compensate the plaintiff. The most common remedy is financial damages; however, plaintiffs sometimes seek other forms of relief such as injunctions.

KEY TERMS

REFERENCES

AI Enterprises Ltd v Bram Enterprises Ltd, 2014 SCC 12, [2014] 1 SCR 177.

Athey v Leonati, 1996 CanLII 183 (SCC), [1996] 3 SCR 458.

Bloor Italian Gifts Ltd v Dixon, 2000 CanLII 14727 (Ont CA).

Cappuccino Affair Ltd v Haraga, 2000 ABQB 750.

Competition Act, RSC 1985, c C-34.

Consumer Protection Act, 2002, SO 2002, c 30, Schedule A.
Crocker v Sundance Northwest Resorts Ltd, [1988] 1 SCR 1186.
David Schnarr v Blue Mountain Resorts Limited, 2017 ONSC 114.
Donoghue (M'Alister) v Stevenson, [1932] All ER Rep. 1, [1932] UKHL 100.
Hutchison v Daredevil Park Inc, 2003 CanLII 25623 (Ont Sup Ct J).
Jordan House Ltd v Menow, [1974] SCR 239.
MacKay v Starbucks Corporation, 2017 ONCA 350.
Mann v Canadian Tire Corporation Limited, 2016 ONSC 4926.
Mustapha v Culligan of Canada Ltd, 2008 SCC 27, [2008] 2 SCR 114.
Negligence Act, RSO 1990, c N.1.
Occupiers' Liability Act, RSO 1990, c O.2.
Palsgraf v Long Island Railroad Co, 248 NY 339, 162 NE 99 (1928).
Parsons and Sons Transportation Ltd v Whelan, 2005 NLCA 52.
Personal Information Protection and Electronic Documents Act, SC 2000, c 5.
Ragoonanan v Imperial Tobacco Canada Ltd, 2005 CanLII 40373 (Ont Sup Ct J).
Rylands v Fletcher (1868), LR 3 HL 330.
Teskey v Toronto Transit Commission, 2003 CanLII 11726 (Ont Sup Ct J).
Thomas v Bell Helmets Inc, 1999 CanLII 9312 (Ont CA).
Trespass to Property Act, RSO 1990, c T.21.
Trew v 313124 Saskatchewan Ltd, 2005 SKQB 79.
Woodhouse v Snow Valley, 2017 ONSC 222.

EXERCISES

True or False?

____ **1.** The standard of proof for tort actions is on a balance of probabilities.

____ **2.** Many actions that were originally torts have become offences under provincial statutes.

____ **3.** To prove that a defendant has committed a tort, a plaintiff must establish that the defendant's actions were the sole cause of the harm.

____ **4.** A fiduciary duty is an enhanced duty of care that flows from a relationship of special trust.

____ **5.** The burden of proving a tort defence, such as voluntary assumption of risk, is on the plaintiff.

____ **6.** The law assesses professional negligence according to the "reasonable professional" standard.

____ **7.** An unlimited right to privacy is constitutionally recognized in Canada.

____ **8.** Defamation in writing is called slander.

____ **9.** The tort of assault involves violent touching.

____ **10.** The *Negligence Act* codified the common law concept of contributory negligence into a statutory provision.

____ **11.** If a business operates in a context of unusual risk and offers an activity to patrons, it may be required to exceed the "normal" or "typical" safety procedures common for that kind of business.

Multiple Choice

1. Contributory negligence:

a. means that the plaintiff was partially at fault for the harm they suffered.
b. must be proven by the defendant.
c. can, if proven, limit the defendant's liability in tort.
d. all of the above.

2. Remedies available for torts include which of the following?

a. Prison sentences and damages.
b. Specific performance and injunctions.
c. Damages and injunctions.
d. Restraining orders and restitution.

3. A properly drafted waiver of liability, when signed by the customer of a business, can form the basis of a defence of voluntary assumption of risk. Which of the following can a waiver do?

a. It can protect the business from claims made under both the *Occupiers' Liability Act* and the *Consumer Protection Act*.
b. It can protect the business from claims made under the *Occupiers' Liability Act* but probably not under the *Consumer Protection Act*.
c. It can protect the business from claims made under the *Consumer Protection Act* but probably not under the *Occupiers' Liability Act*.
d. Waivers have been ruled ineffective in Canada, but may still be useful as a means of communicating risks to customers.

4. Negligence is established only when the plaintiff proves that the defendant could reasonably foresee:

a. that the plaintiff would purchase the defendant's goods.
b. that the plaintiff or someone like them might be harmed or incur loss as a result of the defendant's actions.

   c. that the plaintiff or someone like them might be harmed or incur loss as a result of the defendant's actions, and that the full extent of the harm actually suffered by the plaintiff was also reasonably foreseeable.
   d. that the plaintiff would rely, unjustifiably, on the defendant's warnings.
5. How can a business attempt to limit its liability in tort?
   a. By conducting safety tests on products and services and documenting test results.
   b. By maintaining retail and other premises in good repair and conducting regular safety patrols.
   c. By printing warnings on products advising of potential dangers.
   d. By doing all of the above.
6. To succeed in a defence based on fair comment, a defendant's comment must:
   a. be based on a conclusion that is reasonably supported by evidence.
   b. not be motivated by malice.
   c. be on a matter of public interest.
   d. all of the above.
7. Which is the best strategy for business owners to manage the risk of lawsuits based on the law of nuisance?
   a. Restricting entry to dangerous areas.
   b. Conducting market research before designing new products.
   c. Complying with all land-use laws, such as zoning by-laws, building codes, and environmental laws.
   d. None of the above.
8. To establish that the defendant committed the tort of interference by unlawful means, the plaintiff must prove that:
   a. the defendant's business is a direct competitor of their own and that the defendant has gained an economic advantage over the plaintiff by unlawful means.
   b. the defendant intended to harm the plaintiff's business, that the defendant committed an unlawful act to do so, and that the plaintiff suffered actual harm as a result.
   c. the defendant intended to harm the plaintiff's business and that the harm was done with knowledge on the part of principals of the defendant's corporation.
   d. the defendant committed an unlawful act with the intent to harm the plaintiff's business, whether or not actual harm occurred.
9. An indemnification clause is used to do what?
   a. Prevent suits in nuisance brought by neighbours when a business undertakes a polluting activity.
   b. Require participants to waive their right to sue should they be injured when participating in an activity provided by a business.
   c. Force the employee to assume liability for certain risks associated with their work so that the employer is not exposed to vicarious liability.
   d. Any of the above.
10. Who can sue a manufacturer for injuries related to the negligent design of a ski helmet under product liability law? Choose the *best* answer.
   a. The original purchaser only.
   b. The original purchaser and any second-hand purchaser, as long as the helmet is sold with the original packaging bearing safety warnings.
   c. Any wearer of the helmet, whether or not they purchased it, as long as safety warnings are visible on the helmet.
   d. Any wearer of the helmet.

Short Answer

1. List five business practices that can help reduce losses from product liability lawsuits.
2. What is the difference between negligence and strict liability?
3. Why might a party decide to commence a tort action based on events that also formed the basis of a criminal prosecution?
4. If a defendant is attempting to argue voluntary assumption of risk as a defence to a tort action, what must the defendant prove?
5. Describe an appropriate policy for a business with respect to the handling of trespassers.
6. How can a business protect itself from competitors seeking to pass off their merchandise as that of the business?
7. Explain the "but for" test.
8. Why must a defendant's actions be the cause in fact and also the cause in law of a plaintiff's harm?

Apply Your Knowledge

1. A house fire breaks out late at night on the upper floor of a two-storey house. A 16-year-old boy who had been sleeping on a couch in the study where the fire was believed to have begun and two girls—the boy's 2-year-old and 12-year-old cousins who were sleeping in the next room—are killed in the fire.

   An investigation reveals that the fire was most likely caused by a dropped cigarette. The investigators' theory is that the boy fell asleep while smoking and dropped the cigarette on the couch. The couch was 30 years old and made of highly flammable materials.

   Surprised at how readily the fire started, the investigators inquire about which brand of cigarettes the boy smoked. The boy's parents—who forbade him from smoking—did not know, but his friends reported that he alternated between three brands. Two of those brands were manufactured by the Company.

   The Company's advertising claims that its cigarettes contain 20 percent more tobacco than other brands. Since the 1990s, many, but not all, tobacco companies have changed the way they fill cigarettes, packing the tobacco in a manner that makes the cigarettes "self-extinguishing," so that when put down in an ashtray, they quickly stop burning (which is safer and wastes less tobacco). This packing process also means each cigarette contains about 20 percent less tobacco. These details lead investigators to suspect that the dropped cigarette was not of the self-extinguishing variety; in other words, it was of a brand that is less fireproof than 75 percent of the cigarettes on the Canadian market.

   Answer the following questions from the Company's perspective.

   a. If the bereaved families learn that someone other than the (underage) boy bought the cigarette from the Company, does the Company still owe the boy a duty of care?
   b. Does the Company owe the boy's cousins a duty of care?
   c. Was the cigarette the cause in fact of the damages?
   d. Was the cigarette the cause in law of the damages?
   e. Were there any *other* causes of the damages?
   f. Should the fact that there were other causes affect how the Company handles the case?
   g. Is the type of harm that occurred (death by burning) sufficiently remote from the cause that the Company could deny liability on that basis?
   h. Did the Company breach the required standard of care in the design, manufacture, or distribution of its cigarette product?
   i. If the plaintiffs were to rely on the standard of care argument, what arguments might the Company raise in its defence?

2. Your company makes a spray product designed to remove odours from carpets, upholstery, and curtains. Your public relations department advises that a story is circulating on the Internet specifically naming your product and alleging that it is toxic to house cats. According to the source of the story, an alleged veterinarian in Manitoba, hundreds of cats are reported to have died of liver and kidney failure after being exposed to the product.

   Your product is made mainly of water, baking soda, and mild natural fragrance oils. All the ingredients have been extensively tested, and you know that the product poses no threat whatsoever to house cats. Your own investigation reveals that the person who leaked the story is actually a disgruntled former employee who now works for a competitor.

   Answer the following questions.

   a. Has your former employee committed a tort by starting this story? Which tort?
   b. Did your former employee owe you a duty of care? Would your answer be different had he signed a non-competition clause?
   c. Is your former employee's new employer—your competitor—liable for its employee's actions?
   d. What are your damages?
   e. Would you request any other remedies in this case?

3. You have decided to open a mixed martial arts (MMA) training gym, offering classes for recreational and competitive fighters aged six through adult. It occurs to you that this business may expose you to potential tort liability. Answer the following questions.

   a. What research might you do before offering classes to the public?
   b. What would be the main purposes of your research?
   c. If, after completing your research, you decided to go ahead with the venture, what risk management steps would you need to take?
   d. If you complete the research and risk management tasks you listed in the foregoing questions, are you guaranteed to escape liability if a participant is seriously injured or killed while training at your facility or competing on behalf of your gym? Why or why not?

Understanding Contracts

4

LEARNING OUTCOMES

After reading this chapter, you should be able to:

- Define a contract and recognize when agreements are legal and enforceable and when and why they may not be.
- Explain the importance of contract law for businesses.
- Discuss the advantages of written contracts and the rules by which they are interpreted by courts and tribunals.
- List and explain the purpose of terms that are typical to business contracts.
- Describe the advantages and disadvantages of including or excluding specific contract terms in a variety of business agreements.
- Explain how a business can minimize the risks associated with the inclusion or exclusion of specific terms in a contract.

What Is a Contract?

contract
agreement between two or more parties that is enforceable by law

A **contract** is an agreement between two or more individuals or entities (usually known as the "parties to the contract") that is enforceable by law. Contracts are extremely common in daily life. You may be surprised to learn that you, as a consumer, are generally a party to a contract every time you buy a cup of coffee, shop for groceries, download something from the Internet, take public transportation, use a laundromat, or purchase any other goods or services from a commercial enterprise, either in person or online. A contract may be formed by two or more people communicating with one another (face to face, by telephone, email, or text, etc.), by the interaction of an individual and an electronic agent, or by the interaction of electronic agents. The use of electronic agents is rising with the growth of e-commerce.

Contracts occur with equal frequency in the business world. In fact, mutually beneficial contractual transactions are the sustaining force behind most businesses. They also sustain the economy as a whole. In carrying on business, Val-Nam Generation Limited ("Val-Nam") will likely enter into contracts related to leasing retail or office space, purchasing or supplying inventory, storing or transporting goods, providing or receiving marketing, financial, legal, or IT services, and insuring against losses or damages, among others.

A contract always involves an agreement; however, not every agreement is a contract. For an agreement to constitute a legal and enforceable contract, it must contain four elements:

1. *An intention to create a legal relationship.* The parties to a contract must intend to enter into a relationship with each other that binds them in law.
2. *Offer and acceptance.* A contract requires that one party offer to do something and that the other party accept this offer. A contract cannot be imposed unilaterally on another party without their agreement.
3. *Consideration.* **Consideration** is a legal concept that means each party to a contract must provide something of value to the other. An offer to give someone a gift or to provide services for free does not create a contract—a gratuitous promise can usually be withdrawn without any recourse to the expectant beneficiary.
4. *Legality.* A contract must conform to the law of the land and must not violate public policy.

consideration
something of value given up by each party to a contract

These four essential elements of a contract are discussed in greater detail in Chapter 5 under the heading "Formation of a Contract." Other reasons that agreements may not be legally binding between parties are also discussed in Chapter 5, under the heading "Unenforceable Agreements."

In practical terms, a contract's enforceability is perhaps its principal feature. Parties are expected to live up to the obligations they assume under the contracts they enter into. In other words, if you enter into a business transaction—say, an agreement to purchase inventory—you are expected by the other contracting party, the courts, the business community, and society at large to honour your commitment. Failure on your part to fulfill your contractual obligations is known as a **breach of contract**, and such a breach can result in serious legal and economic consequences for you. The implications of contractual breach are explored in Chapter 5 under the heading "Consequences of a Breach of Contract."

breach of contract
failure to fulfill contractual obligations

Contracts in the Business Context

There are many different types of business contracts, some of which are listed below:

- *Employment contracts*—for example, contracts under which businesses engage the services of staff on a full- or part-time basis.
- *Service contracts*—for example, contracts under which businesses provide or receive services such as financial or legal advice, research, graphic design, social media advertising, marketing analysis, storage, transportation, cleaning, maintenance, catering, and communication or IT services.
- *Leasing contracts*—for example, contracts under which businesses rent office space or equipment.
- *Contracts for the purchase and sale of goods*—for example, contracts under which businesses purchase inventory or supplies.
- *Insurance contracts*—for example, contracts under which businesses insure themselves against claims for personal injury or property damage.

Much of the law that applies to contracts is common law, which has evolved over time in the courts, as discussed in Chapter 1. Sometimes, however, provincial statutes govern particular situations, such as contracts involving consumers and contracts involving the sale of goods, both of which are discussed in Chapter 6. Provincial legislation also governs personal property security contracts, which are discussed in Chapter 8. Contracts governing the employment of staff are subject to federal and provincial human rights legislation, which is discussed in Chapter 9.

This chapter focuses on contract law as it applies to everyday business-to-business transactions. Why, in this context, is it important for businesses to live up to their contractual obligations? One reason is that a single business contract is capable of having far-reaching consequences for many enterprises over a long time. A successful business operator must always be looking ahead and planning for the future. If, as a general rule, businesses can depend on one another to fulfill their contractual obligations, they can run their current operations efficiently and plan for the future confidently. If, on the other hand, they are constantly gambling on whether other businesses will fulfill their contractual obligations, planning becomes impossible and economic chaos becomes likely.

Consider, for example, a retailer that enters into an agreement in June to purchase a large shipment of toys from a manufacturer for delivery in October. The retailer is planning a major toy sale for the holiday season in December. Anticipating that the manufacturer will meet its obligations to deliver the toys on time, in early September the retailer enters into another contract with a supplier of shelving. The supplier agrees to install the shelving in time to display the toys when they arrive in October. Although another supplier offers to sell children's books to the retailer at a good price, the retailer rejects the offer because it will not have room to display both the books and the toys over the holiday season. The retailer also signs contracts for a direct mail flyer and a social media advertising campaign regarding the sale. The flyer distributer and advertising agency insist on payment in advance, so the retailer pays them when the contracts are signed in mid-September. The advertising is scheduled to appear in mid-November. Would the retailer be wise to install shelving, pay for advertising, and turn down another business opportunity if it had little faith that the manufacturer would deliver the toys on time?

This type of interdependence among businesses is standard in most industries. The good news is that, generally, businesses *can* depend on one another to meet their contractual obligations, because businesses know (or should know) that if they fail to meet their contractual obligations,

- they may be sued for breach of contract, which can be very expensive, time-consuming, and stressful; and
- they may quickly obtain a bad reputation in the business community, resulting in the loss of future business opportunities.

Businesses that breach their contracts are likely to find themselves on the losing end of a lawsuit if another party makes a claim against them. Because of the importance of the integrity of business transactions to the business community and the economy as a whole, courts generally rule against parties found to be in breach of their contractual obligations.

The Importance of Contract Law for Business Success

Although most business owners and operators understand the importance of keeping their contractual promises—and do so—it is also helpful for every individual working in business to know about contract law. Why?

- *Contracts can clarify your business dealings.* A contract, if carefully drafted and properly understood, can smooth business dealings by informing both you and the other party of your rights and obligations. Elimination of confusion will benefit both of you by facilitating the efficient performance of your agreement.
- *Contracts can prevent unexpected and undesirable results.* An understanding of frequently used contractual terms can help you avoid surprises. Familiarity with the legal impact of these terms creates certainty about your contract's outcome. Legal terms that are common in contracts are discussed later in this chapter under the heading "Reading the Fine Print: Typical Terms in Business Contracts."
- *Contracts can provide for a dispute resolution process.* Parties can agree beforehand on a process for resolving disputes and include this in the contract. Knowledge of contract law allows you to consider a range of dispute-resolving solutions and mechanisms before any dispute arises. This can increase the chances of maintaining a good working relationship, even in the event of a challenging development. It can also reduce the expense associated with a contractual dispute.
- *Contract law governs disputes.* Despite your best intentions, and those of the other party, contractual disputes can still arise. It is important to understand the rules that have been applied in the past in order to predict the outcome that is likely, in the event that your business contract dispute needs formal resolution.

The Importance of Written Contracts

The law does not require all contracts to be in writing. A mutual exchange of promises by business people over lunch, confirmed with a handshake and an intention to be bound, can constitute a binding contract, provided that the agreement is legal and represents a meeting of minds. A verbal agreement of this sort is every bit as binding as the most detailed of written contracts. In fact, many business contracts are never reduced to writing and are successfully completed without any problems.

However, for businesses, written contracts are usually preferable to verbal contracts for two reasons:

1. *Written contracts provide the parties with a record of their rights and obligations.* Documentary evidence of goods sold, services rendered, and business expenses incurred may be necessary from an accounting and tax perspective.
2. *Written contracts provide proof of the parties' agreement in the event of a dispute.* Should the parties take opposing positions regarding whether a contract exists at all, or should they disagree on the terms of the contract, a written contract provides excellent evidence of their intentions and mutual promises.

There are a number of exceptions to the general rule that contracts need not be in writing to be legally enforceable. Contracts that must be in writing include certain contracts related to consumer transactions (see Chapter 6), most contracts related to the sale or leasing of land (see Chapter 10), and contracts that guarantee the payment of another person's debt if that person defaults on their payment obligations. Some of these exceptions also require that the contract be signed by the parties. Where a signature is a legal requirement, an electronic signature will generally be accepted in Canadian jurisdictions.

If a contractual dispute comes to court, the plaintiff will probably argue that the defendant breached an existing contract. The burden will be on the plaintiff to convince the judge that their version of the case has more merit than the defendant's version (see Case in Point box, below).

CASE IN POINT

Determining What Constitutes a Binding Contract

UBS Securities Canada, Inc v Sands Brothers Canada, Ltd, 2009 ONCA 328

Facts

An agreement was reached through telephone and email exchanges between two companies for the purchase of 100,000 shares of a private company that ran the Montreal Stock Exchange. Following the telephone and email communications, but before the share transaction was finalized, the share price doubled when the company announced its intention to list its shares publicly. The defendant tried to back out of the deal, claiming the contract with the plaintiff had not yet been finalized because a formal written share purchase agreement had not been signed.

Result

The plaintiff was able to introduce the evidence necessary to persuade the court that a contract was formed based on telephone conversations and email messages between representatives of the parties.

Business Lesson

Although this case involved a sophisticated securities transaction, elements of the decision may apply in other contexts. Lessons that businesses can learn from this case include the following:

- In determining whether an oral agreement constitutes a binding contract, a court will consider whether or not it is customary in a particular industry, usually one involving fast-paced transactions, for deals to be completed that way.
- It is important to maintain digital records, because the use of technology creates a time-stamped record of all communications between the parties, which can supplement oral testimony as evidence to help prove when a binding contract was formed.
- Make it a habit to follow up telephone conversations to confirm what was said and respond to messages and notes during negotiations to correct or confirm the essential elements of an agreement.

When there is little evidence beyond the testimony of the parties involved, the case will hinge on whom the judge believes.

If the parties are equally credible—that is, if the judge believes they are both giving their honest, if perhaps mistaken, recollection of the events—and cannot decide whom to believe, the plaintiff will lose the case. Similarly, if the parties are equally incredible—that is, if the judge believes that both are being less than truthful or perhaps exaggerating their evidence—the plaintiff will also lose. A written contract can tip the balance in the plaintiff's favour. *Macatula v Tessier* (see Case in Point, below) is a case that underscores the wisdom of taking time to reduce all financial—and other—agreements to writing.

MINIMIZING YOUR RISK

Remember the Advantages of a Written Contract

- Be aware that you may be legally bound by an oral agreement.
- Avoid committing to a business agreement until the terms have been specified in a written contract. Tell your suppliers and customers that it is your company's policy not to finalize any deals without a signed contract.
- Know the person with whom you are dealing. Formalities may be less important when dealing with long-term business associates than with new business contacts about whom you have little information.
- Do not necessarily refuse to be a party to a verbal contract, but understand the risks involved. Carefully consider whether the benefits of a verbal contract outweigh the problems that might arise in the event of a dispute.

CASE IN POINT

The Advantages of Written Agreements

Macatula v Tessier, 2003 MBCA 31

Facts

A homecare worker purchased a Lotto 6/49 ticket for her employer, a senior who was disabled with arthritis. The worker claimed that she and her employer had an agreement to share the proceeds. When the ticket holder won \$11.4 million, the family of the employer, who was in possession of the winning ticket, claimed the money. The homecare worker sued the employer, claiming that the employer was in breach of their contract to share the proceeds. Although the worker had a credit card receipt to prove she had paid for the ticket, the employer insisted during the trial that she had paid her for the ticket and denied any agreement to divide the winnings.

Result

Without the evidence that a written agreement could have provided, the judge was forced to base his decision on the testimony of the parties. After hearing all the evidence, he concluded that the parties had not been "totally candid" with him. The worker's lawsuit failed because the worker did not succeed in convincing the judge that her version of events was more credible than that of her employer.

Business Lesson

Put your agreements in writing.

Writing a Contract

The terms of a written contract constitute a record of the promises made and exchanged by the contracting parties. It is vital that the contract record these promises with as much precision as possible. Should a dispute arise, the most convenient resolution is to find a solution within the language of the contract itself.

Sometimes, however, a contract is flawed. It may fail to address significant matters, or its drafting may be vague and careless. In these cases, the terms of the contract are unlikely to provide a resolution that is acceptable to both parties in the event of a dispute. The parties may need to look to the courts as a last resort in settling their contractual differences.

Rules of Construction

Over the years, the common law has developed several rules—known as the **rules of construction**—that are used in interpreting disputed contracts. Some of the most significant of these rules are set out below.

rules of construction common law rules used in interpreting disputed contracts

1. *Apply an objective test.* If the parties have used a vague term, such as "durable," in defining, for example, the quality of the portable generator that Val-Nam has agreed to sell to XL Equipment Inc ("XL," a national retail chain), a judge will apply an objective test to interpret the meaning of this term. In doing so, the judge will ask, "What does a reasonable person think 'durable' means?" The judge might consult a dictionary or be guided by earlier decisions of other courts about the meaning of similar words but would probably not be concerned with what the parties themselves think "durable" means. Judges act on the principle that contracts should be strictly enforced according to the ordinary meaning of the words chosen by the parties themselves.
2. *Interpret the contract against the drafter.* Under this rule of construction, a judge will prefer the interpretation offered by the party who did not draft the contract over the interpretation of the party who drafted it. The rationale for this rule may be explained by reference to the Val-Nam/XL example. If Val-Nam drafted the agreement and chose to be satisfied with the term "durable," it ran the risk that XL's interpretation would be different. Because Val-Nam failed to prevent the possibility of conflicting interpretations by being more specific in the language of the contract, it bears the burden of having XL's interpretation prevail if a dispute arises.

3. *Determine the parties' intentions.* Under this rule of construction, a judge will attempt to enforce a contract in accordance with the intention of the parties. However, use of this rule is often problematic when the parties take contrary positions regarding their intention.

What Is in a Contract?

In theory, the content of a contract is limited by nothing but the imagination and creativity of the parties who draft it. In practice, however, contracts within particular industry sectors tend to contain similar or identical terms because these terms have proven, over time, to be expedient for business. A business may choose to create individual contracts for each of its transactions, picking and choosing from an array of terms that are commonly used within its industry. Many of these terms are presented below under the heading "Reading the Fine Print: Typical Terms in Business Contracts." Alternatively, businesses may choose to adopt a standard contract and apply it to all transactions of a similar nature. These contracts are known as standard form contracts.

Standard Form Contracts

standard form contract
contract that is drafted by one of the parties and imposed on the other with little or no opportunity for negotiation

A **standard form contract** is a contract that is drafted by one of the parties and imposed on the other with little or no opportunity for negotiating changes. It is often the party that provides a service or sells a product that dictates the terms of the contract. In contrast, the party that pays for a service or purchases a product may often find itself in a "take it or leave it" situation. The use of standard form contracts is widespread, and you will often encounter the following types:

- *Service agreements*—for example, contracts for office cleaning, equipment maintenance, security, Internet access, cellphone usage, and other information technology.
- *Commercial leases*—for example, contracts for the rental of office space or vehicles.
- *Equipment rental agreements*—for example, contracts for the leasing of photocopiers and telephone systems.
- *Advertising agreements*—for example, contracts for direct mail inserts, print display advertisements (for example, in magazines, newspapers, or on billboards), digital advertising (for example, banner ads on websites, pop-up ads, social media campaigns, and videos), radio or television advertisements, and conference exhibition displays.
- *Insurance policies.*

Although standard form contracts tend to be one-sided, and some of the standard terms may appear to be unfair, these contracts between businesses are just as enforceable as contracts that are the product of extensive negotiations. Most standard form contracts are completed successfully: the business transaction proceeds smoothly, and the terms of the contract never become contentious between the parties. Businesses should, however, exercise caution when using standard form contracts with consumers, because the law holds businesses to very strict standards in their dealings with consumers. This matter is addressed in Chapter 6.

Businesses should be cautious when entering into standard form contracts that are posted online. Some web-based contracts contain terms and conditions that are only accessed through hyperlinks, whereas other contracts can be accessed in their entirety by scrolling down a single web page. To ensure that a web-based contract can be enforced, its terms and conditions should be no more difficult to access than if it existed in printed form. Businesses should also be aware of any provisions regarding updates and amendments to online agreements (see more on issues related to e-commerce in Chapters 6 and 11).

Standard form contracts are often an efficient means of conducting business affairs for the following reasons:

- *Standard form contracts save time.* Rather than draft a separate agreement for every transaction, businesses are able to rely on a familiar and binding statement of their rights and obligations and those of their clients and customers.
- *Standard form contracts reduce costs.* Businesses may be able to lower the prices they charge to their clients or customers if, for example, they can limit their liability by using a standard disclaimer clause. These clauses are discussed in the following section under the heading "Disclaimer (or Limitation of Liability)."
- *Standard terms usually produce standard results in court.* The outcome of a contractual dispute may be more predictable when it is based on a standard form contract whose terms have been previously interpreted by judges. A predictable result may assist the parties in resolving their differences in a timely manner.
- *Standard terms help businesses plan for potentially adverse results.* If a business is familiar with the meaning of a standard term, it can plan for any adverse consequences that the term could produce by, for example, buying insurance or adopting an alternative plan. If it knows that the risk created by the term is too high for its business to assume, it can refuse to enter into the contract.
- *Standard form contracts provide excellent models.* In drafting their own contracts, businesses often review the standard form contracts of others and adopt the terms that are beneficial to them.

Missing and Implied Terms

Contract disputes commonly occur when the parties fail to include essential terms in their agreement. Missing or ambiguous terms are problematic for a number of reasons, several of which are discussed earlier in this chapter under the heading "Rules of Construction."

If the parties fail to express their contractual intentions within the written terms of their agreement, the courts are willing—under certain limited circumstances—to imply terms. An **implied term** is one that a court inserts—or implies—into a contract when it believes that the term is necessary to give effect to the parties' intentions. Examples of situations in which courts may imply contractual terms include the following:

implied term
term that will be inserted by a court into a contract when necessary to give effect to the parties' intentions

- *Custom within an industry.* If, for example, it is customary within the construction industry that interest is payable on accounts that are overdue for 30 days, a court may imply a term allowing an unpaid seller to collect interest from a buyer who refuses to pay within this time.

- *Obligations of good faith.* In a 2014 decision of the Supreme Court of Canada, *Bhasin v Hrynew*, the court recognized a "general organizing principle" that parties must act honestly in the performance of their contractual duties. As stated by the court:

> This means simply that parties must not lie or otherwise knowingly mislead each other about matters directly linked to the performance of the contract. This does not impose a duty of loyalty or of disclosure or require a party to forego advantages flowing from the contract; it is a simple requirement not to lie or mislead the other party about one's contractual performance.

Prior to this ruling, the common law decisions by judges had been inconsistent about whether or not a duty of good faith existed in the performance of contracts and, if so, when and how it should be applied. As an example of the application of this new principle, if Val-Nam has entered into an agreement to purchase property where it intends to build a new manufacturing plant and a condition of the purchase and sale is that Val-Nam obtain financing and receive the necessary property rezoning permit, a court will now imply a term requiring that Val-Nam use good faith or its best efforts to obtain financing and the necessary rezoning. Implying such a term prevents Val-Nam from using inadequate efforts and thus being able to avoid its obligations under the contract (see the discussion later in this chapter under the heading "Condition Precedent").

- *Business effectiveness.* If, for example, the actions of one party undermine the business effectiveness of another party, a court may imply an obligation to refrain from such actions. In *Nickel Developments Ltd v Canada Safeway Ltd*, a case involving a commercial lease, the Manitoba Court of Appeal implied a term that the parties intended the premises to be occupied. In this case, a supermarket was a tenant of a shopping mall under a 20-year lease. Thirteen years into the lease, the supermarket closed because it was operating a more profitable store close by. It continued to pay the rent, allowing the store to remain vacant. This action had a negative impact on attracting customers to the shopping mall. The mall owner successfully sued for breach of contract. The court implied an obligation of continuous operation on the part of the supermarket/tenant in order to give business efficacy to a commercial shopping centre operation.
- *Obvious omission.* If, for example, the price is missing from a contract for the sale of goods or services, a court or tribunal will imply a reasonable price.

Except in the case of the implied obligation of good faith in contractual performance, before a court will imply a term in a contract, the party seeking to have the term included must satisfy the court that

- the term reflects the intention of the parties, and
- the term is reasonable, clear, and does not contradict an **express term** in the contract.

express term
term specified in writing

Whether or not a court chooses to imply a term is completely dependent on the circumstances of a case and the evidence presented by the parties. Because litigation is unpredictable, it is extremely unwise for businesses to rely on courts to imply missing terms. Businesses should take care that their contracts are complete and comprehensive from the outset.

Missing terms can also be imported into contracts by legislation. For example, Ontario's *Sale of Goods Act*, examined in detail in Chapter 6, applies to contracts involving the sale of physical goods. As a result of this Act, all consumer contracts in Ontario contain the following implied terms. Business-to-business contracts will also contain the following implied terms, unless the parties agree otherwise:

- the seller has a right to sell the goods,
- the goods are not subject to any claims by others, such as liens,
- the goods correspond accurately to a description or sample, and
- the goods are of merchantable quality or reasonably fit for a purpose specified by the purchaser.

In order for these terms not to apply to a business-to-business contract, the parties must include a term in their contract that clearly prohibits the application of the Act.

MINIMIZING YOUR RISK

Make Sure Your Contract Is Complete

- Take the time to ensure that your contract addresses all areas of concern to your business.
- Before signing, read the contract again to ensure that nothing is missing.

Reading the Fine Print: Typical Terms in Business Contracts

This section introduces you to a number of terms that commonly appear in business contracts. If the parties turn their minds to each of these terms, their contract should accurately reflect the bargain they have struck. Reasons why you may wish to include each of these terms and how you can avoid the risks they may pose for your business are discussed below.

In the examples below, wherever relevant, the sample terms reflect the Val-Nam/XL contract or other business activities from our fact scenario that Val-Nam may be involved in.

Identification of Parties

Example

AGREEMENT OF PURCHASE AND SALE
BETWEEN
Val-Nam Generation Limited, Seller
AND
XL Equipment Inc, Buyer

In most business transactions, identifying the parties to a contract is fairly straightforward. It is important, however, that you identify the parties correctly because only the parties to a contract may claim benefits under the contract. Conversely, only the parties to a contract can be held responsible for contractual obligations. This legal concept, which restricts the operation of a contract to those who are parties to it, is known as **privity of contract**.

privity of contract
doctrine that restricts the operation of a contract to those who are parties to it

In identifying the parties, ensure that you name them correctly. If the parties are individuals, use the names that appear on official documents, such as drivers' licences. If they are corporations, use the names that appear on the articles of incorporation. Val-Nam Generation Limited and XL Equipment Inc are the names that appear on the respective articles of incorporation of these businesses.

You may also want to include a brief description of the parties' roles in the contractual relationship, such as "Seller" and "Buyer" or "Publisher" and "Advertiser" or "Client" and "Consultant."

MINIMIZING YOUR RISK

Identify the Parties Accurately

- If you are negotiating a contract on behalf of a corporation, ensure that the corporation's name—not yours—appears on the contract. If you are named personally as a party, you may be personally liable if problems arise.
- Accurately name all parties who intend to participate in the benefits and assume the obligations of the contract.

Description of Product or Service

■ Example

The designer will create a website that uses Val-Nam's trademarked stylized "V-N" with an art deco design, five art deco line drawings, and an art deco typeface, and that features the colours black, jade, and salmon.

Precision in description is important. Suppose, instead of using the above phrasing, this contract for the design of Val-Nam's website had stated, "The website is to have a professional appearance in keeping with the professional style of Val-Nam's logo."

Can you see that the website designers and the representatives of Val-Nam might have different opinions about "professional appearance" and appropriate "style"? If these differences lead to a dispute, difficult questions arise:

- Is Val-Nam obliged to pay for a website it does not like?
- Do the designers have to start all over again at their own expense because Val-Nam thinks that the website's appearance is not professional or in the appropriate style?

If the parties cannot reach an amicable resolution to their dispute, they might be forced into costly and needless litigation. If, however, they had put their minds to drafting their requirements in a more specific form, these questions might never have arisen.

If the parties' dispute ends up in court, a judge will apply the rules of construction—with all their difficulty and uncertainty—in interpreting the contract for the parties. (These rules are discussed earlier in this chapter under the heading "Rules of Construction.") The judge is unlikely to allow the parties to produce any evidence of what they agreed upon beyond that set out in the contract itself.

MINIMIZING YOUR RISK

Describe Products or Services Precisely

- Be as precise as possible when describing the products or services covered by your agreement.

Quantity

■ Example 1

Val-Nam agrees to sell, and XL agrees to buy, 100 portable electricity generators per month.

■ Example 2

The seller agrees to sell, and the buyer agrees to buy, 100 cases of Ontario's Best Organic Pea Soup, provided that each case contains 24 28-ounce jars of Ontario's Best Organic Pea Soup.

It is important to specify the quantity of goods or materials that an agreement covers. If, for example, the parties agree to buy and sell a product that comes in cases, ensure that the contract specifies the number of bottles, cans, jars, or other containers within each case. Consider, for example, the difference to the parties between a case containing 24 28-ounce jars and a case containing 12 12-ounce jars.

MINIMIZING YOUR RISK

Specify Quantity Accurately

- Be as accurate as possible when specifying quantity.
- If your industry uses commonly understood measurements, such as "barrel," use them.

Quality

■ Example 1

Val-Nam agrees to deliver CSA-approved portable electricity generators that produce a minimum 6,000-watt charge for a minimum of 30 minutes on a 50 percent load from 24 standard 500 ml plastic water bottles (the "Generators").

■ Example 2

The seller agrees to deliver only inspected and graded beef products that fall into the Canada AA or higher grades.

In the Val-Nam/XL contract, XL will want to clearly set out the performance standard expected of the generators and ensure that the generators meet necessary safety standards in order to minimize the risk of customer harm or dissatisfaction when the generator is sold by XL to its customers. Often, parties will rely on government or other third-party ratings when specifying product standards. For example, if a contract covers the purchase and sale of various cuts of beef to be served at a fundraising gala at your hotel, as in Example 2, you may want to specify that the meat has been inspected and graded in accordance with federal or provincial standards. If the contract includes no description of the quality of meat required to satisfy the supplier's obligations, you cannot assume that you will be supplied with the grade of beef that you are expecting.

As with any other contractual term, specificity regarding quality will not necessarily guarantee that a supplier will deliver satisfactory goods. However, such a term will give the buyer recourse against the supplier for breach of contract in the event that the goods are substandard (various modes of recourse are covered in Chapter 2 under the headings "Civil Court Remedies: Damages" and "Other Remedies").

Another type of contractual term allows for the delivery of substandard goods. If, for example, the parties agree that the buyer will purchase goods "as is"—that is, with existing bumps, dents, and other flaws—they should specify this to be the case in their contract.

MINIMIZING YOUR RISK

Express Your Agreement About Quality

- Where possible, refer to relevant quality control standards, or samples of comparable quality, to eliminate surprises and misunderstandings when a product or service is delivered.

Pricing

■ Example 1

Contract price: $45.00 per Generator
Total price per month: $4,500.00 including all applicable taxes and delivery*
* Note: Price is subject to change on 10 days' notice by Val-Nam in writing to XL.

■ Example 2

In the event of an increase in the price of labour and/or materials necessary for the completion of this project, the supplier reserves the right to increase the project price by up to 10 percent over the original price on reasonable notice to the purchaser.

MINIMIZING YOUR RISK

Allow for Flexibility When Pricing a Product or Service

- Consider tying the price of any product that you distribute or manufacture to a market price, particularly in long-term contracts.
- Negotiate a fixed price if you are the buyer of a product that is prone to fluctuations in price.
- Build in a price cushion to compensate for unexpected costs, or consider a pricing clause that allows for adjustments if you are providing a service.
- Reopen negotiations immediately if pricing problems arise while the contract is in force; do not wait until the contract has been completed before speaking up.

If possible, always incorporate some flexibility into the contract's pricing clause, particularly if your business arrangement extends over a period of time. If there is a chance that Val-Nam's production costs will change significantly over the duration of the contract, Val-Nam will want the ability to adjust the price to XL accordingly. When reviewing your pricing clauses, consider the following: Is there a chance that your costs will increase over the duration of the contract? Is there a chance that you will need additional resources to complete the project if you are running behind schedule? The original contract price may account for these contingencies, but a flexible pricing clause, such as one of the two examples above, may provide greater protection.

A flexible pricing clause must be reasonable from both parties' points of view. If the pricing clause creates too much uncertainty, the vulnerable party should reconsider the wisdom of signing the contract. *MJM Custom Fabrications Inc v Big Drum Inc* illustrates the pitfalls of failing to be specific about the pricing of contractual changes and extras.

CASE IN POINT

Keeping Track of Prices

MJM Custom Fabrications Inc v Big Drum Inc, 2005 CanLII 34584 (Ont Sup Ct J)

Facts

A purchaser contracted with a manufacturer to pay $21,000 for the creation of a chocolate-processing system for a food product business. Because the initial sketches—on which the price was based—were incomplete, the parties implemented a number of design changes during the manufacturing stage at the request of the purchaser. The purchaser knew there would be additional expenses associated with the changes; however, when the manufacturer delivered its final invoice in the amount of $41,363, the purchaser refused to pay the full amount. The manufacturer sued for the balance of $14,597.

Result

The Ontario Superior Court of Justice concluded that the extra work and materials were worth approximately two-thirds of the amount charged, resulting in a judgment in favour of the manufacturer of $6,500. The judge stated, "[T]he only reasonable method of analysis is to start with the fixed price contract, as it was never [revoked], and calculate the value of the extras." He also made the following comments that identify the real costs associated with this dispute:

> Having listened to the evidence, I fail to understand how reasonably intelligent business people would allow their dispute over a small amount of money to proceed to trial. From an economic perspective, it made no sense both in terms of actual expense as well as the time away from their respective businesses. Further, a business relationship of many years has now been destroyed by this dispute.

Business Lesson

Use a flexible pricing clause to predetermine the basis for calculating increases to the initial price, or agree on the price of any changes to the original contract before any extra work is performed.

Payment

■ Example 1

Unless otherwise agreed, payment terms are cash on delivery.

■ Example 2

A down payment of 15 percent of the contract price is due on signing. Balance in full is due within 30 days after completion of the services.

■ Example 3

Terms of payment: Payment in full on delivery of the goods by cash, certified cheque, money order, or credit card only.

■ Example 4

Upon acceptance of the terms of this development agreement, the customer will receive an invoice requiring a minimum deposit of 50 percent of the contract price to commence work. A second invoice for 25 percent will be sent 30 days later. A third and final invoice for the remaining 25 percent will be sent upon completion of the services. Payment is due immediately upon receipt. If payment is not received within 30 days of each invoice date, a late fee of $35.00 will be added to the outstanding amount. Any amounts outstanding 60 days past the invoice date will incur simple interest charges of 10 percent per annum to the date payment is received in full.

■ Example 5

Payment options: The club offers members a pre-authorized payment plan to pay annual fees. The plan consists of 11 equal monthly payments withdrawn from the member's bank account on the first business day of the months of February to December inclusive. A $75.00 administrative fee applies to this option and will be withdrawn at the time of the first payment.

When does a contract require payment? It could be:

- before delivery of a product or service,
- at the time of delivery of a product or service, or
- after delivery of a product or service.

If payment matters to your business (and presumably it does), make sure to include a clause regarding payment terms in your contract.

For new buyers, Val-Nam may require payment on or before delivery, as in Example 1. However, once a commercial relationship is established, and particularly if there are regular shipments of products to a buyer, Val-Nam may be willing to allow for payment after delivery in order to assist the buyer. For example, if XL is able to receive delivery of the generators and pay "net 30 days delivery" (within 30 days of delivery), XL may be able to receive and resell the generators within that time, allowing XL to obtain the funds necessary to pay Val-Nam from XL's own sales of the generators.

MINIMIZING YOUR RISK

Tailor Payment Clauses to Meet Your Needs

- Consider partial payments over the duration of long-term contracts.
- Obtain financing if necessary when payment is required on acceptance or before delivery.

If your business is providing a service over time, can you wait to be paid until the conclusion of the project, or do you need a source of interim revenue to pay for ongoing expenses? Have you any concerns that the other party will pay and/or pay on time? If you answered yes to either of these questions, you would be wise to include a schedule of partial payments.

A schedule of partial payments makes good business sense. If the other party refuses or neglects to make a scheduled payment, you will have recourse against it for breach of contract. You will also have advance warning of potential problems, and you may be able to minimize your losses by pulling out of the project.

Deadline

■ Example 1

Val-Nam shall deliver 100 Generators to XL's warehouse on the first business day of each month.

■ Example 2

A 50 percent deposit for each exhibitor space you request must accompany your signed contract by January 15; payment in full is due by February 15.

■ Example 3

All banner advertising materials must reach the website publishing team at least 24 hours before the date on which the advertisement is to appear. Banner ads cancelled because of a delay or missed deadline will be charged to the client.

■ Example 4

Date work is to begin: ______________________
Date work is to be completed: ______________________

It is particularly important to include a deadline clause that covers delivery or other matters related to a contract's duration when

- a deadline is crucial to a project's effectiveness, or
- several contracts are dependent on one another.

For example, on a construction project, if a cement company is late in pouring the foundation of a building, the later phases of construction may need to be postponed. If the contract between the general contractor and the cement company states a date for completion of the foundation, the cement company should bear the burden of any additional costs associated with the rescheduling of later stages of the project.

MINIMIZING YOUR RISK

Remember the Importance of Timing

- Record all deadlines and set automatic reminders to avoid missing business obligations or opportunities.
- Include enough flexibility in deadline terms to account for unexpected events that may result in delays.
- Remember the risks and costs associated with late completion and be prepared to accept them.

Liquidated Damages

■ Example 1

Should Val-Nam fail to deliver the number of Generators specified, within the time periods set out above, Val-Nam shall pay to XL as liquidated damages and not as a penalty, an amount equal to 30 percent of the purchase price of the Generators that were not so delivered.

■ Example 2

The Advertiser hereby acknowledges that the Display is of a unique and distinctive character and has been expressly designed and manufactured for the Advertiser by the Designer, and that the Designer's design, manufacturing, sales, finance, depreciation, and administrative costs have been amortized over the term of this Agreement. In the event of breach of this Agreement by the Advertiser, the whole of the monthly payments payable hereunder for the balance of the term shall forthwith become due and payable as liquidated damages and not as a penalty (adapted from *32262 BC Ltd v See-Rite Optical Ltd*).

■ Example 3

It is agreed by the Parties to the Contract that in case all the work called for under the Contract is not finished or completed by the final completion date as specified herein, the Contractor will pay to the Owner the sum of $500.00 as liquidated damages for each and every calendar day beyond the final completion date specified that the work remains uncompleted. It is agreed that this amount is an estimate of the actual damage to the Owner that will accrue during the period in excess of the prescribed completion date (adapted from *AWS Engineers and Planners Corp v The Corporation of the Town of Deep River*).

liquidated damages clause
clause in a contract that provides for the payment of money if a certain event—usually a specified breach of contract—occurs

A **liquidated damages clause** allows parties to a contract to set an amount to be paid upon a specified breach of the contract. Reliance on a liquidated damages clause in a contract means the parties should not need to prove the foreseeability and amount of damages. For example, a contract that specifies a deadline for delivering a product or service may also contain a clause that states a sum that will become owing if a party fails to meet the deadline, as in the case of the Val-Nam/XL contract and Example 1. A liquidated damages clause that is tailored to the duration of a breach may state an amount that becomes owing for each hour or day that a payment or delivery is late.

The purpose of a liquidated damages clause is to quantify, in advance of a problem, the compensation that one party will pay to the other in the event that a problem arises. In general, it is wise for parties—while their relationship is still on good terms—to anticipate whatever problems might occur in the performance of the contract and to plan for compensating the party who will suffer loss as a result of such a problem.

Provided that liquidated damages clauses address the matter of compensation for a specified breach of the contract, the courts are generally willing to enforce them. However, if a clause that purports to be a liquidated damages clause is merely a penalty clause in disguise (that is, the amount of liquidated damages is excessive compared to the greatest loss that could possibly result from the breach), the courts will not enforce its application. The court analyzed this matter in the case of *32262 BC Ltd v See-Rite Optical Ltd.*

MINIMIZING YOUR RISK

Negotiate a Liquidated Damages Clause and Use It Sensibly

- Negotiate a liquidated damages clause that fairly estimates the amount of compensation necessary in the event of a breach of contract.
- If there is a breach of contract, use the liquidated damages clause as a starting point for negotiating a fair resolution of your dispute with the other party.
- If there is a breach of contract, also use the liquidated damages clause to determine whether a lawsuit or other formal dispute-resolving procedure is financially worthwhile for your business.

CASE IN POINT

Liquidated Damages as Compensation, Not Penalty

32262 BC Ltd v See-Rite Optical Ltd, 1998 ABCA 89

Facts

The defendant rented a business sign from the plaintiff under a standard form contract that included a liquidated damages clause. When the defendant stopped making monthly rental payments, the plaintiff sued for damages. The liquidated damages clause gave the plaintiff the right to receive an amount equal to the total of all monthly payments owing for the outstanding term of the contract. With 70 months' rental remaining before the contract expired, this was a significant amount.

The primary issue in the case was whether the liquidated damages clause was so oppressive as to amount to a penalty clause, or whether it was a genuine pre-estimate of damages for breach of contract for which the plaintiff was entitled to compensation.

Result

The Alberta Court of Appeal ruled in favour of the plaintiff, concluding that the amount due under the liquidated damages clause "was closely related to the amount to which [the plaintiff] would have been entitled according to principles of general contract law." The defendant was ordered to pay damages amounting to the outstanding 70 months' sign rental, plus interest and legal fees.

Business Lesson

Ensure that a liquidated damages clause addresses compensation and is not a penalty clause in disguise.

Automatic Renewal

■ Example

When this agreement expires, or when any extension of this agreement expires, the parties agree to renew the agreement for a further term of 12 months and automatically to renew the agreement thereafter for a further identical term. If, however, at least 30 days before the expiry of this agreement, or any extension of this agreement, either party gives the other party written notice of its intention to terminate the agreement at the end of the then-current term, the agreement is so terminated.

Many contracts for the provision of a service or the rental of equipment or space extend over a period of time. Examples include contracts for cellphone service, photocopier rental, website hosting, product advertising on public transit, Internet access, and janitorial services. These contracts may contain an automatic renewal clause stating that the contract is to be automatically renewed for a specified period of time, usually one month or one year.

These contracts may include terms that require one party to give the other party notice of an intention to terminate the agreement. If they do contain such a term, it is necessary to comply with the notice requirements to avoid automatic renewal of the contract.

MINIMIZING YOUR RISK

Comply with Notice Requirements

- If you do not intend to renew a contract that contains an automatic renewal clause, take care to give notice within the time and in the manner that the contract specifies.

Cancellation

■ Example 1

Val-Nam may terminate this agreement, in its absolute discretion, by providing 10 business days' notice to XL.

■ Example 2

If you terminate your Service prior to the end of the term (if applicable) you agree to pay us $20.00 times the number of months remaining in the term, to a maximum of $200.

Rogers may allow for the cancellation of your Service without penalty with the following conditions:

- device is returned in complete and original condition to the store where it was purchased (if customer-owned hardware, this condition does not apply) and
- cancellation is requested within 30 days from date of activation and
- your account has incurred less than 30 minutes of airtime usage or 150 kilobytes of data usage.

You will be billed for any local airtime, data, roaming, and long distance charges incurred up to the point of deactivation (adapted from Rogers/AT&T Wireless Agreement, Form #375ONT-51-03—07/02).

■ Example 3

The Purchaser must give written notice of cancellation to the Supplier at the address indicated at the end of this agreement. The Purchaser will be refunded a percentage of the full invoiced amount based on the following schedule:

Table 4.1

Number of days remaining until the event:	Amount refunded:
180 or more	Full amount less $100 administrative fee
90 to 179 days	75% of full invoiced amount
14 to 89 days	50% of full invoiced amount
7 to 13 days	25% of full invoiced amount
Less than 7 days	No refund

A cancellation clause specifies the rights and obligations of the parties in the event that one of them decides to terminate the agreement. Parties often choose to include cancellation clauses in contracts involving services or products to be delivered after the contract is signed or to be delivered over a period of time. Some common examples of contracts that usually include cancellation clauses include:

- contracts for exhibition space at upcoming trade shows
- contracts for advertising in future editions of magazines
- multi-year contracts for cellphone services.

Long-term contracts, or contracts for future services, often come with cost savings for purchasers. However, these contracts may include cancellation penalties, such as those contained in Examples 2 and 3 above. A wise business person should always weigh the benefit of saving money on product or service costs against the risk of losing money on cancellation fees. In some instances, a business may choose to keep its options flexible by refusing to sign a contract until it is ready to receive or provide services or goods. It might prefer to pay a higher price for month-to-month service than to run the financial risk of cancelling a long-term contract. Its choice should be dictated by a clear-headed appraisal of its business's circumstances and prospects.

Cancellation clauses can work to your advantage as well. They can provide a release from a long-term contract at a known and agreeable price. Depending on the situation, it may be beneficial for you to pay the costs of early cancellation in order to take advantage of a better opportunity or to limit even greater losses that would be associated with completing the contract. The cancellation clause above, combined with the clause that allows Val-Nam to adjust the purchase price of the Generators, provides significant protection to Val-Nam in the event of a change in its costs or market conditions or the discovery of a more profitable opportunity.

MINIMIZING YOUR RISK

Be Mindful of Cancellation Penalties

- Weigh the risks of cancellation penalties against the prospect of savings on long-term contracts and contracts covering future events.
- Weigh the cost of completing a contract against the benefits that you could gain through early cancellation, despite having to pay a cancellation fee.

Condition Precedent

■ Example

This agreement is subject to a first mortgage being made available to Val-Nam on or before ________________, in the amount of $ _________ at an interest rate not to exceed ___ percent per annum with a ___-year amortization period, ___-year term, and repayment of approximately $_____ per month, including principal and interest (plus 1/12 of the annual taxes, if required by the mortgagee). This clause is for the sole benefit of Val-Nam.

This agreement is subject to Val-Nam obtaining municipal approval on or before ____________________ of a minor zoning by-law variance to permit construction of a building (not to exceed 40,000 square feet) zoned for industrial use on the subject property.

condition precedent clause in a contract specifying that something must happen before a party is required to perform their obligations under the contract

In a **condition precedent** clause, a contract specifies that something must happen before a party is required to fulfill its contractual obligations.

Conditions precedent are commonly found in agreements to buy and sell real estate. A condition precedent may, for example, make completion of the contract conditional on the purchaser's obtaining financing or permission to rezone a property within a certain time period.

During the waiting period specified in a condition precedent clause, the contract exists as an enforceable agreement, and the parties have certain obligations under it. The purchaser is obliged in law to make a genuine effort to fulfill the condition, and the vendor is obliged to wait and see whether the purchaser succeeds in complying with the condition. In the example above, Val-Nam must try to obtain the necessary financing and rezoning, and the vendor must wait and see whether Val-Nam succeeds in obtaining financing and approval for rezoning; the vendor cannot sell the property to someone else during the waiting period.

If Val-Nam's efforts are ultimately unsuccessful, the condition precedent is not fulfilled. Therefore, the sale falls through because Val-Nam's obligation to buy ceases to exist.

When else might a business want to include a condition precedent in a contract? It may want to do so if it does not want to bind itself to a contractual obligation without knowing that something essential to the contract is available or has occurred. For example, a manufacturer may need to know that it can obtain an adequate supply of a necessary ingredient or part at a fair price in order to commit to a manufacturing project. A computer business may need to know that it has access to the expert personnel essential to performing computer business before undertaking a large job. Both the manufacturer and the computer service would be wise to use a condition precedent to relieve themselves of all obligations under the contract should the essential ingredient, part, or personnel prove to be unavailable.

Condition Subsequent

■ Example

This contract will automatically terminate in the event that XL orders less than the quota for four consecutive months.

A **condition subsequent** terminates a contract when a specified event or circumstance occurs. Until such an occurrence, the parties must perform their obligations under the contract. If the specified event or circumstance never occurs, the contract remains enforceable and the parties are responsible for living up to all obligations they have assumed under it.

condition subsequent occurrence of an event or circumstance that results in the termination of contractual obligations

A business may choose to include a condition subsequent in a contract if it is certain in advance that it no longer wishes to be contractually bound to a business arrangement if a particular circumstance arises. For example, Val-Nam may agree to grant XL the exclusive rights to sell its generators in Ontario provided XL meets certain sales targets. If XL fails to meet those targets, Val-Nam will want to be able to get out of the deal and contract with other retailers in order to increase sales. The sales targets will be a condition subsequent that, if not met, will allow Val-Nam to terminate the exclusive sales arrangement.

The condition subsequent clause has several other useful functions. It clarifies the sales or distribution standards that are required for the contract to remain operative. It also provides a means of terminating the contract in the event that one party's performance falls below a specified standard without the need for resorting to allegations about contractual breach.

MINIMIZING YOUR RISK

Use Conditions Precedent or Subsequent to Terminate Disadvantageous Contracts

- Before contracting, determine preliminary elements that are essential for your business to carry out its obligations under the contract.
- Use conditions precedent to confirm that these elements are in place if the contract is to be binding.
- Before contracting, determine the circumstances that would jeopardize an agreement. Use conditions subsequent to have your contract terminate if these circumstances present themselves.

Deposit

■ Example

This agreement will terminate if the unpaid balance is not paid on or before the purchase completion date, and the deposit paid by the purchaser will be forfeited to the vendor.

A contract may require a deposit of a fixed amount or a percentage of the total contract price. Deposit clauses are commonly found in contracts involving tenders for bids on government projects, as illustrated in the case of *Dhillon v City of Coquitlam*, or contracts for the sale of property. It is important to read deposit clauses carefully because they may specify that a deposit will be forfeited if the purchaser fails to complete the transaction.

MINIMIZING YOUR RISK

Protect Your Deposit

- If missing a deadline may result in your forfeiting a deposit, make sure you have a good reminder system in place.
- If meeting a deadline depends on the performance of work by others, follow up to ensure that all obligations are being fulfilled to avoid having your deposit forfeited.

CASE IN POINT

Forfeiture of Deposit

Dhillon v City of Coquitlam, 2004 BCSC 924

Facts

The City of Coquitlam advertised its intention to offer 22 undeveloped lots for sale through a bid process. A newspaper advertisement invited interested parties to obtain and submit bid packages. The bid packages specified the minimum bid price and required bidders to include a deposit of 10 percent of the total bid amount. The package contained an information sheet that stated, "Deposits will be defaulted if the successful bidders do not complete their obligations by October 14, 2003." It also included a copy of the agreement of purchase and sale that the successful bidders were required to sign. The plaintiffs were the successful bidders. They signed and submitted the agreement of purchase and sale, along with a 10 percent deposit of $23,559. The contract contained the following provision:

> [U]nless the Unpaid Balance is paid on or before the Completion Date, the Vendor [the City of Coquitlam] may, at the Vendor's option, terminate this Agreement and in that case, the amount paid by the Purchaser will be absolutely forfeited to the Vendor.

The plaintiffs intended to sell the property immediately to another purchaser after closing the deal with the City of Coquitlam. Apparently, a dispute arose with this subsequent agreement that prevented the plaintiffs' lawyer from receiving the funds necessary to complete the contract with the City of Coquitlam on time. Since the city did not receive the funds before the October 14, 2003, deadline, it refused to refund the deposit, and the plaintiffs sued to get the money back.

Result

The British Columbia Supreme Court decided in the city's favour. Because the clause calling for forfeit of the deposit was reasonable and did not constitute a penalty, the clause was enforceable.

Business Lesson

When your contractual obligations depend on the actions of a third party, know who you are dealing with and remember that this party's inaction may put your deposit at risk.

Disclaimer (or Limitation of Liability)

■ Example 1

Neither Val-Nam nor XL shall have any liability under this agreement for any punitive or exemplary damages or for any consequential or indirect damages, including for lost profits, lost revenue, or lost business opportunity.

■ Example 2

10.1 The responsibility of the warehouse, unless otherwise stated, is the reasonable care and diligence required by law.

10.2 The warehouse's liability with respect to any one package deposited with it is limited to $40.00 unless the depositor has declared in writing a valuation in excess of $40.00 and paid the additional charge specified to cover the warehouse's liability.

■ Example 3

The Buyer agrees that in no event will the Seller be liable to the Buyer or anyone else for loss of profit, indirect, special, punitive, or consequential damages arising out of any breach of the Agreement, or arising out of the sale, use, or improper functioning of the Equipment, including, without limitation: loss of profit, goodwill, or revenue; and business interruption, even where caused by the negligence of the Seller. In no case shall the Seller's liability exceed the price paid to the Seller by the Buyer for the Equipment at issue (adapted from *Agfaphoto Canada Inc v Overwaitea Food Group Ltd*).

Example 2 above is a simplified version of the limitation of liability clause contained in the case of *London Drugs Ltd v Kuehne & Nagel International Ltd.* In that case, the Supreme Court of Canada held that the clause was effective to limit the liability of the warehouse and its employees after a transformer was damaged while being moved. Although the actual damage suffered by the owner of the transformer was $33,955, liability for the warehouse and its employees was limited to $40.00 as a result of the disclaimer clause.

As stated, a party that fails to fulfill its obligations under a contract can expect to be held liable for breaching the contract. Liability for breach obliges the breaching party to compensate the party that has fulfilled its contractual obligations. Compensation may be provided in a number of ways. The most common is the payment of a sum of money, known as damages. When the parties include a **disclaimer (or limitation of liability) clause** in their agreement, they can limit the amount or the type of damages that they might otherwise be required to pay for a breach, as Val-Nam and XL have done in Example 1.

disclaimer (or limitation of liability) clause
clause in a contract that limits the amount or type of damages that the parties might otherwise be required to pay

Disclaimer clauses are common in business contracts, and they can have a very limiting effect on what a non-breaching party can expect to recover by way of compensation. They differ from exclusion clauses (described below) by capping damages for specified losses rather than barring them entirely. The extent of the limitation of liability depends on the wording of the disclaimer clause. A sensible business person must consider any disclaimer clauses with care and assess the risk of their potential application. Questions that might prove helpful in this regard include:

- How well do you know the party that is protecting itself from potential liability?
- How likely is this party to breach the contract?
- If the contract is breached, what are the likely consequences?
- Is the risk of suffering these consequences acceptable to your business?
- Can you protect your business against these consequences in another way?

Sometimes the clause itself will dictate the wise course of action. For instance, in the warehousing example at the beginning of this section, a business that stores a package whose value exceeds $40.00 would be wise to pay the additional fee required to increase the warehouse's liability.

The purchase of insurance—either by means of the payment of an additional fee, as in the warehouse example, or under a separate contract of insurance—may be all you need to resolve the riskier aspects of disclaimer clauses. The case of *Dryburgh v Oak Bay Marina (1992) Ltd* illustrates the dangers of failing to protect against disclaimer clauses.

MINIMIZING YOUR RISK

Understand the Impact of a Disclaimer Clause

- Include a disclaimer clause in contracts to reasonably limit the potential liability of your business.
- Weigh the risks of signing a contract with a disclaimer clause. How serious an impact might it have on your business? Are there ways to protect your business, such as by purchasing adequate insurance?

CASE IN POINT

Disclaimer Clause? Think Insurance

Dryburgh v Oak Bay Marina (1992) Ltd, 2001 FCT 671

Facts

The plaintiff's yacht was damaged when a dock broke loose at a marina and drifted aground. The plaintiff alleged that the dock broke loose because it was poorly designed, constructed, maintained, and/or supervised. The following is an excerpt from the disclaimer clause contained in the parties' moorage contract:

> All vessels, boathouse and ancillary equipment of the Owner stored or moored on the Company's premises shall be solely at the Owner's risk, and the Company shall not be responsible under any circumstances for any loss or damage caused thereto whether caused by the negligence of the Company, its servants or agents, or the acts of third parties, or otherwise.

The plaintiff sued the marina and one of its employees, claiming damages for negligence and breach of contract.

Result

The Federal Court Trial Division held that the clause was effective to protect both the marina and its employee from any liability for damage to the plaintiff's yacht. The judge commented, "Anyone reading the clause would certainly, if acting reasonably, take out proper insurance to cover the losses which the clause purports to exclude."

Business Lesson

Consider your insurance needs before signing a contract that contains a disclaimer clause.

Entire Agreement

■ Example

This contract constitutes the entire agreement between Val-Nam and XL. There are no representations or warranties—express or implied, statutory or otherwise—and no collateral agreements other than those expressly referred to in this contract.

If a dispute regarding the meaning of a contract comes to trial, a party generally may not introduce evidence of statements made during negotiations unless these statements are included in the written agreement. The Ontario Court of Appeal, in the case of *KPMG Inc v Canadian Imperial Bank of Commerce*, summarized this concept as follows:

> The cardinal interpretive rule of contracts … is that the court should give effect to the intention of the parties as expressed in their written agreement. Where that intention is plainly expressed in the language of the agreement, the court should not stray beyond the four corners of the agreement.

It is worth noting that the prohibition against considering evidence external to a contract refers only to contracts whose terms are clearly expressed. If a contract contains an unclear or ambiguous term, a judge may consider external evidence for the purpose of clarifying the ambiguity.

MINIMIZING YOUR RISK

Write Your Entire Contract Clearly

- Ensure that business contracts state the entire agreement, because any additional statements not contained within them, whether oral or written, may not be allowed as evidence to support your side in a dispute.
- Write contracts clearly to prevent a court from rewriting them for you.

Exclusion

■ Example 1

The service provider shall not be required to provide any services relating to problems arising out of (1) the customer's use of the software in a manner for which it was not designed; (2) operation of the software in a hardware environment not recommended by the service provider; (3) operation of the computer on which the software is installed in environmental conditions outside those recommended by the computer manufacturer; or (4) the customer's negligence, misuse, or modification of the software.

■ Example 2

This service contract DOES NOT COVER repairs or replacements resulting from defects, damage, or deterioration that arise from normal use, wear and tear, exposure, misuse, alteration, negligence, or accidents, and any damage from overheating.

An **exclusion clause** excuses a party from its contractual obligations under certain circumstances. These clauses are frequently seen in insurance contracts, although they appear in other contracts as well, such as service and extended warranty contracts. They differ from disclaimer clauses (although disclaimer clauses are sometimes referred to as exclusionary clauses) by directly affecting the scope of the coverage or services that are the subject of the agreement.

exclusion clause
clause in a contract that excuses parties from their contractual obligations in specified circumstances

It is a good risk management policy for businesses to purchase insurance and, depending on the circumstances, extended service agreements or warranties to cover various potential losses. However, such agreements generally contain exclusion clauses. For example, an insurance contract covering damage to property generally excludes liability for loss or damage resulting from the intentional or criminal acts of the party insured under the contract. Similarly, insurance contracts generally exclude liability for conduct resulting in injury to another party where the insured's intentional or criminal conduct has caused an injury.

You should also be alert to the **endorsements** that insurers often add to insurance contracts either to limit or to expand their coverage. For example, an insurance contract covering a jewellery store may include an endorsement that requires the insured business to install surveillance equipment and security devices in order for the insurance to be effective.

endorsement
additional term added on to a standard form or existing contract

The interpretation of insurance contracts has been the subject of many court decisions and is a topic that is beyond the scope of this book. However, from a business perspective, it is worth knowing that courts generally interpret exclusion clauses strictly against the insurers who drafted them, in accordance with Rule 2 set out earlier in this chapter under the heading "Rules of Construction." Courts also tend to interpret coverage provisions broadly, which means that they give effect to the coverage clauses whenever possible.

MINIMIZING YOUR RISK

Carefully Examine Exclusion Clauses

- Read the contract carefully. Only a thorough reading will reveal restrictions on the insurance or services that may be vital for your business.
- If you are the service provider, review whether the restrictions are sufficiently broad. Would your business benefit from excluding even more from the scope of an agreement?
- Ask yourself: How badly does your business need the contract? How many exclusions is it prepared to accept? How many restrictions will the other party accept?

www.emond.ca/CBL3/links

DIG DEEPER
The federal government assists provincial governments with disaster relief for businesses. Links are included for BC and Ontario programs.

Force Majeure

■ Example

Val-Nam shall not be liable for any losses or damages resulting from acts of God, war, terrorist acts, labour unrest, currency devaluations, government-imposed restrictions on the sale or distribution of the Generators, or any other delays or failure in performance resulting from causes beyond Val-Nam's reasonable control.

force majeure
significant and unanticipated event—such as a natural disaster—that is beyond the control of the parties and makes fulfillment of contractual obligations impossible

A ***force majeure*** is a significant and unanticipated event—such as a war or a natural disaster—that is beyond the control of the parties and prevents them from carrying out the terms of the contract; the effect of a *force majeure* is to terminate the contract. By inserting a *force majeure* clause in a contract, the parties can exempt themselves from liability for damage caused by events beyond their control. For example, the above clause may exempt Val-Nam from liability should it be unable to deliver the Generators within the prescribed timeframe due to a work stoppage at its unionized manufacturing plant.

Like disclaimer clauses, *force majeure* clauses allocate the risk of loss in certain circumstances. They specify that one or both of the parties will not bear the risk of specified losses. As long as the parties are aware of the existence of a *force majeure* clause and its potential impact, they can make wise business choices, such as purchasing insurance or adopting contingency plans. For example, if you are concerned that extreme weather might interfere with the performance of your contractual obligations in a particular place, put a deposit on an alternative location to serve as a backup.

MINIMIZING YOUR RISK

Plan for the Unforeseeable

- Allocate the risk of serious, unexpected events so that the party bearing the risk has the opportunity to protect itself if deemed necessary.

Governing Law

■ Example

Val-Nam and XL agree to construe and enforce this agreement in accordance with the applicable laws of Prince Edward Island and of Canada. The parties also agree to treat this agreement in all respects as a Prince Edward Island contract.

With global trade and e-commerce, it is increasingly likely that parties to a contract are carrying on business in different jurisdictions. Therefore, it is prudent to designate the law that is to prevail in the event of a dispute. While the law is relatively uniform throughout the Canadian provinces and territories, it is not identical in each place. Also, Canadian law may differ from the law of China, Brazil, or the United States, for example, in ways that profoundly affect a contract. Different countries may have different rules about interpreting contracts as well as different procedures for bringing disputes before courts or arbitrators. By including a governing law clause (also known as a "choice of law" clause), the parties can choose the law that they want to govern their dealings. They can thereby eliminate the uncertainty of unexpected (and perhaps unwelcome) legal results.

MINIMIZING YOUR RISK

Let Familiar Laws Govern

- If you are contracting with foreign businesses registered in other countries or provinces, choose laws with which you are familiar to govern any dispute that might arise.

Venue

■ Example 1

Val-Nam and XL agree to submit to the courts of Ontario.

■ Example 2

Val-Nam and XL agree to submit to arbitration in Ontario.

A **venue (or forum selection) clause** states the place where the parties agree to settle any contractual disputes. It is related to, but differs from, a governing law clause, whose purpose is to state the law that governs the parties' contractual relationship. Under a venue clause, the parties could, for example, agree to settle their differences in Ontario. Under a governing law clause, they could agree to apply Prince Edward Island law there.

venue (or forum selection) clause
clause in a contract specifying the place where a contractual dispute will be litigated

It is wise to include a venue clause in a contract because it can be very expensive and time-consuming to travel to a distant place—even within Canada—for the purpose of litigating a dispute. When dealing with disputes in countries other than Canada, a party may be faced with the additional challenges of hiring a foreign lawyer, communicating in a foreign language, and navigating a foreign legal system. The case of *Znamensky Selekcionno-Gibridny Center LLC v Donaldson International Livestock Ltd* illustrates the hardship that can be associated with international disputes involving foreign jurisdictions (see the Case in Point on page 134).

If you succeed in negotiating a venue clause that allows you to resolve your disputes in Canada, you have gained a major contractual advantage. If you fail in your attempt to negotiate such a clause, you may decide that the business risks of submitting to the dispute resolution procedures of another country outweigh the business advantages of entering into the contract.

A venue clause will not necessarily prevent a party to a contractual dispute from starting a lawsuit in a place other than the one specified in the contract. However, if your business is sued in a foreign country, and your contract contains a venue clause stating that Ontario is the appropriate place to resolve any disputes, you have some recourse. You, or lawyers acting on your behalf in the foreign jurisdiction, can argue that the foreign lawsuit should be stayed or dismissed for lack of jurisdiction. Your chances of success probably depend on the foreign jurisdiction. Canadian courts have historically enforced these clauses in business-to-business contracts and stayed lawsuits brought in Canada when the venue clause provides for resolution in another place.

Figure 4.1

Facebook's Terms of Use include a venue (or forum selection) clause stating that lawsuits against Facebook must be pursued in a state or federal court in Santa Clara, California.

Douez v Facebook, Inc, is a recent example of a case involving the enforcement of a forum selection clause. The clause, contained in Facebook's Terms of Use, stated: "You will resolve any claim, cause of action or dispute (claim) you have with us arising out of or relating to this Statement or Facebook exclusively in a state or federal court located in Santa Clara County." The plaintiff commenced a lawsuit in the Supreme Court of British Columbia against Facebook for violation of privacy, alleging that her name and photograph were featured in Facebook's "Sponsored Stories" advertising campaign without her consent. The ads were generated and sometimes displayed on the newsfeeds of "friends" when a Facebook member pressed the "like" button on a post associated with a business or other entity that had paid for the "Sponsored Stories" advertising. Although the plaintiff was successful in the lower court, the Court of Appeal held that she failed to show "strong cause" that the courts of Santa Clara would be unable to preside over a similar claim if brought in California and entered a stay of the proceedings, noting that the plaintiff "is at liberty to bring her action in California." But in a further appeal to the Supreme Court of Canada, the plaintiff was able to convince the majority of justices *not* to enforce the forum selection clause, allowing her case to proceed in British Columbia. The following factors were held to cumulatively establish the "strong cause" necessary to override an otherwise enforceable forum selection clause:

- The contract was a consumer contract between an individual consumer and a large corporation with unequal bargaining power between the parties (i.e., the plaintiff effectively had no choice but to accept Facebook's terms in order to join the social network).
- The claim alleged a breach of quasi-constitutional privacy rights of British Columbians (worthy of a higher level of protection than simple commercial interests), requiring statutory interpretation that would result in better clarity and certainty if decided by a local court.
- The additional existence of a "choice of law" clause in Facebook's terms, designating that the law of California be applied to any dispute, further supported that in the interests of justice a BC court should assess whether or not a consumer customer (as opposed to a business customer) opts out of provincial statutory privacy rights through the application of such a contractual term.
- It would be more convenient (and address concerns about fairness and access to justice) for Facebook to make its books and records available for review in a British Columbia legal action than to require the plaintiff to litigate her claim in California.

Businesses transacting online with Canadian consumers need to be aware that their forum selection clauses may be unenforceable as a result of this decision and factor that risk into their business decisions.

Whatever happens, do not ignore a lawsuit brought against your business in a foreign location. Even if you believe the lawsuit was brought in the wrong jurisdiction and any judgment against your business should be ineffective, it is perilous to ignore the proceedings. As long as there is a real and substantial connection between the foreign jurisdiction and the subject matter of the lawsuit—and assuming that the lawsuit followed procedures that are consistent with Canada's concept of due process and fundamental fairness—it is likely that the foreign judgment can be enforced in Canada.

MINIMIZING YOUR RISK

Designate the Place Where You Will Resolve Contractual Disputes

- Include a venue clause to ensure that disputes will be resolved in a location convenient for your business.
- Before entering into a contract with a foreign venue clause, assess whether the potential risks and costs of foreign procedures are acceptable to your business.

www.emond.ca/CBL3/links

DIG DEEPER
See the full text of the *Arbitration Act, 1991* online.

Arbitration

■ Example 1

Any dispute in connection with this agreement must be settled by arbitration in accordance with the provisions of the Ontario *Arbitration Act, 1991*.

■ Example 2

A.1. In the event of any dispute between the parties arising from the meaning or effect of any clause or matter contained in this agreement, or arising from the rights and liabilities of the parties, the parties will try to settle the matter on an amicable basis.
A.2. If the parties cannot resolve the matter on an amicable basis, they will refer the dispute to an independent third-party mediator.
A.3. If the parties cannot reach a settlement in accordance with the procedures outlined in clause A.1 or A.2 above, they will refer the dispute to arbitration to be settled in accordance with the Ontario *Arbitration Act, 1991* by one arbitrator.
A.4. The arbitration will be held in London, Ontario.

CASE IN POINT

Resolving International Contractual Disputes

Znamensky Selekcionno-Gibridny Center LLC v Donaldson International Livestock Ltd, 2010 ONCA 303

Facts

This case involves a contract providing for the sale of 8,505 pigs by Donaldson, an Ontario-based exporter of purebred pigs, to Znamensky, a Russian agro-industrial company. The contract included the following arbitration clause:

12. Arbitration:
Any dispute, controversy or claim, which may arise out of or in connection with the present contract (agreement), or the execution, breach, termination or invalidity thereof, shall be settled by the International Commercial Arbitration Court at the Chamber of Commerce and Industry of the Russian Federation, in accordance with its Rules and Regulations. The Contract is governed and construed in accordance with the material law of the Russian Federation.

The place of arbitration shall be Moscow, Russia. The language to be used in the arbitral proceedings shall be Russian.

The Contract shall be subject to the Law of Russian Federation.

Before the pigs were shipped, a dispute arose as to their health. Znamensky demanded that Donaldson provide new pigs under the terms of the contract. Donaldson refused, and he alleged that Znamensky's representative uttered death threats. Znamensky demanded that a $1,666,113 advance payment be returned. Attempts to negotiate a resolution failed and Znamensky commenced arbitration proceedings in Russia under the terms of the contract. Donaldson tried to stop the arbitration from proceeding by filing an application for an interim injunction in the Ontario Superior Court of Justice, but was unsuccessful. The arbitration proceeded, but Donaldson chose not to participate in the arbitration. Znamensky was awarded almost $1.7 million in damages and as compensation for the arbitration fees. Znamensky then brought this court proceeding in Ontario seeking an order to recognize and enforce the Russian arbitration award.

Result

The Ontario Superior Court of Justice ordered that the arbitration award be recognized and enforced. The judge rejected Donaldson's argument that it was against public policy in Ontario to enforce the foreign award without a trial to resolve the issue of the death threats, which were the primary reason that Donaldson had refused to participate in the arbitration. The dispute did not end there.

Donaldson appealed to the Ontario Court of Appeal, and the appeal was granted; a trial was ordered on the merits of the application for enforcement of the foreign judgments. This contractual dispute first arose in 2006 and, as of 2017, its status is unknown.

Business Lesson

Before entering into an international contract, give full consideration to the risks associated with terms dictating that disputes be resolved in the other jurisdiction.

An arbitration clause specifies that the parties agree to resolve all disputes that arise under their contract through arbitration, rather than through litigation (a court proceeding). In Ontario, the arbitration process is generally governed by the *Arbitration Act, 1991*.

Some of the advantages of arbitration over litigation are described in Chapter 2. These can include confidentiality, relative flexibility, speed of process, and industry-specific expertise of the arbitrator.

If the parties include an arbitration clause in a contract, they give up the option of bringing a lawsuit. Should a party to such a contract attempt to launch a lawsuit despite the arbitration clause, the other party can ask a court to stay the lawsuit—that is, to put it on hold permanently. There are risks associated with arbitration clauses. The case of *Znamensky Selekcionno-Gibridny Center LLC v Donaldson International Livestock Ltd* is also an example of the problems that can arise when a Canadian business agrees to arbitrate in a foreign jurisdiction.

Example 2 shows an arbitration-mediation clause. It is clearly more detailed than Example 1 and reflects the seriousness of the parties' goal to minimize the costs associated with a contractual dispute. In Example 2, the parties have enlarged the arbitration clause to include an agreement to try to resolve their differences amicably or with the assistance of mandatory mediation first.

As observed in Chapter 2, mediation is another way for businesses to settle their disputes out of court. A neutral third party, the mediator, helps the parties look for a solution that resolves their dispute, ideally leading to a win–win result. Unlike judges or abitrators, a mediator does not have the power to reach a decision and impose it on the parties. The mediator focuses on understanding each party's interests and helping the parties communicate their positions in an effort to reach a mutual agreement.

Mediation is a relatively informal, but confidential, process. It is particularly helpful in maintaining ongoing business relationships when a dispute arises. In Ontario, mediation is now a mandatory component of most civil cases that proceed through the regular court process.

MINIMIZING YOUR RISK

Sue Only If You Have To

- Use an arbitration or an arbitration-mediation clause to increase the likelihood of an early resolution of a dispute and to avoid the high cost of litigation.

Indemnity

■ Example 1

Val-Nam unconditionally guarantees that any elements of text, graphics, photos, designs, trademarks, or other artwork furnished to the website designer for inclusion in the project are owned by Val-Nam, or that Val-Nam has permission from the rightful owner to use each of these elements. Val-Nam also agrees to protect, indemnify, and defend the website designer and its subcontractors from any liability, including any claim or lawsuit (and related legal fees and court costs)—threatened or actual—arising from the use of the elements furnished by Val-Nam.

■ Example 2

The renter shall indemnify and protect the venue from all claims, damages, suits, and actions whatsoever, including any claims for any personal injury (including death resulting therefrom) or any loss of, or damages to, property that arise out of or in connection with the entry onto and use of the venue's facilities on the dates specified in this agreement. If the venue is made a party to any litigation commenced by or against the renter, the renter shall promptly indemnify and hold harmless the venue and shall pay to the venue all costs and expenses incurred or paid by the venue in connection with such litigation (adapted from *Potvin v Canadian Museum of Nature*).

indemnity clause clause in a contract that requires one of the parties to pay for any losses or expenses that the other party may incur as a result of claims related to the contract

To indemnify means to protect another party from loss or legal responsibility, or to compensate that party for losses or expenses. An **indemnity clause** in a contract requires one of the parties to pay for any losses or expenses that the other party may incur as a result of claims related to the contract. Inevitably, the party required to do the indemnifying is the party whose actions or omissions lie at the root of the claim.

For example, consider the position of the website design firm that Val-Nam has hired. It frequently uses many types of text and artwork in creating websites for its clients. Its employees lack the time and knowledge to research the various claims made by Val-Nam in its materials or to check the legitimacy of every photograph, logo, or piece of artwork Val-Nam submits for inclusion in its website.

What if it turns out that a piece of artwork contains something that infringes the copyright of another artist? Or what if the language in a piece of submitted text is defamatory of a competing business or product? The website design firm could be named as a defendant in a lawsuit alleging tort liability and/or copyright infringement. To protect itself from the costs associated with defending such a claim, the website designer can include an indemnity clause in its contract with Val-Nam. This clause requires Val-Nam—who is in the best position to know whether the material is legitimate—to pay for any expenses or losses incurred by the designer as a result of carrying out its contractual obligations.

The following list provides several examples of situations in which indemnity clauses can effectively shift responsibility for risks associated with various business transactions in accordance with the parties' agreement:

- In a contract for the provision of maintenance services in an office building, the maintenance company may agree to indemnify the building owners or occupants against any claims for personal injuries that arise from allegations that the building was improperly maintained.
- In a construction contract, an electrical subcontractor may agree to indemnify the general contractor against any claims for loss or damage that arise from allegations that the electrical work was faulty.

- In a software licensing agreement, the purchaser of the licence may agree to indemnify the software company for any claims that may arise against it from the purchaser's improper use of the software.

It is important to note that an indemnity clause cannot be so broadly worded that it protects a party against its own wrongdoing or negligence. This type of clause will be narrowly interpreted to disallow a party's immunity from responsibility for its own negligence. For example, in *Potvin*, the court ruled that the indemnity clause (see Example 2 above) did not apply when a person suffered injury after falling on the exterior stairs of a rented premises. It found that the injury suffered by the person attending the event hosted by the renter was unrelated to the event itself. The court therefore held that there was insufficient connection between the renter and the injury to invoke the venue's indemnification clause.

MINIMIZING YOUR RISK

Keep Indemnification Obligations in Mind

- Ensure that you have obtained all necessary permissions when providing copy or graphics for an advertisement, website, or brochure.
- Check to see that your commercial liability insurance covers claims for indemnity.

CHAPTER SUMMARY

A contract is an agreement that is enforceable by law. It may be formed by two or more persons communicating with one another (for example, face to face or by telephone, email, or text), by the interaction of a person and an electronic agent, or by the interaction of electronic agents. For an agreement to constitute a contract, it must contain an intention to create a legal relationship, involve an offer by one party and an acceptance of that offer by the other party, involve the exchange of something of value, and conform to the law.

Because business contracts cover employment, services, leases, the purchase and sale of goods, and insurance, among other things, it is preferable that they be written, not verbal, to provide a record of the parties' rights and obligations. In case of a dispute, the most convenient resolution is to find a solution within the language of the contract. Over the years, the common law has developed several rules for interpreting disputed contracts.

In practice, contracts within particular industries tend to contain similar terms because these terms have proven to be expedient for businesses. Standard form contracts are contracts drafted by one party and imposed on the other with little or no opportunity for negotiating changes. Standard form contracts are often an efficient means of conducting business affairs because they save time and reduce costs.

All contracts should contain clauses that identify the parties, the goods or service, the quantity, the quality, the price, payment terms, deadlines, and the amount to be paid upon a specified breach of the contract. Depending on the contract, it may also contain clauses on exclusions, conditions precedent or subsequent, *force majeure*, arbitration, indemnity, governing law, and venue.

KEY TERMS

REFERENCES

32262 BC Ltd v See-Rite Optical Ltd, 1998 ABCA 89.
Agfaphoto Canada Inc v Overwaitea Food Group Ltd, 2008 BCSC 1287.
Arbitration Act, 1991, SO 1991, c 17.
AWS Engineers and Planners Corp v The Corporation of the Town of Deep River, 2005 CanLII 467 (Ont Sup Ct J).
Bhasin v Hrynew, 2014 SCC 71, [2014] 3 SCR 494.
Dhillon v City of Coquitlam, 2004 BCSC 924.
Douez v Facebook, Inc, 2017 SCC 33.
Dryburgh v Oak Bay Marina (1992) Ltd, 2001 FCT 671.
KPMG Inc v Canadian Imperial Bank of Commerce, 1998 CanLII 1908 (Ont CA).
London Drugs Ltd v Kuehne & Nagel International Ltd, 1992 CanLII 41 (SCC), [1992] 3 SCR 299.
Macatula v Tessier, 2003 MBCA 31.
MJM Custom Fabrications Inc v Big Drum Inc, 2005 CanLII 34584 (Ont Sup Ct J).
Nickel Developments Ltd v Canada Safeway Ltd, 2001 MBCA 79.
Potvin v Canadian Museum of Nature, 2001 CanLII 6709 (Ont Sup Ct J).
Sale of Goods Act, RSO 1990, c S.1, as amended.
UBS Securities Canada, Inc v Sands Brothers Canada, Ltd, 2009 ONCA 328.
Zippy Print Enterprises Ltd v Pawliuk, 1994 CanLII 1756 (BCCA).
Znamensky Selekcionno-Gibridny Center LLC v Donaldson International Livestock Ltd, 2010 ONCA 303.

EXERCISES

True or False?

____ **1.** Family members or friends who enter into unwritten business agreements with one another may have difficulty proving they intended the agreement to be legally binding.

____ **2.** When you pay cash for toothpaste at the local corner store and do not receive a receipt from the cashier, the transaction is not a legally binding contract.

____ **3.** Contract law presumes business people understand that their promises to one another may be enforced by courts and tribunals.

____ **4.** It is possible for a business to prove that it did not intend a promise to be legally binding.

____ **5.** If you shake hands on the essential terms of a business transaction, it will not be legally binding until a contract is written up and signed by the parties.

____ **6.** A business should always refuse to deal with businesses that do not put their agreements in writing.

____ **7.** If an essential term of a contract is not precise and results in a contractual dispute that ends up in court, the plaintiff's subjective interpretation of the term will always prevail.

____ **8.** Standard form contracts are one-sided and will not be enforced by the courts.

____ **9.** Legislation can be a source of terms that will be implied into a contract if the parties do not specifically include or exclude them.

Multiple Choice

1. Leigh Miller operates a coffee shop called Coffee Crazed in a trendy area of town. She wants to change coffee suppliers and recently met with Juan Carlos, a sales representative for Columbia Coffee Beans Wholesale Supply Ltd, to discuss the company's products and prices. She agrees to purchase a six-month supply of coffee beans. Which of the following is not an essential term of the contract?

a. Price per unit of the coffee beans.
b. Payment and delivery terms.
c. Signatures of the parties.
d. Description of the quality standards for the coffee beans.

2. If two sophisticated business people enter into a standard form contract, and one of them later wishes to withdraw from it because the terms are one-sided and unfair, a judge will generally:
   a. allow the aggrieved party to withdraw from the contract.
   b. enforce the contract.
   c. add additional terms into the contract to make them fair.
   d. change the terms of the contract to make them fair.
3. Which of the following is an example of a disclaimer or limitation of liability clause?
   a. "This contract will automatically terminate in the event that the purchaser orders less than the quota for four consecutive weeks."
   b. "If the supplier fails to deliver the weekly supply of products to the retailer on or before the first day of each week, the supplier shall pay the retailer $100 for each day that the delivery is late."
   c. "The supplier shall not be liable to the retailer in respect of any losses, damages, costs, or claims resulting from circumstances that are not within the control of the supplier."
   d. "This is the entire agreement between the parties, covering everything agreed or understood in connection with the subject matter of this transaction. No oral promises, conditions, warranties, representations, understandings, or interpretations were relied on by either party to execute this contract."
4. Which of the following is an example of a liquidated damages clause?
   a. "This contract will automatically terminate in the event that the purchaser orders less than the quota for four consecutive weeks."
   b. "If the supplier fails to deliver the weekly supply of products to the retailer on or before the first day of each week, the supplier shall pay the retailer $100 for each day that the delivery is late."
   c. "The supplier shall not be liable to the retailer in respect of any losses, damages, costs, or claims resulting from circumstances that are not within the control of the supplier."
   d. "This is the entire agreement between the parties, covering everything agreed or understood in connection with the subject matter of this transaction. No oral promises, conditions, warranties, representations, understandings, or interpretations were relied on by either party to execute this contract."
5. A party to a contract might choose to include a condition subsequent clause in a contract:
   a. if there is a risk of forfeiting a deposit if a deadline is missed.
   b. if it does not want to be bound to the terms of the contract if a certain situation arises.
   c. to avoid the high cost of litigation if the contract is breached.
   d. to ensure any dispute will be resolved according to the law in a designated jurisdiction.
6. If a term in a contract is ambiguous and the parties disagree on its meaning, how will a judge resolve the dispute?
   a. By applying the interpretation of the party who drafted the contract.
   b. By applying the interpretation of the party who commenced the lawsuit.
   c. By applying their own subjective interpretation of the term.
   d. By applying the interpretation of a reasonable person.

Short Answer

1. Why is it important for business people to know about contract law?
2. Why is it important to uphold the integrity of contractual agreements?
3. Name some situations where a court will imply a missing term into a contract.
4. What are the benefits of a well-written contract?
5. What is a disclaimer clause and how is it different from an exclusion clause?

Apply Your Knowledge

1. Niagara's Best Organic Foods Wholesale Distributors Ltd ("Niagara's Best") distributes organic fruit, vegetables, and other organic products to several stores in Toronto. On September 1, Niagara's Best entered into a one-year contract with Organics for You ("Organics"), an upscale specialty food shop. The contract was negotiated by Anton Kokovski, president of Niagara's Best, and Ying Li, sales manager of Organics. Under the terms of the contract, Niagara's Best is to supply a minimum weekly quantity of products to Organics. Niagara's Best is to deliver two cases each of seven varieties of organic fruit and vegetables, two cases each of two types of packaged organic pasta, and two cases of pasta sauce, for a total of 20 cases of goods (the "quota"), to Organics on the first day of every week. Organics agrees to pay Niagara's Best $500 for each weekly shipment, payable within 14 days of delivery. If Organics wants to add more cases or to order fewer cases than the regularly scheduled quota, it must provide Niagara's Best with notice of the change at least two business days before the scheduled delivery date. Below are a number of additional terms or clauses contained in the contract between Niagara's Best and Organics.
   - **a.** What categories of typical business contract terms does each of the following fall into?
     - "This contract will automatically terminate in the event that Organics orders less than the quota for four consecutive weeks."
     - "If Niagara's Best fails to deliver the weekly supply of products to Organics on or before the first day of each week, Niagara's Best shall pay Organics $100 for each day that the delivery is late."
     - "Niagara's Best shall not be liable to Organics in respect of any losses, damages, costs, or claims resulting from circumstances that are not within the control of Niagara's Best."
     - "This is the entire agreement between the parties, covering everything agreed or understood in connection with the subject matter of this transaction. No oral promises, conditions, warranties, representations, understandings, or interpretations were relied on by either party to execute this contract."
     - "Except as otherwise provided in this contract, Niagara's Best's liability shall include all damages proximately caused by the breach of any condition or warranty in this contract or negligent conduct on the part of Niagara's Best, but such liability shall in no event include any indirect, incidental, or consequential damages, including any loss of profit."
     - "Weekly shipment price = $500* [* Price is set on a sliding scale and will be automatically adjusted to reflect fluctuations exceeding 10 percent in costs associated with delivering the product.]"

   Niagara's Best employs Sam Singh on a part-time basis to help with deliveries. On October 3, Sam accompanies the company president for the weekly delivery of 20 cases of organic foods to Organics. Sam and Anton arrive at Organics at approximately 4:30 p.m. The cases are unloaded into a storeroom at the back of the store. Sam inadvertently stacks the cases too high. They tip over, knocking over a 10-gallon drum of organic cooking oil that spills onto the floor of the storeroom and seeps into the rest of the store, creating a slippery mess. Organics is forced to close down for the remainder of the day while the spill is cleaned up. The cost of cleaning up and replacing products damaged by the oil is $1,200. In addition, Organics estimates that it lost $1,500 in profits because it was closed during its busiest time of the day.
   - **b.** What impact do the problems associated with the October 3 delivery have on the continuation of the contract?
   - **c.** Discuss the terms of the contract. Are they fair? Are they sufficient? Would you suggest any changes or additions to the contract on behalf of either party?
2. After graduating with a diploma in business administration, Tony Nguyen is eager to run his own business. Tony meets with Amira Abebe, a representative of Priority Printing Inc (PPI), a company that franchises a chain of small businesses offering printing services (such as photocopying, colour printing, and sizing and editing of images). Amira tells Tony that an in-depth survey and feasibility study will be conducted to investigate the market size, competition, pricing, and other factors necessary for a successful business in his hometown in Ontario. She meets with Tony again several days later and gives him a printout showing an estimated profit of $30,000 in the first year on estimated gross sales of $320,000. She indicates that, based on her research, it is a "true and accurate financial picture" of the first year of his franchise operation. Amira also tells Tony that PPI offers substantial support in training, advertising, and office management, and that the supplies and equipment

servicing that franchisees are required to purchase from PPI will be cheaper than what he could otherwise source locally. Relying on the positive financial forecast and the information about training support and cost savings, Tony signs a franchise agreement with PPI. The contract does not include the printout of estimated profit, nor does it include specific provisions around support and cost savings associated with supplies and equipment. Tony's financial consideration for the franchise is a one-time payment of $75,000, an ongoing obligation to pay a royalty of 5 percent of gross weekly sales, and a contribution of an additional 5 percent of gross weekly sales to a marketing fund. The franchise agreement is a standard form contract drafted by PPI's lawyers that also contains the following terms:

- **Termination.** This Agreement and the rights conferred upon the franchisee hereunder shall automatically terminate forthwith upon the happening of any of the following events: (i) if the franchisee is delinquent in making royalty or marketing service fund payments to the Company for a period in excess of two (2) weeks; ... (iv) if the franchisee ceases or takes any steps to cease the operation of the franchised business.
- **Entire Agreement.** This Agreement constitutes the entire agreement between the parties and supersedes all previous agreements and understandings between the parties in any way relating to the subject matter hereof. It is expressly understood and agreed that the Company has made no representations, inducements, warranties, or promises whether direct, indirect, collateral, oral, or otherwise concerning this Agreement, the matters herein, or the business licensed hereunder or concerning any other matter that is not embodied herein.

Within a few months of opening his PPI franchise, it becomes apparent that the financial projections were inaccurate; Tony's sales are lower and his costs much higher than anticipated, resulting in a cash-flow problem and an inability to keep up with the weekly royalty and marketing fund payments under the franchise agreement. This is a breach of the ongoing payment clause in the franchise agreement. PPI sends Tony a letter demanding payment of the outstanding amounts and threatens legal action if he fails to pay on the basis of his breach of the franchise agreement (adapted from *Zippy Print Enterprises Ltd v Pawliuk*).

a. What steps could Tony have taken to minimize his risks associated with entering into the franchise agreement?

Working with Contracts

5

LEARNING OUTCOMES

After reading this chapter, you should be able to:

- Explain the essential elements required for the formation of a legally binding contract.
- Describe the consequences of breach of contract.
- Discuss remedies for breach of contract.
- Describe under what circumstances contracts are unenforceable.
- Suggest ways to mitigate the risks and legal expenses associated with your business or another party failing to meet contractual obligations.
- Explain the options available to a business when a contract is breached.

Formation of a Contract

This section revisits and expands on the four essential elements of contract formation that were examined at the beginning of Chapter 4:

1. an intention to create a legal relationship,
2. offer and acceptance,
3. consideration, and
4. legality.

Intention to Create a Legal Relationship

presumption legal assumption that is made, subject to a party proving otherwise

rebuttable capable of being refuted

The law presumes that the parties to a business-to-business transaction understand that the promises they make to each other carry legal consequences. That is, the law presumes that the parties to a business agreement intend that they may sue and be sued by each other if they break the promises that they have made. This **presumption** exists only in the context of the business world and the marketplace, not to agreements between family members or friends.

Even in the commercial world, the presumption that the parties had an intention to form a contract is **rebuttable**, or capable of being refuted. Therefore, if you, as a business owner, sue another business for breaching a commercial agreement, a court will not require you to prove that you intended to enter into a contract: it will presume that both business parties had such an intention. However, if the other business wishes to rebut the court's presumption by presenting evidence that it did not intend to contract—that is, did not intend its promises to be legally binding—it is entitled to do so. However, the other business faces an uphill battle in its attempts to convince the court because the presumption of the law is on your side.

MINIMIZING YOUR RISK

Respect the Presumption to Contract

- Make only the promises that you intend to keep.
- If you do not intend to be legally bound by something you say, make sure the other party understands your intention.

Offer and Acceptance

A contract must demonstrate a "meeting of the minds" between the parties. In other words, both parties must agree to the same thing. In a business-to-business transaction, this requirement is usually straightforward. There must be an offer by one party—for example, an offer to provide a service or product in exchange for a particular sum of money—and unconditional acceptance of that offer by the other party in the form of, for example, a signed document or a verbal agreement.

Disputes can arise when one party believes that a deal is final, while the other party believes that additional negotiations are needed or that additional time is available to reflect on the terms of the deal before it becomes final. Disputes can also arise if one party claims that it had accepted an offer—thus creating an enforceable contract—while the other party claims that the offer was no longer open for acceptance. These types of disputes are essentially about the timing or the formation of the contract, rather than about the contract's terms. Whether a court concludes that there was consensus—and thus that there was a legally binding contract—usually depends on the answer to one of the following two questions:

1. Was the offer still open when it was accepted?
2. Was acceptance of the offer properly communicated?

Was the Offer Open?

It is important for business people to know the rules about when an offer expires, because offers may expire in a variety of ways. Several of the most common ways—lapse, revocation, and counteroffer—are discussed in the following sections.

LAPSE

An offer may itself specify an expiry date and time. If so, once that time has passed, the offer lapses and is no longer open for acceptance. Your business may attempt to accept an offer after there has been a **lapse**, but—in law—your business's "acceptance" is nothing more than another offer. The party that originally extended the offer is free to accept your offer or to reject it. If it accepts your offer, you have a contract. If it rejects it, you have no contractual relationship.

lapse
expiration of an offer

REVOCATION

Whether or not an offer includes either a deadline or a promise to remain open for a particular period of time, the party who extends the offer is entitled to revoke the offer—or take it back—*at any time* before it is accepted. A business that contemplates an offer at its leisure may be unpleasantly surprised to encounter **revocation**—that is, to find that the offer is no longer open by the time the business decides to accept it.

revocation
taking back of an offer

The revocation rule makes sense in view of the voluntary nature of contracts. It allows businesses to reconsider the wisdom of their offers at any time until an offer is accepted; only upon acceptance does an offer become legally binding. Because the marketplace is constantly changing, the revocation rule allows businesses to keep their positions flexible. For example, Val-Nam Generation Limited ("Val-Nam") may offer to sell its portable electricity generators to XL Equipment Inc ("XL") at a price of $35.00 per unit. XL may plan to sell the generators at its retail outlets in Ontario. After making the offer, Val-Nam may discover that its material costs are going to increase due to a global steel shortage and realize that its offer is too low to provide a reasonable profit on the sales. Val-Nam is entitled to revoke the offer so long as XL has not yet accepted it. In the alternative, after Val-Nam makes its offer to XL, Canada Survival Supplies Inc ("CSS"), one of XL's competitors, may approach Val-Nam and offer to purchase double the number of generators that XL would purchase at a price of $50.00 per unit provided Val-Nam grants CSS exclusive distribution rights in Canada. This may be a much more profitable arrangement for Val-Nam. It would then make good business sense for Val-Nam to revoke its offer to XL and accept CSS's offer.

An exception to the revocation rule exists in the option agreement. An **option agreement** is an agreement under which a business that is contemplating an offer commits something of value—usually money—in exchange for a promise from the other party to keep the offer open for a specified length of time. An option agreement is itself a contract, in which the parties exchange mutual promises, which are of value to them both. The exchange of valuable mutual promises is a matter discussed later in this chapter under the heading "Consideration."

option agreement
contract in which a party gives something of value to keep an offer open for a specified period of time

Business people often use option agreements when they need time to conduct market research to determine whether a proposal is sufficiently advantageous to them economically. They also use options when they cannot sensibly accept an offer before determining whether they can line up other related contracts. For example, Val-Nam may need time to consider whether it can fulfill CSS's demand for that many generators. Val-Nam will have to determine whether it currently has the capacity to produce that many generators and, if not, whether it can increase its capacity at a cost and within a time frame that makes the proposed contract profitable. Val-Nam may have to add production lines, hire additional employees, and source additional raw materials. In order to give itself time to consider all of this, Val-Nam might pay for an option agreement to hold the offer open for a specified period of time. If it is important for your business to know that an offer will remain open, to allow you time either to consider it or to negotiate related deals, you must pay for this privilege by entering into an option agreement.

COUNTEROFFER

counteroffer
proposal that accepts an offer on terms differing from those in the offer

By accepting an offer on terms that differ from those proposed in the original offer, a business makes a **counteroffer**. For example, if Val-Nam responds to CSS's offer with the statement "We accept your offer but will only grant CSS exclusive distribution rights in Ontario," Val-Nam has, in fact, *not* accepted CSS's offer but has instead made a counteroffer. Rather than accepting CSS's offer unconditionally, Val-Nam has proposed a modification to it. In law, the effect of this counteroffer is to take CSS's original offer off the bargaining table. By making the counteroffer, Val-Nam now loses the right to accept CSS's original offer. CSS may choose to put its original offer back on the table, but Val-Nam has no power to compel it to do so.

Table 5.1 provides a summary of how contracts are formed.

Table 5.1 Formation of a Contract

Scenario	Contract Formed?	Reason
A makes an offer. B accepts.	Yes	Both offer and acceptance have occurred.
A makes an offer. B rejects the offer. B later accepts the offer.	No	Offer is no longer open after B rejects it.
A makes an offer stating deadline for acceptance. B accepts after this date.	No	Offer has lapsed. B's acceptance is a new offer.
A makes an offer. B makes a counteroffer. A rejects the counteroffer. B accepts the original offer.	No	Offer is no longer open as a result of B's counteroffer.

Table 5.1 Concluded

Scenario	Contract Formed?	Reason
A makes an offer stating the offer remains open until a certain date. A revokes the offer prior to this date. B accepts the offer after revocation but before the original deadline.	No	Offers can be revoked prior to acceptance, even if they include a promise to stay open.
A makes an offer stating the offer remains open until a certain date. B pays money for the right to this time period. A revokes the offer prior to this date. B accepts the offer after revocation but before the date.	Yes	Option agreement operates to keep an offer open.
A makes the same offer separately to B and C. B accepts, then C accepts shortly thereafter.	Yes—two are formed.	Acceptance of offer by one party does not revoke the offer made to another party.

Was Acceptance of the Offer Properly Communicated?

Businesses must also be aware of certain rules that govern the manner in which they must communicate their acceptance of an offer. Unless your contract states that you and the other party to the contract agree to implement different rules, the following are the rules that courts apply in resolving disputes about the formation and timing of contracts:

1. *A contract is formed when the party that accepts the offer communicates acceptance to the party that makes the offer in the manner requested by the offering party.* For example, if, in its offer to XL, Val-Nam specifies that the offer may be accepted by email, written notice delivered by courier, or verbal notice communicated by telephone, a binding contract exists as soon as Val-Nam receives unconditional acceptance of its offer by one of these prescribed modes of communication.
2. *If the offer states that acceptance must be communicated in a specified form, only that form of communication can create a contract.* If, for example, Val-Nam's offer to XL requires that acceptance be communicated by email, when XL sends a text message that purports to accept the offer, a binding contract is not created.
3. *Acceptance can be communicated by action alone, without requiring verbal or written confirmation.* For example, if Val-Nam places an order for delivery of office supplies and requests that the goods be delivered to its warehouse, the supplying company need not acknowledge receipt of the order. Its delivery of the supplies constitutes acceptance of the order and creates a binding contract at the time of delivery.
4. *Acceptance by mail occurs when the party that accepts an offer puts the acceptance in the mail.* The time at which the offering party receives the acceptance is irrelevant to the formation of a contract.

www.emond.ca/CBL3/links

DIG DEEPER
The e-laws website has the full text of the *Electronic Commerce Act, 2000.*

5. *Electronic acceptance occurs when it enters the information system used or designated by the offering party and becomes capable of being retrieved and processed by that party.* This presumption is set out in section 22(3) of the Ontario *Electronic Commerce Act, 2000*. Whether the acceptance is communicated electronically by email or by clicking an "I accept" or "submit" button on a website, once that email message or online acceptance has reached the information system of the offering party's Internet service provider, it is deemed to have been received. This acceptance is presumed to have happened regardless of whether the intended recipient has retrieved and read the electronically transmitted information. See discussions of the *Electronic Commerce Act, 2000* in Chapters 6 and 11.

There are important reasons to be aware of these rules. For example, you would not want to miss out on an opportunity to enter into a beneficial business transaction simply because you failed to convey your acceptance in a timely or appropriate manner.

MINIMIZING YOUR RISK

Observe the Rules of Offer and Acceptance

- You are bound by any offer that you make and that the other party accepts. If you are merely making a proposal that you do not intend to be bound by, ensure that the other party understands that your proposal is a starting point for negotiation, not necessarily a firm offer.
- When making and accepting offers, act with as much speed as required. Do not let an offer lapse or be revoked merely because you have delayed unnecessarily.
- Remove all offers you have made from the bargaining table once you realize they are of no advantage to your business.
- Use option agreements when you need time to consider your position.
- Weigh the usefulness of making a counteroffer against the knowledge that making it will remove an original offer from the bargaining table.
- Communicate your acceptance of an offer in a manner that will bind the other party in law.

Knowledge of these rules will also help you avoid being bound twice by the same offer. This could happen unless you take care to ensure that the offer you make to one business has expired, been revoked, or been subject to a counteroffer before you make the same offer to another business. In the situation above, where Val-Nam has offered to supply generators to XL (assuming that offer was not revoked) and has also, through its counteroffer to CSS, offered to supply generators to CSS, Val-Nam may find that both offers are accepted and that it is a party to two binding contracts. In this case, unless Val-Nam is able to fulfill its obligations under both contracts, it will be in breach of one of them. Given Val-Nam's offer to make CSS its exclusive distributor in Ontario, it will be in breach of its contract with CSS simply by selling generators to XL. If Val-Nam refuses to sell generators to XL in order to honour its agreement to make CSS its exclusive distributor in Ontario, Val-Nam will be in breach of its contract with XL.

Consideration

A valid contract requires consideration. Consideration is effectively the "price" that the parties are each willing to pay for the contractual benefits that they expect to gain. For example, when Val-Nam agrees to supply its generators in exchange for payment, the consideration—from the point of view of Val-Nam—is the generators; from the point of view of XL or CSS, the consideration is the payment. In this situation, the parties' contract has the essential element of mutual consideration that is required to make it valid. Any subsequent changes to the original contract also require a reciprocal exchange of consideration to be legally enforceable.

By contrast, a one-sided promise by one party does not meet the requirement of mutual consideration and therefore is not enforceable as a contract. Anyone who gratuitously promises to give someone a present can usually change their mind; the potential recipient is unlikely to be successful in enforcing the gift in court.

seal
symbol, stamp, etc. on a contract that indicates the intention to be legally bound; takes the place of consideration

Exceptions to the Requirement of Consideration

There are a few situations in which a contract does not need consideration to be valid. If your business agrees to allow another business to pay you less than it owes you in order to satisfy a debt, no consideration is required for your promise to accept the lesser amount. This exception has been created by statute and rests on the philosophy that your business receives the benefit of avoiding the delay and costs associated with collecting the entire debt. An out-of-court settlement of a lawsuit works in much the same way. Both parties give up their right to a trial and its associated risks in exchange for a certain outcome.

Another exception to the consideration requirement applies to contracts made under **seal**. A seal is essentially a special stamp or sticker added to an agreement—including a one-sided promise—to indicate the seriousness of the agreement and an intention to be legally bound by the promise. Contracts made under seal do not require consideration.

Figure 5.1

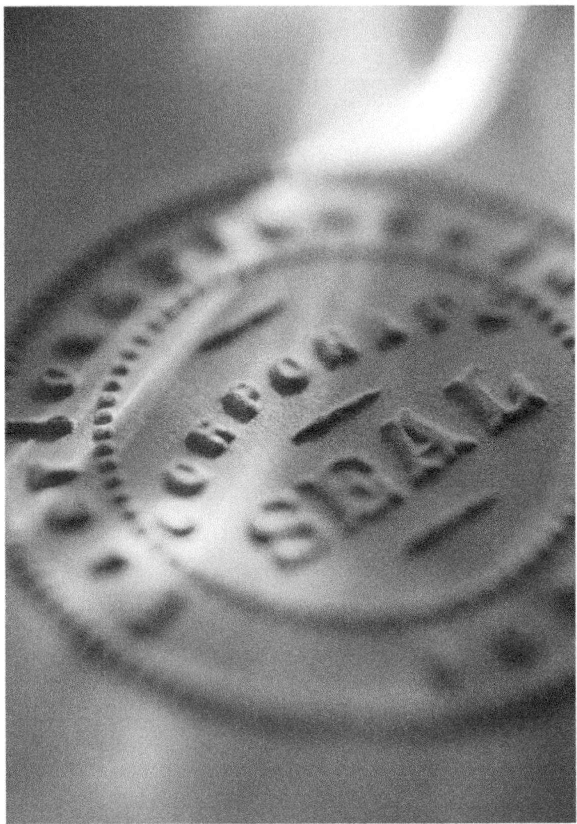

A company's marking of a proposed agreement with its seal indicates the company's intention to be legally bound by the promise.

Changing the Terms of a Contract

If you want to change the terms of a contract before you have carried them out, both parties must provide consideration. If they do not, the law will not enforce the change. One way to avoid problems is to agree with the other party to terminate the original contract and enter into a new one on new terms. The mutual agreement to terminate a contract provides consideration for the termination.

MINIMIZING YOUR RISK

Give and Receive Consideration to Ensure a Contract Is Binding

- Ensure that all parties to an agreement give something in exchange for the benefit they receive.
- Be cautious when asking for or agreeing to changes in contract terms that benefit one party at the expense of another.

Legality

A contract must have a legal purpose. In other words, the parties to the contract cannot agree to do something illegal. A single illegal action or promise can affect a series of business transactions by making all agreements that depend on the illegality unenforceable.

www.emond.ca/CBL3/links

DIG DEEPER
The Canada Border Service Agency offers a step-by-step guide to importing commercial goods into Canada.

Consider the situation if XL knowingly purchases counterfeit generators from a supplier—that is, the generators are copies of Val-Nam's generators and infringe Val-Nam's patent and trademark rights. XL complies with the supplier's request for payment in advance. The deadline for delivery comes and goes, and the supplier fails to deliver the generators. Since trading in counterfeit goods is illegal, XL will probably not be successful in making a claim for the return of the payment against the supplier in a Canadian court. It is likely that a court will rule that the contract is unenforceable because of its illegality.

Now, assume instead that XL pays for the counterfeit generators and receives shipment. XL then sells ten of its newly acquired counterfeit inventory to a small business. The generators are delivered and the small business fails to pay for them. Once again, as a result of the illegality of the transaction, XL will have little success in collecting the money it is owed if it tries to sue the small business.

Similarly, a business that trades in stolen property or sells illegal drugs can hardly expect to be able to enforce its business agreements through the courts. As of 2017 the Canadian government is in the process of legalizing the use and sale of marijuana. Until the legislation and associated regulations are in place, contracts that involve the production, distribution, or sale of marijuana may continue to be unenforceable.

As a word of caution, through legislative changes, some businesses that thought they were dealing in legal products can find themselves faced with unenforceable contracts when those products are suddenly banned. Consider the following examples:

- bans on the shipment of Canadian cattle into the United States,
- bans on pesticide use in some cities, and
- bans on the sale of toys or other children's products that fail to meet safety standards.

If a rancher near Calgary has an ongoing contract with a trucking company to transport cattle to Montana on a weekly basis, what happens when the United States announces a ban on cattle imports? Can a pesticide manufacturer insist that a Toronto lawn care company with a contract to purchase its product in bulk proceed with its contractual obligations after the city declares a ban? Can businesses enforce similar contracts governing other products that are banned?

As you might expect, courts do not enforce contracts if their purpose has become illegal. For example, if the pesticide manufacturer asked a court to enforce its demand that the lawn care company accept delivery of and pay for the shipment of pesticide, the court would probably declare the contract to be **void** (unenforceable). The result for the parties would be the same as if the contract had never existed. The pesticide manufacturer would bear the financial loss incurred by the loss of the market for its product. A court would neither require the lawn care company to fulfill its obligations under the original contract nor order it to compensate the manufacturer through the payment of **damages** for failing to do so. A carefully worded contract can, however, include a term that predetermines which party will bear the risk of this kind of eventuality.

void
unenforceable

damages
losses suffered as a result of the commission of a tort or the breach of a contract, or monetary compensation awarded for these losses

MINIMIZING YOUR RISK

Keep Your Business Dealings Legal

- Know who you are dealing with. If your supplier is not trustworthy, you may end up paying for goods you do not receive or selling goods you do not get paid for. You could also be charged with an offence and fined for infringing patents or copyright or violating trading laws.
- Keep up with political and social developments in your industry. The sooner you know about laws or events that might adversely affect your business, the better you can prepare to minimize their effect. On the bright side, the sooner you know about laws or events that may benefit your business, the sooner you can reap the rewards.

www.emond.ca/CBL3/links

DIG DEEPER
Keeping current with industry regulations and standards is crucial to ensuring a business avoids legal exposure.

Consequences of a Breach of Contract

You should now understand the importance of contract terms and of fulfilling your obligations under a contract. You should also appreciate how you can use specific contract terms to plan for and resolve potential conflicts arising out of the agreement (see Chapter 4). Unfortunately, unanticipated events can still take your business by surprise and interfere with a contractual transaction. This can result in a breach of the contract and the need to assess the possible consequences.

What Constitutes a Breach of Contract?

Although most contracts are successfully completed according to their terms, there will always be occasions when parties fail to live up to their contractual obligations. The following are examples of situations that may constitute a breach of contract:

- A product or service fails to meet the quality or description specified in the contract.
- A product or service is not delivered.
- A product is delivered after the delivery date specified in the contract.
- A project remains incomplete after the deadline specified in the contract.
- No payment is made.

A breach of contract may be intentional or unintentional. Consider the situation in which a significant increase in manufacturing costs makes a contract between

Val-Nam and XL highly unprofitable for Val-Nam (in circumstances where Val-Nam did not include a contract term that would allow a price adjustment, as discussed in Chapter 4). Although Val-Nam may have intended to complete the contract when it was signed, unanticipated events may make it less expensive for the business to breach the contract than to continue fulfilling the contractual obligations at a much higher cost than originally anticipated. Alternatively, consider the situation in which Val-Nam, after signing the contract with XL, receives a more lucrative offer for its generators from CSS. Val-Nam may decide that cancelling the first contract in order to enter into the second is financially irresistible.

An unintentional breach may occur when fulfillment of one contract depends on the successful completion of another. Consider the situation in which Val-Nam relies on a parts manufacturer for components of its generators and that parts manufacturer in turn relies on raw material suppliers. A delay at any stage may create a ripple effect throughout the remaining stages and result in a breach of completion and delivery deadlines. External forces such as governmental bans on fishing for endangered species, natural disasters, political unrest, or labour disputes may also affect the performance of contractual obligations, perhaps making them impossible.

To determine whether a circumstance constitutes a breach of contract—and to predict the consequences of that breach—the parties must look first to the terms of their agreement. For example, a sensible manufacturer will include contractual language that allows for some flexibility in the proposed products and delivery schedule. Terms such as "subject to availability of component parts" or "an equivalent product may be substituted at the manufacturer's discretion" may be useful in this regard. If the Val-Nam/XL contract contains this type of language, the substitution of a different but comparable model of generator is unlikely to be regarded as a breach of contract.

A business that is in the habit of cancelling less lucrative contracts in favour of more lucrative ones may also be in the habit of including cancellation clauses in its contracts. In this case, the terms of the cancellation clause will dictate the consequences of early cancellation. As long as the actions of the business fall within the terms of the cancellation clause, the business will probably have a good defence in an action against it for breach of contract. (Cancellation clauses are discussed in detail in Chapter 4.)

Similarly, if the contract contains a liquidated damages clause, an exclusion clause, or a disclaimer clause, the consequences of one party's breaching the contract—and the remedies available to the non-breaching party—may be clear. These clauses, discussed in Chapter 4, will usually tell the non-breaching party whether starting a lawsuit for breach of contract is a sensible business option.

Breach of Condition or Breach of Warranty?

Does a breach of contract by one party absolve the other party of its obligations under a contract? In other words, does a breach allow the non-breaching party to treat the contract as though it were at an end? The answer depends on the nature of the breach.

condition
important term of a contract whose breach frees the non-breaching party from all further obligations under the contract

If the breach is a serious one that involves an important term—or **condition**—of the contract, the non-breaching party is free of all further obligations under the contract. Breach of a condition allows the non-breaching party to treat the contract as if it were at an end. It also gives the non-breaching party a right to claim compensation for any losses, or damages, that flow from the breach.

However, if the breach is less serious and involves a relatively minor contractual term—or **warranty**—the non-breaching party must fulfill its remaining obligations under the contract. The non-breaching party does, however, have the right to claim damages as compensation for losses it has suffered as a result of the breach.

warranty
minor term of a contract whose breach requires the non-breaching party to continue to fulfill their remaining obligations under the contract

In practical terms, distinguishing between a condition and a warranty is important for one reason only: it allows the non-breaching party to know whether it must continue to live up to its contractual obligations after a breach has occurred. Breach of a condition ends a contract. Breach of a warranty does not end a contract. As long as a contract is in existence, the parties are obliged to honour their contractual obligations. However, once a contract ceases to exist, the parties' contractual obligations cease to exist as well.

It is sometimes difficult to distinguish between a condition and a warranty. Terms that are conditions in some contracts may be warranties in others because their relative importance may vary from contract to contract. Consider, for example, a contractual term that states the parties' agreement about the timing of delivery of a toy shipment. If the timing is crucial to meet a holiday market, the delivery term is probably a condition. This means that the buyer is probably safe in rejecting a late shipment and claiming damages from the supplier. If, however, the delivery is intended for mid-season restocking and the toy market is relatively calm, the term may be a warranty. In this case, the buyer should accept and pay for delivery in accordance with the terms of the contract before making a damages claim against the supplier.

It is extremely wise for parties to specify whether the terms in their contract are conditions or warranties. For example, a delivery term in the toy store situation might read, "It is a condition of this contract that the goods be delivered on or before October 31." If the parties do not specify whether a term is a condition or a warranty, the non-breaching party cannot be certain of how to react to the other party's breach. It will not know whether it can safely consider the contract to be at an end or whether it is still obliged to fulfill its contractual obligations and accept delivery.

Liability of Directors, Officers, and Employees for a Breach of Contract

Generally speaking, a business's contractual obligations are fulfilled on behalf of the business by individuals whom the business employs or retains. In a corporation, that can include the corporation's directors, officers, and employees (see Chapter 7 for a detailed analysis of corporations). For example:

- Packages are delivered by delivery staff, even though the parties to the delivery contract are the customer and the delivery company.
- Advertising slogans or product logos are designed by creative staff, even though the parties to the advertising contract are the customer and the advertising agency.
- Products are manufactured by factory workers, even though the parties to the contract of purchase and sale are the purchaser and the manufacturing company.

In these situations, the delivery staff, the creative staff, and the factory workers perform the tasks on behalf of their employer (as "agents" of the employer). In each of these examples, if the employee fails to perform the work in accordance with the terms of the contract—for example, fails to deliver a package on time, design an acceptable logo, or produce a flawless product—it is the business that is sued, because it is the business's obligation under the relevant contract to deliver the package, design the logo, or produce the product. Note that where the business is a sole proprietorship, it is the sole proprietor who is liable as the "business"; where the business is a partnership, it is the general partners who are liable as the "business"; and where the business is a corporation, it is the corporation that is liable as the "business." This is discussed in detail in Chapter 7.

Generally, as the director, officer, or employee is performing their duties on behalf of the business, they will not be personally liable for any breach of contract between the business and its customer. However, in limited circumstances where the individual acts in a personal capacity (rather than on behalf of the business) or acts outside their authority or not in the best interests of the business, personal liability may attach. Note, however, that the individual may be liable to the business for a breach of their contract with the business, if the individual's performance fell below the standards set out in that contract. For a further discussion of the principles of agency and directors' and officers' liability, see Chapter 7.

MINIMIZING YOUR RISK

Avoid, Plan For, and Respond Sensibly to Breaches of Contract

- Avoid gaining a reputation for habitually breaching your contracts.
- Use cancellation, liquidated damages, exclusion, or disclaimer clauses in your contracts to predetermine the financial cost of a breach.
- In the event of a breach, check the wording of the contract to determine whether the breach is of a condition or a warranty.
- Be prepared to fulfill your obligations in the event of a breach of warranty by the other party.
- Monitor the work of employees to ensure that they do not jeopardize your contractual obligations.

Damages

As discussed, there is much that contracting parties can do to anticipate the possibility of a breach and to address it within the terms of their contract. What happens, however, if a contract is silent about breach and its consequences? The general rule is that any breach, no matter how large or small, entitles the non-breaching party to compensation.

In the commercial world, compensation usually takes the form of monetary damages. The subject of damages eventually evolves into an examination of how much money the breaching party is required to pay to the non-breaching party to compensate for the breach. If a damages claim ends up in court, a judge applies the test set out in the case of *Hadley v Baxendale* to determine the **quantum**, or amount, of the damages:

quantum
amount

> The non-breaching party should be compensated to the extent of the loss of benefits that were within the reasonable contemplation of the parties when the contract was made.

In other words, the damages should be sufficient to put the non-breaching party in the position it would have been in had the contract not been breached, but only to the extent that the damages were foreseeable. For example, if Val-Nam enters into a contract with a website design company for the design of its website and the design company breaches the contract by failing to meet the design specifications, Val-Nam may be entitled to the costs it incurs in hiring another company to complete the website according to the original agreement.

The website design company's breach may in fact lead to other losses to Val-Nam. For example, profits may not be as high as anticipated if the new website had been completed on time. And Val-Nam may lose the opportunity to showcase its products online to potential customers at an upcoming trade show. However, Val-Nam would be unlikely to successfully claim compensation from the website design company for these losses—they are difficult to prove and/or not a foreseeable loss arising from the breach.

As a further example, if an air conditioning system is improperly installed in a shopping mall, the contractor may be liable for any related structural damage, the cost of reinstalling the system correctly, and loss of profit by any businesses that were forced to close during the time of the installation and repair. All of these consequences are reasonably foreseeable.

However, imagine that the air conditioning system was improperly installed in a newly built shopping centre and the need to reinstall it pushed the construction schedule off target by several months. The shopping mall owner could claim the cost of the reinstallation and perhaps the financing costs associated with the delay in construction. It could probably also claim the reasonably anticipated lease payments that it was unable to collect as a result of the delay. But what if there was a significant downturn in the economy during those few months? It is unlikely that the shopping mall owner could also claim the difference between the future lease payments that it could have collected from tenants in a booming economy, had the leases been entered into at the time of the original construction deadline, and the lease payments that it can collect in a now-stagnant economy. The air conditioning contractor could be successful in arguing that it could not reasonably have foreseen these consequences of its breach of contract.

Duty to Mitigate Damages

The non-breaching party has an obligation to keep its losses to a minimum. This obligation is known as the **duty to mitigate**. Because of the duty to mitigate, a breaching party is not required to pay for losses that the non-breaching party could have avoided with reasonable efforts. As noted by the Supreme Court of Canada in the 2012 case of *Southcott Estates Inc v Toronto Catholic District School Board*, an entity sued for breach of contract has the burden of proving "both that the plaintiff has failed to make reasonable efforts to mitigate and that mitigation was possible." As the court also pointed out, "a plaintiff who does take reasonable steps to mitigate loss may recover, as damages, the costs and expenses incurred in taking those reasonable steps, provided that the costs and expenses are reasonable and were truly incurred in mitigation of damages." The duty is one "based on fairness and common sense, which seeks to do justice between the parties in the particular circumstances of the case." Consider the following example.

duty to mitigate
obligation to take all reasonable steps to lessen losses suffered

Assume that a scientific research conference includes an exhibition area where interested businesses can, for a fee, set up booths to demonstrate their products or services. Because exhibition space is limited, exhibitors must reserve a booth and pay a 50 percent deposit at the time of booking. Valery Garza, Val-Nam's CEO, is very interested in demonstrating the technology behind the company's new generator at the conference and reserves a booth on behalf of Val-Nam. One week before the conference, Valery is injured in a skiing accident and has to pull out of the conference. No one else from Val-Nam is available to attend the conference, so Valery notifies the conference organizers that Val-Nam is pulling out of the exhibition. Val-Nam refuses to pay the balance of the booth rental fee. There is no cancellation clause in its contract with the organizers.

Val-Nam is probably in breach of the contract because when it reserved the booth, it entered into a binding agreement to exhibit at the conference and pay the outstanding balance of the booth rental fee. As a consequence, the conference organizers may be entitled not only to keep the 50 percent deposit but also to make a claim for the outstanding balance. This would put the conference organizers in the position they expected to be in had Val-Nam not breached the contract.

In order to mitigate their losses, however, the conference organizers are under a duty to make reasonable efforts to find a replacement exhibitor. If they are able to rent out the space to a different business, they may have no losses and therefore no claim for damages in compensation. Val-Nam's good fortune in avoiding payment of 50 percent of the fee may seem unfair. However, from a business perspective, the conference organizers are also in a much better position than they would have been had they gone to court to attempt to recoup their losses.

Why go to the trouble of making a claim against another party if a more practical solution is available? *Carr v Killam* is a New Brunswick case that illustrates the need for exercising good judgment in mitigating losses after suffering a contractual breach.

CASE IN POINT

Mitigation of Damages

Carr v Killam, 2005 NBQB 260

Facts

The purchaser bought a small building located in Westfield, New Brunswick, for $2,000. He intended to move the building to property he owned in Seeley's Cove. The contract for the sale of the building required that it be removed from the Westfield site by a specified date. The purchaser contracted with a mover to move the building for $8,000. The moving contract indicated that the cost was to be paid in two installments: one of $4,000 paid at the time of execution of the contract and one of $4,000 paid once the house was installed on the Seeley's Cove property. The purchaser paid a deposit of $3,000, which was noted on the contract. As the deadline for moving the building approached, the mover demanded the remaining deposit of $1,000. The purchaser refused to pay the additional $1,000. After the deadline for moving the building came and went, the purchaser sued the mover for breach of contract, claiming the following damages:

- $3,000 deposit,
- $2,000 paid for the building,
- $4,000 for the value of the unmoved building,
- $4,025 for road improvements to his Seeley's Cove property to move the building to an appropriate location on the lot,
- $880 paid to workers who prepared his property at Seeley's Cove,
- $780 for his own time,

- $100 to remove an electrical mast that would have impeded the moving of the building from its original location,
- $260 for miscellaneous expenses (including gas and a tree trimmer), and
- $50,000 for the estimated increased value that would have resulted from the addition of the building to his Seeley's Cove property.

Result

The New Brunswick Court of Queen's Bench rejected almost all of the damages claimed by the purchaser because the purchaser failed to mitigate his losses by hiring another contractor to move the building once he knew that the contract was at an end. The reasonable course of action was for the purchaser to mitigate his losses by retaining another contractor to move the building. All claims—except for the return of the $3,000 deposit—flowed directly from the purchaser's failure to mitigate, rather than from the mover's breach of the contract.

Business Lesson

Following a contractual breach, mitigate your losses immediately.

Punitive Damages

Courts and arbitrators award punitive damages to punish a party who has breached a contract, rather than to compensate a party who has complied with it. To award punitive damages, a court must be satisfied that the conduct of the breaching party is sufficiently reprehensible to warrant monetary punishment. An insurance company's conduct met this standard in *Whiten v Pilot Insurance Co*, a Case in Point in Chapter 2. The jury in *Whiten* evidently believed that the insurance company knew from the outset that its arson claim was contrived and unsustainable and, further, that it was denying the claim to force the plaintiff to settle for less than she was entitled to.

Alternative Methods for Performance

Sometimes a contract specifies that it can be fulfilled in one of several ways—that is, the contract provides for alternative methods for performance. How are damages to be measured if a party breaches such a contract? In *Hamilton v Open Window Bakery Ltd*, the Supreme Court of Canada ruled that the correct test for measuring damages is to apply the method that is least profitable to the plaintiff and least burdensome to the defendant.

MINIMIZING YOUR RISK

Prepare to Justify Your Damages

- Keep all records and documents that pertain to losses flowing from contractual breaches.
- Take immediate steps to mitigate your losses.
- Do not expect compensation for damages that are too remote from a breach.
- Ensure that your conduct toward the other party is honest, reasonable, and businesslike.

CASE IN POINT

Damages for Breach of Contracts with Alternative Performance Methods

Hamilton v Open Window Bakery Ltd, 2004 SCC 9

Facts

An agent contracted with a bakery to be its exclusive sales and marketing representative in Japan for a term of 36 months. The contract allowed the bakery to terminate the contract either

1. "without notice ... if the Agent acts in a manner which is detrimental to the reputation and well being" of the bakery, or
2. "with notice to the Agent effective after the commencement of the 19th month of the term herein, on three (3) months' notice."

Approximately 16 months into the contract, the bakery sent a letter to the agent terminating the agreement immediately on the basis of allegations that she had deliberately falsified ingredient lists and disclosed confidential information to a competitor. Subsequently, the bakery also sent her another letter in accordance with its right to terminate by giving notice as specified under the second item above.

At trial, the judge found no evidence that the agent had acted dishonestly or fraudulently. The bakery had therefore breached the contract by terminating the contract without giving the appropriate notice. The trial judge awarded the agent damages in an amount reflecting the payments she would have received under the remainder of the 36-month contract, less an allowance of 25 percent to reflect the fact that the bakery could have validly terminated the contract on three months' notice, after the commencement of the 19th month.

Result

The Supreme Court of Canada reduced the damages that the bakery was required to pay. The bakery was liable only for the amount that the agent would have received if the bakery had given notice immediately after the 19th month to terminate the contract at the end of the 22nd month.

Because the contract allowed for alternative methods of performance, the court applied the rule that the non-breaching party is entitled to be restored only to the position she would have been in had the least beneficial contractual alternative been performed.

Business Lesson

Keep termination provisions as flexible as possible, particularly in long-term contracts. What seems like a great business relationship at the beginning may sour over time.

Unenforceable Agreements

The great majority of contractual obligations are enforceable. However, in a few limited circumstances, a court or arbitrator (where the parties use private arbitration to resolve the dispute) may relieve a party of the contractual obligations that it has agreed to assume. From a business perspective, it is important to know the factors and conduct that may jeopardize a business transaction. If you can anticipate problems, you can avoid creating them or stumbling into them.

Unenforceable agreements stem from situations in which one party feels that it has been taken advantage of, been misled, or otherwise been unfairly disadvantaged. A party who wants to be relieved of contractual obligations may claim that an agreement is unenforceable in one of two contexts:

1. *Defensively*. A party may raise an objection to the enforceability of an agreement if sued for breach of that agreement.

2. *Assertively*. A party may raise an objection to the enforceability of an agreement by asking a court or arbitrator to declare that an agreement is unenforceable, whether or not the agreement has been breached.

If a party is able to make a convincing claim—or to raise a convincing defence—based on any of the circumstances outlined in the following sections, a court or arbitrator may relieve the party of its contractual obligations.

Misrepresentation of Material Fact

Did one of the parties make a false statement that persuaded the other party to enter into the deal, and was this statement important to the agreement as a whole? The statement at issue is one made outside of the actual terms of the contract. As a general rule, to render an agreement unenforceable, the **misrepresentation**—or false statement—must be a statement of fact, not opinion, on which the deceived party relied when entering into the agreement.

misrepresentation
false statement of fact

The deceived party need not prove that the other party made the misrepresentation intentionally. However, whether the misrepresentation was made innocently, negligently, or fraudulently may affect the remedies available. For example, if a party misrepresents a material fact because it honestly (but mistakenly) believed it to be true, the party who relied on the statement and entered into a contract because of it is only entitled to **rescind** the contract. This means that a judge will attempt to put the parties back to their original positions. However, this may not always be possible, in which case the party who was deceived by the innocent misrepresentation will bear the loss. However, if the misrepresentation is negligent (for example, where the party who made the misrepresentation failed to do the necessary research to back up the claim) or fraudulent (in other words, intentionally deceptive), the party who relied on the statement and entered into the contract may be entitled to monetary damages in tort law (the tort of negligence or deceit) as well as to an order of rescission.

rescind
treat as if the contract were never made

MINIMIZING YOUR RISK

Do Not Make Factual Representations That Cannot Be Supported

- Be careful of what is said both outside of and within the express terms of the contract. If a party relies on your untrue or unchecked factual representations, it may be able to rescind the contract or collect damages.
- If a particular fact about a service or product is important to your decision to enter into a contract, get it in writing as an express term of the contract.

Economic Duress, Undue Influence, and the Unconscionable Agreement

Was one of the parties pressured into making the deal? A business may claim that it was forced to enter into an agreement under **economic duress**—that is, under threat of serious economic harm.

economic duress
pressure to enter into a contract by way of threat of economic harm

Consider a vacation resort that was undergoing renovations on a tight schedule in order to receive booked guests during the busy summer season. What if, midway through the job, the contractor demanded a change to the contract—more money or it would not complete the work? Because of the tight schedule and the threat of not being ready in time for customers, the resort might pay the money. Arguably, this extortionate behaviour by the contractor would amount to economic duress.

A party who claims duress must prove that the pressure exerted exceeded ordinary commercial pressure. A court or arbitrator will not void an agreement unless it is convinced that the threatened party did not freely consent to the terms of the agreement. Economic duress is difficult to prove. It will only be successful if the party claiming that it was under duress can persuade the court that it had no realistic alternative but to submit to the pressure.

undue influence pressure exerted on a weaker party that deprives that party of the ability to exercise their judgment or free will

Undue influence is similar to duress. Individuals may claim to be the victims of undue influence if the pressure exerted by the other parties deprived them of the ability to exercise their free will when they entered into the agreement.

There is a presumption of undue influence where there is a special relationship between the parties that is unbalanced in terms of power—such as that of lawyer and client or doctor and patient. Undue influence may arise in other relationships, such as employer and employee or between spouses, but there is no presumption; the weaker party must prove it.

Consider a wrongful dismissal situation, where an employer fires an employee without a good reason and without providing sufficient notice. The employer might pressure the employee to sign a termination agreement, releasing the employer of all liability (and effectively preventing the employee from suing for wrongful dismissal). The employer might offer a small payment in return for signing the agreement, but threaten that the offer expires in an hour. A distraught employee, worried about paying bills and unaware of any potential entitlement to a much larger sum, might accept this offer. These facts might support an allegation of undue influence.

independent legal advice legal advice regarding a contract obtained from a different lawyer than the lawyer who drafted the contract

To avoid allegations of undue influence, businesses can encourage employees to obtain **independent legal advice** before they sign any contract, including an employment agreement, confidentiality agreement, or termination agreement. Be sure to provide sufficient time for employees to consult with their own lawyer before entering into the transaction.

unconscionable agreement agreement so inequitably one-sided that it is unenforceable

An **unconscionable agreement** is one in which the terms are so unreasonably one-sided that the court will not enforce the agreement. The test for this is strict—a gross inequality of bargaining power coupled with a gross inadequacy of benefit to the weaker party.

MINIMIZING YOUR RISK

Do Not Be Pressured into a Risky Deal

- If you are unsure about a business opportunity, get a second opinion from a trusted source.
- Seek independent legal advice, and make sure the other party has an opportunity to do likewise.
- If it is your position that you were pressured into an agreement against your will, assert this position at the first opportunity.
- Do not exert undue pressure on a business partner or employee—it may give them an excuse to get out of the deal.

CASE IN POINT

Unconscionability and Economic Duress

Upper Valley Dodge Chrysler Ltd v Cronier Estate, 2004 CanLII 34431 (Ont Sup Ct J)

Facts

William Morglan, a successful entrepreneur, lent $160,000 to the unsophisticated Cronier family for their small wood-cutting business. The Croniers had substantial debts already. Morglan took a chattel mortgage on equipment worth about $270,000 but also insisted on taking a mortgage on the Cronier family home. The interest rate charged was 14 percent. The Croniers did not receive independent legal advice. They made payments on the debt sporadically. Years later, after the death of Mr. Cronier, Morglan demanded full payment of the loan, which, with accumulated interest, had grown to over $500,000. Issues raised included unconscionability and economic duress.

Result

The court held that the terms of the loan were not unfair. The rate of interest was reasonable in 1988 when the loan was made. Morglan's insistence on taking a mortgage on the family home was not unreasonable given the size of the loan. The issue of unconscionability must be based upon the nature and terms of the agreement entered into at the time that the agreement was contracted, and based on this, the transaction was not unconscionable. Mrs. Cronier also did not demonstrate that she was coerced into signing the mortgage. The Croniers had an opportunity to obtain independent legal advice but chose not to do so. The Croniers did not take any steps to avoid the contract and claimed economic duress only years later when Morglan demanded payment.

Business Lesson

Unconscionability and economic duress are very hard to prove. If you intend to make allegations like these, it is important to do so as soon as possible. Acquiescence to the contract over a period of time will undermine your argument that you were forced into it.

Minors

Was one of the parties a **minor**—that is, under the age of majority (18 years in Ontario)—when the agreement was entered into? This issue is less likely to arise in a business-to-business context than in a business-to-consumer context, but it is increasingly significant with the prevalence of e-commerce transactions. As a consequence, all businesses should be aware that minors have the option of being excused from most contractual obligations.

minor
person under the age of majority

If you are contracting with a young entrepreneur, obtain confirmation of age before signing the deal. Be aware of and assess the risks associated with contracting with individuals under the age of majority. And do not expect to hold their parents accountable unless they are also parties to the contract or have signed a **guarantee**. A guarantee is an independent contract in which the guarantors (in this example, the parents of a minor) agree to assume liability for the financial obligations of another person (i.e., their child). If the child defaults on obligations under a separate contract, the parents will be obligated to pay the amount owing based on the guarantee.

guarantee
contract whereby a party assumes responsibility for another party's financial obligations if that other party defaults on payment

Capacity

Was an individual suffering from mental health issues, or impaired by drugs or alcohol, such that they did not know what they were doing when entering into an agreement? Persons under the influence of drugs or alcohol, or suffering from a mental health issue, may be able to argue that they lacked the capacity—or legal capability—to contract.

Individuals suffering from impairment as a result of a mental health issue, drugs, or alcohol must prove both that they were incapacitated when they entered into the agreement and that the other party was aware of their condition. Impairment claims are essentially claims that one party has taken advantage of the other as a result of a temporary or permanent mental condition.

MINIMIZING YOUR RISK

Consider Capacity Before Signing a Contract

- If in doubt about someone's capacity to contract due to age, ask for proof.
- Insist on a guarantee before contracting with a minor.
- Avoid finalizing business transactions at social or other events where alcohol and/or drugs may be consumed.

What Can You Do About a Breach of Contract?

If a party breaches a contract to which you are a party, several courses of action are available to you. You can:

- ignore the breach,
- negotiate a compromise that is agreeable to both you and the other party,
- seek alternative dispute resolution services, or
- litigate your differences in court.

Each of these options is discussed briefly below.

Ignore the Breach

A breach of contract may have a very minor effect on your business. For example, if one of Val-Nam's parts suppliers delivers blue casings for the generator when red casings were ordered under the contract, Val-Nam may be wiser to ignore the breach than to expend time and energy in seeking a remedy. If the breaching party is a business with which you have an ongoing relationship, ignoring a breach may work to the advantage of both of you in the long run. By forgiving a breach on one occasion, your business may be forgiven on another.

Negotiate a Compromise

A breach of contract may cause aggravation, perhaps even anger. But as a business person, you must try not to let your emotions interfere with your sound judgment. The most cost-effective and sensible solution to a breach of contract may be to negotiate a resolution with the other party. If possible, work with the other party to understand the reason for the breach and the problems caused by it. Negotiating a reasonable compensation payment may enhance your future relationship with the other party and save everyone money in the long run. Negotiation also allows you to explore creative solutions to the problem and to prevent future breaches.

Once you have resolved your dispute by way of negotiation, the breaching party should ask the non-breaching party to sign a release. A **release** absolves the breaching party of liability for any contract-related claims that the non-breaching party might make in the future. Alternatively, you can draw up a new contract that revokes the original one and sets out the terms of your new agreement. The purpose of the release or the new contract is to bind you both to your compromise agreement and prevent either of you from altering your newly negotiated position.

release
document that absolves the breaching party of liability for any contract-related claims that the non-breaching party might make in the future

Use Alternative Dispute Resolution

The expense and uncertainty of litigation has led to the establishment of the various alternative dispute resolution (ADR) services that are described in detail in Chapter 2. If negotiations with the other party fail to resolve your dispute, you should consider engaging the services of an independent third party to help settle your differences. Two popular forms of ADR are mediation and arbitration. Mediation, the less formal of the two processes, can assist you by pointing out the strengths and weaknesses of both parties' positions. Mediators are skilled in suggesting mutually beneficial compromises. If you succeed in resolving your dispute through mediation, you will want to ensure that a release is signed for the reasons pointed out above. Arbitration, as already discussed, produces a binding result that is enforceable through the courts.

Litigate

Litigation in the courts has become a prohibitively expensive and time-consuming process. It is, however, an option to consider as a last resort.

CHAPTER SUMMARY

It is important for businesses to understand the essential elements necessary to create a legal and enforceable contract. These include the intention of the parties to form a legal relationship (a presumption in business transactions), a mutual understanding among parties of the terms of the contract and the rules of offer and acceptance, the requirement that both parties give and receive "consideration" for the transaction (i.e., not a promise of something for free), and that the agreement does not violate any laws.

Parties are expected to live up to their contractual obligations. Failure to do so is a breach of contract, which can lead to serious legal and economic consequences. To determine whether a circumstance constitutes a breach of contract, the parties must look to the terms of their agreement.

Generally, any breach entitles the non-breaching party to compensation, usually in the form of monetary damages in an amount that is sufficient to put the non-breaching party in the position it would have been in had the contract not been breached. Punitive damages are only awarded for conduct that is sufficiently reprehensible to warrant monetary punishment.

Parties who want to be relieved of contractual obligations may look to whether they have been taken advantage of, misled, or forced to enter into an agreement under duress. Businesses should also be aware that minors have the option of being excused from most contractual obligations.

If a party breaches a contract to which you are a party, you can ignore the breach, negotiate a compromise, use ADR services, or litigate your differences in court.

KEY TERMS

condition, 152
counteroffer, 146
damages, 151
duty to mitigate, 155
economic duress, 159
guarantee, 161
independent legal advice, 160
lapse, 145
minor, 161
misrepresentation, 159
option agreement, 145
presumption, 144
quantum, 154
rebuttable, 144
release, 163
rescind, 159
revocation, 145
seal, 149
unconscionable agreement, 160
undue influence, 160
void, 151
warranty, 153

REFERENCES

Carr v Killam, 2005 NBQB 260.
Electronic Commerce Act, 2000, SO 2000, c 17.
Hadley v Baxendale (1854), 9 Ex. 341, 156 ER 145.
Hamilton v Open Window Bakery Ltd, 2004 SCC 9.
Southcott Estates Inc v Toronto Catholic District School Board, 2012 SCC 51.
Upper Valley Dodge Chrysler Ltd v Cronier Estate, 2004 CanLII 34431 (Ont Sup Ct J).
Whiten v Pilot Insurance Co, 2002 SCC 18, [2002] 1 SCR 595.

EXERCISES

True or False?

____ **1.** If an offer specifies that it must be accepted by fax before a certain deadline, your acceptance by email message before the deadline will result in a legally binding contract.

____ **2.** Your business is running into financial difficulties, and you persuade one of your customers to pay more for your marketing-research services than the original contract specified. If your customer changes their mind and refuses to pay the additional amount, you would likely be successful if you sued them for breach of contract.

____ **3.** Your business purchases a new computer. A week later, you see the same model at a different store at a significantly lower price and realize you paid too much. If you attempt to return the computer to the store where you bought it, the store must refund your money.

____ **4.** It is prudent to avoid finalizing a business transaction over drinks at the local pub.

____ **5.** If they change their mind about a contract, individuals under the age of majority may be excused from their contractual obligations.

____ **6.** Resolving a contractual dispute in court will ensure the fairest result for all parties.

Multiple Choice

1. A property developer is negotiating the purchase of several acres of land from the owner to develop a residential complex. The owner has made an attractive offer that is set to expire within 24 hours. The property developer wants more time to consider the offer before making a final commitment. What should the property developer do to gain additional time?
- **a.** Make a counteroffer on slightly different terms.
- **b.** Allow the offer to lapse and make a new offer later.
- **c.** Enter into an option agreement with the owner.
- **d.** Reject the offer and make a new offer later.

2. When a dispute arises concerning a business contract, the first step the parties should take is:
- **a.** negotiation
- **b.** mediation
- **c.** arbitration
- **d.** litigation

3. If found to be untrue, which of the following statements made by a car salesperson to a potential buyer would constitute a misrepresentation that could render the contract unenforceable?
   a. "The colour of the car matches your eyes—it's perfect for you!"
   b. "In my opinion, this car is the best value for your money."
   c. "This car is accident-free and has had only one previous owner."
   d. "You won't get a better deal anywhere else."
4. A retailer based in British Columbia orders a large quantity of toys from a toy manufacturer in Ontario. The transaction is conducted online. The retailer fills in an online form on the manufacturer's website, pays with a credit card, and clicks a "submit" button to complete the transaction. The contract is formed when:
   a. the retailer purchasing the toys clicks the "submit" button.
   b. the transaction data are processed by the retailer's Internet service provider.
   c. the transaction data reach the toy manufacturer's Internet service provider.
   d. the toy manufacturer sends an email message to the retailer confirming the transaction.

Short Answer

1. What situation might constitute a breach of contract?
2. Explain the remedies available if a breach of contract involves a condition versus a warranty.
3. What is the obligation of a non-breaching party to mitigate its damages?
4. What options does a business have when the other party to a contract breaches it?
5. In what circumstances might a party to a contract be permitted to rescind the agreement?

Apply Your Knowledge

1. You own a small marketing-research consulting business. You entered into a large contract with an American retail chain looking for appropriate locations to expand its market into Ontario and British Columbia. The original contract price was inclusive of travel and other expenses. Unfortunately, airfares have increased dramatically in price, and it has been much more expensive than anticipated to conduct the surveys and focus groups necessary across the two provinces. As a result, your business is running into financial difficulties.
   a. Can you renegotiate the terms of the contract with your American retail client?
   b. If your client agrees to pay more for the same original services, but then changes its mind and refuses to pay, what can you do?
2. Your business enters into a contract for the delivery of a shipment of toys from a manufacturer in Hong Kong. The toys are in high demand for the upcoming holiday season. When they are delivered, you discover that they are counterfeit goods. On reviewing the fine print of the contract, you see that there are governing law and venue clauses specifying that any disputes will be governed by the laws of Hong Kong in the courts of Hong Kong.
   a. If the goods have been paid for, what can you do to get your money back?
   b. If you attempt to deliver the goods to local toy stores and they refuse to accept delivery and pay for the goods, will a court make them pay for the goods, or award damages to your business?
3. You work for a company that manufactures a specialty line of commercial shelving suitable for retail displays. Manufacturing costs have been rising steadily, and you have been negotiating with a new supplier for a key component of the shelving units. The supplier's latest offer is to supply the component for a reasonable, fixed price if your company commits to a minimum monthly purchase for a period of 12 months.
   a. What can your company do to ensure that the offer remains open while you consider whether to accept it?
   b. What are the other risks associated with taking time to consider the offer before accepting it?
   c. If the supplier specifies a deadline for acceptance, can it cancel the offer ahead of the deadline?
   d. If the supplier specifies a deadline for acceptance, can you accept the offer after the deadline expires?
   e. What happens if your company responds by agreeing to a six-month commitment?
   f. If the supplier has made the same offer to both your company and one of your competitors at the same time, what risks does it run?
4. Refer to the case description of Niagara's Best Organic Foods Wholesale Distributors Ltd in Question 1 of Apply Your Knowledge in Chapter 4, on page 140.

a. What options does Organics have to recover its losses? What are the pros and cons of each option?
b. What term(s) of the contract affect(s) the amount that Organics might recover if it sues Niagara's Best for breach of contract as a result of this incident? Who are the proper parties to the lawsuit?

5. Refer to the case description of Tony Nguyen and his ownership of a Priority Printing Inc (PPI) franchise from Question 2 of Apply Your Knowledge in Chapter 4, on page 140. If PPI sues Tony for breaching the terms of the franchise agreement, what arguments can he raise in his defence?

Facilitating Business, Protecting Consumers, and Safeguarding the Marketplace

6

LEARNING OUTCOMES

After reading this chapter, you should be able to:

- Identify key federal and provincial statutes that have been created to facilitate business, protect consumers, and safeguard the Canadian marketplace.
- Explain the effect of the *Sale of Goods Act* on conditions and warranties, transfer of title, and remedies for breach of contract.
- Discuss how the *Electronic Commerce Act, 2000* clarifies the legal status of electronic documents and the legal effect of electronic communications.
- Explain the scope of consumers' rights under the *Consumer Protection Act, 2002*, describe unfair business practices under the Act, and comment on the penalties imposed on businesses that engage in unfair business practices.
- Describe the roles played by the *Food and Drugs Act*, the *Hazardous Products Act*, and the *Canada Consumer Product Safety Act* in protecting the safety of consumers.
- Discuss how consumers' access to adequate and accurate information is protected by the federal *Competition Act* and the *Consumer Packaging and Labelling Act*.
- Examine the criminal and reviewable business practices provisions of the federal *Competition Act* that safeguard the competitive nature of the Canadian marketplace.

A basic overview of the common law relating to torts and contracts is a good first step as Val-Nam Generation Limited ("Val-Nam") tries to understand the scope of legal liability to which its operations may expose the business and those who participate in the business. However, it is only a starting point. Legislation has codified many of the common law principles and then moved beyond those principles in establishing additional legal protections and obligations for Canadian businesses. A familiarity with the range of legislation that imposes obligations on businesses is key.

Moving Beyond the Common Law: The Need to Protect Important Societal Interests

caveat emptor
Latin maxim that translates roughly to "buyer beware"

As noted, to this point we have primarily examined the common law obligations and liabilities that businesses are exposed to. The key distinguishing characteristic of the historical common law approach to contract law was the support of "freedom of contract"—parties were free to negotiate the terms of their bargain, and for the most part, the courts would not question the wisdom of the bargain or its purpose. This philosophy was also expressed in the Latin maxim *caveat emptor*. ***Caveat emptor***, which roughly translates to "buyer beware" or "let the buyer take care of himself," is an expression of the philosophy that dominated the early common law of the marketplace. Under this principle, buyers and sellers were expected to conduct whatever investigations were appropriate and to include whatever contractual terms were necessary to fully protect their own interests. Both of these principles place faith in the ability of a party to do that. In reality, imbalances in bargaining power (related to wealth, experience, or other factors) are common. Significant imbalances in bargaining power can result in the stronger party taking advantage of the weaker party. While these imbalances are seen more frequently in consumer–business transactions, they also occur in business–business transactions. Where such imbalances occur, the general common law position was often insufficient to protect the weaker party's interests, and a case-by-case approach to addressing the imbalance (through, for example, a court challenge to the enforceability of the contract due to unconscionability) was cumbersome and costly.[1] Over time, the common law established a series of exceptions to the general position and read, or "implied," certain terms into contracts. These terms related to issues like the implied quality of the goods sold and when ownership of the goods would transfer to the buyer. These exceptions to the common law were codified in provincial sales of goods legislation in the 19th century.

In addition, the historical common law position relied heavily on the presumption that individuals acting in their own best interests would make decisions that would be of benefit to society as a whole. The justification for freedom of contract relies on this to a certain extent. However, businesses can enter into contracts for many reasons, some of which may be to harm consumers, competitors, or the competitive marketplace. For example they may enter into a contract in order to enhance their market power and suppress competitive conditions so that they can charge consumers higher prices. It became clear that strict adherence to the principles of freedom of contract and *caveat emptor* could hinder rather than facilitate commercial transactions, leave consumers vulnerable in transactions with

1 The bar for finding that a contract was unenforceable was also set very high. Recall that the test for unconscionability is "a gross inequality of bargaining power or a gross inadequacy of benefit to the weaker party." See the discussion in Chapter 5.

businesses, and fail to adequately protect the market system on which the Canadian economic structure depended. In response, legislatures developed laws to address the shortcomings of the common law.

Facilitating Business There is value in establishing clear criteria for contract formation and a baseline against which parties to a contract may negotiate. Clear criteria facilitate contract formation because parties are able to know the legal effect of their actions. Baseline terms can guarantee that a weaker party receives at least a minimum level of value in the bargain and can also provide a clear answer where parties have omitted key contractual terms, thus pre-emptively resolving disputes. Provincial sale of goods acts, which codified the exceptions to the historical common law position, and legislation dealing with e-commerce attempt to provide these benefits to businesses.

Protecting Consumers Generally, consumers are not in a position to bargain with businesses as equals. Consumers are often offered standard form contracts on a "take it or leave it" basis, and these contracts may contain terms that consumers are unaware of or do not understand. Further, the information that is available in the marketplace and that consumers rely on to make their decisions may be incomplete or inaccurate. Provincial consumer protection acts, federal product safety and labelling acts, and the federal *Competition Act* each play key roles in consumer protection.

Safeguarding the Marketplace The Canadian economy is based on a market-oriented economic system that relies on healthy competition for its success. In order to maintain a competitive marketplace, three criteria must be met: (1) buyers must have sufficient accurate information about the products/services being sold and their prices; (2) sellers must have a relatively low market share (or, more accurately, they must not possess significant market power); and (3) competitors must be free to enter or exit the market. These three criteria ensure that buyers make informed decisions, that sellers must compete for sales (thus ensuring the products/services and prices offered are competitive), and that competitors are able to move to high-demand businesses or out of low-demand businesses in response to market changes. Business practices that limit information, or result in misleading information, in the marketplace will hinder competition. Business practices that facilitate the concentration of power (for example, an agreement among competitors to fix prices) reduce competition. Business practices that make it harder for a new entrant to start up (for example, when an existing supplier has required all purchasers in the market to sign exclusivity agreements) also hinder competition. The federal *Competition Act* addresses this behaviour and, through the work of the Competition Bureau and the Competition Tribunal, safeguards the Canadian competitive market system.

Why Is Knowledge of These Laws Important to Your Business?

Knowledge of this area of law will be of particular assistance to you in the following ways:

- *Sale of goods law can assist commercial parties in negotiating deals and resolving disputes.* Contractual terms that the *Sale of Goods Act* implies into contracts concerning the quality of goods and the passage of ownership responsibilities provide a background against which parties can negotiate commercial sales. These statutory terms are mandatory only in contracts involving consumers. Businesses entering contracts with other businesses can choose to waive these terms; however, the terms can provide a default solution for parties that are otherwise unable to reach an agreement.

- *Laws governing competition in the marketplace leave room for innovation and initiative by new businesses.* Competition laws, which protect consumers by eliminating business practices that are designed to restrict trade, also protect young businesses by allowing them to compete for their share of a market that is free of monopoly. By knowing the laws that govern fair competition, you can bring businesses that compete unfairly to the attention of the appropriate authorities and thus create room for your own growing enterprise.
- *By conforming to laws that protect consumers, you contribute to the health of your business.* Laws that enforce fair and open dealings, require services to match promises, and protect vulnerable people from exploitation are codifications of good business practice and attract a loyal customer base.
- *By conforming to laws that protect consumer health and safety, you promote your business's reputation as a good citizen.* Safe food and drugs, properly labelled products (including proper hazard labelling), and public notification of potential product safety concerns—all contribute to a good reputation.

Facilitating Business

Provincial sale of goods acts and statutes dealing with e-commerce provide a clear legal framework for contract formation and set out basic, default protections for parties to a contract. This provides greater certainty and predictability in business dealings, facilitating business transactions.

Sale of Goods Act

title ownership

The Ontario *Sale of Goods Act* and similar statutes that have been adopted through much of the common law world codify the common law rules relating to contract formation and establish a presumptive baseline for key contract terms like the transfer of **title**, basic contractual duties, and remedies for breach.[2] In Ontario, the provincial *Sale of Goods Act* applies to all sales of goods involving consumers and, unless specifically excluded, to business-to-business sales transactions as well.

It is important to remember that a contract for the sale of goods remains a contract, and therefore all the ordinary rules of contract law apply, except where they are modified by the *Sale of Goods Act*. The Act defines a "contract of sale of goods" as "a contract whereby the seller transfers or agrees to transfer the property in the goods to the buyer for a money consideration, called the price." Remedies under the *Sale of*

2 In Quebec, Canada's civil law jurisdiction, the *Civil Code of Québec* addresses these same issues. Note that in international sale of goods transactions the *Convention on Contracts for the International Sale of Goods* will apply if the parties to the contract are from countries that have ratified the Convention, unless the parties contract out of the Convention. The Convention covers many of the same issues as the Canadian sale of goods acts but differs in its treatment of those issues in some cases. For information on which countries have ratified the Convention, see the United Nations Commission on International Trade Law, online: <http://www.uncitral.org/uncitral/en/uncitral_texts/sale_goods/1980CISG.html>.

Goods Act are limited to those persons in privity of contract. Generally, a person may only sue the retailer he or she purchased the goods from and not the manufacturer.[3] However, the retailer could then sue the distributor for indemnity and the distributor could in turn sue the manufacturer for indemnity, all the way up the supply chain.

Application of the Act

The *Sale of Goods Act* applies only to the sale of tangible personal property—that is, goods that you can actually touch, such as automobiles, cellphones, or heads of lettuce. The Act does not apply to goods that represent monetary worth—such as stocks, bonds, or currency—unless they are collected for their aesthetic or historical, rather than financial, value. The goods sold may either already exist, such as merchandise on a store shelf, or be expected to exist in the future, such as merchandise currently being manufactured for future sale. The Act does not apply to the sale of services, even if those services are supplied along with the delivery of goods.

If a buyer purchases something that is a mixture of goods and services, the *Sale of Goods Act* applies only if the contract is primarily for goods. For example, it would not apply to a contract for a tattoo because the consumer's contract with the tattoo artist is for the purchase of services and materials, not merely for the sale of the inks, etc. that the artist uses in the process. The services and goods cannot be separated for practical purposes and it is the design and application of the tattoo (the service component) that are the primary component of the contract. The contract is therefore not covered by the Act. A further limitation is that the Act applies only to contracts in which goods are exchanged for money. It does not apply when goods are traded for other goods or services, as they are in a barter transaction.

As noted above, the Act applies automatically to all sales of goods involving consumers. It also applies to sales between businesses unless the parties to the contract specifically exclude the Act. Any contract that attempts to exclude the operation of the Act must do so clearly, as demonstrated in *IPEX v Lubrizol* (see Case in Point, below).

Conditions and Warranties

The conditions and warranties that the *Sale of Goods Act* implies into contracts significantly soften the harsh doctrine of *caveat emptor*. These conditions and warranties are contractual terms specifically designed to keep commercial dealings fair and honest. In general, a condition is a major contractual term and a warranty is a minor contractual term, although some warranties are extremely significant. The distinction between implied conditions and implied warranties is the same as the distinction between express conditions and express warranties (those written into the contract by the parties)—the breach of a condition brings the contract to an end, and the breach of a warranty does not. A seller's breach of an implied condition in a contract for the sale of goods allows the buyer to repudiate the contract. The buyer may reject the goods (or return them, if they have already been delivered), have the purchase price returned, and ignore all further contractual obligations. Where

3 However, some courts have allowed the consumer/end-user to sue the manufacturer based on *Sale of Goods Act* obligations where the manufacturer has made representations as to the merchantability or fitness for purpose of its products (for example, in its promotional materials) and those representations induced the consumer/end-user to purchase the product from the retailer.

there is a breach of an implied warranty, the buyer may not repudiate the contract. The buyer continues to be bound by the terms of the contract and may only sue for damages arising from the breach. (Conditions and warranties are discussed in detail in Chapter 5 under the heading "Breach of Condition or Breach of Warranty?")

If a seller's product fails to meet the implied conditions or warranties, the seller will be liable for the failure. The buyer does not have to prove that the failure was the seller's fault or the result of the seller's negligence. The seller is strictly liable for the failure.

CASE IN POINT

When Contracting Out of the Sale of Goods Act, Make Your Intentions Clear

IPEX v Lubrizol, 2012 ONSC 2717

Facts

The purchaser bought raw resin material from the seller for use in the manufacturing of thermoplastic piping systems. Customers began to complain that the purchaser's piping systems were failing, and the purchaser sued the seller alleging that the raw material it supplied was defective.

The contract between the purchaser and seller for the purchase of the raw material incorporated terms and conditions from a related contract for the supply of a different product. The incorporated terms stated that the "seller disclaims any implied warranties of merchantability and fitness for a particular purpose." The seller argued that this excluded liability for the implied condition of fitness for purpose contained in the *Sale of Goods Act*.

The purchaser argued that the provision did not exclude liability for the implied condition of fitness for purpose because the provision only excluded liability for implied *warranties*. The purchaser argued that, in Ontario, conditions and warranties have very different legal meanings and that in order to exclude the statutorily implied *condition*, the seller must do so explicitly.

Result

On a motion for summary judgment, the judge agreed with the purchaser. Following Supreme Court of Canada case law in *Hunter Engineering Co v Syncrude Canada Ltd*, the judge held that a disclaimer of liability with respect to implied *warranties* was insufficient to exclude an implied *condition*. The exclusion clause was strictly construed against the party (the seller) seeking to invoke it and only clear and unambiguous language would be sufficient to oust implied statutory liability.

Of note in this case, the disclaimer of liability originated in a contract between two American companies. In the United States, the term "warranties" has a different, more expansive legal meaning. However, the disclaimer as incorporated into the contract between the purchaser and seller was interpreted by the court in accordance with Ontario law.

Business Lesson

If you are a seller who wants to contract outside the *Sale of Goods Act*, do so explicitly and clearly, ensuring that you exclude both implied warranties and implied conditions. Further, if you are using a precedent from a transaction that was governed by a different legal jurisdiction, have legal counsel review the terms. You may not have the same protections in the new jurisdiction.

IMPLIED CONDITIONS

The major conditions implied into contracts by the *Sale of Goods Act* are the following:

- The seller has the right to sell the goods.
- Any goods sold by description will match the description by which they are sold.
- Any goods sold by description are of merchantable quality.

- The goods are fit for the purpose for which the buyer purchases them if the seller is aware of the buyer's purpose.
- Any goods sold by sample will match the sample by which they are sold.

Each of these conditions is examined below.

◇ Right to Sell

Section 13(a) of the *Sale of Goods Act* sets out the implied condition that the seller has the right to sell the goods. The goods must be owned by the seller or will be owned by the seller at a future time, when the seller will be able to transfer ownership in the goods to the buyer. Should the goods turn out to be stolen, the seller has no right to sell them and would therefore be in breach of this implied condition.

◇ Sale by Description

Section 14 of the *Sale of Goods Act* requires goods sold by description to match the description by which they are sold. For example, a buyer who orders goods from a catalogue is entitled to receive the same goods that were ordered, not others of similar quality. This implied condition is also applicable where a buyer specifically picks out an item. For example, if a buyer comes to the pet store where you work, views a tank full of fish, and declares they want "that one," they are entitled to receive the specific fish they agreed to purchase.

◇ Merchantable Quality

Further, Section 15 of the Act requires goods sold by description to be of **merchantable quality**—that is, fit for their common or primary purpose, taking into account their description, price, and other relevant circumstances. For example, if a customer relies on a grocer's sign that says "farm-fresh milk," pays a premium price, and later discovers that the milk is sour, the grocer has breached the implied condition of merchantable quality.

merchantable quality quality sufficiently high to allow goods to be placed for sale as they are, without the need for repairs or other intervention

Determining whether or not something is "merchantable" may also depend on where in the supply chain the transaction occurs. In certain circumstances, merchantability can cover packaging and labelling. Assume, for example, that the goods consist of dolls packed in cardboard boxes with clear plastic display windows. If, when the shipment arrives at the retailer, the dolls are undamaged but the plastic windows have been pierced or ripped during shipping, the goods may not be of merchantable quality as they may not be commercially saleable with ripped packaging. However, a consumer who orders the doll from a retailer and finds that the doll is delivered to them undamaged but with ripped packaging may have a difficult time establishing that the goods are not of merchantable quality as the doll would still be fit for its primary purpose as a toy.

There is an exception to the seller's implied condition of merchantability: the seller is not liable to the buyer for reasonably discoverable defects if the buyer actually inspects the goods before sale and accepts them. If, for example, a buyer examines and purchases a shipment of lumber that, at a quick glance, clearly has noticeable knots in the wood on many boards, the buyer cannot later reject the load based on these defects.

◇ Fitness for Purpose

Section 15 requires that if a buyer makes their purpose in buying certain goods known to the seller—either expressly or by implication—and shows that they are relying on the seller's skill or judgment, the goods must be reasonably fit for the buyer's purpose. This is a more specific obligation than the obligation of merchantability. A lawnmower that cuts grass but cannot cut through thick brush may meet the implied condition of merchantability. However, if the purchaser asked the clerk at Home Depot for advice on what to buy to clear out brush on the purchaser's property, and the clerk directed the purchaser to the lawnmower, the lawnmower's inability to clear the brush may be a breach of the implied condition of fitness for purpose.

◇ Sale by Sample

Section 16(2) of the Act requires goods sold by sample to match the sample. For example, a buyer may come to a seller's shop and order a jacket "just like the one on display." To comply with the requirements of the *Sale of Goods Act*, the jacket delivered to the buyer must match the sample that the seller had on display. A buyer must be allowed a reasonable opportunity to compare any delivered goods with the sample that prompted the sale. Again, the seller bears no liability for reasonably discoverable defects, such as seams that are carelessly finished, if the buyer accepts the goods after inspecting them.

The breach of any of these implied conditions allows the purchaser to repudiate the contract. The purchaser may return the goods (if already delivered) and is entitled to a return of the purchase price.

SCENARIO

XL Equipment Inc. (XL) is a national retailer and has purchased 10,000 of Val-Nam Generation Limited's (Val-Nam) newest portable electricity generators for sale to consumers across Canada. The contract states that Val-Nam will sell 10,000 "7,000-watt" portable electricity generators to XL. The contract also states that "It shall be the obligation of XL to inspect the goods upon delivery. Val-Nam makes no warranties with respect to the goods and no warranty or condition, statutory or otherwise, shall be implied." Approximately two months after delivery of the generators, XL begins to receive complaints from its customers that the generators produce a 3,000-watt charge at best. XL wants to repudiate the contract. Is it able to? On what grounds?

Val-Nam also sells the generators directly to consumers online. On the generator's packaging, it is called a "7,000-watt generator." Val-Nam includes the same exclusion clause described above in its consumer contracts. A customer wants to return the generator and asks for their money back because the generator has never produced more than a 3,000-watt charge. Val-Nam refuses the customer's request, relying on the terms of the exclusion clause. Does the customer have a remedy? Would the outcome be different if the reason Val-Nam refused the refund was because the customer did not return the product within Val-Nam's 30-day return policy deadline?

IMPLIED WARRANTIES

There are a number of implied warranties under the *Sale of Goods Act*, including:

- that the buyer will enjoy quiet possession of the goods;
- that the goods are free of encumbrances;
- that if a time for delivery is not set out in the contract, delivery will be made within a reasonable time;

- that the seller will be paid in accordance with the terms of the contract; and
- that absent lawful excuse, the buyer will accept the goods.

An encumbrance is any form of legal claim against property by a third party. For example, when a farmer purchases a tractor, the farmer may obtain a loan from the bank in order to pay for the tractor. The bank will require the tractor to be pledged to it as security for the loan. If the farmer turns around and sells the tractor without first repaying all of the loan, the tractor will still be subject to the bank's security interest when it is sold. If the farmer fails to inform the purchaser that the tractor is subject to a **lien**, the farmer is in breach of the implied warranty that the tractor is free of encumbrances.

lien
an interest in property that the owner grants to another person, usually to a creditor as security for a debt; it may allow the creditor to sell the property to satisfy the debt if the owner defaults on payment of the debt

A breach of any of these implied warranties does not allow the non-breaching party to repudiate the contract. The party must continue to fulfill its obligations under the contract and seek damages as a remedy.

MINIMIZING YOUR RISK

Comply with or Exclude Implied Conditions and Warranties in a Business-to-Business Sale

- Determine whether there are any implied conditions or warranties that you wish to exclude from your sales transaction.
- Negotiate their exclusion accordingly. Make certain that the exclusion is clear and is brought to the attention of the other party.
- Meet all implied conditions and warranties unless you specifically exclude them from your contract in the clearest possible terms.

Transferring the Rights and Responsibilities of Ownership

The key component of a sale of goods contract is the transfer of ownership of the goods from the seller to the purchaser. This is referred to as the transfer of title to the goods. The person who has title to the goods has the right to sell, lease, give, possess, or dispose of the goods in any manner authorized by law. Therefore, it is important to be able to determine when title transfers from one party to the next.

The physical transfer of property does not necessarily transfer ownership. (The scope of property rights is discussed in detail in Chapter 10.) For example, when you leave your car at a repair shop to have new tires installed, you retain ownership of the car even though the repair shop has physical possession of it. Similarly, the *failure* to physically transfer property does not necessarily mean that ownership has not been transferred. For example, a consumer may purchase a car from a dealership, paying for it in full and thereby gaining title to it under a contract of sale. However, the customer may choose to leave the car with the dealership until the dealer outfits it with, for example, the remote car starter that the customer requires. Even though the customer has not yet picked up the car, the customer owns it.

Why is it important to pinpoint the moment when title to goods passes from a seller to a buyer? Transfer of title determines transfer of risk and responsibility for loss. Thus, if the risk of loss in a sale of lumber has passed to a buyer, the buyer bears responsibility for the loss that occurs when the warehouse in which the lumber is stored burns down. If risk has not yet passed to the buyer, the seller bears the responsibility for the loss. If the goods are insured, transfer of title—and therefore of risk—determines whether the buyer's or the seller's insurance will pay for the goods.

The best way to deal with the question of when title will pass to the buyer is to clearly set out in the contract when title will pass. This allows both parties to properly plan and, in particular, to arrange for insurance to cover any potential loss.

However, if the parties fail to explicitly or implicitly set out when title will pass, section 19 of the *Sale of Goods Act* provides a set of default rules that will apply. A total of five rules determine when title passes. The first four address circumstances where specific goods are the subject of the contract. **Specific goods** are goods that are identified and agreed upon at the time the contract is made. The fifth rule addresses circumstances where the goods are unascertained or future goods. **Unascertained goods** are goods that are not yet set aside and identifiable as the subject of the contract at the time the contract is made. **Future goods** are goods that are not yet made by a factory or craftsperson at the time the contract is made.

specific goods
goods that exist at the time a contract is made and are specifically chosen or pointed out by the buyer

unascertained goods
goods that are not yet separated from the stock of the seller and set aside for a particular buyer

future goods
goods that have not yet come into being at the time a contract is made, such as an agricultural crop, or goods that have not yet been manufactured

deliverable state
condition in which goods are finished, packaged, labelled, and ready to ship

RULE 1: TRANSFER OF SPECIFIC GOODS IN DELIVERABLE STATE

When there is an unconditional sale of specific goods in a deliverable state, title passes to the buyer when the contract is made. It is irrelevant whether the time of payment or the time of delivery is postponed. A **deliverable state** is a state in which the goods are ready to go. Nothing further needs to be done; for example, there is no need for finishing, weighing, or packaging.

RULE 2: GOODS MUST BE PUT IN DELIVERABLE STATE

When a contract for the sale of specific goods requires the seller to do something to the goods to put them in a deliverable state, title does not pass until that thing is done and the buyer receives notice that it has been done.

RULE 3: SELLER MUST DO SOMETHING TO ASCERTAIN PRICE

When a contract for the sale of specific goods in a deliverable state requires a seller to weigh, measure, test, or perform another act to ascertain the price of the goods, title does not pass until the act is performed and the buyer has notice that it has been performed.

RULE 4: GOODS ON APPROVAL

When a seller delivers goods to a buyer on approval or "on sale or return," property passes to the buyer:

- when the buyer signifies approval or acceptance, or otherwise adopts the transaction;
- when the time fixed for return of the goods passes and the buyer keeps the goods without giving notice of rejection; or
- when a reasonable time for the return of the goods passes, the contract contains no fixed time for returning the goods, and the buyer keeps the goods without giving notice of rejection.

RULE 5: UNASCERTAINED GOODS

In a contract that calls for the sale of unascertained or future goods by description, title to the goods passes to the buyer once the goods are unconditionally acquired in a deliverable state—either by the seller with the acceptance of the buyer, or by the buyer with the acceptance of the seller. Acceptance may be express or implied and may be given either before or after the goods are acquired.

SCENARIO

Applying the Rules

Val-Nam and XL have entered into a contract for the sale of 100 portable electricity generators. The contract does not specify when title to the generators will transfer to XL. While the generators are sitting on Val-Nam's loading dock, there is a fire in the warehouse and the generators are destroyed. Consider the following different circumstances and their effect on the transfer of title:

- XL's purchasing manager called Val-Nam stating that XL was in desperate need of 100 generators immediately. Val-Nam's sales manager, Gyan Singh, tells the purchasing manager that he has a pallet of 100 generators sitting on the loading dock that XL can have at the regular price. The purchasing manager says XL will take them. The generators are to be delivered the next day. Who had title to the generators when the fire broke out?
- Under the contract, the purchase price will vary depending on the average wattage of the generators. Val-Nam has agreed to test a random sampling of the generators and the purchase price will be set based on the average wattage of the random sampling. Val-Nam conducted the tests and placed the generators in the loading dock for shipment but has not yet confirmed with XL that the tests were completed and what the final purchase price will be. Who had title to the generators when the fire broke out?
- XL's purchasing manager called Val-Nam and placed an order for 100 generators. Gyan Singh explained that Val-Nam is currently out of stock but that they should be getting new stock the following week. The parties agreed that Gyan would email XL when the generators were ready for shipment to XL. When the generators arrived at Val-Nam the following week, Gyan separated 100 from the shipment and placed them on the loading dock. They were wrapped and labelled for delivery to XL. Gyan emailed XL indicating that the generators were ready for shipment. Who had title to the generators when the fire broke out?
- According to the terms of the contract, Val-Nam was to repackage the generators in XL-branded packaging. The generators had not yet been repackaged when the fire broke out. Who had title to the generators when the fire broke out?

Now consider this circumstance:

Each month, Val-Nam delivers 100 generators to XL. Under the terms of the contract, XL has the right to return any unsold generators within 30 days of delivery. There are no terms in the contract relating to the transfer of title. On April 10, Val-Nam delivers 100 generators to XL. On April 11, XL's store is broken into and 10 of the generators are stolen. Who had title to the generators when they were stolen?

MINIMIZING YOUR RISK

Plan for Passage of Title

- Determine when you and the other party to the contract intend to assume and relinquish the rights and responsibilities of ownership.
- Specify this time in your contract.
- Review your more informal contractual relationships (for example, sales that are recorded by way of invoices only). Be aware that the five rules under the *Sale of Goods Act* will prevail unless you specify an alternative time for the transfer of title in your informal sales contracts.

Remedies

Because sales are contract-based transactions, the parties to a sale have at their disposal the usual common law contract remedies of damages, repudiation, and specific performance in the event of a breach of contract, as discussed in Chapter 2. As discussed earlier in this chapter under the heading "Conditions and Warranties," if a party breaches a condition of a contract of sale—regardless of whether the condition is implied by statute or expressed in the contract—the other party may be entitled to repudiate the contract. This means that if the seller breaches a condition, the buyer has the right to refuse to pay for the goods, or if the seller has already been paid, the buyer can recover their money from the seller. If the buyer breaches a condition, the seller has the right to refuse to deliver the goods, or if they have already delivered the goods, the seller can demand that the goods be returned. If a party breaches a warranty—either one that is expressed in the contract or one that is implied by statute—the other party must continue to perform their obligations under the contract and their only remedy is damages.

In addition to the common law remedies available for breach of contract, the *Sale of Goods Act* creates further protections for buyers and sellers. These protections can be excluded in the terms of a business-to-business contract.

REMEDIES AVAILABLE TO THE BUYER

The remedies set out in the *Sale of Goods Act* that are available to the buyer reflect and reinforce the common law remedies. The remedies relate to a seller's failure to deliver the goods, delivery of the wrong quantity of goods, breach of warranty, and specific performance.

The *Sale of Goods Act* provides that if the seller fails to deliver the goods, the buyer may maintain an action against the seller for damages for non-delivery (s 49). The buyer's duty to mitigate is reflected in the limitation on the amount of damages available. Where there is a market for the goods in question, the amount of damages is limited to the difference between the contract price and the market price, thus effectively requiring the buyer to mitigate their damages by purchasing replacement goods at the market price.

At common law, a small variance in the quantity of goods delivered will not likely amount to a breach of a condition of a contract of sale, unless the contract specifically states otherwise. However, pursuant to section 29(1) of the *Sale of Goods Act*, if the seller delivers a quantity that is less than the buyer agreed to purchase, the buyer has the option to reject the whole shipment or complete the transaction at the contract rate. For example, if XL agrees to purchase 1,000 generators for a total purchase price of $33,595.00, but Val-Nam delivers only 987 generators, XL has two options: it may either reject the entire delivery or purchase the number of generators delivered at the contract rate ($33,595.00 ÷ 1,000 = $33.595 per generator), for a total of $33,158.27 (987 generators × $33.595 per generator). Section 29(2) of the Act also deals with the situation in which Val-Nam delivers a greater quantity to XL than XL ordered. In this case, XL has three options: reject the entire delivery, accept what it contracted to buy (1,000 generators in our example) and reject the excess, or accept the entire order. If XL chooses to accept the entire order, it will pay for the additional generators at the contract rate.

Section 51 of the *Sale of Goods Act* codifies the common law position that a breach of warranty by the seller does not allow the buyer to reject the goods (repudiate the contract). However, in addition to allowing the buyer to maintain an action against the seller for damages for the breach of warranty, the Act allows the buyer to instead reduce (perhaps even to zero) the price to be paid for the goods.

Finally, section 50 of the Act codifies the common law remedy of specific performance, although courts are reluctant to use it. If specific performance is ordered, a seller is required to deliver and a buyer is required to pay for goods in accordance with the terms of the contract of sale. (This remedy is discussed in Chapter 2 under the heading "Other Remedies.") This remedy is usually reserved for goods that are antiques, works of art, or other unique objects whose loss cannot be compensated for by damages.

MINIMIZING YOUR RISK

Buyer Be Wary

- Carefully and promptly inspect—and count—all goods purchased before accepting delivery.
- Know that you can repudiate any contract based on breach of a condition.
- Advise the seller immediately of any problems you discover with respect to a shipment and of your unwillingness to accept the goods.
- Mitigate your losses by finding another supplier.

REMEDIES AVAILABLE TO THE SELLER

For sellers, the *Sale of Goods Act* provides special remedies, including an action for the sale price, a **seller's lien**, and stoppage in transit. While these remedies were very important at one time, they are rarely used now. Modern banking practices—which allow a seller to require assurances of a buyer's solvency before dealing with the buyer—and modern rules with respect to security interests in goods have made reliance on these remedies nearly obsolete in today's commercial world. Modern banking and security interests are discussed at length in Chapter 8.

seller's lien
security interest under the *Sale of Goods Act* that allows a seller to keep and resell goods to discharge an insolvent buyer's debt

Limits on the Protection Offered by the Sale of Goods Act

As noted, the *Sale of Goods Act* is applicable only to the sale of tangible goods, not to the sale of land or the sale of services, and it does not apply to any barter transaction. Because its purpose is to protect contracting parties, the Act and its remedies are not designed to offer retail customers protection from breaches of warranties by the manufacturers of goods.[4]

Over the years, legislatures have recognized the need to provide more comprehensive protection for consumers than the *Sale of Goods Act* affords. Although the Act arguably provides adequate protection for commercial buyers and sellers who are relatively sophisticated in their knowledge of the pitfalls of commerce, consumers are thought to require additional safeguards. Therefore, provincial legislatures and the

4 Although, as noted above, some courts have allowed the consumer/end-user to sue the manufacturer based on *Sale of Goods Act* obligations where the manufacturer has made representations as to the merchantability or fitness for purpose of its products (for example, in its promotional materials) and those representations induced the consumer/end-user to purchase the product from the retailer.

Parliament of Canada have responded with statutes designed to protect the interests of the consuming public in various ways. These will be discussed shortly under the heading "Protecting Consumers."

Electronic Commerce Act, 2000

The ability to transact business over the Internet—that is, to participate in e-commerce (electronic commerce)—is a tremendous development. E-commerce brings together buyers and sellers from all over the world and provides unprecedented opportunities for the exchange of goods, services, and ideas. However, it can also give rise to unforeseen liabilities. Your business can be subject to the laws of many different jurisdictions—for example, the rules of contract formation that apply in New York may govern when and how a sales contract is formed when you sell goods to customers located there, even though you are located in Ontario. New York may even have specific rules for the formation of online contracts. An examination of additional implications of e-commerce for business is undertaken in Chapter 11.

However, a brief review of the provisions of the Ontario *Electronic Commerce Act, 2000* warrants mention here, to the extent that these provisions facilitate business by clarifying the effect of actions taken electronically on the legal validity of documentation and on contract formation when Ontario law applies to the transaction.

Once again, it bears mentioning that the common law rules with respect to contract law apply to Internet transactions as well. The *Electronic Commerce Act, 2000* attempts to provide clarity on how those rules work in the online context.

Application of the Act

The Act addresses the legal recognition of electronic documents and its effect on legal requirements that certain documents be in writing in the Province of Ontario.[5] Its provisions bind the Crown. However, it should be noted that while the Act provides for the legal recognition of electronic documents, it specifically states that no person is required to accept information or documents in electronic form without their consent, although that consent may be inferred from the person's conduct.

The Act does not apply to the following documents or the legal requirement that they be in writing:

- wills and codicils;
- trusts created by wills and codicils;
- powers of attorney for an individual's financial affairs or personal care; or
- negotiable instruments.

Authenticity of Documents

The Act establishes that a document in electronic form and accessible for subsequent usage satisfies the legal requirement that a document be in "writing." So long as

5 Other provincial and territorial jurisdictions have similar legislation: for example, the British Columbia *Electronic Transactions Act*, the Alberta *Electronic Transactions Act*, Nova Scotia's *Electronic Commerce Act*, and Nunavut's *Electronic Commerce Act*.

there is a reliable assurance as to the integrity of the electronic document, providing a person with an electronic document can also satisfy the requirement that an "original" document be provided. In this way, the Act establishes the authenticity and validity of documents in electronic form.

Contract Formation and Electronic Signatures

In addition, the Act provides that any contract that can be entered into in writing and on paper can be entered into electronically. Electronic documents and signatures are the equivalent of written contracts signed by hand. The electronic signature must be sufficient to identify the person and must be clearly associated with the document to be "signed." Courts have held that adding initials or a given name to an email can be a legally effective acceptance of an offer; however, where a name and address block are added automatically to the bottom of emails, the "signed" email was not considered sufficient.

Figure 6.1

Ontario's *Electronic Commerce Act, 2000* provides that any contract that can be entered into in writing and on paper can be entered into electronically, including by signing on a screen with a digital pen, clicking an icon on a screen, or simply adding initials to an email.

Further, any element of the formation of a contract (including the offer and acceptance) can be expressed by any "act that is intended to result in electronic communication" (s 19). So, touching a "√" on a screen or clicking on a shopping cart icon can constitute the legally binding act of acceptance.

The timing of an offer, revocation, counteroffer, or acceptance can also be legally significant. The Act provides that, unless the parties agree otherwise, electronic information is deemed to be sent when it enters an information system outside of the sender's control (s 22(1)). Information is presumed to be received by the addressee when it becomes capable of being retrieved by the addressee (s 22(3)). (The implications of this on transfer of title under the *Sale of Goods Act* were discussed earlier in this chapter under the heading "Transferring the Rights and Responsibilities of Ownership.")

Each of these provisions allows businesses to better understand the legal effect of their electronic actions, thus adding certainty and facilitating business transactions.

SCENARIO

Currently, Val-Nam contracts out the manufacture of its generators to WeSolve Manufacturing Solutions Incorporated (WeSolve). Val-Nam would like to build its own manufacturing plant and is in the market for land suitable for development. Val-Nam heard about two pieces of property in the Ottawa area that might be suitable. On behalf of Val-Nam, Valery visited Property A and was impressed with the size and suitability of the land. The vendor's asking price was a bit high at $1.4 million and Valery would have preferred property on the east side of Ottawa for ease of shipping through the Port of Montreal. However, she was concerned that a better property might not become available and that this property might sell quickly, so she made a written offer on behalf of Val-Nam to purchase the land for $1.1 million.

Later that day, around 3:00 p.m., Valery found out about Property B. It was on the east side of Ottawa, it was the same size as Property A, and the vendor was asking only $800,000. After viewing the property, Valery immediately told the vendor that Val-Nam would take Property B for the asking price. The vendor accepted the offer. As soon as Valery returned to her car, at 4:00 p.m., she called the Property A vendor and left him a voicemail message stating that she had purchased another property and was withdrawing Val-Nam's offer.

When Valery returned to her office, she found an email from the Property A vendor that had arrived in her inbox at 3:15 p.m. The email stated, "We accept Val-Nam's offer to purchase Property A for $1.1 million. Purchase and sale documentation to follow."

Was Valery's revocation of the offer to purchase Property A effective?

What other steps could Valery have taken to try to preserve Val-Nam's right to purchase Property A without the risk that a binding purchase contract would be created before Val-Nam could properly consider it?

MINIMIZING YOUR RISK

Taking E-Commerce Precautions

- Know that you may legally obligate yourself to a contract simply by clicking an icon.
- Remember that an email message or other electronic communication may constitute an offer or acceptance.
- Consider adding boilerplate language after any automatically inserted signature block that clearly states that the electronic signature does not create a legal obligation and does not satisfy the legal requirement that documents be signed.
- Include clear language in your contracts that specifies how modifications to the contract must be made (by email, exchange of faxes, etc.) and use only those methods when modifying the contract.
- Retain all email correspondence so that you have a full record of negotiations and contract terms, should a binding contract form.
- Be aware that an electronic communication is presumed received at the time it is capable of being retrieved, regardless of whether the recipient has actually read the message.

Protecting Consumers

Consumers often face significant disadvantages when entering into transactions with businesses. These disadvantages may include the following:

- Consumers may not be "sophisticated" in the sense that they may not understand the legal significance of the language used during negotiations and in the resulting contract.
- Consumers may have little (or no) bargaining power. Usually, the consumer's interest in purchasing the product or service is of much more importance to the consumer than the single sale is to the business. This means the business is more likely to be able to "play hardball" in negotiations.
- A consumer's lack of bargaining power is emphasized by the fact that many consumer transactions are governed by standard form contracts drafted by the business that the consumer must accept on a take-it-or-leave-it basis.
- The consumer often doesn't have access to full information on the product or service and it is the business that controls access to that information.
- Consumers can feel pressured to enter into transactions in many circumstances; for example, when a pushy salesperson arrives at their door.
- Consumers often don't have the resources (financial and otherwise) to enforce their legal rights.

The scope of legislation created to protect consumers' interests reflects these disadvantages. The most comprehensive legislation is, not surprisingly, the provincial consumer protection acts. These acts focus on ensuring that consumers are provided with sufficient, accurate, and understandable information; are protected from unfair business practices and pressure; and have meaningful, accessible remedies available to them. The Ontario *Collection and Debt Settlement Services Act* also protects consumers from harassing behaviour by those collecting consumer debts. In addition, federal legislation addresses consumer safety concerns through statutes like the *Food and Drugs Act*, the *Hazardous Products Act*, and the *Canada Consumer Product Safety Act*, and it addresses informational concerns through such legislation as the *Competition Act* and the *Consumer Packaging and Labelling Act*. A brief review of this legislation follows.

Val-Nam is currently selling its generators through XL and directly to consumers online. As you examine the legislation protecting consumers, consider what additional liabilities Val-Nam's direct-to-consumer sales attract as compared to its sales through XL. Additional e-commerce liabilities are discussed in Chapter 11.

Consumer Protection Act, 2002

The Ontario *Consumer Protection Act, 2002* is designed to give consumers rights over and above those provided in the *Sale of Goods Act* and the common law of contract. It operates by adding to the existing rights of consumers, not by substituting new rights for the ones that already exist. The Act defines a **consumer** as an "individual acting for personal, family or household purposes and does not include a person who is acting for business purposes." It applies to transactions between consumers and sellers. Therefore, if Val-Nam were to sell its products only to XL (and XL were to then

consumer
purchaser who buys or otherwise obtains goods for his or her own use, not for business purposes

sell the products to consumers), the Act would not apply to Val-Nam's transactions.[6] The Act governs consumer transactions in all forms (including barter transactions and purchases of services) other than those specifically excluded, such as transactions involving professional services (for example, the services of accountants and engineers) and transactions involving the purchase, sale, or lease of most real property.

The Act contains both general provisions that apply to all types of businesses and specific provisions that address conduct in particular business areas (for example, motor vehicle repair and towing services). While businesses operating in these areas must be aware of and comply with the related specific provisions, this review will focus on the Act's provisions that are of more general application.

Clarity

The *Consumer Protection Act, 2002* stresses the principle that clarity is essential in all dealings with consumers. When required by the Act to disclose or deliver information to consumers, a business must present this information in a form that is "clear, comprehensible and prominent" (s 5). To emphasize its concern for clarity, the Act codifies the common law rule that any ambiguous contractual information or provisions drafted by a business are to be "interpreted to the benefit of the consumer" (s 11). This directly addresses some of the concerns with standard form contracts. (The common law rule is discussed in detail in Chapter 4 under the heading "Rules of Construction.")

Consumer Rights and Warranties

Part II of the *Consumer Protection Act, 2002* sets out certain rights of consumers and certain warranties that operate in their favour. The substantive and procedural rights provided for in the Act cannot be waived. Further, the *Consumer Protection Act, 2002* provides that any attempt to contract out of the implied conditions and warranties under the *Sale of Goods Act* when dealing with consumers is void. It also extends protection to services by requiring businesses to warrant that all services supplied to consumers are of a "reasonably acceptable quality."

The Act requires businesses to honour all written price estimates they make to consumers for goods or services within a 10 percent margin of error. A consumer may require any business that exceeds the estimate by more than 10 percent to provide the goods or services at the estimated price.

The Act also makes negative-option marketing—that is, demanding payment for unsolicited goods or services—illegal. For example, a cable company may not unilaterally decide to add new channels and charge customers for them. Rather, each customer must be asked if they would like to purchase access to the new channels.

Unfair Practices

Part III of the Act describes three types of unfair practices:

1. making false, misleading, or deceptive representations,

---

6 Note that consumer protection legislation in Quebec, New Brunswick, and Saskatchewan is broader and includes provisions relating to manufacturer liability. See the *Consumer Protection Act* (Quebec), the *Consumer Product Warranty and Liability Act* (New Brunswick), and *The Consumer Protection and Business Practices Act* (Saskatchewan).

2. making unconscionable representations, and
3. pressuring consumers into renegotiating the terms of a transaction by holding on to their goods.

CASE IN POINT

Watch Your Waivers!

David Schnarr v Blue Mountain Resorts Limited, 2017 ONSC 114

Facts

The plaintiff purchased a 2010–11 season ski pass for Blue Mountain. In order to obtain the season pass, the plaintiff was required to agree to and execute a waiver that barred him from pursuing any legal action against Blue Mountain. In particular, the waiver stated that the plaintiff waived any and all claims "due to any cause whatsoever, including negligence, breach of contract, or breach of any statutory or other duty of care, including any duty of care owed under the *Occupiers' Liability Act*."

In March of 2011, the plaintiff was injured while skiing when he collided with debris from a broken ski pole, lost control, and struck a tree. The plaintiff commenced an action against Blue Mountain for negligence, breach of the *Occupiers' Liability Act*, and breach of the implied warranty under the *Consumer Protection Act, 2002* that supplied services be of a reasonably acceptable quality. Blue Mountain sought to rely on the waiver to avoid liability.

Result

The court held that the provisions of the waiver that purported to exclude liability for *any* breach of contract offended the requirements of the *Consumer Protection Act, 2002*. The Act prohibits the defendant from disclaiming liability for a breach of the implied warranty of reasonably acceptable quality. The waiver was "read down" to exclude this aspect of the disclaimer. The remaining portions of the waiver (relating to negligence claims and *Occupiers' Liability Act* claims) remained enforceable. The plaintiff could move forward with his claim for a remedy for breach of contract.

Business Lesson

When developing your legal risk management plan, remember that you will not be able to contract out of *Consumer Protection Act, 2002* liability.

Examine the language of your waivers carefully. Ensure that they are not overly broad.

Case to Watch

In a similar case, *Woodhouse v Snow Valley*, 2017 ONSC 222, the ski hill had also tried to avoid *Consumer Protection Act, 2002* liability through a broad waiver. In that case, the ski hill asked the court to enforce the waiver because it would be "inequitable in the circumstances" for the consumer not to be bound by the waiver (see s 93(2) of the Act). The court found that the onus is on the ski hill to persuade the court that it would be inequitable. As this decision was in relation to a stated case under Rule 22 of the *Rules of Civil Procedure*, the court did not have a sufficient evidentiary record (nor was it asked) to make a final determination of the issue. The court indicated that the issue would have to proceed to trial to be determined.

This case raises an interesting issue of the "equities" in a consumer transaction. Should it proceed to trial, it will be carefully followed by legal practitioners and businesses alike.

FALSE, MISLEADING, OR DECEPTIVE REPRESENTATIONS

Section 14 of the Act prohibits businesses from making a false, misleading, or deceptive representation to consumers. The Act provides a list of examples of what might constitute a false, misleading, or deceptive statement, including statements

- that the goods or services have sponsorship, approval, performance characteristics, accessories, uses, ingredients, benefits, or qualities they do not have;

- that the goods or services are of a particular standard, quality, grade, style, or model if they are not;
- that the goods are new, or unused, if they are not (this excludes the reasonable use of goods to test or prepare them for delivery);
- that the goods or services are available for a reason that does not exist;
- that the goods or services are available or can be delivered or performed when the person making the representation knows or ought to know they are not available or cannot be delivered or performed;
- that a service, part, replacement, or repair is needed or advisable if it is not;
- that a specific price advantage exists if it does not;
- that use exaggeration, innuendo, or ambiguity about a material fact or fail to state a material fact if the use or failure deceives or tends to deceive;
- where the purpose of any charge or proposed charge is misrepresented; or
- where the benefits that are likely to flow to a consumer if the consumer helps a person obtain new or potential customers are misrepresented or exaggerated.

As is clear from the examples in the list, the provision is intended to promote honest dealings by prohibiting any form of misleading communication with consumers by business people.

UNCONSCIONABLE REPRESENTATIONS

Section 15 of the Act prohibits suppliers from making unconscionable representations. The Act does not specifically define the term "unconscionable," but does provide guidance as to the type of circumstances that should be taken into account when determining whether or not a representation is unconscionable. These circumstances include whether the person who makes the representation—or that person's employer or principal—knows or ought to know

- that the consumer is not reasonably able to protect his or her interests because of disability, ignorance, illiteracy, or inability to understand the language of an agreement;
- that the price grossly exceeds the price at which similar goods or services are readily available;
- that the consumer is unable to receive a substantial benefit from the transaction;
- that there is no reasonable probability that the consumer will be able to pay for the goods or services in full;
- that the consumer transaction is excessively one-sided in favour of someone other than the consumer;
- that the terms of the consumer transaction are so adverse to the consumer as to be inequitable;
- that a statement of opinion is misleading and the consumer is likely to rely on it to his or her detriment; or
- that the consumer is being subjected to undue pressure to enter into the transaction.

This is not an exhaustive list. Other circumstances of an equally serious nature, or those arising from a similarly inequitable balance of power between the parties to the transaction, can render a representation unconscionable. *De Maeseneer v Degamo* is a case in which the conduct of a business person clearly falls afoul of many of the prohibitions in section 15 (see Case in Point, below).

RENEGOTIATION OF TERMS

Section 16 of the Act sets out another form of unfair practice in relation to consumers. Businesses are prohibited from using their custody or control of a consumer's goods to pressure the consumer into renegotiating the terms of a consumer transaction. For example, imagine a situation in which a business runs a computer repair shop and has temporary custody of a customer's malfunctioning computer. A manager cannot negotiate a price for doing the necessary repairs that is higher than the price that the business has specified in its contract by threatening to hold on to the computer for a longer period of time than the customer has agreed to.

CASE IN POINT

An Unconscionable Transaction

De Maeseneer v Degamo, 2002 BCPC 303

Facts

The plaintiff ran a money-lending business whose clientele was primarily women from the Philippines, like the defendant, who were employed in British Columbia as domestic workers.

When the defendant fell behind on loan payments, the plaintiff sued her and her co-signers for the outstanding money. The defendant alleged that the plaintiff was charging a criminal or unconscionable rate of interest and that the loan agreement was therefore illegal and unenforceable.

The plaintiff charged a high rate of interest (24 percent annually to start) that increased if the defendant defaulted. In addition, he charged fees for missed payments, delayed payments, and NSF cheques. He extended loans to borrowers who had defaulted or paid late in the past; the defendant was one of these customers. The plaintiff also extended new loans to existing customers instead of consolidating their loans, so that a customer who was in default would find herself paying multiple sets of late payment/missed payment/NSF fees. The court found that the effect of these business practices was that the defendant was actually paying an effective annual interest rate of 63 percent on her first loan and a rate of 56 percent on her second loan.

Result

The court found that the 63 percent interest rate on the first loan was above the criminal rate of interest (60 percent). After considering the British Columbia *Consumer Protection Act*, among other sources of law, the court found that the 56 percent interest rate on the second loan was an unconscionable rate of interest, particularly since the client was financially unsophisticated, had only a basic grasp of English, and relied on the plaintiff for a full explanation of the borrowing costs; and the plaintiff knew there was no reasonable probability of timely repayment, so it was very likely that the late payment/missed payment/NSF fees would be charged.

The court required that the client repay the principal on her loans. It did not require her to pay fees or interest at the contract rate; instead, it allowed only for the recovery of court order interest from the date of filing the claim to the date of judgment.

Business Lesson

Train your staff to be aware of circumstances that may make it difficult for a customer to understand the legal implications of the transaction (for example, language barriers, disability).

Ensure that contractual terms are explained in full and that the effects of any penalty charges/clauses are clearly described.

Encourage customers to obtain independent assistance/advice with respect to more complex transactions.

Enforcement by Consumers

Section 18 of the *Consumer Protection Act, 2002* gives consumers who have been the victims of an unfair practice the right to rescind a contract—that is, to treat the contract as if it were at an end—within one year from when the contract was entered into. A consumer must notify the business of their intention to rescind. If the business fails to respond, the consumer may commence legal proceedings 30 days later. The consumer also has the right to seek any remedies available to them in law, including compensatory damages and punitive damages. If the sum involved is $25,000 or less, the less expensive and quicker Small Claims Court process can be used.

Staff members at the Ministry of Government and Consumer Services are available to assist consumers. They may ask a consumer to file a formal complaint, which might lead to an investigation into the incident and prosecution of the business or business person involved.

www.emond.ca/CBL3/links

DIG DEEPER
The Ministry of Government and Consumer Services website provides up-to-date information on services that the Ontario government offers consumers.

Penalties

The government is serious about prosecuting business people who engage in unfair practices. An individual convicted of committing an unfair practice faces a maximum fine of $50,000 or a maximum prison term of two years less a day or both; a corporation that commits an unfair practice faces a maximum fine of $250,000.

MINIMIZING YOUR RISK

Be Frank with Consumers

- Ensure that you and your staff communicate clearly and truthfully with consumers when discussing your products and services.
- Resist the urge to make exaggerated or ambiguous claims.
- Take particular care with consumers who have language difficulties or cognitive or other challenges that make them vulnerable.
- Establish a fair price and stick to it.
- Establish a competent customer relations program to deal with complaints and to act as an early warning system for the need to re-educate staff.

Rights and Obligations for Specific Transactions

Part IV of the *Consumer Protection Act, 2002* sets out rights and obligations regarding specific consumer agreements, including the following:

- *Internet agreements.* These are agreements entered into by means of text-based Internet communications, such as on websites where consumers place online orders.
- *Remote agreements.* These agreements, which are usually made by telephone, fax, or mail, are defined as agreements in which consumers and business people "are not present together," for example, when a consumer responds to a telemarketer's call.
- *Future performance agreements.* These are agreements between a consumer and a business (other than Internet or remote agreements) in which delivery, performance, or payment in full is not made at the time the agreement is made. For example, purchases through a "buy now, pay later" deal would be future performance agreements.

- *Direct agreements.* These are agreements (other than Internet agreements, remote agreements, or future performance agreements) negotiated or made with consumers at any place other than a supplier's place of business or a market, trade fair, or exhibition; direct agreements are frequently entered into at a consumer's home with door-to-door sellers.
- *Personal development service agreements.* These are agreements that require payment in advance for such services as fitness or martial arts instruction.

Consumers who enter into any of these agreements have rights concerning disclosure of information. For example, for Internet transactions where the consumer is paying more than $50 for the goods/services, the regulations require that detailed information be set out in the agreement, including a fair and accurate description of the goods/services and all charges, the terms and methods of payment, and the date of delivery or commencement of service, etc. The supplier must give the consumer an express opportunity to accept or decline the agreement. The supplier must also deliver a copy of the agreement in writing to the consumer within 15 days after the consumer enters into the agreement. In certain instances, the Act and regulations also provide a **cooling-off period**—that is, a period (usually 10 to 20 days) during which consumers can cancel their contracts without providing businesses with any justification for doing so. Cooling-off periods are provided for certain direct agreements, personal development services agreements, and other agreements covered by the Act.

cooling-off period
period set by statute during which a consumer who has made a contract can change his or her mind and rescind it

MINIMIZING YOUR RISK

Be Ready to Prove That Consumers Consented to Transactions

- Give consumers the opportunity to decline agreements and correct errors before finalizing deals.
- Obtain signatures to indicate consumers' acceptance.
- When selling over the Internet, provide an order confirmation page before consumers finalize the agreement.
- When selling by telephone, confirm that an order has been placed and that the customer wants to proceed.
- When selling in a store, give consumers a copy of the agreement to review before signing.

Collection and Debt Settlement Services Act

From time to time, businesses may employ agencies to assist them in collecting outstanding debts from consumers, usually in return for a percentage of the amount collected. In Ontario, collection agencies are governed by the *Collection and Debt Settlement Services Act*. If your business is involved in debt collection, you must become thoroughly knowledgeable about this Act and its regulations. The legislation prohibits collection agencies from trying to collect a debt without first informing the debtor, in writing by ordinary mail, that they have been hired to do so. It also prohibits them from harassing debtors, their family members, and their friends, as well as from giving false or misleading information to any person. The regulations under the Act limit the times during which these agencies may attempt to collect debts—for example, collection attempts are prohibited on statutory holidays and must be made between 1:00 p.m. and 5:00 p.m. on Sundays and between 7:00 a.m. and 9:00 p.m. on other days.

MINIMIZING YOUR RISK

Comply with Debt Collection Laws

- If your business collects debts on behalf of others or provides debt settlement services, it must register under the *Collection and Debt Settlement Services Act.*
- Collect debts in a civilized and lawful manner. Even when collecting your business's own debts, at a minimum follow the practices outlined for collection agencies (as to when and how you contact debtors, etc.). These practices set a baseline for appropriate debt collection practices. It is good business practice to meet (or exceed) this baseline.

www.emond.ca/CBL3/links

DIG DEEPER
Consumer Protection Ontario provides consumers with helpful information about debt collection in "Collection Agency: Your Rights," online.

Consumer Safety

All Canadian provinces and the federal government have enacted legislation to protect the health and safety of consumers. In the sections that follow, we examine three such pieces of federal legislation: the *Food and Drugs Act*, the *Hazardous Products Act*, and the *Canada Consumer Product Safety Act.*

Food and Drugs Act

The need for strict and protective food and drug laws has been apparent to governments and the public for years. The thalidomide tragedy of the late 1950s and the early 1960s galvanized public attention after thousands of birth defects resulted from pregnant women ingesting a drug that was touted for its ability to cure morning sickness. Over the years, the subsequent discovery of carcinogenic and other harmful properties of many food additives, artificial sweeteners, and growth hormones have increased the public's concerns about their health and safety. Today, citizens require their governments to monitor the safe production and marketing of the food and drugs available for their consumption.

The *Food and Drugs Act* is one of Canada's oldest statutes. It restricts the advertising, sale, and importation of food, drugs, cosmetics, and medical devices. The Act prohibits advertising (including information on packaging and labels) that is misleading or deceptive or is likely to create an erroneous impression regarding the character, value, quantity, composition, merit, or safety of a food or drug. Where a standard has been established for a food, drug, or cosmetic, the Act prohibits labelling that suggests the product meets the standard where it does not. This indirectly enforces product standards. For example, the *Food and Drug Regulations* specifies that "milk"

- shall be the normal lacteal secretion obtained from the mammary gland of the cow, genus *Bos*; and
- shall contain added vitamin D in such an amount that a reasonable daily intake of the milk contains not less than 300 international units and not more than 400 international units of vitamin D.

Any dairy product labelled as "milk" must meet this standard. The regulations create standards for a very broad range of food, from spices to liquor to cheeses to chicken.

Health- and diet-related claims are strictly regulated. The Act specifically prohibits advertising to the public that any food, drug, cosmetic, or medical device can treat or cure certain diseases or disorders, including arthritis, asthma, cancer, dementia, depression, and diabetes, among others. The Act establishes mandatory labelling standards for food and drug products, including the "Nutrition Facts" table found on most foods.

The Act also prohibits the sale of food, drugs, or cosmetics manufactured, packaged, or stored in unsanitary conditions or the sale of food or drugs that are otherwise adulterated or unfit for human consumption.

The regulation of food, drugs, cosmetics, and medical devices is a complex area of the law, and if your business includes these products, you should obtain guidance from a legal expert in this area. The Food and Drugs Liaison Office receives complaints and inquiries relating to compliance with the *Food and Drugs Act* and will facilitate meetings with Health Canada and provide mediation services between businesses and Health Canada in order to resolve issues that arise. Failure to comply with the requirements of the *Food and Drugs Act* can result in fines and imprisonment. The penalties are particularly harsh if the offence relates to food: the maximum fine is $250,000 and the maximum jail term is three years.

www.emond.ca/CBL3/links

DIG DEEPER

Health Canada provides extensive information on the regulation of food and drugs on its website.

MINIMIZING YOUR RISK

Respect Public Health and Safety

- Institute policies in your manufacturing or retail food business to ensure compliance with all hygiene, health, and labelling requirements under the *Food and Drugs Act* and the *Hazardous Products Act*.
- Keep abreast of changes in the law by consulting a lawyer who specializes in your business's field or by contacting Health Canada.
- Enlist the assistance of managers and other staff in maintaining healthy and safe manufacturing and retailing policies.
- Facilitate and expedite government inspections.

Hazardous Products Act

The *Hazardous Products Act* regulates the importation and sale of hazardous products—such as toxic, flammable, or highly reactive substances—intended for use, handling, or storage in a workplace. The sale and importation of these products is prohibited unless the supplier provides a Safety Data Sheet about the product and labels the product in compliance with the regulations. The Safety Data Sheet includes information that identifies the type of hazard posed by the product, its ingredients, first aid and personal protection measures, instructions on proper handling and storage, and toxicology information.

The Workplace Hazardous Materials Bureau of Health Canada provides assistance to suppliers to ensure compliance with the Act and regulations. Failure to comply with the Act and regulations can result in fines and imprisonment. The penalties are particularly harsh if the contravention is done knowingly or recklessly, in which case there is no maximum fine set and the maximum jail term is five years.

Canada Consumer Product Safety Act

The *Canada Consumer Product Safety Act* imposes obligations on those who manufacture, import, sell, advertise, test, package, or label consumer products. It applies to most consumer products, with the exception of those covered by other legislation (like food, drugs, and cosmetics covered by the *Food and Drugs Act*). The purpose of the Act is to protect consumers from dangerous products. Therefore, the Act

- prohibits the manufacture or sale of certain inherently dangerous products (for example, baby walkers and baby bottles made with bisphenol A);
- establishes standards for certain consumer goods and prohibits the manufacture or sale of goods that do not meet those standards (for example, standards related to children's sleepwear, cribs, and ice hockey helmets);
- prohibits the manufacture or sale of consumer goods that are a danger to human health or safety or that have been recalled; and
- prohibits a person from providing false or misleading information relating to a consumer product, whether on the packaging, on labelling, or in advertising.

www.emond.ca/CBL3/links

DIG DEEPER
Health Canada provides background information about the *Canada Consumer Product Safety Act* in the Consumer Product Safety section of its website.

The Act also requires anyone who manufactures, imports, or sells a consumer product to notify Health Canada of *potential* health or safety concerns.

Failure to comply with the Act and regulations can result in liability for administrative monetary penalties or, in more serious cases, fines and imprisonment. The penalties are particularly harsh if misleading information is provided knowingly or recklessly, in which case there is no maximum fine set and the maximum jail term is five years.

Consumer Information

You can see from the previous discussion that concerns with consumer protection and product safety go hand in hand with concerns that consumers receive adequate and accurate information about products and services. The *Consumer Protection Act*, the *Food and Drugs Act*, and the *Canada Consumer Product Safety Act* all include penalties for providing false or misleading information to consumers. In addition to these protections, two federal statutes directly address concerns with the quality of information available to consumers. The federal *Competition Act* addresses all forms of deceptive marketing while the *Consumer Packaging and Labelling Act* focuses on the accuracy of information contained on packaged goods. Each will be reviewed briefly.

Competition Act: Deceptive Marketing

The *Competition Act* has a number of purposes that will be discussed more fully below under the heading "Safeguarding the Marketplace," but among those purposes is to maintain and encourage competition in Canada in order to provide consumers with competitive prices and product choices. In order for consumers to be able to make appropriate choices, they must have adequate and accurate information. When consumers are misinformed about the products and services they are choosing to purchase, it harms consumers and negatively affects competition. For this reason, significant components of the *Competition Act* deal with sanctions for deceptive marketing practices. The main provisions deal with criminal and civil sanctions for misleading representations and deceptive telemarketing. In addition, a number of individual criminal and civil provisions deal with specific common deceptive marketing practices.

The Act's criminal and civil anti-spam provisions are discussed in Chapter 11.

MISLEADING REPRESENTATIONS

The Act prohibits businesses from making material false or misleading representations to the public when promoting their products or business interests. It does not matter whether anyone is actually misled; making the false or misleading statement is sufficient to violate the Act. The courts[7] will consider not only the literal meaning of, but also the general impression left by, the representation when determining whether it is false or misleading. A representation will be considered to be "material" if it could affect the purchaser's decision to buy the product.

◇ Criminal Offence

When a person makes a false or misleading representation *knowingly or recklessly*, they may face criminal prosecution under the Act (s 52). The decision to pursue a criminal prosecution will be based on a number of considerations, including the nature and scope of the misrepresentation, its impact on consumers and competition, and the need for government intervention to restore competition in the marketplace. All elements of the offence must be proven beyond a reasonable doubt, so prosecutions are pursued only where substantial evidence supports them.

The seriousness with which the government takes this issue is reflected in the maximum penalty on conviction: a fine at the discretion of the court and/or imprisonment of up to 14 years. Consumers harmed by a criminal misrepresentation can also sue the business for any loss or damage caused by the misrepresentation (s 36). Consumers can also recover the costs to them of investigating the misrepresentation.

◇ Civil Provision

Where there is no evidence, or insufficient evidence, that a person has made the false or misleading representation *knowingly or recklessly*, the person may still be subject to civil penalties under the Act (s 74.01). If a person has made a false or misleading representation—even one that the person believed at the time was true—a court can order the person to cease making the representation, to publish a corrective notice, to pay an administrative monetary penalty, and/or to pay restitution to purchasers. Administrative monetary penalties can be as high as $750,000 for individuals and $10,000,000 for corporations in the first instance and higher for subsequent orders.

However, if the person making the misrepresentation can demonstrate that they exercised due diligence to prevent the statements from being false or misleading, even though they were ultimately unsuccessful in achieving that goal, only an order requiring them to cease making the misrepresentation can be made. The other remedies and penalties may not be imposed (s 74.1(3)). This underlines the

7 Criminal proceedings can be heard before the superior courts of criminal jurisdiction and the Federal Court. The provincial superior courts, the Federal Court, and the Competition Tribunal may all hear cases relating to the civil deceptive marketing practices provisions.

importance of a business conducting tests and investigations to verify the accuracy of representations made to the public.

SCENARIO

Failing to Meet Advertised Standards

As discussed earlier, Val-Nam sells its generators directly to consumers online. The online information about the generators indicates that they are "7,000-watt generators." This is also specified on the packaging. However, Val-Nam has received a number of complaints from purchasers who have found that the generators are not capable of producing more than a 3,000-watt charge. Would the statements online and on the packaging constitute a criminal offence?

Perhaps. If the generators do not, in fact, generate more than a 3,000-watt charge, the statement that they are 7,000-watt generators would appear to be misleading. The information that is available online certainly contains statements made "to the public" and it can be argued that advertising the generator as a 7,000-watt generator where it only generates 3,000 watts is a material misrepresentation that would likely affect the consumer's decision to buy the generator.

Whether or not it is a criminal offence will depend on whether Val-Nam knew the generators only produced a 3,000-watt charge (through testing prior to making the representations) or should have known this as a result of the complaints of customers (and presumed follow-up investigations) and still left the representations online and on the packaging. Further, if Val-Nam conducted no tests to determine the wattage of the generators before making the representations, it could be argued that Val-Nam was "reckless" in its representations.

DECEPTIVE TELEMARKETING

According to a recent Ipsos Reid survey, telemarketing is the least-trusted profession in Canada.[8] Public mistrust of, and outrage at, the conduct of telemarketers has led to significant regulation of their business practices. The *Competition Act* regulates their conduct in two ways: first, it establishes mandatory levels of disclosure of information; second, it prohibits certain telemarketing practices.

It is a criminal offence to engage in telemarketing without making the following disclosures in a fair, reasonable, and timely manner:

- the identity of the person on behalf of whom the call is being made;
- the nature of their business and the purpose of the call; and
- the price of the product being promoted and any material delivery conditions or restrictions.

When engaging in telemarketing, it is also a criminal offence to make a false or misleading representation or to

- conduct a contest where the delivery of the prize is conditional upon the prior payment of any amount by the participant or where full and fair disclosure of the chances of winning is not made;

8 Ipsos Reid, "Ipsos Reid and Reader's Digest Release Annual Trusted Brand™ Survey: Canadians Continue to Remain Loyal to Brands They Trust Most" (19 January 2015), online: <https://www.ipsos.com/en-ca/ipsos-reid-and-readers-digest-release-annual-trusted-brandtm-survey>.

- offer one product at no or a low cost to entice a purchaser to buy another product without disclosing the fair market value of the first product; or
- require payment prior to delivery of a product whose price grossly exceeds its fair market value.

However, a person will not be found guilty of these offences if the person can demonstrate that they exercised due diligence. The maximum penalty on conviction is a fine in the discretion of the court or imprisonment for a term not exceeding 14 years or both.

Protect Your Business from Unscrupulous Telemarketers

In May 2017, Thompson Hill Publishing pled guilty to engaging in deceptive telemarketing and making false and misleading representations. The company sold online and hard-copy directory listings to businesses. It employed telemarketers who misled the businesses into believing that the purpose of their call was to renew an existing listing in a business directory. In fact, the telemarketers were selling a new listing in a new directory.

The corporation and the individuals involved were charged with making false or misleading representations regarding prior business relationships, failing to disclose the purpose of the calls, and making false or misleading representations during the call. The corporation must pay fines totalling $180,000 and two of its managers are prohibited from engaging in any telemarketing activities for five years.[9]

Tips to protect your business from telemarketing scams:

- Make sure employees know who your current suppliers are.
- Train employees not to provide any business information or enter into transactions over the phone unless they are certain of the identity of the caller.
- Establish clear procedures with your suppliers as to how orders will be made and processed so that you are alert to someone posing as a supplier who does not follow those procedures.
- Be aware of common cons—business directory sales, business supplies sales, computer virus removal, persons posing as Canada Revenue Agency agents, etc.
- Fraudulent or suspicious activity can be reported to the Canadian Anti-Fraud Centre through its website or by telephone (1-888-495-8501).
- Misleading or deceptive marketing practices can be reported to the Competition Bureau using the online complaint form or by telephone (1-800-348-5358).

SPECIFIC CRIMINAL OFFENCES

In addition to the general criminal provisions relating to misleading representations and deceptive telemarketing, there are more narrow, specific criminal offences relating to common deceptive marketing practices. The following practices are criminal offences:

- deceptive notice of winning a prize (for example, giving a person the impression that they have won a prize and asking the person for money before they can "claim" the prize (s 53));

9 Canada, Competition Bureau, "Telemarketing Company Pleads Guilty to Criminal Charges," news release (24 May 2017), online: <https://www.canada.ca/en/competition-bureau/news/2017/05/telemarketing_companypleadsguiltytocriminalcharges.html>.

double ticketing selling a product at a price that is higher than the lowest price, when there is more than one price on the product

multi-level marketing plan a distribution plan structured such that participants earn money by supplying products to other participants in the plan

pyramid selling a form of multi-level marketing plan that includes one or more of the following: (1) compensation for recruitment; (2) required purchases as a condition of participation; (3) a requirement to purchase excessive inventory; and (4) an inability to return inventory on reasonable commercial terms

- **double ticketing** (where more than one price is on a product, selling the product at a price that is higher than the lowest price (s 54));
- failing to make fair, reasonable, and timely disclosure of compensation in a **multi-level marketing plan** (s 55); and
- establishing, operating, advertising, or promoting a **pyramid selling** scheme (s 55.1).

SPECIFIC CIVIL PROVISIONS

The Act also highlights specific deceptive marketing practices that are not egregious enough to warrant criminal prosecution but which nonetheless harm consumers and competition. The following specific practices are prohibited:

- representations relating to the performance, efficiency, or length of life of a product that are not based on appropriate testing (s 74.01(1)(b));
- misleading representations relating to warranties and guarantees (s 74.01(1)(c));
- misleading representations as to the ordinary selling price of a product (for example, advertising that a product is 50 percent off, when it was never sold at the advertised "original" price) (ss 74.01(2) and (3));
- misleading use of testimonials (for example, by stating that a dog food is the first choice of Canadian veterinarians where no evidence supports the statement) (s 74.02);
- "bait and switch" selling—when one product is advertised at a very low price but stocked in insufficient quantity with the expectation that purchasers will instead buy a similar but more expensive product (s 74.04);
- certain sales above advertised prices (s 74.05); and
- misleading promotional contests (s 74.06).

Consumer Packaging and Labelling Act

Canadian law requires that prepackaged consumer products be labelled accurately and meaningfully to help consumers make informed purchasing decisions and to help them differentiate between products. The federal *Consumer Packaging and Labelling Act* regulates the information that must be provided to consumers on labels affixed to prepackaged products, other than products that qualify as a "device" or "drug" within the meaning of the *Food and Drugs Act*, as that Act addresses the issue for those products.

The *Consumer Packaging and Labelling Act* requires the following information to appear on product labels in both English and French:

- the common or generic name of the product;
- a declaration of the product's net quantity; and
- the identity and address of the person by or for whom the product was manufactured, sold, or imported—that is, dealer identification.

The Act also standardizes certain product containers—such as those for facial tissue, peanut butter, and wine—to prevent consumers from being confused by an undue proliferation of container shapes.

Inspectors under the Act, upon finding a non-compliant label, can seize the mislabelled product and detain it until the dealer or manufacturer brings the packaging into compliance with the law. If the dealer does not do so, the product can be forfeited to the government (usually for destruction) after all appeals of the seizure have been exhausted. The Act imposes fines for serious cases of mislabelling or refusal to comply with labelling regulations. Interfering with an inspector or blocking a search, seizure, or forfeiture constitutes an offence.

Advertising Dos and Don'ts from the Competition Bureau

Dos

- Do avoid fine-print disclaimers. They often fail to change the general impression conveyed by an advertisement. If you do use them, make sure the overall impression created by the ad and the disclaimer is not misleading.
- Do fully and clearly disclose all material information in the advertisement.
- Do avoid using terms or phrases in an advertisement that are not meaningful and clear to the ordinary person.
- Do charge the lowest of two or more prices appearing on a product.
- Do ensure that you have reasonable quantities of a product advertised at a bargain price.
- Do, when conducting a contest, disclose all material details required by the Act before potential participants are committed to it.
- Do ensure that your sales force is familiar with these "dos and don'ts." Advertisers may be held responsible for representations made by employees.

Don'ts

- Don't confuse "regular price" or "ordinary price" with "manufacturer's suggested list price" or a like term. They are often not the same.
- Don't use "regular price" in an advertisement unless the product has been offered in good faith for sale at that price for a substantial period of time, or a substantial volume of the product has been sold at that price within a reasonable period of time.
- Don't use the words "sale" or "special" in relation to the price of a product unless a significant price reduction has occurred.
- Don't run a "sale" for a long period or repeat it every week.
- Don't increase the price of a product or service to cover the cost of a free product or service.
- Don't use illustrations that are different from the product being sold.
- Don't make a performance claim unless you can prove it, even if you think it is accurate. Testimonials usually do not amount to adequate proof.
- Don't sell a product above your advertised price.
- Don't unduly delay the distribution of prizes when conducting a contest.
- Don't make any materially misleading product warranty or guarantee, or promise to replace, maintain, or repair an article.
- Don't use the results of product performance tests and/or testimonials in your advertising unless you are authorized to use them; or, if you are authorized to use them, don't distort test results or the scope of testimonials.
- Don't forget that no one actually needs to be deceived or misled for a court to find that an advertisement is misleading.[10]

10 Canada, Competition Bureau, "False or Misleading Representations and Deceptive Telemarketing Practices" (5 November 2015), online: <http://www.competitionbureau.gc.ca/eic/site/cb-bc.nsf/eng/03133.html>.

Safeguarding the Marketplace

Current Canadian economic policy is based on the assumption that competition is good for the economy and for society as a whole. Competition is believed to promote efficiency and innovation in the economy and therefore should be not only preserved but enhanced. However, determining whether a business's activities are pro- or anti-competitive can be a very complex task. The federal *Competition Act* attempts to identify and prohibit anti-competitive business practices.[11]

Certain activities are inherently anti-competitive. That is, regardless of the type of market, number or nature of competitors in the market, or type of product or service, the activity will harm competition. For example, when two competitors agree on a high price to charge for their similar products, this is an obvious reduction in competition that has harmful effects on consumers and economic efficiency. In these clear circumstances, the provisions of the *Competition Act* are also clear. Activities with inherent anti-competitive effects constitute criminal offences, with significant penalties.

However, other business activities can have anti-competitive effects in certain circumstances, but can have pro-competitive effects in other circumstances. In these cases, a more complex investigation and analysis of the structure of the market, the business's activities, and the effects of those activities must be undertaken. For this reason, activities that fall in this category are not per se, or automatically, prohibited under the Act. It is only once the activity is shown to cause or be likely to cause a significant negative effect on competition that it will be prohibited. These activities are referred to as **reviewable practices**, in contrast to the criminal provisions.

reviewable practices business practices that can have either pro- or anti-competitive effects, depending on market circumstances, and therefore may be subject to review by the Competition Tribunal

The Competition Bureau is responsible for the administration and enforcement of the Act. The Bureau, headed by the Commissioner of Competition, investigates alleged violations of the Act and determines whether or not action should be taken. Where the alleged violation is a criminal offence, the Bureau can refer the matter to the Attorney General of Canada, who then decides whether to prosecute before the courts. Where the alleged violation is in respect of a reviewable matter, the Bureau itself may bring the matter before the Competition Tribunal. The Competition Tribunal, unlike the courts, is composed of members whose expertise is in law as well as members whose expertise is in economics and business. This range of expertise is required in order to assess the competitive effects of the impugned business practices. In this section, we will briefly review the key components of the *Competition Act* including its application, the criminal and reviewable practices provisions, the options for enforcing the Act, and the protections afforded "whistle-blowers."

www.emond.ca/CBL3/links

DIG DEEPER

The Competition Bureau website provides tools and services to help businesses comply with the *Competition Act*.

Application of the Competition Act

The *Competition Act* applies to any "business" operating in Canada. This includes businesses involved in the manufacture, production, transportation, acquisition,

11 As discussed earlier under the heading "Consumer Information," the *Competition Act* also deals with deceptive marketing practices. Those provisions will not be addressed under this heading as they have already been covered in detail in this chapter.

supply, and storage of real or personal property as well as businesses involved in the acquisition and supply of services. It also includes activities relating to the raising of funds for charitable or non-profit purposes.

Criminal Offences under the Competition Act

As mentioned above, the criminal provisions of the Act focus on activities that are widely acknowledged to have anti-competitive effects regardless of market conditions. These activities include certain types of conspiracies and bid-rigging. As they are criminal offences, all elements of the offence must be proven beyond a reasonable doubt.

Criminal Conspiracies (s 45)

The criminal provisions relating to conspiracies aim to address the most egregious forms of **cartel** conduct. A person commits the offence of **conspiracy** when the person "conspires, agrees or arranges" with a competitor to fix prices, allocate markets, or control output or supply levels of a product (under the Act, a "product" includes real and personal property and services). The simple act of agreeing to, for example, fix prices with a competitor will constitute the offence. There is no need to prove that the agreement was acted upon or implemented or that competition was or would have been harmed.

cartel
an association of manufacturers, distributors, or retailers who agree to fix prices or otherwise coordinate efforts in order to limit competition

conspiracy
when one person agrees with a competitor to fix prices, allocate markets, or control output or supply levels of a product

Tackling Cartels

One of the Competition Bureau's top enforcement priorities is the detection and investigation of price-fixing among competitors. Recent cases have involved international cartels in the ocean freight, chocolate bar, air cargo, and grocery bread industries.

One of the most far reaching recent domestic investigations involved the fixing of retail gasoline prices in Victoriaville, Thetford Mines, Sherbrooke, and Magog, Quebec. Between 2008 and 2012, charges were laid against 39 individuals and 15 companies. While some of the cases are ongoing, so far 33 individuals and 7 companies have either pleaded guilty or been found guilty. Over $4 million in fines have been levied and 6 individuals have been sentenced to prison terms.[12]

Bid-Rigging (s 47)

Recent years have seen significant enforcement action relating to **bid-rigging**, which is simply a specific form of conspiracy. A person commits the offence of bid-rigging when, in response to a call for bids, the person enters into an agreement with one or more other persons who agrees

- not to submit a bid,
- to withdraw their bid, or
- to coordinate their bid with the other person(s).

bid-rigging
when, in response to a call for bids, a person enters into an agreement with one or more other persons and the person agrees not to submit a bid, to withdraw their bid, or to coordinate their bid with the other person(s)

12 Canada, Competition Bureau, "Les Pétroles Global Inc fined $1 million for gasoline price-fixing in Quebec," news release (17 April 2015), online: <http://www.competitionbureau.gc.ca/eic/site/cb-bc.nsf/eng/03908.html>.

As with the offence of conspiracy, there is no need to prove that the agreement was acted upon or implemented or that competition was or would have been harmed. The simple act of agreeing to, for example, fix the prices of the bids to be submitted will constitute the offence. However, it is a complete defence to the offence of bid-rigging if the parties to the agreement can prove that they informed the person calling for the bid of the agreement. This allows for the submission of joint bids in more complex projects.

Businesses need to ensure they are not involved in bid-rigging, but they also need to be vigilant to ensure that they are not victims of bid-rigging. If your call for bids is tainted by bid-rigging among your suppliers, you may pay significantly more for goods and services that may also be of lower quality.

MINIMIZING YOUR RISK

Protect Your Business from Bid-Rigging

Val-Nam has purchased property on which it will build a manufacturing plant for its portable generators. Val-Nam will be issuing a call for bids on the construction of the plant. However, Valery has heard rumours that some of the construction firms in the area coordinate their bids, so she is concerned that the company won't obtain a good price for the work. How can Valery better recognize and prevent bid-rigging on this job?

Watch for "red flags":

- bids that are received all together or come from the same source (email or fax number)
- similar errors, bid amounts, terminology, etc. in bids
- similar charges for costs that should be different (for example, the same transportation costs for a firm that is close by and a firm that is far away)
- the winning bidder subcontracts parts of the job to unsuccessful bidders
- a significant price difference between the winning bid and other bids
- one bidder seems to have knowledge of other bids.

Valery should also do her research—get to know the bidders, their suppliers, and market prices. This will allow her to make a judgment as to the reasonableness of the bids she receives. If Valery is suspicious of the bids she receives, she can contact the Competition Bureau to discuss her concerns.

The Competition Bureau provides additional detailed information in its publication "Bid-Rigging: Detecting, Preventing and Reporting."

Penalties

The maximum penalty for criminal conspiracy is a fine of $25 million or imprisonment for up to 14 years or both. The maximum penalty for bid-rigging is a fine at the discretion of the court or imprisonment for up to 14 years or both.

In addition, the Act provides individuals who suffered loss or damage as a result of the conspiracy or the bid-rigging with the right to sue for damages. This can be done regardless of whether a criminal conviction is obtained or even pursued by the government.

Reviewable Practices Under the Competition Act (Part VIII)

We have looked at activities considered to be inherently anti-competitive. However, most business activities can have either pro-competitive or anti-competitive effects, depending on the circumstances. How can that be? Consider when a business decides to expand by purchasing a competitor's business. This can provide many benefits to the business and to the public: (1) the combined business may be able to achieve **economies of scale** that result in lower costs and allow for lower consumer prices; (2) the higher levels of profit of the combined business may allow for higher levels of investment in R&D, resulting in product and process improvements; and/or (3) the combined business may be able to be more efficient and reduce redundancies, again reducing costs. If a significant number of vigorous competitors remain in the marketplace afterwards, the overall effect may be pro-competitive. In contrast, where a business purchases its only competitor and now there is a monopoly in the marketplace, it is likely that prices will increase and other anti-competitive effects will occur because there is no longer a competitive challenge to the business. Therefore, whether or not many business practices have pro or anti-competitive effects depends primarily on how strong the competitive market is.

The Act highlights a number of business practices that may, in circumstances where there is little or no competitive pressure, have significant anti-competitive effects. The following are examples of some of those practices:

- refusing to supply a particular customer with your product (**refusal to deal**, s 75);
- specifying the price at which your customer may resell your product (**price maintenance**, s 76);
- requiring a customer to purchase only your products/loyalty discounts (**exclusive dealing**, s 77);
- providing a discount on one product (for example, a mobile phone) if the customer purchases a second product (for example, a wireless contract) (**tied selling**, s 77);
- requiring a customer to sell your products only in certain geographic areas (**market restriction**, s 77);
- purchasing all or part of another business (mergers, s 92); and
- entering into a joint production agreement with a competitor (competitor collaboration, s 90.1).

Remember, these activities are *not* automatically prohibited by the Act. They are common business activities that most often enhance a business and the economy. It is only when their effect is to harm competition that they are prohibited.

The approach is summed up in the "basket" provision referred to as the abuse of dominance provision (s 78). This provision empowers the Competition Tribunal to prohibit any "anti-competitive practice" if it is engaged in by a person who "substantially or completely" controls a market (meaning where there is little or no competitive pressure) and the practice has, does, or is likely to substantially prevent or lessen competition in the market.

Where the Competition Tribunal finds that any of the above-mentioned practices harms competition, it may order the person to cease the practice and/or pay an

economies of scale
when increased output reduces the average costs of production

refusal to deal
when a supplier refuses to supply a product to a buyer even though there is ample supply of the product, resulting in a substantial negative effect on the buyer's business and an adverse effect on competition

price maintenance
when a supplier prevents a buyer from reselling the product below a minimum price using threats or promises of benefits, or the supplier discriminates against the buyer because of the buyer's low pricing policy

exclusive dealing
when a supplier requires its customer to obtain products only or primarily from the supplier and the practice has caused or is likely to cause a substantial lessening of competition

tied selling
when a supplier requires a buyer to buy one product or service in order to gain commercial access to, or a better price on, another product or service and the practice has caused or is likely to cause a substantial lessening of competition

market restriction
when a supplier forces a buyer to resell its products to only certain customers or only in certain geographic areas and the practice has caused or is likely to cause a substantial lessening of competition

administrative monetary penalty. Where the Tribunal finds that a merger harms competition, it can order that the merger be "undone."[13]

Competition Act Enforcement Options

As discussed earlier in this chapter under the heading "Safeguarding the Marketplace," the Competition Bureau is responsible for the administration and enforcement of the Act. The Bureau has access to a number of investigatory tools such as court-ordered wiretapping, searches and seizures, and the examination of witnesses under oath. The Bureau uses a wide range of enforcement tools to encourage businesses to comply with the Act's provisions. Initial actions may be as simple as an "information letter" or call to a business to explain possible violations of the Act that it may be unaware of. The Bureau may also ask a business for a voluntary undertaking—a binding written promise—to cease a particular business practice. The Bureau can take more formal steps and request a temporary or permanent court order prohibiting

SCENARIO

Business Collaborations: Risks and Benefits

Val-Nam is interested in developing an industrial-sized version of its generator to be used with municipal recycling collection services. Valery envisages a power generation facility located at municipal landfill sites that can both accommodate the biodegradation of plastic and convert landfill gas into electrical power. Valery has discussed engaging in joint R&D with Spotlight Renewables Inc., a firm that has developed a method of capturing landfill gas and using it to generate electrical power. Does this plan raise any *Competition Act* concerns?

R&D cooperation between competitors (or potential competitors) has many benefits, including an ability to share resources, technology, and ideas that can lead to faster progress in product and process developments. However, there are dangers as well:

- Val-Nam and Spotlight will want to limit their cooperation to R&D.
- They will need to ensure that officers and employees do not discuss sensitive competitive information like pricing or marketing strategies, as that may violate the criminal conspiracy provisions of the *Competition Act*.
- They should consider the broader competitive implications of their cooperation, including whether the cooperation will reduce their incentive to compete independently, hinder new businesses from entering the marketplace, or facilitate the exchange of sensitive business information. These outcomes could result in an investigation under the reviewable practices provisions of the Act.

The Competition Bureau provides additional guidance on the permitted scope of collaboration among competitors in its "Competitor Collaboration Guidelines."

---

13 For mergers that exceed certain financial thresholds, the Competition Bureau must be notified in advance of the merger.

a business from engaging in a business practice. With respect to the reviewable practices provisions, the Bureau itself can make an application to the Competition Tribunal for a remedy. With respect to the criminal provisions, the Bureau may refer the matter to the Attorney General of Canada to determine whether or not a criminal prosecution should be pursued.

In addition to these processes, private parties are able to pursue remedies for certain anti-competitive business practices as well. Private parties may apply for leave to bring one of a list of reviewable matters before the Competition Tribunal. These matters include the refusal to deal, exclusive dealing, tied selling, and market restriction provisions. Further, if a person (individual or business) suffers a loss as a result of criminal conduct under the Act, section 36 of the Act grants to the person the right to sue for damages. This includes damages arising from criminal conspiracy, bid-rigging, and criminal misleading advertising, as well as damages arising from a failure to comply with a Competition Tribunal order. This remedy can be sought by the person whether or not a criminal prosecution is pursued by the government.

Whistle-Blower Protections and Immunity from Prosecution

Offences like conspiracy are very hard to detect because they involve secret agreements usually known only to the co-conspirators. Most of the Competition Bureau's successful investigations have been the result of information provided by either an employee of one of the conspirators (a "whistle-blower") or a conspirator who has decided to cease their illegal activity.

The *Competition Act* protects whistle-blowers from retaliatory action by their employers. A whistle-blower cannot be fired, disciplined, or harassed by their employer for providing information to the Competition Bureau in good faith. It is a criminal offence for an employer to do any of these things.

The *Criminal Code* also makes it an offence for an employer to threaten to fire or to fire, discipline, or otherwise adversely affect the employment of an employee because the employee has provided or will provide information to a person whose duties include the enforcement of federal law. This includes providing information to the Competition Bureau.

An individual or business that has engaged in criminal conduct may agree to cooperate with the Bureau in its investigation and, in exchange, the Bureau may recommend to the Director of Public Prosecutions of Canada that immunity from prosecution be granted. However, the Bureau will only consider this if the person requesting immunity is the first to disclose the offence to the Bureau, or, even if the Bureau is aware of the offence, the person is the first to provide sufficient information about the offence to support a criminal prosecution.[14]

14 For additional information on immunity from prosecution, see Canada, Competition Bureau, "Immunity Program under the *Competition Act*," bulletin (7 June 2010), online: <http://www.competitionbureau.gc.ca/eic/site/cb-bc.nsf/eng/03248.html>.

CHAPTER SUMMARY

The federal and provincial governments have both codified common law principles and added to the legal obligations and protections relating to businesses through legislation. These steps were taken to facilitate business transactions, to protect consumers who are vulnerable in many business transactions, and to safeguard the competitive marketplace in Canada in order to promote efficiency and innovation in the economy and provide consumers with competitive prices and product choices. In this chapter, we reviewed a number of key federal and provincial statutes.

In Ontario, the *Sale of Goods Act* facilitates business transactions. It governs the buying and selling of tangible personal property (not services). The Act implies a number of conditions and warranties into contracts to keep commercial dealings fair and honest: for example, that the description of the goods matches the goods sold, that the goods are fit for the intended use, and that they are of a merchantable quality. The Act also provides default rules regarding the transfer of ownership of goods and remedies for breach of contract.

The *Electronic Commerce Act, 2000* governs the purchase and sale of goods over the Internet. It establishes default rules for how contracts can be formed electronically and how electronic documents satisfy the legal requirement that documents be "originals" or "in writing."

The primary legislation protecting consumers in business transactions is the consumer protection statutes in each province and territory. The Ontario *Consumer Protection Act, 2002* applies to services as well as goods and affects areas such as consumer access to accurate information about the products and services they purchase, the protection of consumers from unfair business practices, and the provision of meaningful remedies for consumers. Part II of the Act sets out certain rights of consumers and certain warranties that operate in their favour, such as the quality of goods/services, the accuracy of estimates, and the illegality of demanding payment for unsolicited goods or services.

Part III describes unfair business practices, such as making dishonest representations to consumers, engaging in unconscionable practices, or pressuring a consumer to renegotiate the terms of their transaction by holding on to the consumer's goods.

Part IV sets out rights and obligations regarding Internet, remote, future performance, direct, and personal development service agreements.

Also in Ontario, the *Collection and Debt Settlement Services Act* governs the ways in which collection agencies may collect debts from consumers. It would be a good business practice to follow the baseline set by this Act when collecting debts on behalf of your own business.

All Canadian provinces and the federal government have enacted legislation to protect the health and safety of consumers. The federal *Food and Drugs Act* regulates the importation, sale, preparation, and labelling of food for sale. It also regulates drugs sold in Canada with regard to safety, effectiveness, health claims, etc. The *Hazardous Products Act* provides categories of "restricted" products that must be labelled in a specific manner or meet certain standards to be legally sold in Canada. The *Canada Consumer Product Safety Act* places additional responsibilities on industry to ensure that it is not marketing products that may endanger consumers, especially children.

Many different federal and provincial statutes seek to ensure that the information consumers receive about products and services is accurate and sufficient for making reasoned purchasing decisions. The federal *Competition Act* contains extensive provisions governing misleading representations and deceptive telemarketing by businesses, including criminal sanctions for misleading representations that are made "knowingly or recklessly" or for failing to disclose key information when telemarketing. The *Consumer Packaging and Labelling Act* regulates the information that must be provided to consumers on labels affixed to prepackaged products so that consumers can make informed purchasing decisions.

Finally, the federal *Competition Act* is the statute primarily concerned with safeguarding the competitive marketplace. The Act imposes criminal sanctions for business practices that are inherently anti-competitive, like conspiracies among competitors to fix prices. The Act allows for review by the Competition Tribunal of those business practices that in certain circumstances may be pro-competitive, while in other circumstances may be anti-competitive. Where the Tribunal finds the practice significantly harms competition, the practice can be prohibited.

KEY TERMS

bid-rigging, 199
cartel, 199
caveat emptor, 168
conspiracy, 199
consumer, 183
cooling-off period, 189
deliverable state, 176
double ticketing, 196
economies of scale, 201
exclusive dealing, 201
future goods, 176
lien, 175
market restriction, 201
merchantable quality, 173
multi-level marketing plan, 196
price maintenance, 201
pyramid selling, 196
refusal to deal, 201
reviewable practices, 198
seller's lien, 179
specific goods, 176
tied selling, 201
title, 170
unascertained goods, 176

REFERENCES

Canada Consumer Product Safety Act, SC 2010, c 21.
Civil Code of Québec, CQLR c CCQ-1991.
Collection and Debt Settlement Services Act, RSO 1990, c C.14.
Competition Act, RSC 1985, c C-34.
Consumer Packaging and Labelling Act, RSC 1985, c C-38.
Consumer Product Warranty and Liability Act, SNB 1978, c C-18.1.
Consumer Protection Act, 2002, SO 2002, c 30, Schedule A.
Consumer Protection Act, CQLR c P-40.1.
Consumer Protection and Business Practices Act, SS 2014, c C-30.2.
Criminal Code, RSC 1985, c C-46.
David Schnarr v Blue Mountain Resorts Limited, 2017 ONSC 114.
De Maeseneer v Degamo, 2002 BCPC 303.
Electronic Commerce Act, SNS 2000, c 26.
Electronic Commerce Act, SNu 2004, c 7.
Electronic Commerce Act, 2000, SO 2000, c 17.
Electronic Transactions Act, SA 2001, c E-5.5.
Electronic Transactions Act, SBC 2001, c 10.
Food and Drug Regulations, CRC, c 870.
Food and Drugs Act, RSC 1985, c F-27.
Hazardous Products Act, RSC 1985, c H-3.
Hunter Engineering Co v Syncrude Canada Ltd, [1989] 1 SCR 426, 1989 CanLII 129.
IPEX v Lubrizol, 2012 ONSC 2717.
Occupiers' Liability Act, RSO 1990, c O.2.
Rules of Civil Procedure, RRO 1990, Reg 194.
Sale of Goods Act, RSO 1990, c S.1.
United Nations Commission on International Trade Law, *Convention on Contracts for the International Sale of Goods* (Vienna: United Nations, 1980), online: <http://www.uncitral.org/uncitral/en/uncitral_texts/sale_goods/1980CISG.html>.
Woodhouse v Snow Valley, 2017 ONSC 222.

EXERCISES

True or False?

____ **1.** Leases are governed by the *Sale of Goods Act*.

____ **2.** Fitness for intended purpose is an implied condition under the *Sale of Goods Act*.

____ **3.** Specific performance is a remedy available in special circumstances only.

____ **4.** Unpaid sellers have no statutory remedies.

____ **5.** The *Consumer Protection Act, 2002* requires that ambiguous contract terms be construed in favour of the consumer.

____ **6.** The *Consumer Protection Act, 2002* creates a ten-day cooling-off period for all consumer transactions.

____ **7.** The *Consumer Protection Act, 2002* requires that the final bill for service for which an estimate was given is equal to or less than the estimate.

____ **8.** If an original of a document must be provided, an electronic version of the document will not satisfy that requirement.

____ **9.** The *Competition Act* applies to both goods and services.

____ **10.** An individual has an automatic right to make a complaint to the Competition Tribunal.

____ **11.** Bid-rigging can have a pro-competitive or anti-competitive effect, depending on the circumstances.

Multiple Choice

1. In which of the following areas does the *Sale of Goods Act* not imply terms?
   a. merchantable quality
   b. right to sell goods
   c. fair price for goods
   d. fitness for purpose
2. To which of the following does the *Sale of Goods Act* apply?
   a. the sale of a car
   b. the rental of an apartment
   c. the sale of a house
   d. the rental of a motel room
3. Ashley purchased a used farm tractor for $9,500. She later discovered that the previous owner's bank had a lien on the tractor. Under the *Sale of Goods Act*, this is most likely a breach of ____________, which would allow her the remedy of ____________.
   a. warranty/rescission
   b. condition/rescission
   c. warranty/damages
   d. condition/damages
4. The *Consumer Protection Act, 2002* would *not* cover
   a. a professional manicure
   b. the two-month rental of a summer cottage
   c. the purchase of a car
   d. the delivery of high-speed cable Internet service to a home business
5. An unconscionable representation
   a. is a criminal act
   b. gives a buyer the automatic right to exemplary damages
   c. can be evidence that a transaction is unfair and supports a buyer's right to a remedy
   d. is irrelevant because of the *caveat emptor* rule
6. A main objective of the *Competition Act* is
   a. ensuring a supply that is adequate to meet the demands of consumers
   b. ensuring that inventories held by retailers do not become excessive
   c. protecting consumers from harm caused by misleading information
   d. discouraging businesses from working together to improve their efficiency
7. Jake sells towels at the local beach every summer. The label on his towels reads "100% Egyptian Cotton." In fact, Jake's towels were manufactured in China from 100 percent Chinese materials. Under the *Consumer Protection Act*, Jake may be subject to a maximum penalty of
   a. a $250,000 fine
   b. a $250,000 fine and a three-year prison term
   c. a $50,000 fine and a prison term of two years less a day
   d. a $25,000 fine and no prison term permitted for this crime
8. Jane recently opened a general store that sells hand cream, among other things. Jane advertises the hand cream as being effective in the treatment of arthritis, based on significant tests completed by the manufacturer. Which Act is Jane in violation of?
   a. The *Competition Act*.
   b. The *Food and Drugs Act*.
   c. The *Consumer Packaging and Labelling Act*.
   d. Jane is not in violation of any Act.
9. When a business advertises a product at a very low price but does not stock it in sufficient quantity—in the hope that, once the customer is in the store, the customer will end up buying a similar but more expensive product—it is called
   a. bait and switch selling
   b. tied selling
   c. exclusive dealing
   d. double ticketing

Short Answer

1. When does title to goods pass from the seller to the buyer?
2. If Mario trades his wristwatch for an umbrella at a flea market, can he rely on the *Sale of Goods Act* to ensure that the umbrella will be of merchantable quality?
3. What is a cooling-off period, and how does it differ from the one-year statutory limitation period for repudiation of unfair consumer contracts?
4. Explain why a person might not want to have his or her electronic signature automatically added at the bottom of email messages.

5. Why does the law extend special protections to consumers, as opposed to business parties?
6. What does the Food and Drugs Liaison Office do?
7. What role do private parties play in enforcing the *Competition Act*?

Apply Your Knowledge

1. Sunny Days Foods Ltd is a new business that produces organic herbs and oils. It has been trying to sell its products to the major grocery retailers but has been told by the retailers that they cannot stock any organic herb or oil products other than those produced by Wholesome World Foods Inc or they will lose their product discounts from Wholesome World Foods Inc. This is making it impossible for Sunny Days Foods Ltd to break into the market.
   a. What government body can Sunny Days Foods Ltd contact to file a complaint, and by what means can it be filed?
   b. If the Competition Bureau believes that Wholesome World Foods Inc's actions are significantly harming competition, which provision of the *Competition Act* is likely being violated?
2. Marie is the CEO of Minox Ltée, a small machine shop that does business with several large auto manufacturers. Several years ago, a competitor's CEO asked Marie whether Minox would like to create a trade association to discuss common business issues like marketing practices and pricing. Marie said she was not interested. Shortly after the discussion, Marie heard that a trade association was created among three of her main competitors. Recently, she has noticed that these competitors' products are always priced the same, and she wonders if she should report this to the Competition Bureau.
   a. What *Competition Act* issues does this scenario raise?
   b. Should Marie report the incident? Why or why not?
3. National Women's Fashion is a high-end fashion department store with a number of different locations across Canada. A marketing manager, Shirley Opaque, had price tags placed on garments indicating a "regular" and "sale" price when, in fact, the garments were not sold in any significant quantity or for any reasonable period of time at the "regular" price.
   a. Discuss whether this marketing technique is an acceptable practice in relation to the *Competition Act* and the *Consumer Protection Act*.
   b. If National Women's Fashion's primary supplier decided to limit the locations at which its product could be sold, this would be an example of what type of practice?
   c. In reference to (b), would this be considered an offence?

Forms of Carrying On Business

7

LEARNING OUTCOMES

After reading this chapter, you should be able to:

- Detail the various business forms that business people choose for carrying on business.
- Explain the legal characteristics of and describe the benefits and disadvantages of carrying on business as a sole proprietorship.
- Distinguish between a general partnership, a limited partnership, and a limited liability partnership.
- Discuss the advantages and disadvantages of each type of partnership.
- Describe the contents of a partnership agreement.
- Explain the legal characteristics of a corporation and the advantages and disadvantages of adopting a corporate structure.
- Describe the roles of directors, shareholders, officers, managers, and employees of corporations.
- Distinguish between private and public corporations.
- Describe agency and discuss its application to business.
- Distinguish joint ventures from business forms.
- Discuss the implications of running a franchise.
- Describe the characteristics of licences and provide examples.

What Are Forms of Carrying On Business?

business structure
form of carrying on business that dictates key aspects of a business's creation and operation

Canadian law offers a variety of legal business forms in which a person or a group of people can carry on business. The most common of these forms are the sole proprietorship, the partnership, and the corporation. Each form—or **business structure**—involves a legal regime that governs key aspects of a business's existence: its creation, the manner in which it conducts its internal affairs, its relationship to other businesses, the way in which it pays its taxes, and the extent to which it is legally responsible for its own liabilities, to name a few.

All businesses involve some legal form. For example, if your Uncle Izzy opens his doors to neighbours who pay him to read their fortunes, Uncle Izzy is working within a business form: he is a sole proprietor. By virtue of reading fortunes for money, Uncle Izzy becomes subject to the established body of law related to sole proprietorships. This means he is personally liable to pay tax on the income that his fortune-telling business produces; he may be liable for injuries that his customers suffer while they are on his premises; and, if he decides to adopt a business name other than his own—such as Izzy's Fabulous Fortunes—he is required to register the name. However, although Uncle Izzy will be deemed by law to be a sole proprietor, this may not be the best business form for him or his business.

When Valery, Namid, and Mitchell first developed their business concept, they also needed to consider the best business form to use for Val-Nam, their business. That choice depends on many factors, including how each person wants to be involved in the business, the degree of financial risk they are willing to take, and the business's need for financing. Further, at different stages of the business's development, different business forms may be more appropriate. As we review the most common methods of carrying on business, we will consider the pros and cons of each form for Valery, Namid, and Mitchell.

Every legal form for carrying on business has its advantages and disadvantages regarding, for example, flexibility, cost, complexity, and protection for its owners. In this chapter, we discuss these matters in relation to the most common forms of carrying on business:

- sole proprietorships;
- partnerships, including general, limited, and limited liability partnerships; and
- corporations, including private, public, and, briefly, co-operative corporations.

In addition, we explore the procedures required by law to set up these business forms and maintain their operations smoothly.

After examining these main forms of carrying on business, we will look at some of the different ways that businesses can combine their efforts through use of the following:

- agents,
- joint ventures,
- licensing, and
- franchising.

The various forms of carrying on business offer a business person interesting opportunities for defining significant business relationships: not only the legal relationship between the people who own and run the businesses, but also the legal relationship between their businesses and the people who run, finance, and work for them. A partner in a general partnership, for example, enjoys different rights and obligations in relation to their partner than a director of a private corporation enjoys in relation to other directors and shareholders of the corporation.

www.emond.ca/CBL3/links

DIG DEEPER
The Canada Business Network website provides information on different business forms and government requirements for registration.

The Importance of Choosing a Business Form

There are many reasons why you, as a business person, should understand the legal alternatives available for structuring your business. Choosing the most suitable business form will have a major impact on the smooth operation of your enterprise.

- *Business forms clarify your legal relationships with colleagues and co-workers.* Whether you choose to work alone and engage people to help you on an as-needed basis, to work with a group of trusted colleagues who share the financial burden of your business's ups and downs, or to establish a multinational business empire, the type of business form you adopt dictates the legal roles of all the participants in your enterprise. If you are a director of a private corporation, for example, your rights and responsibilities in relation to the business's officers, managers, and shareholders are defined in detail in statutes and the common law.
- *Choosing the appropriate business form can strike the right balance between the need for simplicity and the need to limit your potential liability.* Your choice allows you to assume, share, or relinquish personal responsibility for your business's liabilities. As a sole proprietor, for example, you assume unlimited liability for your business. On the other hand, as a shareholder in a corporation, your personal assets are generally safe from your business's creditors.
- *Choosing the appropriate business form can help you plan for the future.* Your choice can assist you in planning and implementing future expansions or other modifications of your business. For example, you could incorporate a private company in anticipation of becoming a public company some day.
- *Your choice of business form will affect the amount of professional assistance that is required.* The different legal requirements of business forms will determine whether, and how often, you need to engage the professional assistance of lawyers or accountants, for example.

SCENARIO

To better analyze the form of business that would best meet the needs of Val-Nam, we will quickly review the business's key participants and their interest in the business:

- Valery Garza developed the initial concept for the business and the underlying invention. She wants to be involved in all aspects of the business as it is her "baby."
- Namid Blackburn contributed to the improved efficiency of the underlying invention. His primary interest is continued research and development. He is less

interested in the management side of the business but does want an ownership interest. He requires a steady income as he has a young family.

- Mitchell Wu commercialized the invention (he developed the generator that can be used by consumers). He is involved in a number of different business ventures based on his own inventions. He is interested in helping manage and develop this business and is also interested in investing in the business.
- Angelic Battiste is a wealthy "angel investor," providing start-ups with an initial infusion of capital. She is particularly interested in start-ups developing green technology that could have applications in remote communities.

Sole Proprietorships

sole proprietorship form of carrying on business whereby one person owns and operates the business, with no legal separation between the owner and the business

The **sole proprietorship** is the most basic form of carrying on business. As its name suggests, a single (sole) person owns and operates the business (as its proprietor). There is no legal separation between the owner and the business. The owner is the business, and the business is the owner.

There are thousands of these kinds of businesses across Canada because they are easy to set up, easy to run, and do not involve a great deal of interaction with the government. Your local variety store, the car repair shop up the street, and your favourite neighbourhood restaurant may all be examples of sole proprietorships.

Creation

A sole proprietorship is created as soon as someone opens a business that interacts with the public. For example, if Valery starts selling the portable generators at local agricultural fairs, she becomes a sole proprietor. If the sign she posts on the display at the fairs merely gives her name and adds a title such as "Merchant," she is able to carry on business with minimal legal requirements.

However, if she wishes to use a name for her business other than her own name, she must register that name under the *Business Names Act* in Ontario (or similar legislation in other provinces). If, for example, she decides to call her business "Going Green Generators," she must register that name with the government. This registration requirement exists to ensure that members of the public who interact with the business will know whom to take legal action against if problems arise. If, for example, a purchaser is injured when a generator malfunctions, he can search the government database for Going Green Generators and find Valery's name, as the owner/proprietor. The purchaser will then be able to file a lawsuit against her.

Registering the name of a sole proprietorship involves filling out the appropriate form, paying the required fee (usually less than $100), and submitting both to the appropriate provincial government office. The form includes the name and address of the sole proprietor and the name and address of the business. Failure to register a business name in Ontario may result in a fine of up to $2,000 and also limits the business's ability to maintain a court action until the name is registered.

Although Valery is not required to demonstrate that the name chosen for the business is not confusing with other businesses' names before registering it, she may be liable for damages if it turns out that the name is confused with that of another business and that business suffers harm as a result of the confusion. It is worth noting that registering the business name may not sufficiently protect Valery against others using it. If she wants to prevent a competing business from using the name Going Green Generators, she should consider registering it as a trademark under the *Trade-marks Act*. We discuss this matter in greater detail in Chapter 10.

Legal Characteristics

A sole proprietorship has no legal existence apart from its owner. It therefore cannot, on its own, sue another individual or business, nor can it be sued on its own. The owner—in this case, Valery—is the legal entity that must sue on behalf of the business or that will be sued for the misdeeds of the business.

A sole proprietorship cannot enter into contracts; rather, Valery will enter into contracts on its behalf and is responsible for fulfilling any contractual obligations related to the business. It does not file its own income tax return; instead, Valery will claim income derived from the business and deduct business expenses on her personal tax return.

Conducting Business

In most cases, sole proprietorships are small businesses with few or no employees. They usually operate from a single location (possibly home-based) and offer a limited number of products or services. Many Internet-based businesses are sole proprietorships.

A sole proprietor runs their business on their own or with the help of friends or family members who may or may not be formally paid. Valery could run Going Green Generators and contract with Namid and Mitchell as employees or independent contractors of the business. She could borrow funds from Angelic to help with start-up costs. She might also employ two or three people to help as salespeople. If her business has expanded to that level, she would likely also employ a bookkeeper to maintain her financial records, ensure her taxes are paid and collected, handle her payroll obligations, and pay her suppliers.

Advantages and Disadvantages

Cost, Complexity, and Control

Simplicity is the key advantage of carrying on business as a sole proprietorship. Other than registering her business name with the provincial government (and obtaining business and other licences that the municipality may require for a particular type of operation), Valery has no other requirements to fulfill. She can decide to open the business and be up and running almost immediately.

Valery can make important decisions about the business easily, without changing documentation, obtaining approvals, or consulting others. Therefore, if selling generators does not work out and Valery decides to develop and sell a totally different product, she can do so almost immediately—without having to convince partners, corporate directors, or shareholders that it is a good idea, and without having to revise partnership agreements, articles of incorporation, or other documents.

However, while complete control over business decisions is an advantage to Valery, a sole proprietorship does not account for the extent that Namid and/or Mitchell would like to have a say in the direction the business takes and other important business decisions. Namid and Mitchell may not want to be relegated to roles as employees or independent contractors in a venture that they helped create.

Participation in Profits

As the sole proprietor, Valery will reap the financial benefits (and bear the losses) of the business's successes (or failures). All profits accrue to Valery directly and she alone can decide how to use those profits, whether for her own personal use or to invest back into the business. Namid and Mitchell, as employees or independent contractors, will be paid for their services under an employment contract or other form of service contract. They will not have a right to participate in the profits generated by the business.[1] Again, given that we know both are interested in developing the business and participating in its success (profits), this form of business may not meet their needs.

Tax Implications

The Canada Revenue Agency treats a sole proprietorship as a source of income (or business loss) for its owner. Any profit (income minus legitimate expenses) the business earns is added to any of Valery's other income. Also, business losses can be set off against her income from other sources in order to reduce tax.

As a sole proprietor, Valery will submit her business income and expense information with her personal income tax return. She is required to file a schedule of the income and expenses of the business and to add the net income of the business to her income from all other sources. In other words, the tax department treats income from the sole proprietorship as simply another source of Valery's personal income, along with income from employment, rental property, or investments.

Like other forms of business, a sole proprietorship allows Valery, as owner, to employ people, including members of her family. This can work as an income-splitting arrangement, giving Valery an opportunity to save tax by diverting income from her pocket to that of a family member who pays tax at a lower rate than she does (provided reasonable services are in fact exchanged for the income). In this manner, the business income stays in Valery's family and may be subject to lower tax rates. Note, however, that Valery cannot employ herself in the business. An employment contract cannot be formed unless two separate legal entities are involved (for further discussion of contract formation, see Chapter 5). Because a sole proprietorship does not have a separate existence from its owner, Valery would in effect be entering into a contract with herself, which is not legally possible.

Liability

The main disadvantage of choosing to operate a business as a sole proprietorship is the legal liability of the owner. Because Valery and the business are one in the eyes of the law, Valery is legally liable for any injury (whether physical or financial) that

---

1 Or, if their contract with the sole proprietorship provides for payment of a share of the profits to them, they may be deemed by law to be partners in a partnership and not employees or independent contractors of a sole proprietorship. See the discussion of partnerships later in this chapter.

the business may cause to others. This means that Valery is personally subject to **unlimited liability**.

unlimited liability
full responsibility for any debt incurred or loss caused by a business

As a result, if a purchaser is burned by a malfunctioning generator, he may sue Valery directly for damages. Because the sole proprietorship is unable to enter into contracts, Valery, as owner, becomes responsible for all contractual obligations of the business and personally liable for any breaches of contract. If Going Green Generators fails to pay its suppliers, Valery is personally liable for paying the full amount owing. A creditor can force Valery to sell her personal assets (such as her house and investments) to meet the obligations of the business. And, if Going Green Generators goes into bankruptcy, it takes Valery with it.

However, in contrast, Namid and Mitchell will not be personally liable for the business if this business form is chosen. This protection from liability may be of interest to Namid and Mitchell.

Considerations Concerning Expansion

Only one person can own a sole proprietorship. If Namid or Mitchell wants to participate in the ownership of the business, it will not be possible to start the business as a sole proprietorship. For this reason, a sole proprietorship would probably not be the best choice for the business.

The fact that only one person can own a sole proprietorship has implications for how the business can be financed. Where a business form allows for others to invest in the business through an ownership interest, that business will be able to raise capital through both equity investment and debt. When a sole proprietorship is the business form, it is only able to raise capital through debt. If Angelic were to provide financial support for the business running as a sole proprietorship, she could loan the business money but could not purchase an ownership interest in the business. For additional information on financing a business, see Chapter 8.

www.emond.ca/CBL3/links

DIG DEEPER
The business services page on the ServiceOntario website provides forms and information related to registering a business name as well as other legal compliance reporting.

Even if Valery did start the business as the sole owner and initially used a sole proprietorship for the form of business, she may wish to bring other individuals in as co-owners later—if the business expands significantly, or if it requires a significant infusion of money to continue to operate or to expand. To do this, it would be necessary to convert the business to a structure other than a sole proprietorship: either a partnership or a corporation.

MINIMIZING YOUR RISK

Equip Your Sole Proprietorship for Doing Business

- If you wish to use a business name other than your own name, register it to avoid fines.
- Obtain all licences your municipality requires for operating your type of business.
- Collect and pay all applicable taxes.
- Carry sufficient insurance to cover claims against your business, remembering that a claim against your business is a claim against you.
- Hire a bookkeeper if the complexity of your business (or your personal lack of record-keeping skills) warrants it.
- Prior to starting the business, consider transferring personal assets, such as your home or cottage, to the name of a trusted relative to protect them against creditors.

Introduction to Partnerships

partnership (or firm) form of carrying on business whereby two or more persons operate a business, with no legal separation between the owners and the business

A **partnership (or firm)** is defined in the Ontario *Partnerships Act* as "the relation that subsists between persons carrying on a business in common with a view to profit" but not within a corporate structure. Partners often join together to conduct a business in a manner that is efficient and effective for all of them. Groups of professionals who join together to offer their services to the public, such as lawyers, accountants, and dentists, often use partnerships as a means of carrying on business.

partnership agreement contract signed by all partners that sets out how the partnership will operate and how it will end

Partners have the right to organize their affairs and to determine their rights and obligations within the partnership by way of a partnership agreement. However, a partnership agreement is not mandatory for most partnerships, and where there is no partnership agreement, the relationship will be governed by the relevant provincial partnership act and the common law. A **partnership agreement** is a document signed by all partners that sets out the basic terms of how the business will operate. Some agreements are very simple; others are extremely complex. Many partnership agreements include terms setting out how individual partners may choose (or be required) to leave the partnership, what happens if the partnership ceases to operate, and other important end-of-relationship issues. We discuss these agreements in greater detail later in this chapter under the heading "Partnership Agreements."

Partnerships, like sole proprietorships, are not legally independent from the people who compose them. Partners may be liable for the conduct of other partners. The extent of this liability depends on the nature of the partnership and the terms of whatever partnership agreements the partners have entered into.

In Ontario, partnerships are governed primarily by the *Partnerships Act* and the *Limited Partnerships Act*, which lay out the general requirements of this form of business. The partners can be individuals, corporations, or other partnerships. Generally, a partnership exists where the partners agree to

- pool their capital for a common purpose, that is, running the business;
- share in the profit or loss of the business;
- make decisions and manage the business together;
- exercise authority to bind the partnership to contracts with third parties; and
- share liability.

The three types of partnerships in Canada, which are distinguished by how liability and other responsibilities are shared between the partners, are:

1. the general partnership,
2. the limited partnership, and
3. the limited liability partnership.

This chapter explores each type of partnership separately. Table 7.1 later in the chapter summarizes and compares key aspects of all three types.

General Partnership

The general partnership is the most common form of partnership in Canada. However, limited liability partnerships—recognized in Ontario for the first time in 1998—have become increasingly popular.

Creation

A **general partnership** is created when two or more individuals come together to run an unincorporated business. If Valery, Namid, and Mitchell, together, begin to produce and sell generators to the public and they share in the profits/losses from the production and sales, they will be deemed to be operating a business as a partnership. If no agreement is registered with the appropriate government office specifying that the partnership is a limited partnership or a limited liability partnership, the law assumes that the parties have created a general partnership.

general partnership partnership that is not registered with the government as a limited or limited liability partnership

Valery, Namid, and Mitchell could enter into a partnership agreement that sets out the terms of the relationship among them as partners. If they do not do this, they will equally share responsibility for the business, make decisions on the operation of the business together, and share the profits and losses equally. As noted above, without a partnership agreement, the terms of the relevant provincial partnership act will govern the relationship.

The name of a general partnership is often simply the combined names of the individual partners—for example, Garza, Blackburn, and Wu. However, more inventive names, such as Going Green Generators or coined names like Val-Nam Generation (taken from the first three letters of Valery's and Namid's names), can be used as well. As with sole proprietorships, the name of a partnership must be registered under the *Business Names Act* if it operates under a business name that is different from the names of the partners.

Legal Characteristics

A general partnership, like any other kind of partnership, is not an independent legal entity. It cannot, therefore, enter into legally binding contracts or protect its owners (the partners—Valery, Namid, and Mitchell) from legal liabilities for injuries (either physical or financial) caused by the firm.

joint and several liability financial responsibility requiring all parties to contribute equally, but also making each party responsible for the entire amount owed

As a result, the individual partners in a general partnership have **joint and several liability** for the actions of the firm. This means that they divide liability equally (subject to a partnership agreement) and are also each entirely liable for the firm's actions (see Figure 7.1). Therefore, if a purchaser is injured using the generator,

Figure 7.1 Joint and Several Liability

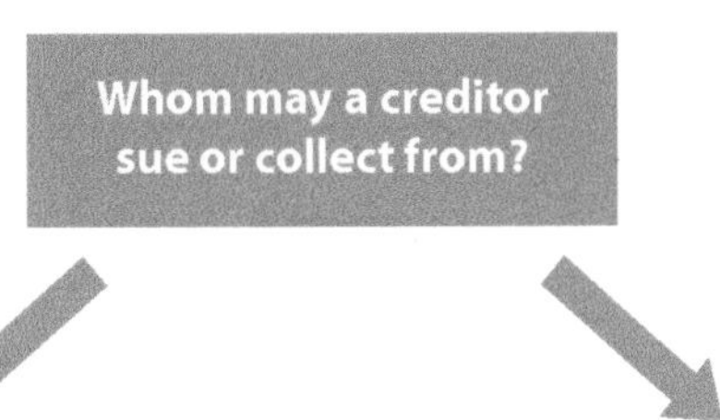
Whom may a creditor sue or collect from?

Joint

A creditor may sue or collect from all partners for a partnership debt. They will contribute equally or as set out in the partnership agreement.

Several

A creditor may sue or collect from one or some of the partners for a partnerhsip debt if the other partners are unable to pay. Partners who have paid the debt can then attempt to obtain reimbursement from the non-paying partner for that partner's share.

and a court orders the firm to make a compensatory payment to the purchaser, Valery, Namid, and Mitchell are each responsible for contributing an equal share of the payment (or their share in accordance with the partnership agreement). If, however, Mitchell is unable to pay his share, the others must make up the difference, because each is individually responsible for paying the entire amount.[2] In seeking a compensatory payment, the purchaser can sue the business in the firm name. Each partner can also be sued individually, but this is not necessary as the provincial rules of court provide for a process to allow plaintiffs to collect against the partners when only the firm is named as a defendant.

If Valery, Namid, and Mitchell decide to run the business as a general partnership, each may be liable for the others' conduct, so long as they are acting in the normal course of the partnership's business. The law views Valery as representing—or as acting as an agent for—both the firm and each partner (Namid and Mitchell) individually. The same is true for how the law views Namid and Mitchell. (We discuss the concept of agency later in this chapter.) As a result, if Valery makes a serious error that harms a customer, both Namid and Mitchell could be legally responsible for compensating the customer for all losses that result from the error.

As in the case of a sole proprietorship, each partner may be liable to the full extent of their personal assets for all debts and other obligations of the partnership. This means Valery, Namid, and Mitchell could lose their homes, their investments, and all their savings if any partner in the firm makes a costly error. It is this effect that most contributed to the creation of the limited liability partnership, which we discuss below.

CASE IN POINT

Know Your Partner

Ernst & Young Inc v Falconi, 1994 CanLII 7237 (Ont Ct (Gen Div))

Facts

Falconi was a lawyer in partnership with Klein. Falconi helped certain clients hide assets from creditors. The trustee in bankruptcy (acting on behalf of the clients' creditors) obtained judgment against Falconi, based on his participation in the fraud. The trustee then went after Falconi's partner, Klein, who was not involved in the fraud.

Result

The law firm was not in the business of committing fraud; however, Klein was held jointly liable. The court concluded that helping clients transfer assets was within the normal scope of the law firm's business, and the fact that it was done fraudulently in this case did not absolve the innocent partner of liability.

Business Lesson

You will pay for your partner's mistakes. Do not enter into a partnership lightly. Keep abreast of your partner's business activities. Make sure your business dealings with partners are transparent.

Conducting Business

In a general partnership, all partners are equal (subject, of course, to the terms of any partnership agreement). Each of Valery, Namid, and Mitchell has equal power

2 Valery and Namid will then be able to sue Mitchell for his missing contribution.

and equal responsibility. The partners generally reach decisions through informal or formal discussion and agreement. Business income is usually used first to pay the expenses of the partnership. It is then allocated to any long-term planning projects the partnership may have, and the rest is then divided among the partners. Unless a partnership agreement provides otherwise, profits of the business are divided equally.

Depending on the size of the partnership—some can become huge enterprises—decisions about the day-to-day operations of the firm may be made by all the partners or by a small group of partners specifically chosen to make these decisions.

In a three-person firm, for example, the partners would typically discuss day-to-day, and even major, decisions affecting the firm over their morning coffee or over lunch. In a firm with 400 partners, however, a representative group of, say, five partners would make day-to-day decisions, and similar committees would make more specialized decisions—for example, decisions about the firm's computer resources, the hiring and firing of support staff, and the allocation of profits.

Advantages and Disadvantages

Cost, Complexity, and Control

As noted above, as soon as two or more persons begin to carry on a business in common with a view to profit, a general partnership is created. No forms must be filed or fees paid before the law will recognize the creation of a general partnership. The relevant provincial partnerships act and the common law will establish the terms of a general partnership created in this manner. However, it is rare that partners are satisfied with these "default" provisions and often experts, including lawyers and accountants, are engaged to ensure the partnership is structured in a way that reflects how the partners wish to operate. The creation of a partnership agreement that reflects this will add to the cost and complexity of the structure.

However, the fact that a partnership agreement can be flexible and can reflect different interests, power, and liabilities of the partners is of value. Valery, Namid, and Mitchell could agree that business decisions must be made unanimously or that agreement by two of the three partners can result in binding decisions. Valery could be granted a higher percentage of any profits (and losses) and, in return, accept a higher degree of liability for the obligations of the partnership, protecting Namid and Mitchell to some degree. Each partner can negotiate agreement terms that best represent how they would like to contribute to the business and the degree of risk that they are able to assume.

The general partnership has the advantage of simplicity when smaller groups of people choose to work together. A general partnership is for the most part inexpensive, easy to set up, and easy to run. As long as it remains small, its operations can be flexible.

Participation in Profits

A sole proprietorship has only one owner, and only the owner has the right to participate in the profits of the business. A general partnership allows the business to have more than one owner and to add owners as there is a need for additional capital. Each owner will have a right to participate in the profits of the business in accordance with the terms of the partnership agreement or, if there is no agreement, they will participate equally in the profits. Thus, a general partnership will allow Valery, Namid, and Mitchell to all participate in the profits of the business.

Tax Implications

Like the sole proprietorship, business profits of the partnership become part of the personal income of its owners—the partners (Valery, Namid, and Mitchell)—for the purpose of income tax. The firm keeps accounts of its income and expenses in order to calculate its annual profit (or loss). The profit (or loss) is then apportioned to each partner either equally or otherwise in accordance with the terms of the partnership agreement. Each partner then includes their share of the firm's profits as business income in their personal tax returns.

Given that Mitchell has income from a number of other ventures, he may want to be able to take a portion of the losses from this new business to offset income from his other ventures. If the business is run as a sole proprietorship, with Valery as the sole proprietor, this would not be possible. A general partnership structure provides this benefit to Mitchell.

Liability

Not surprisingly, the biggest disadvantage of the general partnership is unlimited liability. Valery, Namid, and Mitchell will each be personally liable for the debts and obligations of the firm. If the firm cannot pay its employees or its bills, the individual partners must do so. If a purchaser slips and falls in the firm's sales office, the individual partners may be liable for the purchaser's injuries. Each partner's liability is limitless, which means that each partner will have to honour the firm's obligations until all personal assets are depleted.[3]

This liability exists even if the firm is sued as a result of a single partner's error. In this regard, every partner acts as a sort of insurer for the mistakes of the others.

Limitless liability may be less of a concern in a three-person firm, where the partners trust and are able to monitor one another, than in a larger firm. Of course, the larger the firm, the more partners there are to share the cost of mistakes.

Considerations Concerning the Pooling of Resources

One of the greatest advantages to Valery, Namid, and Mitchell of carrying on business as a partnership is that they can work together—they can draw on each other's expertise, share expenses (like the cost of manufacturing space, research and development, and marketing), and pool their individual capital. "Economies of scale" increase as the firm grows larger. With these financial savings, the firm may also be able to offer its clients lower prices for its services while still maintaining an adequate profit margin.

In addition, the three friends working in partnership might be able to pursue and attract large clients whose needs are beyond the capacity of one of them working alone or to develop products beyond the expertise of only one of them.

---

3 Note that a partnership agreement may specify that one partner will be responsible for a higher percentage of liability (perhaps Valery will agree to assume 50 percent of the firm's liabilities in exchange for a higher percentage of the profits and Mitchell and Namid will assume 25 percent each). This agreement is valid among the partners (Mitchell could sue Valery for contribution if he paid more than his specified share of the partnership debt) but will not change the liability that the partner has to third-party creditors. The partner remains jointly and severally liable to third parties for the full amount of the debt but will then be able to sue the other partners for the return of any overpayment based on the terms of the partnership agreement.

Each partner has different strengths—personal, financial, and professional—that they can pool to better provide service to their clients and better develop the business. Each partner also has the comfort of knowing that the other partners are there for support when he or she is obliged to deal with—and pay for—problems. Beyond this, the flexibility of the partnership structure can allow for the addition of new partners should there be a need to add resources, whether they be managerial, financial, or product related.

MINIMIZING YOUR RISK

Choose Your Partners Carefully

- Know the people with whom you enter a partnership.
- Ensure that their personal ethics, professional abilities, and styles of doing business are similar to your own.
- Register your partnership's name if it differs from the personal names of the individual partners.
- Carry sufficient insurance to cover liabilities that may arise in the course of doing business.
- Create a partnership agreement to ensure that your expectations and those of your partners are the same.

Limited Partnership

A **limited partnership** has one or more general partners and one or more limited partners. The limited partners provide the firm with money and other property (but not services) in exchange for a share in any profits. The main purpose of a limited partnership is to provide a method for the partnership to raise capital.

limited partnership partnership composed of a minimum of one general partner and one limited partner who provides money or property to the firm and shares in the profits, but who does not participate in the business affairs of the firm and whose liability is limited to exclude any personal assets

As their name suggests, limited partners are limited in their level of participation in the firm. Their names generally cannot be included in the name of the firm and they cannot take part in the management of the firm, but their liability for the firm's obligations is also limited. If the firm accumulates debts or is sued, the only thing a limited partner can lose is their investment in the firm and any profits to which they might be or might become entitled. Their personal assets are not at risk. Given this, Angelic may be interested in becoming a limited partner as it allows her to invest in the firm without attracting unlimited liability.

The general partners, meanwhile, have the same rights, responsibilities, and liabilities as the partners in a general partnership. They operate the firm, take profits from the firm, and are liable for the debts and obligations of the firm. Their liability is, once again, limitless. Because Valery and Mitchell are interested in taking part in the management of the firm, they would have to be general partners in a limited partnership. As Namid is *not* interested in taking part in the management of the firm, he may prefer to be a limited partner if this form of business is used.

Creation

Unlike a general partnership, which can form without any government involvement, a limited partnership is formed when a partnership declaration is filed under a provincial limited partnership statute—in Ontario, the *Limited Partnerships Act*.

The declaration must include basic information, such as the names and contact information of all general and limited partners.

Legal Characteristics

Like all partnerships, a limited partnership is not a separate legal entity. It is not separate from the partners. The general partners operate and sign on its behalf; they are personally liable for its debts and obligations in an unlimited fashion. Valery and Mitchell will be exposed to unlimited personal liability for the debts and obligations of the business. As limited partners, Namid and Angelic's liability is limited to their investment in the firm and their share of the firm's profits.

The law views all general partners as agents of the firm with the legal authority to bind the firm and all its general partners to an agreement with third parties such as suppliers and customers. Provided that a partner is acting in the normal course of the partnership's business, third parties can generally rely on their reasonable belief that a general partner has this authority.

Limited partners may also be agents in circumstances described in the partnership agreement. However, if a limited partner takes on a managerial role with respect to the partnership's business, they risk losing their "limited" status and open themselves up to the liability of a general partner. This may be a risk for Namid if, in the course of his active involvement in the firm, he begins to provide advice and direction on the management and development of the business.

Conducting Business

A limited partnership usually conducts its business in the same manner as a general partnership of similar size and focus. As mentioned above, the limited partners may not take part in the management of the firm without risking the loss of their protected status.

A limited partner may require the return of their investment in the firm under certain circumstances. These circumstances are set out in the governing statute or in the partnership agreement. If the firm is unwilling or unable to return the limited partner's investment as required, the limited partner could force the firm to dissolve and distribute its assets.

Advantages and Disadvantages

Cost, Complexity, and Control

The limited partnership is a more complex business structure than the general partnership, and it requires more documentation. For example, the *Limited Partnerships Act* in Ontario requires that a current record of the limited partners be kept on the premises and be made available for inspection by the public. This record includes names and contact information of all limited partners and the amount of money or value of property contributed to the partnership by each limited partner.

A carefully drafted partnership agreement—though a significant business expense when drafted by a lawyer—is particularly important in outlining the obligations and rights of both types of partners. All partners must be careful to follow the rules applicable to their roles in the firm—that is, general partners must adhere to the rules relating to general partners, and limited partners must adhere to the rules relating to limited partners. A limited partner who steps over the boundaries of their role, as described in the partnership agreement or *Limited Partnerships Act*, runs the risk of losing the protection of their limited partner status and gaining the liabilities of a general partner.

Participation in Profits

As with a general partnership, each general and limited partner will have the right to participate in the profits of the business in accordance with the limited partnership agreement, if there is one, or the relevant provincial limited partnerships statute.

Tax Implications

The tax implications for a limited partnership are basically the same as for a general partnership. Each partner's share of the profits is combined with that partner's other income in calculating taxes.

Liability

As discussed above, the general partners have unlimited liability for the debts and obligations of the partnership. The liability of the limited partner is usually limited to their investment in the firm.

Considerations Concerning Financing

A limited partnership has many of the advantages of a general partnership. It has the additional advantage of allowing people to become involved in the business without assuming the risks or responsibilities of a full general partner. This increases the firm's ability to attract investors, or "silent partners," as an inexpensive and low-risk method of obtaining capital. While individuals can provide financing for a partnership through loans and not attract personal liability for the obligations of the partnership, the ability to invest and participate in the profits/losses of the firm as a limited partner is often a more attractive option.

Attracting investment from limited partners also reduces the financial risk of the general partners. For example, if Val-Nam as a limited partnership borrows money to finance the purchase of a new manufacturing plant and the business fails, Valery and Mitchell will be personally liable for the unpaid loan. However, if the purchase is financed through investment by Angelic and Namid as limited partners, and the business fails, Angelic and Namid are entitled to the return of their investment only to the extent that the assets of the business can cover it. Valery and Mitchell will not be personally liable for any shortfall.

MINIMIZING YOUR RISK

Consider Taking On a Silent Partner If You Need to Raise Capital

- Before raising capital on riskier terms, weigh the advantages of taking on a limited partner to finance your business operations.
- If you are a limited partner, be careful not to jeopardize your status by assuming management responsibilities.
- File a limited partnership declaration that includes all the information required by the *Limited Partnerships Act*.

- Maintain records and make them available for inspection as required by the *Limited Partnerships Act*.
- Clarify the rights and obligations of all partners in a limited partnership agreement.
- Define the circumstances under which a limited partner expects the return of their investment in the limited partnership agreement.

Limited Liability Partnership

limited liability partnership (LLP) partnership composed of partners in certain professions, such as lawyers and accountants, who have the same liabilities as those in a general partnership except that partners are not liable for the professional negligence of other partners or employees supervised by other partners

The **limited liability partnership (LLP)** is the newest type of partnership in Canada, available only to certain professionals (such as lawyers and chartered accountants) whose governing bodies allow their members to use the limited liability option. It is designed to offer the flexibility and simplicity of a general partnership while avoiding the disadvantage of unlimited liability for all partners. In essence, it is a midway point between a general partnership and a corporation in terms of liability.

Valery, Namid, Mitchell, and Angelic are not able to use an LLP for their business as they will not be carrying on business in one of the qualifying professions.

Creation

A limited liability partnership is created in Ontario when two or more people enter into a written partnership agreement that designates the partnership as an LLP and states that the *Partnerships Act* governs the agreement. An LLP must also register its name under the *Business Names Act* before it may legally conduct business.

Legal Characteristics

The legal characteristics of the LLP are similar to those of a general partnership, with one crucial difference: in an LLP, a partner is *not* liable for the professional negligence of the other partners. Therefore, if a lawyer provides negligent advice to a client resulting in financial harm to the client, the other lawyers in the firm will not be liable. This limitation on liability is not only in respect of negligent acts or omissions of other partners in the firm, but also of any person who is under the control and supervision of other partners of the firm, such as an associate lawyer or law clerk.

A partner in a limited liability partnership is liable only for the following:

- the general debts and obligations of the firm that do not arise from negligent acts or omissions (for example, unpaid loans made to the partnership, unpaid supplier bills); and
- the debts and obligations that arise from the partner's own negligent acts or omissions or the negligent acts or omissions of any person (employee, agent, or representative) who is under that partner's direct control and supervision.

Conducting Business

LLPs conduct their business in the same manner that general partnerships of similar size and focus conduct their business. The firm must, however, include the words "limited liability partnership" or the initials "LLP" in its name.

Advantages and Disadvantages

Cost, Complexity, and Control

The LLP offers greater simplicity than the corporation, which we discuss at length below. Further, the LLP offers professionals at least some of the protection from personal liability that the corporation offers.

In order for an LLP to be created, there *must* be a written limited liability partnership agreement and its name *must* be registered. This adds to the complexity and cost of creating this business form. However, the relationship among the limited liability partners can be customized in a manner that reflects the different degree of control over the business that partners may desire.

Tax Implications

The tax implications for a limited liability partnership are substantially the same as for a general partnership and a limited partnership.

Liability

As mentioned above, each partner in an LLP is liable for the general debts and obligations of the firm and for their own professional negligence. However, each partner is protected from liability for the negligence of the other partners in the firm.

Table 7.1 Comparison of the Three Types of Partnerships

	General Partnership	Limited Partnership	Limited Liability Partnership
Typical example	Two friends go into business together; they share capital costs, debts, work, profit, and liability.	A sole proprietor needs capital and finds investors who become limited partners; they provide capital, share losses, and are entitled to profit, but they do not manage the business and have limited liability. The sole proprietor becomes a general partner.	A group of accountants form a partnership; they share capital costs, debts, work, and profit; and they are not liable for one another's professional negligence.
Liability	All partners are jointly and severally liable for each other's debts and negligence, including professional negligence. Liability is unlimited.	At least one general partner must be fully liable for the debts of the firm and any negligence of the other partners. Liability of general partners is limitless. Limited partners are liable for the debts of the firm and any negligence of the other partners only to the extent provided in the partnership agreement (usually to the extent of their capital investment).	Limited liability partners are liable only for the general debts of the firm and their own professional negligence and not for the professional negligence of the other partners.

(The table is concluded on the next page.)

Table 7.1 Concluded

	General Partnership	Limited Partnership	Limited Liability Partnership
Decision-making and profit taking	Partners often make decisions and share profit equally. A partnership agreement may provide that some partners have more decision-making power and are entitled to more profit (usually because of a larger initial investment) than others.	The general partners will manage the business and make business decisions. Limited partners have no decision-making powers. If they become involved in business decisions, they risk losing their status as limited partners and could become liable as general partners. General and limited partners are entitled to profit according to the terms of the partnership agreement.	Limited liability partners may have decision-making powers and are entitled to profit according to the terms of the partnership agreement.

Partnership Agreements

A partnership agreement is the contract on which a partnership is founded. It is enforceable through the courts by any of the parties who sign it. With the exception of LLPs, which require a partnership agreement, other partnerships may operate without an agreement, in which case the terms of the *Partnerships Act* or the *Limited Partnerships Act*, as applicable, govern the operation and dissolution of the partnership. However, it is generally unwise to rely on the Acts: they are not comprehensive, and the partners are in a better position than the government to tailor their agreement to their circumstances and the needs of their business.

A partnership agreement allows the members of a partnership—at the beginning of their business relationship, when goodwill is strong among them—to come to an agreement on all issues that are relevant to their business. This includes day-to-day management and more potentially contentious issues that may cause problems for the business in the future.

The business's lawyer usually drafts the partnership agreement. In many cases, individual partners obtain independent legal advice before signing the agreement. Once signed, the agreement governs how the business will operate, how disputes will be resolved, and, if necessary, how the partnership will come to an end. The following are some of the matters that a comprehensive partnership agreement usually covers:

- *financial matters*, such as bank accounts, signing authority for cheques and other documents, accountants and auditors, and borrowing privileges and limits;
- *compensation matters*, such as division of profits, allocation of vacation time, and provisions governing illnesses;
- *business matters*, including scope of and limits on the firm's areas of business;
- *management matters*, such as responsibility for hiring and managing employees, property management, or management of inventory and receivables;
- *membership*, such as adding new partners and removing existing ones; and
- *dissolution of the partnership*, with or without the consent of all partners.

Agreements can be amended from time to time as the needs of the partnership change. An amendment process that is satisfactory to the partners can be included in the agreement itself.

A well-drafted partnership (or limited partnership) agreement can allow Valery, Namid, Mitchell, and Angelic to create a business relationship that reflects their different skills, contributions, interests, responsibilities, and appetites for risk. But for their business, choosing a partnership as the business form will require at least one of them to take on unlimited personal liability for the obligations of the business. Only the corporate form can provide limited liability to all involved.

Corporations

The creation of a **corporation** involves the birth of a distinct legal entity, one that has almost all the rights and obligations of an individual and that enjoys an existence independent of its creators. If the people who created the corporation die, the corporation continues to exist.

corporation
form of carrying on business by means of a legal entity that is distinct from its creators and enjoys almost all the rights and obligations of an individual

The subject of corporations is incredibly complex. Numerous voluminous statutes and regulations govern corporations, both at the provincial and federal level. Entire books have been written on very small areas of corporate law, and it is not possible to present more than a brief overview of the subject here.

A corporation, familiarly called a company, can be created to run almost any type of business, large or small.[4] Corporations can themselves create other corporations. They can buy or sell other businesses, enter into contracts, own property, and exert influence. They are very useful in many ways, but the complexity of their creation and operation can make them too expensive and too difficult to be useful for extremely small businesses.

We will explore the differences between private corporations and public corporations later in this chapter. These terms are no longer included in most Canadian statutes, but they are popularly used to indicate whether the company's shares are available for sale to the public. The statutes now use the term "offering corporation," or "distributing corporation," to refer to a public corporation. The shares of a **private corporation** are held by a small group of people who usually know one another, such as family members or business associates. **Public corporations** sell their shares to the public at large and are subject to a much greater degree of government regulation as a result.

private corporation
corporation whose shares are held by one person or a small group of people and are not offered to the public

public corporation
corporation whose shares are offered for sale to the public

The Players

A corporation is distinct from the people who create it, the people who own it, the people who work for it, and the people who manage and run it. We discuss the roles that people play throughout the existence of a corporation in the sections that follow. A diagram of these players appears in Figure 7.2.

As we explore the roles played by incorporators, shareholders, directors, and officers, it should be remembered that while many people may fulfill these roles in a corporation, a single individual can also fulfill all of these roles as the sole incorporator, sole shareholder, sole director, and sole officer.

4 Many professions are either prohibited from carrying on business in corporate form or must use a "professional corporation" if they incorporate. There are special rules that relate to professional corporations—in particular, the allocation of liability for professional negligence. A discussion of professional corporations is beyond the scope of this text.

Figure 7.2 Corporate Players

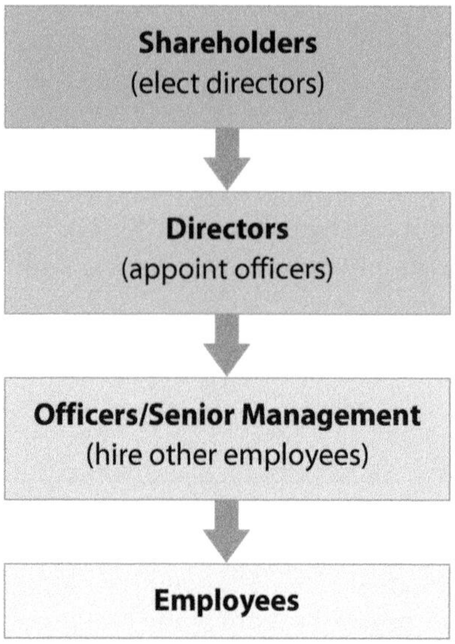

Shareholders (elect directors)
↓
Directors (appoint officers)
↓
Officers/Senior Management (hire other employees)
↓
Employees

Incorporators

incorporator
individual or other corporation that causes a corporation to come into existence by filing the required documentation

The creators of a corporation are called its incorporators. There may be one or more incorporators. An **incorporator**—who may be an individual or another corporation—completes and files the required documents, assembles the initial capital (money), and causes a corporation to come into existence and begin operations. The incorporators are likely to be the initial officers and directors of the corporation, and they are also likely to be its shareholders. The incorporators may remain a part of the corporate structure throughout the life of the corporation, or they may part ways with the corporation at some point during its existence. The corporation, in such a case, continues without them. Incorporators are not legally liable for the debts and obligations of the corporation unless they are also directors of the corporation and, even then, in only limited circumstances.

Shareholders

shareholder
owner of a corporation who shares in the profits of the business; a shareholder may be an individual or another corporation

A **shareholder** is an owner of a corporation. A shareholder may be an individual or another corporation. The vehicle of ownership is a share: by owning shares in a corporation, a shareholder owns an interest in the assets of the corporation and may have a voice in how the corporation operates. The rights of share ownership differ according to the type (class) of shares that the shareholder owns and the terms of any shareholders' agreement that may exist.

The rights of a shareholder may include the following:

- the right to vote in the election of the directors of the corporation,
- the right to share in the profits of the corporation in the form of dividends,
- the right to sell some or all of their shares to others, and
- the right to share in the assets of the corporation if it is wound up.

Where there is only one class of shares, the rights attached to those shares *must*, at a minimum, include the equal right to vote in the election of the directors of the corporation and the equal right to the remaining assets of the corporation if it is wound up.

Shareholders are guaranteed the following rights by statute:

- the right to be protected from oppressive acts of the directors or other shareholders,
- in respect of certain fundamental changes, the right to vote, and
- the right to review the corporation's records.

Shareholders are generally not liable for a corporation's debts and obligations.

Directors

A **director** of a corporation is responsible for making major decisions regarding the affairs of the corporation. The directors are the minds of the corporation. Because of this special relationship between corporations and their directors, directors owe a duty—called a **fiduciary duty**—to act honestly and in good faith with a view to the best interests of the corporation. This duty requires directors to put the corporation's interests before their own personal financial interests. Directors are also required to exercise care, diligence, and skill when carrying out their duties.

Directors are elected by shareholders and must report to shareholders at regular shareholders' meetings. Directors are generally protected against liability for the debts and obligations of the corporation, with a few exceptions, which we discuss later in this chapter under the heading "Directors' and Officers' Liability."

director
person who makes major decisions regarding the business of the corporation; the director is elected by, and accountable to, the shareholders

fiduciary duty
duty to act honestly and in good faith, with a view to the best interests of the corporation

Officers

An **officer** of a corporation is responsible for its day-to-day operation under the supervision of the directors. Officers are members of senior management and may have titles such as chief executive officer, president, chief financial officer, and chief operations officer. Like directors, officers owe a fiduciary duty to the corporation and have the duty to act with reasonable care and competence. They are also generally protected against liability for the debts and obligations of the corporation, with a few exceptions.

officer
person responsible for the day-to-day operation of a corporation; the officer is appointed by and reports to the board of directors

SCENARIO: FOR DISCUSSION

Consider which roles Valery, Namid, Mitchell, and Angelic should take in a business that is incorporated to develop, manufacture, market, and sell the generators they have invented. Who among them is likely to want to be:

- a shareholder?
- a director?
- an officer?

Given the size that the business is expected to grow to, what other types of expertise might they need? What roles would individuals with this expertise likely want to play in the corporation?

Creation

Let's assume that Valery, Namid, and Mitchell decide to incorporate their business. While all three of them could be incorporators together, they decide to ask Valery to act as the sole incorporator for the sake of simplicity. In order to create the corporation, Valery (as the incorporator) must submit an application to the appropriate government office. In Ontario, the application must include draft **articles of incorporation** and a NUANS name search report (discussed later in this chapter) if a non-numbered name will be used for the corporation. Included in the articles are:

articles of incorporation document that creates a corporation

- the name of the corporation(if a non-numbered name will be used),
- the location of the head office,
- the name(s) and address(es) of the incorporator(s),
- the number (which can be a range), name(s), and address(es) of the corporation's first director(s),
- the number (which may be unlimited) and types of shares that are to be sold,
- a statement of any restrictions placed on the rights associated with each type of share,
- a statement of the corporation's business purpose (optional), and
- the signature(s) of the incorporator(s).

Once the articles of incorporation are registered with the relevant government office, a certificate of incorporation is issued and the corporation is born!

The directors named in the articles of incorporation are responsible for "organizing" the corporation. Even though a corporation exists once its certificate of incorporation is issued, additional steps must be taken before it will be able to fully operate. These steps are completed through a series of directors' and shareholders' meetings.

When a corporation is first incorporated, it has no shareholders. So, one of the first tasks of the directors is to issue shares to those who want to be shareholders. If Valery and Mitchell are listed as the corporation's directors in the articles of incorporation, they will hold a first meeting of directors to authorize the issuance of shares and to call the first shareholders' meeting. It is likely that Valery, Namid, Mitchell, and Angelic will all want to invest in the corporation as shareholders, but they may not all wish to hold voting shares. Often, if an investor is not interested in becoming involved in the business, the investor will opt for non-voting "preferred" shares that provide a preferential higher return. Let's assume that Valery, Namid, and Mitchell are issued voting shares while Angelic and Mitchell (Mitchell makes an additional capital investment) are issued non-voting preferred shares.

At the first shareholders' meeting, the voting shareholders—Valery, Namid, and Mitchell—will then elect the directors who will manage the business going forward. These directors may be the same directors listed in the incorporation documents or they may be different. The voting shareholders may elect the directors based on the votes allocated to their shares or they may enter into a shareholders' agreement in which they agree among themselves on how they will vote their shares, effectively agreeing on how the directors will be chosen. Valery, Namid, and Mitchell may agree that they will elect Valery and Mitchell as directors and that all three will then vote freely to elect a third "outside" person as a director.[5] At the first shareholders'

5 It is often considered good governance practice to have at least some "outside" directors on the board to ensure an added perspective is brought to decision-making.

meeting, the voting shareholders will also likely appoint an accountant or auditor for the business.

Now that the directors of the corporation have been elected by its shareholders, the directors will hold a meeting to complete the organization of the corporation. The meeting may address the following issues:

- appointing officers,
- making bylaws,
- making banking arrangements,
- establishing signing authorities,
- approving a corporate seal and form of share certificate,
- authorizing significant business transactions, and
- authorizing a business plan.

Directors are required to call annual meetings of shareholders at which the shareholders will consider minutes of earlier meetings, the financial statements, and auditor's report (if any); elect directors; and appoint the auditor or accountant, as the case may be. Directors may also call "special" meetings of shareholders at any time to consider special business, which is essentially any business other than that covered by the annual meeting.

Statutes such as the *Canada Business Corporations Act* and the Ontario *Business Corporations Act* require corporations to keep corporate records, including a corporate **minute book** that keeps track of all the corporation's important papers, such as the articles of incorporation and amendments, the names and contact information for directors and shareholders, details of share transactions (when shares are issued, bought, or sold), minutes of directors' and shareholders' meetings, copies of any resolutions passed at these meetings, bylaws and amendments, and copies of any unanimous shareholders' agreements. The minute book must be kept up to date and available for review by directors, shareholders, and other interested parties.

minute book
book that holds corporate records, such as minutes of meetings

The **corporate seal** is a mechanism that was historically used by corporations to communicate their intention to be bound by a written contract. The use of the seal made it clear that it was the corporation, rather than the individuals acting on its behalf, that was binding itself to the terms of the contract. Physically, the seal is a device—usually kept with the minute book in the offices of the corporation or its legal adviser—that is used to create an imprint on paper documents. The use of a corporate seal is no longer required by many corporate statutes, such as the *Canada Business Corporations Act* and the Ontario *Business Corporations Act*, but some corporations choose to use it anyway.

corporate seal
imprint made on corporate contracts and other documents that communicates the intention to bind the corporation

A **share certificate** is a document that represents the ownership of shares in the corporation. It is signed by the officers or directors of the corporation and is given to shareholders to represent their rights within the corporation. The Ontario *Business Corporations Act* (and other business corporations legislation) severely restricts the advertisement and sale of shares in a private corporation.

share certificate
document that represents the ownership of shares of a corporation

The cost of creating and setting up a corporation is not insignificant. Valery, Namid, and Mitchell likely consulted a lawyer and an accountant during the process. They would have to pay for those services, the cost of the name search, the registration fee (about $500), and the costs of organizing the corporation. The corporation would then need to hire and pay an auditor or accountant to review the books as required by the corporation's shareholders.

It bears repeating that the corporation could have been created with a single person in all of the roles outlined above. Valery could have decided to be the sole first director and to issue shares only to herself at the outset to maintain control of the corporation. As the sole shareholder, she could also name herself as the corporation's sole director. By keeping things this simple, she could basically run the business as if she were a sole proprietor, with the exception that she would have to maintain the corporate minute book and pay corporate taxes. Namid, Mitchell, and Angelic could then interact with the corporation as employees, independent contractors, creditors (providing loans), or non-voting shareholders without affecting Valery's control of the business.

Federal or Provincial Incorporation

You can choose to file articles of incorporation with a province or with the federal government. There is no longer a significant difference in the complexity or cost of a provincial or federal incorporation. Provincial incorporation gives the corporation full legal rights only in the province of incorporation; however, a corporation may file "extraprovincial" registrations in other provinces in which it wishes to carry on business. Federal incorporation, on the other hand, gives the corporation full legal rights across Canada. This includes the right to use the corporation's name and to stop other businesses from using it.

Federal corporations are governed by the *Canada Business Corporations Act*, and provincial corporations are governed by provincial statutes, such as the *Business Corporations Act* in Ontario. The provisions of these corporate statutes are similar, but there is some variation.

Naming the Corporation

If the corporation is going to use a non-numbered name, the articles of incorporation must be accompanied by proof that the incorporators have searched the appropriate government databases to ensure that the name they propose to give the corporation is not currently being used by any other corporation in the province or across Canada. This is known as a NUANS (newly updated automated name search) report. If you propose a name that is too similar to the name of an existing business and is likely to cause confusion, the government will not accept your articles of incorporation.

Searching for the Perfect Name

It can be difficult and expensive finding an appropriate name for a new business. Before paying for a NUANS search, it is wise to conduct some free searches to see if the proposed corporate name might be confused with the name of an existing business. Using various online search engines to research your proposed name can be a "quick and dirty" way of excluding names that may be problematic. For example, consider the name suggested for Valery's sole proprietorship: "Going Green Generators." A quick search reveals the website gogreengenerators.com, for a company that provides generators and climate control equipment in New York

State. Valery thought that "EcoPlas Generation" might be a good name, but found the website ecoplastic.net, which markets a product with the registered trademark "ecoplas." While the existence of a similar name is not fatal—the similar name may not be confusing with your proposed name if it applies to a different type of business in a different geographic area, for example—it is often wise to steer clear of names that could, even in the future, be problematic. You do not want to spend years developing goodwill related to a business name only to be barred from using it when you expand to a new market (like New York) and it is deemed confusing with a business in that market.

Coined names like Val-Nam Generation tend to be unique and are less likely to cause confusion with existing business names. For this reason, it is quite common for businesses to use coined words, such as FedEx, IKEA, or PetroCan, as the distinctive elements in their names.

You can order a NUANS report for federal corporations directly from the Government of Canada, at www.nuans.com. The cost is less than $25.00 including HST. Only private businesses, called NUANS Members, can conduct provincial searches. You can find a list of members in your area on the same government website.

You will not be permitted to incorporate your business without a NUANS report unless you propose to use a numbered name (discussed below). However, you can register a business name for your sole proprietorship or partnership without a NUANS search. That said, it is still wise to verify that proposed sole proprietorship or partnership names are not confusing with other existing business names, as your business could then be subject to passing-off or trademark actions. For less than $10.00, you can search business names in Ontario and obtain a Detailed Business Names Report. This search reports only exact matches. Unlike the NUANS search, it will not report names that are similar. If your business is unincorporated, you must renew its business name registration every five years.

Instead of naming your corporation, you may accept a number issued to your corporation by the government (for example, 2873346 Ontario Inc). In this case, your corporation becomes known as a "numbered company." If, subsequent to incorporation, your numbered company decides to adopt a name, you must then obtain the NUANS report and register the name.

Once a corporation is registered with a particular name, it has the right to protect that name from being used by any other business operating where the corporation was incorporated or where the corporation has registered its name. Valery could, therefore, incorporate Val-Nam Generation in New Brunswick, register its name in Manitoba and Alberta, and then stop any other business from using that name in all three provinces. Alternatively, Valery could incorporate Val-Nam Generation federally, giving it the right to do business and to protect the business name in all Canadian provinces and territories.

The corporation must include a form of the words "corporation," "incorporated," or "limited" (or their French equivalents) in its name. These words can appear in full or abbreviated form. Valery's business might therefore be known as Val-Nam Generation Limited.

Figure 7.3 How to Create a Corporation

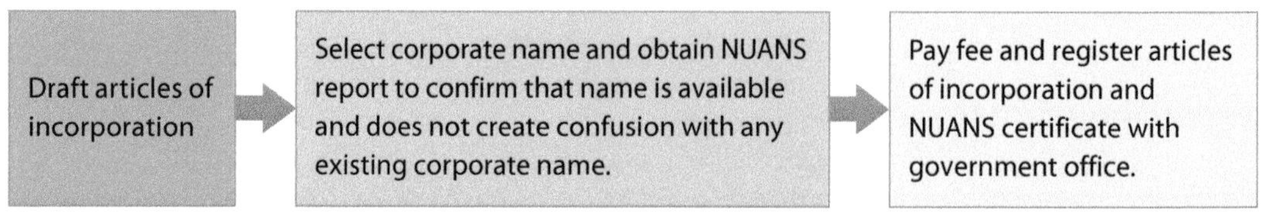
Draft articles of incorporation
Select corporate name and obtain NUANS report to confirm that name is available and does not create confusion with any existing corporate name.
Pay fee and register articles of incorporation and NUANS certificate with government office.

Figure 7.3 sets out the steps involved in the creation of any corporation.

Legal Characteristics and Liability Issues

A corporation is a distinct legal entity that has almost all the rights and obligations of an individual. A corporation can enter into and be bound by contracts; it can own property; and it can sue and be sued in its own right. A corporation exists independent of its shareholders, directors, officers, and employees.

Because a corporation is an independent legal entity, it is responsible for its own debts and obligations. Except in certain, very limited circumstances, a corporate structure protects shareholders, employees, officers, and directors from personal liability of any kind for the debts and obligations of the corporation. Whereas a sole proprietor or a general partner faces unlimited liability for the debts and obligations of their business, the shareholder, employee, officer, and director are generally protected.

This is a huge advantage. If the corporation is forced into bankruptcy for any reason (as a result of, for example, poor earnings, insurmountable debt, or losses from lawsuits), generally no asset of its shareholders, directors, officers or employees can be used to pay the debts of the corporation. The corporation fails on its own.

This principle of corporate law dates back to 1897 and the landmark case of *Salomon v A Salomon & Co Ltd*, where a court established that a corporation is a legal entity separate from its shareholders. See the Case in Point below for a discussion of this case.

However, creating a corporation is not a simple and foolproof method of protecting yourself from the debts and liabilities of your business. In the case of a small start-up business, loans from financial institutions, such as banks and trust companies, are usually needed as a source of capital. In order to approve a loan, a bank or trust company generally requires collateral. If the corporation has no assets, this means that the business people involved in the corporation must provide the financial institution with personal guarantees.

For example, Valery, Namid, and Mitchell may decide to operate through a corporation, Val-Nam Generation Limited. They anticipate that one of the benefits will be protection against liability and debts. However, to receive the bank loan of $50,000 that they need to expand research and product development, they are each required by the bank to sign a personal guarantee. Should Val-Nam Generation Limited run into financial difficulties, the bank could demand payment of the loan from each of them personally. That said, Valery, Namid, and Mitchell would still be protected from any debts and liabilities of the corporation that they did not personally guarantee (for example, payments to suppliers or arising from a lawsuit against the corporation).

CASE IN POINT

Corporations Are Separate Entities

Salomon v A Salomon & Co Ltd, [1897] AC 22 (HL)

Facts

Aron Salomon was the sole proprietor of a successful shoe manufacturing business. For the purpose of eventually transferring the business to his children, he decided to create a corporation, called A Salomon & Co Ltd, to operate his business. He issued nearly all the shares to himself, with only a very few to his wife and children, giving him complete control of all business decisions.

Aron Salomon intended to sell the shoe manufacturing business to A Salomon & Co Ltd, but the newly created company had no money. Therefore, he personally loaned the money to the company and took security over the company's assets. He was now a secured creditor of A Salomon & Co Ltd.

Labour troubles eventually led to the business becoming insolvent, and there was a dispute among the company's creditors. As a secured creditor, Aron Salomon claimed that he was entitled to repayment of his loan before the other creditors, such as suppliers, who were unsecured. This would have left nothing for the other creditors. These creditors claimed that Aron Salomon should be held personally liable for the company's debts, to the extent that the company assets were not sufficient to cover them.

Result

The (British) House of Lords held that A Salomon & Co Ltd was a legal entity separate from Aron Salomon. Therefore, Aron Salomon was not personally liable for the debts owed by the company. He was also entitled to payment of his loan ahead of the unsecured creditors from the sale of the company's assets.

Business Lesson

When seeking to limit your personal liability, a corporation may be your best choice of business structure.

Application of Charter Protections and Criminal Law to Corporations

What other implications flow from the special legal status of corporations? What treatment do corporations receive under laws such as the *Canadian Charter of Rights and Freedoms* or the *Criminal Code* that were primarily designed to apply to people? Generally, whether the special legal status of corporations entitles them to the protections of the Charter depends on the type of right or freedom under consideration. For example, freedom of expression has been interpreted as extending to corporations in the case of *Irwin Toy Ltd v Quebec (Attorney General)*, but the right to equality and the freedom of religion have been restricted to human beings.

Does criminal law apply to corporations? A corporation cannot be sent to jail for criminal acts, but governments are more and more willing to create offences (criminal offences or quasi-criminal offences such as environmental offences) for which corporations can be found guilty and punished through substantial fines. But how does a corporation commit an offence? Where an individual who is acting as an agent or employee of the corporation commits an act that constitutes an offence, the corporation may be found guilty of the offence if the individual was a "directing mind" of the corporation. This has generally been interpreted by the courts to mean that the individual has sufficient authority in the corporation to be considered its "alter ego." If a directing mind of the corporation commits an offence, the corporation is deemed to have committed the offence.

In some cases, the directors or officers of a corporation may be jailed for serious criminal offences perpetrated by the corporation where they direct the corporation to commit the offence or are personally involved in the commission of the offence.

CASE IN POINT

Charter Protections Are Limited for Corporations

Irwin Toy Ltd v Quebec (Attorney General), [1989] 1 SCR 927

Facts

Certain sections of Quebec's *Consumer Protection Act* impose restrictions on advertising to children. The Act includes various penalties, such as fines and terms of imprisonment, for those found guilty of committing an offence. Corporations can be subject only to fines under the Act, but the Act deems corporate directors to be liable and subject to imprisonment in appropriate cases.

A corporation was charged under the *Consumer Protection Act* for violations of the restricted advertising provisions. (Its individual directors were not charged.) The corporation challenged the validity of the legislation on numerous grounds, including that it offended two Charter guarantees: (1) freedom of expression and (2) the right to life, liberty, and security of the person. It argued that freedom of expression included the right of a business to advertise to children as well as adults. It also argued that the Act contained vague and uncertain provisions, and, since one of the penalties for breach of the Act was imprisonment, this gave rise to a potential deprivation of liberty in circumstances that violated principles of fundamental justice.

Result

The Supreme Court of Canada agreed that freedom of expression applied to a business's right to advertise and that the Act violated this freedom. However, it held that the limits on this freedom were justifiable because children can suffer significant harm as a result of advertising directed at them and the limitation on freedom of expression was minimal. With respect to the right to life, liberty, and security of the person, the court decided that, given the context of the Charter provision, it does not extend to artificial persons, such as corporations.

Business Lesson

The rights and freedoms guaranteed by the Charter have limits. Not all Charter provisions will apply to corporations. Even when a court is willing to protect a corporate right or freedom—such as the freedom of expression—it may find that limiting the right or freedom is justifiable to protect a larger public interest, such as the well-being of children.

Directors' and Officers' Liability

As discussed above, directors and officers owe their corporations a fiduciary duty. In addition, every director and officer of a corporation must use reasonable care, diligence, and skill in the course of carrying out their duties. This duty is a general duty of "reasonableness"; however, if a director or officer possesses special skills (for example, the person is also a lawyer), they will be expected apply those special skills in carrying out their duty. This duty of care, originating in the common law, is codified in corporate statutes such as the *Canada Business Corporations Act* and the Ontario *Business Corporations Act*.

In carrying out their duties, directors and officers must ensure that they gather the information that they need in order to make an informed decision. They must carefully assess this information and they must critically probe management's recommendations. Generally, it is not enough for a director or officer to simply say that they tried their best. However, a director who relies in good faith on a report by a professional—for example, incorrect financial statements prepared by an auditor—is not usually held liable for a breach of duty. A director is also entitled to rely on reports by officers or employees if it is reasonable to do so in the circumstances.

It should be noted that if a unanimous shareholders' agreement transfers a director's power to the shareholders, the director will no longer be responsible for the exercise of that power and therefore cannot be liable for a breach of duty related to the exercise of that power.

Directors and officers also have obligations, and are subject to liability, under legislation intended to protect the public, such as environmental protection statutes and workplace statutes that protect employees. This liability can be substantial—as high as hundreds of thousands of dollars in fines—and can even result in prison terms. Table 7.2 illustrates the statutory obligations of directors and officers under three Ontario statutes.

Most regulatory offences are strict liability offences, meaning that the Crown need not prove intent or even negligence. Once the prohibited act is proven by the Crown—for example, if it was proven that toxic chemicals were released into a river by a corporation—the onus is then on the corporation to prove that those in control did everything reasonable in the circumstances to prevent the act from occurring. This defence of **due diligence** can be supported by evidence of corporate policies and

due diligence
defence that claims a person did everything reasonable to prevent an offence from occurring

Table 7.2 Statutory Obligations of Directors and Officers

	Occupational Health and Safety Act	*Employment Standards Act, 2000*	*Environmental Protection Act*
Duty	Every director and officer of a corporation must take all reasonable care to ensure that the corporation complies with the Act, regulations, and ministerial orders made under the Act.	The directors of an employer corporation are jointly and severally liable for wages if the corporation is insolvent and certain conditions have been met.	Every director or officer of a corporation has a duty to take all reasonable care to prevent the corporation from polluting contrary to the Act, or otherwise violating the Act, regulations, or orders made under the Act.
Liability	The penalty on conviction is a fine of up to $25,000 and/or imprisonment for up to one year.	The maximum amount that directors are liable to pay is an amount equivalent to six months' wages and 12 months' vacation pay, plus interest.	Depending on the offence, the penalty on conviction may be a fine of up to $50,000 per day that the offence occurs (for first conviction) and up to $100,000 per day (for each subsequent conviction) and/or imprisonment for up to one year. Penalties for other offences include fines of up to $4 million on first conviction (increasing for subsequent convictions) and/or imprisonment for up to five years.
Defence	For certain offences, the accused may prove due diligence—that every precaution reasonable in the circumstances was taken. Those offences are strict liability offences.	There is no defence. This is an absolute liability offence.	The onus is on the accused to prove due diligence—that they took all reasonable care to prevent the offence from occurring. This is a strict liability offence.

procedures in place to prevent these events. Where a director or officer is charged personally, the director or officer will have to prove that they personally did everything reasonable in the circumstances to prevent the prohibited act from occurring.

Some statutes impose absolute liability on corporations, directors, and officers. In an absolute liability offence, there is no defence—once the prohibited act is proven by the Crown, guilt is established. *Employment Standards Act, 2000* offences include absolute liability offences.

CASE IN POINT

Officers and Directors Can Be Liable for Corporate Pollution

R v Bata Industries Ltd, 1993 CanLII 8677 (Ont Ct (Gen Div))

Facts

A storage site for containers of chemical waste at a corporation's shoe manufacturing facility had been neglected to the point that more than 200 containers, in various sizes and stages of decay, sat rusting and exposed to the elements. One of the directors, who was also president, visited the facility only twice a year, and another director visited about once a month. At some point, however, both directors had personal knowledge of the problem, but failed to take effective steps to remedy the situation.

When the corporation was convicted of causing or allowing the discharge of liquid industrial waste, the two directors were also found personally liable for failing to take "all reasonable care" under the *Ontario Water Resources Act* and the *Environmental Protection Act*. The directors were fined $12,000 each. The judge prohibited the corporation from reimbursing (indemnifying) the directors for the amounts they were required to pay in fines. The directors appealed their sentences.

Result

The court confirmed the personal liability of the directors, although it reduced their fines to $6,000 each. Environmental legislation obliges corporate officers and directors to establish a pollution prevention system. This includes being aware of industry standards, supervising the program established for the company, and reviewing environmental compliance reports submitted by other corporate officers. Although directors are entitled to place reasonable reliance on those to whom various tasks are delegated, ultimately they remain responsible for ensuring that the company complies in full with its environmental responsibilities. The standard of care expected of them varies according to their degree of personal contact with the plant and their knowledge of the environmental problems on site.

In a further appeal, the Ontario Court of Appeal struck out the prohibition order preventing the corporation from indemnifying the directors.

Business Lesson

As a director, you are ultimately responsible for ensuring your company's compliance with environmental laws. You cannot insulate yourself from liability by delegating compliance tasks to others.

Remedies for Shareholders and Others

The previous section explored how directors can be held accountable for their actions as directors of a corporation. However, there is also a range of statutory protections provided to shareholders and others that seek to ensure their fair treatment vis-à-vis the corporation. The three main remedies are the oppression remedy, appraisal rights given to minority shareholders, and derivative actions. Each is briefly described below.

Where a corporation acts in a manner that is oppressive or unfairly prejudicial to, or that unfairly disregards the interests of, a shareholder, creditor, director, or officer of the corporation, that person may apply to the court for an oppression remedy to rectify the matter. For example, if Valery and Mitchell as directors of Val-Nam vote to grant unjustified bonuses to officers of the corporation (particularly if one or more of the officers are related to Mitchell), this could prejudice Angelic's interests as a preferred shareholder. The bonuses will reduce the profits available for distribution to preferred shareholders. Although this reduces the amount of profits available to both Mitchell and Angelic, the bonuses may be a backdoor means of transferring profits to Mitchell (through his relations) without allowing Angelic to take part. In such a circumstance, Angelic may be able apply to the court for an oppression remedy.

CASE IN POINT

Oppression Remedy

Downtown Eatery (1993) Ltd v Ontario, 2001 CanLII 8538 (Ont CA)

Facts

Grad and Grosman owned and operated two nightclubs in Toronto. Alouche, who worked as a manager of one of the clubs, received his paycheque from Best Beaver, a related company controlled by Grad and Grosman. When Alouche was fired, he sued Best Beaver for wrongful dismissal. In the midst of the lawsuit, there was a major reorganization of the Grad-Grosman companies, and Best Beaver ceased to do business. Alouche was awarded $59,906.76 in damages, but was unable to collect the money from the defunct Best Beaver. Alouche sued Grad and Grosman personally, on the basis of the oppression remedy.

Result

Harm caused to the complainant by oppressive conduct need not be intentional for the oppression remedy to apply. Although the winding up of Best Beaver was not designed to deprive Alouche of the damages awarded to him, that was the result. Grad and Grosman, as the only shareholders of Best Beaver, benefited from this restructuring. As a result, the court ordered them to pay Alouche the amount of the judgment against Best Beaver.

Business Lesson

Parties other than minority shareholders, such as creditors, may also use the oppression remedy in certain circumstances. The protection against liability enjoyed by the shareholders of a corporation is not absolute. Shareholders who control a corporation may find themselves liable for decisions made in the name of the corporation and should consider this risk when making decisions that result in direct economic harm to others.

Appraisal rights are particularly useful to minority shareholders in private corporations where there is not a ready market for the shareholders' shares. A fundamental principle of corporate law is that the "majority rules": the holders of the majority of the voting shares are able to control the decisions of the corporation. This can sometimes lead to situations where decisions are made that minority shareholders do not agree with. When the decision involves certain fundamental changes to the corporation (for example, the approval of the sale of all or substantially all of the corporation's assets), corporate statutes provide minority shareholders who voted against the resolution with the right to require the corporation to buy back their shares for fair value. This allows minority shareholders to escape with their investment when the fundamental nature of the corporation changes.

Finally, a derivative action is an action where a shareholder, director, officer, or other person may bring or defend an action in the corporation's name, where the board of directors declines to do so. A derivative action could be used, for example, to allow a shareholder to bring an action in the corporation's name against a director for breach of the director's duty to the corporation. The board may not want to launch a lawsuit against "one of their own." In such a case, the court may allow a shareholder to launch the action against the director and obtain compensation for the corporation for the breach of duty.

Sale of a Corporation

Because ownership of a corporation is represented by the ownership of shares, a corporation is never really sold. Its assets can be sold, and some or all of its shares can be sold, but the corporation itself remains intact. For example, Val-Nam Generation Limited may sell its head office building or its manufacturing plant, or even one of its product lines, such as the generator, to another business. However, the corporation called Val-Nam Generation Limited continues to exist, even though the plant and the manufacturing line are no longer its assets.

Angelic might disagree with management's decision to sell the plant and the generator line and thus choose to sell her shares. If the company is a public company, with shares traded on a stock exchange such as the Toronto Stock Exchange or the New York Stock Exchange, she will simply sell the shares through the exchange to a willing buyer. The buyer will become a shareholder.

It is extremely rare for one person to own all of the shares in a large public corporation. That said, a single person may acquire a controlling interest in the corporation by, for example, buying more than 50 percent of the voting shares from the previous owners. A controlling interest allows the person to control who is elected to the board of directors and, through the board, how the corporation is operated. However, having a controlling interest in a corporation does not mean the shareholder "owns" the corporation; they simply own the majority of the corporation's shares.

In a smaller, private business, if the directors/shareholders wish to sell their business, they can find an interested purchaser who will then purchase either all the assets of the corporation or all its shares.

Dissolution

Because a corporation continues to exist even when its assets or shares are sold, a corporation is said to have a "perpetual" existence. This doesn't mean that a corporation's existence cannot be terminated. A corporation's existence ends (it is "dissolved") through its liquidation or winding up, which is generally governed by the same statute (such as the *Canada Business Corporations Act* or the Ontario *Business Corporations Act*) that created the corporation. However, if a corporation begins bankruptcy proceedings, the provisions of the federal *Bankruptcy and Insolvency Act* dictate how the corporation's affairs must be terminated. (Bankruptcy and insolvency are discussed in Chapter 8.) A corporation is required by statute to maintain its corporate records for a fixed period after dissolution. Any legal proceedings by or against the corporation that were begun before the corporation's dissolution are allowed to continue as though the corporation still exists.

Conducting Business

Officers, managers, supervisors, and other employees of a corporation carry out a corporation's day-to-day business. If Valery were the sole shareholder and director of Val-Nam Generation Limited, for example, she could make all the business decisions and may, in fact, do all the corporation's work. She may wear all the hats: shareholder, director, officer, and employee.

However, because there are other shareholders, and other people who help Valery with the corporation's day-to-day business, the process is more complicated. She cannot make decisions unilaterally about running the business of Val-Nam Generation Limited. Large companies with many employees have very complex corporate structures because so many people are involved in the corporation's day-to-day affairs.

Tax Implications

Corporations have a more complex tax structure for carrying on business than non-corporate vehicles. The corporation generates income of its own, pays its own expenses, assumes its own liabilities, and ends up with its own profit or loss in each fiscal year. The government taxes a corporation on its own income in much the same way that it taxes an individual. A corporation is required to prepare and file its own tax returns each year and to pay taxes on its profit.

The corporation may also be required to pay business taxes to the local municipality and to collect and pay GST or HST on the goods and services that it uses and provides. These other taxes are expenses of the corporation for the purpose of calculating its federal income tax.

Shareholders must include dividends (representing a share of the profits) as income in their personal income tax returns. Thus, in essence, the government taxes the profits of corporations twice: once as corporate income and then again as personal income of the shareholders. A dividend tax credit available to shareholders partially offsets this double taxation.

Profits

Once all tax is paid, the corporation can use the remainder of its profit as its board of directors sees fit: to expand, replace existing equipment and buildings, pay bonuses to directors and officers, provide raises or bonuses to its employees, save for future plans, or pay dividends to its shareholders. The law requires the board of directors to act fairly and reasonably in deciding what to do with any profits the corporation earns.

For example, growth companies (companies whose revenue is growing quickly) usually reinvest heavily in expansion, and may not pay dividends. Shareholders may be satisfied with this situation if the company's growth is reflected in rising share prices. Mature companies that do not enjoy substantial revenue and profit growth are more likely to pay their profits directly to shareholders by way of dividends. Ultimately, the shareholders who elect the directors will have a voice in how the profits are used.

Shareholders' Agreements

A **shareholders' agreement** is an enforceable contract designed to govern how two or more shareholders conduct their relationship with the corporation or how the corporation itself conducts its business. Some shareholders' agreements are signed by all shareholders or, in the case of a more complex corporation where not all shares are voting shares, by all shareholders who are entitled to vote on the affairs of the corporation. These are known as "unanimous shareholders' agreements."

shareholders' agreement contract that governs the relationship between shareholders, or between shareholders and a corporation, or governs how the corporation conducts its business

Unanimous shareholders' agreements can be comprehensive—covering most or all matters concerning how the corporation is run—or they may be limited to one or a few issues related to the relationship among the shareholders or between the shareholders and the corporation.

These limited scope agreements often involve issues around the ownership of shares rather than the operation of the corporation. For example, all shareholders in a corporation can agree to ensure that shares in the corporation are not transferred to third parties without the consent of the other shareholders. A unanimous shareholders' agreement can, for example, require each shareholder to take legal steps to ensure that the shares are protected from division of property in the event of a marriage breakdown, are not included in the estate of a deceased shareholder, and cannot be pledged as security for a debt. (The latter requirement would help to avoid the possibility of a lender becoming the owner of the shares in the event that a shareholder defaulted on the debt.)

A comprehensive unanimous shareholders' agreement has a different use. In it, the shareholders of a corporation can set out in detail how they wish the corporation to be managed and operated. This agreement, which is usually kept in the corporate minute book, effectively limits the ability of the directors of the corporation to run the business. If a unanimous shareholders' agreement exists, the directors cannot make decisions that run contrary to the terms of the agreement. The comprehensive unanimous shareholders' agreement can be used to help the close-knit shareholders of a private corporation ensure that no outsider becomes an owner of shares in the corporation, or ensure that the corporation will operate in a fashion that is acceptable to all shareholders, rather than leaving decisions to individual votes at different meetings.

The comprehensive unanimous shareholders' agreement is similar in its scope to the partnership agreement discussed above. It would include clauses that address such issues as:

- the creation, issuance, and transfer of shares by the corporation or the shareholders;
- the business of the corporation;
- the day-to-day operation of the corporation;
- payment of dividends to shareholders;
- compensation for directors;
- the scheduling and running of shareholders' meetings; and
- financial matters, such as banking, accountants and auditors, reports to shareholders, and borrowing limits.

A unanimous shareholders' agreement allows a private corporation to enjoy the flexibility that a partnership offers, while still taking advantage of the benefits of incorporation.

Agreements that involve only some of the shareholders with voting shares are known as "non-unanimous shareholders' agreements." A non-unanimous shareholders' agreement is, by definition, limited in its scope. In it, certain shareholders might agree to vote on specific corporate issues in specific ways. For example, imagine a corporation in which six individuals own voting shares. One individual owns 40 percent of the voting shares and the other five shareholders each own 12 percent of the voting shares. The 40 percent shareholder will be able to control, for example, who is elected to the board of directors as long as she gets any one of the other five to vote with her or if she is able to split the votes of the other five members in some other way. The five smaller shareholders may not like this state of affairs and may decide, as a group, to enter into a shareholders' agreement in which they agree to vote together in the election of the board. As a result, the five smaller shareholders can effectively control the vote and elect a board that pleases them.

MINIMIZING YOUR RISK

Understand the Limits of Corporate Protection

- Remember that a corporation does not always enjoy the same protections as an individual under the Charter.
- Be aware that directors and officers are personally responsible for a corporation's compliance with environmental and other laws that protect the public.
- Be aware that personal guarantees for loans will erode the liability protection offered by incorporation.
- Remember that directors are answerable for their actions to their corporation's owners: its shareholders.

Private Versus Public Corporations

As noted earlier, a private corporation's shares are not offered for sale to the general public. For this reason, it is sometimes referred to as a "closely held corporation" or a "non-offering corporation." It differs from a public corporation (also known as an "offering corporation"), which does issue shares for public sale.

The law imposes fewer requirements on private corporations than on public ones. A private corporation is simpler to create and to operate than a public corporation, but its ability to raise capital for operations and growth is more limited. At any point in its existence, a private corporation can "go public" if it follows the steps set out in the applicable legislation.

Creation

Private and public corporations are created in much the same way; there are, however, some differences. The single most significant difference is that before shares in a public corporation are offered for sale to the public, the incorporators (in the case of a new public corporation) or the corporation (in the case of a private corporation going public) must prepare and distribute a document called a prospectus.

A **prospectus** is a document about the corporation that includes information about the directors and officers, the type and numbers of shares that have been or will be sold, the financial history, the current and past audited financial statements, assessments of the corporation's future financial situation, reasons for issuing the shares, and lists of assets, debts, and/or liabilities.

prospectus
document containing detailed financial information about a corporation that is required before sale of shares to the public

A prospectus is a very complex, highly regulated document. Its purpose is to ensure that any member of the public who is contemplating spending their money to purchase shares in the corporation has sufficient reliable information about the corporation, its financial health, and its future prospects to make the decision wisely. Governments require that potential investors have access to reliable information before investing.

Corporate statutes obligate corporations to prepare and circulate a prospectus to potential investors before offering any of their shares to the public. The corporation and the individuals who create and distribute its prospectus are legally responsible for the accuracy of the information contained in the prospectus. If it contains false or misleading information, whoever circulated the prospectus may be sued by anyone who suffers a loss as a result of relying on it.

Advantages and Disadvantages

Raising Capital

The major advantage of a public corporation over a private corporation is its ability to raise capital by selling shares to the public. As any corporation grows, it may require an influx of money to take advantage of a new business opportunity or to add to its production capacity. The group that owns a private corporation may not have enough money to meet the corporation's needs. By going public, a corporation can attract investment by all kinds of people.

The public corporation is the method of carrying on business best suited to larger enterprises that require a great deal of capital to operate. By providing access to the pockets of the investing public, the public corporation allows a business to grow.

Share Ownership and Control

The disadvantage of a public corporation, clearly, is loss of control: the more voting shares owned by different members of the public, the less control any one shareholder or group of shareholders has. It is often more difficult to convince members of the public to invest in a corporation that is controlled by a small, fixed group than it is to attract them to a corporation in which they will have a say in operations.

Ownership of a public corporation is potentially volatile. Because any member of the public can buy shares in the corporation, there is the possibility that any person can—at any time—become the controlling shareholder. In some cases, a takeover of ownership of a public corporation is "hostile"—that is, the person buying shares in an effort to gain control is doing so contrary to the wishes of the directors, officers, and (perhaps) some of the corporation's existing shareholders.

Cost and Complexity

Setting up and running any corporation is significantly more costly and complex than setting up and running either a sole proprietorship or a partnership. However, a public corporation is by far the most expensive and complex. The potential involvement of members of the public as shareholders creates a whole new set of requirements with regard to financial record-keeping, auditing, and reporting, which contribute to the cost of running this type of corporation.

Tax Implications

Sometimes a private corporation is created for the operation of a family business, with minimizing tax as a primary goal. For example, the corporation's share structure can be used to divert income to the lowest earners in the family business, thereby taking advantage of the low earner's low marginal income tax rate.

The structuring of income flow is an extremely complex subject, well beyond the scope of this chapter.

Liability and Accountability

The protection against liability that incorporation offers to business owners generally applies to both private and public corporations. However, because a public corporation, by definition, involves members of the public in the ownership of the business, the activities and decisions of its directors and officers may be more closely scrutinized by shareholders and securities commissions (the government bodies that regulate the sale of shares of public companies). The law demands greater care with regard to reports of meetings and to audit and budgeting requirements.

A director of a public corporation may be more likely to be called to task for their decisions than is a director of a private corporation, who is likely a major shareholder or the relative of a major shareholder. The statutory remedies for shareholders and others will apply to both private and public corporations (see "Remedies for Shareholders and Others," above).

Responsiveness

The corporation is a complex, highly regulated form of carrying on business. It has many advantages, but, when numerous people are involved as directors and shareholders, it can become very difficult to control and manage. Changes to the corporation's structure, mandate, business process, or operations cannot be made quickly and easily. Meetings must be held, approvals obtained, and votes taken. In many cases, significant changes must be discussed and voted on at shareholders' and directors' meetings and must be recorded in the corporate minute book. This can adversely affect the business's ability to respond rapidly to changes in a competitive climate.

On the other hand, the corporate form can accommodate the growth of a small business into a massive enterprise. Even with the simplest of articles and the most conservative of share structures, a corporation can become both immense and immensely powerful. It can create other corporations under its own control (subsidiaries), amalgamate with other corporations, and enter into partnerships with other corporations or with individuals.

Corporations of any size require the services of legal, accounting, and other advisers to meet their obligations under the law, to compete effectively in business, and, if necessary, to terminate operations.

Table 7.3 provides a comparison of some aspects of private and public corporations. Figure 7.4 represents the cost, complexity, and liability exposure factors of various business structures, including private and public corporations.

MINIMIZING YOUR RISK

Understand the Complexities of Going Public

- Consult an experienced lawyer before undertaking the responsibilities of steering a corporation through the process of going public.
- Ensure that your company's prospectus is professionally drafted to comply with statutory requirements.
- Expect and prepare for ongoing monitoring by government regulators.

Table 7.3 Comparison of Private and Public Corporations

	Private Corporation	Public Corporation
Typical example	A sole proprietorship or small partnership wants the liability protection of a corporation; the owner(s) wants to maintain control and does not need to raise a large amount of capital.	A successful business needs a large amount of capital to grow; its owners are willing to forgo a degree of control to raise money by selling shares to the public.
Raising capital	More difficult to raise capital.	Can continually raise capital by issuing more shares, provided that buyers are interested.
Regulation	Less regulation because its shares are not sold to the public.	More regulation—particularly regarding public financial disclosure—because its shares are sold to the public.
Cost and complexity	Less complex and expensive because there is less regulation.	More complex and expensive because of onerous regulation, especially regarding public financial disclosure.
Share ownership and control	One shareholder or a small group of shareholders retain control.	Because more shares are issued, sold, and traded, control is less concentrated and more susceptible to change.

Figure 7.4 Cost, Complexity, and Liability Exposure in Business Structures

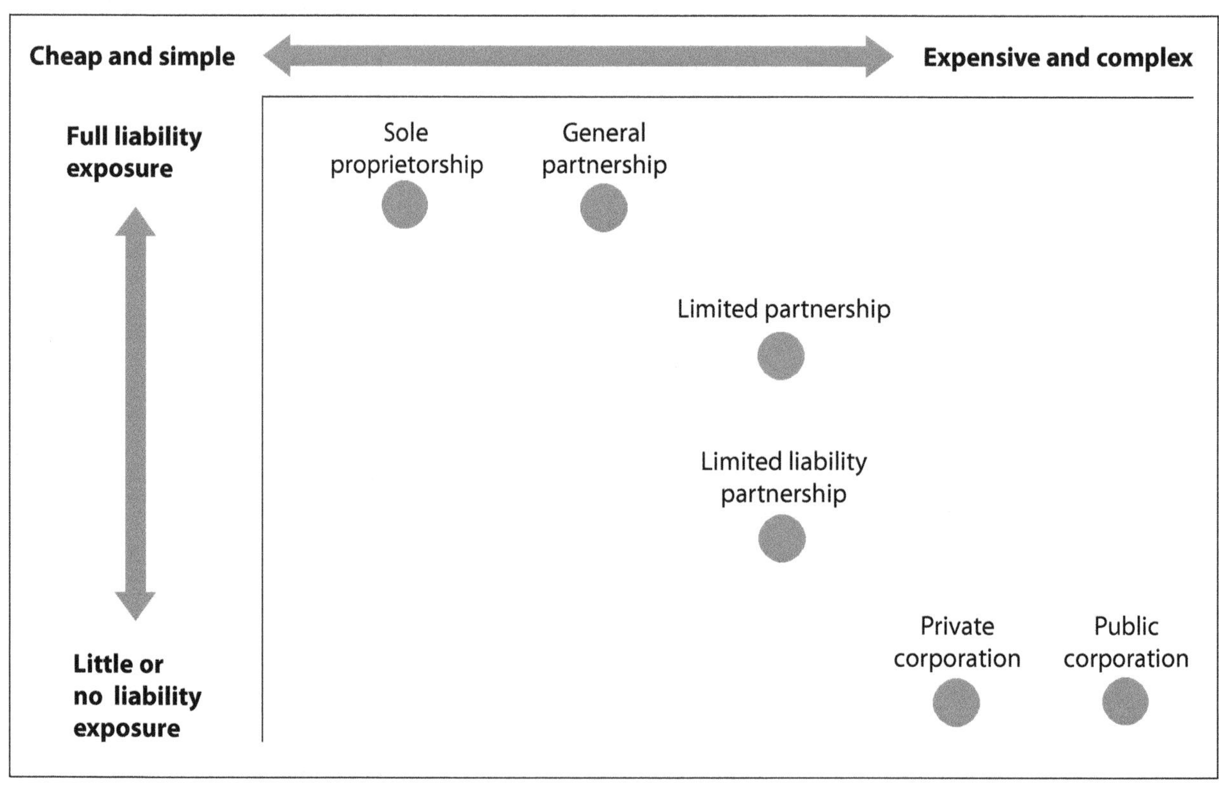

Co-operatives

Co-operatives are business organizations that operate in virtually every sector of the economy and are owned by their members, who either use the co-op's services or work at the co-op, or both. Co-operatives provide members (who can be consumers, producers, buying groups, etc.) with an alternative type of organization—one that meets their needs and is owned and controlled by them. Rather than aiming to create the maximum profit for shareholders, co-operatives are generally concerned with the needs of their members and the quality of life in their communities. They allocate their profits differently than corporations, dividing them among their member-owners based on how much the members use the co-op. Co-operatives often invest their profits in ways that can enrich the community and improve services for their members.

Co-operatives can be established as either federal co-operative corporations (under the *Canada Cooperatives Act*) or provincial co-operative corporations (under, for example, the Ontario *Co-operative Corporations Act*).

The types of co-ops are virtually limitless; they include workers' co-ops, housing co-ops, retail co-ops (for example, food or clothing), childcare co-ops, and credit unions. Well-known Canadian co-ops include Mountain Equipment Co-operative (MEC) outdoor recreation equipment stores (Figure 7.5), Gay Lea Foods Co-operative Ltd dairy farmers' co-operative, and The Co-operators Group Limited insurance co-operative.

Figure 7.5

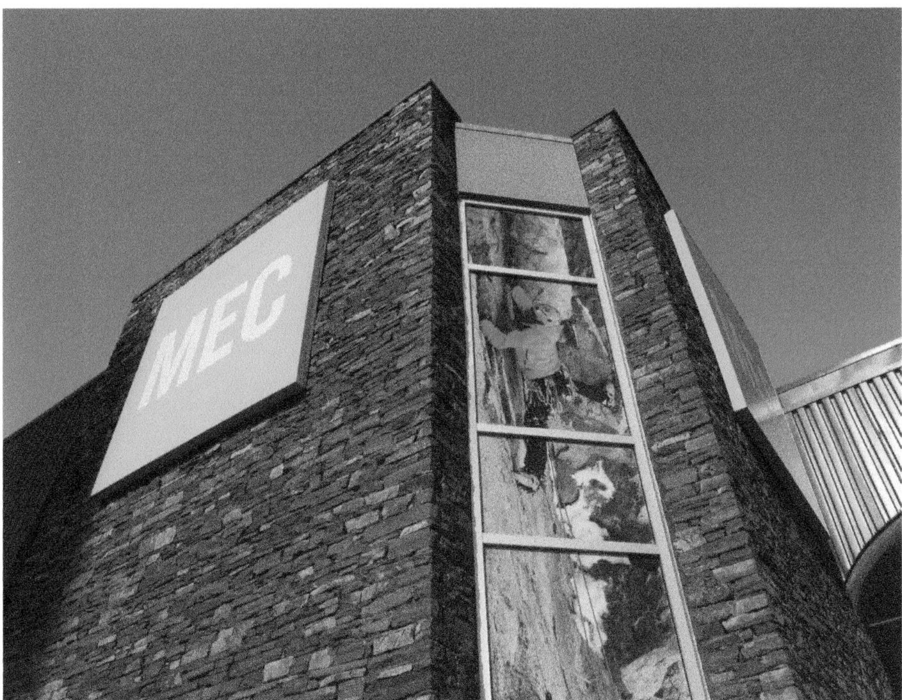

MEC, an outdoor recreation gear and clothing retailer, is one of Canada's most recognizable co-operatives.

Agency

We are now familiar with the three main forms of carrying on business: sole proprietorship, partnership, and corporation. However, before we go further, we need to explore how these forms of business take action. It is clear that a sole proprietor is the one who legally binds their business, but could someone else also bind the business to a contract? We know that partners can bind the partnership (and the other partners) to contracts. We know that directors, officers, and employees bind the corporation to contracts. But how is this done? When we talk about one person being bound to a contract through the actions of another, we are discussing issues of agency law.

Agency law can be very useful when you want to delegate responsibility so that you are not the only one who can make decisions in your business. Agency law is *required* in order to allow artificial legal entities like corporations to act, because they are not capable of acting on their own (a corporation doesn't have a hand to sign a contract; it relies on its agents to sign the contract on its behalf). So what does an agency relationship look like? An agency relationship is created when one person gives the other person the power to represent him or her and affect his or her legal relationships. The person given the power to act is the **agent**. The person who is represented by the agent is the **principal**. The agent acts on the principal's behalf in an interaction with a third party, legally binding the principal to commitments made to the third party by the agent. Generally, provided the agent informs the third party that they are acting on behalf of the principal, the agent is not personally liable for the commitments made, for example, in contracts negotiated and signed on behalf of the principal. Figure 7.6 demonstrates this situation.

agent
person who has the authority to act on another's behalf

principal
person who has given another the authority to act on their behalf

There are many different types of agents—some with extensive powers to bind the principal and some with very limited powers. You may have heard the terms "signing agent" or "signing authority." These terms apply to an agent who has the authority to sign contracts or cheques on behalf of a principal. These documents are signed "per" the principal.

Figure 7.6 Contractual Relationship Between Principal, Agent, and Third Party

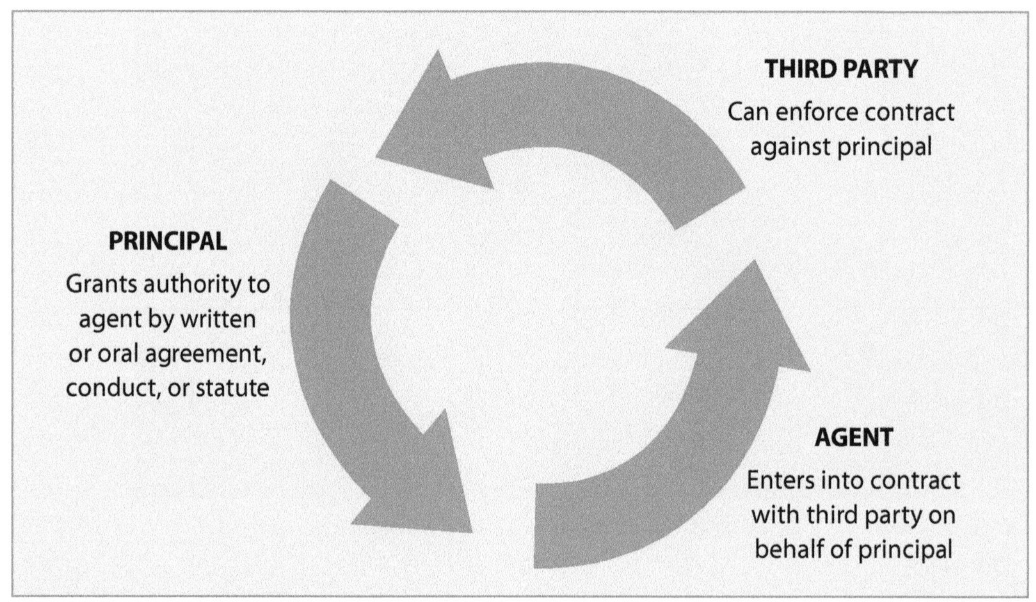
THIRD PARTY
Can enforce contract against principal
PRINCIPAL
Grants authority to agent by written or oral agreement, conduct, or statute
AGENT
Enters into contract with third party on behalf of principal

In the business world, an agency relationship commonly arises in contractual situations. For example, an employee may be able to act as an agent for their employer when negotiating a contract with a customer. In this case, the employer, as a principal, may be obliged to fill the customer's order at the price negotiated by the employee. Binding contracts may also be signed by partners as agents of partnerships and by incorporators as agents of soon-to-be-incorporated businesses.

Characteristics of Agency

The basic characteristics of an agent-principal relationship are as follows:

- The agent has the authority (either actual or apparent) to represent and bind the principal to a contract with a third party.
- The agent has a duty to represent the principal fairly and to act in the best interests of the principal while representing him or her.
- Any third party with whom the agent deals has the right to rely on the agent's apparent authority and to hold the principal legally responsible for their dealings with the agent.

Creating an Agency Relationship

An agency relationship is generally created in one of four ways: (1) the principal and the agent enter into a contract that expressly sets out the agent's powers and duties, including any restrictions; (2) the common law or statute law creates the agency relationship (for example, both the common law and statute law establish that partners are agents of each other); (3) the principal appoints the agent to a position that carries with it the authority to act on behalf of the principal (for example, appointing a CEO to a corporation); or (4) the principal makes representations to a third party that suggest an individual is an agent of the principal.

The first three of these ways that an agency relationship can be created are examples of granting an agent what is referred to as "actual authority." This is authority that has been authorized either by the principal or by operation of law. The fourth way of creating an agency relationship is an example of "apparent authority." In that case, the principal does not mean to authorize the purported agent to act on its behalf but, through the principal's action or inaction, the principal creates the impression in a third party that the purported agent is a true agent.

Actual or Apparent Authority: What's the Difference?

Let's assume that Valery is appointed chief executive officer of Val-Nam Generation Limited by the board of directors. The bylaws of the corporation state that the CEO has the power to enter into contracts on behalf of the corporation for the purchase of machinery and equipment up to a total value of $80,000, but for any contracts above that value, both the CEO and chief financial officer must sign the contract in order to bind the corporation. Valery, as CEO, has *actual authority* (based on the third method of creating an agency relationship) to sign a contract on behalf of the corporation for the purchase of equipment valued up to $80,000, but she is not authorized to sign contracts of a higher value on her own.

What happens if Valery signs a contract on behalf of Val-Nam for the purchase of $100,000 worth of equipment? Will Val-Nam be bound by that contract?

The answer is probably yes. If Val-Nam represented that Valery is its CEO (through letterhead, business cards, etc.) but did not inform the seller that there was a limit on the value of contracts the CEO can sign on behalf of the corporation, the seller may have relied on the reasonable expectation that a CEO would have the authority to bind the corporation in this instance. The seller would be relying on Valery's *apparent authority* and may be able to enforce the contract against Val-Nam.

Business Lesson

If there are unusual limitations to the authority of an agent, the principal must ensure that third parties are aware of these limitations.

Val-Nam should put in place procedures to ensure third parties are aware of any limitations to its agents' authority.

Thus, principals must be aware of the risk that they will be bound by contracts that are entered into by an agent who acts outside of their actual authority but within their apparent authority. Agents acting outside of their actual authority may be sued by the principal for breaching their duty to the principal.

Third parties must also be wary when dealing with agents. As the *LeRuyet v Stenner* case demonstrates, third parties will want to be certain that the agent has the required authority to bind the principal.

CASE IN POINT

When Dealing with an Agent, Do Your Homework

LeRuyet v Stenner, 2001 BCSC 1129

Facts

LeRuyet asked the defendant, Stenner, to help him with his investments. Stenner recommended buying a Great West annuity and showed him documents bearing the Great West logo. LeRuyet gave Stenner $130,000 to buy this annuity. LeRuyet then discovered that Stenner had not bought the annuity and that none of the documents shown to him had been legitimate. Stenner was convicted of fraud. LeRuyet sued Stenner. He also sued Great West, claiming that the company was vicariously liable for Stenner's actions, because he had been its agent. The agency agreement between Stenner and Great West allowed Stenner to solicit applications for annuities and to receive commission on sales of Great West products. But it did not give Stenner express authority to bind Great West. Great West itself would have to accept any offer to purchase by customers such as LeRuyet. Stenner did not have Great West business cards, did not work out of Great West's premises, nor did he display any connection to Great West.

Result

The action was dismissed. Evidence did not support the claim of vicarious liability against Great West for Stenner's acts. The agency contract did not give Stenner actual authority to bind Great West, nor did Great West represent through words or conduct that Stenner had authority to bind it. Accordingly, Stenner was not acting within apparent authority. Stenner's use of the Great West logo was not sufficient to establish the link with Great West necessary to show apparent authority.

Business Lesson

When you are dealing with someone holding themselves out as an agent, and where a great deal is at stake, ask for evidence of the agency relationship and make inquiries of the principal directly to determine the limits of its liability for acts of the agent.

Now that we understand the legal framework for the principal-agent relationship, we will look at three common agency relationships found in the business context.

Agency and Soon-To-Be-Incorporated Businesses

Before a corporation comes into legal existence, its incorporators often wish to set the business in motion. They may, for example, want to sign leases on buildings, sign contracts to purchase equipment and materials, and even enter into sales contracts with customers of the future corporation. Because the corporation does not yet exist, it does not itself have the legal standing to do these things.

However, the incorporators can sign **pre-incorporation contracts**, advising the other parties that they are doing so as agents for the soon-to-be-created corporation. The corporation can then **ratify**—or adopt—the contracts after incorporation. Once the newly formed corporation has officially ratified the contract—or, in the language of agency law, once the corporation has acknowledged its incorporators' authority to act as its pre-incorporation agent—the corporation becomes legally liable for the contracts as principal in the agency relationship.

It must be noted, however, that the incorporator who signed the contract will be personally liable for the contract if the corporation does not come into existence, or if it refuses to adopt the contract after its incorporation.

pre-incorporation contract
contract entered into between a third party and the incorporators of a soon-to-be-incorporated business

ratify
acknowledge corporate liability for a contract entered into on behalf of a business before incorporation

Agency and the Employment Relationship

Employees who are carrying out the business of their employer and acting within the scope of their authority (or apparent authority) are agents of the employer. The agency relationship usually involves executives, such as officers of a corporation, who make major decisions that affect the business. It is reasonable for third parties who deal with these executives to rely on the representations that they make on behalf of the business.

As was evident in our discussion of the $100,000 equipment contract that Valery purported to sign on behalf of Val-Nam, if there are any restrictions on the authority of executives—such as procedures they must follow before striking a deal with a third party or additional approvals or signatures that must be obtained—it is the business's responsibility to communicate these limitations to the third party. Otherwise, it will be bound to any contract, written or not, because the executive has apparent authority. In the context of corporate management, this concept is sometimes called the "indoor management rule," and it has been codified in corporate statutes.

Employees other than executives may also act as agents for their employer. For example, cashiers in clothing stores enter into simple contracts with customers every day on behalf of their employers. These employees can also bind their employer, even when they act beyond the scope of their actual authority. For example, even if it is against store policy, a cashier may act within the scope of her apparent authority in making an agreement with a customer that the customer can return a sweater and repurchase it the next week during a scheduled sale. In this case, the store is probably legally required to fulfill this commitment to the customer.

CASE IN POINT

Is an Employer Criminally Responsible for the Acts of Its Employees?

R v Goyal, [2001] MJ No 585 (QL)

Facts

Goyal, owner of a convenience store, was charged with selling tobacco products to a minor. One of his employees sold the cigarettes without his knowledge or consent. Goyal was not present at the time. The employee testified that Goyal instructed her to ask for identification from customers wanting to buy cigarettes who appeared to be under the age of 18, and that she did this. Her evidence was that the purchaser looked older than 18. Goyal also posted signs indicating that it was illegal to sell tobacco products to young persons.

Result

An acquittal was entered. Goyal showed that the offence was committed without his knowledge or consent. He had exercised due diligence to prevent such an offence being committed. Having demonstrated that he did everything he reasonably could to prevent the offence from happening, he is not liable for the act of his agent, the employee. This is a criminal offence of strict liability, where due diligence is a defence. In a civil case, it is much more likely that an employer will be held liable for the acts of an employee since, as principal, an employer is vicariously liable for civil wrongs done by an agent/employee in the course of employment, even where the employer itself has done nothing wrong.

Business Lesson

Employers may be responsible for the acts of their employees who are their agents. To reduce risk, be sure your employees are carefully instructed and trained, particularly with respect to activities that are likely to expose you to legal liability.

Agency and Partnership

All partners are agents of their partnership. This common law rule has been codified in the *Partnerships Act*. It means that any contract made by a partner in the course of the partnership business generally binds the other partners. It is therefore important that partners not act beyond the scope of their authority as defined in their partnership agreement.

MINIMIZING YOUR RISK

- Avoid personal liability by ensuring that recently incorporated businesses ratify all pre-incorporation contracts.
- Use a partnership agreement to define and clarify the roles of all members of a partnership.

Relationships Among Businesses

When starting a business, you must determine whether it is most advantageous for your business to operate as a sole proprietorship, partnership, or corporation. Choosing the form of business is a key initial decision. However, this is only one of many decisions you will make that shape how your business operates and the liabilities that it may be exposed to. Another key decision you will need to make is how you will structure your relationships with other businesses that you encounter. In the next sections, we will look at four common options for structuring relationships with other businesses: agency in the context of a business relationship, joint ventures, franchises, and licences.

Agency as a Business Relationship

Two or more businesses (they can be sole proprietorships, partnerships, or corporations) can enter into an **agency agreement** in order to provide services to and receive services from each other. A person may choose to become an agent as a method of earning money. In fact, one can create a business whose sole role is acting as an agent for another business. Val-Nam, for example, may hire a sales agent to market its products in new territories and enter into contracts with distributors and retailers. The sales agent, who may operate as a sole proprietor or corporation, may derive their only business income from this undertaking.

agency agreement
contract between principal and agent that describes the agent's rights and authority

An agent may have a number of clients. Val-Nam's sales agent, for instance, may also represent other manufacturers around the world. The principal in an agency relationship may also have several agents. For example, Val-Nam may have different sales agents representing it in different parts of the province, the country, or the world. Each agent enters into an agency agreement that sets out the sales territory (the geographic area in which the sales agent is to operate), the commission rate, the time period covered by the agreement, the scope of the agent's authority (the agent may, for example, be allowed to approach local retailers but not national retailers), and how the agency relationship is to be governed.

The advantage for Val-Nam is that it can assemble a devoted and enthusiastic sales force without assuming all the legal obligations of hiring full-time employees. The advantage for the agents is that they have flexibility in setting their own schedules and in choosing how to approach clients; they can also control their incomes, earning as much as they need or want in a particular year.

MINIMIZING YOUR RISK

Take Care in Creating and Defining Agency Relationships

- Provide written clarification of all agency relationships to ensure that agents act only within the scope of their defined authority.
- Advise third parties with whom your business contracts of any limitations on the authority of your agents.
- Consider agency as a cost-efficient means of obtaining services on an as-needed basis.

Joint Ventures

A **joint venture** is not a form of carrying on business; rather, it is a temporary relationship between two or more people or businesses that come together for the purpose of completing one or a series of specific projects. The members of a joint venture can be sole proprietorships, partnerships, or corporations. A joint venture need not be registered with the government or undergo any other official process, and it rarely has a name.

joint venture
temporary relationship created to complete one or more business projects

If Val-Nam wanted to develop a large-scale generator with the assistance of Spotlight Renewables Inc, a corporation that captures landfill gas and uses it to generate electricity, it could enter into a joint venture with Spotlight Renewables. Val-Nam would have no legal relationship with Spotlight Renewables, apart from the relationship created for this one project. The relationship could be defined and governed by a written agreement between Val-Nam and Spotlight Renewables. It would cover all matters related to the development of the large-scale generator, such as who does what, who pays for what, and who is entitled to any patents developed during the project; it would also address matters such as insurance, equipment, leasing of research space, and how long the project will last.

The joint venture, as an approach to a particular project or series of projects, has its advantages. It is fairly simple and quick to put together, and it has a natural end. It allows businesses to work together for a brief period to their mutual advantage, then to go their separate ways at the end of the project with no impact on their individual operations or legal status.

However, there are some disadvantages. If a joint venture agreement is not carefully and properly prepared, problems can arise among the members regarding how to share profits (or losses) and how to deal with liabilities. There is also the possibility that members of the venture may not put their full efforts into the project. Val-Nam might find, for example, that it is too busy refining its initial portable generator and expanding its market share to put much effort into the development of this new product; the joint venture would suffer as a result, and Spotlight Renewables could end up losing money on a project that goes nowhere.

MINIMIZING YOUR RISK

Create Written Agreements Before Entering Joint Ventures

- Determine the legal requirements of your joint venture, such as permits and security, and satisfy them.
- Obtain adequate insurance coverage to protect you from liability.
- Draft and sign a written agreement that defines the responsibilities of participants in the venture.
- Devise a formula or other method for sharing profits and losses, and include it in your written agreement.
- Include a method of resolving any disputes that arise (for example, a mandatory arbitration clause) in the written agreement.

Franchises

franchise
right to operate a business using the name, products, business methods, and advertising of another business

A **franchise** is a right to operate a business using the name, products, business methods, and advertising of another business. Franchises exist all over Canada, particularly in the fast-food and convenience store industries. Sometimes it is difficult to tell whether a particular business is simply a member of a chain of stores all owned by the same corporation or a franchise of a larger corporation.

In a typical franchise situation, a large and established corporation enters into agreements with smaller business enterprises (sole proprietorships, partnerships, or other corporations). For a fee (or a percentage of the profit), the large corporation (the franchisor) allows the small enterprise (the franchisee) to operate in a particular location and sell the products of the franchisor.

The franchise agreement between the two businesses is often extremely detailed. It governs almost every aspect of the business relationship and usually favours the franchisor. In essence, the prospective franchisee knows that the franchisor is successful and well known; the franchisee is therefore willing to have the franchisor control the franchisee's business in order to profit from the franchisor's success.

A franchise agreement usually includes the following requirements:

- that the franchisee sell only products supplied by the franchisor in the form in which they are supplied, and to the standards set by the franchisor;

- that the franchisee set up and decorate the business premises exactly as required by the franchisor so that the outlet resembles all other franchises;
- that the franchisee pay both an initial franchise fee and a periodic royalty to the franchisor, often a percentage of the profit of the franchise;
- that the franchisee provide audited financial statements to the franchisor on a regular basis;
- that the franchisee contribute a certain amount of money to the franchisor's advertising fund, which the franchisor then uses to advertise the franchise across its territory (national, provincial, or local);
- that the franchisee offer specials and discounts only as directed by the franchisor;
- that the franchisee limit their business to a given territory (when, for example, delivering fast foods);
- that the franchisee maintain the business premises, the service offered to the public, and the products offered for sale to the standards of the franchisor;
- that the franchisee establish and maintain sufficient liability insurance on the business and protect the franchisor from any legal liabilities that may arise; and
- that the franchisee participate in any group scheme or organization that the franchisor might set up (for example, the call centre of a pizza business).

The agreement also usually includes an acknowledgment that the franchisor may, at any time, revoke the franchise agreement if the franchisee fails to live up to any of its obligations under the agreement.

CASE IN POINT

Souring of a Sweet Deal

Facts

Franchisees expect franchise agreements and arrangements to be weighted heavily in favour of the franchisor; however, when that balance is tilted too far in the franchisor's favour, the franchisor can face a franchisee revolt. Recently, the relationship between Tim Hortons and some of the iconic company's franchisees has been challenging. Franchisees have alleged that product changes have lowered quality (the switch from fresh-baked doughnuts to partially-baked products that had been flash-frozen was the focus of an unsuccessful lawsuit in 2012).[6] They also allege that increased costs imposed on franchisees and brand mismanagement are negatively affecting their profits.

In June 2017, a Toronto franchisee of Tim Hortons filed a $500 million class action lawsuit against Restaurant Brands International Inc (RBI) on behalf of approximately 3,500 franchisees. The lawsuit alleges that the parent company has misused money collected from franchisees for marketing purposes.[7] As of writing, this lawsuit is still underway.

Business Lesson

Disputes with franchisees can be expensive to resolve and can have a negative effect on brand image. Fostering strong franchisor-franchisee relationships can be key to long-term success.

6 Barbara Shecter, "Tim Hortons Franchisees File Lawsuit Against Restaurant Brands for Breach of Contract," *Financial Post* (19 June 2017), online: <http://business.financialpost.com/news/retail-marketing/tim-hortons-franchisees-file-lawsuit-against-restaurant-brands-for-breach-of-contract>.

7 CBC News, "Tim Hortons Franchisees Launch $500M Class-Action Suit Against Parent Company," *CBC News* (19 June 2017), online: <http://www.cbc.ca/news/business/tim-hortons-class-action-1.4167739>.

Many Canadian jurisdictions have taken an active approach to regulating franchises in recent years. More regulations are appearing, requiring franchisors to provide reliable information to prospective franchisees about the business, its products, the terms of the franchise agreement, and the franchisor's financial situation. The increased disclosure requirements make it easier for a prospective franchisee to make an informed and intelligent decision about entering into a franchise agreement with a particular franchisor.

The franchise method of carrying on business has many advantages for both parties. The franchisee enjoys some of the advantages of running their own business while knowing that they are offering a popular product and that they are supported by strong advertising and the guidance of experts from the franchisor. A franchisee who is inexperienced in running a business may benefit greatly from the guidance of an experienced franchisor. If, at a later time, the franchisee chooses to run their own business, they can take the lessons learned from the experience of operating the franchise and apply them at their new business.

The sale of franchises allows the franchisor to expand quickly into new territories while not taking the full risk and cost of the new ventures upon itself. By choosing its franchisees wisely, the franchisor obtains the services of strong local managers with a powerful interest in making the business succeed. Both the local franchisee and the large franchisor can profit from the arrangement.

On the other hand, a franchise has disadvantages, especially for the creative franchisee. In most cases, the franchisor hands the franchisee a business package and expects the franchisee to operate their business to the rigorous standards of the franchisor. There is no room for creativity. The franchisor believes that the success of the entire franchise business depends on customers finding consistent quality and

Figure 7.7

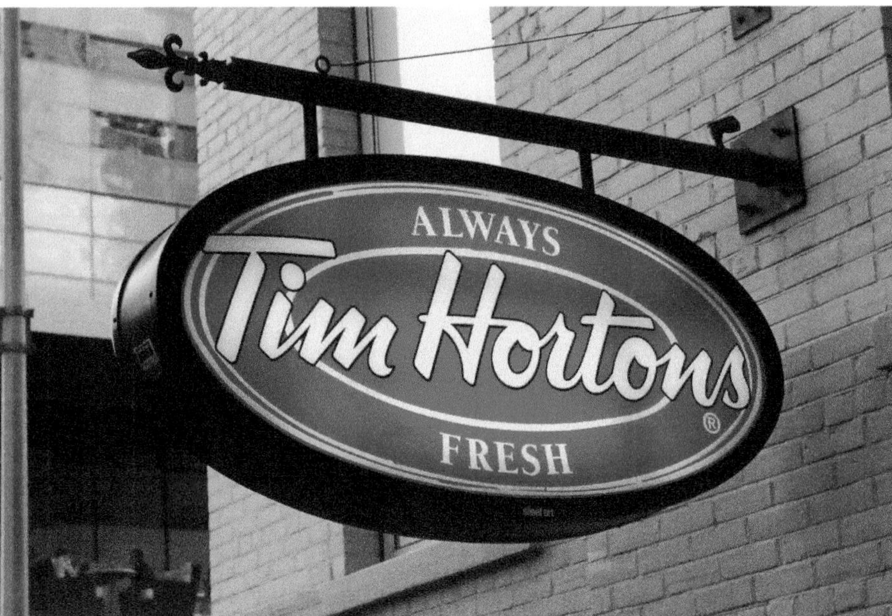

With its longstanding ties to Canadian culture, Tim Hortons remains one of Canada's most popular options for franchisees.

service in every location. It will usually not, therefore, allow franchisees to exercise their creative judgment in response to local conditions or personal preference.

And, unfortunately, the franchisor often keeps for itself sweeping powers to cancel the franchise agreement. From time to time, it exercises these powers to the detriment of a blameless franchisee. For example, there have been cases where a franchisee has succeeded far beyond the expectations of the franchisor in a particular location, only to have their store taken from them. At the height of an outlet's success, some franchisors have used the powers given to them by the franchise agreement to revoke the franchise in order to take over the business and enjoy the profits themselves.

MINIMIZING YOUR RISK

Investigate Potential Franchisors Thoroughly

- Take advantage of disclosure requirements to conduct a thorough investigation of a franchisor's products, franchise terms, and financial situation.
- Investigate a potential franchisor's track record, and refuse to do business with franchisors that unexpectedly and unjustifiably revoke successful franchises.
- Take the franchise agreement to a lawyer specializing in franchise law for review *before* you sign it.

Licences

A licence is a contract that confers rights from one party to another in accordance with the terms of the licence. Usually, the word "licence" is used when the rights relate to intellectual property, such as patents, copyright, and trademarks. A licence is not a sale in the ordinary sense—it is limited in scope. It may be time-limited and include other conditions of use.

Nearly everybody is familiar with software licences. Some software licences are time-limited or limit updates for a fixed period. Most software licences are non-exclusive, which means that the licensor (the business that owns the copyright in the software) will sell licences to numerous licensees (the businesses or individuals that purchase the software). Standard software licences include restrictions or "conditions of use," such as a prohibition on making copies of the software.

Trademarks are also commonly licensed, for example, the use of Disney characters on toys and clothing. The licensor, such as Disney, is often paid by royalty—a percentage of per unit sales of the toys or clothing.

Trademark licences are a component of franchise agreements, as the franchisee is paying a royalty to the franchisor for the use of the business and product names, as well as the other elements shared with the franchisee as outlined above.

SCENARIO: FOR DISCUSSION

1. What type of licences might Val-Nam be interested in granting to a third party?
2. What are some of the advantages of granting a licence to use a patent to a third party?
3. Why might Val-Nam prefer to licence its products rather than enter into franchise agreements with third parties?

CHAPTER SUMMARY

The most common business structures are sole proprietorships, partnerships, and corporations. A business person must weigh the flexibility, cost, complexity, and protection from liability of each structure before deciding which is best for their business.

Sole proprietorships are easy to set up and run. A single person owns and operates the business, and any profit the business earns is added to the owner's other income for tax purposes. Since there is no legal separation between the owner and the business, the owner is fully liable for any injury the business may cause to others.

A partnership is a relationship between two or more people or corporations who join together in a common business. Like sole proprietorships, partnerships are not legally independent from their owners, the partners. In addition, partners may be liable for the conduct of other partners. In Canada, there are three types of partnership—general, limited, and limited liability—that differ depending on how liability and other responsibilities are shared among the partners.

A corporation is a distinct legal entity that has almost all the rights and obligations of an individual and exists independently of its creators. The shares of private corporations are held by a small group of shareholders. The shares of a public corporation are for sale to the public and, because of this, public corporations are subject to more record-keeping and government regulation. Public corporations are best suited to larger enterprises that require a lot of capital to operate. Because a corporation is an independent legal entity, it is responsible for its own debts and obligations; it files its own tax returns, collects GST or HST, and can sue and be sued. Its structure protects shareholders, employees, officers, and directors from personal liability. It is often far more expensive and complex to set up and run a corporation than a sole proprietorship or a partnership.

An agency relationship exists when an agent has the authority to bind its principal by, for example, signing contracts or cheques on behalf of the principal. Agency relationships are frequently used in soon-to-be-incorporated businesses, employment relationships, and partnerships, and they can be a means of creating a business relationship among businesses. Agents usually act within the scope of the authority granted by their principals. However, if they exceed it, the principal may be bound by the agent's actions where the agent has apparent authority to bind the principal.

A joint venture is a temporary relationship formed between two or more people or businesses to complete one or more projects. Joint ventures do not have to be registered with the government or undergo any official process. They allow businesses to work together to their mutual advantage, then to go their separate ways with no impact on their individual operations or legal status.

A franchise agreement grants to a franchisee the right to operate a business using the name, products, business methods, and advertising of a franchisor for a fee or a percentage of the profits or, more likely, both. Franchise agreements govern almost every aspect of the business relationship and usually favour the franchisor. Franchises are particularly visible in the fast-food and convenience store industries.

KEY TERMS

agency agreement, 253
agent, 248
articles of incorporation, 230
business structure, 210
corporate seal, 231
corporation, 227
director, 229
due diligence, 237
fiduciary duty, 229
franchise, 254
general partnership, 217
incorporator, 228
joint and several liability, 217
joint venture, 253
limited liability partnership (LLP), 224
limited partnership, 221
minute book, 231
officer, 229
partnership agreement, 216
partnership (or firm), 216
pre-incorporation contract, 251
principal, 248
private corporation, 227
prospectus, 243
public corporation, 227
ratify, 251
share certificate, 231
shareholder, 228
shareholders' agreement, 241
sole proprietorship, 212
unlimited liability, 215

REFERENCES

Bankruptcy and Insolvency Act, RSC 1985, c B-3.
Business Corporations Act, RSO 1990, c B.16.
Business Names Act, RSO 1990, c B.17.
Canada Business Corporations Act, RSC 1985, c C-44.
Canada Cooperatives Act, SC 1998, c 1.
Canadian Charter of Rights and Freedoms, Part I of the *Constitution Act, 1982*, being Schedule B to the *Canada Act 1982* (UK), 1982, c 11.
Consumer Protection Act, CQLR, c P-40.1.
Co-operative Corporations Act, RSO 1990, c C.35.
Criminal Code, RSC 1985, c C-46.
Downtown Eatery (1993) Ltd v Ontario, 2001 CanLII 8538 (Ont CA).
Employment Standards Act, 2000, SO 2000, c 41.
Environmental Protection Act, RSO 1990, c E.19.
Ernst & Young Inc v Falconi, 1994 CanLII 7237 (Ont Ct (Gen Div)).
Irwin Toy Ltd v Quebec (Attorney General), [1989] 1 SCR 927.
LeRuyet v Stenner, 2001 BCSC 1129.
Limited Partnerships Act, RSO 1990, c L.16.
Ontario Water Resources Act, RSO 1990, c O.40.
Partnerships Act, RSO 1990, c P.5.
R v Bata Industries Ltd, 1993 CanLII 8677 (Ont Ct (Gen Div)).
R v Goyal, [2001] MJ No 585 (QL).
Salomon v A Salomon & Co Ltd, [1897] AC 22 (HL).
Trade-marks Act, RSC 1985, c T-13.

EXERCISES

True or False?

_____ **1.** A sole proprietorship is a corporation with only one shareholder.

_____ **2.** The name of a sole proprietorship must include the name of the owner.

_____ **3.** A partnership is a legal entity.

_____ **4.** A general partnership does not require a partnership agreement.

_____ **5.** A corporation is a "person" in law.

_____ **6.** Shareholders are liable for the debts and obligations of the corporation in which they hold shares.

_____ **7.** A private corporation does not offer shares for sale to the public.

_____ **8.** Many principals may work for one agent.

_____ **9.** Before a company is officially incorporated, the incorporators often act as agents for the corporation.

Multiple Choice

1. Which of the following is not an advantage of a sole proprietorship?
- **a.** Liability is limited.
- **b.** It is inexpensive to set up.
- **c.** Losses incurred by the business can be set off against the owner's income from other sources to reduce income tax.
- **d.** Changes to the owner's business plan can be made easily.

2. The word "firm" is most appropriately used to describe which business structure?
- **a.** A limited partnership only.
- **b.** A partnership of lawyers or accountants only.
- **c.** Any partnership.
- **d.** A privately held corporation.

3. Limited partners are best described as:
- **a.** partners that make only a limited financial contribution.
- **b.** partners in a general partnership.
- **c.** partners that receive a smaller portion of the partnership's profits.
- **d.** investors in a partnership.

4. Which of the following activities may a corporation carry out?
- **a.** Creating other corporations.
- **b.** Buying or selling other business entities.
- **c.** Entering into contracts.
- **d.** All of the above.

5. Which of the following statements is most correct?
- **a.** Shareholders report to directors.
- **b.** Directors report to officers, and officers report to shareholders.
- **c.** Directors report to shareholders, and officers report to directors.
- **d.** Directors report to incorporators.

6. Which of the following are responsible for the day-to-day operation of a corporation?
- **a.** shareholders
- **b.** directors
- **c.** officers
- **d.** incorporators

7. Which one of the following is not necessarily a characteristic of an agent-principal relationship?
   a. The agent's authority may be general, or it may be restricted in some way.
   b. The agent has a duty to fairly represent the principal and to act in the best interests of the principal.
   c. Any third party with whom the agent deals has the right to rely on the agent's authority and to hold the principal legally responsible for its dealings with the agent.
   d. The agent is an employee of the principal.
8. Which of these descriptions of a joint venture is false?
   a. It is a temporary relationship designed to allow participants to complete one or a series of projects.
   b. Participants may be individuals or businesses, including sole proprietorships, partnerships, and corporations.
   c. The joint venture must have a name that combines the names of all of its participants.
   d. A joint venture need not be registered with the government.
9. Which of the following is not an advantage to a franchisee?
   a. Selling of a known, popular product.
   b. Advertising and marketing support paid for by the franchisor.
   c. Business advice from a franchisor with a successful track record.
   d. Quick expansion into new territories.

Short Answer

1. What are the legal requirements in creating a sole proprietorship?
2. Is it mandatory to register a name for a sole proprietorship?
3. Must a sole proprietor file a separate income tax return for their business?
4. Can two people co-own a sole proprietorship?
5. What are the three types of partnerships in Canada?
6. How are a sole proprietorship and a partnership similar?
7. What does "jointly and severally liable" mean?
8. A partnership agreement is a contract that sets out the rules governing the partnership. What are some of the issues it may cover?
9. What are some of the rights that shareholders enjoy?
10. What is a comprehensive unanimous shareholders' agreement?
11. What is the main advantage of a public corporation over a private corporation?
12. Describe the contents and purpose of a prospectus.
13. What matters are covered in a franchise agreement?

Apply Your Knowledge

1. Joe is shopping for a new TV at Big Screen City Ltd. The company's return policy applies to regularly priced products only. The salesperson, who is new to the job, mistakenly tells Joe he may return *any* TV within seven days if he returns the box and packaging materials as well. Joe relies on this representation when he chooses a very large plasma television on sale for 10 percent off the regular price.

   When Joe returns home, he learns his wife just lost her job. He immediately returns to Big Screen City with the TV and the packaging materials. The manager tells him the store policy does not allow for returns of sale merchandise.
   a. In this example, who is the agent, who is the principal, and who is the third party?
   b. Is this an example of actual or apparent authority? Explain your answer.
2. Siblings Jack and Jill own a house-cleaning business. One day, Jack forgets to lock the door of a client's house when he leaves. The house is robbed, and the owners suffer a loss of approximately $20,000. The homeowners decide to seek damages in the Small Claims Court.
   a. Who will the owners name as defendants in their lawsuit, and why?
   b. Other than ensuring the door was locked, what steps might Jack and Jill have taken to protect themselves against such a lawsuit?

3. Big Burping Burgers is a successful and well-known fast-food operation run by Rory Rib. Rory started as a sole proprietor, and he still runs the business that way because it gives him total control and oversight of the business. The store is always busy. It is open long hours and has many employees and a broad customer base. People come from out of town to try Rory's burgers. Rory is also innovative and has developed burgers made with products other than beef that appeal to customers across cultural lines. He is thinking about expanding his business.
   a. With respect to the form of business organization Rory is using, is there anything he should do before he considers expansion options?
   b. For expansion, what are the pros and cons of franchising Big Burping Burgers?
   c. What other forms of business organization should he consider for expansion?

4. Well, it happened. Big Burping Burgers is in trouble. At one of its new branches, an employee mixed a batch of burgers that contained bacteria. The burgers were not cooked enough to kill off the organisms. As a result, 40 people became gravely ill, and four of them died. The municipal health unit shut the location down. The business is going to be fined a large sum of money, and there are civil suits by victims whose combined claim is in the millions of dollars.

   What will the financial consequences be for Rory if:
   a. the branch is a franchise and Rory is the franchisor?
   b. the business is a sole proprietorship?
   c. the business is a partnership?
   d. the business is a corporation?

5. Brickbats Ltd is in the business of cleaning and restoring the brick exteriors of buildings. It had a longstanding relationship with Weatherchem Ltd, a supplier of the materials used in restoring brick. Brickbats had a running account with Weatherchem. The company was constantly ordering material from Weatherchem, often having Seamus O'Rourke, one of its key restorers, place orders in his own name for Brickbats in the course of his employment. O'Rourke would deliver the bills to Brickbats, which always paid them. Unknown to both Brickbats and Weatherchem, O'Rourke decided to run a small brick restoration business of his own on the side and also ordered his supplies from Weatherchem. He ordered in his own name, as always, but said nothing about ordering for himself. Weatherchem simply assumed that the order was on behalf of Brickbats. O'Rourke did not present these bills to Brickbats, but neither did he pay them, and eventually the scheme collapsed. Weatherchem made a demand on Brickbats to pay the outstanding bills. Brickbats discovered what O'Rourke had done and refused to pay.
   a. How would you argue in favour of Brickbats's position?
   b. How would you argue in favour of Weatherchem?

Banking, Financing, and Debtor-Creditor Law

8

LEARNING OUTCOMES

After reading this chapter, you should be able to:

- Understand how financial institutions can assist business people.
- Describe the different types of negotiable instruments and their uses.
- Define an account agreement and describe its main provisions.
- Explain how and why a business might borrow for the short and long term.
- Understand how to negotiate a credit agreement.
- Describe how businesses use equity financing.
- Explain the remedies available to secured and unsecured creditors.
- Explain a debtor's options under bankruptcy legislation and the *Companies' Creditors Arrangement Act*.
- Describe bankruptcy requirements and proceedings under the *Bankruptcy and Insolvency Act*.

What Is Banking, Financing, and Debtor-Creditor Law?

Banking, financing, and debtor-creditor law concerns the borrowing and lending of money, the types of loans available, and the consequences of failure to repay these loans. All these areas of law are governed principally by statutes passed by both the federal and the provincial governments.

The federal government regulates chartered banks. Much of the governing legislation relates to inspecting and auditing bank operations and ensuring that banks do not fail or go bankrupt. The provinces regulate other financial institutions, such as provincially chartered trust companies and credit unions; much of this legislation also concerns inspections and audits. Recently, regulators have also begun to focus on maintaining adequate levels of service to consumers.

Financial institutions operate by taking deposits from customers and then lending the funds to others. Rather than simply handing over bags of coins and bills, they make and receive payments by electronic funds transfer (EFT) or by using negotiable instruments. There are three types of negotiable instruments currently in use in a business context: cheques, bills of exchange, and promissory notes. Today, these negotiable instruments are often used in electronic format.

When it comes time to raise money, you will have additional financing decisions to make. Whether you need capital to start up your business or to enlarge its operations, you will have to consider whether you want to use debt or equity financing. If you decide to raise money with debt, you will be borrowing money and paying it back over time. If you decide to use equity, you will be attracting investors to invest in your business. You will probably need expert advice in deciding which type of financing is best for you.

If your business borrows money, it becomes a debtor, and the lender becomes a creditor of your business. This debtor-creditor relationship becomes particularly important if your business ever suffers serious financial setbacks—that is, becomes insolvent or goes bankrupt. Depending on the type of loan your business has taken out, the creditor must consider its options. These may include assisting your business by extending further credit in the expectation that it will again become profitable. However, if your business is insolvent and unable to pay its creditor, the creditor may petition your business into bankruptcy under the *Bankruptcy and Insolvency Act*. It can also sue your business for the amount that it is owed. Businesses that are heavily in debt, and unlikely ever to recover, may also choose to voluntarily make an assignment in bankruptcy.

Businesses will be both creditors and debtors and they may also be investors (shareholders) in other businesses. The table below provides a few examples of how Val-Nam Generation Limited ("Val-Nam") may find itself in these varied roles.

SCENARIO

Varied Roles for Val-Nam

Financial Activity	Roles Played by the Parties Involved	
Val-Nam borrows money from a bank in order to finance its purchase of land and construction of a new manufacturing facility	The bank becomes a creditor of Val-Nam when it advances the funds to Val-Nam	Val-Nam becomes a debtor of the bank
Val-Nam allows one of its customers to pay for generators "net 30 days" of delivery	Val-Nam is a creditor of the customer until the customer pays for the generators	The customer is a debtor of Val-Nam until the customer pays for the generators
Val-Nam hires warehouse employees	The employees are creditors of Val-Nam each day/week/month until they are paid for work completed	Val-Nam is a debtor of each employee until it pays the employees for work that has been completed
Val-Nam invests in a corporation that will be jointly owned by itself and Spotlight Renewables Inc to manufacture and manage landfill-based generators	Val-Nam is a shareholder of the corporation in exchange for financial investment	The corporation (through its board of directors) issues shares to Val-Nam
Angelic Battiste provides additional funds to Val-Nam to help it finance the new manufacturing facility	Options	
	Angelic purchases shares in Val-Nam and becomes a shareholder	Val-Nam (through its board of directors) issues shares to Angelic
	Angelic lends money to Val-Nam and becomes a creditor of Val-Nam	Val-Nam is a debtor of Angelic
	Or Angelic and Val-Nam could choose a combination of debt and equity investment to provide the necessary funds	

The Importance of Banking, Financing, and Debtor-Creditor Law for Business People

Banking, financing, and debtor-creditor law provide the legal framework for the financial operations of businesses. These branches of law not only provide the rules under which money changes hands; they also address the assignment of economic risk by providing schemes under which losses are allocated between businesses and their creditors when businesses find themselves in financial difficulty. Business people should familiarize themselves with these areas of law for many reasons, three of which are set out below:

- *Knowledge of how financial institutions work can strengthen your position when dealing with them.* Understanding that there is room for negotiation with banks and other financial institutions when, for example, signing account and loan agreements may assist you in obtaining the services of these institutions on the terms most favourable to your business.
- *A sound mixture of debt and equity financing may be your business's recipe for success.* At some point your business will very likely need to acquire funds for operations or expansions. Should you borrow? Should you seek investors? There are advantages and disadvantages to both. Knowing your options will help you obtain the financial balance that you need, in both the short and the long term.
- *If your business falls on hard times, sensible treatment of your creditors may keep you out of bankruptcy.* Bankruptcy is not the only option if times get tough for your business. The law provides various opportunities to restructure your debt, such as the relatively inexpensive procedure of making a proposal to your creditors. You may have much more leverage than you think, because banks and other creditors like to avoid suing their customers and spending money on enforcing their rights, if possible.

caisse populaire credit union based primarily in Quebec but also operating for francophone clientele in other parts of Canada

negotiable instrument financial document, such as a cheque, that promises to pay the bearer a specified amount and that can be transferred to a third party

promissory note document in which the maker, or promisor, promises to pay the promisee the sum indicated in the note, either on demand or on a later fixed date

Banking

In practical terms, it is not possible to operate a business without the backing of a financial institution to help meet the business's monetary needs and to provide the financial services required on a day-to-day basis. To accomplish any of these goals, your business—or the business you work for—needs an ongoing relationship with a financial institution. In Canada, that institution is likely to be a federally chartered bank, a federally or provincially chartered trust company, or a provincially chartered credit union or ***caisse populaire***.

Negotiable Instruments

In the modern business world, many people use negotiable instruments to make and receive payments for goods and services. A **negotiable instrument** is a document that promises to pay the bearer a specified amount and that can be transferred to a third party. Negotiable instruments in Canada take three forms: cheques, bills of exchange, and promissory notes. A **promissory note** is a document in which the maker, or promisor, promises to pay the promisee the sum indicated in the note, either on demand or on a later fixed date. A **bill of exchange** is a document signed by a **drawer** ordering a drawee to pay a specified sum to a payee immediately or on a later fixed date. While still used in international business transactions, they are otherwise rarely used. A cheque is a particular type of bill of exchange and, as cheques remain the most common form of negotiable instrument used by businesses, we examine them in some detail below.

bill of exchange
document signed by a drawer ordering a drawee to pay a specified sum to a payee immediately or on a later fixed date

drawer
person who drafts and sends the bill of exchange to the drawee for acceptance

Negotiable instruments have certain advantages over money. They are more portable than large sums of cash, and they reduce the risk of theft because only the named payee can cash them. They can create credit by deferring the payment of funds from the date the instrument is created to another date specified in the instrument (consider a postdated cheque, for example). They can also be transferred to third parties. With EFT, these transactions can be done quickly and relatively securely. Negotiable instruments are regulated under the federal *Bills of Exchange Act*. The rules that govern negotiable instruments in Canada are similar to those in the United States and the United Kingdom, which is important when enforcing rights to payment in those international markets.

Cheques

The parties involved in writing a **cheque** consist of a drawee, a payer, and a payee. The **drawee** of a cheque is always a financial institution. The **payer** is always an account holder at that institution. The payer uses the cheque to direct the drawee bank to pay the payee, who is the person named on the cheque. However, the drawee bank is required to pay the **payee** only if there are sufficient funds in the payer's account to cash the cheque. If there are insufficient funds in the account, the drawee bank may refuse to honour the cheque by returning it to the payee. The drawee bank is not liable to the payee for the amount of the cheque; the payee's only recourse is against the payer.

cheque
negotiable instrument under which the drawee banking institution pays the payee from the bank account of the payer

drawee
the person or institution to whom a negotiable instrument is sent for payment

payer
person who pays, or honours, a negotiable instrument

payee
person who receives payment on a negotiable instrument

For example, suppose Val-Nam buys a truckload of steel from Smelter Inc to be used in the production of Val-Nam's generators. Smelter Inc carries on business in Hamilton, while Val-Nam is located in Ottawa. If Smelter Inc requires payment before it ships the steel, Val-Nam can write a cheque in which Val-Nam is the payer, the bank is the drawee, and Smelter Inc is the payee. Smelter Inc will deposit the cheque with its bank. This bank, acting on Smelter Inc's behalf, will present the cheque for payment to Val-Nam's bank. If there are sufficient funds in Val-Nam's account, Val-Nam's bank will pay Smelter Inc's bank, which will pay the amount into Smelter Inc's account. If not, it will return the cheque to Smelter Inc's bank marked NSF (non-sufficient funds). Such an event will alert Smelter Inc to the risk that it might not be paid if it ships the steel to Val-Nam. Figure 8.1 is a copy of Val-Nam's cheque.

Cheques are payable on demand anytime after the date that appears on the cheque, provided that the cheque is presented for payment within a reasonable time. In Canada and the United States, the time is usually six months, after which the cheque is stale-dated and therefore no longer negotiable.

While most businesses accept company cheques, some do not. If Smelter Inc does not want to accept Val-Nam's cheque, Val-Nam may have to provide cash, use a bank cheque, or use a bank money order. Val-Nam could also make payment by electronic transfer, if it is set up for e-banking. These methods of payment are more secure than a simple company cheque because, in our example, Val-Nam must pay the required

Figure 8.1 Negotiable Instruments: Val-Nam's Cheque to Smelter Inc

* Signature of authorized signing officer for payer, Val-Nam Generation Limited

funds to the bank before the bank will issue the cheque or money order. A certified cheque offers similar security, because the bank certifies it only after withdrawing the funds from the customer's account.

Once the drawee bank honours Val-Nam's cheque, Val-Nam's debt to Smelter Inc is extinguished. Val-Nam, or any payer, may choose to note details about a transaction on a cheque so that there is clear evidence that the debt has been paid. For example, Val-Nam may write "payment for steel ordered May 2, 2017, invoice 1234" for the purpose of its own records. Banks either retain cancelled cheques for a certain time or return them immediately to the customer.

Since a cheque is a negotiable instrument, the payee may assign or transfer the right of payment to someone else. Smelter Inc, for example, might wish to transfer its right to payment to Scoop Mines Ltd, one of its creditors. In this case, Scoop Mines becomes the holder and may present the cheque to Val-Nam's bank for payment. To transfer its right to payment to Scoop Mines, Smelter Inc must endorse the cheque. Endorsement can occur in either of the following ways:

1. *In blank.* Smelter Inc signs the back of the cheque and passes it to Scoop Mines, in which case Scoop Mines or anyone else can cash it.
2. *By restrictive endorsement.* Smelter Inc writes "pay to Scoop Mines Ltd only" and signs the back of the cheque. In this case, only Scoop Mines can cash the cheque; it cannot further endorse it for someone else to cash.

Consumer Bills and Notes

Businesses often use promissory notes when their customers purchase expensive consumer items, such as cars or large appliances, on installment. The notes are documents that set out the terms and conditions for repayment of the loan. Like other bills of exchange, promissory notes often provide for the payment of interest after their due date; they may also require the payment of interest before the due date.

In the past, the use of negotiable instruments in consumer purchases sometimes created problems. The fact that a promissory note is a negotiable instrument that can be transferred to a third party meant that consumers who bought defective goods could sometimes be held responsible for paying an innocent third party who had purchased the note from the seller. For example, Kyle might give a promissory note for part of the purchase price of a used car to Ed's Car Lot. Ed might sell the promissory note to his bank at a discount, in return for cash. The bank now holds the note and is entitled to enforce it against Kyle. What if the car is defective? The bank still has the right to collect the debt from Kyle, even if the car was defective. Kyle's only right with respect to the defect was to sue Ed's Car Lot. If Ed had gone bankrupt or disappeared, the bank, as a **holder**, is still entitled to payment. To address this problem, the *Bills of Exchange Act* now provides consumers with some protection. The legislation modified the rules governing traditional bills and notes. First, the bank that purchases a promissory note from the original seller no longer has an automatic right to collect from a consumer like Kyle who bought a defective product. Now, a consumer may raise any defence they could have raised against the original seller of a defective product against the bank as a defence to any claim by the bank for payment. Second, the legislation requires that a consumer bill or note be marked "consumer purchase." This provides notice to purchasers of consumer notes that they will be subject to claims and defences that a consumer could raise against the original creditor. Note that, with respect to business debtors who have signed promissory notes, the bank still has the right to repayment by the business debtor, regardless of any disputes between the business debtor and the original lender on the note.

holder
person who is assigned the right to be paid on a promissory note by the creditor originally entitled to be paid

MINIMIZING YOUR RISK

Use Bills of Exchange Wisely

- Try to negotiate the interest rate and the timing of payments for large purchases.
- Check whether you can obtain more favourable interest and repayment terms by using a line of credit with a bank for ongoing business operations instead of using a promissory note or other bill of exchange.
- In a non-consumer purchase, negotiate terms that prevent or limit the creditor from assigning or transferring payment rights to a third party.
- Negotiate to pay a lesser sum than owed if you are in default. Creditors are usually not interested in lawsuits.

Credit Cards

The use of credit cards has increased astronomically since they were introduced in the 1960s by banks and some businesses. Credit cards are not negotiable instruments. Nor can they be construed as money in the ordinary sense because they do not necessarily bear any relationship to currency in the hands of the cardholder. Rather, they are a form of money substitute that allows purchasers to buy now and (presumably) pay later.

General card issuers, such as Visa or MasterCard, sometimes charge an annual fee. In addition, they charge participating businesses a fee on each transaction and may charge other fees as well. Their biggest profits, however, come from cardholders who do not pay their monthly balances in full. Those who have unpaid balances may pay anywhere from 10 to 20 percent interest. This easy but expensive credit, critics say, has led to an increase in consumer bankruptcy and a decline in consumers' personal savings rates.

Businesses also use credit cards, but not in the way consumers do. They would not use a credit card to purchase a major asset where they could make this purchase by obtaining a loan from a financial institution or using a negotiable instrument. The reason for this is that the interest rate on the purchase is much higher on a credit card than on a negotiable instrument, or almost any other type of business credit. Businesses use cards to buy small items and to cover employees' business-related expenses. For example, employees who travel on business often use a company credit card to cover hotel and meal expenses. The monthly statement goes directly to the business, which usually pays the account promptly to avoid high interest charges. It is a convenient way of paying expenses.

Electronic Banking

Electronic banking (e-banking) is a term that describes the use of computers, public automated teller machines (ATMs or bank machines), and telephones, including wireless phones, by bank customers to perform many of their banking transactions instead of having to complete paper documents and attend bank branches in person. E-banking, particularly online banking and ATMs, has had a great impact on consumers.

Businesses can also conduct day-to-day transactions by bank machine, online, or by telephone, and they can monitor their accounts, including payments on loans. Many use telephones or computers for receivables when customers pay by credit cards. As with consumers, a business needs an online account name or number and password to access e-banking and must ensure that this information can be kept secure to prevent unauthorized use and fraud. As well, because many of these transactions are done on the Internet, they are vulnerable to hackers. If you intend to rely on e-banking, it is wise to invest in anti-virus, anti-spyware, and other specialized security software. Many financial institutions have separate account agreements for e-banking. Be sure to look at these carefully to see how the cost of e-banking fraud is apportioned, keeping in mind that financial institutions tend to resort to standard form contracts that they draft and on which they may not be prepared to negotiate.

One form of e-banking, EFT, is seeing dramatically increased use by Canadian businesses. EFT is a bank-account-to-bank-account transfer of funds that is instantaneous and secure. It is commonly used to pay employee wages (direct deposit transactions), make automatic electronic bill payments, and allow customers to pay through use of a debit card.

However, in more complex arrangements—such as negotiating business loans—face-to-face transactions prevail. And e-banking is of limited use to businesses such as convenience stores and coffee shops, because businesses that operate on a cash basis still need to physically take the cash to the bank. However, many small businesses do now use various forms of e-banking, offering the option to pay using devices that accept both credit cards and debit cards from customers. Because financial institutions using credit cards, such as Visa or MasterCard, charge businesses a fee on each electronic transaction, some businesses only accept debit cards, where there is either no fee or a very low fee. For the same reason, some businesses will

Figure 8.2

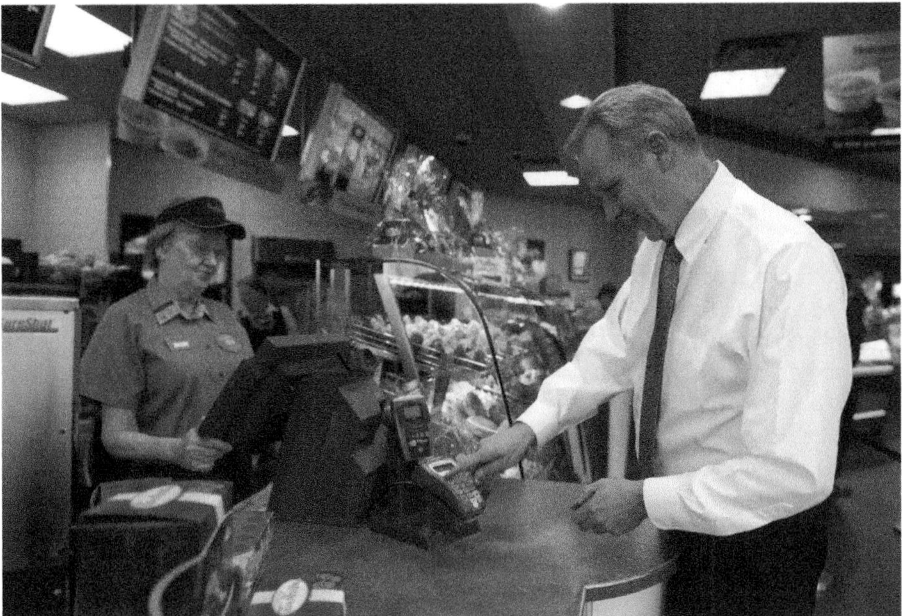

After resisting for many years, Canada's popular coffee chain Tim Hortons finally allowed customers to pay by debit card in 2010.

offer a discount if a purchase is made by cash rather than by credit card, though this is much more common in the United States than in Canada.

Account Agreements

Before the government made changes in the financial services sector, when your business opened a bank account, you signed an account agreement that set out the bank's rules about the operation of the account and apportioned risk resulting from errors or negligence between your business and the bank. Account agreements, which were drawn up by the bank, were often composed in legal language and were not negotiable. Not surprisingly, they usually favoured the bank and required a business to accept most of the risk and liabilities that could arise from the use of its account.

Since 2001, the Financial Consumer Agency of Canada (FCAC) has been encouraging banks to establish codes of conduct and to become more business- and consumer-friendly. One of the results of the FCAC's work is a reshaping of the old account agreement into a general financial services agreement. This general agreement, usually drafted in everyday language, covers all the services that a bank offers to its customers. However, these terms often still favour the interests of the bank over those of its customers, both businesses and consumers. General agreements often contain terms such as the following:

- The agreement covers all services that the bank offers at the time the business signs the agreement, whether or not the business uses them. Should the business decide to use these services in the future, it is bound by the terms applicable on the signing date.

CASE IN POINT

Account Agreement Works in Bank's Favour

Don Bodkin Leasing Ltd v The Toronto-Dominion Bank, 1998 CanLII 1101, 40 OR (3d) 262 (CA)

Facts

For about four years, the plaintiff's accountant forged a number of cheques and gave fraudulent instructions with respect to cheques payable to the plaintiff's accounts at the defendant bank. The company failed to notify the bank of any error in the bank statements. When the fraud was discovered, the plaintiff demanded that the bank reimburse the lost funds on the grounds that the bank had delivered the cancelled cheques and bank statements to the dishonest accountant even though he was not an authorized officer named in the plaintiff's banking resolution. The bank relied on the verification clause in the account agreement with the plaintiff. The clause required that the plaintiff notify the bank of any errors within 30 days of receiving statements, after which time the bank statements are deemed to be correct. The trial judge ruled in favour of the bank on the basis that the plaintiff had sufficient information to discover the fraud. The plaintiff appealed.

Result

The appeal was dismissed. The company held out the accountant as the person responsible for the banking. It was reasonable for the bank to suppose that he had actual or apparent authority to pick up the bank statements, so that the plaintiff received the statements and cancelled cheques within the meaning of the verification clause of the account agreement. Having failed to notify the bank of any errors within 30 days, the plaintiff was deemed to have released the bank from any claim with respect to the fraudulent cheques.

Business Lesson

Make sure you exercise due care and diligence in your internal financial operations and have an appropriate system of internal control and oversight of finances. Banks are entitled to assume that this is being done, and they may rely on their verification clause for all cheques received without taking any special steps to detect fraud.

- The bank may hold cheques—that is, refuse to make money available—for a specified period of time or until the cheque has been honoured by the drawer's bank.
- The bank can require seven days' notice of a withdrawal from any account.
- The bank takes no responsibility for verifying signatures on a business's cheques. It will cash all cheques, even if they are fraudulent, unless the business can show that it took reasonable care to safeguard against fraud and checked its transactions against its statement or passbook. The business must report all errors or incidents of fraud within 30 days of receipt of the bank statement.
- If the bank makes an error, or its account machinery malfunctions, or if a business suffers loss through any failure in the bank's service—even if the bank knew the loss was likely and even if the loss resulted from the negligence of the bank or its employees—the bank is not liable for any damages.
- The business is responsible for reimbursing the bank for any legal or other costs it incurs in recovering money owed by the business.
- The bank can close all of a business's accounts and can terminate the agreement without notice to the business.

www.emond.ca/CBL3/links

DIG DEEPER

For an example of a financial services agreement, check the TD Canada Trust website.

Resolving Problems with Your Business's Bank

As a business person, what can you do if you have a complaint about a bank's treatment of your financial affairs? Suppose, for example, that the bank negligently makes an error in crediting your account and, thinking you have insufficient funds, refuses to honour cheques you have written to creditors. Your creditors sue you for non-payment. Under the provisions of its account agreement, the bank may exempt itself from any liability for its error. In a situation like this, the answer depends on whether the financial institution you are dealing with is federally or provincially regulated. If you wish to complain about a bank, particularly if it has breached a regulatory requirement, go to the FCAC. If the financial institution operates under provincial regulation, you may make your complaint to a provincial body; in Ontario, the Financial Services Commission of Ontario handles complaints.

In the past decade or so, regulators have been paying attention to the growing friction between consumers of financial services and the financial institutions that supply them. Regulators have made provision for informal resolution of disputes and for review of decisions by banks to reduce customer services, particularly in rural areas. These services are designed for individual consumers, however, not for businesses. Businesses are basically on their own.

This is not a problem for large corporations. Because they are major customers, and a source of great profit for financial institutions, the institutions are responsive to their needs. But small businesses are more like individual consumers from the bank's point of view: it is more expensive to provide services to them than to large corporations, and small businesses generally pose much higher risks as borrowers than large corporations. Many small businesses complain about the cavalier treatment they receive from banks, the complicated procedures, and the resistance to extending credit on acceptable terms. If a business finds itself in a dispute with a bank, existing government agencies are of little use in the absence of outright fraud by the bank. The only real recourse, if a business cannot work out its problems with the bank, is to sue, either for negligence if the bank has been derelict in its duty or for breach of contract if the bank is in breach of its account agreement.

MINIMIZING YOUR RISK

Get the Best Possible Deal from Your Financial Institution

- Try to negotiate some of the terms of your account agreement, despite the fact that the agreement is a standard form. If, after signing the agreement, the bank offers more favourable terms on a particular service, renegotiate.
- Ensure you understand the terms of your account agreement before you sign it; consult a lawyer if necessary.
- Train your employees, particularly those responsible for accounts payable and receivable, to understand what the bank requires from your business.
- Be vigilant about checking your monthly statements and accounts for errors.
- Report all errors immediately in order to hold the bank responsible for them. This can be done online.
- Shop around. Financial institutions offer a variety of services, at a range of costs, and on different terms.

Financing a Business

All successful businesses ultimately meet their expenses out of the income that they generate from selling their goods or services. However, circumstances may require a business to borrow funds to finance or expand its operations, on either a short- or a long-term basis. Most businesses arrange for short-term financing by means of loans secured through banks or other financial institutions. There are a number of ways in which businesses obtain long-term financing: arranging loans from financial institutions, issuing and selling long-term company bonds with fixed interest rates, or selling shares in the business to investors.

Generally, in making a decision about how to finance a business, a business person must decide between two forms of financing: equity and debt (or a combination of the two). With **debt financing**, the business borrows capital, usually from a financial institution. The business's obligation is to repay the loan, including interest, in accordance with the terms of the loan agreement. Debt financing may also be accomplished through the sale of bonds. Individual investors buy a business's bonds, thereby providing the business with capital in exchange for a fixed or variable rate of return over a number of years.

debt financing borrowing money from a lender

Equity financing, on the other hand, is arranged through the sale of shares in a business corporation. The shares give investors an interest in the business in exchange for providing capital. The value of a company's shares generally depends on how successful the business becomes. Shareholders must accept the risk that their shares may turn out to be valueless if the business fails. They cannot sue a company for the return of their capital in the same way that a lender can sue for repayment of a loan.

equity financing raising money by issuing and selling shares in a corporation or using retained earnings to meet short- or long-term financial needs

A business person who is considering debt financing must also consider whether the debt is to be secured or unsecured. An unsecured debt is a simple promise by the debtor to repay the loan. If a debtor breaches their promise by failing to repay a loan, the lender must first sue the debtor and then enforce the judgment.

If the debt is secured, the debtor—in addition to promising to repay the debt—backs up the promise by giving the lender a security interest in something of value the debtor owns. The right or thing given as security is called **collateral**, and if the debtor fails to repay, the lender has the right to seize and sell the collateral and use the sale proceeds to pay down the loan. Examples of collateral include land, machinery, the right to collect on accounts receivables, royalties, and inventory.

collateral property that a borrower makes available to a lender to sell in order to repay the amount due on a loan if the borrower defaults

Where a creditor has an interest in collateral owned by the debtor, the creditor is known as a **secured creditor**. A secured creditor can often register their interest in a public registry system. Registration gives notice to the world that the secured creditor has an interest in the debtor's property. This means that others who have no collateral interest in the debtor's property—or who have an interest but who registered or acquired it after the secured creditor's interest was acquired and registered—cannot interfere with the secured creditor's right to seize and sell the collateral to pay down the debt. The secured creditor in this example is said to have **priority** over secured creditors who acquired or registered interests at a later date or who had no security interest at all. In situations where there are multiple creditors and few valuable assets, a creditor's place in the priority sequence can make the difference between collecting on the debt and not.

secured creditor lender who has the right to sell an asset owned by the borrower to pay a loan if the borrower defaults

priority position in a ranking system that creates the order in which competing creditors can satisfy their claims against a debtor's property

Debt Financing

Borrowing money from a lender is called debt financing, a concept that can include both short- and long-term borrowing. Val-Nam will need to decide how to finance its business by meeting its short- and long-term needs as they arise. Val-Nam may discover that its income is cyclical. It may find that it has large income receipts at the beginning of the spring, when consumers purchase generators for use at cottages, and in the early fall, when small businesses purchase generators as backup power supplies in preparation for winter storms. But in the periods between, when Val-Nam is buying supplies and manufacturing stock that is not moving as quickly, it may have very little income. Val-Nam will likely need to borrow money during these quieter periods, on a short-term basis to cover operating expenses, and repay the loan out of the profits that Val-Nam generates during the busier times in the year.

Val-Nam may also wish to increase its manufacturing capacity by buying additional land and building a new manufacturing facility. For these capital expenditures, it will need long-term financing—that is, Val-Nam may need to incur debt that it will repay over several years. If this is the case, Val-Nam should be knowledgeable about secured and unsecured credit, general credit agreements, and corporate bonds. We examine these types of debt financing in the sections that follow.

Unsecured and Secured Credit

As we have already noted, a lender can extend credit to a business on a secured or an unsecured basis. In an **unsecured loan**, a lender advances funds to a borrower in exchange for a simple promise to repay the loan. If the borrower does not repay the loan, the lender's only legal recourse is to sue the borrower on the promise to repay. With a **secured loan**, the borrower promises the lender that they will repay the loan *and* provides the lender with rights in collateral. If the borrower does not repay the loan, the lender can still sue the borrower, but the lender may also seize the collateral, sell it, and use the money from the sale to pay down the loan.

unsecured loan
loan given without collateral in exchange for a simple promise to repay

secured loan
loan for which a borrower provides collateral that the lender may sell to pay the loan if the borrower defaults

A lender rarely provides unsecured credit unless there is

- an ongoing relationship between the parties,
- a high degree of trust,
- a small loan,
- a short repayment period, and
- a high expectation that the loan will be repaid.

If one or more of these criteria is absent, the lender is likely to insist that the loan be secured because security increases the likelihood of repayment. Depending on the relationship between Angelic Battiste and Val-Nam, Angelic may be willing to extend an unsecured loan to Val-Nam. However, if she does that, her only recourse if she is not paid is to sue Val-Nam on its promise to repay the debt, and she may never get her money back. She can obtain a judgment—that is, a court order that Val-Nam repay her; however, collecting the debt can quickly become very costly, and she may have little to show for her efforts. Furthermore, if Val-Nam goes bankrupt, Angelic cannot enforce the judgment at all, but must claim against Val-Nam's estate along with all the other unsecured creditors. If she is lucky, she may collect 25 cents on each dollar owed.

However, if the loan is secured, Angelic will have additional remedies at her disposal if there is a default. Failure to pay an installment and bankruptcy are obvious acts of default, but the secured loan agreement may include other acts of default. For example, some agreements define an act of default to include failure to pay another creditor, even though payments to the secured lender under the loan agreement are in good standing.

On default, most secured loan agreements permit the lender to seize control of the collateral and sell it without having to obtain a court order. In such a case, Angelic may recover the funds that she loaned Val-Nam—and the money she spent on selling the collateral—from the proceeds of the sale. If the funds obtained from the sale do not cover the loan, Angelic can then sue Val-Nam for the balance still owing. If the funds obtained from the sale exceed what is owed to Angelic, Val-Nam is entitled to the excess amount.

Declaring bankruptcy constitutes a default under the terms of most secured loan agreements. Therefore, if Val-Nam goes bankrupt, Angelic would be entitled to take steps to recover her investment by seizing the collateral, which gives her interest in Val-Nam's property priority over the interests of its unsecured creditors. This is why an unsecured creditor often recovers little or nothing from a bankrupt: the secured creditors are first in line and take the bankrupt's most valuable assets.

Negotiating a Credit Agreement

The decision of an individual or a financial institution to advance credit to a business will depend on their assessment of the business's prospects for making a profit. It is therefore important for businesses to consider their credit options in relation to their projected profitability and to prepare carefully when negotiating a credit agreement.

When dealing with a financial institution, you must first determine which institution you want to deal with. In making your choice, you should consider the following factors:

- *How willing is the financial institution to assume risk?* If an institution is willing to assume some risk, it will be more likely to grant a loan, but the risk that it assumes may be reflected in a relatively high interest rate.
- *Can the institution give you useful financial advice?* Some financial institutions offer financial analysis, provide assistance with cash flow planning, and make helpful suggestions based on their experience with businesses similar to your own.
- *Does the institution understand your business and your market?* It is helpful to have a bank manager, or loans officer, who is familiar with your type of business and understands its particular needs.
- *Does the institution have loan limits?* Many new businesses fail because they are inadequately financed. The ability to obtain adequate funding when you need it is important to your business's ultimate success.

In order to persuade a bank to finance Val-Nam, it will need a written business plan. An effective plan accomplishes the following:

- *It tells potential lenders why the business needs money.* For example, it explains that green energy has become very fashionable and demand for sources of green energy has surged across Canada. Val-Nam seeks to expand its business by opening new manufacturing facilities in key cities.

- *It explains how the business intends to use the money to improve operations and profitability.* It describes Val-Nam's intention to use the capital to purchase land, build a manufacturing plant, buy machinery, and purchase raw materials to meet the increased market demand.
- *It describes the competence and industry experience of key company employees.* It identifies key managers and employees in terms of their skills, their experience, and the length of time they have been with the company. Val-Nam may attach resumés for each person.
- *It sets out the amount of money needed.* It sets out Val-Nam's capital needs, estimating the amount required for land, construction, new equipment, staff, staff training, and inventory. It also provides projected revenue estimates.
- *It describes the sources and types of collateral that are available.* It identifies those assets that are available as collateral and estimates the value of each asset. Val-Nam should arrange the assets by class: land, buildings, machinery, vehicles, inventory, and accounts receivable, for example.
- *It states when the business will repay the loan.* On the basis of revenue estimates, it presents several options for repayment. To do this, Val-Nam must calculate various credible estimates based on different installment amounts and payment dates.

In addition—particularly if Val-Nam is an established company—it should provide the financial institution with a cash flow analysis that shows the times in the fiscal year when income exceeds expenses and when expenses are higher than income and explains this cycle. An intelligent analysis is especially important in a seasonal business such as Val-Nam's, which will need short-term loans to cover some of its slow periods.

The financial institution will also expect to see that Val-Nam has a risk management program to safeguard its investment in the company. It may require that Val-Nam carry risk management insurance as well as life insurance for key personnel.

Once Val-Nam has gathered the necessary information, it is ready to negotiate a credit agreement. Val-Nam's mission is to obtain the highest possible credit limit at the lowest possible interest rate. The more solid Val-Nam appears to be, and the better its profit record, the more likely the financial institution will be to offer the terms that it gives to its most creditworthy commercial borrowers.

General Security Agreements

A financial institution will often require a borrower to enter into a **general security agreement**. Such an agreement, whose purpose is to secure the institution's loan, is usually required before financial institutions will extend short-term credit to cover operating expenses and cash flow fluctuations, and in some cases before they will extend credit to cover capital loans (loans of relatively large sums usually used for expansion or improvement of a business). In a general security agreement, a borrower pledges all or most of its assets as collateral or security for a loan. Financial institutions may also require that the officers and directors of small businesses pledge their personal assets—their homes, for example—as security for the business's loan. Early on it its development, Val-Nam may need to have key personnel like Valery Garza (director, president, and CEO), Namid Blackburn (vice-president, research and development), and Mitchell Wu (director and vice-president, marketing) guarantee the loan and pledge their personal assets.

general security agreement
pledge, often used by a debtor's bank, of most of a debtor's assets to cover short-term loans made over an extended period

Because loans may be advanced in the future and may be in amounts not yet known, the general security agreement requires that Val-Nam—and possibly its officers and directors—pledge a pool of assets sufficiently large to cover its future debt. This pool of assets will vary from time to time. This pledge is called a **floating charge**. It is created because Val-Nam needs to be free to use its assets to earn income. For example, Val-Nam may pledge its heavy machinery, inventory of supplies, and accounts receivable as collateral. However, it may need to sell or replace machinery. Supplies will be used up, inventory will be sold, and customers will pay their bills, thus replacing accounts receivable with company income. The floating charge permits individual assets in the listed categories to be used up, sold, or replaced.

floating charge
class of collateral, such as inventory, where a creditor allows a debtor to dispose of items in the class

If Val-Nam defaults on its loan, the floating charge over all of these assets "crystallizes"—that is, the charge attaches to all of the specific assets in the various pledged classes at the time of default. The charge crystallizes only to the extent of the debt, of course, because the financial institution is not able to recover more than Val-Nam owes it.

Potential lenders often want to know if other lenders already have a security interest in a business's assets. For this reason, a security agreement can be registered under provincial legislation. Registration is public notice of a creditor's security interests. If Val-Nam pledges assets as security for one loan when it has already pledged these assets as security for another loan, the earlier lender takes priority over the later lender in seizing and selling the collateral, provided that the earlier lender has registered its security agreement.

In practical terms, this means that the later lender must stand back and allow the registered lender with a prior interest to seize and sell the collateral. Regardless of which lender seizes and sells the collateral, if there is nothing left after the earlier lender is repaid, the later lender is out of luck. Generally, whoever registers first has priority, and it does not matter that the second lender did not search the registry before advancing funds. Registration is notice, whether a lender checks the registry or not.

Corporate Bonds

corporate bond
company's written promise to repay the buyer (of the bond) both principal and interest at specified intervals

A **corporate bond** is a company's written promise to repay the buyer of the bond—who is also the lender—both principal and interest at a fixed rate at specified intervals. Bonds are often used by large public companies to raise capital, with repayment periods spread over long periods—for example, 10, 20, or 30 years. Should the company become bankrupt, bondholders are entitled to recover their capital investment in a company ahead of all of the company's shareholders.

A company may use more than one class of bond to raise money. Differences in the terms of individual bonds—for example, the interest rate payable on the bond—may affect both the bond's initial price and its price on resale. In general, secured bonds (bonds backed by collateral) make safer and more expensive investments than unsecured bonds. Unsecured bonds issued by a company in poor financial condition are often called junk bonds, and the interest rates offered are higher to compensate for the increased risk.

Although bonds are a form of debt financing, they are not arranged between a business and an individual lender, as a loan is. Bonds are often issued in amounts far too large to be attractive to an individual lender, and a successful bond issue needs to attract many investors. For these reasons, bonds are issued in a manner that is similar to the way that shares are sold. Several financial institutions or a brokerage house may be given the task of marketing a company's bonds to the general public or to institutional investors. Those who wish to invest may buy units of the bond offering. After bonds have been initially offered to the public, investors who buy them may also sell them to other investors, in the same way that shareholders may sell their shares.

Once a bond has been issued, its resale value will be governed by its rating and also by the economy generally. If interest rates are rising, the value of bonds tends to fall. To minimize risk, bond investors scrutinize a bond's terms, the bond market generally, future market trends, and the performance of the company that issued the bond. To assist investors, bond-rating services, such as Moody's, Standard & Poor's, and Canadian Bond Rating Services, rate both government and corporate bonds, assessing them as high-grade, medium-grade, speculative, or poor-grade investments. These assessments are often expressed in letter grades: AAA is a high-grade investment; C or D is considered a high risk.

MINIMIZING YOUR RISK

Use Debt Financing Wisely

- Distinguish between the amount you want to borrow and the amount you can afford to repay. They may not necessarily be the same. Your objective is to borrow capital, not to end up in bankruptcy.
- Estimate projected income and profits conservatively to ensure that you can meet the debt obligations you are incurring.
- Consider whether you can get someone to guarantee your loan. If someone who is creditworthy guarantees repayment, a lender may extend funds to you on more favourable terms or may forgo security.
- Decide whether you have collateral that you wish to give as security for the loan. Collateral may increase the amount of the loan and lower your interest rate.
- In giving security, try to use valuable assets that are not closely tied to production. If, for example, a business owns land that is not central to its operations, the land could provide valuable security for a lender, the seizure of which would not hamper the company's operations.
- Try to avoid giving inventory or accounts receivable as collateral because both directly affect cash flow and the ability to repay debts.
- If you default on a loan, try to renegotiate to extend the time for payment or reduce or defer the interest. Your lender may be amenable if there is any prospect that your fortunes will improve.

Equity Financing

So far, we have been talking about debt financing—that is, borrowing funds from financial institutions and bondholders. A second approach is equity financing. Equity financing involves the contribution of funds by the shareholders. In the case of a privately held corporation, this may involve a contribution by the founders or it may involve an "angel investor," like Angelic, who invests in the business but is not otherwise involved. In the case of public companies, equity financing involves issuing and selling shares to institutional investors and the public.

Shares

initial public offering (IPO) first offering of shares by a corporation to the public through a brokerage firm to raise capital for use by the company

Suppose Val-Nam wishes to raise funds by issuing shares and selling them to members of the public. If Val-Nam is issuing new shares, it will sell them by making an **initial public offering (IPO)** on a stock exchange. To do this, Val-Nam will enter into a contract with a brokerage house. Often the brokerage house, either alone or in combination with investment banks, will buy the shares—thus providing Val-Nam with capital—and will then sell them to the general public. Before Val-Nam's shares can be sold to the public, Val-Nam will have to issue a detailed prospectus, providing information about ownership of the company, its assets, performance, the purpose for which the shares were issued, and any other data that will allow purchasers to make an informed decision about whether to buy the shares. We provide further information about the contents of prospectuses in Chapter 7 under the heading "Private Versus Public Corporations."

common shares shares whose dividends are paid at the discretion of a corporation's management on the basis of the company's profits after dividend payments have been made on preferred shares

Common shares are the most widely traded shares. They can produce a return on investment for shareholders in two ways:

1. through dividends, that is, a company's distribution of its profits to its shareholders, and
2. through resale by shareholders to new investors at a higher price than originally paid.

preferred shares shares for which dividends are paid before any dividends are paid on common shares

Unlike interest that is paid to a bondholder, payment of dividends is always at the discretion of the board of directors of the corporation. Some shares, called **preferred shares**, provide that, should the corporation choose to distribute dividends, the preferred shareholders must be paid before the common shareholders. This makes the price of preferred shares less volatile than the price of common shares and makes them somewhat more certain of producing some benefit for shareholders. However, shareholders will pay a premium price for preferred shares.

MINIMIZING YOUR RISK

Use Equity Financing Wisely

- Calculate your capital needs, and analyze the reasons you need this amount and your company's prospects.
- Take great care in preparing a fair and accurate prospectus to avoid lawsuits for fraudulent or negligent misrepresentation, and prosecution by securities commissions.
- Because the brokerage house or financial institution that is managing the sale stands to make a large commission on sales, negotiate the terms of an initial public offering.
- If you are concerned about restless shareholders or hostile takeovers, remember that common shares have voting rights, but preferred shares do not.

The Pros and Cons of Equity Versus Debt Financing

A company's "capital structure" refers to its mix of debt and equity financing. Achieving an appropriate capital structure usually requires consideration of a number of factors, some of which are listed in Table 8.1.

Table 8.1 Equity Versus Debt Financing

	Debt Financing	Equity Financing
Timing of repayment	Accurate prediction of a company's future performance is required to meet a repayment schedule.	No payment plan is required.
Cost of financing	Regular principal and interest payments are required.	Payments are made in the form of dividends only when the company generates profits and when other financial needs (i.e., growth) are not considered a priority.
Effect on company's assets	Assets are usually required as collateral and will be sold in the event of default.	Shareholders accept the risk of loss if the company does poorly and take assets only after all creditors are paid.
Tax implications	Interest payments are deductible from business income.	Dividends paid to shareholders are not tax-deductible.
Control of the company	Lenders have no direct influence over the management of the company, but payment of principal and interest at regular intervals reduces the amount of profit available for such things as new equipment and advertising. In case of default, secured creditors can seize assets and may be able to take over management.	Profits can be used for growth rather than dividends, subject to shareholders' right to remove directors and seize control or influence management. One company can take control of another by buying up shares on the stock market. This may be friendly (encouraged by management) or hostile (not encouraged by management), and a bidding war for shares may occur.

From this discussion, it might appear that a business can minimize its risk by preferring equity financing over debt financing. However, a company may need to sell a lot of shares—thereby greatly expanding its ownership base—in order to raise the funding that it needs. In smaller businesses like Val-Nam, key shareholders control the management of a company, and they may not be willing to share control with a group of dissatisfied shareholders, nor do they wish to set the scene for a successful takeover of the company. For these reasons, most companies opt for a mix of both debt and equity financing.

Debt Collection and Insolvency

In the sections that follow, we examine the legal relationship between creditors and debtors. How do creditors go about assessing risk before they extend credit? What do they do when a debtor fails to pay them back? When do they send a defaulting debtor into bankruptcy?

Creditor Protection

When a creditor extends credit, the aim is to make a profit and avoid loss. The interest rate the creditor will decide to charge depends both on market rates and on the assessment of the risk in lending money to a particular debtor in particular circumstances: the higher the risk, the higher the interest rate.

If, for example, Val-Nam seeks to raise capital by obtaining credit from a credit union, the credit union will examine Val-Nam's business plan to see if Val-Nam's proposal makes economic sense. The lender may also assess Val-Nam's credit application against economic trends and other factors relevant to the green energy sector in which Val-Nam is active. The lender will also examine Val-Nam's credit history to see how diligent it was in repaying past debt. If the company has a good track record, both as debtor and as participant in a profitable industry, the credit union will likely advance the loan at a relatively low interest rate. If Val-Nam's credit record is bad, if the green energy sector is unstable, or if Val-Nam's business performance has been average despite a generally profitable market, the credit union will likely demand a higher interest rate or may refuse to lend Val-Nam money.

Credit History

The credit union can inquire into Val-Nam's credit history in a number of ways: through credit reporting agencies and through bankruptcy, execution, and secured transaction searches. We examine each of these methods in the following sections. We also take a detailed look at the ranking of interests of both secured and unsecured creditors.

CASE IN POINT

The Importance of Correct Credit Information

Dimov v Equifax Canada Co, 2017 NSSM 1

Facts

Dimov claimed that Equifax had compiled and placed on its files incorrect information about his creditworthiness. As a result, he claimed he was unable to acquire credit cards or obtain a car loan and generally suffered refusals to advance him credit based on information lenders had obtained from Equifax on his creditworthiness. He complained about this to Equifax and asked the credit reporting agency to correct its credit report.

Equifax's position was that it had contacted the creditor that had supplied the information, and that the creditor had verified the information it had supplied, although there were inconsistencies that indicated the report was full of errors, as Dimov had tried to point out. Equifax argued that having made the inquiry and received confirmation of the information on record from the creditor, there was nothing further it was obliged to do, and the record would remain as it was. Equifax did not provide Dimov with contact information about the creditor so that Dimov could contact the creditor directly to try and correct the information it had supplied to Equifax.

Result

Dimov's action against Equifax was successful. The court held that while Equifax had made an inquiry as required by the Nova Scotia *Consumer Reporting Act*, it had not carried out its duties with "skill and diligence" as the statute required. In effect, this imposes on a credit reporting agency a duty of care requiring a careful and diligent check on credit reports when there is a complaint, with a finding of negligence with damages to follow if the credit reporting agency fails to exercise care and diligence. Although the creditor who had supplied erroneous information to Equifax was not sued, it is likely that it could have been sued and been found liable.

Business Lesson

Credit reporting agencies rely on creditors to supply information about a debtor. Such information can contain errors. Because these errors can damage someone's reputation and finances, credit reporting agencies allow individuals to check their credit information and suggest corrections. Wise business persons will check and review their own credit reports to ensure they are accurate. As well, a debtor has a right to see the detailed report on which their credit rating is based and to contact not only the credit reporting agency, but the supplier of the report. If information should be corrected but is not, the debtor could bring an action against both the credit reporting agency and the provider of the incorrect information. In addition to an action for negligently posting inaccurate and damaging information, this fact situation could also, in some circumstances, give rise to an action for libel and slander if the negligence results in the circulation of false information that damages the debtor's reputation.

CREDIT REPORTING AGENCIES

If Val-Nam has ever issued corporate bonds, potential lenders can check indexes such as Canada Bond Rating Services to see how these bonds have been rated (bonds and their ratings were discussed above under the heading "Corporate Bonds"). Let us assume, though, that Val-Nam is a relatively small company, with a relatively small amount of capital, and therefore is unlikely ever to have issued bonds as a means of raising funds.

In this case, the credit union can look to its own informal information networks based on information gathered by its loan officers, or it may use a commercial credit reporting agency, such as Equifax. These agencies are clearinghouses for information about credit transactions, and they can provide Val-Nam's credit transaction history. The credit union can use this information to contact other creditors and obtain details about Val-Nam's repayment of debt. Some credit reporting agencies have inexpensive online search facilities where clients either pay on a per-search basis or pay an annual fee to use an agency's database.

All credit reporting agencies have an obligation to correct inaccurate information about a debtor if the debtor demands it. Businesses that become aware that inaccurate information is being held about them may call the agency and provide the correct information or file a complaint with the relevant regulatory agency, such as a provincial consumer and business relations ministry.

www.emond.ca/CBL3/links

DIG DEEPER

Learn more about Equifax and TransUnion, two of the larger credit reporting agencies, from their websites.

BANKRUPTCY, EXECUTION, AND SECURED TRANSACTION SEARCHES

Potential creditors may also search public databanks for information about a debtor's past repayment performance and conduct any of the following inexpensive searches:

1. *Bankruptcy searches.* A lender can search online at www.strategis.gc.ca to determine if the debtor has gone bankrupt in the past, is being petitioned into bankruptcy, or is currently involved in the bankruptcy process.
2. *Execution searches.* Anyone who has obtained a judgment against a defendant (in a lawsuit concerning debt or anything else) is likely to have filed a **writ of seizure and sale**—also referred to as a writ of execution. Such a writ directs a sheriff to seize and sell a defendant's assets and to use the money from the sale to pay the judgment that a plaintiff has obtained against the defendant. An execution search would tell the credit union whether there are any judgments against Val-Nam, and if so, it would identify Val-Nam's judgment creditors, as well as specify the amount of the judgments and how much remains to be paid.

writ of seizure and sale
court order directing a sheriff to seize and sell assets belonging to a judgment debtor and pay the money from the sale to a judgment creditor; also called a "writ of execution"

3. *Secured transaction searches.* The credit union will likely ask Val-Nam for security in the form of collateral. It needs to know that any property that Val-Nam offers as collateral is not already pledged to other creditors. It also needs to know that Val-Nam actually owns the collateral that it will be pledging as security. Secured transaction searches will show whether Val-Nam is the owner of the collateral, whether there are others with an interest in it, and the nature and extent of these interests. It is essential that the credit union perform these searches because, if another creditor has already registered an interest in Val-Nam's collateral, the interest of the earlier-registered creditor will take priority over any later-registered interest of the credit union. Important registries include the following:

    a. *Land titles or registry search.* In Ontario, registries maintained under the *Land Titles Act* and the *Registry Act* contain a record of interests in land—for example, ownership interests, mortgage interests, and construction liens (a security interest that can be taken by contractors for unpaid work).
    b. *Personal property security registry search.* In Ontario, a registry maintained under the *Personal Property Security Act* allows a creditor to register its interest in any personal property (property other than land) that a debtor has pledged as collateral. Registered security agreements will describe the collateral that a debtor has pledged and the amount of the loan at the time the agreement was registered. Potential creditors may contact existing security holders to obtain details about their security interests.
    c. *Bank Act search.* Certain Canadian businesses—usually large ones in specific commercial sectors, such as mining and manufacturing—can obtain long-term loans from chartered banks to finance their operations. Under section 427 of the *Bank Act*, if the business gives the bank a collateral interest in an asset to secure continued financing, the bank acquires an ownership interest in the asset. The bank keeps title to the asset until the business repays the loan. The business retains possession of the asset and can use it in the usual course of its operations, as long as it keeps making payments on its loan. A potential creditor can conduct a search to determine the extent of a bank's interest in the property of a potential debtor.

Priority Among Creditors

Suppose Fly By Night Finance gave credit to Val-Nam last year, and Venture Fund gave it a loan this year. If Val-Nam cannot pay either of its creditors in full because it has insufficient assets to cover its debts, which creditor has the right to be paid first? The answer depends on which creditor's debt was secured, whether the security interest was registered, and when.

UNSECURED CREDITORS

As we have discussed earlier in the section entitled "Unsecured and Secured Credit," unsecured creditors are those who extend credit in exchange for a simple promise by the debtor to repay the debt. If the debtor fails to repay the debt, the creditor's only remedy is to sue the debtor for repayment. Suppose that Val-Nam defaults on a debt and Smelter Inc, one of its unsecured creditors, obtains a judgment against it for $50,000. If Smelter Inc takes action to enforce the judgment—that is, finds one of Val-Nam's assets that is valuable and has the sheriff seize and sell the asset (note that this asset cannot be subject to the claim of a secured creditor)—Smelter Inc will use the proceeds of the sale first to pay the costs of the sale and then to pay Val-Nam's debt.

But what happens if more than one unsecured creditor obtains a judgment against Val-Nam? If other judgment creditors have filed writs of seizure and sale with the sheriff against Val-Nam—and have thereby become **execution creditors** of Val-Nam—the sheriff must pay them all on a pro rata basis. Figure 8.3 demonstrates such a payment.

execution creditor
creditor who has obtained a judgment and seeks to enforce (execute) it

Figure 8.3 Pro Rata Payment of Unsecured Execution Creditors

Val-Nam has three execution creditors:

- **It owes creditor A $50,000.**
- **It owes creditor B $20,000.**
- **It owes creditor C $10,000.**

Val-Nam's total judgment debt is therefore $80,000.

Creditor C is successful in having the sheriff seize and sell one of Val-Nam's assets, recovering $30,000.

Each creditor is entitled to payment in accordance with the following pro rata payment formula:

$$\frac{\text{amount recovered in sale} \times \text{amount owing to creditor}}{\text{amount owing to all creditors}} = \text{share paid to creditor}$$

Therefore:

Creditor A receives $$\frac{\$30{,}000 \times \$50{,}000}{\$80{,}000} = \$18{,}750$$

Creditor B receives $$\frac{\$30{,}000 \times \$20{,}000}{\$80{,}000} = \$7{,}500$$

Creditor C receives $$\frac{\$30{,}000 \times \$10{,}000}{\$80{,}000} = \$3{,}750$$

SECURED CREDITORS

How does a secured creditor get priority over another secured creditor? The general rule is that the secured creditor with the earliest registered interest in a particular item of collateral takes priority over other secured creditors with interests in the same collateral. This means that if the debtor defaults, any secured creditor can seize and sell the collateral, but money from the sale must be paid out to the creditor with the earliest registered interest first, after which the next most senior secured creditor is paid, and so on. Once all secured creditors are paid from the proceeds, the remaining amount is available for distribution pro rata among any unsecured creditors. However, if there is not enough money from the sale to pay all of the secured creditors, the most junior creditor may not be paid at all.

CASE IN POINT

Ownership of Property During Bankruptcy Proceedings

Business Development Bank of Canada v S and S Mobile Refrigeration, [1996] OJ No 4680 (QL) (Sup Ct J)

Facts

This was an application for a declaration that the creditor bank held a prior security interest over S and S Mobile. The applicant bank was a creditor of a bankrupt restaurant. The bank held a personal property security agreement with a floating charge on all the assets and a realty mortgage on the land. The respondent, S and S Mobile Refrigeration, supplied the bankrupt business with a heating-cooling unit for its building after the registration of the bank's interests. The bank gave notice to other creditors that it was appointing a receiver with respect to its floating charge against all of the bankrupt business's property and that it was exercising its mortgage remedies against the property, including fixtures on the property. S and S denied it had notice of the impending action by the bank. It removed the unit.

S and S did not register a security agreement. Its interest was perfected by repossession of the refrigeration unit. The unit was attached to the bankrupt's real property by its own weight and by gas and electricity lines. The bank argued the unit was a fixture and was covered by the realty mortgage. It also argued that the floating charge under the security agreement crystallized on the notice of appointment of the receiver. S and S argued that the bankrupt business's principal operated the restaurant as an agent of the receiver after bankruptcy. It claimed that the principal had the authority to authorize the unit's removal.

Result

The application was granted. The bank's realty mortgage did not include the cooling unit; it was attached after the mortgage was executed and registered. However, the bank had priority under the floating charge of the security agreement. The charge crystallized on the notice of appointment of the receiver, and it covered all property, including property acquired after the security agreement was registered. S and S had real knowledge of the notice and impending sale. S and S removed the unit after receiving notice. It wilfully ignored the bankrupt principal's lack of authority to permit removal of the unit.

Business Lesson

Businesses extending secured credit must be aware that sorting out claims of competing security interests can be legally very complex. Where large amounts are involved, it is advisable to use a lawyer's services to conduct necessary searches and draft the loan agreement. Businesses must also exercise care in giving notice properly to all other secured creditors when there is a default.

Creditors' Remedies

What should you do if your business becomes an unpaid creditor—if, for example, your business has supplied goods to a retailer that seems unlikely to pay for them? Most creditors are wise in pausing a moment before they seize and sell collateral or proceed with a lawsuit against the debtor. These proceedings are expensive and may not yield the desired result. Creditors who have existing relationships with defaulting debtors may want to preserve these relationships if they can.

Rather than taking aggressive action immediately, your business may choose to send a payment reminder to the debtor and, if that fails, a demand letter. A **demand letter** is a document stating that the debtor has defaulted and that the full amount owing must be paid, including interest, by a given date, or the debtor will face legal action. You must take care to phrase such a letter carefully. Do not threaten criminal proceedings for fraud or theft if the debtor does not pay; threatening to bring criminal proceedings to collect a debt constitutes the criminal offence of extortion.

demand letter
letter, usually written by a creditor's lawyer, stating that the debtor to whom the letter is addressed has defaulted and that the debtor must pay the full amount, including interest on the principal sum owing, by a given date or face legal action

A debtor may respond to your demand letter by offering to pay you all or some of the amount owing. You should consider this offer carefully. If the debtor is in financial difficulty, a negotiated settlement in which you agree to accept less than the amount you are owed may be preferable to an expensive lawsuit followed by a failed attempt to enforce a judgment after the debtor has gone bankrupt. This is particularly important for an unsecured creditor, whose interests might be near the bottom of a lengthy list of other creditors' interests. If demand letters or attempts to negotiate a compromise are unsuccessful, however, you may choose to take legal action to collect the debt.

Debt Collection for Unsecured Creditors

If your business is an unsecured creditor and a debtor does not pay you what it owes, your only remedy is to sue the debtor for failure to pay the debt and then to enforce your judgment. Depending on the amount of the debt, you can sue the debtor either in the provincial Superior Court or the Small Claims Court. Factors to consider in choosing an appropriate court, and how the litigation process works, are discussed in Chapter 2.

Debt Collection for Secured Creditors

If you are a secured creditor, the recovery methods at your disposal are simpler than if you are an unsecured creditor. You have the right to seize and sell the assets in which you have a security interest to recover what the debtor owes you. Once the sale is over, however, you have exhausted your security rights. If the sale of the security does not yield enough to pay the debt, you can still sue the debtor for the balance owing. In this suit, however, you are in the same position as any other unsecured creditor. You have no better claim against the debtor's remaining assets than anyone else.

As a secured creditor, you enjoy a number of advantages over unsecured creditors. Often, you can take action to recover the debt sooner than other creditors because your security agreement will allow you to seize and sell property as soon as the debtor defaults. You do not need a judgment or a writ of seizure and sale.

The security agreement may also define default as including actions other than non-payment of the debt. For example, it may define default as including misuse of the collateral by the debtor or the debtor's failure to pay a debt to another creditor. You are not required to obtain a court order to decide that a default has occurred. In the event that you choose to exercise a quick, self-help remedy, you can hire a private bailiff to seize and sell the collateral. Take care, however: where a secured creditor acts unfairly or oppressively, a court can void the security agreement between the creditor and debtor, and the creditor can be liable for damages. Consider the case of *Burns v Financial Bailiff Services Ltd* in this regard.

CASE IN POINT

Punitive Damages for Trespassing Bailiffs

Burns v Financial Bailiff Services Ltd, 2000 SKQB 546, [2000] SJ No 794 (QL)

Facts

Acting under a warrant of seizure, two bailiffs went to a First Nations reserve with the intention of seizing a van that was subject to a chattel mortgage. While one bailiff knocked at the door of the residence of the debtors, the other bailiff entered the van. The second bailiff also entered the van later to avoid physical confrontation with one of the debtors.

Result

The court found that seizure of the van would have been unlawful under the federal *Indian Act*, which prohibits creditors from entering a reserve to seize the property of an Indigenous person or band on a reserve. As professionals, the bailiffs knew, or are deemed to have known, this. The bailiffs therefore committed trespass, and the debtors were entitled to $3,000 in punitive damages awarded against the bailiffs and the company for which they worked.

Business Lesson

Employ reliable bailiffs who know the law and are trained to act within their legal authority.

MINIMIZING YOUR RISK

Collect Your Debts Efficiently

- Send a polite reminder, usually after 60 days from the due date.
- Search for writs of seizure and sale, registration of personal property security interests, and bankruptcy to see if there are signs of financial collapse.
- Approximately 90 days after the due date, send a demand letter.
- If you have security, use the self-help remedies to seize collateral.
- If you are an unsecured creditor, commence legal proceedings as soon as possible to stay ahead of any bankruptcy proceedings.
- If you obtain a judgment, file writs of seizure and sale immediately and carry out a judgment debtor examination to find out what assets may be available for seizure.
- Be ready to negotiate a settlement for less than what is owing, based on the likelihood of recovery of the debt and the costs of litigation. There is practical wisdom in the saying that a bird in the hand is worth two in the bush.
- If you fail to recover the debt, remember that a bad debt is a business expense that is deductible from business income for tax purposes.

Bankruptcy and Insolvency

act of bankruptcy inability to pay debts as they come due or commission of fraudulent or evasive acts to avoid creditors

Suppose Val-Nam is unable to pay its debts, has been sued by creditors, and has a number of outstanding judgments against it that it is unable to pay. It may be time to consider bankruptcy. In law, Val-Nam is in a position to go into bankruptcy if its debts exceed $1,000 and it has committed one or more acts of bankruptcy, as defined in the *Bankruptcy and Insolvency Act*. One commits an **act of bankruptcy** either by being unable to pay debts as they come due (and not having assets that can be sold to pay them) or by committing fraudulent or evasive acts to avoid creditors.

If Val-Nam decides to declare bankruptcy, what happens? The general purpose of the *Bankruptcy and Insolvency Act* is to distribute a bankrupt's assets fairly among its creditors, and then to discharge the bankrupt from further responsibility and allow it to start afresh. The Act operates by requiring bankrupt individuals and companies to turn over their assets to a trustee, who sells them and distributes the money from the sale to the bankrupt's creditors. A bankrupt who has not committed a fraud or other bankruptcy offence will be released from bankruptcy, with many of their assets gone, but with most of their debts discharged and cancelled. The bankrupt is then free to begin again, relieved of their load of debt.

You might ask why bankrupts should be able to escape their debts in this way. A short answer is that a discharged bankrupt, if freed of old debt, will be able to resume the commercial activity that ultimately benefits the economy and the consuming public as a whole. Creditors will recover at least some portion of what is owed to them, and they too will be able to continue engaging in useful economic activities and contribute to economic growth.

www.emond.ca/CBL3/links

DIG DEEPER

You can find information on bankruptcy, obtaining a trustee, and bankruptcy searches on the Bankruptcy Canada website and the Innovation, Science and Economic Development Canada website.

Bankruptcy Proceedings

If Val-Nam is in a financial position that is sufficiently insolvent for it to consider bankruptcy, it has a number of options. It may make a proposal to its creditors, make a voluntary assignment in bankruptcy, or wait for a creditor to petition it into bankruptcy. We examine each option in the following sections.

PROPOSAL TO CREDITORS

A **proposal to creditors** is an arrangement put forward on behalf of a debtor to creditors under the provisions of the *Bankruptcy and Insolvency Act*. If, for example, Val-Nam finds itself unable to pay its debts as they become due, it may decide to make a proposal in order to avoid bankruptcy and continue to carry on business. To do this, it will retain the services of a **trustee in bankruptcy** or a proposal administrator who is licensed by the Office of the Superintendent of Bankruptcy. The trustee or administrator will review Val-Nam's financial affairs with Val-Nam's management and prepare a proposal. The proposal will then be sent to the **official receiver**, a government official in the Office of the Superintendent of Bankruptcy. Once the proposal has been reviewed and approved by the official receiver, it is sent to Val-Nam's creditors. The creditors then vote as a group to accept or reject Val-Nam's proposal.

If the creditors accept Val-Nam's proposal, the proposal is then binding on Val-Nam and on all of its unsecured creditors. Secured creditors are still at liberty to seize Val-Nam's collateral, provided that Val-Nam has committed an act that amounts to a default under the security agreement between Val-Nam and the creditor. An accepted proposal means that Val-Nam will not go bankrupt and is not subject to other bankruptcy proceedings, so long as it abides by the terms of the proposal.

If the creditors reject Val-Nam's proposal, Val-Nam may make an assignment in bankruptcy and voluntarily go bankrupt, or any creditor may petition Val-Nam into bankruptcy. If, after a proposal is accepted, Val-Nam does not abide by its terms, it may also be forced into bankruptcy.

The proposal procedure we have just described should not be confused with the more complex and formal proposal procedure that is available to debtors under the *Companies' Creditors Arrangement Act*. The latter is a court procedure and is described later in this chapter.

proposal to creditors
debt restructuring proposal made under the *Bankruptcy and Insolvency Act* or the *Companies' Creditors Arrangement Act* that allows the business to continue operating and—if accepted—delays or avoids bankruptcy

trustee in bankruptcy
individual, usually an accountant, who is licensed under the *Bankruptcy and Insolvency Act* to administer a bankrupt's assets for the benefit of the bankrupt's creditors

official receiver
government official in the Office of the Superintendent of Bankruptcy who receives proposals, examines bankrupts under oath, and chairs meetings of creditors

VOLUNTARY ASSIGNMENT IN BANKRUPTCY

If Val-Nam determines that its financial position is so precarious that bankruptcy proceedings are its only sensible option, it can voluntarily declare bankruptcy. By doing so, it assigns its assets (which are called its "estate," as though it has died) for the benefit of its creditors. It then files its assignment in bankruptcy with the official receiver, at which time it officially becomes a bankrupt. The trustee in bankruptcy then takes control of Val-Nam's estate and will sell Val-Nam's assets and distribute the proceeds to its creditors.

INVOLUNTARY BANKRUPTCY PETITION

If Val-Nam remains optimistic about its financial future despite evidence that it is sinking further and further into debt, its creditors can take action. Any creditor to whom Val-Nam owes more than $1,000 (after deducting the value of any security that Val-Nam has given it), and who can identify an act of bankruptcy by Val-Nam that occurred within the last six months, may petition Val-Nam into bankruptcy. The most common act of bankruptcy that Val-Nam is likely to have committed is failing to pay its debts as they become due. The other act of bankruptcy, fraud, is difficult to prove and is alleged relatively rarely.

Therefore, if Val-Nam owes Smelter Inc $10,000 and the account has been past due for three months, Smelter Inc is in a position to file a "petition for a receiving order" with the registrar of the Bankruptcy Court (a branch of the Superior Court in the province where Val-Nam carries on business). If the petition succeeds, which it will if Smelter Inc proves the debt, the court will make a receiving order. The **receiving order** appoints a trustee, who is usually nominated by a creditor. The trustee takes control of Val-Nam's property and takes steps to sell the property on behalf of Val-Nam's creditors.

receiving order
order that appoints a trustee in bankruptcy to take control of the bankrupt's property following a creditor's successful bankruptcy petition

A petition for a receiving order can be risky and expensive for a creditor. If Smelter Inc's petition fails, Smelter Inc will probably be responsible for court costs. However, Smelter Inc may have sound reasons for taking a risk. If Val-Nam is insolvent and refuses to go bankrupt voluntarily, it will continue to deplete whatever business assets it has left. The sooner it is declared bankrupt, the sooner the trustee gets control of its assets. Assets of an insolvent company may disappear rapidly prior to bankruptcy, leaving even less for creditors later on.

Smelter Inc may also be concerned about Val-Nam giving preference to another creditor over it. For example, Val-Nam's management may have an especially close relationship with Angelic Battiste, and Val-Nam may therefore prefer to pay the amount it owes Angelic on the unsecured loan she provided to Val-Nam before it pays Smelter Inc's invoices. Such an activity is known as a fraudulent preference and is illegal under the *Bankruptcy and Insolvency Act* and provincial statutes, such as Ontario's *Assignments and Preferences Act*. Rather than trying to recover funds diverted to Angelic in a fraudulent preference scheme, Smelter Inc may be wise to take proactive steps to gain control of Val-Nam's remaining assets by means of the supervisory powers of the trustee in bankruptcy and the official receiver.

Viva Developments Inc v Icarus Properties Ltd is a case that involved a fraudulent preference and a fraudulent conveyance under British Columbia legislation. The principles demonstrated in this case that prohibit fraudulent activity are analogous to those embodied in the *Bankruptcy and Insolvency Act*.

CASE IN POINT

Mortgage for Shareholders Equals Fraudulent Conveyance

Viva Developments Inc v Icarus Properties Ltd, 2004 BCSC 1176, [2004] BCJ No 1858 (QL)

Facts

Between the time that the plaintiff corporation was awarded judgment against the defendant corporation and the time that the court quantified damages, the defendant granted a mortgage over land to its shareholders. The mortgage purported to secure shareholders' loans and management fees payable. The payment of management fees was approved by a resolution of the board of directors after judgment was granted. The amount of the shareholders' loans was inflated.

The defendant corporation also transferred property to its majority shareholder. The defendant claimed that the dominant intention of the transfer was to keep the company in business and to avoid foreclosure proceedings.

Result

The court found that the granting of the mortgage was void because it was a fraudulent conveyance, intended to "delay, hinder, or defraud creditors and others of their just and lawful remedies." It also found that the dominant intent of the transfer of property was to ensure the shareholders' loans and management fees were paid, not to keep the company in business. The mortgage was therefore void as a fraudulent conveyance and the transfer was void and set aside as both a fraudulent conveyance and fraudulent preference.

Business Lesson

Be aware that schemes to divert funds from creditors and others who are entitled to receive them may be fraudulent and illegal.

Companies' Creditors Arrangement Act

The *Companies' Creditors Arrangement Act* is a federal statute that provides an alternative to bankruptcy, particularly for large businesses with many creditors. The Act allows a company to make a proposal for paying its debts—through the courts—to its creditors, both secured and unsecured. Companies use the Act's protection in an effort to hold off creditors and bankruptcy proceedings by obtaining a court order.

Should Val-Nam obtain such an order, it will not go into bankruptcy; it will not be broken up and sold. Instead, while under the court's protection, Val-Nam will attempt to restructure its debt by proposing revised repayment terms to creditors. If Val-Nam's creditors accept Val-Nam's debt restructuring, they will usually receive less than they are legally entitled to, or they will agree to postpone their right to payment for a longer time than they are legally required to wait. Val-Nam's creditors will make these concessions if they feel that they will fare better under a *Companies' Creditors Arrangement Act* proposal than under a bankruptcy, or if they believe that Val-Nam can be returned to financial health with a promise of eventual repayment of their debt. If the creditors refuse to accept the proposal, bankruptcy usually follows.

When Air Canada fell into financial difficulties after absorbing Canadian Airlines International, it took refuge under the *Companies' Creditors Arrangement Act*, which prevented bankruptcy proceedings from being initiated while it negotiated a proposal with its creditors. Negotiations were complex and prolonged. Creditors, such as airline employees, had to consider whether accepting pay reductions to keep the company in business was preferable to the company's bankruptcy and their resulting job losses. After consideration—and considerable bargaining—employee groups, lenders, and other secured and unsecured creditors eventually achieved a deal that permitted the airline to continue in operation and pay its creditors over time.

MINIMIZING YOUR RISK

Use Bankruptcy Proceedings When Necessary

- If you are a debtor, consider going voluntarily into bankruptcy only when it is clear that your company's debts cannot be paid when they are due and there is no realistic hope that the business's prospects will improve.
- If there is some hope of saving your business, use the relatively inexpensive proceedings available under the *Bankruptcy and Insolvency Act* to make a proposal to your creditors to restructure your debt.
- If you are an unsecured creditor, consider petitioning a debtor into bankruptcy only if the debt is large, there is ample evidence that the company is insolvent, and there is some prospect that you may be paid after secured creditors have seized collateral.
- Remember that there may be less reason for a secured creditor to push a debtor into bankruptcy because seizing collateral may satisfy much of the debt.

CHAPTER SUMMARY

Banking, financing, and debtor-creditor law provides the legal framework for the financial operations of businesses: the borrowing and lending of money, the types of loans available, and the consequences of failure to repay these loans. Business people should be familiar with these laws so they can deal with banks knowledgeably, find the best blend of debt and equity financing for their business, and provide their creditors with alternatives to bankruptcy if the business is in financial difficulty.

In Canada, the three types of negotiable instruments used to pay and receive payment for goods are bills of exchange, promissory notes, and, most commonly, cheques. The parties involved in writing a cheque consist of a drawee, a payer, and a payee. The drawee is always a financial institution where the payer has an account. While the types of transactions involving negotiable instruments are still in common use, electronic transactions between financial institutions and both businesses and consumers are steadily growing in importance for making and receiving payments as well as for transferring capital.

With debt financing, the business borrows capital and repays the loan with interest. If the debt is secured, the debtor provides collateral that the lender (or secured creditor) may seize if the debtor defaults. These debts should be registered so that the order of secured creditors is established in the event that a sale of the collateral in a bankruptcy procedure does not raise enough funds to repay them all. A creditor will decide the interest rate depending on the risk the debtor poses. The debtor's credit history can be checked through credit reporting agencies and public databanks. Unpaid creditors may consider sending a demand letter. If that fails, and depending on the amount of the debt, creditors can sue in the provincial Superior Court or the Small Claims Court.

Equity financing involves issuing and selling shares to institutional investors and the public. New shares are sold by issuing a "prospectus" of information about the company and making an initial public offering (IPO) on a stock exchange. Common shares are the most widely traded shares. Holders of preferred shares are always paid their dividends before common shareholders.

Businesses can go into bankruptcy if their debts exceed $1,000 and if they have committed one or more acts of bankruptcy, such as not paying their debts or committing fraudulent or evasive acts to avoid creditors. After a legal bankruptcy procedure, a bankrupt company will have lost most of its assets, but is free to start over without a debt load.

KEY TERMS

act of bankruptcy, 288
bill of exchange, 267
caisse populaire, 266
cheque, 267
collateral, 274
common shares, 280
corporate bond, 278
debt financing, 274
demand letter, 287
drawee, 267
drawer, 267
equity financing, 274
execution creditor, 285
floating charge, 278
general security agreement, 277
holder, 269
initial public offering (IPO), 280
negotiable instrument, 266
official receiver, 289
payee, 267
payer, 267
preferred shares, 280
priority, 274
promissory note, 266
proposal to creditors, 289
receiving order, 290
secured creditor, 274
secured loan, 275
trustee in bankruptcy, 289
unsecured loan, 275
writ of seizure and sale, 283

REFERENCES

Assignments and Preferences Act, RSO 1990, c A.33.
Bank Act, SC 1991, c 46.
Bankruptcy and Insolvency Act, RSC 1985, c B-3.
Bills of Exchange Act, RSC 1985, c B-4.
Burns v Financial Bailiff Services Ltd, 2000 SKQB 546, [2000] SJ No 794 (QL).
Business Development Bank of Canada v S and S Mobile Refrigeration, [1996] OJ No 4680 (QL) (Sup Ct J).
Companies' Creditors Arrangement Act, RSC 1985, c C-36.
Consumer Reporting Act, RSNS 1989, c 93.
Dimov v Equifax Canada Co, 2017 NSSM 1.
Don Bodkin Leasing Ltd v The Toronto-Dominion Bank, 1998 CanLII 1101, 40 OR (3d) 262 (CA).
Indian Act, RSC 1985, c I-5.
Land Titles Act, RSO 1990, c L.5.
Personal Property Security Act, RSO 1990, c P.10.
Registry Act, RSO 1990, c R.20.
Viva Developments Inc v Icarus Properties Ltd, 2004 BCSC 1176, [2004] BCJ No 1858 (QL).

EXERCISES

True or False?

____ **1.** Bills of exchange are no longer used in Canada.
____ **2.** A company's capital structure reflects its balance of debt and equity financing.
____ **3.** A bankrupt emerges from bankruptcy free of most, but not necessarily all, debts and stripped of most, but not necessarily all, assets.
____ **4.** A registers an interest in collateral owned by B in 2010. C sues B and obtains a judgment in 2010. C will be able to enforce the judgment against all of B's assets.
____ **5.** If a business signs a financial services agreement with a bank, it will cover services the business does not use at the time the agreement is signed.
____ **6.** Generally, if interest rates are rising, the value of bonds tends to fall.
____ **7.** A characteristic of common shares is that if dividends are to be paid on the shares, the common shareholder is paid ahead of other shareholders.
____ **8.** The share price of preferred shares tends to be more stable than the price of common shares.
____ **9.** Common shares have voting rights while preferred shares do not.
____**10.** If a credit reporting agency has incorrect information about you that is damaging, your only recourse is to sue them.
____**11.** All retail businesses offer to accept payment from customers using credit and debit cards.

Multiple Choice

1. A cheque endorsed in blank is cashable:
a. by the payee named on the front of the cheque only.
b. by the payer only.
c. within 30 days.
d. by anyone.

2. Which of the following is true about a consumer note?
   a. It bears no interest prior to the payment date.
   b. It is not transferable.
   c. It sometimes offers the maker a defence against payment.
   d. It is not a negotiable instrument.
3. A floating charge:
   a. crystallizes when a debtor defaults.
   b. is used by unsecured creditors.
   c. is a form of equity financing.
   d. is a form of security held jointly by multiple creditors.
4. Before it is eligible for a loan, what may a new business need to do?
   a. Pledge security.
   b. Prepare a written business plan.
   c. Provide a cash flow analysis.
   d. All of the above.
5. What is covered by a general security agreement?
   a. The ranking of a debtor's various creditors.
   b. The details of a company's capital structure.
   c. A description of the security pledged, and a description of the actions that constitute a default.
   d. All of the above.
6. How can creditors obtain information about potential debtors?
   a. By conducting a search for security interests through public registries.
   b. By conducting an execution search.
   c. By conducting a bankruptcy search.
   d. All of the above.
7. What is a proposal to creditors?
   a. A business plan presented to a bank to obtain a loan.
   b. Part of the petition of a debtor into bankruptcy.
   c. An arrangement by the debtor to pay creditors without going bankrupt.
   d. A voluntary assignment in bankruptcy.
   e. c and d

Short Answer

1. How does secured credit differ from unsecured credit?
2. What is an initial public offering?
3. What is the difference between common and preferred shares?
4. What are the advantages and disadvantages of debt and equity financing?
5. What methods are available to unsecured creditors to enforce their rights?
6. How does a business's use of a credit card differ from a consumer's use?
7. What general steps should you take if you are in the business of extending credit to businesses?

Apply Your Knowledge

1. Liz Singh graduated with a diploma in computer science with a specialty in programming. She worked for several years for a well-known software company, but felt her full talents were not being used. On her own time she has been working on some very sophisticated communications software that is likely to be better than anything currently on the market. She has written a business plan and figures the development costs to bring the product to market, and to market it, will be about $1 million. She currently rents an apartment, leases a car, and is still repaying her student loan. She needs some advice on how to finance the venture. Advise her.
2. Miss Fyshe Ltd is a chain of retail stores launched in 2010 that specializes in organic seafood. With consumer interest in natural foods, the company was very successful initially, rapidly expanding to 31 stores in prime areas across Canada. In order to expand, however, it regularly had to borrow money. In 2017, business started to fall off—consumers became interested in other foods, and various supply sources started to dry up as fish stocks became depleted. Profits declined sharply, and the chain now appears to be running at a loss. An examination of its debt situation reveals the following:
   - The chain has had a line of credit—which is currently showing a debt of $30,000—with the Caring Bank since 2010.
   - There is a secured loan from Fly By Night Finance for $100,000 in 2011 for the purchase of freezers for the stores. The creditor has a collateral interest in the freezers, and it registered its interest in 2011 under the *Personal Property Security Act*. The amount outstanding on the loan is $25,000.
   - There is a further secured loan from Freebee Investments in 2012 for $20,000, with the freezers again taken as security along with security in accounts receivable. Freebee also registered its

interest. The amount outstanding on the loan is $5,000.

- Chen's Garage Ltd repaired one of Miss Fyshe's delivery vans in February 2016. The invoice, in the amount of $2,000, still has not been settled.

Suppose you act for Chen's Garage.

a. What searches would you carry out in order to advise Chen about whether or not to sue to recover the debt owing from Miss Fyshe?

b. Tell Chen what the priority rights are among the known debtors, starting with the most senior.

c. Tell Chen what the chances of his getting paid are likely to be if Miss Fyshe goes bankrupt.

3. Catwatch Ltd, a cat-sitting service, has just started up business and wants to open a commercial bank account with the Caring Bank. Before signing an account agreement, what does Catwatch need to consider?

Workplace Law

9

LEARNING OUTCOMES

After reading this chapter, you should be able to:

- Discuss how the common law affects hiring and other employment decisions.
- Analyze the common law that governs the dismissal of non-unionized employees.
- Explain how to run a business in conformity with human rights legislation.
- Identify key rights and obligations under employment standards, workplace safety and insurance, and health and safety legislation.
- Analyze various types of equity requirements in the workplace.
- Discuss privacy in the workplace.
- Describe a business's obligations in relation to unionized employees and employees who are in the process of unionizing the workplace.

What Is Workplace Law?

Workplace law regulates the day-to-day relationships between you and the employees who work for your business. It affects these relationships from the time you recruit an employee until the time an employee resigns, retires, or is dismissed. Workplace law is an extremely broad branch of business law. It includes human rights law, contract law, employment standards law, health and safety law, equity law, privacy law, labour relations law, and tort law.

In order to deal with any of the following situations, you must be familiar with the laws that govern the workplace. As Val-Nam Generation Limited carries on and expands its business, a number of different workplace issues may arise:

- An applicant for an administrative job at Val-Nam's head office is qualified and has excellent references; during his job interview, it is apparent that his vision is extremely poor and that he would need special equipment to do the work required. Val-Nam is concerned that if he is hired, the company may be required to purchase expensive equipment.
- Fearing that equipment is unsafe at Val-Nam's new manufacturing plant, two certified members of the joint health and safety committee issue a stop-work order. Val-Nam needs to get everyone back to work as quickly as possible to fulfill a significant contractual obligation.
- A plant manager confidentially advises Val-Nam's head of research and development, Namid Blackburn, that certain employees are interested in forming a union to improve their benefits and working conditions. When Namid tells the CEO, Valery Garza, about this, she indicates she would like to speak directly to these employees about their union activities but is unsure whether this would violate her obligations under the *Labour Relations Act, 1995*.
- Val-Nam must restructure its operations quickly in order to remain competitive in the marketplace. It is necessary to dismiss a non-unionized long-term employee and several new recruits. Val-Nam wants to avoid the expense of being sued for wrongful dismissal. How should it structure a severance package?

non-unionized employee
employee whose terms and conditions of employment are based on an individual employment contract rather than a collective agreement negotiated between an employer and a union

unionized employee
employee whose terms and conditions of employment are based on a collective agreement negotiated between an employer and a union rather than an individual contract of employment

In Canada, laws governing the workplace rights of employers and employees are found both in statutes and in common law. The employment relationship between an employer and a **non-unionized employee** is contractual, and therefore the common law principles of contract apply. (The terms and conditions of employment for a **unionized employee** are set out in collective agreements, which are discussed later in this chapter under the heading "The Unionized Workplace.")

That said, the employment relationship is a highly regulated one and there are also numerous statutes that provide employees with a "floor of rights" below which the parties cannot negotiate. Although both the federal and provincial levels of government can pass employment-related statutes, about 90 percent of employees in Canada are governed by provincial employment legislation. Which one applies depends on the industry the employer is in. Federal employment laws cover the 10 percent of employees who work in national industries, such as airlines, broadcasting, banks, and interprovincial transportation. Since approximately 90 percent of workplaces are provincially regulated, this chapter focuses on Ontario's employment legislation. (Employment laws in other provinces are often similar, although not identical, to the laws discussed below.) Where statutory standards differ, employers that operate in several provinces have a choice: they can either adopt different policies in each province or adopt the most generous standard and apply it across the country.

The Importance of Workplace Law for Businesses

The law of the workplace is diverse and can be complex. It is nevertheless essential for business people to understand and be able to identify the key legal issues that can arise on a day-to-day basis. Why?

- *Understanding workplace law can help you reduce business risks and minimize time-consuming and costly legal problems.* If you are unaware of the laws that govern your workplace, your business is at a disadvantage. It may be subject to government fines and penalties for failing to comply with statutory employment, human rights, and health and safety standards of which you are unaware. It may also be sued by employees who are becoming increasingly knowledgeable and insistent about their rights and your obligations.
- *Infringement of workplace law can impair your business image.* Without knowing the prohibited grounds of discrimination under the *Human Rights Code*, for example, you may find—to your surprise—that your business is guilty of practising discrimination in the workplace. The costs to your reputation in the business community—and the community at large—of a well-publicized human rights complaint could be formidable.
- *A business's relationship with its employees can have far-reaching effects on an organization's public image, profitability, and survival.* If you comply with workplace laws, develop effective policies, and constructively manage disputes in your workplace, the resulting good relations with employees, unions, and the public can go a long way to ensuring the future success of your business and its place in the larger community.

Threshold Issue: Independent Contractor or Employee?

Historically, the employment relationship was governed by the notion of "freedom of contract": the parties were free to "negotiate" any terms of employment they chose. However, given the employer's greater bargaining power in most situations, and the employee's reliance on employment, this often resulted in employees receiving very low wages and poor working conditions. For this reason, both common law and statutory protections have been developed to protect employees. That said, most of the protections for workers that we will discuss are available only to individuals who are legally "employees." Therefore, one threshold question that a business person must ask is whether an individual is being hired as an "employee" or as an independent contractor. An **independent contractor** is a self-employed worker who accepts specific projects, usually from several businesses. Although it is sometimes difficult to distinguish an employer-employee relationship from a principal-independent contractor relationship, the two are treated very differently in law. For example, an independent contractor is not covered by employment standards legislation and therefore is not entitled to receive vacation pay, pregnancy or parental leave, or the

independent contractor
self-employed worker who accepts specific projects, usually from several businesses

termination notice specified in statutes. Conversely, independent contractors receive tax benefits that are not available to employees. For example, they may deduct business expenses, and income tax is not withheld and submitted by the business that hires them.

What makes an individual an independent contractor rather than an employee? Generally, courts and tribunals apply the common law test: Is the individual an independent entrepreneur in business for herself (an independent contractor), or is she under the control and direction of the hiring organization (an employee)? No single fact determines the matter; a court or tribunal will assess the substance of the relationship, including whether the business controls where, when, and how the work is performed and whether the individual is free to have other clients. A statement in the contract that the relationship is one of principal and independent contractor, rather than employer and employee, indicates the parties' intentions. However, it will not be the only evidence considered and does not bind courts or tribunals.

SCENARIO

Investor? Employee? Contractor?

Mitchell Wu is a mechanical engineer who helped develop Val-Nam's prototype portable electricity generator. He has commercialized a number of his own inventions and is currently involved in two other business ventures. He is interested in using his experience to help Val-Nam develop, but is unsure of which type of relationship he should have with the business. He is considering each of the following:

- investing,
- part-time employment,
- full-time employment,
- short-term employment, and
- contract work as an adviser or as an agent.

If Mitchell wants to continue to be involved in other business ventures and to continue to develop his own inventions, he will likely want to consider an investor/independent contractor relationship with Val-Nam. An employment relationship may not be compatible with his other business interests.

What is the risk if your business makes a mistake in determining whether workers are employees or independent contractors? There is a risk that a court or tribunal may re-characterize the relationship to your business's detriment. For example, if Val-Nam treats Mitchell as an independent contractor, Val-Nam is justified in not paying him employment standards benefits and in not providing him with statutory notice of dismissal. However, if a court or tribunal subsequently determines that Mitchell is, in fact, Val-Nam's employee, Val-Nam may have to remit thousands of dollars to various government agencies for outstanding statutory premiums—such as Canada Pension Plan and Employment Insurance—payable on behalf of employees. Val-Nam may also have to pay Mitchell, newly characterized as an "employee," significant amounts of money for employment standards benefits (such as vacation pay). And Val-Nam may even be liable for wrongful dismissal damages that are available to employees only (wrongful dismissal is discussed later in this chapter under the heading "Wrongful Dismissal Damages").

More recently, courts have recognized a third category: dependent contractors. These are individuals whom the courts find are self-employed but who, because they are economically dependent on a single "employer," are entitled to wrongful dismissal damages.

Note that under the 2017 amendments to the *Employment Standards Act, 2000* (Bill 148), misclassification of employees as independent contractors is expressly prohibited and the *onus is on the employer* to prove that a worker is an independent contractor.

MINIMIZING YOUR RISK

Respect the Independence of Independent Contractors

- Encourage independent contractors to work for other businesses, and never restrict their ability to do so.
- Specify in a written contract that both you and the independent contractor intend your relationship to be that of principal and independent contractor.
- Take no statutory deductions from the money you owe independent contractors, and make no income tax remittances on their behalf.
- Do not reimburse independent contractors for their expenses.
- Do not provide employee benefits such as vacation time and pay, holiday pay, or overtime pay.
- Avoid setting hours of work.
- Encourage independent contractors to work offsite as much as possible.
- Have independent contractors supply their own tools and equipment.

The remainder of this chapter will focus on the employer-employee relationship. We will start with workplace issues related to the common law, followed by key statutory requirements.

The Common Law

Hiring

When hiring an employee, there are a number of common law issues that are of concern to businesses even before employment begins. It is important to act with honesty and integrity and to check candidates' references thoroughly. Furthermore, a carefully crafted contract of employment provides a solid basis for a successful employer-employee relationship. In the sections that follow, we explore these and related issues.

Honesty and Good Faith in the Hiring Process

During the hiring process, business owners and job candidates should interact honestly with one another. Misrepresentations, including deliberate lies, can result in legal consequences.

Courts have held that misrepresentations by candidates for jobs may justify dismissal after they have been hired if the misrepresentations go to the root of a candidate's qualifications or suggest an inherent lack of honesty. This may be of particular concern where the job is one that requires a high degree of trust. For example, if an applicant for a nursing job claims that he has a nursing degree and the nursing home that employs him subsequently discovers that he has completed only the first year, the nursing home may be entitled to dismiss him, even if he is performing his job satisfactorily.

Similarly, if a business owner makes inaccurate statements to a job candidate during the hiring process, she may be legally liable if the candidate relies on the misrepresentation and suffers damages as a result. For example, imagine a situation in which a company recruiter states that the position being offered involves heading up a major new innovative project; however, the recruiter fails to mention that the project is still subject to final board approval. The candidate accepts the offer—leaving a secure job and relocating their family—only to be terminated shortly thereafter when final approval for the project is denied. In this situation, the employer could be liable for the *tort of negligent misrepresentation*, with possible damages including loss of income and the cost of obtaining new employment and relocating, as well as general damages for emotional stress. The fact that the recruiter did not intentionally mislead the candidate is not relevant. The employer has an obligation to ensure that all material statements made during the recruitment process are accurate.

Employers must also take care not to be overly aggressive in "luring" prospective employees, especially ones that are currently in secure employment. For example, if the recruiter repeatedly calls a candidate, urging her to leave her current job, or makes inflated promises about what the new position will offer, that employee may be awarded a longer termination notice period if she is later dismissed from the new job without just cause.

Similarly, hiring employers need to be aware that they can be liable for *inducing breach of contract* if they knowingly induce the breach of an existing contract between two other parties. In the employment context this can happen where, for example, an employer offers a position to an individual knowing they must break an employment contract—such as by failing to provide contractually required advance notice of resignation—to accept the new position. In that situation, the *new* employer may be liable to the *former* employer for damages suffered as a result of the induced breach.

MINIMIZING YOUR RISK

Be Frank with Candidates

- Include in job application forms an acknowledgment by the applicant that all information provided is true and complete to the best of the applicant's knowledge and that a false statement may be cause for dismissal.
- Know exactly what duties the job you are offering entails, and be honest about them with the candidate.
- Do not make specific promises with respect to long-term job security or the possibility of career advancement.
- Have written employment contracts state that all oral representations are void on signing of the contract.
- Include a carefully drafted and balanced termination clause in the employment contract.
- Avoid overly aggressive recruiting methods such as repeatedly contacting a prospective employee and encouraging them to leave a current job.

Hiring Due Diligence

Finding out whether a prospective employee is subject to a restrictive covenant and checking references are both legally advisable practices.

RESTRICTIVE COVENANTS

A **restrictive covenant** is a clause in an employment contract that restricts the legal right of employees to engage in certain types of activities during employment and after it ends, such as competing with the ex-employer, soliciting customers from the ex-employer, and disclosing confidential information about the ex-employer. Before hiring a candidate, determine whether the candidate signed an employment contract with an enforceable restrictive covenant with their previous employer. The terms of such a covenant might affect the candidate's ability to do the job that you are offering.

Your business might be wise to include in employment contracts a clause in which a candidate verifies that they have no existing contractual obligations that prevent them from accepting a job at your business. We return to restrictive covenants in the context of employment contracts later in this chapter under the heading "Contractual Restrictive Covenants."

restrictive covenant clause in an employment contract that restricts an employee's activities, especially after employment ends; for example, a restrictive covenant might prohibit an ex-employee from disclosing confidential information about the employer

MINIMIZING YOUR RISK

Inquire About Restrictive Covenants

- Find out if job candidates have signed a restrictive covenant with their current or previous employers.
- If they have, have the clause(s) reviewed by a lawyer to get a legal opinion concerning enforceability.
- Ensure written employment contracts designate which party will be legally responsible if a former employer successfully enforces the restrictive covenant.

CHECKING REFERENCES

At the hiring stage, an employer must keep in mind potential obligations related to checking employment references. Although the law imposes no general obligation to check references, an employer may nevertheless be liable for "negligent hiring" if it fails to verify the references of applicants for jobs that could expose others to harm.

Employers who hire employees to fill positions of trust (such as daycare workers) or employees who may be required to use force (such as security guards) are required to exercise a high standard of care in checking references.

In addition to being liable for its own negligent hiring, the employer may also be liable for the wrongful actions of the hired employee. We discuss an employer's liability for the actions of an employee, even in the absence of the employer's own negligence, in Chapter 3 under the heading "Vicarious Liability."

MINIMIZING YOUR RISK

Check Candidates' References

- Obtain candidates' written permission to check references through a statement on the application form.

- Check references thoroughly, particularly if the job could result in harm to others.
- Make the same general inquiries about all applicants.
- Record details of all steps taken when investigating candidates, including references who did not respond and the information provided by those who did.
- Keep information confidential.

Employment Contracts

As noted above, under the common law the relationship between an employer and an employee who is not a member of a union is basically a contractual one. Subject to any statutory requirements, the terms and conditions that apply to non-unionized employees generally are those that the employer and the employee themselves negotiate. The essence of an employment contract is the following:

- the employer makes a job offer ("offer") that the employee accepts ("acceptance"), and
- the parties mutually promise to exchange wages for work ("consideration").

While oral agreements are legally binding, a well-drafted written employment contract offers crucial advantages. These include greater certainty about the contractual terms, reduced risk of misunderstanding, and the ability to ensure that important terms, such as a termination clause, are expressly incorporated into the contract. In most employment relationships, the written contract is not lengthy or formal. It often consists of a letter from the employer offering an employee a job and setting out the key terms, such as salary, benefits, starting date, title, job duties, and termination provisions. If your business has a policy manual—and it is a good idea to develop one if you are going to be hiring many employees—refer to this manual in your letter and provide a copy *before the employee starts work*. Such a reference incorporates your policies about matters such as discipline, probationary periods, absence, safety, and harassment into the employment contract.

Sometimes a more formal employment contract is needed. If you are hiring a senior employee or one who will be doing a specialized job, ensure that you draft the contract carefully—perhaps seeking professional assistance—and customize it to reflect the issues that are important to both parties.

In the following sections, we examine some terms that are of particular interest to business people in drafting contracts: notice of termination, fixed-term contracts, probationary periods, and restrictive covenants.

MINIMIZING YOUR RISK

Customize Your Employment Contracts

- Ensure that all employees have written contracts of employment—even if they are only a one- or two-page letter of hire.
- Use plain, clear language.
- Customize the contract so that it reflects what is important to the parties involved.
- Seek legal assistance, if necessary, in negotiating and drafting more complex or specialized contracts.
- Make sure the contract is signed before work begins.

- Make sure the contract refers to the employee policy manual and that the employee receives a copy of the manual *before* starting work.
- Negotiate and include a carefully drafted notice of termination clause in the contract—even in a fixed-term contract.
- If hiring someone on a fixed-term contract, do not mislead that employee into believing that renewal is automatic or a mere formality.
- Include a probationary period clause in the contract.
- Use restrictive covenants where necessary, but limit restrictions to those absolutely necessary to protect your legitimate business interests.

TERMINATION CLAUSE

Typically, the most contentious clause in an employment contract relates to notice of termination. Without a termination provision, an employee who is dismissed without **just cause** (justification based on conduct) is entitled to "reasonable notice" of termination (that is, working notice or **pay in lieu of notice**) *under the common law*. Depending on the circumstances, **reasonable notice** may be very lengthy—as much as a month or more per year of service. If you, as an employer, fail to provide reasonable notice, you may be required to pay the employee an amount equal to the wages plus the benefits that the employee would have earned during this period of time.

just cause
justification for dismissal without notice based on an employee's conduct

pay in lieu of notice
payment as a substitute for receiving adequate notice where an employee is dismissed without just cause

reasonable notice
period of time an employee should be given between notification of dismissal and end of employment

If you address what will happen upon termination at the beginning of the employment relationship while you and the employee are on good terms, you reduce the costs and uncertainty of relying on a court to determine what constitutes reasonable notice. In *Mesgarlou v 3xs Enterprises Inc*, for example, the employment contract included a termination clause that limited the employee's entitlement on termination to the amount of notice required under Ontario's *Employment Standards Act, 2000* (ESA). The court found that because the termination clause was clear enough to rebut the common law presumption of entitlement to reasonable notice, the employee's entitlement was limited to the ESA amount, which was $2,477. Had there *not* been an enforceable termination clause in the contract, that same employee would have been entitled to three months' salary (or $32,000) in lieu of reasonable notice under the common law.

Employers should negotiate a termination provision with prospective employees and draft the term clearly in a written contract of employment.

FIXED-TERM CONTRACTS

Employers may hire employees on a permanent basis (full-time or part-time), called an indefinite hire, or for a fixed term (full-time or part-time). Employees hired for a fixed term are sometimes called "contract workers," but they are not independent contractors—they are employees. They are entitled to all the rights conferred on workers under the ESA, including the right to receive vacation pay. Because the date of termination is known in advance, an employer generally need not give the fixed-term employee further notice of termination if the employee works for the entire fixed term. However, where the term is for 12 months or more, the ESA requires that statutory notice still be given.

Note that workers who are hired through a temporary employment agency ("temps") are typically employees of that agency. The agency is liable for providing them with their employment standards entitlements, such as vacation and overtime pay. The employer simply pays the agency.

Employers should not use a series of fixed-term contracts to cover what is, in substance, an indefinite contract of employment in an attempt to avoid notice of termination obligations. In these circumstances, courts and tribunals have looked beyond the actual provisions in the contract and found that the employee is entitled to reasonable notice based on total years of service.

Moreover, fixed-term contracts should contain a termination clause in case the employer wants to terminate the contract early. Otherwise the employer could be legally required to continue to pay the individual for the entire term of the contract. An example of this is seen in the case of *Ballim v Bausch & Lomb Canada Inc.*

CASE IN POINT

Don't Forget the Termination Clause

Ballim v Bausch & Lomb Canada Inc, 2016 ONSC 6307

Facts

The employer emailed Ballim an offer of employment to replace an employee who was going on maternity leave. The email cover letter included the following statement: "It is a one-year contract." The attached employment agreement itself did not contain a termination clause. When Ballim was dismissed after only three months, she sued the employer, arguing she was hired for a one-year term and was therefore entitled to be paid for the remaining 38.5 weeks in that term. The employer countered that Ballim was hired for an indefinite term.

Result

The court found for the employee. The cover letter was held to be part of the employment contract and as such supported Ballim's position that she was hired for a fixed term of one year. She was therefore entitled to be paid for the remainder of that contractual one-year term.

Business Lesson

Include a termination clause in all your employment contracts, even fixed-term contracts. The potential liability in early termination of a fixed-term contract extends to continuing to pay the employee for the remainder of the term. This could significantly exceed the "reasonable notice" period an indefinite employee is entitled to, especially for a short-service employee.

PROBATIONARY PERIODS

If you, as an employer, want to monitor an employee's suitability for a job by instituting a probationary period, you must provide for a probationary period in your contract of employment. Probationary periods typically last from three to six months, depending on the nature of the job. Business owners and managers usually determine the length of the probationary period based on how long it will take them to assess an employee's on-the-job ability.

Note that under Ontario's *Employment Standards Act, 2000* statutory notice *is* required after three months of service. Therefore, where the probationary period under a contract exceeds three months, the employer must give *statutory* notice to an employee who is dismissed after three months unless the dismissal occurs for reasons exempted from the statutory notice requirement (for example, if the employee's poor job performance constitutes "wilful neglect of duty").

CONTRACTUAL RESTRICTIVE COVENANTS

Three main types of restrictive covenants are included in employment contracts:

- *non-competition clauses*, which restrict an ex-employee's ability to work in a competing business for a certain period of time and within a certain geographic area after employment ends (very difficult to convince a court to find enforceable);
- *non-solicitation clauses*, which restrict an ex-employee's ability to solicit employees or customers of a former employer (difficult to convince a court to find enforceable); and
- *non-disclosure clauses*, which restrict an ex-employee's ability to use a former employer's confidential information (often enforced).

Courts are extremely reluctant to find *non-competition* clauses—and to a lesser extent, non-solicitation clauses—enforceable, as they restrict a former employee's ability to work in their field for the period of time indicated in the contract. To be enforceable the onus is on you, the employer, to prove the non-competition clause is reasonable in duration and geographic scope, that it is absolutely necessary to protect your legitimate business interests, and that a non-solicitation clause or non-disclosure clause would not be sufficient.

Enforceability of Employment Contracts

Like any other contracts, contracts of employment may be challenged because they are ambiguous or because they were made under duress (see Chapter 5 for a general discussion of when contracts will be unenforceable). A party who is unhappy with the terms of an employment contract may also challenge its enforceability on the basis that it lacks consideration or because it fails to meet minimum statutory standards.

LACK OF CONSIDERATION (AND CHANGING TERMS MID-CONTRACT)

An employment contract lacks consideration when an employer fails to provide something of value in exchange for an employee's promise to work. Consider, for example, an employer who presents an employee with a contract that contains a termination clause *after* the employee has already started to work. As soon as the employee started work, an unwritten employment contract existed. The later written contract likely constitutes an amendment to that initial unwritten contract. Therefore, the termination clause is probably unenforceable unless it is supported by new *consideration* for signing it, such as a signing bonus or an additional week of vacation. In these circumstances, continued employment does not constitute consideration.

Similarly, an employment contract that is fully enforceable at the time an employee is hired may become problematic in the future if the employer wants to change its employment policies. If the proposed change is minor (for example, a small change in break times), it probably presents no legal problem. However, if the change is significant and the employee will not agree to it, it may constitute constructive dismissal (that is, a fundamental breach of the contract). To avoid this result, the employer has two choices:

1. Obtain the employee's consent and provide fresh "consideration" in the form of, for example, a one-time bonus or raise in salary or a promotion that depends on signing a revised employment contract.

2. Provide the employee with reasonable notice of the change, which may be determined in the same way as reasonable notice of termination (unfortunately, this may be impractical if the employer has to make adjustments to the workplace in a hurry). However, where an employee clearly rejects the proposed new term, the employer must take the extra step of letting the employee know the consequences of that rejection. An example would be a situation where an employer gives an employee the required notice that it intends to reduce the length of the termination notice the employee is entitled to under the current employment contract. If the employee clearly indicates a refusal to accept that change, the employer must advise that the employee's employment under the terms of the existing contract ends at the end of the working notice period. It may then offer to rehire the employee under the new terms, starting at the end of the working notice period.

FAILURE TO MEET MINIMUM STATUTORY STANDARDS

The terms of an employment contract must be at least as favourable to employees as the minimum standards set by legislation (we address some of these standards later in this chapter under the heading "Employment Standards"). If a contract fails to meet these minimum standards in relation to wages or notice of termination provisions, for example, the relevant clause of the contract is void and unenforceable.

In this situation, a court will not simply substitute statutory notice provisions; instead, it will apply the common law. This means that if the contract contains an inadequate termination notice provision, the employer must compensate an employee by providing reasonable notice of termination or pay in lieu of notice, which is usually significantly more than the statutory entitlements. The decision in *Wood v Fred Deeley Imports Ltd* demonstrates the high standard courts apply to ensure that contractual termination provisions clearly provide employees with at least their minimum statutory entitlements.

CASE IN POINT

Court Provides Employers with Added Incentive to Comply

Wood v Fred Deeley Imports Ltd, 2017 ONCA 158

Facts

Wood, the plaintiff, was hired in April 2007 as a sales and event planner for the defendant, a Harley-Davidson distributor. Her employment agreement contained the following termination provision:

[The Company] is entitled to terminate your employment at any time without cause by providing you with 2 weeks' notice of termination or pay in lieu thereof for each completed or partial year of employment with the Company. If the Company terminates your employment without cause, the Company shall not be obliged to make any payments to you other than those provided for in this paragraph. … The payments and notice provided for in this paragraph are inclusive of your entitlements to notice, pay in lieu of notice and severance pay pursuant to the *Employment Standards Act, 2000*.

In April 2015 the employer was bought out by Harley-Davidson and its employees were given notice of termination. The employer provided Wood with 13 weeks' working notice (continuing full benefit coverage throughout), plus a lump sum representing 8 weeks' pay. The payments met and even exceeded those required under the ESA. However, Wood sued, alleging, among other things, that the

termination clause was unenforceable because it violated the ESA by:

- not *specifically* requiring the employer to make benefit contributions during the notice period, and
- not clearly requiring the employer to provide statutory severance pay.

Result

The Court of Appeal held that the termination provision was unenforceable because it did not comply with the ESA. First, it failed to mention the obligation to continue benefits during the notice period. The fact that the employer *did* continue benefits during the notice period does not remedy this failure because it is the clause's own wording that matters, not what the employer actually did. Second, by combining the requirement for statutory notice and severance pay, along with the wording "*the Company shall not be obliged to make any payments to you other than those provided for in this paragraph*," the clause did not unambiguously require payment of statutory severance pay and was therefore not in compliance with the ESA. The Court of Appeal awarded Wood nine months' reasonable notice or pay in lieu of reasonable notice.

In reaching its conclusion, the court pointed to the inherent inequality of bargaining power between employers and employees and the importance of interpreting the law in a way that encourages employers to comply with the minimum requirements of the ESA. It stated that if an employer can remedy illegal termination clauses by making additional, voluntary payments upon termination, it will have little incentive to draft legal and enforceable ones at the beginning of the employment relationship.

Business Lesson

This case underscores the importance of carefully drafting termination clauses so they clearly meet or exceed the minimum requirements of the *Employment Standards Act, 2000* in every way. Seek legal advice in this area.

MINIMIZING YOUR RISK

Ensure Enforceability of Your Contract

- Have contract terms represent a reasonable balance between the interests of both parties.
- Avoid ambiguous wording.
- Point out complex or potentially contentious clauses and have the candidate initial them.
- Have the candidate sign the contract *before* work begins.
- Give the candidate plenty of time to review the contract.
- Advise the candidate to seek independent legal advice before signing.
- Obtain the employee's agreement and provide additional consideration or give the employee reasonable notice of the change if you want to introduce significant new terms that are disadvantageous to the employee after employment starts (for example, a restrictive covenant). If the employee rejects the change, be sure to advise them of the consequences of this rejection.
- Regularly review all contracts to ensure they are current.
- Update contracts whenever there is a promotion or other significant change in job duties.
- Ensure that the contract clearly meets, at the very least, the minimum requirements of the *Employment Standards Act, 2000* regardless of the length of employment.

Ending the Employment Relationship

In the following sections, we consider the three most common ways in which employment relationships come to an end: resignation, retirement, and termination (dismissal). Each of these partings of the ways brings with it legal implications that you, as a business person, should consider.

Resignation

Under the common law, employees have an obligation to provide notice of resignation, just as employers have a duty to provide notice of dismissal. However, in practice, employers rarely find it worthwhile to sue former employees for breaching this obligation.

One of the most common legal issues regarding resignation involves answering the following question: Did an employee quit, or was the employee fired? The answer is significant because employers who dismiss employees without cause—that is, without a reason based on the employee's conduct that is justifiable in law—must provide notice or pay in lieu of notice under the *Employment Standards Act, 2000* and the common law. Depending on the employee's length of service and the circumstances of the dismissal, an employer can owe a dismissed employee a substantial sum of money.

If an employee resigns after being offered a "choice" between resigning or being dismissed, a court or tribunal will probably find the resignation was not voluntary. The employer will therefore be obliged to provide pay in lieu of reasonable notice or to show just cause for dismissing the employee. Similarly, an employee who resigns from a job because an employer changes a fundamental term of the employment contract may be able to raise a successful argument that they were constructively dismissed (we discuss this concept later in this chapter under the heading "Constructive Dismissal").

To be effective, an employee's resignation must be intentional and voluntary. If a supervisor requires an employee to work through lunch and break times, and the employee, in frustration, walks off the job site saying, "I quit," it is unclear whether the employee has resigned. Even the words "I quit" are not considered to be a voluntary resignation if an employee is provoked, obviously distressed, or acting in the heat of the moment.

Figure 9.1

The words "I quit" are not usually considered to be a voluntary resignation if the employee was provoked, obviously distressed, or acting in the heat of the moment.

Similarly, if an employee quits during a heated exchange but apologizes later that day, indicating that they did not intend to resign, in law there is probably no voluntary resignation.

Retirement

The Ontario government has amended the Ontario *Human Rights Code* to generally prohibit employers from having a mandatory retirement policy at age 65. Effective December 12, 2006, the definition of "age" in the Ontario *Human Rights Code* was changed so that discrimination in employment because of age became illegal in Ontario for people aged 18 years or over (the previous definition had allowed age discrimination against employees who were 65 or older). This change will almost certainly require more accommodation of age-related disabilities.

MINIMIZING YOUR RISK

Know Your Obligations Regarding Resignations and Retirement

- Before acting on a resignation, consider all the circumstances in which it was given.
- Confirm your acceptance of an employee's resignation in writing as soon as possible after receiving it.
- Include a notice of resignation clause in the written employment contract (usually two to four weeks).
- Conduct "exit" interviews to get feedback on reasons for leaving and to ensure that company property is returned.
- Never fire an employee who provides notice of resignation. If you do not want that employee to stay in the workplace during the notice period, accept their resignation but tell them that, while they will be paid throughout the notice period, they should not attend work.
- Implement a consistent performance review program, with relevant documentation, for all workers (not just older workers).
- Accommodate employees with age-related disabilities up to the point of undue hardship.

Termination

In most situations, employers in non-unionized workplaces may dismiss employees as long as they provide advance notice or pay in lieu of notice. If, however, an employer has just cause for dismissing an employee, no notice is necessary. Because of its potential cost, the termination of employment is one of the most important workplace issues facing all employers. Two types of termination—for cause and without cause—are discussed below.

TERMINATION FOR (JUST) CAUSE

As an employer, if you can prove that you had just cause to dismiss an employee, you are no longer bound by the common law obligation to provide reasonable notice or pay in lieu of notice (wrongful dismissal damages). Proving just cause, however, is extremely difficult.

Under the common law, an employer has just cause to dismiss an employee when the employee's conduct is so serious that it fundamentally breaches the employment contract (whether written or oral) and thereby justifies dismissal without notice. Note that "good" cause, such as economic necessity, does not constitute just cause and as such an employee who is permanently laid off due to lack of work is still entitled to notice or pay in lieu of notice.

Some of the more common grounds of just cause include dishonesty, insubordination, disobedience, sexual harassment, and intoxication at work. Some misconduct, such as premeditated theft, or serious incidents of assault or sexual harassment, so seriously undermines the employment relationship that it may constitute just cause even if it occurs only once. However, most other types of misconduct or performance-related incidents must usually occur more than once to support dismissal for cause. This is especially true in the case of a long-term employee who has an otherwise excellent performance and disciplinary record. It is also true in the event of extenuating circumstances that cause an employee to act out of character. Furthermore, courts are increasingly requiring employers to use progressive discipline before resorting to dismissal for just cause (progressive discipline is discussed below).

While incompetence is one of the most common reasons for dismissing an employee, it is also one of the most difficult grounds to justify on the basis of just cause. An employer must show that the employee fell below an objectively determined level of performance, that that standard was reasonable, and that the problem lies with the employee, not with other factors, such as lack of adequate training. Generally, it must also show that it gave the employee sufficient time to improve their performance.

It is important in this regard for employers to have a consistent and objective performance appraisal process and to involve employees in the process. Performance reviews should be fair—never vindictive—and they should be accurate; they should neither ignore nor exaggerate problems. You would be wise to document performance reviews, including your employee's response to the review. If alleging just cause for dismissal, you should be prepared to prove that you took all reasonable steps to facilitate the employee's improvement and to help the employee meet your expectations.

Table 9.1 provides very brief summaries of several cases that show how Canadian courts interpret just cause. Keep in mind that the circumstances of every case are different and that each case must be interpreted on its own merits.

◇ Progressive Discipline

If you raise a defence of just cause in a wrongful dismissal action, you may be required to demonstrate that you first implemented progressive discipline.

progressive discipline discipline imposed by an employer in steps that increase in severity

Progressive discipline involves gradually increasing levels of discipline—for example, from a verbal warning to a written warning, a final written warning, and finally dismissal. In unionized workplaces, progressive discipline steps are codified in the collective agreement and usually include an unpaid suspension after a written warning. However, an unpaid suspension can pose legal problems where the employee is not unionized, since unless it is specifically provided for in the employee's contract, it could constitute constructive dismissal, a concept that we discuss below.

Table 9.1 Interpreting Just Cause

Case Name and Allegation	Facts	Result
McKinley v BC Tel (2001) Allegation: dishonesty	Employer argued just cause after finding out that, while on medical leave, the employee deliberately withheld information that he could safely return to work if he took certain medication.	Employer lacked just cause for dismissal. The employee's dishonesty did not go to the root of the employment relationship.
Henry v Foxco Ltd (2004) Allegations: insolence and insubordination	An auto body shop employee quarrelled with a supervisor who had said he took too long working on vans. During the confrontation, the employee repeatedly challenged the supervisor to "go ahead and fire" him.	The employer lacked just cause for dismissal. Given the employee's length of service and previous work record, this single incident did not warrant immediate dismissal. The employer should have observed a "cooling-off period" before deciding on an appropriate course of action.
Chaba v Ensign Drilling Inc (2002) Allegation: disobedience	A drilling-rig employee was told to remove ice using a crowbar and pickaxe, but when this was unsuccessful, he used and damaged a front-end loader that he knew he was not authorized to use.	The employer lacked just cause for dismissal. The employee's failure to follow instructions was an error in judgment, not a wilful act of disobedience or defiance. The employee had experience using the equipment and had seen it used before to accomplish the same task.
Bannister v General Motors of Canada Ltd (1994) Allegation: sexual harassment	An employee in a supervisory position made unwanted sexual comments and gestures to a student employed for the summer. Five other employees lodged similar complaints about the employee's conduct. The employee insisted his conduct was not harassment.	The employer had just cause for dismissal. The employee abused his power by condoning or creating a poisoned working environment for women. His repeated denial that his actions constituted misconduct raised a question as to whether he would change his behaviour.

SCENARIO

Hard-Headed About a Hard Hat

Val-Nam's "personal protective equipment standard" requires all employees to wear a hard hat when in the manufacturing plant, and two months ago, it expanded the policy to include the warehouse area attached to the plant. Jon Aubin is a forklift operator who has worked in the warehouse for over two years. Jon was told by his manager about the new policy but he is refusing to wear his hard hat while driving the forklift in the warehouse. Jon argues that he doesn't need the hard hat because the forklift itself has overhead protection; he also says that, due to his height, wearing a hard hat requires him to crouch over when driving and that the hard hat limits his peripheral vision, posing a safety hazard. Jon's manager believes Jon is being insubordinate and unsafe. The manager wants to know what steps should be taken.

The manager should consider the following initial steps:

- Engage in an open discussion with Jon to address his concerns and to explain the purpose of the safety standard.
- Examine options (seat height adjustments, modified hard hat that does not sit as high and/or does not block peripheral vision, added mirrors to enhance peripheral vision, etc.).
- Provide Jon with a verbal warning that all safety standards must be followed.

If Jon persists in not wearing his hard hat, the manager should consider the following steps, in order:

- Provide a written warning explaining the steps that have been taken to address Jon's concerns and the consequences of a failure to follow all safety standards.
- Issue a final written warning indicating that no further warnings will be provided.
- Terminate Jon's employment for failure to follow safety standards.

As an employer, it is very important that you meticulously document all disciplinary actions that you take so there will be reliable written evidence of what has occurred. You should also give your employees the opportunity to respond to any allegations that you make about them or their work before you take disciplinary action of any kind. Always act in a fair and even-handed manner.

If you apply progressive discipline, you can also prevent an employee from later arguing that you have condoned their misconduct by failing to respond to it within a reasonable period of time. **Condonation** of misconduct occurs when an employer overlooks misconduct or takes no action against it; it gives employees the impression that their employer will tolerate the misconduct in the future. If you condone a particular form of misconduct, you may be unable to rely on that incident in imposing discipline for future incidents.

condonation
implied acceptance by an employer of the conduct of an employee by permitting the conduct to continue without warning, discipline, or corrective action

TERMINATION WITHOUT (JUST) CAUSE

Employers can find themselves in a position where they want to dismiss employees for reasons that clearly do not constitute just cause under the law, such as a restructuring of the workplace or changing needs. If you find yourself in this position, you must provide your employees with advance notice or a comparable severance (sometimes called "separation") package so that they have time to look for a new job while still on your payroll. If you fail to live up to this legal obligation, your employees could successfully sue you for wrongful dismissal.

Even if an employee's conduct has been poor, unless the misconduct has been extreme, many employers choose to provide dismissed employees with a severance package rather than face the potential cost and uncertainty of a wrongful dismissal lawsuit. As noted above, unless you can prove that an employee fundamentally breached the terms of their employment contract through serious misconduct or performance problems, you owe the employee advance notice or payment in lieu thereof.

Employees are entitled to working notice or a severance package (that is, pay in lieu of notice) based on three possible sources:

- an employment contract that includes an enforceable termination provision that governs notice of dismissal;
- the *Employment Standards Act, 2000*, which provides fairly short notice based solely on length of service; and,
- in the absence of an enforceable termination provision, the common law, which requires the usually significantly longer "reasonable notice."

The rationale behind both the statutory and the common law notice obligations is to provide employees with an opportunity to find new employment while still receiving an income.

Why are there two types of notice periods—statutory and common law? The *Employment Standards Act, 2000* provides a minimum notice period that employers cannot override by contract. Employers and employees may, however, override the longer common law notice obligations by clearly setting out an alternative notice period in a written employment contract. As noted above, to be enforceable, the contractual notice *must* meet at least the minimum standards provided in the ESA. However, a contractual notice period that is shorter than common law notice *does bind* the employer and the employee if the contract is otherwise valid (as discussed earlier in this chapter under the heading "Enforceability of Employment Contracts").

The ESA provides employees with a simple process for enforcing their rights. Rather than commencing a lawsuit for wrongful dismissal, they may simply file a claim with the Ministry of Labour, and the ministry will investigate. This is a much less expensive and less risky process for an employee than launching a lawsuit. Employees who are not offered any notice or pay in lieu of notice and who wish to enforce their right to notice must choose between filing a complaint under the ESA and commencing a lawsuit for wrongful dismissal under the common law. In Ontario, employees cannot do both (we discuss an employee's termination entitlements under the ESA later in this chapter under the heading "Termination Notice and Pay Entitlements Under the Employment Standards Act, 2000").

In terms of the *common law* requirement, how much notice is reasonable? This depends on the circumstances of each case, including factors such as an employee's length of service, their age, their job, their salary, and the availability of similar employment (called the "Bardal" factors). Reasonable notice is usually a lengthy period under the common law, amounting to up to 24 months'—or even more—notice or pay in lieu of notice for long-term employees. Historically, some commentators have pointed to a rough rule of thumb for estimating reasonable notice, consisting of one month per year of employment and then modified up or down by the other factors (for example, someone aged 63 will be awarded a longer notice period than someone who is 32, all other factors being equal). However, courts have warned that this so-called rule of thumb can be misleading because, for example, someone with a short length of service may be entitled to a significantly longer period of notice due to other circumstances. For example, in *Sciancamerli v Comtech (Communication Technologies) Ltd*, a 57-year-old senior account executive whose employment was terminated after only 10 months was awarded 5 months' notice because of the specialization of his position and the lack of availability of similar employment.

Courts also consider whether an employee has fulfilled the common law **duty to mitigate** damages. This means that employees are required to take all reasonable

duty to mitigate
obligation to take all reasonable steps to lessen losses suffered

steps to find comparable alternative employment during the reasonable notice period. Employees must undertake serious job searches or risk being awarded a shorter notice period by a court. If an employee is successful in finding new employment before the end of the notice period, the employee's earnings from the new job are usually deducted from the wrongful dismissal award (but not from their entitlement under the ESA). Also, where there is a fixed, or easily calculable, notice period in the contract, the employee will only have a duty to mitigate where the contract expressly says so.

◇ Wrongful Dismissal Damages

wrongful dismissal dismissal without just cause in which an employer breaches its common law duty to provide reasonable notice to an employee

As noted above, **wrongful dismissal** occurs when an employer fails to meet its contractual duty to provide adequate advance notice of termination (the length of such notice being either what is expressly specified in the employment contract or, if no enforceable termination provision exists, the amount of reasonable notice implied under the common law). If an employee decides to sue for wrongful dismissal and is successful against the employer, a court will award the employee an amount equal to the wages and benefits that the employer would have owed during the period of notice, as well as court costs. These are called wrongful dismissal (or reasonable notice) damages. In practice, most employees and employers settle their cases without going to court for an amount that approximates what a court would order, because neither party wants to incur the expense of going to court.

In addition to seeking damages for failure to provide reasonable notice of termination, an employee can ask for additional damages if they have suffered actual losses as a result of the *manner* in which they were terminated (these are called "aggravated" or "moral" damages). In wrongful dismissal cases, an employee can also ask for punitive damages. Awards of punitive damages are rare but occur when the employer's conduct is particularly reprehensible and deserving of punishment.

The case of *Boucher v Wal-Mart Canada Corp* is a good illustration of wrongful dismissal damages as it discusses all three types, as well as damages for the tort of intentional infliction of mental suffering.

CASE IN POINT

The High Cost of Bad Behaviour

Boucher v Wal-Mart Canada Corp, 2014 ONCA 419

Facts

Boucher, aged 43, was an assistant manager at a Walmart store in Windsor, Ontario. A good worker, Boucher got along well with her manager, Pinnock, until May 2009, when he asked her to falsify a temperature log and she refused. After this, Pinnock started belittling Boucher in front of co-workers. In June, Boucher availed herself of Walmart's Open Door Communication Policy by asking to meet with the district people manager to discuss this issue; however, in breach of that policy, Pinnock was told of this meeting and thereafter he became even more abusive toward Boucher. In October, Boucher asked to meet with senior management representatives, who said they would investigate her concerns. However, they warned her that she could suffer negative consequences if her concerns were found to be unjustified and, in mid-November, after finding that her complaints were "unsubstantiated," they told Boucher she would be "held accountable for making them." A few days later, Pinnock again humiliated her in front of other employees, this time by grabbing her by the elbow and telling her to prove to him that she could count to ten—he prompted her by initiating the count and then told her to count out loud along with him. Boucher was so humiliated that she left the store and soon after tendered her resignation. As one witness later testified, Pinnock seemed "overjoyed" when he heard she had quit.

Boucher sued Walmart and Pinnock for constructive dismissal and related damages. In a jury trial, Boucher was awarded:

- 20 weeks' salary, as required under her employment contract (2 weeks' salary per year of service);
- $1.2 million against Walmart ($200,000 in aggravated damages for the manner in which she was dismissed, and $1 million in punitive damages); and
- $250,000 damages against Pinnock ($100,000 for the tort of intentional infliction of mental distress and $150,000 for punitive damages).

The defendants appealed.

Result

With respect to Walmart, the Court of Appeal upheld the $200,000 award for aggravated damages on several grounds: it failed to take Boucher's complaints seriously; it failed to discipline or stop Pinnock's mistreatment of her; it failed to follow its own workplace policies; and it threatened Boucher with retaliation for making her complaints. However, the appellate court reduced the punitive damages award from $1 million to $100,000, because the high aggravated damages award already contained an element of punishment and denunciation.

The Court of Appeal upheld the award of $100,000 against Pinnock for committing the tort of intentional infliction of mental suffering; his actions were flagrant and calculated to harm the plaintiff. However, it similarly reduced the punitive award from $150,000 to $10,000 on the basis that the tort award already carried a "strong punitive component."

Business Lesson

Despite the reduction in the punitive damage awards, the total amount awarded for aggravated damages and intentional infliction of mental distress remains a significant sum. This case holds several important lessons for employers:

- Create fair workplace anti-harassment policies and follow them.
- Conduct workplace investigations promptly, thoroughly, and in an unbiased manner.
- Deal effectively with all employees, including managers and supervisors, who breach the workplace's violence, harassment, or discrimination policies.
- Do not impose or threaten to impose sanctions against an employee who lodges a complaint, except in the most obvious cases of bad faith.

◇ Constructive Dismissal

constructive dismissal fundamental breach by an employer of an employment contract that entitles an employee to consider themselves dismissed and to sue the employer for wrongful dismissal

Essentially, **constructive dismissal** can be claimed in two circumstances. One is where, as in the *Boucher* case, the employer's treatment of the employee (or its tolerance of offensive conduct) makes continued employment intolerable and the employee is justified in leaving and claiming constructive dismissal. This is because the employer has breached its implied obligation to provide a workplace that is safe and non-hostile.

The other situation occurs when an employer makes a fundamental change to an employment agreement without the employee's consent or without providing the employee with reasonable notice of the change. Fundamental changes include significant changes in job responsibilities or working conditions. When an employer makes such a change, the law treats the situation as if the employer had fired the employee from their old job and rehired them in a new job. Under these circumstances, the employee is entitled to reasonable notice of dismissal or payment in lieu of notice.

Although claims for constructive dismissal are relatively rare, employers should be aware of workplace changes that could initiate a constructive dismissal claim, including the following:

- significant changes to benefit packages,
- relocation of employees,

- alteration of duties and responsibilities of employees,
- changes in employees' reporting structure, and
- imposition of new obligations, such as restrictive covenants, on employees.

Usually, an employee who rejects a fundamental change to the terms of employment leaves the job and sues the employer for constructive dismissal damages. However, in *Russo v Kerr*, the employee sued the employer successfully even though he continued to work under the new terms of employment. In that case, Russo had been told that his annual compensation was being reduced from $144,000 to $60,000 (a decrease of about 60 percent), due to the difficult economy. The court held that because the employer allowed Russo to continue to work under the new terms, even after he made it clear that he did not accept the change, he was entitled to the difference in pay between the old and new terms during what would have been the reasonable notice period. During that period, he was in effect fulfilling his duty to mitigate. However, where the employee stays beyond the reasonable notice period, they are deemed to have accepted the lower pay from that point forward.

Note that a much smaller decrease (of, say, 5 percent) in an employee's salary due to economic conditions probably would not constitute constructive dismissal, especially if it were an across-the-board decrease.

Employers may gain some protection by building flexibility into a written employment contract. If the employer anticipates changes to the job description over time, the employment contract should state that duties and responsibilities may vary in response to changing business needs.

RIGHT TO REINSTATEMENT

right to reinstatement employee's right, provided by statute in some circumstances, to return to the job; for example, an employee who is terminated for going on pregnancy leave may be reinstated by an order of the Ministry of Labour

The **right to reinstatement** refers to an employee's right to be returned to their job. This extreme remedy is not available under the common law. It is available only in particular circumstances dictated by a collective agreement or statute. Unionized employees may be entitled to reinstatement if their employer dismisses them in contravention of the governing collective agreement. Non-unionized employees may be entitled to reinstatement if their employer dismisses them for exercising their rights under the ESA or various other statutes.

PROVIDING REFERENCES

You as an employer are not liable for defamation when providing references for former employees as long as the information provided is truthful. Moreover, employers providing a negative reference are further protected by the defence of "qualified privilege." This means that an employer providing a reference will not be liable if the views expressed are honestly held, based on reasonable grounds, and provided without malicious intent.

Note that there also is no legal obligation to provide a dismissed employee with a letter of reference, but an employee who lacks a reference will probably find it more difficult to obtain a new job and this could result in a higher wrongful dismissal award.

If you dismiss an employee for cause and provide the employee with too positive a reference, however, you are leaving yourself open to a lawsuit for negligent misrepresentation from a new employer who relies on your reference and suffers harm as a result. Moreover, if you take the position that you dismissed an employee for cause, you must be careful not to undermine that position by providing too glowing a letter of reference. One approach is to give the employee a letter that confirms the period of employment, position, and salary but does not comment on the employee's performance.

MINIMIZING YOUR RISK

Reduce the Potential for Dismissal Claims from Non-Unionized Employees

- Never dismiss or otherwise retaliate against an employee for exercising their legal rights.
- Include a notice of termination clause in the written employment contract.
- Include in the employment contract a clause allowing you some flexibility to make changes, such as to job duties.
- Make effective use of probationary periods by monitoring suitability and performance carefully.
- Provide employees with as much notice as possible of any significant changes to their duties and compensation.
- Carefully document any problems with employees as soon as they occur.
- Implement and consistently apply an objective performance evaluation program that provides employees with regular, balanced feedback on their performance, guidance on ways to improve, and a reasonable time in which to make these improvements.
- Apply progressive discipline in all but the most serious instances of misconduct.
- Allow employees an opportunity to respond to any allegations of misconduct.
- Do not appear to condone misconduct by failing to respond to it within a reasonable time.
- Put notice of termination in writing, clearly specifying the termination date.
- Unless you are certain that you have just cause for dismissing an employee (and this should be reviewed with expert legal counsel first), provide an employee with advance notice of dismissal.
- Ensure that advance notice of dismissal meets at least the mandatory minimum requirements of the *Employment Standards Act, 2000*.
- If there is no notice of termination clause in the employment contract, provide the dismissed employee with reasonable notice of termination.
- Consult an employment lawyer to determine the appropriate notice period and the best form of severance package for a particular employee.
- Be fair and courteous to dismissed employees.
- Obtain a written release from employees indicating their acceptance of your separation package and their agreement not to sue for more. Urge employees to obtain independent legal advice first.
- Provide job search support for employees where appropriate.
- Make sure that any negative statements made in the course of a job reference are accurate and provided in good faith.

Statute Law

While the non-union employment relationship is grounded in the common law of contract, there are a significant number of statutes that apply to the employer-employee relationship as well. The primary purpose of these laws, as they have evolved over the years, is to provide employees with greater rights and protections than they would otherwise have based on their ability to negotiate individual employment terms with their employer.

Arguably, the most significant of these statutes is human rights legislation: it affects every phase of the employment relationship, from the initial hiring stage through to the end of employment.

Human Rights in the Workplace

discrimination negative or singular treatment of a person or group on the basis of a prohibited ground of discrimination under the *Human Rights Code*

The Ontario *Human Rights Code* states that it is "public policy in Ontario to recognize the dignity and worth of every person and to provide for equal rights and opportunities without discrimination." The Code prohibits workplace **discrimination** and harassment on specified prohibited grounds.

Prohibited Grounds of Discrimination

The Ontario *Human Rights Code* prohibits discrimination in employment on the following grounds:

- race
- ancestry
- place of origin
- colour
- ethnic origin
- citizenship
- creed (religion)
- sex (including the right to equal treatment without discrimination because of pregnancy)
- sexual orientation
- age (where the person is at least 18 years old)
- record of offences (provincial offences or pardoned federal offences)
- marital status
- family status (this ground covers parent and child relationships and includes biological parents, adoptive parents, and legal guardians)
- gender identity
- gender expression (how a person publicly presents or expresses their gender)
- disability (this ground includes physical, mental, and psychiatric disabilities; drug or alcohol addiction; perceived disabilities; and disabilities for which workers' compensation benefits were claimed or received; it excludes minor, temporary illness to which the general public is susceptible, such as the flu or common cold).

If your business makes an employment decision in which a discrimination based on prohibited ground plays *any* part, unless one of the exceptions described below applies, you have infringed the Code. It is irrelevant whether the prohibited ground was the only, or even the primary, factor that you took into account. It is irrelevant that you did not know you were discriminating or that the motives for your decision were not malicious. The crucial factor is the effect of the discrimination on the job applicant or employee. For example, a retail store's requirement that all full-time employees be available to work Saturdays may not intend to discriminate against members of religious groups who observe Saturday as a day of rest, but this will be the result.

OHRC's Report Says Sexualized Dress Code Requirements May Violate the Human Rights Code Based on Gender

Figure 9.2

Under recent amendments to the *Occupational Health and Safety Act* (Bill 148), employers in Ontario are now prohibited from requiring a worker to wear footwear with an elevated heel unless doing so is required to safely perform their work or where they are employed as a performer in the entertainment and advertising industry.

According to an Ontario Human Rights Commission (OHRC) report, the following are possible examples of gender-based discrimination in dress codes:

- Women staff being required to wear revealing skirts or dresses featuring short hemlines, low necklines, sleeveless tops, and/or very tight-fitting and/or thin fabric.
- Women not being allowed to wear pants, being given a pants option not equivalent to that for men (such as yoga pants versus jeans), or being told they can't wear pants in certain roles or locations (such as hosts or servers in lounge areas).
- Women staff being prohibited from covering up, in the following ways:
  - requiring them to have bare/exposed legs—that is, prohibiting them from wearing stockings or pantyhose, tights, or leggings under dresses or skirts;
  - not allowing them to wear another layer (sweater, jacket, long sleeves, etc.) with revealing outfits, or limiting when or where they may do so.

Discrimination Not Covered by the Human Rights Code

The Code's prohibited grounds now cover many, but not all, situations that involve discriminatory conduct. For example, an employee who suffers discrimination in the workplace on the basis of their political convictions or social status cannot file a complaint under the Code because neither political convictions nor social status are prohibited grounds of discrimination in employment in Ontario.

The Code also sets out specific, narrow exemptions where discrimination on the basis of a prohibited ground is permissible (s 24). For example, a faith-based organization can stipulate that counsellors must be of that faith. However, it probably cannot insist that custodial staff be of that faith because such a requirement is not related to a custodial job. Similar exemptions from the Code apply in the case of sex discrimination in hiring. For example, a recreational club may hire only male attendants to work in the men's locker room.

nepotism policy
employment policy that allows an employer to discriminate in favour of, or against, their close relatives or the close relatives of employees

There is also a **nepotism policy** exemption that allows an employer to give preferential consideration to, or to discriminate against, job applicants who are closely related to the employer or to a current employee. In other words, as an employer, you may choose to have a hiring policy that gives preference to the close relatives of employees, or you may choose to have a hiring policy that prohibits the hiring of close relatives of employees (or you may choose to have no such policy at all). The list of relatives that can be covered by a nepotism policy is short: spouse, children, or parents of an employee or of the employer.

The Duty to Accommodate

What constitutes "discrimination" has expanded greatly since Ontario enacted its first comprehensive human rights laws in 1962. Initially, the term referred to intentional discrimination or discriminatory actions perpetrated on purpose. For example, if an employer advertises a sales position and states that only married men between ages 18 and 40 will be considered for the job, the discriminatory intent is obvious. The employer's hiring policy clearly discriminates on the basis of sex, age, and family status and is a violation of human rights law. Such blatant instances of discrimination are unlikely today, although not unheard of. More commonly, discrimination is less direct and is unintentional.

adverse impact discrimination
workplace policy that unintentionally affects certain groups in a detrimental way

accommodation
human rights concept that refers to making changes that allow a person or group protected by the *Human Rights Code* to participate in the workplace

A workplace policy that unintentionally affects certain groups in a detrimental, or negative, way is called **adverse impact discrimination** (also known as constructive discrimination). For example, a security guard company whose hiring policy requires all applicants be a certain minimum height may not intend to discriminate against women or certain racial groups, but this will be the result. The duty to provide **accommodation** is based on the belief that it is unfair to exclude people from the workplace in a discriminatory fashion because their needs are different from those of the majority of workers.

bona fide occupational requirement (BFOR)
reasonably necessary job qualification or requirement imposed because it is necessary for job performance

A rule or qualification that has a negative impact on a person or group based on one of the Code's prohibited grounds is generally considered to be discriminatory, and thus unlawful, unless a business can prove that it is a legitimate job requirement that cannot be modified or eliminated without creating a very severe burden for the employer. This type of qualification is called a **bona fide occupational requirement (BFOR)** or qualification (BFOQ). For example, a trucking business would have no problem proving that the absence of its rule against hiring blind truck drivers would create a severe burden; the qualification of sight is therefore a BFOR for a trucking job.

To be a BFOR, a job qualification must be:

- rationally connected to job performance,
- adopted in good faith, and
- reasonably necessary to accomplish a legitimate work-related purpose.

To prove that a requirement is reasonably necessary, an employer must prove that it cannot accommodate a person who lacks this requirement without experiencing what the Code refers to as "undue hardship" (the "Meiorin" test). For example, an employer cannot refuse to hire someone with very poor eyesight for a clerical position if, by making certain workplace modifications, such as purchasing a special computer screen or software program, the employer could enable that person to perform the job satisfactorily.

The case of *Canadian Union of Public Employees, Local 4400 v Toronto District School Board* demonstrates how the test for showing that a job requirement is a BFOR is applied. In that decision, several female job candidates successfully challenged the employer's physical demands requirements for the position of cleaner (see the Case in Point below).

CASE IN POINT

Discrimination on the Basis of Sex Found in Pre-Employment Fitness Test

Canadian Union of Public Employees, Local 4400 v Toronto District School Board, [2003] OLAA No 514 (Howe)

Facts

The employer school board offered three women part-time cleaning jobs on the condition that they pass a physical demands assessment. They began work but were dismissed when they failed to complete the part of the assessment that required them to lift 50 pounds (23 kilograms) from bench to shoulder height. The employees filed grievances challenging the lifting requirement. They got their jobs back after they were given strength training that helped them meet the lifting requirements, but they pursued their grievance, claiming that the requirement was discriminatory.

Result

The arbitrator found that the lifting requirement indirectly resulted in the exclusion of a group identified by a prohibited ground (sex) since evidence showed that female candidates initially failed the strength test 16 times more often than male candidates. Because the job requirement had a *prima facie* (on the face of it) discriminatory effect, the onus shifted to the employer to show that the requirement was a BFOR. The employer failed the third part of the Meiorin test because it failed to demonstrate that it could not accommodate the employees without incurring undue hardship. For example, the employer could have ordered supplies in smaller containers, reduced the height to which supplies are stacked, or arranged for the heavier lifting to be done by others.

Business Lesson

Where a rule or requirement has a negative impact on one group based on a protected ground, consider whether it is essential. If it is, consider how that individual or group could be accommodated up to the point of undue hardship.

Note that the duty to accommodate has two dimensions: procedural and substantive. The procedural dimension requires an employer to explore accommodation options; the substantive dimension requires the employer to then show it fulfilled its duty to accommodate to the point of undue hardship.

Employees and their unions must cooperate in the accommodation process by taking reasonable steps to facilitate solutions to problems. In other words, accommodation is a shared responsibility. For example, it is up to the employee seeking accommodation to answer questions or provide information regarding relevant restrictions or limitations, including providing information from health care professionals. Similarly, unions have a legal obligation to help find solutions when accommodation potentially conflicts with the collective agreement. In one case, a union was ordered to pay damages to an employee after it refused to allow the disabled employee to transfer his full seniority to a new, accommodated position.

undue hardship difficulty beyond that which an employer is required to endure when accommodating the needs of an individual or a group protected under the *Human Rights Code*

UNDUE HARDSHIP

According to the Ontario Human Rights Commission's policy, **undue hardship** is the point at which the cost of accommodating an employee substantially affects the economic health of the business or produces a substantial health and safety risk that outweighs the benefit of accommodation. In considering the economic impact, a business should try to obtain outside sources of funding, such as government grants, to help pay for an accommodation. Tax writeoffs may also be available.

SCENARIO

A Solution Within Sight

The most qualified applicant for the administrative job at Val-Nam's head office should be offered the job. If it turns out that the applicant has poor eyesight and requires specialized equipment (additional lighting, larger computer screen, screen-reading technology, etc.), Val-Nam will be required to provide that equipment for the applicant to the point of undue hardship.

While this is Val-Nam's legal obligation, it can also make good business sense. Accommodating the applicant may impose an initial cost on the business, but the opportunity to retain a highly qualified and (based on the applicant's references) dedicated employee can far outweigh those initial costs in the long run.

Any business that claims it is unable to fulfill its obligation to accommodate is fighting an uphill battle. Inclusive workplaces are the order of the day. That said, the Supreme Court of Canada has reaffirmed the principle that the exchange of work for remuneration still lies at the heart of the employment relationship. This principle was clearly articulated in *Hydro-Québec v Syndicat des employées de techniques professionnelles et de bureau d'Hydro-Québec, section locale 2000 (SCFP-FTQ)*. In that case, the court found that where the employer had taken all reasonable measures to accommodate an employee, but the employee still remained unable to do her essential job duties, now and into the reasonably foreseeable future, the employer had established undue hardship. The standard of reasonable accommodation is not whether accommodation is impossible but whether accommodation short of undue hardship is impossible.

MINIMIZING YOUR RISK

Accommodate Employees in Good Faith

- Accept employee requests for accommodation in good faith and respond promptly.
- Obtain expert opinion or advice where necessary.
- Diligently investigate accommodation solutions.
- Where one solution would create undue hardship, investigate alternative approaches.
- Keep a record of accommodation requests, decisions made (with reasons), and actions taken.
- Maintain employees' confidentiality.
- Implement accommodation strategies in a timely manner unless they create undue hardship.
- Where possible, seek grants and tax writeoffs to fund accommodations.

SITUATIONS COMMONLY REQUIRING ACCOMMODATION

◇ Disabilities

A significant percentage of the human rights claims filed in Ontario are based on disability in employment. As noted above, "disability" is broadly defined and includes both physical and mental disabilities. The *Human Rights Code* states that employers may require an employee to perform only those duties that are "essential" to their job. For example, if a sales job depends on an employee's driving to customers' premises, then having a valid driver's licence is essential. On the other hand, if driving is necessary only to get to an occasional meeting, the requirement for a valid licence is not justifiable. Why? It unnecessarily disqualifies people who cannot obtain a driver's licence as a result of a disability.

Even if a job duty is essential, a business must tailor its workplace to meet the special needs of a disabled employee up to the point of undue hardship. This may require, for example, changing the layout of the workplace to make it barrier-free, modifying equipment and vehicles, providing modified seating and special computer hardware or software, modifying work hours, or reassigning disabled employees to vacant jobs that they are better able to perform.

Generally speaking, employers are not entitled to an employee's diagnosis, but they are entitled to know the limitations that are placed on the employee's ability to do their job. A Functional Abilities Form can be filled out by the employee's doctor to indicate what the person can and cannot do. However, the employee needs to authorize the employer to contact the doctor. (New OHRC guidelines detail obligations in accommodation requests.)

Accessibility for Ontarians with Disabilities Act, 2005

The *Accessibility for Ontarians with Disabilities Act, 2005* (AODA) was passed in 2005 with the goal of making Ontario fully accessible to people with disabilities by 2025. It is meant to complement the *Human Rights Code* by obliging organizations to address accessibility issues proactively rather than on a case-by-case, complaint-driven basis.

Requirements have been phased in over time, based on sector (for example, private or public) and organization size (by number of employees). However, as of 2018 even small private and not-for-profit organizations must be in compliance with most of its provisions.

There are five accessibility standards, one of which is the Employment Accessibility Standard: it generally requires employers to establish and implement employment policies, procedures, and training related to accessibility in recruiting, hiring, retaining, and accommodating people with disabilities. For example, when recruiting, an organization has to make applicants aware that accommodations are available to allow them to participate in the recruitment process and that assessment and selection materials are available in an accessible format on request.

The AODA standards do not take away from rights available under the *Human Rights Code*. All employers, regardless of size, still have the duty to accommodate an individual employee to the point of undue hardship under the Code.

www.emond.ca/CBL3/links

DIG DEEPER
More detailed information on the Integrated Accessibility Standards Regulation is available on e-Laws.

The definition of "disability" includes alcohol and drug abuse, as well as perceived abuse. Therefore, the Code requires businesses to accommodate employees who are disabled by a drug or alcohol problem, unless doing so creates undue hardship. This requirement usually obliges an employer to implement an employee assistance program or to allow an employee time off work to attend a rehabilitative program. However, it does not require an employer to accept lengthy, ongoing absences unrelated to rehabilitation, as demonstrated in the case of *Chopra v Syncrude Canada Ltd.*

CASE IN POINT

Alcohol Abuse and the Duty to Accommodate

Chopra v Syncrude Canada Ltd, 2003 ABQB 504

Facts

An employee's performance was adequate for most of the 14-year period during which he worked for his employer. In the eight months preceding his retirement, however, the employee's alcoholism and depression created problems in the workplace. On one occasion, he was found to have consumed so much alcohol while on the job that his supervisor had to escort him home.

The employee agreed to accept mandatory referral to the employer's assistance program, to never again violate the employer's drug and alcohol policy, and to attend supervisory and follow-up meetings as required. Both parties understood that failure to follow this plan would result in a termination hearing.

The employee attended a treatment program but was soon asked to leave for violating its policies. He was, however, admitted into a relapse prevention program to help him deal with his disability. Another disruptive incident occurred a short time later, resulting in the employee's absence from work because of intoxication. The employer then required the employee to submit to a medical tracking process and random drug and alcohol testing. After he was again found to be under the influence of alcohol while at work, the employer dismissed him. The employee then filed a wrongful dismissal lawsuit against the employer.

Result

The court found that the employer had fulfilled its duty to accommodate the employee's disability. The employee was not entitled to any further accommodation, and the employer was justified in dismissing him.

Business Lesson

Before dismissing an employee for problems arising from alcoholism or drug problems, provide counselling services, necessary leaves of absence, and appropriate warnings in writing.

◇ Religious Beliefs and Practices

The *Human Rights Code* refers to religious belief and practice as "creed." The requirement to accommodate an employee's creed may arise in a number of ways, including dress codes, break policies, work schedules, and religious leave. As a business person, you must implement flexible policies in your workplace. For example, break policies should be sufficiently fluid to accommodate daily periods of prayer for employees whose religion requires them. Employees who are unable to work on particular days of religious observance must be given the day off unless doing so would cause undue hardship for your business. The Ontario Human Rights Tribunal has held that an employer does not have to pay an employee for time taken off for religious holidays as long as it offers reasonable options allowing the employee to make up for wages lost through other means, if possible, such as rescheduling.

◇ Pregnancy

Your duty to accommodate a pregnant employee might include the need to relocate her temporarily from a work area that might endanger her pregnancy. For example, you might need to move her from an area that is close to chemical fumes. You may also need to provide her with a flexible work schedule, increase her break times, and, once she has the baby, give her a private and comfortable place to breastfeed her child or pump breast milk.

An employee who requires time off before or after her pregnancy or parental leave arising from pregnancy-related health concerns is entitled to benefits under an employer's workplace sick or disability plan.

Note that according to the OHRC's updated policy (2014) on preventing discrimination because of pregnancy and breastfeeding, it is not only illegal to discriminate because a woman is pregnant or has chosen to breastfeed (or not to breastfeed) her child. Discrimination is also prohibited against someone because she *was* pregnant, was trying to get pregnant, has had an abortion, miscarriage, or stillbirth, is going through fertility treatments, or experiences complications or has specific needs related to pregnancy.

◇ Family Caregiving Obligations

Since 2000, courts and tribunals increasingly have been asked to consider the extent to which employers have a duty to accommodate employees for their general family caregiving obligations, including childcare and eldercare. The law in this area is evolving. In *Canada (Attorney General) v Johnstone*, in 2014, the Federal Court of Appeal set out a four-part test to determine whether an employer has a duty to accommodate an employee's request based on family status and childcare. The four elements are:

- The child is under the employee's care and supervision.
- The childcare obligation at issue engages the individual's legal responsibility for that child, as opposed to a personal choice (for example, the obligation to take care of a child's basic needs versus the desire to attend a child's school concert).
- The employee has made reasonable efforts to meet those childcare obligations through reasonable alternative solutions, and no such alternative solution is reasonably available.
- The impugned workplace rule interferes with fulfilling that obligation in a way that is not trivial.

Note that this test places an onus on the employee to "self-accommodate" to some extent by showing that reasonable efforts have already been made to meet their childcare obligations.

More recently, in 2016, the Ontario Human Rights Tribunal held in *Misetich v Value Village Stores Inc* that this test is too restrictive. For example, in requiring that a "legal responsibility" be engaged, the test could not easily be modified to cover eldercare. The Tribunal also held that an employee should not have to show that she attempted to "self-accommodate"; she only needs to demonstrate that the workplace rule in question results in a "real disadvantage to the parent-child relationship."

While the practical differences between these two approaches have yet to be determined, under either approach employers need to be open and flexible when responding to requests for family-related accommodation. At the same time, employees still have an obligation to provide supporting information concerning their accommodation request and to cooperate in identifying possible solutions.

MINIMIZING YOUR RISK

Accommodate Special Needs

- Design workplace policies and standards with everyone in mind, including those with special needs.
- Apply dress codes and other requirements in a way that is sensitive to people who have special needs for religious reasons.
- When assessing a disabled employee's or applicant's ability to do the job, consider only duties that are essential to the job and make reasonable adjustments to work processes and tools to accommodate the individual's disability.
- Implement and consistently apply a policy to assist in the rehabilitation of employees who suffer from substance abuse.
- Be prepared to provide pregnant employees with increased breaks, a temporary relocation, or a flexible work schedule if required.
- Be flexible with respect to breastfeeding requirements, including providing a comfortable, private place in the workplace for breastfeeding.
- Be flexible when facing an employee's request for accommodation of family obligations by exploring options available to meet this need to the point of undue hardship.

Recruitment and Selection

As noted above, the Code's protections begin even before an employment relationship exists. Job advertisements, application forms, the interview process, and pre-employment testing all must comply with human rights law. You should remember that you are in violation of the Code if *any* of your reasons for making a hiring decision involve a discriminatory ground. In other words, you cannot successfully claim in your defence that you based your decision mainly on non-discriminatory factors.

JOB ADVERTISEMENTS AND APPLICATION FORMS

The intention of the Code is to have employers consider a broad range of qualified candidates in the early part of the recruitment process so that they do not eliminate suitable candidates inadvertently. The Code therefore prevents employers from advertising or requesting information in a discriminatory fashion. For example, in a job application form, employers can generally ask only for an applicant's name, address, education, and previous employment history.

Table 9.2, which is based on the OHRC guidelines, sets out the prohibited grounds of discrimination and provides examples of questions that the Commission believes should be avoided on job application forms (including online forms) because they directly or indirectly touch on those prohibited grounds. In some cases, acceptable alternative wording is suggested.

JOB INTERVIEWS

At the job interview stage, the employer may expand the scope of job-related questions to include questions that touch on prohibited grounds where these relate to either:

- one of the exceptions to the rule against discrimination, such as a nepotism policy, or
- a BFOR.

Table 9.2 OHRC's Guidelines for Designing Application Forms

Prohibited Grounds	Examples of Unacceptable Questions	Examples of Acceptable Questions
Race/Colour/ Citizenship/ Place of origin/ Ethnic origin/ Religion	• Are you a Canadian citizen? • What is your social insurance number? (This may indicate place of origin or citizenship status, and employers should request it only following a conditional offer of employment.) • Where are you from originally? • What schools have you attended? (This may indicate a candidate's place of origin.) • Are you a member of any clubs or other organizations? (This could indicate sex, race, or religion.) • What is your height and weight? • What is your Canadian work experience? • Are there any days of the week you are unable to work? • What is your religion? • What religious holidays or customs do you observe? • Are you willing to work on Saturdays?	• Are you legally entitled to work in Canada? • What is the highest level of education you have reached? • What professional credentials and diplomas have you received? • Are you fluent in English, French, or another language? (This question is acceptable only if fluency is a BFOQ.)
Sex	• What was your family name before marriage? • What form of address do you prefer: Ms, Mrs, Miss, or Mr? • What is your relationship with the person to be notified in case of emergency?	None
Sexual orientation	• Are you a member of any clubs or other organizations?	None
Marital status	• Are you married? • What was your family name before marriage? • What form of address do you prefer: Ms, Mrs, Miss, or Mr? • Is your spouse willing to transfer? • What is your relationship with the person to be notified in case of emergency?	• Are you willing to travel or relocate? (This question is acceptable only if travel or relocation is a BFOQ.)
Family status	• Are you married, divorced, single, or living in a common-law relationship? • What is your birth name? • What form of address do you prefer: Ms, Mrs, Miss, or Mr? • Do you have children? • How many children do you have? • Do you plan to start a family soon? • Are you pregnant? • Do you have appropriate childcare arrangements? • Is your spouse willing to transfer? • What is your relationship with the person to be notified in case of emergency?	• Are you willing to travel or relocate? (This question is acceptable only if travel or relocation is a BFOQ.)

(The table is continued on the next page.)

Table 9.2 Concluded

Prohibited Grounds	Examples of Unacceptable Questions	Examples of Acceptable Questions
Record of offences	• Have you ever been convicted of a crime?	• Have you ever been convicted of a criminal offence for which a pardon has not been granted?
Age	• What is your date of birth? • Attach a copy of your driver's licence. • Provide an educational transcript. (This could include dates that indicate the age of the applicant.)	• Are you 18 years of age or older? (As of December 2006, it is no longer acceptable to ask a person whether he or she is less than 65 years of age.)
Disability	• Do you have any physical or mental disabilities? • Have you ever claimed or received workers' compensation benefits? • Do you have a history of substance abuse? • Are you physically or mentally capable of performing this job? • Do you require any accommodation to perform this job? • This job requires heavy lifting. Will you be able to do it? • Are you a member of Alcoholics Anonymous?	None

Source: Compiled in part from information contained in Ontario Human Rights Commission, *Hiring? A Human Rights Guide* (Toronto: OHRC, 1997), pp. 3–6.

An employer should not ask any BFOR questions that relate to a prohibited ground unless they are directly related both to a candidate's ability to perform the essential duties of the job and to the nature of any necessary accommodation.

The following interview questions are allowed in certain circumstances:

- What languages do you speak? (This question is acceptable if multilingualism is a BFOR, as it is for a customer service job in a business that serves clients who speak languages other than English and French.)
- Are you a Canadian citizen? (This question is permitted *only* in limited circumstances, such as where the job is a senior executive position.)
- Are you bondable? (Record of offences may be relevant where an applicant's capacity to be bonded is a BFOR, as it is for a security guard job.)
- Do you have a valid driver's licence? (Driving may be an essential job duty, as it is for truck drivers, whose convictions under the *Highway Traffic Act* are relevant.)
- Do you have a spouse, parent, or child employed here? (The employer may have a nepotism policy that prevents or favours the hiring of these family members.)

CONDITIONAL OFFERS OF EMPLOYMENT

conditional offer
offer subject to the fulfillment of one or more conditions

A **conditional offer** of employment is an offer subject to the fulfillment of one or more conditions. For example, a transport company may offer a truck driving job to a candidate and attach the condition that she provide a copy of a valid driver's licence or other documentation to prove that she is qualified and meets government criteria. Should the candidate fail to satisfy the condition, the company is justified in revoking its offer of employment.

The Inclusive Workplace

The same anti-discrimination and accommodation principles that apply during the recruitment and hiring process continue to apply throughout your workplace relationship with your employees. You must make all decisions concerning promotions, training opportunities, rewards, job assignments, discipline, layoffs, and terminations on a non-discriminatory basis.

MINIMIZING YOUR RISK

Recruit, Select, and Hire Job Candidates Fairly

- Advertise jobs widely to draw candidates from diverse backgrounds.
- Follow the Human Rights Commission's guidelines when designing application forms.
- Standardize your interview questions to ensure consistent treatment of candidates.
- Accommodate job candidates who are unable to attend a job interview because of a disability.
- Educate staff involved in the hiring process about the Code's requirements.
- Use interview teams to reduce the risk of individual bias and to facilitate the taking of detailed notes.
- Document reasons for decisions made throughout the hiring process.
- Unless disability is obvious or the job candidate raises the issue, leave accommodation issues until after a conditional offer of employment is made.
- Where relevant to the job, have the candidate undergo a pre-employment medical examination after a conditional offer of employment is made.

On-the-Job Drug and Alcohol Testing

As noted above, under human rights law, substance abuse is viewed as a disability, and employment-related drug and alcohol testing is severely restricted. According to the OHRC's policy on drug and alcohol testing, the Commission takes the position that testing as part of the *initial* applicant screening process is prohibited and—although case law has not ruled out the possibility—it recommends against testing *after* a candidate receives a conditional offer of employment for a safety-sensitive position.[1]

Historically, on-the-job testing has been acceptable only in very limited circumstances—for example, where an employee is involved in a workplace accident that reasonably suggests impairment (that is, "post-incident"), as part of a rehabilitation plan, or where an employer has "reasonable grounds" for believing that an employee is impaired. This could be based, for example, on the way they are behaving or the fact that their breath smells like alcohol. Even then, a positive test result should not automatically result in termination; testing should be part of a broader medical assessment and substance abuse policy that includes counselling and rehabilitation.

With respect to random testing, courts and tribunals have traditionally made a distinction between randomly testing for alcohol and for drugs. It has been more

1 Ontario Human Rights Commission, *Policy on Drug and Alcohol Testing* (7 April 2016), online: <http://www.ohrc.on.ca/en/policy-drug-and-alcohol-testing-2016>.

Figure 9.3

In April 2017, an Ontario court rejected an application by the TTC's union for a temporary injunction to stop the Toronto Transit Commission from instituting random drug and alcohol testing pending an arbitrator's final decision on the issue.

difficult for an employer in Ontario to defend a random drug-testing program because such tests were considered overly intrusive (a urine sample was usually required) and not indicative of current impairment.

However, partly in response to improvements in drug-testing technology, the law in this area is evolving. More recent case law suggests that random, on-the-job drug or alcohol testing *may* be a justified intrusion on worker privacy for *safety-sensitive* jobs where the employer can show that impairment is a general problem in the workplace.

Harassment

harassment
course of vexatious comment or conduct that is known or ought reasonably to be known to be unwelcome

sexual harassment
course of vexatious comment or conduct based on sex that is known or ought reasonably to be known to be unwelcome

In addition to outlawing workplace discrimination on the prohibited grounds, the Code also prohibits harassment. **Harassment** is defined as "a course of vexatious comment or conduct that is known or ought reasonably to be known to be unwelcome." The term "harassment" potentially includes a broad range of conduct, including verbal threats, intimidation, jokes, unwelcome remarks, and offensive pictures and posters.

Courts have found that the term **sexual harassment** includes unwelcome expressions of sexual or romantic interest or physical contact, offensive remarks, ostensibly flattering remarks about physical appearance, inappropriate staring, offensive jokes, displays of offensive pictures or other materials, questions or discussions about sexual activities, and paternalistic comments that undermine the recipient's authority.

Businesses may be liable for the human rights infringements of their employees, so it is important to have clear policies in place with fair and effective complaint procedures and to foster a corporate culture that encourages victims of harassment to come forward and have their complaints dealt with internally.

Another type of prohibited harassment relates to creating or allowing a **poisoned work environment**. This term refers to a workplace that feels hostile because of insulting or degrading comments or actions related to a prohibited ground of discrimination. It is not necessary that a particular complainant be the target of offensive comments or actions to create grounds for a human rights complaint. A poisonous workplace may be one that, for example, tolerates the display of pornographic images or racial slurs that undermine and humiliate employees.

poisoned work environment
workplace plagued with insulting or degrading commentary or actions related to a prohibited ground of discrimination under the *Human Rights Code*

The employer must be alert to the atmosphere of the workplace, since the employer is ultimately responsible for keeping the environment inclusive and humane. For example, an employer who fails to erase offensive graffiti as quickly as possible may be liable for harassment for allowing a poisoned work environment. Where harassment is extreme and ongoing, a human rights tribunal may order systemic remedies aimed at changing a workplace culture.

It should be noted that 2016 (Bill 132) amendments to Ontario's *Occupational Health and Safety Act* place a number of new obligations on employers regarding workplace harassment. These include the requirement to investigate "incidents," as well as complaints, of workplace harassment and to inform the parties of the results of the investigation and any corrective action (Bill 132's requirements are discussed below under the heading "Occupational Health and Safety Act").

Enforcement of the Human Rights Code

All applications (formerly known as "complaints") alleging discrimination or harassment are filed directly with the Ontario Human Rights Tribunal unless the application arises in a unionized workplace. In that case, applications are usually filed as grievances and heard by an arbitrator under the collective agreement.

www.emond.ca/CBL3/links

DIG DEEPER
The Ontario Human Rights Commission's guidelines and policy papers are available on its website.

The Ontario Human Rights Commission's role is to advocate for human rights and to promote public understanding of, and compliance with, human rights requirements. The OHRC may also file its own application or intervene in an application in particular cases of interest, such as those involving systemic discrimination. It also develops policies on human rights issues that, while not binding on the Tribunal, the Tribunal must consider in making its decisions.

A third human rights body, the Human Rights Legal Support Centre, provides free legal advice and assistance to people making a human rights application. Respondents (such as employers) must pay for their own legal representation.

Remedies for human rights violations may include orders such as the following against an employer:

- Pay compensation to the employee for actual lost earnings.
- Pay compensation to the employee for injury to dignity, feelings, and self-respect. (There is no upper limit for damages awarded under these headings.)
- Pay the employee's legal costs.
- Hire or reinstate the employee.
- Undertake staff training, such as in cross-cultural communications or sexual harassment.
- Implement an anti-harassment policy.

REPRISALS FOR EXERCISING RIGHTS

Like other employment statutes, the Ontario *Human Rights Code* specifically prohibits reprisals, or actions taken against anyone who asserts their rights under the Code. Reprisals are a violation of the Code and subject to the same orders as above.

MINIMIZING YOUR RISK

Prevent and Eliminate Harassment

- Prepare an anti-harassment policy that explains the types of behaviour that are considered harassment.
- Communicate this policy to all staff—before they begin employment.
- Hold awareness programs to emphasize the policy's importance.
- Encourage employees to report instances of harassment.
- Train supervisors to recognize harassment and respond quickly.
- Clearly explain the process for making internal complaints as well as how these complaints will be investigated.
- Encourage applicants to bring their concerns to the employer's attention.
- Advise employees either to inform harassers that their behaviour is unwelcome or to inform their supervisor (or another identified individual if the supervisor is the alleged harasser) of the harassment.
- Treat complaints confidentially and inform employees in advance about the confidentiality policy.
- Maintain a written record of all complaints.
- Require a prompt and thorough investigation by an impartial person who is knowledgeable in human rights law.
- Post the anti-harassment policy in a prominent place.
- Conduct a workplace investigation of all incidents or complaints of workplace harassment in compliance with the Bill 132 amendments to Ontario's *Occupational Health and Safety Act*.

Employment Standards

The Ontario *Employment Standards Act, 2000* sets out *minimum* terms and conditions of work required for employees in provincially regulated businesses. An employer is free to create standards of work that are more favourable to employees than the statutory minimums, but generally speaking, no employer can impose working conditions that are less favourable to employees than those imposed by the Act, even if an employee agrees to accept them.

Where an employer offers a term that exceeds the ESA minimum, that enhanced term applies to the employment contract: it replaces the statutory standard for that particular term.

General Standards

The ESA requires employers to keep accurate and specific records about employees and to make them available to inspectors from the Ministry of Labour on request. Employers are also required to provide employees with a copy of a poster prepared by the Ministry of Labour that contains a brief summary of key standards and information about enforcement and to display it conspicuously in the workplace.

The Act also sets out specific requirements concerning the payment of wages, including the information that must be contained on each pay statement. As an employer, you may not make deductions from an employee's wages except in clearly defined and limited circumstances that are authorized by law, such as the deduction of Employment Insurance premiums. Even with specific written authorization from the employee, you may not make deductions for faulty workmanship or for cash shortages unless an employee has sole access and total control over the property or cash.

www.emond.ca/CBL3/links

DIG DEEPER
A copy of the employment standards poster is available on the Ontario Ministry of Labour's website.

Specific Standards

As a business person, you have the option of hiring various types of employees—for example, permanent (full-time or part-time) or temporary (full-time or part-time). Employment laws rarely distinguish between these different categories of employees, although their statutory benefits, such as vacation or holiday pay, reflect the number of hours worked.

The ESA does make some distinctions based on occupations and industries. For example, managers and supervisors are not covered by the hours of work and overtime pay provisions. Some industries, such as construction, are exempt from certain employment standards as well. This information is available by industry on the Ministry of Labour's website (note that the Ontario government is currently reviewing these exemptions).

www.emond.ca/CBL3/links

DIG DEEPER
The Ministry of Labour website is constantly updated with new information on employment standards.

In November 2017, the Ontario legislature passed Bill 148, the *Fair Workplaces, Better Jobs Act*, which makes significant changes to the ESA as well as to the *Labour Relations Act, 1995*. The ESA changes are meant to address the growing number of workers whose employment status is precarious (for example, part-time, temporary, contract, casual, and seasonal). One of the most significant of these changes is that employers must now pay the same rate to employees who are performing the same work *regardless of employment status*. Exceptions would be allowed if differences in pay are based on seniority, merit, quantity or quality of production, or any other objective factor other than gender or employment status.

Table 9.3 sets out an overview of the general standards in effect before and after the passage of Bill 148.

Termination Notice and Pay Entitlements Under the Employment Standards Act, 2000

TERMINATION NOTICE OR PAY IN LIEU OF NOTICE

Under the ESA and its regulations, employees (both non-union and union) are entitled to receive notice of termination (or pay in lieu of this notice) unless the termination falls within one of several limited exceptions, including the following:

- The employee has engaged in *wilful* misconduct, disobedience, or *wilful* neglect of duty that is not trivial and has not been condoned by the employer.
- The employee has refused reasonable alternative employment with the same employer.
- The employee is on temporary layoff (as defined in the Act).

Individual notice periods are based entirely on an employee's length of service: typically one week per year of service to a maximum of eight weeks. It is up to the

Table 9.3 Summary of General Minimum Employment Standards (Ontario), Including Changes Made Under Bill 148

Standard	ESA Entitlements, Including Bill 148 Changes	Comments
Employee versus independent contractor classification	Misclassification of employees as independent contractors is expressly prohibited; onus is on employer to prove worker is an independent contractor.	New – Bill 148 amendment. 175 ESA inspectors are being hired; more proactive enforcement expected. No definition of "independent contractor" set out, so common law tests will apply.
Minimum wage (lowest hourly wage an employer may pay an employee)	The general minimum wage in Ontario is: • $14.00 per hour effective January 1, 2018 • $15.00 per hour effective January 1, 2019. Thereafter, wage rates will be adjusted for inflation. Special wage rates apply to some employees, such as students under 18 and workers who serve liquor.	Before passage of Bill 148 in November 2017, the general minimum wage in Ontario was $11.60.
Work hours (maximum number of hours an employee may be required to work)	8 hours per day (or, if employer has established a regular workday longer than 8 hours, the number of hours in that day) and 48 hours per week.	The Ministry of Labour has indicated that it will be reviewing current ESA exemptions for this and other standards, including those for managers and supervisory employees.
Overtime	Employers must pay non-managerial employees overtime pay at the rate of 1.5 times their regular rate of pay after they work 44 hours in a week. Under Bill 148 amendments, employees who work different jobs at different rates for the same employer will be paid an overtime rate based on the rate of the work being performed at the time overtime hours are accrued.	Provision relating to overtime rate when different jobs are worked is new under the Bill 148 amendments.
Vacation	Employees are entitled to at least 2 weeks' vacation time (4% pay) after they have worked for an employer for 12 months. After 5 years this changes to 3 weeks' vacation time (6% pay). Employer is entitled to decide when an employee can take vacation time; however, an employee is entitled to receive it within 10 months of earning it.	Bill 148 added requirement to increase vacation time from 2 to 3 weeks after 5 years.

Table 9.3 Continued

Standard	ESA Entitlements, Including Bill 148 Changes	Comments
Public holidays	Most employees are entitled to 9 paid public holidays per year. Employees in certain industries (e.g., hotels, restaurants, hospitals) may be required to work on a public holiday and take a substitute day off. Public holiday pay is calculated by taking the total regular wages the employee earned in the pay period immediately preceding the public holiday divided by the number of days worked in that period.	Before Bill 148 amendments, holiday pay was calculated as pay earned in the 4 work weeks before the week in which the holiday fell, divided by 20. This meant that an employee working one day a week would earn holiday pay of 1/5 their regular daily pay. Now that same employee will earn full wages for that holiday.
Statutory leaves of absence	Types of (mostly unpaid) leaves include: • pregnancy leave (17 weeks) • parental leave (61–63 weeks) • personal emergency leave (10 days per calendar year—*first 2 days must be paid*) • family medical leave (up to 28 weeks in a 52-week period) • family caregiver leave (up to 8 weeks) • military reservist leave • organ donor leave (13 weeks with possible extension) • death of a child leave (up to 104 weeks) • crime-related child disappearance leave (up to 104 weeks) • critical illness leave (up to 17 weeks to care for critically ill adult family member, up to 37 weeks for critically ill child under 18) • domestic or sexual violence leave (up to 10 days AND 15 weeks per calendar year—*first 5 days must be paid*) Employees may receive employment insurance benefits while on leave, if they qualify. Employees who take statutory leave have the right to return to the *same job at* the end of their leave period unless it no longer exists for reasons unrelated to the leave. During leave, employees have the right to retain benefits (e.g., health insurance) provided they continue to contribute to the benefit plan and to accrue seniority.	Under Bill 148 amendments, parental leave is extended from 35 to 61 weeks if pregnancy leave is taken and, if it is not, from 37 to 63 weeks. Before Bill 148 amendments, personal emergency leave was available only to employees whose employer had 50 or more employees, and it was entirely unpaid.

(The table is concluded on the next page.)

Table 9.3 Concluded

Standard	ESA Entitlements, Including Bill 148 Changes	Comments
Equal pay for equal work	*Gender-based:* Employers must pay men and women the same for performing substantially the same work (unless difference in pay is based on seniority, merit, quantity or quality of production) *Employment status–based:* Casual, part-time, temporary, seasonal, and temporary help agency employees have to be paid equally to full-time employees when performing substantially the same job for the same employer (unless difference in pay is based on seniority, merit, quantity or quality of production, or any other objective factor other than gender or employment status).	 New – Bill 148 amendment.
Pay for being on call or for shift cancellation with less than 48 hours' notice	Employees are entitled to a minimum of 3 hours' pay if: • their employer cancels their scheduled shift within 48 hours of the start of that shift • they are "on call" and not called in to work or are called in for less than 3 hours • they regularly work more than 3 hours a day and are required to come to work but work less than 3 hours. Some exceptions apply.	New – Bill 148 amendment. This amendment greatly reduces employer's incentive to have employees "on call." Employers will want to take great care in shift scheduling.
Refusal to work on short notice	Employees can refuse to accept shifts without repercussion if their employer asks them to work with less than 4 days' notice.	New – Bill 148 amendment.
Requests for change of schedule or location	Employees have right to request schedule or work location changes without reprisal after 3 months of service.	New – Bill 148 amendment. Employer must provide reasons if request is denied.
Temporary help agencies	Temporary help agencies must provide an assignment employee with 1 week's written notice or pay in lieu if an assignment that was supposed to last for 3 months or more is terminated before the estimated end date, unless another assignment lasting at least 1 week is offered to that employee.	New – Bill 148 amendment.

The scheduling-related changes under Bill 148 generally take effect January 1, 2019. The equal pay for equal work provisions take effect April 1, 2018. See Ontario Ministry of Labour website for list of exemptions from various standards.

employer whether to provide the employee with advance notice of termination and let the employee work throughout the notice period or to give the employee pay in lieu of notice. The employer may provide an employee with a combination of written notice and termination pay as long as together they equal the number of weeks set out in the Act. The employer must continue to pay the employee's benefits during the statutory notice period.

MASS LAYOFFS

In the unhappy event of a mass layoff, in which an employer dismisses many employees at once, different—lengthier—notice entitlements under the ESA may apply. If an employer lays off 50 or more employees in a period of four consecutive weeks, the mass notice requirements under the Act generally replace the Act's individual notice requirements.

SEVERANCE PAY

The term "severance pay," or "severance package," is often used synonymously with "termination pay." However, under the ESA, **severance pay** is a separate entitlement: a one-time lump-sum payment made in defined circumstances on the basis of an employee's years of employment. This payment is made in addition to any minimum termination notice or pay in lieu of notice requirements under the Act.

severance pay
one-time lump-sum payment made to a terminated employee in circumstances set out in the Ontario *Employment Standards Act, 2000*

To qualify for severance pay under the ESA, an employee must have worked for an employer for five or more years. In addition, the employer must have an Ontario payroll of at least $2.5 million or must have terminated the employment of 50 or more employees in a six-month period because all or part of the business closed. Qualifying employees are entitled to receive severance pay in the amount of one week's pay for each year's—or partial year's—service (dating from the start of their employment), to a maximum of 26 weeks.

SCENARIO

Restructuring Costs

Val-Nam must restructure its operations quickly in order to remain competitive. As part of that restructuring, it will need to dismiss a non-unionized, long-term employee and three relatively new employees. When evaluating the cost of the restructuring and its feasibility, Val-Nam will have to include consideration of:

- common law notice/pay in lieu of notice requirements if there is no provision in the employment agreements that limits these requirements,
- ESA minimum notice/pay in lieu of notice requirements,
- the cost of benefit payments during the notice period, and
- the conditions in which ESA severance must be paid and whether they apply to the long-term employee.

As with termination pay, there are a number of exceptions to the obligation to pay severance. For example, employers are not required to pay severance to employees who engage in wilful misconduct, who refuse to accept a reasonable alternative position, or who are on temporary layoff.

Table 9.4 Summary of Employer's Legal Obligations to Employee When Employment Ends

Circumstances	Employer's Legal Obligations
Unionized or non-unionized employee resigns.	• No notice or severance payment to employee required (unless otherwise specified in employment contract, which is rare).
Employer dismisses unionized employee with or without cause.	• Collective agreement and *Employment Standards Act, 2000* govern employer's obligations.
Employer dismisses non-unionized employee with legal just cause.	• No notice or severance payment to employee required.
Employer dismisses non-unionized employee with under five years' employment, without legal just cause.	• Minimum termination notice under *Employment Standards Act, 2000* applies. • Employer must provide reasonable notice under common law (or payment in lieu of notice) unless notice specified in employment contract.
Employer dismisses non-unionized employee with over five years' employment, without legal just cause.	• Minimum termination notice under *Employment Standards Act, 2000* applies. • Severance pay requirements under *Employment Standards Act, 2000* may apply if requirements are met (that is, generally speaking, where the employer has an Ontario payroll of at least $2.5 million). • Employer must provide reasonable notice under common law (or payment in lieu of notice) unless notice specified in employment contract.
Employer dismisses over 50 employees during four-week period.	• Mass termination provisions in the *Employment Standards Act, 2000* with respect to notice generally apply, replacing individual notice requirements.
Employer constructively dismisses non-unionized employee.	• Same as dismissal without legal just cause (see above).

Enforcement

The ESA is typically enforced when an employment standards officer from the Ministry of Labour responds to a claim filed by an employee who believes that their employer has infringed their rights under the Act. An employment standards officer can order an employer to reinstate an employee and/or to compensate the employee for, among other things, lost wages, job search expenses, and emotional pain and suffering as a result of the violation.

Health and Safety

The key health and safety statutes in Ontario are the *Occupational Health and Safety Act* and the *Workplace Safety and Insurance Act, 1997*. The *Occupational Health and Safety Act* (OHSA) has very broad coverage, including all workers and independent contractors. It sets the standards for employers in preventing workplace illness and injury. It requires employers to "take every precaution reasonable in the circumstances for the protection of a worker." The *Workplace Safety and Insurance Act, 1997*, on the other hand, addresses the financial consequences of workplace illness and injuries when they do occur. It is essentially an insurance system paid for entirely by employers, which guarantees compensation to workers for work-related injuries or diseases. This is a no-fault system, and workers cannot sue employers for work-related injuries or disease.

Occupational Health and Safety Act

The purpose of OHSA is to protect workers from work-related health and safety hazards. It assigns responsibilities to all parties in the workplace (workers, supervisors, and employers); sets out the rights of workers; establishes procedures for dealing with hazards; and provides for enforcement where an employer is not in compliance with the Act.

Workers' Rights

The *Occupational Health and Safety Act* gives workers four key rights: the right to participate in the health and safety of their workplace, the right to refuse to do unsafe work, the right to stop unsafe work, and the right to know about workplace hazards. These rights encourage workers to take a proactive approach to their own health and safety and are intended to encourage cooperation between employers and the people who work for their businesses.

Front-line workers are often the people most aware of the health and safety risks they face, and their knowledge and expertise is invaluable to business owners. Employers cannot penalize workers in any way for exercising their rights under the Act.

THE RIGHT TO PARTICIPATE

The *Occupational Health and Safety Act* places duties on everyone involved in the workplace, including business owners, suppliers, workers, and supervisors.

The **joint health and safety committee** is one of the cornerstones of the system of internal responsibility created by OHSA. The committee is an advisory group composed of equal numbers of worker and management representatives. Members meet regularly to discuss health and safety concerns, review progress, and make recommendations to the employer on health and safety issues. Every workplace where 20 or more workers are regularly employed generally requires a joint health and safety committee (special rules apply to construction projects). Workplaces with 6 to 19 employees must have a health and safety representative.

joint health and safety committee
committee composed of equal numbers of management and worker representatives generally required by the *Occupational Health and Safety Act* in workplaces with 20 or more workers

THE RIGHT TO REFUSE UNSAFE WORK

Every worker has the right to refuse unsafe work, although this right is restricted for some occupations—such as police officers—where danger is an inherent part of the job. The statute sets out a specific procedure for both the employer and the worker to follow when a worker chooses to exercise this right.

An inspector from the Ministry of Labour must be called in when the issue cannot be resolved between the workplace parties.

SCENARIO

Safety First

Delia Panchyk operates one of the metal presses in Val-Nam's manufacturing facility. She notices that one of the sensors that prevents the press from closing if a worker's hand is within the press area has been working only intermittently. She wants to refuse to work at that press until it is fixed. In order to do this, the following steps must be taken:

- Delia has to report the issue to her supervisor.
- She, together with her supervisor and a representative of the joint health and safety committee, has to investigate the issue.
- If they are able to resolve the issue, Delia can resume work.
- If not, and if Delia still believes the press is unsafe, one of the parties must call the Ministry of Labour to investigate the refusal.

THE RIGHT TO STOP UNSAFE WORK

The right to stop work is distinct from the right to refuse work. Only members of a joint health and safety committee who have undergone health and safety training and certification may initiate a stop-work order, according to the provisions of the statute.

WHMIS (workplace hazardous materials information system) national information system designed to provide essential information about hazardous materials in the workplace

THE RIGHT TO KNOW ABOUT WORKPLACE HAZARDS

Under OHSA, workers have the right to know about potential hazards to which they may be exposed. This includes the right to receive training about the safe use of machinery, equipment, and processes, as well as the right to know about hazardous substances at the workplace. Employers and workers also must comply with the requirements of the **WHMIS (workplace hazardous materials information system)**, a nationwide system designed to provide workers with essential information about using, handling, and storing hazardous materials in the workplace.

www.emond.ca/CBL3/links

DIG DEEPER
The Ministry of Labour website provides information on workplace health and safety requirements.

Accident Reporting

The *Occupational Health and Safety Act* requires employers to report all workplace accidents to the Ministry of Labour. In the case of critical injuries or fatalities, the employer must notify the ministry immediately and provide a written report within 48 hours. Non-critical injuries must be reported within four days of the occurrence. Separate accident-reporting obligations exist under the *Workplace Safety and Insurance Act, 1997* (discussed later in this chapter).

Enforcement

Safety inspectors from the Ministry of Labour are available to provide specialized safety advice and expertise. In addition to investigating work refusals, work stoppages, and serious injuries or fatalities, inspectors also conduct random, unannounced inspections of workplaces. They have broad powers, including the power to enter any workplace without a search warrant, except where the workplace is also a personal dwelling.

MINIMIZING YOUR RISK

Fulfill Your Health and Safety Obligations

- Designate a senior manager to be responsible for compliance with the *Occupational Health and Safety Act*.
- Prepare a written health and safety policy.
- Provide a safety orientation for all new employees and existing employees with new job assignments.
- Ensure that members of the joint health and safety committee (or the health and safety representative in smaller workplaces) receive the necessary health and safety training.
- Have senior executives actively support the joint health and safety committee.
- Identify workplace hazards through internal and external safety audits.
- Support and respond to concerns of the joint health and safety committee.
- Hold regular safety meetings to update workers.
- Discipline all workers and managers who fail to follow safety requirements.
- Implement a system of recognition and rewards for departments and individuals who reach safety goals.
- Keep equipment in good working condition.
- Investigate accidents promptly and thoroughly.
- Do not tamper with the site of an accident.
- Report accidents as required by the Act.
- Document all your efforts to ensure a healthy and safe workplace as part of proving due diligence.

Every offence under the *Occupational Health and Safety Act* is a **strict liability offence**, which means that the ministry does not need to prove that an employer intended to commit an offence to obtain a conviction under the Act. Once a prosecutor establishes that an offence occurred, the onus is on the employer to prove that it took every precaution that was reasonable in the circumstances to prevent the occurrence. This is called the **due diligence defence**. If, for example, a worker is injured by unguarded machinery, the employer may successfully defend itself by proving that it took all reasonable care to ensure that the machinery was guarded, including training employees about the importance of guards and disciplining employees who remove them. If, on the other hand, the employer cannot prove due diligence and is convicted, they may be fined up to $100,000 per charge and imprisoned for up to 12 months. Corporations now may be fined up to $1,500,000 per charge (these fines reflect increases made pursuant to the *Stronger, Fairer Ontario Act (Budget Measures), 2017* and are effective as of December 14, 2017.)

strict liability offence
offence in which proof that an accused performed the prohibited act is sufficient to sustain a conviction, regardless of intention, unless the accused demonstrates that they took all reasonable care to avoid committing the prohibited act

due diligence defence
defence to strict liability offence requiring accused to demonstrate that they took all reasonable steps to avoid committing a prohibited act

The due diligence defence was at issue in the case of *Ontario (Ministry of Labour) v Cementation Canada Inc* (see the Case in Point).

Canada's *Criminal Code*, a federal statute, also imposes duties on anyone who directs work to take "reasonable steps" to prevent bodily harm arising from that work. Failure to adhere to the duty may result in life imprisonment and unlimited fines.

CASE IN POINT

Failure to Supervise Undermines Employer's Due Diligence Defence

Ontario (Ministry of Labour) v Cementation Canada Inc, 2008 ONCJ 135

Facts

A mine worker was given conflicting instructions on how to repair a machine called a cactus clam. Attempting to follow one set of instructions, the worker borrowed a forklift from another worker to flip over the machine to get access to the damaged part. While using the forklift, for which he had not been properly trained, the worker got into an accident and broke his leg. The employer was charged under the OHSA for several safety violations.

Result

The Ontario Court of Justice found that the employer had not exercised due diligence. Among other things, the injured worker had no direct supervision while he was repairing the damaged machine. It was clearly foreseeable that the worker had not been given enough information, instruction, or supervision to perform the task safely.[2]

Business Lesson

When assigning work to an employee, ensure that they have been adequately trained on all related procedures and equipment and that instructions are clear, consistent, and unambiguous. Particularly with new and unfamiliar tasks, it is important to provide enough supervision to allow the employee to perform the task safely.

Workplace Violence and Harassment

Ontario's *Occupational Health and Safety Act* also requires employers to specifically address workplace violence (including threats of violence) and workplace harassment (including sexual harassment). Requirements include assessing the risk, developing policies, training employees, and implementing programs to deal with workplace violence and harassment.

Ontario's workplace violence requirements also require employers to address domestic violence in the workplace. If an employer is aware, or ought reasonably to be aware, that domestic violence may occur in the workplace, the employer must "take every precaution reasonable in the circumstances" for the protection of the worker.

Moreover, in certain circumstances, an employer must provide a worker with information about a person with a history of violent behaviour. This duty arises if the worker can be expected to encounter a person with a history of violent behaviour in the course of their work, and if the risk of workplace violence is likely to result in physical injury.

Effective September 2016, employers also have a statutory duty to investigate "incidents," as well as complaints, of workplace harassment in a manner "appropriate to the circumstances." The Ministry of Labour's new Code of Practice provides some guidance on how such investigations should be conducted. For instance, the investigator must be impartial (not the respondent or someone under the respondent's direct control) and the investigation must be completed within 90 days, unless there are extenuating circumstances.

Note that if an inspector finds that an employer failed to conduct an appropriate investigation, the inspector may, among other remedies, order an employer to retain an independent investigator, at the employer's expense, to conduct such an investigation and provide a written report.

2 "Due Diligence Scorecard," *Safety Compliance Insider* 4, no 2 (December 2008): 4.

MINIMIZING YOUR RISK

Address Workplace Violence and Harassment

- Prepare a policy to prevent and address workplace violence and harassment, as required by the legislation.
- Train all employees in violence and harassment prevention.
- Conduct a violence risk assessment and take measures to control the risks it identifies.
- Implement procedures for reporting incidents or threats of violence.
- Thoroughly investigate all incidents, complaints, or threats of workplace violence.
- Implement procedures for summoning immediate assistance when violence occurs or is likely to occur, or when threats of violence are made.
- Maintain accurate and detailed records of such incidents and the related investigations, such as the disciplining of employees for failing to adhere to policies and the contacting of law enforcement, as appropriate.

Conduct Workplace Investigations Appropriately

- Choose an investigator who is unbiased, competent, and knowledgeable about both the law and investigatory best practices.
- Ensure that both the respondent and the complainant are interviewed thoroughly and that the respondent has an opportunity to respond to the specific allegations.
- Ensure witnesses are interviewed separately.
- Ensure a written report is prepared, including a summary of the investigation, findings of fact, and a conclusion.
- Ensure both the complainant and respondent receive the results of the investigation.

www.emond.ca/CBL3/links

DIG DEEPER
The Workplace Safety and Insurance Board website and the Canadian Centre for Occupational Health and Safety website have information on addressing workplace violence.

Workplace Safety and Insurance Act, 1997

In the following sections, we examine the Ontario *Workplace Safety and Insurance Act, 1997*. This Act is of particular interest to business people because it puts in place a scheme, funded entirely by employers, to compensate workers for injuries or diseases that they suffer on the job.

Employers can consider the workplace safety and insurance system as a method of managing risk. It eliminates lawsuits by workers who have suffered workplace injuries and illnesses in the course of their employment. Workers may no longer sue their employers for this type of harm. However, unlike most other risk management strategies, workplace safety and insurance is a government program in which most employers are required to participate.

www.emond.ca/CBL3/links

DIG DEEPER
The Workplace Safety and Insurance Board website contains useful fact sheets on occupational diseases.

Eligibility for Benefits

The *Workplace Safety and Insurance Act, 1997* insures workers against injuries or diseases that "arise out of and in the course of employment," such as injuries resulting from workplace accidents or diseases caused by exposure to toxic chemicals at work. The Act does not apply to non-occupational injuries or illnesses.

The presumption that an injury incurred on the job is work-related does not apply to disability cases. For example, with a repetitive strain injury, it is up to the worker to show a relationship between the disability and the work. However, it is not necessary that the work be the primary or dominant cause of a worker's injury, provided that it contributed to the injury in a significant way.

The *Workplace Safety and Insurance Act, 1997* compensates workers for occupational diseases if there is a causal relationship between the disease and the employment. Industrial diseases known to arise from specific industrial processes are set out in the schedules to the Act.

Types of Benefits

Types of compensation available under the Act include the following:

- health care costs resulting from the injury,
- loss of earnings benefits,
- non-economic losses (such as loss of the enjoyment of life),
- loss of retirement income benefits, and
- death and survivor benefits.

Workers are compensated by the Workplace Safety and Insurance Board (WSIB) for lost earnings after the day of the injury. The employer must pay the worker the wages and benefits they would have earned for the day or shift on which the injury occurred. Benefits for loss of earnings are calculated at 85 percent of net earnings—that is, earnings after deductions for income tax, Canada Pension Plan premiums, and Employment Insurance.

Workers are encouraged to return to work as soon as they are safely able to do so, even if only on a part-time basis or with reduced responsibilities. Under the *Workplace Safety and Insurance Act, 1997*, employers have a duty to cooperate with injured workers and facilitate their return to work. Employers with 20 or more employees have specific obligations related to re-employment of an injured worker with one or more years of service. The *Workplace Safety and Insurance Act, 1997* covers most industries in the province, both union and non-union, including manufacturing, construction, hospitals, hotels, restaurants, and theatres. Some industries, such as financial institutions and law firms, are not required to participate in the legislative scheme. However, many of these low-risk businesses choose to apply for coverage since it protects them from lawsuits for work-related injuries at a relatively low cost.

www.emond.ca/CBL3/links

DIG DEEPER
The Workplace Safety and Insurance Board website provides information on how to maintain a healthy and safe workplace environment.

Funding the System

Employers pay the full cost of the compensatory system through premiums paid to the WSIB. These premiums are based on the employer's industry class and rate group. For example, low-risk industries, such as technical services, pay a low rate, while high-risk industries, such as demolition, pay a high rate. The employer's assessment is calculated as a percentage of the employer's payroll to a maximum amount per worker.

The *Workplace Safety and Insurance Act, 1997* provides financial incentives to employers to reduce the cost of injuries, with experience rating—a system that compares the claim rates and costs of businesses in the same or similar industries. Employers receive a refund or pay a surcharge on the regular premium rate, depending on how their claims measure up against those of other employers in the same rate group.

MINIMIZING YOUR RISK

Reduce Your Workplace Safety and Insurance Costs

- Report work-related injuries and diseases to the WSIB as required.
- Effectively manage insurance claims: document all claims, even those that seem minor; keep notes of all contacts; establish a return-to-work plan; and make necessary accommodation short of undue hardship.
- Cooperate fully in efforts to return a worker to their pre-injury job or attempt to provide suitable work.
- Find out if your business is in the appropriate rate assessment group or whether all or part of your employees could be in a group with lower premiums.

Equity in the Workplace

Equity in the workplace refers to both fairness in terms of pay and fairness in terms of employment opportunities. While human rights legislation prohibits discrimination in the workplace, it generally depends on the lodging of complaints and usually focuses on individual instances of unfairness. In contrast, employment equity addresses the broad social problem of the underrepresentation of certain groups of people, such as visible minorities and people with disabilities, in most workplaces, especially in better paid and higher-level jobs.

In this section, we discuss and distinguish between three related topics:

- equal pay for equal work under the *Employment Standards Act, 2000*,
- equal pay for work of equal value under the *Pay Equity Act*, and
- fair and representative employment practices under the *Employment Equity Act*.

Equal Pay for Equal Work

The Ontario *Employment Standards Act, 2000* requires that women and men receive **equal pay for equal work**. To fall within the scope of this law, the work need not be identical as long as it is substantially similar. For example, male and female cooks who work in the same restaurant must receive the same rate of pay. Different rates of pay can apply if based on factors unrelated to gender, such as merit and seniority.

Under the 2017 (Bill 148) amendments to the ESA, discussed earlier under the heading "Employment Standards," the concept of equal pay for equal work is now much broader. Extended beyond requiring gender equality in pay, these amendments require employers to compensate part-time, temporary, casual, or limited-term contract employees at the same rate as full-time employees doing substantially the same work, subject to certain exceptions such as differences in pay related to seniority.

equal pay for equal work concept obliging employers to pay female and male employees who perform substantially the same jobs in the same workplace at the same rate, unless a legislated exception applies (since passage of Bill 148 amendments to the *Employment Standards Act, 2000*, this concept also refers to requiring employers to provide equal pay for equal work regardless of employment status)

Equal Pay for Work of Equal Value

The Ontario *Pay Equity Act* also addresses the issue of fair pay, but it goes further than the *Employment Standards Act, 2000* by requiring employers to provide **equal pay for work of equal value (pay equity)**. This is a relatively recent concept that

equal pay for work of equal value (pay equity) concept obliging employers to pay female- and male-dominated jobs at the same rate based on an assessment of job value rather than job content requires employers to compare jobs performed mostly by female workers with those performed mostly by male workers (for example, clerical workers and truck drivers, respectively) within a workplace to determine whether they are of equal value to the business. Pay equity legislation is intended to reduce—and eventually eliminate—systemic gender discrimination and the wage gap between women and men by requiring employers to compare job value, rather than job content.

gender-neutral job evaluation system system that evaluates the relative value of jobs in a manner that does not favour factors found in jobs traditionally performed by men

The *Pay Equity Act* requires an employer to use a **gender-neutral job evaluation system** to make the comparison, based on a composite of skill, effort, responsibility, and working conditions. If two jobs are found to be of equal value, an employer must raise the pay for the women's job classes to match that of comparable men's job classes. There are statutory exceptions to this obligation. For example, no pay adjustment is required if the pay differential results from a formal seniority system.

The *Pay Equity Act* applies to all Ontario public sector (government) employers and to all provincially regulated private sector (non-government) employers with ten or more employees. Employers must keep the requirements of the *Pay Equity Act* in mind when making changes in the workplace that might affect the value assigned to a job or the job comparisons required under the Act (for example, eliminating or adding a job).

Employment Equity: Fair and Representative Employment Practices

employment equity range of measures promoting a representative workforce; federal employment equity legislation and programs focus on four designated groups: women, visible minorities, people with disabilities, and Indigenous peoples

While the purpose of human rights legislation is to prevent discrimination, **employment equity** legislation goes a step further: its purpose is to encourage fair and representative hiring and promotion practices for certain historically disadvantaged groups. Many workplaces do not reflect the external workforce from which they recruit because some employment practices, such as having a height and weight requirement, have the effect of excluding certain groups.

Ontario does not have an employment equity law that applies to private sector employers. Canada has the *Employment Equity Act*, which applies only to federally regulated companies—such as banks, railways, airlines, and broadcasting companies—with 100 or more employees. It requires employers to implement employment equity programs to address the underrepresentation and lower job status of four designated groups—women, visible minorities, people with disabilities, and Indigenous peoples—in their workplaces.

The federal government has also implemented a federal contractors' program that affects some Ontario employers. Businesses with at least 100 employees that wish to bid on federal government contracts worth at least $1 million must certify that they will develop and implement a formal employment equity plan. This plan includes collecting and analyzing workforce data; reviewing employment systems to identify barriers to hiring, promoting, and retaining members of the four designated groups; and adopting special measures to achieve employment equity. There are many different kinds of barriers. For example, when businesses need to hire additional staff, they often turn to current employees and ask them whether they know anyone who could do the job. This "word-of-mouth" recruitment may be faster and less expensive than advertising a job in the newspaper or hiring a recruiting agent to do a thorough search. However, the candidates suggested by current employees are likely to have backgrounds and cultures similar to theirs, thereby perpetuating the makeup of the business's current workforce.

In recent years, the concepts of **workplace diversity** and inclusiveness have gained prominence. These terms are now widely used to connote the importance of fairness in the workplace and the value of employing individuals from different backgrounds in a workplace where all feel welcome, respected, and productive.

www.emond.ca/CBL3/links

DIG DEEPER

The Pay Equity Commission website provides information about pay equity in Ontario.

workplace diversity employment of people from diverse backgrounds in a workplace where all feel welcome and respected

MINIMIZING YOUR RISK

Ensure Equity in Your Workplace

- Review your pay equity responsibilities when there are changes in the workplace that may affect job comparisons (such as a job being eliminated or added, new technology, a sale or merger, or a union certification).
- Review your recruitment practices to ensure there are no barriers to increasing diversity.
- Analyze workforce data to see if your employees reflect the diversity of the external workforce in the relevant occupational groups.
- Review employment systems to identify barriers to hiring, promoting, and retaining members of the designated groups.
- Implement proactive employment equity programs (for example, a mentoring program that makes the workplace more welcoming to diverse groups).

Privacy in the Workplace

New technologies have increased concerns about privacy. Computers allow personal information to be compiled and transferred in seconds. Employee monitoring, at low cost, is now possible in a multitude of ways, including video cameras and email monitoring. Employers have an interest in maintaining productivity as well as a duty to prevent the downloading of offensive material as part of their effort to maintain a workplace free of discrimination and harassment. Balancing those business interests with an employee's privacy interests is a challenge, and this is an area in which the law is evolving.

PIPEDA and the Protection of Personal Information

In recent years, legislation such as the *Personal Information Protection and Electronic Documents Act* (PIPEDA) has been passed to address concerns about privacy. PIPEDA is a federal statute that applies to federally regulated employers, such as banks, telecommunications companies, and airlines. Its requirements are based on ten "fair information principles" that relate to the collection, use, protection, and disclosure of personal information.

At present, provincially regulated businesses in Ontario, including restaurants, retail stores, and manufacturing companies, are not required to apply PIPEDA's provisions to their employees. (They are, however, required to comply with PIPEDA in relation to customers and clients.)

Nevertheless, as an employer in Ontario, you should be aware that disclosure of personal information that relates to a prohibited ground of discrimination under the *Human Rights Code*, such as religious affiliation or marital status, can be the subject of a human rights complaint. Moreover, in 2012, Ontario's Court of Appeal issued its landmark decision in *Jones v Tsige* wherein it became the first appellate court in Canada to recognize a common law right to sue for the tort of "intrusion upon seclusion."

CASE IN POINT

Ontario's Appellate Court Recognizes New Tort: "Intrusion upon Seclusion"

Jones v Tsige, 2012 ONCA 32

Facts

Jones, an employee of the Bank of Montreal, discovered that another bank employee, Tsige, had accessed her (Jones's) bank account at least 174 times over the previous four years. Tsige admitted doing this because she had formed a common law relationship with Jones's ex-husband and was checking to see whether Jones was receiving support payments from him. When the employer found out about this breach of its privacy policy, it disciplined Tsige. However, Jones decided to also bring a court action directly against Tsige, suing her for damages for breach of privacy. Jones lost at trial on the basis that there was no independent tort action based on privacy. Jones appealed.

Result

Signalling that it was time for the common law to catch up with technological developments, the Ontario Court of Appeal awarded Jones $10,000 damages on the basis of a new tort called "intrusion upon seclusion." The court set out three elements that a plaintiff must prove to receive damages for this tort:

- The defendant's conduct must be intentional (which includes reckless conduct).
- The defendant must have invaded, without lawful justification, the plaintiff's private affairs or concerns.
- A reasonable person would regard the invasion as highly offensive, causing distress, humiliation, or anguish. (para 71)

The court stressed that this tort will apply only where there are "deliberate and significant invasions." Where, as here, the plaintiff has suffered no monetary loss, the award will be in a range up to $20,000. Relevant factors include the frequency and nature of the defendant's wrongful act, the level of distress caused to the plaintiff, and whether an apology had been offered.

Business Lesson

Employers should have policies that respect employees' privacy. Video surveillance should be a last resort. At the same time, email and Internet use policies should reduce employee expectations of privacy so it is clear the employer has a right to monitor such use to prevent illegal or improper activities.

MINIMIZING YOUR RISK

Respect Privacy

- Limit collection of personal information to what is necessary.
- Obtain the consent of employees and independent contractors before collecting, using, or disclosing personal information about them.
- Use personal information only for the purpose for which the consent was given.
- Keep personal information safe from loss, theft, or unauthorized access.
- Securely dispose of personal information when it is no longer required.
- Unless certain statutory exceptions apply, allow employees access to personal information about them and encourage them to correct any misinformation.

- If you use a third-party payroll or other service provider, specify in writing that the service provider can use personal information only for the purpose of fulfilling its contract with you.
- Use video surveillance only as a last resort and make sure it is conducted in a reasonable manner.
- Prepare and broadly communicate a policy on email and computer use that details what uses are, and are not, permitted and that reduces employee expectations of privacy. As always, be consistent in the enforcement of this policy.

Ontario's Personal Health Information Protection Act, 2004

Although Ontario does not have general privacy legislation comparable to PIPEDA that covers personal employee information, it does have comparable legislation that covers personal *health* information. Ontario's *Personal Health Information Protection Act, 2004* (PHIPA) regulates how health information custodians (HICs) may collect, use, and disclose personal health information within the Ontario health care system.

Although employers are not the target of the legislation, they are covered in certain circumstances, such as where they receive personal health information from HICs with respect to administering sick leaves. HICs may only disclose personal health information about an employee where that employee has given express, informed consent or where it is necessary to carry out a statutory or legal duty. Moreover, an employer is restricted to using or disclosing the health information solely for the purposes for which the employee authorized disclosure.

The Unionized Workplace

Canada, like many other democratic countries, has a long-established history of freedom for workers to form or join a **union**. Over the years, unions have significantly advanced the rights of workers by negotiating **collective agreements**—which set the terms and conditions of employment—and by providing collective representation for workers in dealings with their employers. Workers usually join unions with a view to bargaining with their employers for higher wages, more benefits, better working conditions, and greater job security than they currently have in their non-unionized workplace.

union
organization of workers that negotiates wages and working conditions as a group with an employer

collective agreement
contract between a union and an employer that governs the terms and conditions of employment for union members

Despite the trend to a more cooperative relationship between unions and employers, most non-unionized businesses prefer to stay that way. They do not want to assume the additional administrative costs of dealing with a union, and they prefer to retain maximum flexibility in communicating and dealing with employee relations. Many non-unionized employers offer pay and benefits that are comparable to those offered by unionized employers in the hope that their employees will not seek union membership.

In Ontario, the statute that governs unionized workplaces is the *Labour Relations Act, 1995*. The Act allows most, but not all, employees to form unions; it creates exceptions for managers, human resources personnel, and professionals, such as architects and lawyers, who are employed in a professional capacity. The Act also sets out the process by which a group of employees may become unionized and the rules for collective bargaining. Disputes arising from the application of the Act are

Ontario Labour Relations Board (OLRB)
tribunal that mediates and adjudicates labour relations (and other matters) arising in Ontario

ratification
approval by union members of a collective agreement

heard by the **Ontario Labour Relations Board (OLRB)**, a government tribunal that specializes in labour law.

Once a collective agreement is negotiated between a union and an employer, it is ratified. **Ratification** involves approval by workers, as evidenced by a vote (that is, more than 50 percent *of those who vote* must vote in favour). The collective agreement then governs the employer-employee relationship in much the same way as an employment contract does for individual employees in a non-unionized workplace. Disputes arising from the application of the collective agreement are heard by an arbitrator, as described in the collective agreement itself.

Union Organizing

unfair labour practice
actions by employers that interfere with the formation and activities of a union, including intimidation

The *Labour Relations Act, 1995* strictly prohibits employers from interfering with the right of employees to join the union of their choice and to participate in its lawful activities. **Unfair labour practices** prohibited by the Act include the following:

- questioning employees individually about union activities,
- firing union organizers or other employees who are in favour of union activity,
- threatening (even subtly) that unionization will jeopardize employees' job security, and
- promising to increase wages if employees reject the union.

The Act prevents employers from disciplining, firing, or harassing employees for pro-union campaigning or activities. Any employer that the OLRB finds to have committed an unfair labour practice faces substantial damage awards. Moreover, under amendments made in 2017 under Bill 148, the OLRB must now order automatic certification of the union without a vote where it determines that an employer has committed an unfair labour practice that impacted its employees' support for a union.

bargaining unit
group of the employer's employees whom the trade union is entitled to represent

certification
approval by a labour relations board that gives a union the right to negotiate on behalf of a bargaining unit

Typically, a group of employees, called a **bargaining unit**, becomes unionized when a union applies to the OLRB for **certification**. Certification gives the union the right to represent the bargaining unit by showing that it has the support of the majority of employees within the unit. *When certified, the union has exclusive authority to bargain collectively with the employer* on behalf of all the employees in the bargaining unit. As an employer, therefore, you may not negotiate with your employees individually with respect to matters covered by collective agreements, such as raises, work hours, promotions, and job security. Instead, you must deal only with the certified union.

In Ontario, for most industries, the process for applying for certification requires a secret ballot vote. To hold a vote, a union must first show that at least 40 percent of employees in the proposed bargaining unit have signed union membership cards. The OLRB certifies the union if it wins the support, in an election by secret ballot, of more than 50 percent *of the employees who vote*. The vote is usually held within five to seven business days from the filing of the union's application for certification. If it occurs within your workplace, you must remember that it is your employees' right to join the union of their choice. You must be particularly careful about any communications you have with employees during this period to avoid any suggestion that you are interfering with the process and thus committing an unfair labour practice.

Note that for the construction industry—and now, as a result of 2017 amendments to the *Labour Relations Act, 1995*, also for temporary help agencies, companies in the building services sector, and organizations that provide home care or community services—certification is *card-based.* This means that if a certain percentage (i.e., at least 55 percent) of the members in the potential bargaining unit sign union membership cards, the union may apply to the OLRB for certification and may be certified *without a secret ballot vote.*

Unions can lose their right to represent a bargaining unit in several ways. Generally speaking, dissatisfied members of a bargaining unit may bring an application for decertification during the "open period" that occurs in the final three months of the term of every collective agreement. Alternatively, another union may succeed in convincing workers that they should join it instead; once it obtains certification, the first union is automatically decertified. This also must occur during the "open period."

Negotiating a Collective Agreement

Once a union is certified, both the union and you as an employer have a "duty to bargain in good faith" and use every reasonable effort to reach a collective agreement. As a unionized employer, you may, of course, communicate with your unionized employees, but you must be careful not to do so in a way that reveals an attempt to bargain directly with them.

Generally, it is the responsibility of the parties—the employer and the union—to negotiate a collective agreement. However, with respect to the *first* collective agreement only, the OLRB provides binding arbitration in the event that you and the union are unable to reach an agreement. This removes the incentive some employers may have when faced with a newly certified union to "dig in its heels" and refuse to bargain.

Subject to the first contract provisions of the *Labour Relations Act, 1995*, and a small number of compulsory terms such as a required provision that recognizes the union as the exclusive bargaining agent for the employees, you and the union are left to negotiate whatever terms and conditions of employment you both choose, as long as the terms are lawful.

Administration of the Collective Agreement

A dispute arising from the administration of a collective agreement—called a **grievance**—is resolved through the grievance process. For example, if you suspend a worker for one day without pay for being late, the worker may file a grievance against you; the grievance will be heard through the multi-step grievance process that you negotiated with the union and specified in the collective agreement. If the grievance cannot be resolved through the internal grievance process, it may go to an outside arbitrator to decide how the grievance is to be resolved, based on the wording of the collective agreement.

Strikes, during which employees collectively refuse to work, and **lockouts**, during which employers refuse to allow employees to work, are prohibited while a collective agreement is in effect. These bargaining tactics are legal only after a collective agreement expires and certain other procedural requirements are met.

During a lawful strike or lockout, employers may hire replacement workers. However, it is illegal under the *Labour Relations Act, 1995* for employers to use professional strike breakers—outsiders who are not involved in the dispute and whose primary objective is to interfere with or disrupt a lawful strike or lockout. Also, as a result of Bill 148's amendments, there is no longer a six-month limitation on employees being able to apply to return to work. Now, employees must be reinstated to their former job when a lawful strike or lockout has ended.

grievance
dispute arising in a unionized workplace with respect to matters covered in the collective agreement

strike
collective refusal to work by a group of unionized employees that usually occurs while an employer and a union attempt to negotiate a new collective agreement

lockout
refusal by an employer to let unionized employees into a workplace; usually occurs while an employer and a union attempt to negotiate a new collective agreement

The passage of Bill 148 (discussed earlier under the heading "Employment Standards") has resulted in several other changes to the *Labour Relations Act, 1995*, including the following:

- Granting unions access to employee lists and certain contact information with proof that at least 20 percent of employees in the proposed bargaining unit have signed union membership cards.
- Authorizing the OLRB to consolidate bargaining units after a successful certification if the existing bargaining units are no longer appropriate.
- Making it easier to access first agreement mediation and arbitration.

MINIMIZING YOUR RISK

Know Your Responsibilities as a Unionized Employer

- Understand and respect your employees' right to unionize.
- If you become aware of an organizing drive, speak to legal counsel before communicating with your employees about related issues.
- Once a union is certified, negotiate in good faith to reach a collective agreement.
- Treat the union with respect.

www.emond.ca/CBL3/links

DIG DEEPER

To learn more about unions, visit websites for labour relations boards for several provinces, including the Ontario Labour Relations Board website.

Responsible Business Strategies to Avoid Unionization of Your Workforce

grievance arbitration
an external process for resolving disputes that arise under the collective agreement

Many businesses find that day-to-day management and workplace relations can be much more flexible, informal, and collaborative in a non-unionized setting. As a business person, you may also want to save the time and money necessary to negotiate collective agreements and defend at **grievance arbitrations**. You may prefer to institute ethical hiring and firing policies on your own without having to follow job security provisions in a collective agreement. You are, of course, prohibited by the *Labour Relations Act, 1995* from participating in unfair labour practices during a union drive, and changing workplace conditions at such a time could amount to this type of practice.

By managing your workplace proactively, however, and engaging the loyalty of the people who work for you, your business may avoid a union drive. For example, if working conditions and wages in your place of business are comparable to those in unionized workplaces, employees are less likely to seek the benefits of union membership because they would be paying union dues for no purpose.

SCENARIO

There are murmurings around the manufacturing plant that some of Val-Nam's employees want to unionize. They are upset with their wage rate and benefits package, particularly given the wages and benefits provided by Val-Nam's unionized competitor, Off-Grid Real Energy Solutions Ltd.

Now that employees are mobilizing, Val-Nam will be restricted in its ability to respond to employee concerns as it must ensure that it does not interfere with the unionization process. However, Val-Nam might have avoided this situation if it had initially adopted proactive strategies to ensure that it:

- communicates openly and regularly with employees about the business, their working conditions, and any other workplace issues that are important to employees;

- listens to employees' concerns and takes their advice and recommendations seriously;
- ensures that employees' wages and benefits at least match those in similar types of businesses that have unions;
- creates an internal complaint procedure for employees (Val-Nam can use the same process to address human rights complaints);
- provides training and professional development opportunities for its employees;
- promotes employees fairly;
- fosters an atmosphere in which employees feel they are important members of the team; and
- introduces profit-sharing or share distribution plans so that employees actually have a stake in the profitability of the business.

CHAPTER SUMMARY

Workplace law regulates the day-to-day employer-employee relationships. It affects these relationships from the time employees are recruited until they resign, retire, or are dismissed.

When hiring employees, it is important to be honest, to check candidates' references, and to consider whether the business needs a full- or part-time employee or an independent contractor, since this status affects the person's statutory benefits. Businesses should have clearly worded employment contracts that cover a variety of management or other situations and set out key terms such as salary, benefits, duties, and termination provisions.

Most employee relationships end through resignation, retirement, or dismissal. Each has its own legal implications, especially in non-unionized workplaces where employee rights are covered by the common law.

To be valid in law, a resignation must be intentional and voluntary. It must not involve a "choice" of resigning or being dismissed, and it must not be given in haste or frustration. Employees must provide notice of their departure according to the terms agreed to in their hiring contract.

In Ontario, it is no longer legal in most workplaces to require employees to retire at age 65. This change is likely to increase the number of older workers in the workplace. Businesses should accommodate employees with age-related disabilities up to the point of undue hardship.

In most situations, employers dismiss employees by providing reasonable notice or pay in lieu of notice (a separation package). If an employer has just cause for dismissing an employee, no notice is necessary; otherwise, the employer must provide notice or, if it wants the employee to leave the premises immediately, pay in lieu of notice. Employees who feel they have not received the required advance notice may file a claim with the Ministry of Labour for their statutory notice entitlements or launch a lawsuit for wrongful dismissal damages under the common law, but not both.

Ontario's employment legislation covers discrimination, harassment, the duty to accommodate to the point of undue hardship, working standards, working conditions, health and safety, equity in the workplace, and the formation of unions. Federal statutes, which apply to the approximately 10 percent of Ontario workplaces that are federally regulated, also cover the use and disclosure of employee personal information and the obligation of large employers to have their workforce better reflect the proportion of women, visible minorities, people with disabilities, and Indigenous peoples in the labour force.

In Ontario, most employees have the right to form unions. Employers are not allowed to interfere with that right. The union and the employer are responsible for reaching a collective agreement regarding wages, benefits, and other elements of the employment relationship. Labour disputes are handled through a grievance arbitration process set out in the agreement. Strikes and lockouts are not permitted while the agreement is in effect. Many businesses try to avoid spending the resources to negotiate collective agreements, instead promoting more flexible and collaborative workplaces.

KEY TERMS

accommodation, 322
adverse impact discrimination, 322
bargaining unit, 352
bona fide occupational requirement (BFOR), 322
certification, 352
collective agreement, 351
conditional offer, 330
condonation, 314
constructive dismissal, 317
discrimination, 320
due diligence defence, 343
duty to mitigate, 315
employment equity, 348
equal pay for equal work, 347
equal pay for work of equal value (pay equity), 347
gender-neutral job evaluation system, 348
grievance, 353
grievance arbitration, 354
harassment, 332
independent contractor, 299
joint health and safety committee, 341
just cause, 305
lockout, 353
nepotism policy, 322
non-unionized employee, 298
Ontario Labour Relations Board (OLRB), 352
pay in lieu of notice, 305
poisoned work environment, 333
progressive discipline, 312
ratification, 352
reasonable notice, 305
restrictive covenant, 303
right to reinstatement, 318
severance pay, 339
sexual harassment, 332
strict liability offence, 343
strike, 353
undue hardship, 324
unfair labour practice, 352
union, 351
unionized employee, 298
WHMIS (workplace hazardous materials information system), 342
workplace diversity, 349
wrongful dismissal, 316

REFERENCES

Accessibility for Ontarians with Disabilities Act, 2005, SO 2005, c 11.
Ballim v Bausch & Lomb Canada Inc, 2016 ONSC 6307.
Bannister v General Motors of Canada Ltd, 1994 CanLII 7390 (Ont SC).
Bardal v Globe & Mail Ltd, 1960 CanLII 294 (Ont SC).
Bill 148, *Fair Workplaces, Better Jobs Act*, SO 2017, c 22 (first reading 1 June 2017).
Boucher v Wal-Mart Canada Corp, 2014 ONCA 419.
British Columbia (Public Service Employee Relations Commission) v BCGSEU (sub nom Meiorin), [1999] 3 SCR 3, 1999 CanLII 652.
Canada (Attorney General) v Johnstone, 2014 FCA 110.
Canadian Union of Public Employees, Local 4400 v Toronto District School Board, [2003] OLAA No 514 (Howe).
Carnegie v Liberty Health, [2003] OJ No 4101 (Div Ct)
Chaba v Ensign Drilling Inc, 2002 ABPC 131.
Chopra v Syncrude Canada Ltd, 2003 ABQB 504.
Criminal Code, RSC 1995, c C-46.
Employment Equity Act, SC 1995, c 44.
Employment Standards Act, 2000, SO 2000, c 41.
Henry v Foxco Ltd, 2004 NBCA 22.
Highway Traffic Act, RSO 1990, c H.8.
Human Rights Code, RSO 1990, c H.19.
Hydro-Québec v Syndicat des employées de techniques professionnelles et de bureau d'Hydro-Québec, section locale 2000 (SCFP-FTQ), 2008 SCC 43.
Jones v Tsige, 2012 ONCA 32.
Labour Relations Act, 1995, SO 1995, c 1, Schedule A.
McKinley v BC Tel, 2001 SCC 38, [2001] 2 SCR 161.
Mesgarlou v 3xs Enterprises Inc, 2001 CanLII 6268 (Ont Sup Ct J).
Misetich v Value Village Stores Inc, 2016 HRTO 1229.
Occupational Health and Safety Act, RSO 1990, c O.1.
Pay Equity Act, RSO 1990, c P.7.
Personal Health Information Protection Act, 2004, SO 2004, c 3, Schedule A.
Personal Information Protection and Electronic Documents Act, SC 2000, c 5.
Ontario (Ministry of Labour) v Cementation Canada Inc, 2008 ONCJ 135.
R v Cole, 2011 ONCA 218.
Russo v Kerr, 2010 ONSC 6053.
Sciancamerli v Comtech (Communication Technologies) Ltd, 2014 BCSC 2140.
Stronger, Fairer Ontario Act (Budget Measures), 2017, SO 2017, c 34.
Wood v Fred Deeley Imports Ltd, 2017 ONCA 158.
Workplace Safety and Insurance Act, 1997, SO 1997, c 16, Schedule A.

EXERCISES

True or False?

____ 1. The Ontario *Human Rights Code* prohibits employers from discriminating against a job applicant with tattoos.

____ 2. The obligations of employers under the Ontario *Human Rights Code* begin even before an applicant is interviewed.

____ 3. If a business wishes to hire an independent contractor rather than an employee, a well-worded contract describing the nature of the relationship will always hold up in court.

____ 4. The court views restrictive covenants strictly—if they are unclear or more restrictive than necessary, the court will not enforce them.

____ 5. The principles of contract law apply to employment contracts, but not to unionized workers who are governed by a collective agreement.

____ 6. The *Occupational Health and Safety Act* requires all employers with 20-plus employees to create a joint health and safety committee made up of management and employee representatives.

____ 7. Equal pay for equal work is the same as equal pay for work of equal value.

____ 8. The right of employees to form or join a union is governed by the *Human Rights Code*.

____ 9. Employee incompetence is often successfully argued by employers to defend against wrongful dismissal claims.

____10. Accident reports written immediately following the event will be useful evidence if an employer ends up in court.

____11. Unlike random alcohol testing, random on-the-job drug testing is prohibited because it is seen as a violation of an employee's human and privacy rights.

____12. Employment contracts must be in writing to be enforceable.

____13. Where an employment contract is silent concerning a probationary period, there is no probationary period under the common law.

Multiple Choice

1. What is the duty to accommodate?
   a. The obligation to provide room and board to migrant workers.
   b. The obligation to satisfy the demands of unionized workers.
   c. The obligation to assist an employee who has special needs.
   d. The obligation to help workers suffering from undue hardship.

2. When are conditional offers of employment useful to the employer?
   a. When there is a bona fide occupational qualification.
   b. When the employer anticipates dismissing the employee without cause.
   c. When a union is about to be certified.
   d. When a probationary period is appropriate.

3. Which of these behaviours might be considered sexual harassment?
   a. Holding a co-worker briefly by the waist while squeezing through a small space, such as behind a cash register.
   b. Pinning up magazine pictures of men in bathing suits in the lunch room.
   c. Asking a subordinate on a date.
   d. All of the above.

4. Why is addressing "reasonable notice" in an employment contract before work begins a useful strategy for employers?
   a. It permits the employer to circumvent the *Employment Standards Act, 2000*.
   b. It reduces the risk of human rights claims against the employer for acting unreasonably.
   c. It reduces the costs and uncertainty of relying on a court to determine what constitutes reasonable notice under the common law.
   d. It clearly demonstrates that the employee is a fixed-term employee.

5. Which of the following issues is not governed by the *Employment Standards Act, 2000*?
   a. vacation pay
   b. equal pay for work of equal value
   c. minimum wage
   d. work hours and overtime

6. Which rights do employees have under the *Workplace Safety and Insurance Act, 1997*?
   a. The right to participate in the health and safety of their workplace, the right to refuse to do unsafe work, the right to stop unsafe work, and the right to know about workplace hazards.
   b. The right to benefits in the event that a disability or illness makes it impossible for them to continue working.

c. The right to compensation for injuries and illness sustained at work.
d. Both b and c.

7. When may a worker refuse to do work according to the *Occupational Health and Safety Act*?
   a. When danger is an inherent part of the job.
   b. When a worker has a sincere and reasonable belief that the equipment or the physical condition of the workplace is likely to endanger them or another worker.
   c. When the joint health and safety committee has refused to initiate a stop-work order.
   d. When a worker is aware that hazardous materials, as described in the WHMIS (workplace hazardous materials information system), are present in the workplace.
8. Which of the following statements is false in regard to a union that has been certified?
   a. The union has the right to prohibit union members from communicating with other unions.
   b. The union has the right to negotiate a collective agreement with the employer.
   c. The union may apply to the Ontario Labour Relations Board for a remedy if the employer fails to bargain in good faith.
   d. The employer may not enter into employment contracts with new employees who would be part of the bargaining unit.
9. Factors that may be considered by a court when determining the common law notice period include:
   a. length of employment, age of employee, progressive discipline, salary, and job market conditions
   b. length of employment, age of employee, disability of employee, salary, progressive discipline, and job market conditions
   c. length of employment, age of employee, intoxication, absenteeism, and insubordination
   d. length of employment, age of employee, salary, position, and job market conditions
10. For employers, documenting their policies and their responses to particular incidents is important in the context of:
    a. progressive discipline
    b. harassment in the workplace
    c. workplace accidents
    d. all of the above
11. Which of the following is unlikely to result in a successful claim of constructive dismissal?
    a. significant changes to benefit packages
    b. relocation to a different city
    c. reconfiguration of office cubicles
    d. change in duties or responsibilities
12. Which one of the following statutes requires an employer to provide paid statutory holidays?
    a. Ontario *Human Rights Code*
    b. *Labour Relations Act, 1995*
    c. *Pay Equity Act*
    d. *Employment Standards Act, 2000*
13. Which of the following statements related to the privacy rights of Ontario employees is true?
    a. Ontario has general privacy legislation comparable to PIPEDA.
    b. Ontario has privacy legislation specifically covering personal health information.
    c. The new tort of "intrusion upon seclusion" provides Ontario employees with privacy rights similar to those held by federally regulated employees.
    d. PIPEDA's ten privacy principles apply to the personal information of customers, suppliers, and employees held by organizations in Ontario.
14. What will happen if the termination clause in an employment contract is found to be unenforceable?
    a. Courts will apply the minimum statutory entitlements found under the *Employment Standards Act, 2000* instead.
    b. The employer will be required to provide reasonable notice (or pay in lieu of notice) under the common law.
    c. The employer does not have to provide notice of termination (or pay in lieu of notice) because the parties failed to properly negotiate such a requirement.
    d. The courts will determine which party had the greatest bargaining power and settle on a result that protects the weaker party.
15. Most secret ballot certification votes in Ontario take place:
    a. within 3 to 5 days of the application for certification
    b. within 5 to 7 days of the application for certification
    c. within 8 to 12 days of the application for certification
    d. within 15 to 20 days of the application for certification

Short Answer

1. Your company offices are on the ground floor, but your operations and storage areas cover three levels, with two full sets of stairs. A candidate for an inventory clerk job mentions that she cannot climb more than three or four steps because of a long-term knee condition. She is well qualified for the job and most of the work can be done in the office; however, previous inventory clerks visited the other floors regularly to monitor supplies. What factors must you take into account in deciding whether to hire her?
2. An employee at your company has four years' experience in a manual labour job. During this time, he has twice required time off to participate in a drug rehabilitation program. Now he wants to apply for training to operate a lift truck. You have concerns about his taking on such a high-risk job. What should you do?
3. Since Ted started work in your plant, he has kept to himself. Some of the other employees have formed the impression that he is gay and have written derogatory messages to that effect outside the lunch room. A supervisor has told you that, although Ted is doing a good job, "things would go smoother around here" if Ted found another job. What can you, as a business owner, do to address this situation?
4. Penny is an accounts payable clerk who has just returned from a pregnancy leave. During her leave, her employer hired a substitute, Zhang, who has mastered the job and has become a permanent employee. Without consulting Penny, the employer assigns her to a different job that requires similar skills and has the same level of pay, hours of work, and general working conditions. What are the employer's legal obligations and workplace options in this situation?
5. Job applicants frequently list references on their application form, resumé, or covering letter. Should the employer construe this as permission to contact the references for information about the applicant's experience?
6. Chantal has been the manager of corporate communications for four years. Her new boss feels that the "chemistry" is not right between them and has hired a new person to head the corporate communications department, with the title "director." She tells Chantal that she values her talents and will use them on various special communications projects, with no reduction in her pay and benefits. What considerations does the employer need to take into account?
7. Beverley was employed by her employer under a five-year fixed-term employment contract that did not contain an enforceable termination clause. She was subsequently terminated on a "without cause" basis less than two years into the contract. The employer provided her with eight weeks' pay in lieu of notice of termination—an amount well in excess of the two weeks' pay required under the *Employment Standards Act, 2000* for an employee with two years of service. It also continued her benefits throughout the notice period. Could Beverley still successfully sue the employer in this situation?

Apply Your Knowledge

Scenario 1: Is It Discrimination Under the Code?

Mr S had a PhD and extensive work experience in environmental science. However, after he immigrated to Canada from India he was unable to get a job in keeping with his background. He ended up taking a job in landscaping to pay the bills. So when he heard that the provincial government was advertising several entry-level environmental positions, he immediately applied for one of them. His interview went well, and he was very hopeful that he would receive an offer. Despite being one of the best-qualified candidates, the interview team decided to not offer him the job. The team was concerned that he was overqualified, that the job would bore him, and he would leave as soon as he found something more suitable. High turnover rates were already a problem. When Mr S found out that he did not get one of these entry-level positions despite his extensive qualifications and the positive interview, he was very disappointed. He decided to file a human rights application.

1. On what possible ground(s) of prohibited discrimination can Mr S base his claim?
2. Assuming that the employer acted in good faith and that "overqualification" was the actual basis for not offering Mr S a position, did the employer discriminate against him contrary to the *Human Rights Code*? Explain your answer.

Scenario 2: Independent Contractor or Employee?

Icarus, a house painting company, had about 40 workers but only 3 "employees" (the owner and two directors)—the other 37 were characterized as "independent contractors" with whom Icarus had signed commercial contracts that clearly indicated them as such. These workers were paid by the project, not the hour. Icarus found the customers and provided the materials. When Icarus refused to pay several workers one week on the basis that their work was unsatisfactory, those workers filed claims for unpaid wages with the Ministry of Labour. Icarus responded that since they were not "employees," they could not file such claims.

1. Under what employment statute would the workers file their claims for unpaid wages?
2. Can an employer withhold wages for poor workmanship from an employee under this statute?
3. Were the unpaid workers "employees" or "independent contractors"? Explain your answer by referencing the arguments that both parties might make.

Scenario 3: Employment Contracts and Restrictive Covenants

When Hasim was hired as a salesperson by a large company that manufactured chemical products, he was required to sign a confidentiality agreement that contained the following clause:

> I agree that if my employment is terminated for any reasons by me or by the Company, I will not, for a period of one year following the termination, directly or indirectly, for my own account or as an employee or agent of any business entity, engage in any business or activity in competition with the Company by providing services or products to, or soliciting business from, any business entity that was a customer of the Company during the period in which I was an employee of the Company, or take any action that will cause the termination of the business relationship between the Company and any customer, or solicit for employment any person employed by the Company.

Hasim's sales territories were mostly in North America, but he had access to information related to clients' international operations as well as access to his own employer's sales, marketing, and business opportunities. After 17 years of employment, Hasim was dismissed, allegedly for cause. He applied to the court for a declaration that the provision he signed when he was hired was unenforceable.

1. What is this type of clause called?
2. What arguments could Hasim make to support his application that this clause is unenforceable?
3. What arguments could the company make to defend the clause's enforceability?
4. Do you think this clause is legally enforceable? Explain your answer.
5. Would a non-solicitation clause (prohibiting solicitation of customers) have been sufficient to protect the employer's proprietary interest?

Scenario 4: Dismissal in a Unionized Workplace

ABC Company had recently become unionized after a highly contentious organizing drive. Two employees (Bob and Jeff), who had been very active in the organizing campaign, started posting derogatory statements on their Facebook accounts about their supervisor. Over the course of two months, the comments became increasingly negative, implying violence and homophobia.

Together, the employees had hundreds of "friends" on Facebook, including several co-workers and a manager at ABC, who alerted the employer about these postings. After monitoring the postings for several weeks, ABC spoke to Bob and Jeff to hear what they had to say. Both initially denied their involvement, saying that their accounts had been hacked. Finding their explanation not credible, ABC decided it had just cause to dismiss them despite their previously clean disciplinary records.

Their union alleged that their dismissal was an unfair labour practice and that the employer did not have "just cause" to dismiss them.

1. With what adjudicative body would the union file its complaint of an unfair labour practice?
2. Describe the arguments that both the employer and Bob and Jeff could make to support their position regarding the alleged just cause. Who do you think would be successful and why?

Scenario 5: Workplace Investigations: What Is "Just Cause"?

Karen was a training engineer at a trucking firm. Her job was to take trainee drivers on the road for a one-to-two-week trip to teach them various aspects of the job. At the end of each trip, trainees were required to complete a critique of the training program. All of Karen's reviews were positive. However, six months after she started doing this training, two trainees, Shanez and Kate, got talking about their training sessions with Karen. Based on that conversation, they approached management together, alleging that Karen had sexually harassed them both during their respective training sessions with her. The alleged harassment included Karen initiating conversations that focused on sadism, masochism, and domineering behaviour; displaying herself in various stages of nudity; swearing excessively; and inviting each of them to participate in submissive relationships.

Shortly after receiving the written complaints, management called Karen in for a meeting. They did not tell her the reason for the meeting and, fearing she would retaliate against the complainants, they did not tell her their identities or the specific allegations against her. In response to their general allegations, Karen claimed that she slept nude in the truck's cab because her obesity made it more comfortable, but she denied the other allegations. At the end of the meeting, the employer terminated Karen on the grounds that she had created a hostile work environment. Karen sued for wrongful dismissal; the employer responded that it had just cause under the common law.

The employer policy regarding harassment was brief. It simply stated: "Harassment is prohibited and will not be tolerated."

1. Do you think the employer will be successful in establishing just cause under the common law? Explain your answer.
2. Assuming that the employer did *not* have just cause, what is the amount of reasonable notice that the employee would be entitled to receive?

Property Law 10

LEARNING OUTCOMES

After reading this chapter, you should be able to:

- Define property law and discuss its purpose.
- Distinguish ownership from possession of real and personal property.
- Define personal, real, and intellectual property.
- Explain the differences between lucrative, constructive, special, and gratuitous bailment.
- Describe conditions and warranties that are useful when buying or selling real property.
- Discuss the rights and obligations of mortgagors and mortgagees.
- Explain the rights and obligations of landlords and tenants under commercial leases.
- Describe the types of property insurance commonly used by businesses.

What Is Property Law?

property law
collection of rules that confer rights of ownership, possession, and transferability over things

property
something in which one has a legal interest with right to possess or use it to the exclusion of others

Property law confers rights over things. The term **property** refers not to the thing itself but rather to the rights a person has over the thing. Property law, therefore, allows the owners of these things to enforce their rights against others. Without laws to define property rights, people could not own things; they could merely possess them. Anyone who had or took possession of an item could use it until they lost possession—until, for example, someone stole the item, or the person gave it away or left it behind inadvertently. Because of the conflict and uncertainty that such a situation would produce, all societies have devised rules to govern property. In Canada, property ownership generally includes the right to:

- possess and use property,
- prevent others from possessing it, and
- transfer property rights to others.

public property
things owned by the government for the benefit of society

private property
things owned by individuals, businesses, or other organizations

real property
immovable things, including land, buildings, and fixtures

personal property
movable, tangible things (including physical objects that are not attached to land or buildings) and intangible property

tangible property
physical things

chattels
movable, tangible property

intangible property
things whose value does not arise from their physical attributes

choses in action
intangible personal property, such as negotiable instruments, insurance claims, and shares in a corporation

Types of Property

Property may be classified as **public property**, which is owned by the government for the benefit of society as a whole, or **private property**, which is owned by individuals, businesses, or other organizations, to the exclusion of others.

Property is most commonly categorized into three types: real property, personal property, and, although technically a subcategory of personal property, intellectual property.

Real property, commonly known as real estate, is immovable property and includes land, buildings, and any physical structures attached to land. Fixtures that are attached to land or buildings are also categorized as real property. Real property is tangible property.

Personal property includes items that are tangible (also known as chattels) and items that are intangible (also known as choses in action).

Tangible property consists of things that are physical, that can be seen and touched. Real property is tangible property but so are forms of personal property that are movable. Personal property includes movable tangible goods that are not attached to land or buildings. We call these tangible forms of personal property **chattels**. Examples of chattels include cars, computers, office equipment, furniture, clothes, and all other items that can be picked up and taken from one place to another. The transfer of ownership in movable tangible goods was considered in Chapter 6's review of the *Sale of Goods Act*.

Intangible property describes something one can own or have rights to but that has no physical substance. Intangible property has value, but its value does not arise from its physical attributes. Intangible personal property is also referred to as **choses in action**. These intangible assets include **goodwill**, which is a business's good reputation with its customers and others, and negotiable instruments, such as cheques, money orders, and promissory notes that have no value in and of themselves but represent rights or claims to something of value. Like other types of property, negotiable instruments are important assets that are included in the balance sheet of any business (see Chapter 8).

Intellectual property, which refers to the rights that arise from the product of a person's mental efforts and comes in many forms, is another type of intangible property. Intellectual property is generally dealt with as a separate category of property because the rules, and the rationale behind them, are quite different from those that govern other types of property. Intellectual property is broken down into numerous categories, including copyright, patents, trademarks, and trade secrets. Intellectual property law will be examined in Chapter 11.

It is important to remember that whether tangible or intangible, real, personal, or intellectual, "property" refers to a person's right to, or interest in, an item, and not to the item itself. This chapter will focus primarily on chattels, which are commonly called goods, and real property.

goodwill
a business's good reputation

intellectual property
things created by the mind or intellect, such as logos and inventions

SCENARIO

The business of Val-Nam Generation Limited ("Val-Nam") will be affected on a daily basis by property law considerations. To effectively manage the legal risks of the business, Val-Nam will require a familiarity with real, personal, and intellectual property law. Consider the following examples.

Val-Nam rents photocopy machines from Kangaroo Copy Inc ("Kangaroo Copy"). One of the machines is located on the warehouse floor just outside the receiving office because there isn't enough space in the office. An employee backed a forklift into the photocopy machine. Who is responsible for the damage? How can Val-Nam protect itself from liability?

Val-Nam leases an additional warehouse from Suki's Storage Limited ("Suki's Storage"). Val-Nam uses part of the space to store inventory of raw materials and packaging and part of the space to store archived business records. Suki's Storage appears to take no care of the property. There are roof leaks, resulting in water damage to Val-Nam's raw materials, and an infestation of mice is currently gnawing its way through Val-Nam's business records. Is Suki's Storage responsible for fixing these problems?

The synthetic enzyme that Valery Garza created is the foundation of Val-Nam's business. How can Val-Nam protect it so that a competitor doesn't acquire it, use it, and harm Val-Nam's business opportunities?

Val-Nam wants to expand and build a second manufacturing plant. Does it have any options other than purchasing additional land and building the plant itself?

Table 10.1 Types of Property

Real Property	Personal Property		Intellectual Property
• Land • Buildings • Garages • Fences • Bridges • Fixtures (e.g., sinks, lighting fixtures, built-in shelving)	• Chattels o automobiles o furniture o computers o inventory o office supplies o machinery	• Choses in action o shares in corporations o goodwill o negotiable instruments (e.g., cheques, promissory notes)	• Copyrights • Trademarks • Patents • Industrial designs • Trade secrets
↑ Tangible Property ↑		↑ Intangible Property ↑	

The Importance of Property Law for Business People

It is practically impossible to think of a business that could operate without property. Every day, businesses buy supplies and materials, manufacture goods, lease or own buildings, or develop new processes or products. The names of these businesses, their product names, and the goodwill they have built up are often very important and valuable assets. Property law affects all businesses that own or deal in property by defining the risks assumed by the ownership or possession of property.

Different types of property pose different risks of loss. Buildings and personal property may be destroyed by fire or storm damage. Personal property is at risk of being stolen or damaged. Intellectual property, such as patents and copyrights, could be used without payment. The value of goodwill and trademarks may be diminished by unauthorized use. Property law helps you manage these risks and offers several advantages:

- *It defines areas where your business may be vulnerable to loss.* For example, assume that you are in the business of storing other people's property. Property law defines the rights of both you and your customers in relation to this property. It indicates which of you is responsible if the property is damaged. It tells you when, how, and to what extent you need to protect yourself by, for example, purchasing insurance.
- *It sometimes allows ownership and possession to be split.* Because property law distinguishes between ownership and possession, it is not always necessary to buy property; for instance, it is possible to rent an office or equipment from the owner. This frees your business from the capital outlay that a purchase requires.
- *It promotes the lending and borrowing of money.* Businesses need money to grow, and borrowing is an important source of capital. Ownership of property, including land, buildings, machinery, and inventory, facilitates borrowing, because lenders can take the property as security for the loan. In the case of land and buildings, this security is called a mortgage. For machinery and inventory, it is called a security interest. Personal property held as security for a debt means that if a business borrows money, the lender may require the business to secure the loan by giving the lender the right to seize and sell the personal property if the loan is not repaid. Use of property to be held as security for debt is explored in greater detail in Chapter 8.
- *It allows innovation to flourish.* By protecting creators and inventors from having their work misappropriated by others, intellectual property law promotes artistic expression and encourages technological advancement. It allows a business to support projects and enterprises that can respond innovatively to challenges by ensuring that the benefits and rewards of those efforts can be protected.

Distinguishing Ownership from Possession

Different people may have different property rights in the same piece of property. The primary distinction is between ownership and possession. For example, when Kangaroo Copy rents photocopy machines to Val-Nam, Kangaroo Copy continues to own the machines while Val-Nam has possession of them. Val-Nam has the right to possess and use the photocopy machines according to the terms of the rental agreement with Kangaroo Copy. Similarly, if Val-Nam sends one of its machine presses to a repair shop for repair, it does not transfer ownership of the machine press to the repair shop. The repair shop only has temporary possession of the press. These two examples relate to the division of personal property interests. Real property interests can also be divided, as when Val-Nam leases a warehouse from Suki's Storage. Val-Nam has the right to the use and enjoyment of the warehouse, but Suki's Storage retains its ownership of the warehouse (the division of real property interests is discussed later in this chapter under the heading "Real Property").

Personal Property

A key ownership right is that of possession. Owners of property may grant this right to others by giving them permission to possess their property. When ownership and possession of goods (personal property) are split in this manner, the legal relationship between the owner and the possessor is called bailment.

Bailment

A **bailment** is created when a person is in possession of personal property owned by another. The law of bailments addresses important legal obligations in the business context, including the storage and movement of goods from manufacturer to the end user, as well as the rightful possession of the goods for purpose of service or repair. Instances of bailment occur when goods are borrowed, rented, stored, or found by a person other than the owner of the property. The owner is known as the **bailor** and the person who is in temporary possession of the property—but who does not own it—is called the **bailee.**

bailment
legal relationship that arises when personal property is borrowed, rented, stored, or found by a person other than its owner

bailor
party in a bailment that owns the personal property

bailee
party in a bailment that is in temporary possession of the bailor's personal property

A bailee has a legal duty of care when in possession of goods belonging to another. Where a bailment is part of a business relationship, a bailee has the responsibility to take such proper care of the goods as a prudent owner may reasonably be expected to take of their own goods. If the goods are damaged while in the bailee's possession, the bailor may sue the bailee for the tort of negligence (see Chapter 3). If the bailor can establish the harm (damage or destruction of goods), the onus will shift to the bailee, who will have to prove that the damage was not the result of negligence. In other words, in order to avoid liability, the bailee will have to show that they exercised due diligence with respect to the goods while in possession of them. A bailor also has a duty of care to the bailee to take care that the bailor's goods do not cause harm to those using them and to warn the bailee of any defects or inherent dangers in the goods.

It is useful to keep in mind that when bailment occurs in a business context, it is usually governed by a contract. The common law rules of bailment apply only in the absence of a contract or to the degree that such a contract is silent on matters relevant to liability. In a bailment, the standard of care—that is, the degree to which the bailee must be careful with the goods, or the degree to which the bailor must be careful that the goods will not cause harm—varies depending on the type of bailment and other circumstances, including the terms of any contract between the parties and the application of any statutory provisions that may apply in the situation.

The most common type of bailment in business situations is known as lucrative bailment, where both the bailee and bailor receive a benefit from the bailment. We will also look at other types of bailment: constructive bailment, where the bailee comes into possession of goods involuntarily; special bailment, where a statute will govern the relationship; and gratuitous bailment, where only one party (either the bailee or the bailor) receives a benefit from the bailment. The standard of care imposed on the bailee in these types of bailments will vary according to the specific relationship. We discuss the various types of bailment and their accompanying standards of care in the following sections. Table 10.2 provides a summary.

Lucrative Bailment

Lucrative bailment, also known as bailment for reward, is the most common form of bailment in the business world. It includes transactions such as renting storage units or warehouse space, leasing vehicles or equipment, and using mail or couriers

Table 10.2 Comparison of Different Types of Bailment

Type of Bailment	Description	Examples	Liability of Bailee	Liability of Bailor
Lucrative	Money or other payment changes hands.	The bailee pays the bailor for renting personal property, or the bailor pays the bailee for storing or repairing property.	The bailee must conform to the standard of care of a reasonably diligent person. A higher standard may exist if the bailed item is particularly valuable or fragile.	The terms of the contract may dictate the standard of care owed by the bailor. If the bailor rents defective equipment to the bailee, the bailor may be liable for harm suffered by the bailee as a result.
Constructive	The bailor loses personal property, which comes into the possession of the bailee.	A customer inadvertently leaves keys behind at a grocery store.	The bailee has an obligation to return the property to the bailor, if possible.	A person who loses personal property is generally not liable to the finder of the lost object. However, liability could arise if the object is inherently dangerous, such as a loaded gun.
Special	Particular obligations are imposed by statute on certain bailment relationships, such as those undertaken in the hotel business.	A hotel guest deposits jewellery in a hotel safe.	The bailee hotel is required to receive the property for "safe custody" and is liable if the property is damaged, lost, or stolen.	The bailor is required to deposit the property in a fastened and sealed box or other receptacle if the hotel requires him to do so.
Gratuitous	No money or other payment changes hands.	The property may be borrowed, to the benefit of the bailee, or it may be stored, to the benefit of the bailor.	When the bailment benefits the bailor, the standard of care is low: gross negligence. When the bailment benefits the bailee, the standard of care is very high: slight negligence.	Even when the bailment benefits the bailee, such as where the bailor lends property to a friend, the bailor has an obligation to be aware of any defects or potential injury that could be caused by the property, and to caution the bailee.

to send a package. In each of these circumstances, both the bailor and the bailee receive a benefit.

Three other types of lucrative bailment are worth particular mention:

1. *Bailment for repair or service.* This is a form of bailment in which the bailor pays the bailee for repairing or servicing the bailor's goods. For example, suppose that one of Val-Nam's production machines breaks and Val-Nam is not able to repair it onsite. Val-Nam will take it to a repair shop and leave it there until the repair can be completed. Val-Nam is paying the repair shop not to store the machine but to repair it. Nevertheless, the situation qualifies as a lucrative bailment—Val-Nam gets its machine repaired and the repair shop is paid for the repairs.
2. *Consignment.* The form of lucrative bailment called "**consignment**" is used by many antique and used-clothing shops. Owners of clothing and antiques (bailors) approach these shops and ask if their goods can be sold there. Instead of buying the goods, the shops agree to display and sell them on behalf of the owners in return for a commission. The shops are never the owners of the goods: they are lucrative bailees. The compensation they receive for their services is the commission they earn if they sell the goods. Manufacturers and distributors also use this type of arrangement. Val-Nam may have a sales contract with certain of its retailers that allows the retailer to return unsold stock within a certain number of days of delivery. Until this date passes, Val-Nam retains ownership of the stock even though it is in the retailer's possession.
3. *Parking lots.* One of the most common types of short-term bailment relationships is formed when a bailee is in possession of a car for the purpose of parking it. The law of bailment applies to valet parking, where the bailee takes possession of the vehicle and parks it, or where the bailee accepts the keys to the vehicle after it has been parked. The transfer of possession of the vehicle in these instances is essential to create bailment. However, there is no transfer of possession in cases where a vehicle is parked in a lot and the owner of the vehicle holds on to the keys. In those cases, the vehicle owner is merely renting a parking space on a short-term basis. The rental of the parking spot in these cases is akin to a licence agreement, and the legal relationship is governed by the contract (the express and implied terms of the agreement to park the car in the spot). Parking lot operators use exemption clauses to limit their liability for any damage to the vehicle. These limitations on liability are generally contained on the back of the parking stub and in clearly visible signage.

consignment
act of giving over possession of goods to another but retaining legal ownership in them until they are sold

LIABILITY FOR LUCRATIVE BAILMENT

In most cases of lucrative bailment, a contract dictates the terms of the bailment relationship and liability. The parties will resort to common law bailment rules only if the contract is silent on an issue. Most standard contracts for the commercial rental of goods, for example, will set out some limits to the bailor's liability for defective goods by using exemption clauses. Similarly, most standard contracts for the commercial storage of goods, for example, will set out limits to the bailee's liability for their care in exemption clauses. An exemption clause is a term in the contract by which one party attempts to limit the other party's right to damages or remedies for a breach of contract. Note, however, that there may be limits to the enforceability of these clauses (for a review of the application of clauses that limit liability, see Chapter 4). A contract provides an opportunity to set out the expectations of both parties, including the obligations on the bailee for maintenance of the goods and return of the goods in a particular condition.

If you are involved in a lucrative bailment, it is wise to record your expectations in a written contract. This reduces the risk of misunderstanding, conflict, and lawsuits. Because the terms of a contract generally override common law principles, a contract provides you and the other party with the opportunity to make your own rules. It is very likely that Kangaroo Copy and Val-Nam's photocopy machine lease agreement specifies that Val-Nam is liable for any damage to the machine while it is in Val-Nam's possession. Where there is no contract and common law tort principles prevail, the standard of care applicable to a bailee in a lucrative bailment is usually the care that an ordinary or reasonably diligent person would take of the goods in the circumstances.

CASE IN POINT

Licence Versus Bailment

Heffron v Imperial Parking Co, 1974 CanLII 801 (Ont CA)

Facts

The owner of a vehicle left his car in a parking lot that required him to leave his keys with a parking attendant. The back of the ticket and signs in the lot stated that the parking lot operator was "not responsible for theft or damage of car or contents, however caused." When returning to the lot, the owner of the vehicle found that the keys and car had been stolen. The parking lot operator argued that use of the parking spot was a licence agreement, not bailment.

Result

The Ontario Court of Appeal held that while use of a parking spot may be a bailment or a licence, depending on the circumstances, the facts of this case established a bailment: the vehicle owner delivered up the keys to an attendant and there was an expectation of supervision of the vehicles parked there.

Business Lesson

Be aware of conduct that can create a bailment relationship where none may be intended. Bailment creates legal responsibility over goods in one's possession.

◇ Effect of Payment to Bailee on Standard of Care

Under the common law, if the bailee receives payment to possess the bailed goods, the bailee has a duty to preserve the value of the goods. The bailee is obliged to care for the goods at least as well as—and probably better than—if the bailee owned the goods.

An even higher standard of care exists if the goods are particularly valuable (an antique necklace, for example), if they are easily damaged (for example, glassware), or if they are perishable (for example, fresh produce). It is reasonable to assume that all such goods require extra care. The bailee may be liable for even slight negligence. On the other hand, if the loss occurs as a result of a defect in the bailed goods (such as a defective clasp on the antique necklace), then the bailee may not be liable for the loss.

◇ Liability of Bailor in Rental Situation

Suppose Martina's Equipment Rental Ltd ("Martina's") enters into a contract with Val-Nam to lease a forklift. Even if the contract is silent about the condition of the forklift, there is likely an implied term that the forklift is in usable condition. If the forklift is defective, Val-Nam would have a claim, based on contract and on tort, against Martina's. Martina's could be liable for any damage caused by the defect. For example, if the lift mechanism is defective and as a result a load of generators is dropped and significantly damaged, Martina's may be required to compensate Val-Nam for the damage. If Val-Nam loses clients or breaches its own delivery contracts as a result of the damage to the generators, Martina's may also be liable for those losses.

◇ Lien Against Bailor Who Refuses to Pay

Where there is a bailment for repair or service, the bailee has the right to a **lien** on the bailed property in the event that the bailor refuses to pay the bill. For example, if Val-Nam takes its broken machine press to a repair shop for repairs but then refuses to pay for this service, the repair shop could refuse to return the machine. Ultimately, the repair shop might have the right to sell the machine in order to be paid from the money received from the sale. (The remainder of the money would go to Val-Nam.) Businesses engaged in automobile repairs commonly exercise their lien rights if customers fail to pay for their services.

lien
legal claim on the property of another until a debt has been paid back

Constructive Bailment

A **constructive bailment** is involuntary. It usually arises when a bailor accidentally loses an item that the bailee finds. Suppose Avery goes to a restaurant wearing a necklace, but the catch on the necklace breaks and the necklace falls off. Avery eats her meal and leaves without noticing that the necklace has fallen under the table. When the restaurant is closing, Avery's waiter notices the necklace and turns it over to the restaurant manager. This is a constructive bailment because Avery did not intend to leave the necklace with the restaurant: she left it there accidentally.

constructive bailment
custody of property that has come into possession accidentally

Once the waiter finds the necklace, the restaurant has an obligation to return it to Avery, its owner. If the restaurant is unable to locate Avery, then it may keep the necklace, subject to Avery's right to claim it in the future. Avery's ownership rights do not end until she abandons her claim to the necklace. Purchasing a new necklace or stopping the search might be considered abandonment of her claim. If Avery claims her necklace and finds that it has been damaged, the restaurant will be liable only if it has been grossly negligent.

Special Bailment

A bailment relationship that is created by statute, rather than by common law principles, is called a special bailment. By statute, governments have imposed particular obligations on certain bailees, including those involved in the business of transporting goods (railway or trucking companies) and innkeepers. These businesses generally have special obligations in relation to the property in their charge. For example, an innkeeper, or hotel owner, must allow guests to deposit their goods for "safe custody." The Ontario *Innkeepers Act* limits a hotel's liability for valuables that are lost or stolen from a room to $40.00. In order to benefit from this limitation of liability, the statute requires the hotel to also accept guests' goods for "safe custody." For example, the hotel may furnish a safe in which the guests can store their valuable belongings. Information about the hotel's limited liability must be posted in each hotel room. If goods that were held in safe custody are lost or stolen, or if the hotelier refuses to accept the guest's goods for safekeeping, the hotel may be liable for an amount exceeding $40.00. But if the goods were in the room, liability will be limited as set out in the statute. Statutory provisions, therefore, can create special rules for some forms of bailment.

Gratuitous Bailment

gratuitous bailment possession of property where the benefit flows to only one party (i.e., only the bailor benefits or only the bailee benefits)

Gratuitous bailment, in which no payment changes hands between bailor and bailee, is uncommon in the business world. However, we discuss this type of bailment briefly for the purpose of comparison with commercial bailments. In a gratuitous bailment, either the bailor or the bailee can receive the benefit of the bailment. For example, Avery might create a gratuitous bailment by leaving her necklace with her friend Yasmin while she goes on a trip, thus saving herself the cost of renting a safety deposit box. She might also create a gratuitous bailment by lending her necklace to Yasmin to wear on a special occasion.

LIABILITY WHEN BAILOR BENEFITS FROM GRATUITOUS BAILMENT

If a gratuitous bailment benefits the bailor—Avery, for example, when she stores her necklace with Yasmin—the standard of care expected of Yasmin is relatively low because the bailee is doing the bailor a favour. The bailee is liable only for gross negligence—or negligence that involves recklessness—such as leaving the necklace on a table beside the front door while hosting a party for 200 guests.

LIABILITY WHEN BAILEE BENEFITS FROM GRATUITOUS BAILMENT

If the gratuitous bailment benefits only the bailee—Yasmin, for example, when she borrows Avery's necklace to wear on a special occasion—the standard of care expected of the bailee is high. She is liable even for slight negligence, such as failing to notice that the necklace has slipped from her neck while she is dancing. If, however, the clasp was defective and Avery, the bailor, knew or ought to have known about the defect, she has an obligation to tell Yasmin before lending the necklace. Avery has an obligation to check the necklace for obvious problems, such as a defective clasp, that could result in its loss. If she fails to do so, or fails to inform Yasmin, Avery is liable for any damage or loss that results. Avery's failure to notice the defect would not be considered reasonable in these circumstances.

MINIMIZING YOUR RISK

Be a Responsible Bailor and Bailee

- Ensure that all bailed goods are well maintained, safe, and in good repair.
- Describe the responsibilities of bailor and bailee in a written contract.
- Include exemption clauses where appropriate.

Real Property

Real property, also called realty or real estate, is generally defined as land, buildings, and fixtures. Land includes the minerals and water below its surface as well as the airspace above it. **Fixtures** are items such as shelving, sinks, or equipment that are attached to buildings. When real estate is sold, all fixtures are included in the sale unless specified otherwise.

fixtures
property, such as shelving or sinks, that is attached to buildings

Unless a business operates purely on the basis of a cellphone and laptop computer, it likely owns or rents real property. Offices, stores, factories, farms, parking lots, and even hot dog stands require real property to conduct business. There are a number of ways in which businesses can meet their needs for real property. We discuss the legal implications of each below.

Interests in Land

An interest in land is a property or ownership right that is obtained in or over land. The interests you should be familiar with are explored in the following subsections.

Fee Simple

Technically, only the government owns real property. What we commonly call ownership is really an interest in the property called a "**fee simple**," which provides ownership rights. A fee simple estate is granted by the government (the Crown). These rights include the right to possess the real property, exclude others from it, use it, build on it, sell it, give it away, and transfer it by will. However, as the true "owner" of all property, the government may impose taxes on property owners, and an owner's failure to pay may result in the loss of the property to the government. The government also has the right to limit how an owner uses land by imposing zoning bylaws or through environmental regulations.

fee simple
ownership rights in land where the owner can do what they want, including transfer, sell, and dispose of it

To hold an interest in fee simple, then, means "to have the maximum interest in the land." An owner in fee simple may do virtually anything with the land because they own it "in its entirety." Despite the technical distinction between the terms "ownership" and "fee simple," we will use the term "ownership" in this chapter because it is the commonly used term. An owner may decide to transfer all of their interest in the land to someone else (by granting a fee simple absolute to another), to transfer some of it temporarily (by granting a leasehold in the property), or even to transfer some of it for a lifetime (by granting a life estate in the property).

Life Estate

When someone has a **life estate** interest in a piece of land, they have the ability to retain a limited interest in the property for the duration of their lifetime. The person granted a life estate (the "life tenant"), not the owner of the fee simple (the grantor of the life estate), has the right to possession of the property for the duration of the life estate. Upon the death of the life tenant, full ownership returns to the grantor. This means that the life tenant is not considered an "owner" in the sense of having full fee simple ownership rights (like the right to sell the property or to use it as they desire). A life tenant is required to use the land that was "loaned" to them in a reasonable manner. This means maintaining the land in accordance with how the grantor desired the land to be maintained. Think of a life estate as a loan of an interest in

life estate
interest in land for the duration of a person's life and where, upon death, ownership rights transfer automatically to another

land to another person; it is not theirs to keep and they have to give it back in good condition. For example, Bob owns a piece of land in fee simple absolute on which he runs his vegetable farm. Bob transfers his interest in this property as a life estate to Judy. Judy now has an interest in this property until she dies; however, because Judy does not have ownership of this property, she must ensure that the farm is maintained in good condition, just as Bob would have done. This means that Judy cannot start a totally different business or build a commercial mall on Bob's property. Why? The land is not hers to keep, and she must give it back in the condition Bob desired unless he explicitly authorizes (in his will, for example) that she may use the property as she wishes or in a different fashion.

Easement

easement
right to use the land of another for a specific purpose

An **easement** creates a temporary interest or right in another's land. It is important to note that the interest created by an easement is granted in the *land*. A new owner of a piece of land can benefit from an easement if the time limit on its use has not expired because the land that was transferred to the new owner has this benefit or right attached to it. An example of an easement is consent to use a portion of or "right of way" (the benefit to reasonably pass or use the pathway of another's land) over someone's property, roadway, or gateway. For example, if Brian, the owner of a chicken farm in a rural area, has an easement to use Kevin's pathway that has better access to the roadway, when Natalie (a new buyer) buys Brian's home she may be entitled to use this easement if it "runs with the land," meaning it passes on to the next person who owns the land.

Leasehold Interest

leasehold interest
temporary right to occupy real property

lessor
person who leases property to another; landlord

lessee
person who leases property of another; tenant

A primary example of a **leasehold interest** is demonstrated in a situation where someone has rented a property or unit for a specific duration and sometimes for a specific purpose. Leases can be residential or commercial. A residential leasehold interest would apply to a place of residence where someone has ownership of the property and is allowing another to use it for a specific duration and with certain conditions, such as payment of rent. For example, Drew rents apartment B1 from Diana, who is both the landlord and the owner of the apartment building. Diana would therefore be considered the **lessor** (an owner of property who leases or rents to another) and Drew would be considered the **lessee** (a user or renter of the leased property). Before occupying the apartment, Drew signs a lease specifying that he must pay $500 a month for a period of 12 months. Drew is now paying $500/month in exchange for complete possession of the property Diana outlined in the lease. Although Diana still has ownership of the property, she has given up her possession rights in the property to Drew until his leasing period has expired. Commercial leases are discussed in more detail later in this chapter.

Agreements of Purchase and Sale

agreement of purchase and sale
legal contract that obligates the buyer to buy and the seller to sell

An **agreement of purchase and sale** is the usual first step in transferring ownership in real property. Like any contract, an agreement of purchase and sale may be negotiated to suit the needs of the parties. These contracts must be in writing to be enforceable. They set out all the terms that form the legal relationship between the buyer and the seller, including the selling price and the closing date, and may include conditions and warranties that usually protect the buyer.

Many people rely on a real estate agent to help execute an agreement of purchase and sale and then retain a lawyer to help finalize the transfer in ownership. However, the legal rights and obligations that arise from the transaction are created at the time that the contract is entered into, so retaining a lawyer after the fact may be too late if an issue arises because a matter has not been adequately addressed. Although real estate agents can help broker the deal, only a lawyer can provide legal advice. Purchasers, in particular, can help minimize legal risks associated with buying property by obtaining legal advice prior to entering into an agreement and ensuring their rights are suitably protected in the contract.

There are some exceptions to the rules governing the law of contracts when it comes to contracts relating to real property. Two notable exceptions are as follows: (1) a contract involving the transfer in ownership of or interest (i.e., mortgage) in real property must be evidenced in writing; and (2) unlike common law rules regarding liquidated damages in contracts (where a deposit represents a prepaid amount to be forfeited in the event of a breach in place of suing for damages) in a real estate transaction where the purchaser breaches the contract, the seller can forfeit the deposit and still sue the buyer for the full extent of the damage caused by the breach.

SCENARIO

Loss of Deposit Despite No Loss to Vendor

Val-Nam has been looking for property on which to build a new manufacturing plant. It entered into a purchase and sale agreement with Vendor 1 for the purchase of property in the south end of Ottawa. As a condition of the agreement, Val-Nam paid a $10,000 deposit to Vendor 1. A week later, an even better location was put up for sale in Ottawa's east end. Val-Nam informed Vendor 1 that it was not going to go through with the deal. Vendor 1 informed Val-Nam that it was keeping Val-Nam's deposit due to the breach.

Vendor 1 then found another purchaser for its land and ended up selling the land for $50,000 more than the price negotiated with Val-Nam. Val-Nam wants its deposit back, since Vendor 1 is actually better off after Val-Nam's breach of the purchase and sale agreement. Does Val-Nam have the right to get its deposit back?

Probably not. While there is some inconsistency in the case law, the general position appears to be that a purchaser that backs out of a real estate deal loses its deposit regardless of whether the vendor suffers any actual loss, provided the deposit is not so large as to be unconscionable.

Conditions Precedent

In Chapter 4, we discussed conditions precedent in the context of standard form contracts. These conditions—which specify that something must happen before a party is required to fulfill contractual obligations—often arise in agreements of purchase and sale. The following are examples of conditions precedent that you are likely to encounter when buying and selling real property.

1. *Conditional on financing:* a condition that the buyer is not required to complete the sale unless the buyer is able to arrange a mortgage or other financing by a specified date (we discuss mortgages in detail later in this chapter).

2. *Conditional on zoning approval:* a condition that the buyer is not required to complete the sale unless the buyer is able to obtain the zoning approval required to use the land in the manner intended.
3. *Conditional on inspection:* a condition that the buyer is not required to complete the sale unless a building inspection indicates that there are no hidden structural problems with the building.
4. *Conditional on environmental audit*: a condition that the buyer is not required to complete the sale unless an environmental audit indicates that there are no hidden environmental hazards on the property. This condition is particularly important to protect buyers of industrial land. Environmental laws can hold buyers responsible for the high costs of cleaning up toxic wastes, even if they were unaware that environmental problems existed at the time of purchase.

Recalling concepts related to contract law from Chapters 4 and 5, condition precedent clauses like the ones above create a conditional contract. In the context of agreements of purchase and sale, conditional contracts mean that the property is not "sold" until the conditions are met or otherwise removed by the purchaser (within the time set out in the contract to do so). If, for example, a purchaser is unable to successfully change the zoning where doing so is a condition of sale, the purchaser is not obligated to go through with the agreement. It is important to note, however, that the purchaser has a good faith obligation to make an application for rezoning and cannot use an unfulfilled condition as an excuse to try to get out of an agreement.

Warranties

Warranty in contract law refers to a clause in a contract that creates an obligation that, if breached, does not terminate the agreement. In a purchase and sale agreement, therefore, when a warranty is breached, the non-breaching party is not excused from fulfilling the obligations under the contract; the contract remains in place but the non-breaching party is entitled to sue the breaching party for damages. The following two warranties are commonly found in agreements of purchase and sale:

1. *Warranting no toxic wastes on property.* The vendor may warrant that there are no toxic wastes, such as oil tanks, buried under the surface of the property. If toxic waste is found years later, the buyer can sue the vendor for breach of contract. The vendor would likely be required to reimburse the buyer for the costs of restoring the environment to a non-toxic state.
2. *Warranting no asbestos in buildings.* The vendor may warrant that there is no asbestos in the building. If asbestos is later discovered to be present, the buyer's remedy is to sue the vendor for damages.

Of course, depending on whether the vendor can be found years later, and depending on whether the vendor has money to pay damages, the buyer's ability to enforce the warranty may be limited.

Closing

Real property is not legally transferred when the parties sign an agreement of purchase and sale; rather, it is transferred at a time specified in the agreement, called the "closing date." On closing, the buyer pays the vendor the purchase price and title transfers. This requires that the transfer in ownership be filed formally with the government. We will look next at how title is transferred under the land titles system. On closing, the buyer takes possession of the property.

MINIMIZING YOUR RISK

Protect Yourself Against Environmental Cleanup Costs

- Ensure that the land you buy does not subject you to unexpected liability for environmental cleanup by inserting appropriate conditions in your agreement of purchase and sale and by carrying out appropriate inspections and environmental audits.
- Ensure that if you discover environmental or health issues associated with the property, you have the right to seek reimbursement of the cleanup costs from the vendor by having inserted appropriate warranties into the agreement of purchase and sale.

Transfer of Ownership

The historical system for keeping track of the status of title to property involved a paper registration of deeds, known as the land registry system. The **land registry system** put the onus on the prospective purchaser of the land to ensure that the current registered owner's title was good by tracing the history of title through all the registered deeds on that property at the land registry office. The title search process was complicated and carried greater risk for the purchaser than the system now in place.

land registry system
system for the registration of title to lands that required a historical search of deeds to establish valid ownership

Ontario, like many other parts of Canada, now uses a system known as the **land titles system** (also known as Torrens title system), which has significantly simplified the administration of land registration. The land titles system does not require a prospective buyer to make a historical search of the title; the system ensures that the chain of title is established and that the last registered owner appearing on the registry is certified as being the correct and legal owner. The government, therefore, guarantees title. In the event that title as set out in this system is incorrect, the party who suffers a loss from this error is entitled to seek compensation from the (provincial) government for the mistake.

land titles system
system for the registration of land where the government certifies valid title to and interest in the property

The land titles system has been modernized into an electronic registry. Different terminology is used to avoid confusion with the previous system: a deed is referred to as a **transfer** and a mortgage is referred to as a **charge**. A transfer of ownership of a parcel of land is completed by the land registrar, whose duty it is to ensure that transfers are legally valid. Transfer in ownership may come about because of the sale of the property or by other means, such as court order, or due to the death of the registered owner. Also noted in the register are any interests in the property such as charges (mortgages) or liens.

transfer
term used for a deed under the land titles system

charge
term used for a mortgage under the land titles system

Mortgages

A **mortgage** is a loan secured by real property; it gives the lender the right to sell the property, and recoup any loss, if the borrower fails to repay the loan. Mortgages

mortgage
loan secured by real property

therefore operate in relation to real property the way security agreements operate in relation to personal property (security agreements are discussed in Chapter 8 under the heading "Unsecured and Secured Credit").

It is helpful to remember the terminology: the owner of the property who borrows funds is the **mortgagor**, and the lender (usually a financial institution) is the **mortgagee**. While the mortgage is in effect, the mortgagor keeps possession of the real property and may make full use of it, provided that the obligations, included in all standard mortgage agreements, are fulfilled. The mortgagor must:

mortgagor
owner of real property who borrows funds from a mortgagee

mortgagee
party that loans funds to a mortgagor; usually a financial institution

- make periodic mortgage payments (usually monthly or biweekly),
- pay all property taxes,
- insure the property against loss, and
- make all repairs necessary to ensure that the property does not lose value.

Failure to fulfill any of these obligations results in **default**, which allows the mortgagee to take possession of the property and avail itself of other remedies, which we discuss below.

default
mortgagor's failure to fulfill their obligations under a mortgage

Like most loan payments, mortgage payments consist of a combination of principal (the amount of money loaned) and interest. The **amortization period** is the length of time it will take to pay off the debt entirely, based on the regular payment of a fixed amount. The amortization period is usually long—25 years, perhaps. However, the **mortgage term** is considerably shorter, usually between 1 and 5 years. The negotiated interest rate applies only during the mortgage term. At the end of the term, the mortgagor and the mortgagee must negotiate a new interest rate. If another lender is offering lower rates, the mortgagor can switch lenders. Once the debt is paid in full, the mortgagor takes clear title.

amortization period
length of time required to pay entire mortgage debt

mortgage term
period, usually between one and five years, during which a stipulated interest rate applies

Purchasers often obtain mortgages to finance the purchase of real property. Sometimes, however, property owners mortgage the property they already own as a method of raising funds for some other purpose. For example, a small business owner might mortgage their own home to finance the growth of the business. A large corporation with numerous real estate holdings, such as factories and office buildings, might mortgage some of these properties to raise needed capital.

It is possible to have several mortgages on the same property. Mortgagees, like personal property security holders, hold their interests in a priority sequence. In the event of a default, a first mortgage takes priority over a second mortgage, which takes priority over a third mortgage, and so on. The terms "first," "second," and "third" refer to the time when the mortgages are registered. Also, like personal property security holders, mortgagees must register their mortgages to preserve their position in the priority sequence.

Default

What happens if a mortgagor defaults by failing to make mortgage payments, pay property tax, insure the property, or make necessary repairs to the mortgaged property? Most mortgage agreements include an **acceleration clause**, which provides that full payment of the entire debt becomes due on default.

acceleration clause
contractual term providing that payment of an entire debt becomes due on default

If the mortgagor defaults, the mortgagee may simply sue the mortgagor for payment of the debt. Alternatively, the mortgagee may seek an order for possession of the property and then obtain relief in one of three different ways:

1. *Sell the property under the power of sale authorized by the mortgage.* Most mortgage agreements give the mortgagee the power to sell the property in the event of default by the mortgagor. This form of sale is the most commonly used remedy because it is relatively quick and easy. In less than two months from the date of default, title to the property may be transferred directly to a new purchaser, who receives clear title, free of the mortgage. The mortgagee uses the proceeds of sale to pay the debt that the mortgagor owes. Any surplus goes to subsequent mortgagees and other registered creditors in priority based on the dates that the subsequent mortgages and interests were registered. Finally, anything left over is returned to the mortgagor. If the proceeds of sale are insufficient to satisfy the entire debt, the mortgagor is liable for the shortfall.
2. *Obtain title in a foreclosure action.* An action for foreclosure is more complicated than a sale under the power of sale clause in the mortgage agreement because it involves transferring legal title to the property from the mortgagor to the mortgagee. Once title is transferred, the mortgagee has the choice of selling or keeping the property. Some mortgagees may choose to keep the property, renting it to a tenant and recouping their losses over time.

   Unlike a sale under power of sale, a final order of foreclosure extinguishes the debt owed by the mortgagor to the mortgagee. The mortgagor is not liable for any shortfall, nor are they entitled to any of the proceeds of sale, even if the proceeds exceed the amount owed under the mortgage.
3. *Sell the property in a judicial sale action.* A judicial sale is a sale by court order. The sheriff sells the property by tender or public auction, and the proceeds are distributed in the same manner as a sale under power of sale. The mortgagees and other registered creditors are entitled to payment of the debts owed to them, in priority sequence, and anything left over is returned to the mortgagor.

MINIMIZING YOUR RISK

Fulfill Your Mortgage Responsibilities

- If you are a mortgagor, make your payments on time, pay your property taxes, and insure your property and keep it in good repair.
- If you are a mortgagee, search the registry for prior mortgages and liens and register your own mortgage without delay.

Commercial Leases

Many businesses choose to rent the commercial property they occupy rather than buy it. There are many reasons for this choice. For example, renting

- does not tie up capital,
- increases a business's flexibility to change locations, and
- may decrease maintenance responsibilities (depending on the terms of the lease).

Figure 10.1

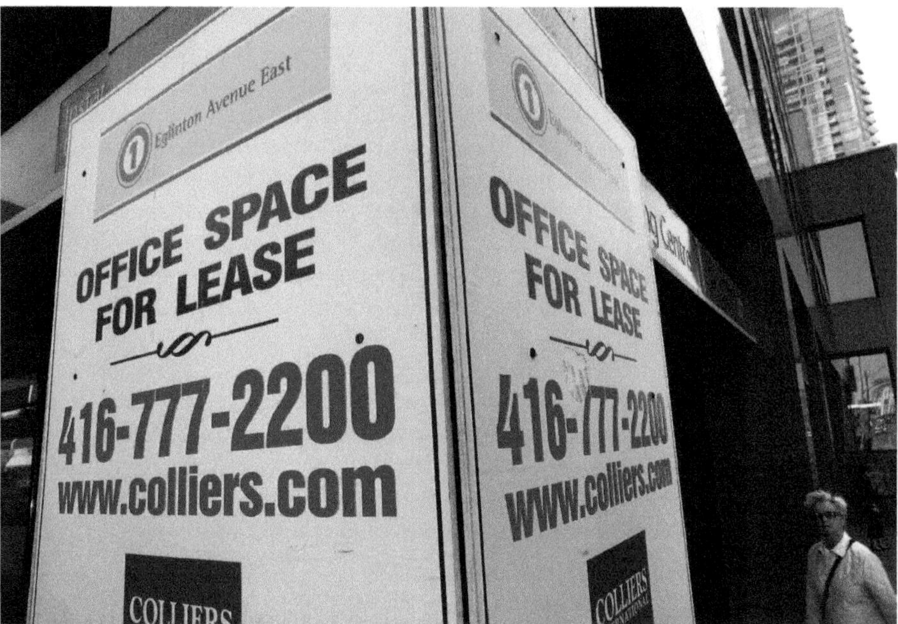

Many businesses will have the option of leasing the premises they occupy rather than buying it.

Some businesses, such as property management companies, make their living from renting properties to others. Our focus here, however, is primarily on the needs and risks of the commercial tenant. It is also very important for businesses to remember that the law governing commercial tenancies is significantly different from the law governing residential tenancies. Legislation such as the *Residential Tenancies Act, 2006* provides protection for residential tenants that greatly exceeds the protection provided for commercial tenants. Our discussion is limited to commercial tenancies.

Just as a bailment separates possession from ownership of personal property, a lease separates possession from ownership of real property. Under a commercial lease, a commercial tenant enjoys possession of property for the purpose of conducting business there, while the landlord continues to own the property. The **lease** is the contract that sets out the rental terms that the parties have agreed to, such as the length of the lease, the amount of rent to be paid, the timing of rental payments, obligations of maintenance and repair, and any restrictions on the tenant's use of the premises. When the lease comes to an end, the right of possession reverts to the landlord.

lease
contract that sets out terms of property rental

While the lease is in operation, the tenant is entitled to **exclusive possession** of the property. This means that the tenant may exclude all others from the property, including the landlord, except in unusual circumstances such as emergencies. The tenant may also use the property without interference by the landlord, subject to any agreed-upon restrictions provided in the lease. For example, a lease agreement may prevent a tenant from doing major renovations or making changes to the structure of a building without the landlord's prior consent.

exclusive possession
possession of real property to the exclusion of others

Common Lease Provisions

TERM OF THE LEASE

In a **fixed tenancy**, a lease exists for a fixed term, such as 1 year, 5 years, or even 99 years. At the end of the term, the landlord and tenant have no obligation to each other to continue the lease arrangement. They may part ways without legal consequence or they may negotiate a new term. In a **periodic tenancy**, the lease does not specify a rental term or a termination date. Instead, the lease continues to operate indefinitely, unless one of the parties gives notice to the other to terminate the lease. Both fixed and periodic tenancies require the periodic payment of rent. Fixed tenancies may become periodic tenancies if, after the termination date, no new term is negotiated, but the tenant continues paying rent and the landlord continues to collect it.

fixed tenancy
right to rent real property for a specified period of time

periodic tenancy
right to rent real property for an indefinite period of time, where both landlord and tenant have the right to terminate the tenancy after providing notice

RENT

The amount of rent payable under most commercial and industrial leases is determined on the basis of the square footage of the space leased. The rate charged per square foot varies depending on the building's attributes and location and is negotiated by the parties. Because the term of commercial leases is often long, and market rates for commercial premises change unpredictably over time, most long-term commercial leases provide for renegotiation of the rate at specified intervals—every five years, for example. If the parties are concerned about their ability to renegotiate a mutually agreeable rate, they may include an arbitration clause in the lease agreement.

Under the common law, a tenant's obligation to pay rent continues even if the property is rendered unusable by, for example, a devastating fire. This is a serious concern for tenants. If you lease premises, it is important that you include a provision in your lease that permits you to stop paying rent under certain circumstances. Otherwise, you may find yourself paying rent for premises that your business cannot use.

If a tenant fails to pay rent, a landlord has several remedies available. The landlord may sue for payment of the debt, most likely in the Small Claims Court. Commercial landlords also have the right of **distress** against their tenants' goods. This means they may seize and sell a tenant's personal property—such as computers and office equipment—located on the leased premises to cover the amount of the tenant's debt. Note that the right of distress is not available to residential landlords.

distress
remedy allowing a landlord to seize and sell a tenant's personal property when rent is unpaid

Finally, commercial landlords have the right of re-entry, or **forfeiture**, which allows them to regain possession of the premises when a tenant fails to pay the rent. Changing the locks is the most common method of regaining possession. A tenant that has been locked out has the option of applying to a court to reinstate the lease after paying the full amount of rent owing. Once a landlord uses the forfeiture remedy, the landlord no longer has the right of distress. Therefore, landlords should consider their options carefully before changing the locks. If a tenant has enough personal property on the leased premises that can be sold to cover the debt, a landlord may be wise to use the distress remedy before resorting to forfeiture.

forfeiture
remedy allowing a landlord to regain possession of leased premises when rent is unpaid

REPAIRS AND MAINTENANCE

A well-drafted lease sets out both a landlord's and a tenant's responsibilities for repairing and maintaining the premises. Apart from a lease, commercial tenants have very little protection because legislation requires landlords only to maintain basic safety. The common law does not oblige a landlord to make repairs, only to warn tenants of any dangers.

Commercial tenants are generally not entitled to withhold rent for any purpose, even if their landlord breaches a provision in a lease. If a landlord refuses to make repairs according to the requirements of the lease, a commercial tenant must seek other remedies, such as suing the landlord for breach of contract. If successful in such a suit, the tenant may be awarded a rent abatement, which is a reduction in the amount of rent payable.

SCENARIO

Val-Nam leases a warehouse from Suki's Storage. Suki's Storage appears to take no care of the property. There are roof leaks resulting in water damage to Val-Nam's raw materials and a mice infestation. What can Val-Nam do?

- Review the terms of the lease. What are Suki's Storage's obligations with respect to maintenance and repair? Can Val-Nam require repairs according to the lease?
- If not, does Val-Nam have the right to effect repairs? Does Val-Nam have to obtain consent from Suki's Storage first? Is Val-Nam entitled to be compensated for repairs made?
- Will a breach of Suki's Storage's obligations with respect to maintenance and repair be a breach of condition or a breach of warranty? Can Val-Nam get out of the lease due to the condition of the property?
- What is the cost and procedure for Val-Nam to terminate the lease? Is this the least-cost means of getting out of a bad deal?

Val-Nam should review the lease with legal counsel in order to determine the options available to remedy the situation.

In the future, Val-Nam should ensure that its leasing contracts clearly set out its rights as a tenant and the landlord's obligations with respect to the maintenance and repair of the premises. It may also want to include termination provisions that allow it to get out of the lease quickly, and at no cost, should the landlord fail to adequately maintain the premises.

USE OF PREMISES

quiet enjoyment tenant's right to use leased property for the intended purpose without interference from the landlord or others under the landlord's control

Tenants have the right to **quiet enjoyment** of the premises. This means that a tenant is entitled to use the property for its intended purpose, without interference from the landlord or others that are under the control of the landlord (such as other tenants). To avoid a misunderstanding about the tenant's intended purpose, the lease agreement should specify this purpose in the clearest terms.

For example, if Val-Nam decides to lease a premises for its new manufacturing plant—which involves noise 24 hours a day and will probably damage the interior of the building—it is important that the landlord accept this usage in the lease. The lease should also clarify both the landlord's and Val-Nam's responsibilities for maintaining the premises in a condition agreeable to both. In addition, the lease should set out Val-Nam's responsibilities for its potential interference with the quiet enjoyment of the premises by other tenants.

SUBLETS

Tenants have the right to sublet the premises unless the lease states otherwise. This means that a tenant may find a new tenant to take possession of the premises. However, the original tenant remains responsible for fulfilling all of the obligations under the lease, such as paying the rent and maintaining the property. The new tenant, or subtenant, is responsible only to the original tenant; the subtenant has no contractual obligations to the landlord.

If a tenant has a long-term lease and it wants to change location, it may find a subtenant. The original tenant will collect rent from the subtenant and pay the landlord. The sublet allows the original tenant to move out without losing money.

A tenant may charge as much rent as the market will bear; it need not be the amount specified in its lease. If a subtenant is willing to pay a higher rent, the tenant may be able to make a profit—that is, the difference between the amount the subtenant pays to the tenant and the amount the tenant pays to the landlord under its lease.

ASSIGNMENT

Tenants also have the right to assign the lease, unless the provisions of the lease provide otherwise. In an assignment, a new tenant becomes a party to the lease and deals directly with the landlord according to the terms of the lease. However, unless the landlord releases the first tenant from its obligations under the lease, the landlord may still sue the first tenant in the event that the new tenant fails to pay the rent or otherwise abide by the lease.

FIXTURES

If a tenant adds fixtures to the rented premises, what happens to the fixtures when the tenant leaves? Generally, fixtures stay on the premises and tenants are not permitted to remove them. The law creates an exception for trade fixtures, which are specific to the tenant's business—for example, washing machines in a laundromat, machinery in a factory, shelving in a store, or dental chairs in a dentist's office. It is wise to specify, when signing the lease, which fixtures the parties intend to be trade fixtures to avoid confusion and disagreement later.

MINIMIZING YOUR RISK

Customize Your Commercial Lease

- Include an arbitration clause in long-term leases to avoid rent hikes that exceed market rates.
- Specify the tenant's intended use of the property and the landlord's agreement to this use.
- Include a provision exempting the tenant from paying rent if the premises becomes unusable.
- Include detailed provisions about maintenance and repair obligations of both landlord and tenant.
- Specify which party will keep any fixtures installed by the tenant.

Shopping Centre Leases

Shopping centre leases are complicated because they include space that is shared among many tenants, such as space for parking, storage, and shipping, as well as public space for shoppers. The common interests of the tenants and landlord are reflected in the special obligations that they all assume under shopping centre leases. For example, a lease may require the landlord to promote the shopping centre with advertising. Tenants may be required to keep their stores open during specified business hours for the convenience of shoppers, which provides a benefit for all tenants. Also, because of the parties' shared interest in the shopping centre's success, rental payments are usually arranged so that the landlord shares in the profits of the tenants. The lease may require a minimum monthly rental payment, but it also usually requires the tenant to pay the landlord a percentage of gross sales.

Licences

Some uses of real property involve licences, such as:

- a licence from a municipality or an amusement park owner to operate a hot dog stand on a city street or on the grounds of the amusement park
- a licence from a hotel to hold an office party in a banquet hall
- a licence from a provincial government to extract oil or minerals from real property
- a licence from a building owner to attach an antenna or satellite dish to a building.

A licence does not create an interest in land; rather, it creates a contractual right. The rights of both parties are entirely dictated by the terms of the contract. Unlike a lease, there are no additional common law principles (such as the right to exclusive possession) or special statutes to govern the relationship.

Insurance

Every business owner and most people have had some experience with insurance because it is an important part of any risk management plan. Car insurance, home insurance, life insurance, tenants' contents insurance, and liability insurance are all commonly obtained for prevention of loss. Insurance limits the risk of future loss by spreading the risk among a large group.

Suppose that, statistically speaking, one house in your neighbourhood will sustain damages of $200,000 as a result of fire or water damage in the next year. There are 2,000 houses in your neighbourhood. Each household may choose to contribute $100 to a fund, with the understanding that the $200,000 collected will go to the household that sustains the damage. The result is that everyone enjoys peace of mind for the price of $100, and the owners of the damaged house will have the money they need for repairs. Insurers manage the pooled fund, which is called the "float." The float is the total of all premiums paid by those who are insured, less administrative expenses.

A person or business that seeks insurance typically applies to an insurer for insurance coverage. Once the insurer approves the applicant and after the applicant pays a premium, the insurer issues an insurance policy. The **policy** is a contract that describes the types of losses covered as well as the reasons why the insurer may deny coverage. If a loss occurs, the insured obtains compensation from the insurer according to the terms of the policy.

policy
insurance contract describing the rights and obligations of an insurer and an insured

Types of Insurance

The different types of insurance are generally divided into two main categories: (1) life and health, and (2) property and casualty. Life and health insurance may be of interest to businesses that create benefit plans for their employees. Beneficiaries of this sort of insurance are generally the employees and their families. Property and casualty (or liability) insurance protects against the loss of both real and personal property and against the costs of being sued for negligence, including professional negligence. (We discuss the tort of professional negligence in Chapter 3. Businesses that employ professionals, such as architects or lawyers, should ensure that their professional employees are covered by appropriate levels of errors and omissions insurance.)

Sensible businesses usually carry the following types of property-related insurance:

1. *Property loss.* Businesses carry property loss insurance to protect themselves against the risk of loss from catastrophes such as fire, flood, theft, accident, and extreme weather. Property loss insurance protects businesses against losses of real property, such as factories, and personal property, such as machinery and equipment inside these factories.
2. *Liability for property loss.* Businesses carry property liability insurance to protect themselves against the financial consequences of failing to take adequate care of the property of customers and others. This form of insurance is particularly important for businesses that act as bailees where property in their possession may be damaged. Bailment is not the only situation in which liability insurance protects a business against damage to the property of another. If, for example, a delivery driver rear-ends another vehicle, the business that employs the driver can look to its liability insurance for protection.
3. *Occupiers' liability.* The occupier of real property—that is, the owner or tenant, depending on who is using the premises—owes a duty of care to customers and others who venture onto the property (see Chapter 3). An occupier who is found to be negligent because of, for example, failing to shovel snow or to clean up a spill quickly is liable for injuries sustained by those on the premises. Occupiers' liability insurance protects an occupier against negligence lawsuits by covering legal costs and any damage awards. Business tenants of shared spaces, such as shopping malls, should review their leases carefully to determine the extent of their responsibility for maintenance and insurance.
4. *Business interruption.* After suffering the loss of real or personal property, a business may find that its operation is seriously impaired or shut down entirely. If, for example, a business is temporarily shut down when a fire devastates its premises, business interruption insurance compensates it for the loss of its operating income.

www.emond.ca/CBL3/links

DIG DEEPER

The Insurance Bureau of Canada website has detailed checklists that help businesses manage insurance risks.

Insurable Interests

insurable interest interest that causes the insured to benefit from the existence of the property and to suffer from its loss

To obtain insurance for property, you must have an **insurable interest** in that property—that is, an interest that causes you to benefit from the existence of the property and to suffer from its loss. This is unlike insurance against liability for property loss. For example, only a tenant, not the landlord, can insure the tenant's computers. This is because the landlord does not have an insurable interest in the tenant's computers; however, the landlord could purchase liability insurance that would cover the cost of replacing the computers if they were stolen due to the landlord's negligence.

The insurable interest is limited by the fair market value of the property. For example, a computer system worth $50,000 may not be insured for $60,000.

Where ownership and possession are split—as they are in situations involving tenancy and bailment—it is not always clear who should insure real or personal property. Generally, the party whose property is at risk should obtain insurance. In a tenancy, for example, the landlord usually insures the real property and the tenant usually insures the personal property. However, a landlord with obligations to repair the premises would be wise to obtain liability insurance to protect against a loss to a tenant's property that results from the landlord's negligence. For example, a roof that leaks because a landlord neglects to maintain it could damage a tenant's valuable computer system, and an insured landlord could look to the insurer for protection from the financial fallout.

Following the risk principle, a bailor usually insures against loss or damage to the goods that are rented to a bailee. However, the bailee is liable if the bailed goods are damaged or lost as a result of the bailee's negligence. Therefore, a bailee might want to obtain liability insurance to protect against such a loss. To avoid double insurance of the same goods, bailors and bailees may want to include a term in their contract that assigns the responsibility for obtaining insurance to one party or the other.

Ensure You Insure

Val-Nam rents photocopy machines from Kangaroo Copy. Who should insure the machines?

Val-Nam leases a warehouse from Suki's Storage. The roof leaks, resulting in water damage to Val-Nam's raw materials, and an infestation of mice has damaged Val-Nam's business records. Who should insure the real and personal property in this scenario?

Coverage

When deciding on the insurance coverage appropriate for your business, it is wise to consider two things:

- the types of loss that you want to insure against, and
- the value of coverage that you are willing to pay for.

Both parties (the "insurer" and the "insured") are expected to exercise a duty of good faith. Therefore, they must act in an ethical and honest manner and disclose any material facts (i.e., a fact that is so important, it may affect the parties' decision-making process regarding the insurance contract).

It is also important to note that not all losses are necessarily covered by standard insurance policies. For example, property insurance may cover losses that arise from a variety of events, such as fire, flood, accident, and theft, but each type of loss must be specified in the policy. This issue was highlighted in New Orleans after Hurricane Katrina, when some insurers denied coverage by taking the position that storm coverage does not include floods, thereby leaving policyholders with no protection. As a business person, you should review your insurance contracts carefully to ensure that they specify all of the losses that you intend to insure against. If necessary, you may need to purchase additional coverage.

An insurance contract is considered to be "unilateral," meaning that only the insurer is legally bound to fulfill the promises of the contract. The insurer is the one who has to pay when damages occur that fall within the insurance policy. However, the insured person must pay premiums (payments made each month or year depending on the agreement terms) in order to secure payment from the insurer for any damages or losses they intend to claim. The value of insurance coverage may not exceed a business's insurable interest in its insured property. However, it is possible to insure property for less than its market value and thereby partially self-insure it. Businesses use this strategy to save money because it reduces the premium payable to an insurer. When partially self-insuring, a business buys enough insurance to cover part—but not all—of a potential loss. For example, a business that owns a factory worth $800,000 might insure the factory for $600,000. In the event that the factory is completely destroyed by fire, the business receives only $600,000 in compensation. It bears the additional $200,000 loss itself.

Another method of reducing insurance premiums is to include a higher deductible in the policy. The **deductible** is an out-of-pocket payment that an insured must contribute and that is deducted from the insurance payment. For example, if your deductible is $500, you must pay the first $500 of any claim yourself. Therefore, if you suffer property damage in the amount of $1,500, your insurer is obliged to only pay out the remaining $1,000. The higher your deductible, the lower your premium payment because the insurer takes a smaller risk in insuring your interest.

deductible
out-of-pocket payment that an insured must make that is deducted from the insurance payment

MINIMIZING YOUR RISK

Purchase Adequate Insurance

- Carefully assess all your real and personal property risks.
- Check that your insurance policies specifically mention these risks and cover them adequately.
- Consider partial self-insurance or high deductibles to reduce premiums.
- Comply with building and safety codes.
- Inspect your premises and equipment regularly, and keep them in good repair.
- Train employees with respect to fire, safety, and emergency procedures.
- Advise your insurer of any material change in the risk.

CHAPTER SUMMARY

Property law confers rights over goods. It allows the owners of goods to enforce their rights against others. Without laws to define property rights, people could not own goods; they could merely possess them.

Property is commonly categorized into three types: real (land, buildings, fixtures, etc.), personal (tangible items that are not attached to land or buildings), and intellectual (copyright, patents, trademarks, etc.).

Personal property (including intellectual property) may be held as security for a debt. If a business borrows money, the lender may require the business to secure the loan by giving the lender the right to seize and sell the personal property if the loan is not repaid. Possession is a key ownership right. Owners of property may grant this right to others by giving them permission to possess their property. When ownership and possession of personal property are split in this way, the legal relationship between the owner and the possessor is called bailment.

A bailment exists when goods are borrowed, rented, stored, or found by someone other than the owner. In a business context, lucrative bailments are usually governed by contracts for rental, lease, repair, or consignment. Every possessor has a duty to take care of the owner's goods, especially if they pay to possess them or if the goods are valuable. The owner of the goods has a duty to ensure that the goods are not defective and that the possessor is warned of any inherent dangers.

Technically, only the government owns real property. What is commonly called ownership is really an interest called a "fee simple," which provides the right to possess the real property, exclude others from it, use it, build on it, sell it, give it away, and transfer it through a will. Other interests in real property include life estates, easements, and leases. Real property is legally transferred on the "closing date" specified in the agreement of purchase and sale.

Property and casualty (or liability) insurance protects against the loss of both real and personal property and against the costs of being sued for negligence, including professional negligence. Businesses usually carry insurance against property loss, liability for property loss, occupiers' liability, and business interruption. When deciding on appropriate insurance coverage, businesses should consider the types of loss they want to insure against and the value of coverage they are willing to pay for.

KEY TERMS

REFERENCES

Heffron v Imperial Parking Co, 1974 CanLII 801 (Ont CA).
Innkeepers Act, RSO 1990, c I.7.
Residential Tenancies Act, 2006, SO 1996, c 17.
Tercon Contractors Ltd v British Columbia (Transportation and Highways), [2010] 1 SCR 69.

EXERCISES

True or False?

____ 1. Real property is the same as real estate.
____ 2. Chattels are fixtures attached to real property.
____ 3. Different people may have different property rights in the same piece of property.
____ 4. Bailors are always responsible for insuring the bailed property.
____ 5. Provincial statutes govern all lucrative bailments.
____ 6. A limited liability clause in a bailment contract will ensure that the bailee will carry no legal risk for loss of, or damage to, property in the bailee's possession.
____ 7. Breach of environmental audit conditions terminates agreements of purchase and sale.
____ 8. Before title can be registered to the purchaser of land using the land titles system, a historical search of the deeds registered for that property must be conducted to ensure that the seller is the valid owner at the time of sale.
____ 9. The owner of a commercial property is responsible to insure the chattels in the premises belonging to the tenant.
____10. Property loss insurance can protect businesses against fire, theft, accident, and weather damage.

Multiple Choice

1. Personal property does *not* include which one of the following?
   a. a car
   b. a home
   c. a computer
   d. a promissory note
2. Lucrative bailments do *not* include:
   a. bailment for repair or service
   b. consignment
   c. lease of a photocopy machine
   d. lending of money
3. Which of the following does not create a bailment?
   a. Leaving a coat to be dry cleaned.
   b. Sending a package by courier.
   c. Parking a car at a meter.
   d. Borrowing a friend's lawnmower.
4. Louise is the owner of a laptop computer. Thelma is in possession of the computer. In which of the following situations would Thelma have the lowest standard of care in relation to the computer?
   a. Louise left her computer at Thelma's shop for repairs.
   b. Louise is paying Thelma to deliver the computer to Louise's aunt.
   c. Louise asked Thelma to store her computer while Louise goes on vacation.
   d. Louise let Thelma borrow her computer to finish a school project.
5. Which of the following does *not* create a temporary interest in another person's land?
   a. easement
   b. life estate
   c. fee simple
   d. leasehold interest
6. Which of the following is a condition precedent in an agreement of purchase and sale?
   a. The condition that the purchaser arrange financing by a specified date.
   b. The condition that the purchaser have the property inspected.
   c. The condition that the purchaser obtain zoning approval.
   d. All of the above.
7. Consider advantages and disadvantages of leasing commercial space versus owning it. Which of the following is *not* an advantage of a commercial lease?
   a. A commercial lease does not tie up capital as the purchase of property would.
   b. A commercial lease will have fewer maintenance responsibilities.
   c. A commercial lease carries no legal risk for hazards on the property.
   d. A commercial lease provides more flexibility in relocating business.
8. To obtain insurance, you must have:
   a. an insurance policy
   b. an insurable interest
   c. sufficient float
   d. possession of the insured property

Short Answer

1. In Canada, what rights do property owners have?
2. What is bailment?
3. What is the key component of any risk management plan involving a business's real and personal property?
4. What is a periodic tenancy?

5. Do commercial landlords have a remedy when dealing with a tenant who has an unpaid debt? Please explain.
6. List two types of property-related insurance that a sensible business should carry.

Apply Your Knowledge

1. Karl, a potter, owns property in the country where he has a workshop and two large kilns. He supplies his high-quality pottery to various shops across Canada and also fills orders directly from people who order on his website. The stores that sell Karl's pottery do so on a consignment basis. When an item is sold, Karl receives payment, less the store's selling fee. Karl stores his pottery in his friend Larry's barn before shipping it to stores or Internet customers.
   a. Describe the legal relationship between Karl and the stores that sell his work.
   b. What is the legal relationship between Karl and Larry?
   c. What risks might Karl want to insure against?
   d. What risks might Larry want to insure against?
   e. Do the stores need to insure Karl's pottery? Why or why not?
2. Janet is selling her business after 20 years. She has been asked to provide a list of her real and personal property (including tangible and intangible property). Classify the following as either real or personal property (intangible/tangible).
   a. Janet's company towers (buildings).
   b. Janet's delivery truck.
   c. The goodwill and reputation of Janet's company.
   d. The photocopy machines used in Janet's office.
   e. The trademark of Janet's company.
4. Ali is excited to buy a commercial property to start up his new business and investment initiative. He is suspicious about a particular property and does not want to go ahead with the purchase until he is certain that the property is in good condition. Georgiana is drawing up the agreement of purchase and sale on Ali's behalf. What specific terms should Ali seek to have included in the contract? Discuss.

Intellectual Property and Business Law in the Digital Age

11

LEARNING OUTCOMES

After reading this chapter, you should be able to:

- Distinguish between copyrights, patents, trademarks, industrial designs, and trade secrets.
- Explain how the law applies in protecting each type of intellectual property.
- Identify ways to minimize legal risks related to the infringement of various intellectual property rights.
- Discuss legal aspects and protection of confidential business information.
- Explain the importance of legal compliance with respect to collection, use, and disclosure of personal customer information.
- Discuss legal risks associated with commercial electronic messages and ways to minimize those risks.

Intellectual Property

Creativity, new ideas, and advances in science and technology are all drivers of a strong economy. Governments that want to encourage innovation by businesses and individuals must ensure that there is benefit for those businesses and individuals by helping to protect the products of their innovation. As we discussed in Chapter 10, intellectual property is intangible—that is, its value is distinct from any physical object. Although intellectual property may be associated with an object, its real value lies in its owner's right to prevent others from copying it. For example, when you buy a CD or a prescription drug, you get a copy of the music or a bottle of pills. The physical item is a chattel that you own. But you do not get the right to copy the CD or to manufacture a version of the pills and sell them to others. These rights belong to those who own the intellectual property rights associated with the CD and the drug.

Society has an interest in both protecting intellectual property and ensuring a free flow of creative and innovative work. Intellectual property law recognizes that there are competing interests in intellectual property—the owner's private interests in the work and the public's interest in innovation—and attempts to balance these interests. Intellectual property laws are designed to provide exclusive rights and legal protection to the owners of innovative, creative, and original works and inventions in exchange for disclosing and sharing these works and inventions with the world.

Intellectual property rights can be claimed by creators, such as inventors, authors, engineers, and scientists, or—more commonly—they may be transferred to and claimed by others, for example, by the businesses that employ the creators. Intellectual property law recognizes the value inherent in creating software programs, books, photographs, and scientific inventions, and it provides remedies for those who own the property rights in these things. There are laws that protect copyright, trademarks, patents, and industrial designs by preventing the unauthorized copying of a protected work, invention, design, or brand.

As we saw in Chapter 1, the authority to make law in relation to intellectual property is granted to the federal government under the Constitution. Where legislation is enacted to govern various forms of intellectual property—copyrights, trademarks, patents, and industrial designs—it is federal law applicable across Canada. Trade secrets are protected in the common law. Here is an overview of what each of these types of intellectual property protects:[1]

- Copyright in an original work grants the owner an exclusive right to use, reproduce, sell, or perform the original artistic, literary, musical, photographic, or other work. For example, a musician owns the copyright in an original sound recording, and an author owns the copyright in their written work. Val-Nam Generation Limited ("Val-Nam") will own the copyright in its product manuals and advertising copy.
- A patent is a government-issued monopoly right to make, sell, or use a novel, innovative, and useful invention. For example, Apple owns many patents for the unique functionality and interface of its iPhone. Valery Garza will likely want to patent the synthetic enzyme she invented. She may be willing to transfer the patent rights to Val-Nam, for a fee.

1 Adapted from May Cheng, "Intellectual Property Law and Work" in David Doorey, *The Law of Work: Common Law and the Regulation of Work* (Toronto: Emond, 2016) 423.

- A trademark is a unique identifier or brand used to distinguish one company's products or services from those of another company. For example, Nike and Starbucks are trademarks. Val-Nam's stylized "VN" (see margin) is a distinctive mark that identifies Val-Nam's products from those of its competitors.
- An industrial design is a government-granted exclusive right to make, sell, and use an ornamental feature, shape, or configuration. For example, the distinctive design of a fancy pair of eyeglasses or piece of jewellery can be registered as an industrial design. The distinctive casing around Val-Nam's generators may also be registered as an industrial design.
- A trade secret is the recipe, method, process, data, or know-how of a business that is confidential and that has actual or potential value in not being generally known. Efforts must be made to keep it a secret. For example, KFC's secret mix of herbs and spices is a trade secret, as may be a company's market research data. The improvements that Namid Blackburn has made to the plastic biodegradation process may be patentable, but the business may decide to protect the process improvements as a trade secret instead.

We will examine these major forms of intellectual property and the applicable law that governs them. Table 11.1 sets out a summary that compares the various forms of intellectual property and the manner in which they can be protected. In business, many types of intellectual property may need to be protected, including formulas or designs for products, logos, advertising slogans, brand names, and trade secrets. It is fair to say that virtually every business has some type of intellectual property to protect.

Assignment and Licences

The key to understanding the legal aspects of intellectual property is to first regard them as, indeed, forms of property. As such, the property owner has legal means available to protect it. Protecting it, however, does not necessarily mean that owners of intellectual property will prevent others from using it. It does mean that owners can, in accordance with the protections afforded by law, determine when and how they will allow others to use their intellectual property. Further, the fact that these are types of property also means that the rights in them can be transferred or sold to a new owner.

Assignment and licences are ways in which rights to intellectual property can be transferred to another in whole or in part, permanently or for a specific use or purpose. "**Assignment**" means transfer in ownership, and—with the exception of moral rights to copyrights, which are discussed below—all forms of intellectual property are assignable. **Licences** grant permission to use intellectual property according to the terms and conditions of the licence. Assignment and licences are forms of agreements and, therefore, are governed by contract law.

assignment
transfer of ownership in intellectual property

licence
permission to use intellectual property in accordance with terms and conditions

Copyright Law

Copyright law is concerned with the right to copy and recognizes the right of the copyright owner or original creator to control the use and reproduction of the work. It prevents people from reproducing a creative work without the permission of the

Table 11.1 Various Forms of Intellectual Property

	Copyright	Patent	Trademark	Industrial Design	Trade Secret
Matter protected	Creative work: artistic, literary, musical, dramatic, photographic works; recordings, software	Inventions: new or improved useful composition of matter or process	Brands: names, logos, symbols, slogans, pictures, product containers	Visual design: shape, pattern, ornamental features	Commercial information: plans, data, recipes, technology
Examples	Books, plays, films, videos, electronic games, architectural drawings, website content, music	iPhone interface, pharmaceuticals	Nike name, swoosh logo, "Just Do It" slogan	Design of sunglasses, pattern on wallpaper or fabric	A company's foreign market entry plan; recipe for Coca Cola
Governed by	Common law *Copyright Act*	*Patent Act*	Common law *Trade-marks Act*	*Industrial Design Act*	Common law
Prohibits	Copying, modifying	Use, manufacture	Use	Use, manufacture	Disclosure, use
Essential qualities	Original work, fixed form	New, useful, not obvious	Unique, distinguishes goods or services	Original, novel, visually appealing	Secret with economic value (actual or potential)
Symbol	© Registered or unregistered	Patent number	® Registered ™ Unregistered	Ⓓ Registered	Not applicable
Term of protection	Life of creator plus 50 years; sound recordings: 70 years	20 years from registration; not renewable	As long as used (common law) If registered: 15 years; renewable	10-year registration; not renewable	Indefinite
Registration	Optional	Required	Optional	Required	Not applicable

copyright holder. Illegal reproduction includes copying or plagiarizing part or all of a work. The *Copyright Act* is a federal statute, applicable across the country. It protects a broad range of works, including:

- books, magazines, and newspapers
- music, both recorded and written
- computer programs
- plays and movies
- paintings, drawings, charts, maps, and photographs
- sculptures and architectural works.

The various types of works protected by copyright have different rights attached to them. Generally, however, copyright law gives the copyright holder the exclusive right to produce or reproduce the protected work in any form. This includes photocopying, file sharing, and other modes of copying. Additional rights—such as the right to translate a work, to convert it to another medium, to adapt it, and to publicly perform it—are also protected by copyright law.

Scope of Copyright Protection

Copyright applies to the expression of ideas but not to the ideas themselves. A writer, for example, can protect the arrangement of words in an article through copyright but cannot prevent others from writing on the same subject matter. Copyrights are protected in the common law, which means that registration is not necessary to protect them, although they may be registered pursuant to the *Copyright Act*. Whether registered or unregistered, copyright protection does not last forever. Even when protected, there are a number of exceptions and defences to infringement. We discuss these matters in the sections that follow.

copyright
exclusive right to use, reproduce, sell, or perform the original artistic, literary, musical, photographic, or other work

Copyright holders may, of course, agree to permit others to reproduce their works in whole or in part. Authors, for example, can profit financially when their books are made into movies because film companies are required to compensate them for giving their permission to produce their work in film.

Canadian copyright law is enforceable outside Canada in countries that are signatories of the *Berne Convention*, a multinational treaty. Therefore, an international bestseller written by Canadian author Margaret Atwood is protected in Canada and also in other countries where the book is published, provided that those countries have signed the *Berne Convention*.

Length of Protection

Copyright law protects copyright for a fixed period of time. Once copyright protection expires, a work is said to be "in the **public domain**." This means that the public is free to use it. Anyone may exercise the rights that were formerly held exclusively by the copyright owner.

public domain
works not copyright protected, can be used freely

In general, unless the *Copyright Act* contains a specific provision to the contrary, a work becomes part of the public domain 50 years after the calendar year following the creator's death. This explains why the music of Mozart may be freely used and copied and why new versions of fairy tales by Hans Christian Andersen and the Brothers Grimm may be freely published and adapted into movies and plays.

Canada recently amended the legislation concerning copyrights of sound recordings and performances. Beginning in June 2015, the term of protection for sound recordings is 70 years after the release date of the recording. Note that this is only in relation to copyright of a particular artist's performance in a sound recording. It does not apply to the copyright of the music itself, which may be much longer in duration (that is, it remains protected for 50 years after the death of its composer).

Originality and Fixation

Two requirements must be met before the creator of a work may enjoy copyright protection: originality and fixation. Originality demands that the work be new in some way and come from the creator. Fixation demands that the work be more than simply an idea. Ideas themselves are not protected by copyright. To enjoy copyright protection, ideas must be fixed in a material form, such as written pages, digital data, or a video or audio recording. For example, a speech given at a conference may not be protected unless it is written down or recorded. Text on a computer monitor may not be considered fixed until it is saved. If a film company has an idea for a movie but never commissions a script or produces a film, copyright law will not protect the unrealized idea.

Copyright Symbol

The copyright symbol © is a mark used by the owner to alert others that the work is copyright protected. There is no requirement to use it; a work is protected by copyright whether it is accompanied by the symbol or not. However, it functions to remind potential violators that copying the work is illegal and, because it is universally recognized, it can enhance protection of the work internationally.

Copyrights Protected in Common Law: Registration Optional

Copyrights are governed by the common law in Canada, which recognizes that creative works are automatically protected in Canada when created. This remains true even if the work remains unpublished. Copyrights can, however, be registered with the Copyright Office, which is part of the Canadian Intellectual Property Office (CIPO). Registration creates a presumption that the person who registered the copyright is the owner. The advantage in registering the copyright is that it provides an evidentiary advantage: the person who registered it is presumed to be the owner and the burden to disprove this would be on anyone who has infringed the copyright or otherwise wishes to challenge it.

CASE IN POINT

Testing the Limits of Fair Dealing

CCH Canadian Ltd v Law Society of Upper Canada, 2004 SCC 13

Facts

Canadian publisher CCH Canadian Ltd ("CCH") was in the business of publishing materials such as law reports, textbooks, and various legal publications. CCH filed a lawsuit because it believed that the Law Society of Upper Canada (now the Law Society of Ontario) violated its copyright by allowing users of the Law Society's Great Library to copy CCH's materials. This claim was based on the fact that the Law Society had free-standing photocopiers for users and a notice disclaiming any liability for copyright violations above each copier. CCH also claimed that the Law Society violated its copyrights by permitting a service where its employees could copy materials for a fee. In trial court, it was found that the Law Society had violated some of CCH's copyrights. The Federal Court of Appeal held that all of CCH's copyrights were being violated by the Law Society's Great Library and its users.

Result

The Supreme Court of Canada held that the Law Society did not violate CCH's copyrights because allowing its users to utilize its photocopiers did not encourage them to violate copyright. The fact that the Law Society had a disclaimer above each copier was given special consideration; the court viewed this as further discouragement provided by the Law Society to its users. The court also determined that an exemption under the *Copyright Act* applied: materials are permitted to be reproduced for the "purpose of research or private study" without infringing copyright.

It is worth noting that the issue of fair dealing with respect to photocopying in academic institutions has not been put to rest. In *Canadian Copyright Licensing Agency v York University*, in July 2017, the Federal Court of Canada ruled against York University in a legal dispute with Access Copyright, an organization that compensates authors and publishers for photocopied works. In this case, the court ruled that York University had overstepped the boundaries of fair dealing by allowing extensive photocopying of copyrighted works.

Business Lesson

If you are a provider of published materials and resources, be sure that copies are made in compliance with section 29 of the *Copyright Act*. Also, to avoid any issues when it comes to having individual copiers in your place of business, always provide a disclaimer, such as a notice stating that your company is "not liable for any copyright violations that might take place."

Fair Dealing and Other Exemptions

Copyright owners control the right to copy; thus, use of their work without permission is a copyright **infringement**. It is important to note that copyright infringement is not tied to commercial gain. Copyright can be infringed even where copying the work is not done for monetary gain. For instance, software piracy is illegal even when software is duplicated and shared without exchange of money. However, copyright infringement for commercial gain presents a greater legal risk because the damages can be significantly higher.

infringement
unlawful interference with someone's legal rights

Despite the legal protections afforded to copyright owners, control over the use of copyright is not absolute. The law recognizes that there is a public interest in creative works and attempts to balance the rights between copyright owners and the interest that the public may have in the work. As a result, the *Copyright Act* sets out a long list of exemptions or defences to infringement.

Copyright owners have rights over public performance of their work, which means that private performance of certain works is permissible. For example, singing a song at home does not infringe copyright, but a licence would be needed to perform it publicly.

The chief defence to infringement is **fair dealing**. The fair dealing defence allows copying of the work if the purpose is to research, privately study, criticize, review, parody, or report on the work. Where the work is used in research, review, or news reporting, it needs to be attributed, which means the source has to be sufficiently acknowledged. The statute does not set out specific limits as to how much of a work may be copied but, depending on how it is used, it can be neither all nor a "substantial part" of a work; it is not fair dealing if use of the work is a thinly disguised means of actually distributing the work.

fair dealing
defence to copyright infringement that allows copying in some circumstances

Other exemptions apply to educational institutions, museums, archives, and libraries, and to the conversion of works for the perceptually disabled. More recent amendments to Canada's copyright law provide exemptions for "user-generated content," created by integrating or building on the copyright-protected work of another. Examples include uploading a video of a wedding couple dancing to a copyrighted song, or fan fiction. This so-called mash-up exception is not one that can be relied on in a business context, however, because the exemption applies only if the new work is used solely for non-commercial purposes.

Software and Digital Media

A person or business that purchases software does not become the owner of the copyright. Rather, the purchaser is given the right to use the software, with certain conditions or restrictions imposed by the copyright owner. Typically, the software publisher is the copyright owner and the terms and conditions are set out in the licence.

Software **piracy**—the illegal copying, distribution, or use of software—poses significant legal risk to business operators. Installing unlicensed copies of software exposes a business to legal risk even if the illegal software is installed by an employee without the business owner's knowledge. Canadian copyright law permits a user to make a copy of software for backup purposes, to safeguard against damage to the original copy. Beyond that, it is illegal to copy or distribute the software in any way prohibited by the licence. It is also illegal to tamper with or break digital locks that are used to prevent unauthorized duplication of software, DVDs, or other digital media.

piracy
illegal copying or distribution of another's intellectual property

Infringement of software copyrights carries the risk of civil liability and, in cases where it is done for commercial gain, may lead to criminal prosecution with risk of fines and/or imprisonment if convicted.

MINIMIZING YOUR RISK

Use Software Responsibly

- Purchase only legitimate software products.
- Install and use software products in accordance with software licences.
- Do not use more copies of the software product than you have licence for.
- Do not bypass or tamper with digital locks or encryptions.
- If you are outsourcing your information technology needs, ensure that your contractor provides you with properly licenced products.
- Establish employee policies and protocols for installation of software on business computers and devices.

Ownership and Assignment of Copyright

The author or creator is deemed to be the first owner of a work and is entitled to its copyright. However, where work is created during the course of employment by an employee whose job it is to create the work, the copyright in the work will belong to the employer. These are the common law rules of ownership in copyright and can be varied by the terms of a contract between the parties. For example, where a freelance writer produces an article, a newspaper can pay the writer to publish it. The freelance writer will own the copyright to the work (unless a contract between them says otherwise). Conversely, the work of a writer who is employed by the newspaper will belong to the employer (unless a contract between them says otherwise). If a book publisher wanted to include the articles in a collection, the publisher would need the permission of the (freelance) writer in the first case but the permission of the (employer) newspaper in the second case.

Independent contractors, like the freelance writer in the example above, own the copyright to their work. This may present a legal risk to businesses that use independent contractors to create copyrights. Where a business contracts with a software developer, for example, to create a software application for the business, the business may want to ensure that the contract suitably addresses the issue of ownership of the software. Conversely, the copyright in photographs taken by a commercial photographer belongs to the photographer. Once again, this highlights the need to ensure that the contract that governs the relationship of a business with an independent contractor hired to do work addresses intellectual property rights. Copyrights, like all forms of property, can be sold. Transfer in ownership of copyright is called assignment. Although not required, it may be prudent for a business that acquires copyright ownership through assignment to register the copyright with CIPO.

Copyright Collectives

The *Copyright Act* permits copyright holders to form collectives for the purpose of administering their rights. Several collectives operate in Canada to administer rights to music, dramatic works, and published works. These collectives negotiate licences with users, collect fees, and distribute royalties to the copyright holders. A business that wishes to use copyrighted materials belonging to others—such as a nightclub that wants to play music or a school that wants to distribute photocopies of a textbook—may contact the appropriate copyright collective to arrange for a licence and pay a fee. Two notable collectives that manage licensing are:

- Access Copyright, which represents many publishers and authors and negotiates with copy centres, libraries, and educational institutions, providing for payment of royalties for photocopying of copyrighted works; and
- SOCAN (Society of Composers, Authors and Music Publishers of Canada), which administers the performing rights of its music industry members by collecting fees in exchange for providing licensing rights to use or perform musical works publicly.

Moral Rights

Moral rights are separate from copyright. They belong to the creator alone. Moral rights may not be assigned to anyone, including an employer or publisher. The following are the three moral rights to the work that the creator has:

moral rights
creator rights to have work properly attributed, not to be altered prejudicially, and not to be used in connection with a product, service, or cause where the use might dishonour the creator's reputation

1. The right to be identified as the author or creator and, if preferred, the right to remain anonymous or use a pseudonym.
2. The right to prevent changes to the work that might dishonour the creator's reputation, such as drawing a moustache on a portrait.
3. The right to prevent the work from being used in association with a product, service, cause, or institution where the association might dishonour the creator's reputation.

While moral rights may not be assigned, they may be waived. In other words, a creator can agree not to enforce their moral rights. Consider an architect's moral rights to a building that is constructed according to the architect's plan. What happens if the owner of the building later decides to renovate and build an addition? If the change dishonours the architect's work, the owner may be prevented from renovating. To preserve future options, business people who hire architects should negotiate a waiver of moral rights. To minimize legal risk, a waiver of moral rights should be part of a written contract.

MINIMIZING YOUR RISK

Protect Your Copyrights

- Use the copyright symbol to remind others to respect your copyright.
- Fix your creations—for example, by recording your conference speech.
- Ensure that those who create works on behalf of your business assign their copyright and waive their moral rights in writing.
- Consider registering important works with the CIPO Copyright Office to establish a presumption that your business is the owner of the work.

Patent Law

A pharmaceutical or technological company would not be willing to invest millions of dollars in research and development if its competitors were free to use and sell the new drugs or technology that it produced. Patent law protects the rights of inventors and the companies that employ them. It encourages individuals and businesses to invest in the research and development necessary to pursue ideas, innovate, and invent.

Patent law prevents others from manufacturing, using, or selling inventions without the permission of the patent holder. However, permission is commonly granted pursuant to licensing agreements, which allow others to use the patented invention in return for a fee.

Scope of Patent Protection

Like the *Copyright Act*, the *Patent Act* is a federal statute enforceable across Canada. Unlike the *Copyright Act*, the *Patent Act* requires that an application be made to the government before it will grant a patent for an invention. There is no automatic right to one's inventions. Inventions require registration. Patent protection demands more effort than copyright protection. Protection of a **patent** is limited to the country in which it is registered. Generally, in order to protect a patent in other countries, a separate application must be filed in each of those countries. However, for those in states that are signatories to the *Patent Cooperation Treaty*, a single international application can be filed and that single application can activate national patent applications in the other PCT states.

patent
government-issued monopoly right to make, sell, or use a new, innovative, and useful invention

The *Patent Act* contains numerous restrictions and complex procedures for obtaining a patent. An expert, such as a patent agent, is generally needed to help guide an applicant through the process.

Length of Protection

A patent is protected for 20 years from the day on which the patent application is filed. In exchange for a patent, the patent holder must disclose the invention to the public in its entirety. Patent applications become public 18 months after they are filed. The requirement to disclose the information about the patent is how patent law attempts to balance the private and public interests in the invention. Although having access to the patent information can provide inspiration for other innovations, the patent protects the invention from being used, sold, or manufactured by others without permission. At the expiration of the 20-year period, however, the invention enters the public domain and can be freely used by anyone.

SCENARIO

Do You Have a Remedy?

Valery is considering applying for a patent for the synthetic enzyme that she developed. However, one of her colleagues from university has horror stories of a patent he registered that was then used by a foreign company to develop a competing product. Her colleague spent many thousands of dollars trying to stop the infringement but got nowhere as the jurisdiction where the foreign company was located had very lax intellectual property laws.

There is a saying in law: "no right without a remedy." Essentially, it means that a legal right protects only so far as there is an effective remedy available to enforce that right. In some countries, weak enforcement of patent infringement can pose a significant risk to businesses. In most countries, it can be very expensive to bring patent infringers to justice. Because the details of the patent must be made public as part of the patent process—and competitors then have access to this information—some businesses are reluctant to patent. Unscrupulous competitors may take advantage of this information and the patent holder may not be able to do much about it without expending considerable resources.

Patent Eligibility

Patents protect inventions that are defined in the *Patent Act* as "an art, process, machine, manufacture or composition of matter." To be eligible to be patented, the invention must be new, useful, and not obvious. Patents will also protect a new and useful improvement of an existing invention.

To be considered new, the invention must not have been published by the applicant more than one year before the applicant submits the patent application. "Publishing" the invention includes displaying it at an invention convention or giving media interviews about it.

Unlike copyrights, for example, which need not have a purpose beyond artistic expression, patents must have some utility. This means that an invention has some "use" as set out in the patent application. A recent Supreme Court decision (see Case in Point, below) has determined that the threshold for utility is quite low, but the invention must be capable of a use specified or predicted in its application.

CASE IN POINT

Utility of a Patent

AstraZeneca Canada Inc v Apotex Inc, 2017 SCC 36

Facts

Pharmaceutical company AstraZeneca had sued generic drug-maker Apotex for infringing the Nexium patent with Apotex's generic version of a stomach-acid drug. Apotex argued that the patent filed by AstraZeneca was invalid because the patent lacked utility on the basis that when AstraZeneca filed its patent application, the patent specification contained a promise for its use that was not demonstrated. The Federal Court ruled in Apotex's favour, basing its decision on a long-standing "promise doctrine": that a patentee's invention should do what it promises and that AstraZeneca's patent was invalid because it fulfilled only one of the two promises of "use" that were specified in its application. AstraZeneca appealed the decision, and the issue of the "promise doctrine" went all the way to the Supreme Court of Canada.

Result

In a unanimous judgment, the Supreme Court overturned the decision and held that application of the "promise doctrine" was inconsistent with the words and scheme of the *Patent Act*. The court held that in granting a patent, once the subject matter of the invention is identified, the issue is whether that subject matter is capable of a practical purpose. Claiming several potential uses in the specifications of a patent application does not set a higher bar for utility. It is sufficient to meet the criteria of utility if a single use related to the subject matter is established (through demonstration or sound prediction). As stated in the decision, the *Patent Act* "does not prescribe the degree or quantum of usefulness required, or that every potential use be realized—a scintilla of utility will do."

Business Lesson

Usefulness is a requirement that must be established and either demonstrated or soundly predicted when an application for patent is filed, but a single use related to the nature of the invention is sufficient. This is helpful to applicants and holders of Canadian patents in research-intensive and patent-heavy fields (including computer technology, household products, natural resources, and biotechnology).

It is important to note that determination of usefulness by the Patent Office does not mean that the product is safe for use, nor does the granting of a patent minimize risk of being sued in tort for injury or harm caused by the invention. Furthermore, usefulness is not measured by market value. For example, a digital salt shaker that measures the portion of salt dispensed to the exactness of a grain could be patentable. The fact that the general public would not have much use for such an invention does not prevent it from passing the "useful" test.

In addition to being new and useful, an invention also must not be obvious. Many patent applications fail this test. For example, in order to be patentable, an improvement in the manufacturing of maple syrup must not be obvious to someone skilled in maple syrup manufacturing.

In summary, patentability requires inventiveness (being something new or improved) and utility (having a useful function) and that the invention not be obvious. Patents can take several forms, as shown in Table 11.2 regarding inventions related to door locks.

Improvements Are Patentable

As noted above, to be patentable an invention must be new in relation to what was known or used previously. This does not mean it must be entirely new. In fact, most inventions build on earlier inventions. This is why the *Patent Act* provides that "improvements" are patentable.

To be patentable, improvements cannot be superficial or cosmetic. The improvement must involve an inventive step. It is important to keep in mind that if an improvement is made on an invention where a patent is still in force, there can still be an infringement of the original patent. If a business invents an improvement to a patented process or machine, it may be required to negotiate a licensing agreement with the owner of the original patent. The *Patent Act* does provide a process by which the original patent owner may be mandated to provide a compulsory licence to the inventor of the improvement. To avoid the legal risks that may arise from improving an existing patent, it is advisable to obtain the assistance of a patent agent.

Not Eligible for Patent Protection

Although processes and methods can be patented, a theory cannot. For example, a patent will not be granted for a new theory of aeronautics. However, a patent can be obtained for the design of an aircraft, the product that results from the practical application of the theory. Scientific principles and mathematical formulas are also not patentable. Consider that while a mathematical formula may be newly discovered, it has always "existed." Similarly, the "discovery" of something that exists in nature, like a new species of plant, is not patentable (whereas new plants invented in a lab are capable of being patented).

Table 11.2 Example: Form of Patentability

Form	Example
Product	A new kind of door lock
Composition of matter	Chemical composition used in lubricant for door lock
Machine	Apparatus for building door locks
Process	A method for making door locks

Source: Canadian Intellectual Property Office, *A Guide to Patents* (Ottawa: Industry Canada, 2010).

Some things in Canada are not patentable as a matter of public policy. A new method of administering medical treatment, for example, may not be patentable on the basis that it should be available for others who may benefit from it (contrast this, however, to the fact that drugs as a form of medical treatment are patentable). As a matter of public policy, Canada does not allow the patenting of "higher life forms." Although Europe, the United States, and Japan allow businesses to patent "higher life forms"—including the genetic material of animals—in Canada, "animals at any stage of development, from fertilized eggs on, are higher life forms and are thus not patentable subject matter." Similarly, although artificial organ-like or tissue-like structures may be patented on a case-by-case basis, organs and tissues themselves are not patentable.

Application for a Patent

As mentioned earlier, unlike copyright law, patent law does not automatically protect an invention. A patent must be registered, and the process starts with the filing of an application with the CIPO Patent Office.

The Patent Office grants a patent to the party who is first to file an application. For example, assume that Lydia and Padma are independently working on a design for a garbage can with a childproof locking mechanism that releases automatically when an adult passes a hand over the bin in a particular manner. The businesses for which Lydia and Padma work each test prototypes of the products. Lydia's company files a patent application on June 13, 2017, and Padma's company files a patent application two days later, on June 15, 2017. Since Lydia's company was first to file the application, Lydia's invention is entitled to patent protection, and Padma's is not. This is the case even if Padma actually invented her garbage can several months before Lydia did.

Efficient filing is often essential to avoid having a competing invention take priority. Consulting a patent agent can help minimize the extensive delays that an applicant may encounter when filing a patent application. Once filed, a patent application can take several years to complete. The process is concluded with a patent examination, which ensures both that the invention complies with the requirements of the legislation and that it has not already been invented. Once the invention successfully passes the examination stage, the Patent Office issues a patent.

Once patented, manufactured goods can use the word "patented" and display the patent number. It is not necessary to do so, but alerting others to the existence of the patent may minimize some risk in potentially having one's patent infringed.

www.emond.ca/CBL3/links

DIG DEEPER

The Canadian Intellectual Property Office website has a database of patent descriptions and images for over 90 years of patents.

Ownership of Patent Rights

Generally, the inventor of the process or product is the first owner and is entitled to the protection of patent law. This means that rights to patents should be expressly addressed in contracts with consultants or other independent contractors who are hired to do research or development work. Even where works are created in the course of employment, the employee inventor may claim rights to the patent as first owner. However, the employer can claim ownership if:

- the invention was made in the course of employment where the employee was specifically hired for that purpose, or
- there is a contract, express or implied, indicating that the employer has rights to the invention of an employee.

Infringement of Patent Rights

A patent grants the owner the exclusive right to make, construct, and use the invention. It also grants the patent owner the right to let others use it or to sell it. Patent infringement claims are the manner in which patent owners enforce these exclusive rights over their invention. Where the nature of one's business exposes it to the possible risk of patent infringement, legal risk management is crucial. The costs and resulting damages of patent litigation can be fatal to a business.

MINIMIZING YOUR RISK

Respect and Protect Inventions

- Negotiate contracts with employees and independent contractors that clearly set out ownership rights to inventions.
- If you determine that your invention is viable, file a patent application without delay.
- Consult a patent agent, because the application process is complex and the stakes may be high.
- Negotiate licensing agreements with patent holders if you intend to use their inventions.

Trademark Law

trademark
unique identifier of brand used to distinguish one company's products or services from those of another

Trademarks are the form of intellectual property most closely tied to commercial activity. **Trademarks** protect the words, symbols, and pictures associated with a business's name, brand, or product. A trademark protects the trademark owner's name (where the name is itself a brand), its brand recognition, and the reputation that accompanies its name and brand recognition. Consider a successful fast food, or soft drink, and the slogans associated with it. As you think of the slogans connected to this product, an image may also come to mind—maybe it is an advertising device, such as Ronald McDonald, or the distinctive colour and design of a soft drink can. Each of these marketing symbols or logos can be protected by trademark law.

Arguably, trademark law is not "intellectual." It does not protect creativity so much as it protects marketing and advertising clout. Trademark rights have more to do with who uses a trademark, and how this leads to brand identification, than with who creates the trademark. Unlike other types of intellectual property law, the primary purpose of trademark law is to facilitate commerce, not to promote innovation.

Types of Trademarks

The following types of marks are covered by the *Trade-marks Act*:

1. *Ordinary marks.* Trademarks may include the name, word or words, letters, numbers, symbols, sounds, slogans, and designs—or any combination of these—that distinguish a business's goods or services. The key feature of these, and of every other trademark, is that they brand the product or service in a way that distinguishes it from its competitors.

2. *Distinguishing guise.* The appearance, shape, colour, and packaging of a product can be characterized as a trademark if these attributes distinguish the product from those of its competitors. Examples of distinguishing guise include a bell-shaped bottle of scotch, gold foil-wrapped chocolates, and pink insulation.
3. *Certification marks.* This type of mark is licenced to businesses for the purpose of showing that their goods or services have met a particular standard, be it the safety or quality of the goods, the place where the goods were produced, or the working conditions of the workers who made them. For example, a product approved by the Canadian Standards Association may be labelled as such. Unions may also permit the labelling of products to indicate that they were produced by unionized labour only. Similarly, certification marks may be used by franchisors to label the products sold by franchisees.

Scope of Trademark Protection

Similar to copyrights, trademarks are afforded protection both in common law and by statute. In other words, both registered and unregistered trademarks are legally protected. Both methods require that a trademark be used in order to claim protection.

Unlike copyrights, ownership of a trademark is not tied to the creator. Ownership of a trademark is determined by usage.

Canadian trademark protection, like patent protection, does not apply in other countries. Therefore, if you own a Canadian trademark and want to protect it in Mexico, for example, you must obtain protection in Mexico as well.

Unlike copyrights, patents, and industrial designs, there is no mandated cut-off for the protection of a trademark in Canada. A trademark can be protected indefinitely as long as it is in use.

Common Law Trademarks

Trademarks do not need to be registered to protect their exclusive use. Unregistered trademarks are also referred to as common law trademarks. A common law trademark is protected where the mark is adopted by the business and is associated with the product or service. Violation of an unregistered trademark is addressed by an action for "passing off," an intentional tort described in Chapter 3. Passing off involves the misrepresentation of a product or business by using a name or mark that is associated with another, similar product or business. To succeed in a lawsuit based on passing off, the plaintiff must prove each of the following elements:

- use of the trademark for sufficient time to demonstrate a market association between the mark and the product or business;
- confusion between a business's trademark and the use of it by a competitor, or misrepresentation by a competitor in connection with the trademark; and
- damage to brand reputation or a loss of sales.

Recall from Chapter 3 that infringement of a trademark does not require that the copy used by a competitor be exactly the same as the original. It need only be sufficiently similar so that confusion may result. Although no symbol needs to be used in relation to a trademark in order for it to be protected, an unregistered trademark can be marked with "TM" to alert others of the intention to protect it. The duration of protection of an unregistered trademark lasts for so long as the trademark is in use in association with the product or service.

Registered Trademarks: Trade-marks Act

The option to register a trademark is governed by the *Trade-marks Act*, a federal statute. A registered trademark is one that has been entered in the Register of Trademarks through the Canadian Intellectual Property Office. Registration of a trademark grants the sole right to use the mark across Canada. Although it is not necessary to do so, the symbol® can used for a registered trademark to indicate that the owner intends to protect against infringement. The Office of the Registrar of Trademarks does not police trademarks. Registrants are responsible for enforcing their rights in the event of any trademark infringement.

Use of a trademark without the owner's consent constitutes trademark infringement. Infringement includes use of a trademark that is confusingly similar to a registered trademark. Where an action for trademark infringement is successful, a court may make any order "appropriate in the circumstances," including an order for damages and an order for destruction of the goods.

Like patent law, trademark law is an extremely specialized area; it would be in an applicant's best interest to look to the guidance of a trademark agent. Applications for registration are processed by the Trademarks Office examiner, who ensures that there are no other applications for a similar trademark and that the mark is registrable.

www.emond.ca/CBL3/links

DIG DEEPER
You can search registered trademarks in Canada at the website of the Canadian Intellectual Property Office.

Registration Is Renewable

Registration of a trademark is valid for 15 years, but with continued use, it can be renewed indefinitely.[2] Trademarks are the only form of registered intellectual property that is renewable.

Advantages of Trademark Registration

Registration requires an application process and payment of fees but doing so provides greater protection over common law trademarks. If a trademark is properly registered under the statute, the owner can bring an action for infringement and prevent others from using the mark, whereas owners of unregistered trademarks must sue for the tort of passing off. The following are some of the advantages of registering a trademark:

- Registration provides a presumption that the trademark is owned by the party that registered it; the duty to disprove this lies with the party that wishes to challenge it.
- Trademark infringement is easier to prove than passing off; passing off requires the plaintiff to prove that use by another has caused market confusion.

2 Note that at the time of this writing, the Government of Canada has introduced a bill to amend the *Trade-marks Act* to harmonize Canada's trademark registration period with that of other countries. If the proposed amendments become law, the renewal period will be reduced from the current 15 years to 10 years (for trademarks registered or re-registered after the legislation comes into effect).

- A registered owner of a trademark needs only to establish use of the trademark, but an owner of a common law trademark needs to prove both use and connection to market reputation.
- Establishing registration infringement does not require proof of damage; unauthorized use of a registered trademark is sufficient to establish infringement. Damages in a passing off action require the plaintiff to prove damage to brand reputation or loss of sales.
- Registration protects trademarks across Canada; common law trademarks are protected only in the geographic area where the business has established a reputation associated with the mark.

Distinctiveness

To qualify for registration, a trademark must be distinctive. A mark is generally something that is visible and separate from the product itself. A chocolate bar would not be subject to trademark protection; however, its name and the logo on the wrapper probably would be. The distinctiveness of made-up words, phrases, and symbols is often straightforward. However, more common words and even colours can be subject to trademark protection if their use over time has associated them exclusively with a particular product or brand.

Trademark: Use It or Lose It

To benefit from protection under the statute, trademarks must be used. As a result, a registered trademark can be expunged from the trademark registry if ongoing usage cannot be established. This "use it or lose it" requirement ties into the notion that the purpose of trademarks is to facilitate commerce and marketing.

Ineligible for Registration

Not all marks are eligible for registration. The following are examples of the types of marks that may be denied registration:

- an official government symbol
- an offensive mark
- the given or family name of someone who is living—including the applicant—or has died within the previous 30 years unless such a given or family name is directly related to the particular good or service (made-up names are acceptable)
- a mark that causes confusion in relation to another registered trademark
- a deceptive or misleading description of the product or its place of origin
- a generic descriptive word that is regularly used to describe the type of product (such as "firm" mattress) and that does not distinguish it from competitive products
- the name of a product that is simply the word for the product in a language other than English or French.

Trademark Infringement: Causing Confusion

The underlying principle in trademark law is that trademarks protect how businesses distinguish their products or services from their competitors. Trademarks are protected from misuse and imitation of the mark by others. The owner of the trademark is entitled to prevent another business from using or registering any trademark so similar that it would confuse members of the public.

The test regarding confusion is whether the similar mark would cause confusion in an ordinary purchaser. An ordinary purchaser is one who is looking to make a purchase in a relatively hurried manner (as opposed to a sophisticated purchaser who deliberates on the product or service). A number of factors may be considered in determining whether a mark may cause confusion in its similarity, including the following:

- Do the marks look or sound alike?
- Is the mark used in a similar market?
- Would an ordinary purchaser think the products or services came from the same source?

It is important to remember that not all similar marks will result in a successful action for trademark infringement. Consider the result in *Mattel, Inc v 3894207 Canada Inc.*

CASE IN POINT

Barbie Doll or Barbie-Q?

Mattel, Inc v 3894207 Canada Inc, 2006 SCC 22

Facts

A toy manufacturer that produces a well-known doll with the trademark "Barbie" opposed the application of the owner of a small chain of restaurants in the Montreal area to register its "Barbie's" trademark and a related design. The restaurant owner had used "Barbie's" as a trademark since 1992 to designate its restaurant, takeout, catering, and banquet services. The Trade-marks Opposition Board allowed the registration on the basis that use of the trademark "Barbie's" was unlikely to create confusion in the marketplace. Both the trial and appeal divisions of the Federal Court upheld the board's decision. The toy manufacturer appealed to the Supreme Court of Canada.

Result

The Supreme Court dismissed the toy manufacturer's appeal. Although trademarks are now recognized as among the most valuable of business assets, their legal purpose is to distinguish their owner's wares or services from those of others. A mark is both a guarantee of origin and an assurance to consumers that the quality of goods or services will be what they have come to expect. In the circumstances, the board acted reasonably in deciding that there was no possibility that a hypothetical purchaser—that is, a casual consumer in somewhat of a hurry—would be confused by the marks in the marketplace.

Business Lesson

Be aware that trademarks that resemble those of famous products may be open to expensive challenges before the courts. However, also consider that the relevant test is confusion and that the use of even famous trademarks is open to analysis on a case-by-case basis.

Loss of Protection: Trademarks That Become Generic

In addition to ensuring that the trademark is in use, businesses need to ensure that they take steps to prevent others from using the trademark when it occurs without authorization. Not enforcing one's trademarks may result in losing rights, even if the trademark is registered, if others are using the term to describe similar products.

Figure 11.1

Google is continuously taking steps to protect its trademark and prevent "googling" from becoming a generic term for Internet searching.

When this happens, the original trademark loses its claim of distinctiveness. For example, "zipper," "trampoline," "linoleum," and "escalator" are examples of words that were originally trademarks but that have lost protection by becoming generic terms used to describe the item instead of the specific brand. Interestingly, Google has taken steps in an effort to prevent its trademark from becoming a generic term used to describe Internet searches conducted by any search engine.[3]

Trademark Versus Trade Name

The terms "trademark" and "trade name" are often thought to be the same but there is a distinction between the two. A **trade name** is the name in which a business operates. Not all business names are trademarks. However, a trade name may be a trademark if the name is used to identify goods or services. A business or trade name can have great value for a business by linking the business's reputation with the quality of its goods or services. Trademark law protects the business name where it is used in this way. For example, if XYZ Ltd is a business that produces frozen pizzas and the product is identified with this name (that is, XYZ Ltd is on the product's packaging), then the trade name can also be a trademark. However, if the consumer does not identify this pizza with the trade name because the pizzas are called "Pop-A-Pizza," then "Pop-A-Pizza" is the trademark and XYZ Ltd is the trade name. Generally, registration of a business name is under provincial jurisdiction. Registration of a business name does not, in and of itself, warrant against trademark infringement.

trade name
name in which a business operates

3 See Suzanne Choney, "No Googling, Says Google—Unless You Really Mean It," *NBC News* (26 March 2013), online: <https://www.nbcnews.com/tech/internet/no-googling-says-google-unless-you-really-mean-it-f1C9078566>.

Adoption of a trademark may prevent the use of an identical or similar trade name. The reverse is also true: a trade name may prevent someone from using the same or similar name as a trademark. Even where registered, a trademark may be cancelled if someone else in Canada has made use of a similar trade name (or trademark) in the past. To understand this, it helps to think of trademarks as a form of consumer protection in that they help prevent confusion in the public. A key question to consider is the similarity of the product or service and whether use of the name will cause confusion. Because a trade name can be an unregistered trademark, a business should search trade name registries as well as the trademark registry before deciding on a name. Since trade names are registered provincially, there is no single list of trade names in Canada. Hiring a trademark agent to ensure a thorough search of trademark and trade name registries can help reduce legal risk.

Trademarks and Domain Names

domain name
unique address of a website

Domain name refers to the unique address of a website. A legal dispute can arise from the registration of a domain name that is another's trademark.

Domain names are issued on a first come, first served basis by the administering authority. There are country-specific domains; for example, ".ca" denotes a Canadian website and is administered by the Canadian Internet Registration Authority (CIRA). Additionally, there are generic domains (for example, ".com," ".org," ".net") that are controlled by a US non-profit corporation known as ICANN (Internet Corporation for Assigned Names and Numbers).

cyber-squatting
registering trademarks as domain names in bad faith

Registering a domain name for an illegitimate purpose is known as **cyber-squatting**. Cyber-squatting is the registration of a domain name that is the trademark of another, done in bad faith for the purpose of either preventing the trademark owner from using the domain name or for the purpose of selling the domain name to the trademark owner. Often, cyber-squatters use the website as a means of advertising their own products or services directly or to redirect traffic to another website for that purpose.

In cases where a domain name has been registered in bad faith, the trademark owner can use a dispute resolution process available through the domain name issuing authority (CIRA or ICANN). A successful complaint can result in the cancellation of the domain name or the transfer of the domain name to the complainant. The complainant will need to establish that:

- the domain name is identical to the trademark or similar enough to cause confusion,
- the registrant of the domain name did not have a legitimate interest in it, and
- the registrant is using the name in bad faith.

MINIMIZING YOUR RISK

Respect and Protect Trademarks

- Be original in your packaging, brand names, and slogans; search trademark and trade name registries to minimize legal risk of infringing the trademarks of others.
- Keep your trademarks in use; trademarks that are abandoned are not protected.
- Use your trademark properly to prevent it from becoming generic: do not use your trademark as a verb or noun or in any manner that makes it a general term to describe the product.

- Use the symbol ® or ™ after your mark, as appropriate (particularly as you begin to establish its use in association with your product or service).
- Police your trademarks: ensure that your marks are not being used without permission, and take action to prevent use of your trademark if this occurs.
- Consider whether your trademarks should be registered; consult a trademark agent.
- Do not use the trademarks of another in any way, including digital platforms, without authorization.

Industrial Design Law

Industrial design law protects the visual appearance of a product, including its shape, pattern, ornament, or configuration, or a combination of these.

The law that governs **industrial design** fills a gap left by copyright law, which does not generally cover mass-produced goods. The difference between a copyright and an industrial design, therefore, is that industrial design applies where the design is reproduced by an industrial process. The *Industrial Design Act* offers creators of artistic works that are mass-produced an opportunity to protect their designs from use by others. Like the other intellectual property statutes discussed in this chapter, the *Industrial Design Act* is a federal statute enforceable across Canada.

industrial design
government-granted exclusive right to make, sell, and use an ornamental feature, shape, or configuration

Scope of Industrial Design Protection

Like patents, industrial designs must be registered, and protection is time-limited. An industrial design cannot be registered until six months after the application is filed. A registered industrial design is protected for ten years.

Because industrial design is based on visual appearance, it contains a non-functional element. For example, the basic shape of a potato peeler is dictated by its function and does not create an industrial design. However, the distinctive curves, angles, and other decorative features of the particular potato peeler may qualify for protection as an industrial design if these features are sufficiently novel. Similarly, a standard rectangular swimming pool may not qualify as an industrial design, but a pool shaped like a poplar leaf might.

The owner of a registered industrial design has the sole right to use it when manufacturing the product and can prevent others, when manufacturing a competing product, from copying or imitating the design. A business that wants to own the industrial designs created by its employees and consultants can establish its ownership rights contractually. Such a contractual arrangement eliminates the risk that an employee or consultant will later claim ownership of a design that the company believes to be its own.

Once registered, industrial designs can carry the symbol Ⓓ followed by the design owner's name. There is more reason to use the industrial design symbol than in other forms of intellectual property protection. Whereas the symbol is not necessary to legally prevent others from infringing the industrial design, use of the symbol allows the owner to claim damages as well as an injunction.

Registration

To be protected, industrial designs must be registered with the Industrial Design Office, which, like other offices that register various forms of intellectual property, is part of the Canadian Intellectual Property Office. The office will not register industrial designs that have been disclosed previously or used before the one-year period preceding the application. The design must be original and not similar to a previously registered design.

An industrial design must be applied to a finished product. This means that the application must describe not only the design but also the product or products to which the design is applied. For example, to register a poplar leaf design for a swimming pool as an industrial design, the application must also describe the pool. Registration will apply to a pool only. It will not prevent another company from manufacturing plates shaped like a poplar leaf.

Functional aspects of a design are not protected by industrial design law. If a functional component of a design is a new invention, the creator can apply for industrial design for the visual aspect but should apply for patent for the new mechanism.

Infringement

Infringement of industrial design occurs when anyone copies, sells, rents, imports, or manufactures a registered industrial design without permission. An injunction is the most common order made for industrial design infringement. A successful civil action for industrial design infringement can also result in an award for damages where the product was properly marked with the industrial design symbol on its label or packaging.

MINIMIZING YOUR RISK

Respect and Protect Industrial Designs

- If your business creates designs intended for mass production, be original in your designs; employ consultants and staff who prefer to work creatively than to recycle thinly veiled copies of the work of others.
- Don't wait too long to apply for industrial design protection, as eligibility for registration will be lost after one year of the design becoming public.
- Ensure that employment or consultant contracts set out ownership of the industrial designs created in those relationships.
- Register your industrial designs—it is your only way to protect them.
- Properly mark design packaging or labels with the industrial design symbol.

Trade Secrets and Confidential Business Information

trade secret
recipe, method, process, data, or know-how of a business that is confidential, that has actual or potential value in not being generally known, and where efforts are made to keep it a secret

confidential business information
information that provides a business advantage by being kept secret

Trade secrets are categorized as intellectual property because they take the form of intangible assets deserving of legal protection. **Trade secrets** include technical information—such as recipes, formulas, or methods—that provides a business advantage over competitors who do not have it. Trade secrets are a form of confidential business information and, over time, these terms have come to be used interchangeably. **Confidential business information** is a term that more broadly includes supplier pricing, customer lists, planned advertising campaigns, designs, blueprints, financial information, business plans, and other types of strategic business information that is not generally known.

Confidential business information, including trade secrets, is information a business does not want disclosed to the public (or to competitors). Unlike with the other forms of intellectual property discussed above, no specific statutory provision sets out rules for confidential business information. The protection of confidential information and trade secrets is recognized in the common law principles that have developed over time in court decisions.

Confidential information, including trade secrets, has value to a business. Its value is often monetary and depends—at least in part—on it remaining confidential. **Breach of confidence** is a tort and will hold a party liable for violating the duty to keep information confidential. The law, however, will not protect information that a business has not itself taken efforts to protect. In this section, we will examine how confidential business information can be protected and what gives rise to the duty of confidentiality.

breach of confidence disclosure of information that one was legally required to keep confidential, resulting in harm

Scope of Protection

Confidential business information and trade secrets may be protected indefinitely as long as the following conditions are met:

- The information is not generally known in the industry.
- The information represents a business advantage; generally, it has economic value (or potential economic value) as a result of not being commonly known.
- Efforts have been made to keep the information from becoming generally known.

Secret recipes are examples of confidential business information that can be maintained for a long time. For example, the formula for Coca Cola has been a trade secret for over 130 years. Other types of information may be protected as confidential for a relatively short period of time. Confidential business information loses its legal protection when the information is no longer secret either because the business has failed to protect it or because it has become generally known. For example, the design of a new model vehicle by a car manufacturer may be confidential business information during its development; however, once the new model is revealed at a car show, the car company can no longer claim it as secret. Similarly, research and development work will often be done with a great deal of protection for its secrecy, but if the work leads to application for a patent, the nature of patent law will require its disclosure, at which point it will no longer have the protection of a trade secret.

Duty of Confidentiality

The legal obligation to maintain confidential information can arise in a number of ways, for example:

- expressly stated in contract
- implied by contract
- arising from a fiduciary relationship
- created by nature of special relationship or circumstances.

Businesses that want to claim protection over confidential information must take steps to maintain its secrecy. On the other hand, it is sometimes necessary to share information in confidence in order to conduct business. Investors, contractors, and

SCENARIO

Patent or Trade Secret?

Should Valery patent the synthetic enzyme she created or guard it as a trade secret? Here are some of the issues she will want to consider:

	Advantages	However . . .
Patent	Valery will have an intellectual property right in the patented enzyme. She will be able to control how it is used in the countries in which she obtains a patent.	It can take years to complete the review and approval process to obtain a patent and it can be expensive, particularly if she wants patent protection in many countries.
	The patented enzyme cannot legally be manufactured, copied, or sold without Valery's permission.	It can be expensive and time-consuming to enforce patent rights. Enforcement may not be effective in jurisdictions with limited intellectual property rights protections or weak enforcement.
	The patent can be sold (to Val-Nam, for example) or licensed. This can be a significant source of income.	Because the details of the invention must be publicly disclosed as part of the patenting process, this information is made available to the world. Unscrupulous competitors can use this information without obtaining a licence, etc. and Valery's only remedy may be an expensive legal challenge.
	Public disclosure of the details of the invention may encourage additional improvements and requests for licences.	Because a patent is very specific, an unscrupulous competitor could modify the synthetic enzyme with just enough differences to allow it to patent that product, thus getting around Valery's patent.
	The patent lasts for 20 years.	Once it expires, anyone can use the invention.
Trade secret	It can be very cheap to protect. If only Valery needs to know the details, she could keep them secret from the world.	As the business expands, additional individuals may need to know the details of the invention. As more individuals know this confidential information, there is a greater risk that it will be disclosed.
	The trade secret can be immediately protected simply by keeping it a secret.	That protection can also immediately be lost if the secret is disclosed. Once control over the information is lost, there is no protection.
	A trade secret never "expires." As long as it is kept a secret, it is protected from use by others.	If someone else develops the invention and then patents it before Valery, she will lose the right to use it.

Valery will want to discuss these and other implications with a patent agent or other expert before making a decision on how best to protect her invention.

consultants, as well as higher-level employees, are examples of business associates with whom information may need to be shared. Express contractual terms regarding confidential information can be a vital tool in minimizing legal risk. Confidentiality may be a term of a broader contract, including an employment contract, or of a stand-alone **non-disclosure agreement** (NDA). Either way, contracts provide an essential mechanism for protecting information from being shared by the recipient (confidentiality clauses are discussed in Chapter 9 under the heading "Contractual Restrictive Covenants").

non-disclosure agreement
contract that legally obligates a party to confidentiality

Although expressly setting out the duty of confidentiality in a contract is a best practice, confidentiality can also be an implied term of a contract. Businesses that do work for other companies that disclose confidential information to them should be careful with such information and not rely on the fact that there is no written contract or confidentiality clause. Similarly, there is generally an implied duty of confidentiality for higher-level employees who are entrusted with sensitive business information. Note that express or implied confidentiality terms do not prevent an employee or consultant from using the skills they have acquired in the course of their work for another employer or client. The general nature of the skills they have acquired is transferable to their next job—but the confidential information is not.

The obligation to maintain confidentiality exists in all **fiduciary** relationships and other positions of trust. Professionals who provide consulting, advice, and professional services may be in a position of trust in relation to the client. Partners are fiduciaries to each other and officers of a corporation have a fiduciary obligation to the company. An agent has a fiduciary relationship with the principal. Fiduciaries have a common law duty not to disclose confidential information and not to use it for their own benefit.

fiduciary
based on trust and confidence

Beyond fiduciary relationships, the common law has expanded to recognize that the obligation to maintain confidentiality exists where the circumstances themselves create the legal duty. The Case in Point, below, demonstrates that the duty of confidentiality can arise during the process of negotiating a business deal and continues even if the business deal falls through.

Breach of Confidence

Breach of confidence can result in damages, injunction, and other remedies, including punitive damages. Three factors are needed to establish breach of confidence:

1. The information was confidential.
2. The information was communicated to the recipient in confidence.
3. The information was misused by the recipient to the detriment of the party that disclosed it.

CASE IN POINT

Information Obtained in Confidence

Lac Minerals Ltd v International Corona Resources Ltd, [1989] 2 SCR 574

Facts

Corona was a mining company investigating the gold mining potential on a property in northwestern Ontario adjacent to property it already owned. Lac Minerals was a mining company that heard about Corona's geological explorations and arranged to visit the site. Detailed information was disclosed by Corona to Lac's representatives about the adjacent property, including geological findings, drilling plans, and potential of large gold reserves over a wide area of the property. Corona and Lac entered into discussions about a joint venture. Corona shared financial information with Lac. The issue of confidentiality was not raised. Lac advised Corona to aggressively pursue purchase of the property, but shortly after, negotiation for the joint venture broke down. Having received the confidential information, and without the knowledge of Corona, Lac proceeded to make a much higher offer and purchase the property itself. Lac went on to develop the property, which turned out to be the biggest gold mine in Canada, resulting in huge profits for Lac. Corona sued and the matter ultimately reached the Supreme Court of Canada.

Result

Despite there being no confidentiality agreement between the parties, the court found that the circumstances in which the information was communicated gave rise to a duty of confidentiality, that the information shared was confidential, and that it was misused by Lac for its own gain at the expense of Corona. The Supreme Court of Canada found Lac liable for breach of confidence and transferred the property to Corona.

Business Lesson

A duty of confidentiality can arise not only by way of contractual obligation but also from the nature of the relationship between the parties. Parties should not misuse confidential information that is disclosed to them in confidence. Negotiation of a business deal can create the circumstances in which a duty of confidentiality exists even without a non-disclosure agreement in place.

MINIMIZING YOUR RISK

Respect and Protect Confidential Business Information

- Include confidentiality clauses in employment contracts.
- Execute non-disclosure agreements when engaging outside contractors or consultants (including IT professionals).
- Safeguard your confidential information by limiting who has access to it and establishing strict access protocols for secret information.
- Do not misuse the confidential information entrusted to you in your business relationships.

Privacy: Safeguarding Personal Information

In discussing intellectual property, we examined the legal aspects of confidential business information and how a business can protect its business secrets. In this section, we turn to the legal risks a business can be exposed to when it comes into possession of personal information belonging to others. Businesses are custodians of any personal information they collect. They have legal obligations related to the collection, use, disclosure, and general safeguarding of the personal information of others. The law governing privacy is of critical concern to all businesses, particularly in the age where electronic data collection has become an essential aspect of doing business.

PIPEDA and the Collection, Use, and Disclosure of Personal Information

Canada has federal legislation that regulates the protection of privacy and applies to all jurisdictions that don't have substantially similar legislation of their own. Some provinces (Quebec, British Columbia, Alberta) have enacted their own legislation.

All other provinces and territories are governed by the federal legislation: the *Personal Information Protection and Electronic Documents Act* (PIPEDA). Ontario has provincial legislation that applies to personal information collected in the health care sector, but otherwise, PIPEDA applies to how businesses collect, use, and disclose consumers' personal information (the obligations of businesses with respect to the personal information of its employees is dealt with in Chapter 9).

PIPEDA defines "personal information" as any information about an identifiable individual. This includes information—in any form—such as name, age, identification numbers of any kind, ethnic origin, blood type, opinions, and social status; it also includes records of an individual including medical, credit, employment, and so on. PIPEDA requires that businesses obtain the consent of individuals in collecting their personal information and that the information be used only for the pre-identified purpose consented to. PIPEDA applies to all personal information collected, used, or disclosed in the course of "commercial activities" (i.e., customer/consumer information) and it applies to small businesses as well as major corporations, even where business is conducted wholly online.

PIPEDA was established to promote best practices, but a complaint by a customer about the handling of their personal information may be made to the Office of the Privacy Commissioner of Canada, an agent of government, so there is a risk of legal sanction for any business that fails to comply with the regulations. The Privacy Commissioner has the power to investigate complaints, and issues can end up in federal court, where damages can be awarded to a complainant. A **privacy breach** occurs when personal information is collected, used, or disclosed in a manner that was not authorized. Privacy breaches can cause personal harm; result in financial loss; effect damage to reputation, credit, business relationships, and opportunities; and lead to identity theft.

privacy breach unauthorized access to, or disclosure of, personal information

Information Security and Compliance

Businesses that handle information electronically need to manage the security of the data they possess and pay particular attention to the risk of information being intercepted during transmission. Businesses that do not have in-house information technology specialists should seek professional assistance from consultants to establish protocols for safely managing data and protecting it from hackers. Where data is transmitted electronically, encryption and other security measures should be implemented.

Individuals from whom personal information has been collected have the right to request access to their information, to challenge its accuracy and completeness, and to know how it is being used or disclosed. PIPEDA requires business organizations to designate an individual who will be accountable for compliance with the regulatory framework for protecting personal information. These requirements include:

- identifying and documenting the purpose for which personal information is collected;
- obtaining consent from individuals for the collection, use, and/or disclosure of personal information;
- limiting the collection of information to that which is necessary for the purpose that has been pre-identified and consented to, and ensuring that it is not used or disclosed for any other purpose;

- keeping accurate, up-to-date, and complete records of information collected, and retaining information only for so long as is necessary to fulfill the purpose for which it was collected;
- safeguarding the security of the information; and
- informing individuals of the organization's policies and practices for managing personal information and developing and implementing complaint procedures.

Where a privacy breach occurs through theft, unauthorized disclosure, or a violation of the business's security safeguards, steps to minimize risk must be taken immediately and may require self-reporting of the breach to the Privacy Commissioner.

MINIMIZING YOUR RISK

Protecting Personal Information

- Use knowledgeable and capable information technology specialists to establish and securely maintain data management systems.
- Establish policies and protocols for the proper handling of personal information by employees.
- Use encryption and other mechanisms to safeguard electronic transmission of data.
- Appoint a PIPEDA compliance officer who is responsible for ensuring that personal information is being used, collected, and disclosed lawfully.

Electronic Communications: Complying with the Law

Canada's Anti-Spam Legislation

Businesses that use electronic forms of messaging need to be aware of Canada's Anti-Spam Legislation (CASL), which addresses unwanted commercial electronic messages sent by email, text, or social networking platforms. Despite its name, the legislation's reach goes well beyond what would typically be considered "spam"; sending an electronic message with any amount of commercial content to someone who has not consented to receiving it can present significant risk to a business. Organizations that don't comply with CASL can face penalties of up to $10 million.

commercial electronic message
message sent electronically that contains commercial promotion of any kind

A **commercial electronic message** (CEM) is one that encourages participation in a commercial activity, even in a minor way. Emails, for example, that contain information about promotions, events, offers, or business opportunities (and that may include links to websites that contain commercial promotions) are CEMs. Messaging is not limited to text but includes sound, voice, images, and video. Generally, CASL prohibits the sending of CEMs unless the sender has the recipient's consent. Note that the law applies to communications sent directly or indirectly; businesses that use a third-party agent to market or promote their goods and services will be responsible for communications sent on their behalf. In the event of a complaint, the CASL requires that the sender prove consent. Compliance with CASL requires that:

- all messages must be permission-based; recipients need to have opted in to receive communications;
- all messages must contain an easy-to-find unsubscribe link; recipients who ask to be unsubscribed must be removed from the message distribution list within ten days;
- the subject line of the message must pertain to the content of the message; it should not be misleading or false; and
- the message must identify the sender's name, business, and contact information.

CASE IN POINT

Porter Airlines Inc Undertakes to Pay $150,000 for CASL Violations (2015)

Canadian Radio-television and Telecommunications Commission, "Undertaking: Porter Airlines" (29 June 2015), File No 9109-201500402-001, online: <http://crtc.gc.ca/eng/archive/2015/ut150629.htm>.

Facts

Porter Airlines Inc ("Porter") was investigated by the Canadian Radio-television and Telecommunications Commission ("CRTC") for (1) alleged violations of the CASL concerning the sending of CEMs that did not set out an unsubscribe mechanism "clearly and prominently" or were missing an unsubscribe mechanism and (2) failure to honour an unsubscribe request within ten business days. Porter also did not provide complete identification information in email messages and was unable to provide proof of consent for some of the email addresses it had sent messages to.

Result

Porter agreed to an undertaking to pay $150,000 and consented to update its compliance program. Porter's cooperation with the CRTC and prompt remedial action to address the violations led to a resolution and was a mitigating factor in the outcome.

Business Lesson

This case underscores the importance of complying with the CASL requirements. Businesses should ensure they keep records of consent to send electronic communications. The onus of demonstrating proof of consent will be on the sender.

Exceptions to CASL

There are a number of exceptions to the consent requirements for electronic communications. The regulations do not apply to messages sent within an organization or between organizations with an existing business relationship. Other exceptions include:

- communications sent in response to requests, inquiries, or complaints, or to satisfy legal obligations;
- communications providing a quote or estimate for products or services, where requested by the recipient;
- communications providing product updates or upgrades, warranty, product recall, or safety information relating to a product the recipient has purchased.

MINIMIZING YOUR RISK

Ensure Commercial Electronic Communications Comply with the Law

- Do not send commercial electronic communications to recipients unless you have their consent.
- Have a system in place to store and retrieve consents.
- Ensure commercial electronic communications have an unsubscribe link and that it works.
- Do not use misleading or false messaging in subject lines; the subject line should correspond to the purpose of the message.
- Make sure those operating your email and other messaging programs are trained to understand the legal requirements of sending commercial electronic messages.

CHAPTER SUMMARY

Intellectual property law provides opportunity to individuals and businesses to generate value from the product of their ideas, creations, and innovations. Intellectual property laws protect copyrights, trademarks, patents, and industrial designs by providing remedies for those who own these property rights, should their rights be violated by others.

Similarly, the law recognizes that confidential business information and trade secrets that provide businesses with a competitive advantage require legal protection against disclosure. Contractual terms and business relationships can give rise to legal obligations relating to confidentiality with corresponding legal risks for breach of confidence.

Privacy law regulates the collection, use, and disclosure of personal information. The *Personal Information Protection and Electronic Documents Act* protects personal and sensitive information about consumers by requiring businesses to comply with rules and procedures regarding such information. Consumers may complain about the handling of their personal information to the Office of the Privacy Commissioner of Canada. Statutory requirements also impose legal obligations in relation to commercial electronic messages.

The way business is conducted will continue to be affected by innovative technologies in an ever-expanding digital society, and the law will continue to evolve with these advancements. Identifying and managing legal risk, therefore, must be a continuous process.

KEY TERMS

assignment, 393
breach of confidence, 413
commercial electronic message, 418
confidential business information, 412
copyright, 395
cyber-squatting, 410
domain name, 410
fair dealing, 397
fiduciary, 415
industrial design, 411
infringement, 397
licence, 393
moral rights, 399
non-disclosure agreement, 415
patent, 400
piracy, 397
privacy breach, 417
public domain, 395
trademark, 404
trade name, 409
trade secret, 412

REFERENCES

An Act to promote the efficiency and adaptability of the Canadian economy by regulating certain activities that discourage reliance on electronic means of carrying out commercial activities, and to amend the Canadian Radio-television and Telecommunications Commission Act, the Competition Act, the Personal Information Protection and Electronic Document Act and the Telecommunications Act, SC 2010, c 23 [the Act that implemented changes to a range of other Acts that together are referred to as "Canada's Anti-Spam Legislation"].

AstraZeneca Canada Inc v Apotex Inc, 2017 SCC 36.

Berne Convention for the Protection of Literary and Artistic Works, 9 September 1886, S Treaty Doc No 99-27 (1986) (as revised at Paris on 24 July 1971 and amended in 1979).

Canadian Copyright Licensing Agency v York University, 2017 FC 669.

Canadian Radio-television and Telecommunications Commission, "Undertaking: Porter Airlines" (29 June 2015), File No 9109-201500402-001, online: <http://crtc.gc.ca/eng/archive/2015/ut150629.htm>.

CCH Canadian Ltd v Law Society of Upper Canada, 2004 SCC 13.

Copyright Act, RSC 1985, c C-42.

Industrial Design Act, RSC 1985, c I-9.

LAC Minerals Ltd v International Corona Resources Ltd, [1989] 2 SCR 574.

Mattel, Inc v 3894207 Canada Inc, 2006 SCC 22.

Patent Act, RSC 1985, c P-4.

Personal Information Protection and Electronic Documents Act, SC 2000, c 5.

Trade-marks Act, RSC 1985, c T-13.

EXERCISES

True or False?

____ **1.** In order to be protected, copyrights must be accompanied by the © symbol.

____ **2.** In exchange for the monopoly given under the *Patent Act*, the owner of the patent must disclose the invention in its entirety.

____ **3.** It is possible for a trademark to lose protection if it is not being used, even if it is registered.

____ **4.** The most advantageous way to protect the distinctive design of a product container is by registration of industrial design.

____ **5.** The most effective way to protect a recipe or formula is to register it under the *Trade Secrets Act*.

____ **6.** A trademark infringement can occur by use of a mark that is not exactly the same but is similar enough to cause confusion.

____ **7.** Registered trademarks can be searched at the Canadian Intellectual Property Office's database, which is available online.

____ **8.** In order to sue for breach of confidence, a confidentiality agreement must exist between the parties.

____ **9.** Even though PIPEDA is federal legislation, it applies to the private sector in Ontario.

____ **10.** Commercial electronic messages are regulated provincially, which means businesses must comply with the anti-spam legislation of the province in which the business is registered.

Multiple Choice

1. Which of the following forms of intellectual property are protected in the common law, as well as by statute?
- **a.** trademarks and industrial designs
- **b.** patents and copyrights
- **c.** copyrights and trademarks
- **d.** industrial designs and patents

2. Which of the following forms of registered protection is renewable?
- **a.** copyrights
- **b.** trademarks
- **c.** industrial designs
- **d.** patents

3. In order for copyrights to be protected, creative works must …
- **a.** be original works that are expressed in some fixed form.
- **b.** be original ideas.
- **c.** be registered with the Copyrights Office.
- **d.** be in use.

4. Which of the following is not a moral right to copyright?
- **a.** The creator of the work is entitled to have their name associated with it.
- **b.** The creator of the work can prevent the work from being in a way that harms its reputation.
- **c.** The creator of the work can prevent the work from being used in association with a cause.
- **d.** The creator of the work can prevent the owner from making excessive profits from it.

5. Which statement is incorrect?
   a. Industrial designs are decorative, not functional.
   b. Inventions that are improvements to other inventions may be patented.
   c. Patents must be useful and have market value.
   d. Trademark law is based on a tort.
6. Which of the following statements about patentable inventions is not correct?
   a. The rightful owner of the invention is, in all cases, the inventor.
   b. The invention may be a significant improvement of another invention.
   c. Registration expires after 20 years and is non-renewable.
   d. The invention must have some useful purpose.
7. In regards to the advantages of registering a trademark, which of the following statements is not correct?
   a. Registration of a trademark provides registrant with the presumption of ownership in the trademark.
   b. The Canadian Intellectual Property Office monitors use of trademarks for infringement by third parties.
   c. Registration of a trademark protects it across Canada.
   d. Infringement of a registered trademark is easier to prove than passing off.
8. Which of the following is not correct in regards to confidential business information?
   a. A company's shareholders owe a duty of confidentiality to its corporate officers.
   b. Information that is generally known in the industry cannot be protected as a trade secret.
   c. Confidentiality may be an implied term of an employment contract.
   d. A successful claim for breach of confidence can result in damages as well as an injunction.
9. Which of the following is not a harm that is associated with a privacy breach resulting from the unauthorized disclosure of personal information:
   a. financial loss
   b. identity theft
   c. loss of business opportunity
   d. infringement of copyright
10. Consider Canada's anti-spam legislation (CASL) and select the statement that is incorrect:
   a. Compliance with CASL requires consent from the recipient of commercial electronic messages.
   b. Unlike emails, commercial electronic text messages do not require an unsubscribe option.
   c. Subject lines that are false or misleading may infringe the CASL.
   d. Consent is not required to send emails regarding product recalls to a customer who has purchased the product.

Short Answer

1. If copyright law applies to sculptures, what is the point of industrial design law?
2. Name two types of marks covered by the *Trade-marks Act*.
3. Explain the difference between copyright and patent in terms of the types of property that each protects.
4. Explain the concept of fair dealing.

Apply Your Knowledge

1. Explain whether the law protects confidential information in the following situations:
   a. Uncle Bill's Bonbons is a family business that uses secret recipes passed down from the founder's grandmother. Its employees know that these recipes are not to be disclosed to customers or competitors. One of the chefs leaves to found a company that produces strikingly similar products using identical ingredients.
   b. Uncle Bill's Bonbons holds a contest asking its customers to submit their best cookie recipe. The winning recipe is posted in its store. A competitor begins to sell cookies based on the recipe.
   c. Emily's Edibles independently arrives at a manufacturing process that exactly duplicates the creamy texture of Uncle Bill's chocolate pudding.
2. Ricky owns a music production company with his partner, Alyssa. Ricky is a huge fan of Mozart and would like to start reproducing his work in the form of a dance music track. Alyssa explains to Ricky that she can no longer be a part of the project as she firmly believes that they will violate the *Copyright Act* by using Mozart's work. What should Alyssa be advised of and why?

Glossary

acceleration clause contractual term providing that payment of an entire debt becomes due on default

accommodation human rights concept that refers to making changes that allow a person or group protected by the *Human Rights Code* to participate in the workplace

act of bankruptcy inability to pay debts as they come due or commission of fraudulent or evasive acts to avoid creditors

administrative agency government body that administers and enforces a particular area of law

administrative law body of rules applied to monitor decision-making powers of government agencies

administrative tribunal government body that has decision-making power regarding an administrative matter

adverse impact discrimination workplace policy that unintentionally affects certain groups in a detrimental way

agency agreement contract between principal and agent that describes the agent's rights and authority

agent person who has the authority to act on another's behalf

aggravated damages a subcategory of non-pecuniary damages awarded for intangible harm, such as harm to reputation or humiliation

agreement of purchase and sale legal contract that obligates the buyer to buy and the seller to sell

alternative dispute resolution (ADR) settlement of conflict through a process other than the court system

amortization period length of time required to pay entire mortgage debt

articles of incorporation document that creates a corporation

assault tort in which the defendant threatens the plaintiff with physical harm

assignment transfer of ownership in intellectual property

bailee party in a bailment that is in temporary possession of the bailor's personal property

bailment legal relationship that arises when personal property is borrowed, rented, stored, or found by a person other than its owner

bailor party in a bailment that owns the personal property

balance of probabilities standard of proof in civil (as opposed to criminal) law indicating that one version of events is more probable than another

bargaining unit group of the employer's employees whom the trade union is entitled to represent

battery tort in which the defendant engages in unwanted physical contact with the plaintiff

beyond a reasonable doubt standard of proof that the prosecutor must meet in a criminal trial in order for a defendant to be found guilty

bid-rigging when, in response to a call for bids, a person enters into an agreement with one or more other persons and the person agrees not to submit a bid, to withdraw their bid, or to coordinate their bid with the other person(s)

bill of exchange document signed by a drawer ordering a drawee to pay a specified sum to a payee immediately or on a later fixed date

bona fide occupational requirement (BFOR) reasonably necessary job qualification or requirement imposed because it is necessary for job performance

breach of confidence disclosure of information that one was legally required to keep confidential, resulting in harm

breach of contract failure to fulfill contractual obligations

burden of proof requirement that a certain party prove a particular fact at trial

business structure form of carrying on business that dictates key aspects of a business's creation and operation

caisse populaire credit union based primarily in Quebec but also operating for francophone clientele in other parts of Canada

cartel an association of manufacturers, distributors, or retailers who agree to fix prices or otherwise coordinate efforts in order to limit competition

caveat emptor Latin maxim that translates roughly to "buyer beware"

certification approval by a labour relations board that gives a union the right to negotiate on behalf of a bargaining unit

charge term used for a mortgage under the land titles system

chattels movable, tangible property

cheque negotiable instrument under which the drawee banking institution pays the payee from the bank account of the payer

choses in action intangible personal property, such as negotiable instruments, insurance claims, and shares in a corporation

civil law system system of law where all rules are established in statute and courts lack authority to act without a statute; judges in civil law systems are not bound by the doctrine of precedent and have the freedom to interpret statutes independently of previous decisions; another way to refer to "private law"

collateral property that a borrower makes available to a lender to sell in order to repay the amount due on a loan if the borrower defaults

collective agreement contract between a union and an employer that governs the terms and conditions of employment for union members

commercial electronic message message sent electronically that contains commercial promotion of any kind

common law system system of law that recognizes court decisions with the same force of law as statutes, where statutes mean what courts interpret them to mean and where courts have the authority to make law where no legislative statute exists and to establish precedent

common shares shares whose dividends are paid at the discretion of a corporation's management on the basis of the company's profits after dividend payments have been made on preferred shares

condition important term of a contract whose breach frees the non-breaching party from all further obligations under the contract

condition precedent clause in a contract specifying that something must happen before a party is required to perform their obligations under the contract

condition subsequent occurrence of an event or circumstance that results in the termination of contractual obligations

conditional offer offer subject to the fulfillment of one or more conditions

condonation implied acceptance by an employer of the conduct of an employee by permitting the conduct to continue without warning, discipline, or corrective action

confidential business information information that provides a business advantage by being kept secret

consideration something of value given up by each party to a contract

consignment act of giving over possession of goods to another but retaining legal ownership in them until they are sold

conspiracy when one person agrees with a competitor to fix prices, allocate markets, or control output or supply levels of a product

constitution supreme law that establishes the basis upon which all other laws are created

constructive bailment custody of property that has come into possession accidentally

constructive dismissal fundamental breach by an employer of an employment contract that entitles an employee to consider themselves dismissed and to sue the employer for wrongful dismissal

consumer purchaser who buys or otherwise obtains goods for his or her own use, not for business purposes

contract agreement between two or more parties that is enforceable by law

contributory negligence role that a plaintiff may play in negligently contributing to the cause or aggravation of their own injury

cooling-off period period set by statute during which a consumer who has made a contract can change his or her mind and rescind it

copyright exclusive right to use, reproduce, sell, or perform the original artistic, literary, musical, photographic, or other work

corporate bond company's written promise to repay the buyer (of the bond) both principal and interest at specified intervals

corporate seal imprint made on corporate contracts and other documents that communicates the intention to bind the corporation

corporation form of carrying on business by means of a legal entity that is distinct from its creators and enjoys almost all the rights and obligations of an individual

costs court fees and the fees and expenses charged by a legal representative

counteroffer proposal that accepts an offer on terms differing from those in the offer

criminal law rules established by the federal government that govern the standard of acceptable behaviour in society, the breach of which results in fines and imprisonment

Crown all aspects of the state in a commonwealth nation; the Monarch is the symbolic embodiment

cyber-squatting registering trademarks as domain names in bad faith

damages losses suffered as a result of the commission of a tort or a breach of contract, or monetary compensation awarded for those losses

debt financing borrowing money from a lender

deductible out-of-pocket payment that an insured must make that is deducted from the insurance payment

defamation tort based on harm to a person's or a business's reputation through false statements made by the defendant

default mortgagor's failure to fulfill their obligations under a mortgage

defendant party who is sued in a lawsuit; person accused of an offence

deliverable state condition in which goods are finished, packaged, labelled, and ready to ship

demand letter letter, usually written by a creditor's lawyer, stating that the debtor to whom the letter is addressed has defaulted and that the debtor must pay the full amount, including interest on the principal sum owing, by a given date or face legal action

director person who makes major decisions regarding the business of the corporation; the director is elected by, and accountable to, the shareholders

disclaimer (or limitation of liability) clause clause in a contract that limits the amount or type of damages that the parties might otherwise be required to pay

discovery procedure after exchange of pleadings where both parties disclose all information, including producing documents, relevant to the case

discrimination negative or singular treatment of a person or group on the basis of a prohibited ground of discrimination under the *Human Rights Code*

distress remedy allowing a landlord to seize and sell a tenant's personal property when rent is unpaid

doctrine of paramountcy rule that establishes that where there is a conflict between federal and provincial law, the federal law will prevail and, where it conflicts, the provincial law will be inoperative

doctrine of precedent principle requiring that a rule set out by a court in a decided case be applied to a new case

domain name unique address of a website

double ticketing selling a product at a price that is higher than the lowest price, when there is more than one price on the product

drawee the person or institution to whom a negotiable instrument is sent for payment

drawer person who drafts and sends the bill of exchange to the drawee for acceptance

due diligence defence defence to strict liability offence requiring accused to demonstrate that they took all reasonable steps to avoid committing a prohibited act

duty of care legal duty owed by one person to another based on a relationship or on the doctrine of foreseeability

duty to mitigate obligation to take all reasonable steps to lessen losses suffered

easement right to use the land of another for a specific purpose

economic duress pressure to enter into a contract by way of threat of economic harm

economies of scale when increased output reduces the average costs of production

employment equity range of measures promoting a representative workforce; federal employment equity legislation and programs focus on four designated groups: women, visible minorities, people with disabilities, and Indigenous peoples

endorsement additional term added on to a standard form or existing contract

equal pay for equal work concept obliging employers to pay female and male employees who perform substantially the same jobs in the same workplace at the same rate, unless a legislated exception applies (since passage of Bill 148 amendments to the *Employment Standards Act, 2000*, this concept also refers to requiring employers to provide equal pay for equal work regardless of employment status)

equal pay for work of equal value (pay equity) concept obliging employers to pay female- and male-dominated jobs at the same rate based on an assessment of job value rather than job content

equity financing raising money by issuing and selling shares in a corporation or using retained earnings to meet short- or long-term financial needs

exclusion clause clause in a contract that excuses parties from their contractual obligations in specified circumstances

exclusive dealing when a supplier requires its customer to obtain products only or primarily from the supplier and the practice has caused or is likely to cause a substantial lessening of competition

exclusive possession possession of real property to the exclusion of others

execution creditor creditor who has obtained a judgment and seeks to enforce (execute) it

executive branch branch of government at both the federal and provincial levels responsible for implementing and enforcing the laws made by the legislative branch

express term term specified in writing

fair dealing defence to copyright infringement that allows copying in some circumstances

false imprisonment tort in which the defendant unlawfully restricts the freedom of the plaintiff

federal system of government system whereby law-making powers are divided between the federal and provincial governments according to subject matter

fee simple ownership rights in land where the owner can do what they want, including transfer, sell, and dispose of it

fiduciary based on trust and confidence

fiduciary duty duty to act honestly and in good faith, with a view to the best interests of the corporation

fixed tenancy right to rent real property for a specified period of time

fixtures property, such as shelving or sinks, that is attached to buildings

floating charge class of collateral, such as inventory, where a creditor allows a debtor to dispose of items in the class

force majeure significant and unanticipated event—such as a natural disaster—that is beyond the control of the parties and makes fulfillment of contractual obligations impossible

foreseeability expectation of whether a reasonable person could predict that a certain result might follow from their actions

forfeiture remedy allowing a landlord to regain possession of leased premises when rent is unpaid

franchise right to operate a business using the name, products, business methods, and advertising of another business

fundamental fairness principle encompassing the right to be heard, the right to hear the case against you, and the right to reply to the case

future goods goods that have not yet come into being at the time a contract is made, such as an agricultural crop, or goods that have not yet been manufactured

gender-neutral job evaluation system system that evaluates the relative value of jobs in a manner that does not favour factors found in jobs traditionally performed by men

general damages pecuniary damages for pain, suffering, and future economic loss, including future loss of life expectancy or quality of life

general partnership partnership that is not registered with the government as a limited or limited liability partnership

general security agreement pledge, often used by a debtor's bank, of most of a debtor's assets to cover short-term loans made over an extended period

goodwill a business's good reputation

gratuitous bailment possession of property where the benefit flows to only one party (i.e., only the bailor benefits or only the bailee benefits)

grievance dispute arising in a unionized workplace with respect to matters covered in the collective agreement

grievance arbitration an external process for resolving disputes that arise under the collective agreement

guarantee contract whereby a party assumes responsibility for another party's financial obligations if that other party defaults on payment

harassment course of vexatious comment or conduct that is known or ought reasonably to be known to be unwelcome

holder person who is assigned the right to be paid on a promissory note by the creditor originally entitled to be paid

implied term term that will be inserted by a court into a contract when necessary to give effect to the parties' intentions

incorporator individual or other corporation that causes a corporation to come into existence by filing the required documentation

indemnity clause clause in a contract that requires one of the parties to pay for any losses or expenses that the other party may incur as a result of claims related to the contract

independent contractor self-employed worker who accepts specific projects, usually from several businesses

independent legal advice legal advice regarding a contract obtained from a different lawyer than the lawyer who drafted the contract

industrial design government-granted exclusive right to make, sell, and use an ornamental feature, shape, or configuration

infringement unlawful interference with someone's legal rights

initial public offering (IPO) first offering of shares by a corporation to the public through a brokerage firm to raise capital for use by the company

injunction court order requiring a party to discontinue an action or prohibiting a party from taking a proposed action

insurable interest interest that causes the insured to benefit from the existence of the property and to suffer from its loss

intangible property things whose value does not arise from their physical attributes

intellectual property things created by the mind or intellect, such as logos and inventions

intentional tort injury deliberately caused to a plaintiff by a defendant

joint and several liability financial responsibility requiring all parties to contribute equally, but also making each party responsible for the entire amount owed

joint health and safety committee committee composed of equal numbers of management and worker representatives generally required by the *Occupational Health and Safety Act* in workplaces with 20 or more workers

joint venture temporary relationship created to complete one or more business projects

judicial branch courts at the federal and provincial levels responsible for interpreting and applying the law passed by the legislative branch; also responsible for determining that law is valid within the authority set out in the Constitution

judicial review process whereby a court reviews the decision of an administrative tribunal

judiciary term used to describe judges, collectively

jurisdiction authority to make or enforce the law

just cause justification for dismissal without notice based on an employee's conduct

land registry system system for the registration of title to lands that required a historical search of deeds to establish valid ownership

land titles system system for the registration of land where the government certifies valid title to and interest in the property

lapse expiration of an offer

lease contract that sets out terms of property rental

leasehold interest temporary right to occupy real property

legal risk management plan plan that allows businesses to take action to prevent or reduce loss

legislative branch branch of government at both the federal and provincial levels that has the power and responsibility to pass legislation

lessee person who leases property of another; tenant

lessor person who leases property to another; landlord

liability legal responsibility for injuries or losses suffered by another

liable legally responsible

licence permission to use intellectual property in accordance with terms and conditions

lien an interest in property that the owner grants to another person, usually to a creditor as security for a debt; it may allow the creditor to sell the property to satisfy the debt if the owner defaults on payment of the debt

life estate interest in land for the duration of a person's life and where, upon death, ownership rights transfer automatically to another

limitation period time period in which a lawsuit must be commenced, after which the right to sue is lost

limited liability partnership (LLP) partnership composed of partners in certain professions, such as lawyers and accountants, who have the same liabilities as those in a general partnership except that partners are not liable for the professional negligence of other partners or employees supervised by other partners

limited partnership partnership composed of a minimum of one general partner and one limited partner who provides money or property to the firm and shares in the profits, but who does not participate in the business affairs of the firm and whose liability is limited to exclude any personal assets

liquidated damages clause clause in a contract that provides for the payment of money if a certain event—usually a specified breach of contract—occurs

litigation process of resolving disputes through a formal court process

lockout refusal by an employer to let unionized employees into a workplace; usually occurs while an employer and a union attempt to negotiate a new collective agreement

market restriction when a supplier forces a buyer to resell its products to only certain customers or only in certain geographic areas and the practice has caused or is likely to cause a substantial lessening of competition

merchantable quality quality sufficiently high to allow goods to be placed for sale as they are, without the need for repairs or other intervention

minor person under the age of majority

minute book book that holds corporate records, such as minutes of meetings

misrepresentation false statement of fact

moral rights creator's rights to have work properly attributed, not to be altered prejudicially, and not to be used in connection with a product, service, or cause where the use might dishonour the creator's reputation

mortgage loan secured by real property

mortgage term period, usually between one and five years, during which a stipulated interest rate applies

mortgagee party that loans funds to a mortgagor; usually a financial institution

mortgagor owner of real property who borrows funds from a mortgagee

multi-level marketing plan a distribution plan structured such that participants earn money by supplying products to other participants in the plan

negligence failure of a person to act reasonably, resulting in harm to someone else

negotiable instrument financial document, such as a cheque, that promises to pay the bearer a specified amount and that can be transferred to a third party

nepotism policy employment policy that allows an employer to discriminate in favour of, or against, their close relatives or the close relatives of employees

neutral individual a person who has no personal interest in a dispute between the parties and can help them resolve a dispute, such as a mediator or arbitrator

non-disclosure agreement contract that legally obligates a party to confidentiality

non-pecuniary damages damages that cannot be readily quantified in financial terms

non-unionized employee employee whose terms and conditions of employment are based on an individual employment contract rather than a collective agreement negotiated between an employer and a union

nuisance tort in which the defendant interferes with the use and enjoyment of the plaintiff's property

occupier person or company that has control over land or buildings, including owners and tenants

occupiers' liability subcategory of negligence that imposes liability on occupiers of land or buildings for any harm caused to visitors, invitees, or trespassers

officer person responsible for the day-to-day operation of a corporation; the officer is appointed by and reports to the board of directors

official receiver government official in the Office of the Superintendent of Bankruptcy who receives proposals, examines bankrupts under oath, and chairs meetings of creditors

omission failure to act

Ontario Labour Relations Board (OLRB) tribunal that mediates and adjudicates labour relations (and other matters) arising in Ontario

option agreement contract in which a party gives something of value to keep an offer open for a specified period of time

parliamentary supremacy constitutional convention that holds the legislative branch of government supreme over the other branches, thus allowing new legislation to override judge-made law

partnership (or firm) form of carrying on business whereby two or more persons operate a business, with no legal separation between the owners and the business

partnership agreement contract signed by all partners that sets out how the partnership will operate and how it will end

passing off tort based on one party's attempt to distribute its own knock-off product or service on the pretense that it is the product or service of another party

patent government-issued monopoly right to make, sell, or use a novel, innovative, and useful invention

pay in lieu of notice payment as a substitute for receiving adequate notice where an employee is dismissed without just cause

payee person who receives payment on a negotiable instrument

payer person who pays, or honours, a negotiable instrument

pecuniary damages damages that are actual monetary losses

periodic tenancy right to rent real property for an indefinite period of time, where both landlord and tenant have the right to terminate the tenancy after providing notice

personal property movable, tangible things (including physical objects that are not attached to land or buildings) and intangible property

piracy illegal copying or distribution of another's intellectual property

plaintiff party who commences a lawsuit (the suing party)

poisoned work environment workplace plagued with insulting or degrading commentary or actions related to a prohibited ground of discrimination under the *Human Rights Code*

policy insurance contract describing the rights and obligations of an insurer and an insured

pre-incorporation contract contract entered into between a third party and the incorporators of a soon-to-be-incorporated business

preferred shares shares for which dividends are paid before any dividends are paid on common shares

presumption legal assumption that is made, subject to a party proving otherwise

price maintenance when a supplier prevents a buyer from reselling the product below a minimum price using threats or promises of benefits, or the supplier discriminates against the buyer because of the buyer's low pricing policy

principal person who has given another the authority to act on their behalf

priority position in a ranking system that creates the order in which competing creditors can satisfy their claims against a debtor's property

privacy breach unauthorized access to, or disclosure of, personal information

private corporation corporation whose shares are held by one person or a small group of people and are not offered to the public

private law rules that govern the relationship between individuals (including corporations) where there is no government involvement

private property things owned by individuals, businesses, or other organizations

privity of contract doctrine that restricts the operation of a contract to those who are parties to it

procedural law rules that establish the process of how substantive law will be enforced

product liability subcategory of negligence based on a defendant's liability for harm caused to others because of his or her defective or dangerous products

professional negligence tort based on a professional's failure to provide services that meet that profession's standards

progressive discipline discipline imposed by an employer in steps that increase in severity

promissory note document in which the maker, or promisor, promises to pay the promisee the sum indicated in the note, either on demand or on a later fixed date

property something in which one has a legal interest with right to possess or use it to the exclusion of others

property law collection of rules that confer rights of ownership, possession, and transferability over things

proposal to creditors debt restructuring proposal made under the *Bankruptcy and Insolvency Act* or the *Companies' Creditors Arrangement Act* that allows the business to continue operating and—if accepted—delays or avoids bankruptcy

prosecutor representative of the government who is responsible for presenting the government's case in public law matters against an accused person charged with an offence; also known as Crown attorney

prospectus document containing detailed financial information about a corporation that is required before sale of shares to the public

public corporation corporation whose shares are offered for sale to the public

public domain works not copyright protected, can be used freely

public law rules that govern the relationship between individuals (including corporations) and government

public property things owned by the government for the benefit of society

punitive damages sum added to a damage award that is intended to punish a defendant and discourage similar behaviour by others where the behaviour is particularly outrageous

pyramid selling a form of multi-level marketing plan that includes one or more of the following: (1) compensation for recruitment; (2) required purchases as a condition of participation; (3) a requirement to purchase excessive inventory; and (4) an inability to return inventory on reasonable commercial terms

quantum amount

quiet enjoyment tenant's right to use leased property for the intended purpose without interference from the landlord or others under the landlord's control

ratification approval by union members of a collective agreement

ratify acknowledge corporate liability for a contract entered into on behalf of a business before incorporation

real property immovable things, including land, buildings, and fixtures

reasonable notice period of time an employee should be given between notification of dismissal and end of employment

reasonable person fictional person who, in negligence law, applies the appropriate standard of care in a given situation

rebuttable capable of being refuted

receiving order order that appoints a trustee in bankruptcy to take control of the bankrupt's property following a creditor's successful bankruptcy petition

refusal to deal when a supplier refuses to supply a product to a buyer even though there is ample supply of the product, resulting in a substantial negative effect on the buyer's business and an adverse effect on competition

regulations rules created by the executive branch of government that have the force of law

regulatory offence breaking of a rule contained in a statute that can result in fines or other penalties but is not a criminal offence

release document that absolves the breaching party of liability for any contract-related claims that the non-breaching party might make in the future

rescind treat as if the contract were never made

restrictive covenant clause in an employment contract that restricts an employee's activities, especially after employment ends; for example, a restrictive covenant might prohibit an ex-employee from disclosing confidential information about the employer

reviewable practices business practices that can have either pro- or anti-competitive effects, depending on market circumstances, and therefore may be subject to review by the Competition Tribunal

revocation taking back of an offer

right to reinstatement employee's right, provided by statute in some circumstances, to return to the job; for example, an employee who is terminated for going on pregnancy leave may be reinstated by an order of the Ministry of Labour

rule of law legal principle that every person has equal rights before the law and that the law is supreme; it safeguards citizens from arbitrary actions of government

rules of construction common law rules used in interpreting disputed contracts

rules of natural justice principle encompassing the right to be heard, the right to hear the case against you, and the right to reply to the case; also known as fundamental fairness

seal symbol, stamp, etc. on a contract that indicates the intention to be legally bound; takes the place of consideration

secured creditor lender who has the right to sell an asset owned by the borrower to pay a loan if the borrower defaults

secured loan loan for which a borrower provides collateral that the lender may sell to pay the loan if the borrower defaults

seller's lien security interest under the *Sale of Goods Act* that allows a seller to keep and resell goods to discharge an insolvent buyer's debt

severance pay one-time lump-sum payment made to a terminated employee in circumstances set out in the Ontario *Employment Standards Act, 2000*

sexual harassment course of vexatious comment or conduct based on sex that is known or ought reasonably to be known to be unwelcome

share certificate document that represents the ownership of shares of a corporation

shareholder owner of a corporation who shares in the profits of the business; a shareholder may be an individual or another corporation

shareholders' agreement contract that governs the relationship between shareholders, or between shareholders and a corporation, or governs how the corporation conducts its business

sole proprietorship form of carrying on business whereby one person owns and operates the business, with no legal separation between the owner and the business

solicitor–client privilege protection that prevents a solicitor from revealing in court communications between that lawyer and the client

special damages pecuniary damages that have already been incurred and that can be precisely measured (out-of-pocket losses)

specific goods goods that exist at the time a contract is made and are specifically chosen or pointed out by the buyer

specific performance requirement by a court that a party complete its obligations under a contract

standard form contract contract that is drafted by one of the parties and imposed on the other with little or no opportunity for negotiation

standard of care degree of care that a person must take to prevent harm to others

standard of proof degree to which a party must convince a judge or jury that the allegations are true

stare decisis principle that requires judges to follow decisions of higher courts in similar cases

statement of claim court document notifying a defendant of a lawsuit against him or her and the reasons for the proceedings

statement of defence court document notifying the plaintiff in a lawsuit that the defendant is denying the claim and identifying the defendant's arguments

strict liability offence offence in which proof that an accused performed the prohibited act is sufficient to sustain a conviction, regardless of intention, unless the accused demonstrates that they took all reasonable care to avoid committing the prohibited act

strict liability tort unintentional tort that requires no proof of negligence

strike collective refusal to work by a group of unionized employees that usually occurs while an employer and a union attempt to negotiate a new collective agreement

substantive law rules that establish rights and limits

tangible property physical things

tied selling when a supplier requires a buyer to buy one product or service in order to gain commercial access to, or a better price on, another product or service and the practice has caused or is likely to cause a substantial lessening of competition

title ownership

tort civil wrong, other than a breach of contract, for which damages may be sought to compensate for any harm or injury sustained

tort action lawsuit based on tort

trade name name in which a business operates

trade secret recipe, method, process, data, or know-how of a business that is confidential, that has actual or potential value in not being generally known, and where efforts are made to keep it a secret

trademark unique identifier of brand used to distinguish one company's products or services from those of another

transfer term used for a deed under the land titles system

trespass to land tort in which the defendant, without the permission of the plaintiff, comes onto land occupied by the plaintiff

trustee in bankruptcy individual, usually an accountant, who is licensed under the *Bankruptcy and Insolvency Act* to administer a bankrupt's assets for the benefit of the bankrupt's creditors

ultra vires beyond the level of power of a government or corporation

unascertained goods goods that are not yet separated from the stock of the seller and set aside for a particular buyer

unconscionable agreement agreement so inequitably one-sided that it is unenforceable

undue hardship difficulty beyond that which an employer is required to endure when accommodating the needs of an individual or a group protected under the *Human Rights Code*

undue influence pressure exerted on a weaker party that deprives that party of the ability to exercise their judgment or free will

unfair labour practice actions by employers that interfere with the formation and activities of a union, including intimidation

unintentional tort injury inadvertently caused to a plaintiff by a defendant

union organization of workers that negotiates wages and working conditions as a group with an employer

unionized employee employee whose terms and conditions of employment are based on a collective agreement negotiated between an employer and a union rather than an individual contract of employment

unlawful means tort based on intentional harm, through illegal acts, to a party's means of earning money

unlimited liability full responsibility for any debt incurred or loss caused by a business

unsecured loan loan given without collateral in exchange for a simple promise to repay

venue (or forum selection) clause clause in a contract specifying the place where a contractual dispute will be litigated

vicarious liability liability imposed on one party (often an employer) for the harmful actions or omissions of another (often an employee)

void unenforceable

voluntary assumption of risk defence based on proof that a plaintiff knowingly entered into a risky situation and thereby assumed responsibility for any injuries

waiver of liability acknowledgment of the risks in an activity and an agreement to assume them

warranty minor term of a contract whose breach requires the non-breaching party to continue to fulfill their remaining obligations under the contract

WHMIS (workplace hazardous materials information system) national information system designed to provide essential information about hazardous materials in the workplace

without prejudice stipulation indicating that statements made either orally or in writing may not be disclosed to the court if attempts at settlement are unsuccessful

workplace diversity employment of people from diverse backgrounds in a workplace where all feel welcome and respected

writ of seizure and sale court order directing a sheriff to seize and sell assets belonging to a judgment debtor and pay the money from the sale to a judgment creditor; also called a "writ of execution"

wrongful dismissal dismissal without just cause in which an employer breaches its common law duty to provide reasonable notice to an employee

Index

Credits

Figure 1.1, House of Commons: © jiawangkun/Shutterstock

Figure 1.3, Supreme Court of Canada: © meunierd/ Shutterstock

Figure 2.2, Ontario Court of Appeal: © NiKreative / Alamy Stock Photo

Figure 3.4, skydivers: © Sky Antonio/Shutterstock

Figure 4.1, Facebook: © Denys Prykhodov/Shutterstock

Figure 5.1, corporate seal: © Tetra Images / Alamy Stock Photo

Figure 6.1, onscreen signature: © huePhotography/iStock

Figure 7.5, MEC: © Felix Choo / Alamy Stock Photo

Figure 7.7, Tim Hortons: © Niloo/Shutterstock

Figure 8.2, Tim Hortons debit machine: © Carlos Osorio/ Toronto Star via Getty Images

Figure 9.1, I quit: © Fuzzbones / Alamy Stock Photo

Figure 9.2, dress code: © Andriy Popov / Alamy Stock Photo

Figure 9.3, TTC streetcar: © Ken Gillespie Photography / Alamy Stock Photo

Figure 10.1, office space for lease: © Deborah Baic/The Globe & Mail/CP Images

Figure 11.1, Google: © achinthamb/Shutterstock

Table 11.2: Industry Canada, *A Guide to Patents* (2010).